GUINNESS
BOOK OF
SPORTS RECORDS, WINNERS & CHAMPIONS

NORRIS McWHIRTER

PETER MATTHEWS
Sports Editor

DAVID A. BOEHM
American Editor

STAN GREENBERG
Associate Editor

STEPHEN TOPPING
Associate American Editor

BANTAM BOOKS
TORONTO · NEW YORK · LONDON · SYDNEY

GUINNESS BOOK OF SPORTS RECORDS, WINNERS AND CHAMPIONS

*A Bantam Book / published by arrangement with
Sterling Publishing Co., Inc.*

PRINTING HISTORY

Sterling edition published August 1980

Bantam edition / December 1981

*Bantam Books are published by Bantam Books, Inc. Its trademark, consisting of
the words "Bantam Books" and the portrayal of a rooster, is Registered in U.S.
Patent and Trademark Office and in other countries. Marca Registrada. Bantam
Books, Inc., 666 Fifth Avenue, New York, New York 10103.*

PRINTED IN THE UNITED STATES OF AMERICA

0 9 8 7 6 5 4 3 2 1

CONTENTS

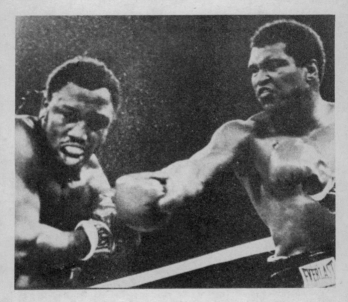

INTRODUCTION

The greatest efforts in sports vary in nature from the brute strength of weightlifting to the planning and guile of a finesse in bridge; from the explosive speed of the short sprints to the timing and grace of figure skating. Yet, every sport has its outstanding performers, its strongest and cleverest, fastest and most graceful, who stand out from the rest and leave their mark in the record books. In these pages you will find the all-time greatest athletes in over six dozen sports. Here are the men and women who have attained superlative achievement, either through great individual effort, as exemplified by the perfect scores of gymnast Nadia Comaneci, or precision teamwork, as so awesomely demonstrated by the Pittsburgh Steelers.

In an attempt to make our already unique reference book even more comprehensive, this edition of the *Guinness Book of Sports Records, Winners and Champions* presents a greatly enlarged coverage of the world of sports competition. All of the sports information from the *Guinness Book of World Records,* representing a quarter of a century of research, has been updated and included. This material has been expanded and supplemented to provide greater interest to North American readers with the inclusion of new sections on, for example, marathon runs, fast and slow pitch softball, and North American Soccer League records.

Perhaps the most significant additions are the lists of winners in Olympic, world, and national championships and tournaments. Besides increasing the usefulness of this book as a reference source, these lists capture the names and achievements of competitors whose records may have been broken over the years, but who dominated their sports in their time. In many cases it has been necessary to limit these lists to a roll of recent champions (the last 20 or 30 years), as complete listings of all past winners in every sport and event would make the size and price of this volume prohibitive, and would be impractical in such a general work. However, many of the lists are complete, especially those involving competitions of major significance, such as the winners of the World Series and Stanley Cup.

A further area of increased coverage is the inclusion of collegiate records and team champions in a number of sports, most notably those sports, such as football and basketball, where the college competition represents the highest level of amateur play in the United States.

While this introduction illustrates many of the major additions and new directions to be found in this volume, the description is by no means complete. The only way to fully appreciate the wealth of information in this book is to turn the pages and read. There you will find all of the best, and sometimes the worst, in athletic achievement.

The editors wish to thank and acknowledge the many people whose contributions to this book were invaluable. The national and international sports organizations and teams that graciously and enthusiastically supplied updates, revisions and new material are simply too numerous to mention individually, but their support is greatly appreciated. In addition, the following individuals provided outstanding assistance: Jim Benagh, of *The New York Times*, helped locate, compile and check records in American professional and N.C.A.A. sports, and his pleasure in digging up unusual sports stories was contagious; Jane Habiger willingly worked overtime to collect records of the tournaments supervised by the Association for Intercollegiate Athletics for Women, an organization that has significantly aided the growth and recognition of women's sports; Roger Gynn in Great Britain and Dr. David Martin in the United States contributed much of the material on the marathon; and Elizabeth Hawley of Katmandu, Nepal, supplied information on the successful ascents of Mount Everest.

Evolution of Sports Records in the 20th Century

	Start of the Century—January 1, 1901	*Middle of the Century—January 1, 1951*	*Present-Day Record—December, 1979*
Greatest Weight Lift	4,133 lbs.—Louis Cyr (Canada), 1896	4,133 lbs.—Louis Cyr (Canada), 1896	6,270 lbs.—Paul Anderson (US), 1957
Fastest 100 Meters	10.8 secs.—Luther Cary (US) and 4 others, 1891–1900	10.3 secs.—Percy Williams (Canada) and 6 others, 1930–1935	9.95 secs.—James Ray Hines (US), 1968
Fastest One Mile	4m 12.8s—W. G. George (UK), 1886	4m 0.13s—Gunder Hägg (Sweden), 1945	3m 49.0s—Sebastian Coe (GB), 1979
One Hour Running	11 miles 932 yds.—W. G. George (UK), 1884	12 miles 29 yds.—Viljo Heino (Finland), 1945	13 miles 24⅔ yards—Jos Hermens (Netherlands), 1976
Highest High Jump	6′ 5⅝″—M. Sweeney (US), 1895	6′ 11″—Lester Steers (US), 1941	7′ 8″—Vladimir Yashchenko (USSR), 1978
Highest Pole Vault	11′ 10½″—R. Clapp (US), 1898	15′ 7¾″—Cornelius Warmerdam (US), 1942	18′ 8¼″—David Roberts (US), 1976
Long Jump	24′ 7¾″—P. O'Connor (UK), 1900	26′ 8¼″—Jesse Owens (US), 1935	29′ 2½″—Robert Beamon (US), 1968
Longest Shot Put	48′ 2″—D. Horgan (UK), 1897	58′ 10¾″—Jim Fuchs (US), 1950	72′ 8″—Udo Beyer (E Germany), 1978
Longest Discus Throw	122′ 3½″—R. Sheldon (US), 1899	186′ 11″—Fortune Gordien (US), 1949	233′ 5″—Wolfgang Schmidt (E Germany), 1978
Longest Hammer Throw	169′ 4″—J. J. Flanagan (US), 1900	196′ 5″—Imre Németh (Hungary), 1950	263′ 6″—Karl-Heinz Riehm (W Germany), 1978
Longest Javelin Throw	161′ 9¾″—E. Lemming (Sweden), 1899	258′ 2″—Yrjo Nikkanen (Finland), 1938	310′ 4″—Miklos Németh (Hungary), 1976
One Hour Walking	8 miles 270 yds.—W. J. Sturgess (UK) (Amateur), 1895	8 miles 1,025 yds.—John Mikaelsson (Sweden), 1945	9 miles 1,383 yds.—Daniel Bautista (Mexico), 1979
Longest Ski Jump	116½′—O. Tanberg (Norway), 1900	442¾″—Dan Netzell (Sweden), 1950	593′ 10″—Bogdan Norcic (Yugoslavia), 1977
Fastest 500 meters Ice Skating	45.2 sec.—P. Ostlund (Norway), 1900	41.8 sec.—Hans Engnestangen (Norway), 1938	37.00 sec.—Evgeni Kulikov (USSR), 1975
Fastest 100 meters Swim (long course)	1m. 14.0s (no turn)—J. Nutall (UK), 1893	55.8 sec.—Alexandre Jany (France), 1947	49.44 sec.—Jonty Skinner (S Africa), 1976
Cycling Paced (m.p.h.)	62.27—C. M. Murphy (US), 1899	>80—L. Vanderstuyft (Belgium), 1928	140.5—Allan V. Abbot (US), 1973
Fastest 1 mile Racehorse (excluding straightaways)	1m. 35.5s.—*Salvator* in U.S., 1890	1m. 33.4s.—*Citation* in U.S., 1950	1m. 32.2s.—*Dr. Fager* in U.S., 1968
Highest Mountain Climbed (feet)	22,834—Aconcagua, Argentina, 1897	26,492—Annapurna I, Nepal, 1950	29,028—Everest, Nepal-Tibet, 1953

THE SPORTS WORLD

Earliest. The origins of sport stem from the time when self-preservation ceased to be the all-consuming human preoccupation. Archery was a hunting skill in Mesolithic times (by *c.* 8000 B.C.), but did not become an organized sport until about 300 A.D., among the Genoese. The earliest dated evidence for sport is *c.* 2450 B.C. for fowling with throwing sticks and hunting. Ball games by girls, depicted on Middle Kingdom murals at Beni Hasan, Egypt, have been dated to *c.* 2050 B.C.

Fastest

The highest speed reached in a non-mechanical sport is in sky-diving, in which a speed of 185 m.p.h. is attained in a head-down free-falling position, even in the lower atmosphere. In delayed drops, a speed of 614 m.p.h. has been recorded at high rarefied altitudes. The highest projectile speed in any moving ball game is 188 m.p.h. in pelota (jai-alai). This compares with 170 m.p.h. (electronically timed) for a golf ball driven off a tee.

Slowest

In amateur wrestling, before the rules were modified toward "brighter wrestling," contestants could be locked in holds for so long that a single bout once lasted for 11 hours 40 min. In the extreme case of the 2-hour 41-minute pull in the regimental tug o'war in Jubbulpore, India, on August 12, 1889, the winning team moved a net distance of 12 feet at an average speed of 0.00084 m.p.h.

Longest

The most protracted sporting test was an automobile duration test of 222,618 miles by Appaurchaux and others in a Ford Taunus. This was contested over 142 days in 1963. The distance was equivalent to 8.93 times around the equator.

The most protracted non-mechanical sporting event is the *Tour de France* cycling race. In 1926, this was over 3,569 miles, lasting 29 days. The total damage to the French national economy due to the interest in this annual event, now reduced to 23 days, is immense, and is currently estimated to be in excess of $2,000,-000,000.

Largest Field

The largest field for any ball game is that for polo with 12.4 acres, or a maximum length of 300 yards and a width, without side-boards, of 200 yards.

Most Participants

The *Stramilano* 22-kilometer run around Milan, Italy, attracted over 50,000 runners on April 16, 1978.

In May, 1971, the "Ramblin' Raft Race" on the Chattahoochee River at Atlanta, Georgia, attracted 37,683 competitors on 8,304 rafts.

According to a report issued in 1978, 55 million people are actively involved in sports in the USSR, using 3,282 stadiums, 1,435 swimming pools and over 66,000 gymnasiums. It is estimated that some 29 per cent of the East German population participates in sports regularly.

Worst Disasters

The worst disaster in recent history was when an estimated 604 were killed after some stands at the Hong Kong Jockey Club race course collapsed and caught fire on February 26, 1918. During the reign of Antoninus Pius (138–161 A.D.) the upper wooden tiers in the Circus Maximus, Rome, collapsed during a gladiatorial combat, killing 1,112 spectators.

Most Versatile Athletes

Charlotte (Lottie) Dod (1871–1960) won the Wimbledon singles title (1887 to 1893) five times, the British Ladies' Golf Championship in 1904, an Olympic silver medal for archery in 1908, and represented England at hockey in 1899. She also excelled at skating and tobogganing.

Mildred (Babe) Didrikson Zaharias (US) was an All-American basketball player, took the silver medal in the high jump, and gold medals in the javelin throw and hurdles in the 1932 Olympics.

VERSATILITY: "Babe" Didrikson Zaharias (1914–1956) was an Olympic medalist in track and field, won 19 golf tournaments, was an All-American basketball player, and set the woman's record for the longest throw of a baseball.

SIXTY MILLION DOLLAR MAN: Three-time heavyweight champion Muhammad Ali had the greatest earnings in the history of sports. Here, he scores a right to the head of Ken Norton while earning a record $6.5 million for defending his title.

Turning professional, she first trained as a boxer, and then, switching to golf, eventually won 19 championships, including the US Women's Open and All-American Open. She holds the women's world record for the longest throw of a baseball—296 feet.

Youngest and Oldest Sports Recordbreakers

The youngest age at which any person has broken a world record is 12 years 298 days in the case of Gertrude Caroline Ederle (born October 23, 1906) of the United States, who broke the women's 880-yard freestyle swimming world record with 13 minutes 19.0 seconds at Indianapolis, Indiana on August 17, 1919.

The oldest person to break a world record is Irish-born John J. Flanagan (1868–1938), triple Olympic hammer throw champion for the US, 1900–1908, who set his last world record of 184 feet 4 inches at New Haven, Connecticut, on July 24, 1909, aged 41 years 196 days.

Youngest and Oldest Internationals

The youngest age at which any person has won international honors is 8 years in the case of Joy Foster, the Jamaican singles and mixed doubles table tennis champion in 1958. It would appear that the greatest age at which anyone has actively competed for his country is 72 years 280 days in the case of Oscar G. Swahn (Sweden) (1847–1927), who won a silver medal for shooting in the Olympic Games at Antwerp on July 26, 1920. He qualified for the 1924 Games, but was unable to participate because of illness.

Youngest and Oldest Champions

The youngest person to have successfully participated in a world title event was a French boy, whose name is not recorded, who coxed the winning Netherlands pair at Paris on Aug. 26, 1900. He was not more than 10 and may have been as young as 7. The youngest individual Olympic winner was Marjorie Gestring (US), who took the springboard diving title at the age of 13 years 9 months at the Olympic Games in Berlin in 1936. Oscar G. Swahn (see above) was aged 65 years 258 days when he won the gold medal in the 1912 Olympic Running Deer team shooting competition.

Most Prolific Recordbreaker

Between January 24, 1970, and November 1, 1977, Vasili Alexeyev (USSR) (b. January 7, 1942) broke a total of 80 official world records in weightlifting.

Longest Reign

The longest reign as a world champion is 33 years (1829–62) by Jacques Edmond Barre (France, 1802–73) at real (royal) tennis.

Heaviest Sportsmen

The heaviest sportsman of all time was the wrestler William J. Cobb of Macon, Georgia, who in 1962 was billed as the 802-lb. "Happy Humphrey." The heaviest player of a ball game was Bob Pointer, the 487-lb. tackle, formerly on the 1967 Santa Barbara High School team.

Greatest Earnings

The greatest fortune amassed by an individual in sport is an estimated $60,000,000 by the boxer Muhammad Ali Haj to August, 1979. The most for a single event is a purse of $6,500,000 won by Ali in his title fight against Ken Norton, fought in New York City on September 28, 1976.

The highest-paid woman athlete in the world is ice skater Janet Lynn (*née* Nowicki) (US) (born April 6, 1953) who in 1974 signed a $1,500,000 three-year contract. In 1974 she earned more than $750,000.

Largest Trophy

The world's largest trophy for a particular sport is the Bangalore Limited Handicap Polo Tournament Trophy. This massive cup is 6 feet tall and was presented in 1936 by the Raja of Kolanka.

Most Expensive

The most expensive of all sports is the racing of large yachts— "J" type boats and International 12-meter boats. The owning and racing of these is beyond the means of individual millionaires and is confined to multi-millionaires or syndicates.

Largest Crowd

The greatest number of live spectators for any sporting spectacle is the estimated 2,500,000 who lined the route of the New

ONE BILLION FANS: The greatest number of viewers for a televised event is an estimated 1,000,000,000 each for the live and recorded transmissions of the XXth Olympic Games in Munich, from August 26 to September 11, 1972, and the XXIst Games in Montreal (opening ceremony shown above), from July 17 to August 1, 1976.

York City Marathon on October 21, 1979. The race was won by Bill Rogers (US) for the fourth consecutive time. However, spread over 23 days, it is estimated that more than 10,000,000 see the annual *Tour de France* along the route.

The largest crowd traveling to any sporting event is "more than 400,000" for the annual *Grand Prix d'Endurance* motor race on the Sarthe circuit near Le Mans, France. The record stadium crowd was one of 199,854 for the Brazil *vs.* Uruguay match in the Maracaña Municipal Stadium, Rio de Janeiro, Brazil, on July 16, 1950.

Television. The largest television audience for a single sporting event (excluding Olympic events) was the 400,000,000 who watched the final of the 1978 World Cup soccer competition.

The highest TV advertising rate was reportedly $468,000 per minute for CBS network prime time during the transmission of Super Bowl XIV on January 20, 1980. The game was viewed by an estimated 105,000,000 fans.

Largest Stadiums

The world's largest stadium is the Strahov Stadium in Praha (Prague), Czechoslovakia. It was completed in 1934 and can accommodate 240,000 spectators for mass displays of up to 40,000 Sokol gymnasts.

The largest football (soccer) stadium in the world is the Maracaña Municipal Stadium in Rio de Janeiro, Brazil, which has a normal capacity of 205,000, of whom 155,000 may be seated. A crowd of 199,854 was accommodated for the World Cup soccer final between Brazil and Uruguay on July 16, 1950. A dry moat, 7 feet

LARGEST STADIUM: Strahov Stadium in Prague, Czechoslovakia, can accommodate 240,000 spectators for mass displays of up to 40,000 gymnasts.

wide and over 5 feet deep, protects players from spectators and *vice versa*. The stadium also has facilities for indoor sports, such as boxing, and these provide accommodation for an additional 32,000 spectators.

The largest covered stadium in the world is the Azteca Stadium, Mexico City, opened in 1968, which has a capacity of 107,000, of whom nearly all are under cover.

Largest One-Piece Roof. The transparent acrylic glass "tent" roof over the Munich Olympic Stadium, West Germany, measures 914,940 square feet in area. It rests on a steel net supported by masts. The roof of longest span in the world is the 680-foot diameter of the Louisiana Superdome (see below). The major axis of the elliptical Texas Stadium, completed in 1971 at Irving, Texas, is, however, 784 feet 4 inches.

LARGEST INDOOR ARENA: New Orleans' 13-acre Superdome can seat 97,365 conventioneers. The stadium cost $173,000,000 to build (left), and is outfitted with luxurious box suites and six large TV screens, as well as electric message boards that exult a score by the home football team, the New Orleans Saints (right).

Largest Air-Supported Structure. The world's largest air-supported roof is the roof of the 80,600-capacity octagonal Pontiac Silverdome Stadium, Michigan, measuring 522 feet wide and 722 feet long. The air pressure is 5 lbs. per square inch, supporting the 10-acre translucent fiberglass roofing. The structural engineers were Geiger-Berger Associates of New York City.

Largest Indoor Arena. The world's largest indoor stadium is the 13-acre $173,000,000 273-foot-tall Superdome in New Orleans, Louisiana, completed in May, 1975. Its maximum seating capacity for conventions is 97,365 or 76,791 for football. Box suites rent for $35,000, excluding the price of admission. A gondola with six 312-inch TV screens produces instant replay.

The Sullivan Award

An award instituted in 1930 by the A.A.U. in the memory of James E. Sullivan, for the "amateur athlete who, by performance, example and good influence did the most to advance the cause of good sportsmanship during the year." The winner is selected on the basis of votes cast by sports authorities throughout the United States.

1930	Bobby Jones, Golf	1940	Greg Rice, Track
1931	Bernard Berlinger, Track	1941	Les MacMitchell, Track
1932	James Bausch, Track	1942	Cornelius Warmerdam, Track
1933	Glenn Cunningham, Track	1943	Gil Dodds, Track
1934	Bill Bonthron, Track	1944	Ann Curtis, Swimming
1935	Lawson Little, Golf	1945	Felix "Doc" Blanchard, Football-Track
1936	Glenn Morris, Track		
1937	Don Budge, Tennis	1946	Arnold Tucker, Football, Basketball, Track
1938	Don Lash, Track		
1939	Joseph Burk, Rowing	1947	John Kelly, Jr., Rowing

SULLIVAN AWARD WINNERS: Bobby Jones (left) was honored with the A.A.U.'s first Sullivan Award in 1930. That year, he won golf's grand slam, which then consisted of the British and US Amateur and Open championships. Tracy Caulkins (right) became the youngest recipient of the award when, at 16 years of age, she broke or tied 27 world and American swimming records in 1978. Her autograph was in great demand on the night of the award ceremony. (See also Golf and Swimming)

The Sullivan Award (continued)

1948	Bob Mathias, Track	1964	Don Schollander, Swimming
1949	Dick Button, Figure Skating	1965	Bill Bradley, Basketball
1950	Fred Wilt, Track	1966	Jim Ryun, Track
1951	Bob Richards, Track	1967	Randy Matson, Track
1952	Horace Ashenfelter, Track	1968	Debbie Meyer, Swimming
1953	Sammy Lee, Diving	1969	Bill Toomey, Track
1954	Mal Whitfield, Track	1970	John Kinsella, Swimming
1955	Harrison Dillard, Track	1971	Mark Spitz, Swimming
1956	Patricia McCormick, Diving	1972	Frank Shorter, Track
1957	Bobby Morrow, Track	1973	Bill Walton, Basketball
1958	Glenn Davis, Track	1974	Rick Wohlhuter, Track
1959	Parry O'Brien, Track	1975	Tim Shaw, Swimming
1960	Rafer Johnson, Track	1976	Bruce Jenner, Track
1961	Wilma Rudolph, Track	1977	John Naber, Swimming
1962	Jim Beatty, Track	1978	Tracy Caulkins, Swimming
1963	John Thomas, Track	1979	Kurt Thomas, Gymnastics

Sports Illustrated Sportsmen of the Year

(Awarded for symbolizing in character and performance the ideals of sportsmanship.)

1954	Roger Bannister	1967	Carl Yastrzemski
1955	Johnny Podres	1968	Bill Russell
1956	Bobby Morrow	1969	Tom Seaver
1957	Stan Musial	1970	Bobby Orr
1958	Rafer Johnson	1971	Lee Trevino
1959	Ingemar Johansson	1972	John Wooden and Billie Jean King
1960	Arnold Palmer	1973	Jackie Stewart
1961	Jerry Lucas	1974	Muhammad Ali
1962	Terry Baker	1975	Pete Rose
1963	Pete Rozelle	1976	Chris Evert
1964	Ken Venturi	1977	Steve Cauthen
1965	Sandy Koufax	1978	Jack Nicklaus
1966	Jim Ryun	1979	Terry Bradshaw and Willie Stargell

GOOD SPORTS: Billie Jean King (left) was the first woman to receive *Sports Illustrated's* **"Sportsman" of the Year award. In 1972, she won the Wimbledon, US, and French singles titles. One year earlier, she led all American tennis players in earnings. Steve Cauthen (middle) was honored in 1977 when he became the first jockey to win more than $6 million in prize money. He is here astride "Affirmed," the horse he rode to racing's triple crown in 1978. Sprinter Bobby Morrow (right) captured three gold medals in the 1956 Olympics and is one of three men who have received both the Sullivan Award and the** *Sports Illustrated* **title. (See also Tennis, Horse Racing, and Track and Field)**

AEROBATICS

Earliest. The first aerobatic maneuver is generally considered the sustained inverted flight in a Blériot of Célestin-Adolphe Pégoud, at Buc, France, on September 21, 1913, but Lieut. Peter Nikolayevich Nesterov, of the Imperial Russian Air Service, performed a loop in a Nieuport Type IV monoplane at Kiev, USSR on August 27, 1913.

World Championships

Held biennially since 1960 (excepting 1974), scoring is based on the system devised by Col. José Aresti of Spain. The competitions consist of two compulsory and two free programs.

Most Titles

The world championships team competition has been won on four occasions by the USSR. No individual has won more than one title, the most successful competitor being Igor Egorov (USSR) who won in 1970, was second in 1976, fifth in 1972 and eleventh in 1968. The most successful in the women's competition has been Lidia Leonova (USSR) with first place in 1976, second in 1978, third in 1972 and fifth in 1970.

LONG SHOT: Harry Drake holds the flight shooting record in the footbow class with a distance of 1 mile 268 yards in 1971. Drake is also the crossbow record-holder at 1,359 yards 29 inches in 1967.

Inverted Flight

The duration record for inverted flight is 2 hours 15 minutes 4 seconds by John Leggatt in a Champion Decathlon on May 28, 1974, over the Arizona Desert.

Loops

John "Hal" McClain performed 1,501½ inside loops in a Pitts S–2A over Long Beach, California, on December 16, 1973. He also achieved 180 outside loops in a Bellanca Super Decathlon on September 2, 1978, over Houston, Texas.

ARCHERY

Earliest References. The discovery of stone arrowheads at Border Cave, Northern Natal, South Africa, in deposits exceeding the Carbon 14 dating limit, indicates that the bow was invented *ante* 46,000 B.C. Archery developed as an organized sport at least as early as the 3rd century A.D. The world governing body is the *Fédération Internationale de Tir à l'Arc* (FITA), founded in 1931.

Flight Shooting

The longest flight shooting records are achieved in the footbow class. In the unlimited footbow division, the professional Harry Drake of Lakeside, California, holds the record at 1 mile 268 yards, shot at Ivanpah Dry Lake, California, on October 24, 1971. The crossbow record is 1,359 yards 29 inches, held by Drake and set at the same venue on October 14–15, 1967. The unlimited handbow class (*i.e.* standing stance with bow of any weight) record is 1,164 yards 2 feet 9 inches by Don Brown (b. 1946) at Wendover, Utah, on September 18, 1977. April Moon (US) set a women's record of 870 yards 1 foot 2 inches at Ivanpah Dog Lake, October 7, 1979.

Sultan Selim III shot an arrow 1,400 Turkish *pikes* or *gez* near Istanbul, Turkey, in 1798. The equivalent English distance is somewhere between 953 and 972 yards.

STRAIGHT ARROW: Darrell Pace (US) achieved the highest score ever for a Double FITA round to capture the gold medal at the 1976 Olympics in Montreal. He also holds the record for a single FITA round (36 shots each at distances of 90, 70, 50, and 30 meters) with 1,341 points of a possible 1,440.

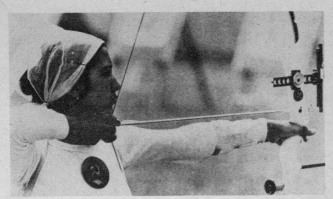

BEAR ARMS: Russia's Zebiniso Rustamova was the 1975 women's world champion and captured the bronze medal in the 1976 Olympic Games. She held the women's record for a single FITA round from October, 1977, until August, 1979.

Highest Scores

The world records for a single FITA round are: men, 1,341 points (of a possible 1,440) by Darrell Pace (US) at Kumamoto, Japan, November 4, 1979; and women, 1,321 points (possible 1,440), by Natalia Butuzova (USSR) in Poland, August 1979.

There are no world records for Double FITA rounds, but the highest scores achieved in either a world or Olympic championship are: men, 2,571 points (possible 2,880) by Darrell Pace (US) posted at the 1976 Olympics at Montreal, Canada, July 27–30, 1976; women, 2,515 by Luann Ryon (US) at Canberra, Australia, February 11–12, 1977.

Most Titles

The greatest number of world titles (instituted 1931) ever won by a man is four by Hans Deutgen (Sweden) in 1947–48–49–50. The greatest number won by a woman is seven by Mrs. Janina Spychajowa-Kurkowska (Poland) in 1931–32–33–34, 1936, 1939 and 1947.

Oscar Kessels (Belgium) (1904–1968) participated in 21 world championships beginning in 1931.

Olympic Medals

Hubert van Innis (Belgium) (1866–1961) won 6 gold and 3 silver medals in archery events at the 1900 and 1920 Olympic Games.

Greatest Pull

Gary Sentman of Roseburg, Oregon, drew a longbow weighing a record 176 lbs. to the maximum draw on the arrow (28¼ inches) at Forksville, Pennsylvania, on September 20, 1975.

Highest 24-Hour Score

The record over 24 hours by a pair of archers is 51,633 during 48 Portsmouth Rounds (60 arrows at 20 yards with a 2-inch-diameter 10 ring) shot by Jimmy Watt and Gordon Danby at the Epsom Showgrounds, Aukland, New Zealand, on November 18–19, 1977.

Archery World Records

(as ratified by the FITA as of January 31, 1980)

WOMEN

Event	Name	Record/Maximum	Year
FITA	Natalia Butuzova (USSR)	1321/1440	1979
70 m.	Natalia Butuzova (USSR)	328/360	1979
60 m.	Valentina Kopvan (USSR)	334/360	1978
50 m.	Natalia Butuzova (USSR)	330/360	1980
30 m.	Natalia Butuzova (USSR)	350/360	1979
Team	USSR (Natalia Butuzova, Keto Lossaberidze, O. Rogova)	3878/4320	1979

MEN

Event	Name	Record/Maximum	Year
FITA	Darrell Pace (US)	1341/1440	1979
90 m.	Richard McKinney (US)	318/360	1980
70 m.	Sante Spigarelli (Italy)	338/360	1978
50 m.	Sante Spigarelli (Italy)	340/360	1976
30 m.	Darrell Pace (US)	354/360	1975
Team	United States (Richard McKinney, Darrell Pace, R. Baston)	3868/4320	1979

World Champions

World Championships were first held in 1931, and were held annually from 1931 to 1939 and 1946 to 1950. From 1959 they

MOST TITLES: Hans Deutgen (Sweden) won 4 consecutive world championships from 1947 through 1950. His 4 titles are a men's record.

have been held every other year, while they were also held in 1952, 1953, 1955, 1957 and 1958. Since 1957 both team and individual competitions have been held with competitors shooting Double FITA rounds. That is 72 arrows each, at four different distances.

Winners since 1957 of Target Archery championships:

Men's Individual		Women's Individual	
1957	O. K. Smathers (US) 2231	Carole Meinhart (US) 2120	
1958	S. Thysell (Swe) 2101	Sigrid Johansson (Swe) 2053	
1959	James Caspers (US) 2247	Ann Weber Corby (US) 2023	
1961	Joseph Thornton (US) 2310	Nancy Vonderheide (US) 2173	
1963	Charles Sandlin (US) 2332	Victoria Cook (US) 2253	
1965	Matti Haikonen (Fin) 2313	Maire Lindholm (Fin) 2214	
1967	Ray Rogers (US) 2298	Maria Mazynska (Pol) 2240	
1969	Hardy Ward (US) 2493	Dorothy Lidstone (Can) 2361	
1971	John Williams (US) 2445	Emma Gapchenko (USSR) 2380	
1973	Viktor Sidoruk (USSR) 2185	Linda Myers (US) 2204	
1975	Darrell Pace (US) 2548	Zebiniso Rustamova (USSR) 2465	
1977	Richard McKinney (US) 2501	Luann Ryon (US) 2515	
1979	Darrell Pace (US) 2474	Jin-Ho Kim (S Kor) 2507	

Team Competitions				Team Competitions		
	Men	*Women*			*Men*	*Women*
1957	US 6591	US 6187		1969	US 7194	USSR 6897
1959	US 6634	US 5847		1971	US 7050	Poland 6907
1961	US 6601	US 6376		1973	US 6400	USSR 6389
1963	US 6887	US 6508		1975	US 7444	USSR 7252
1965	US 6792	US 6358		1977	US 7444	US 7379
1967	US 6816	Poland 6686		1979	US 7409	S Korea 7314

Olympic Champions

Archery was included in the Olympic Games of 1900, 1904, 1908 and 1920 and re-introduced in 1972 and 1976 when the winners were:

Men		*Women*	
1972	John Williams (US) 2528	1972	Doreen Wilbur (US) 2424
1976	Darrell Pace (US) 2571	1976	Luann Ryon (US) 2499
1980	Tomi Poikolainen (Fin) 2455	1980	Keto Lossaberidze (USSR) 2491

AUTO RACING

Earliest Races. There are various conflicting claims, but the first automobile race was the 201-mile Green Bay-to-Madison, Wisconsin, run in 1878, won by an Oshkosh steamer.

In 1887, Count Jules Felix Philippe Albert de Dion de Malfiance (1856–1946) won the *La Vélocipède* 19.3-mile race in Paris in a De Dion steam quadricycle in which he is reputed to have exceeded 37 m.p.h.

The first "real" race was from Paris to Bordeaux and back (732 miles) June 11–13, 1895. The winner was Emile Levassor (1844–97) (France) driving a Panhard-Levassor two-seater with a 1.2-liter Daimler engine developing 3½ h.p. His time was 48 hours 47 min. (average speed 15.01 m.p.h.). The first closed-circuit race was held over 5 laps of a mile dirt track at Narragansett Park, Cranston, Rhode Island, on September 7, 1896. It was won by A. H. Whiting, who drove a Riker electric.

MEN OF LE MANS: Jacky Ickx (left) is one of two men to achieve four
victories in the Le Mans 24-hour race. He recorded the fastest practice
lap in 1978, averaging 146.97 m.p.h. Jean Pierre Jabouille (right) holds
the race lap record of 3 minutes 34.2 seconds for an average speed of
142.44 m.p.h. over the 8.475-mile lap.

The oldest auto race in the world still being regularly run is the
R.A.C. Tourist Trophy (40th race held in 1976), first staged on
the Isle of Man on September 14, 1905. The oldest continental
race is the French Grand Prix (57th in 1979) first held on June
26–27, 1906. The Coppo Florio, in Sicily, has been irregularly
held since 1900.

Fastest Circuits

The highest average lap speed attained on any closed circuit is
250.958 m.p.h. in a trial by Dr. Hans Liebold (b. October 12,
1929) (Germany) who lapped the 7.85-mile high-speed track at
Nardo, Italy, in 1 minute 52.67 seconds in a Mercedes-Benz
C111-IV experimental coupe on May 5, 1979. It was powered by
a V8 engine with two KKK turbochargers with an output of 500
h.p. at 6,200 r.p.m.

The highest average race lap speed for a closed circuit is 214.158
m.p.h. by Mario Gabriele Andretti (US) (b. Trieste, Italy, February 28, 1940) driving a 2.6-liter turbocharged Viceroy Parnelli-
Offenhauser on the 2-mile 22-degree banked oval at Texas World
Speedway, College Station, Texas, on October 6, 1973.

The fastest road circuit was the Francorchamps circuit near
Spa, Belgium, then 14.10 kilometers (8 miles 1,340 yards) in
length. It was lapped in 3 minutes 13.4 seconds (average speed of
163.086 m.p.h.) on lap seven of the Francorchamps 1,000-kilometer
sports car race on May 6, 1973, by Henri Pescarolo (b. Paris,
France, September 25, 1942) driving a 2,933-c.c. V12 Mantra-
Simca MS 670 Group 5 sports car. The race lap average speed
record at Berlin's AVUS track was 171.75 m.p.h. by Bernd
Rosemeyer (Germany) (1909–38) in a 6-liter V16 Auto Union in
1937.

The fastest world championship Grand Prix circuit in current use is the 2.932-mile course at Silverstone, Northamptonshire, England (opened 1948). The race lap record is 1 minute 14.40 seconds (average speed 141.87 m.p.h.) by Gianclaudio (Clay) Regazzoni (Switzerland) (b. September 5, 1939) driving a Saudia-Williams FW07 on July 14, 1979. The practice lap record is 1 minute 11.88 seconds (146.84 m.p.h.) by Alan Jones (Australia) (b. November 2, 1946) in a Saudia-Williams on July 12, 1979.

Fastest Races

The fastest race in the world is the NASCAR Grand National 125-mile event (a qualifying race for the Daytona 500) on the 2½-mile 31-degree banked tri-oval at Daytona International Speedway, Daytona Beach, Florida. The record time is 40 minutes 55 seconds (average speed 183.295 m.p.h.) by William Caleb "Cale" Yarborough (born March 27, 1939) of Timmonsville, South Carolina, driving a 1969 Mercury V8, on February 19, 1970.

The fastest road race was the 1,000-kilometer (621-mile) sports car race held on the Francorchamps circuit (8 miles 1,340 yards) near Spa, Belgium. The record time for this 71-lap (622.055-mile) race was 4 hours 1 minute 9.7 seconds (average speed 154.765 m.p.h.) by Pedro Rodriguez (1940–71) of Mexico and Keith Jack "Jackie" Oliver (b. Chadwell Heath, Essex, England, Aug. 14, 1942), driving a 4,998-c.c. flat-12 Porsche 917K Group 5 sports car on May 9, 1971.

Toughest Circuits

The Targa Florio (first run May 9, 1906) was widely acknowledged to be the most arduous race in the world. Held on the Piccolo Madonie Circuit in Sicily, it covered eleven laps (492.126 miles) and involved the negotiation of 9,350 corners over severe mountain gradients and narrow rough roads.

The record time was 6 hours 27 minutes 48.0 seconds (average speed 76.141 m.p.h.) by Arturo Francesco Merzario (b. Civenna, Italy, March 11, 1943) and Sandro Munari (Italy) driving a 2,998.5-c.c. flat-12 Ferrari 312 P Group 5 sports car in the 56th race on May 21, 1972. The lap record was 33 minutes 36.0 seconds (average speed 79.890 m.p.h.) by Leo Juhani Kinnunen (born Tampere, Finland, Aug. 5, 1943) on lap 11 of the 54th race in a 2,997-c.c. flat-8 Porsche 908/3 Spyder Group 6 prototype sports car on May 3, 1970.

The most gruelling and slowest Grand Prix circuit is that for the Monaco Grand Prix (first run on April 14, 1929), run through the streets and around the harbor of Monte Carlo. It is 3.312 km. (2.058 miles) in length and has 11 pronounced corners and several sharp changes of gradient. The race is run over 76 laps (156.4 miles) and involves on average about 1,600 gear changes.

The record for the race is 1 hour 55 minutes 22.48 seconds (average speed 81.338 m.p.h.) by Jody Scheckter (b. South Africa, January 29, 1950) driving a Ferrari 312T4 on May 27, 1979. The race lap record is 1 minute 28.65 seconds (average speed 83.67 m.p.h.) by Andreas-Nikolaus "Niki" Lauda (b. Austria, February 22, 1949) driving a Brabham-Alfa Romeo BT46 on May 7, 1978. The practice lap record is 1 minute 26.45 seconds (average speed

85.69 m.p.h.) by Jody Scheckter in a Ferrari 312T4 on May 26, 1979.

Le Mans

The greatest distance ever covered in the 24-hour *Grand Prix d'Endurance* (first held on May 26–27, 1923) on the old Sarthe circuit (8 miles 650 yards) at Le Mans, France, is 3,315.208 miles by Dr. Helmut Marko (b. Graz, Austria, April 27, 1943) and Jonkheer Gijs van Lennep (b. Bloemendaal, Netherlands, March 16, 1942) driving a 4,907-c.c. flat-12 Porsche 917K Group 5 sports car on June 12–13, 1971. The record for the current circuit is 3,134.52 miles by Didier Pironi (b. March 26, 1952) and Jean-Pierre Jaussaud (b. June 3, 1937) (average speed 130.60 m.p.h.) in an Alpine Renault, June 10–11, 1978. The race lap record (8.475 mile lap) is 3 minutes 34.2 seconds (average speed 142.44 m.p.h.) by Jean Pierre Jabouille (b. France, October 1, 1942) driving an Alpine Renault on June 11, 1978. The practice lap record is 3 minutes 27.6 seconds (average speed 146.97 m.p.h.) by Jacques-Bernard "Jacky" Ickx (b. Belgium, January 1, 1945) in a turbo-charged 2.1-liter Porsche 936/78 on June 7, 1978.

Most Wins. The race has been won by Ferrari cars nine times, in 1949, 1954, 1958 and 1960–61–62–63–64–65. The most wins by one man is four by Oliver Gendebien (Belgium), who won in 1958, 1960–61–62, and by Jacky Ickx (Belgium), who won in 1969, 1975–76–77.

Indianapolis 500

The Indianapolis 500-mile race (200 laps) was inaugurated on May 30, 1911. The most successful driver has been Anthony Joseph "A.J." Foyt, Jr., who won in 1961, 1964, 1967 and 1977.

The record time is 3 hours 4 minutes 5.54 seconds (average speed 162.962 m.p.h.) by Mark Donohue (b. New Jersey, March 18, 1937, d. 1975) driving a 2,595-c.c. 900-b.h.p. turbocharged Sunoco McLaren M16B-Offenhauser on May 27, 1972. The rec-

MAKING TIME IN INDIANAPOLIS: Mark Donohue recorded the fastest time ever for the Indianapolis 500 when he completed the 500 miles in 3 hours 4 minutes 5.54 seconds to win the race in 1972.

ord prize fund was $1,271,954 for the 63rd race on May 27, 1979. The individual prize record is $290,363 by Al Unser (b. Albuquerque, New Mexico, May 29, 1939) on May 28, 1978.

The race lap record is 46.71 seconds (average speed 192.678 m.p.h.) by Danny Ongais (b. Hawaii, May 21, 1942) driving a 2.6-liter turbocharged Parnelli-Cosworth DFX on lap 42 of the race held on May 29, 1977. The 4-lap qualifying record is 2 minutes 58.08 seconds (average speed 202.156 m.p.h.) by Tom Sneva (b. US, June 1, 1948) driving a Penske-Cosworth DFX turbocharged PC6 on May 20, 1978.

Fastest Pit Stop. Bobby Unser (US) took 4 seconds to take on fuel on lap 10 of the Indianapolis 500 on May 30, 1976.

Duration Record

The greatest distance ever covered in one year is 400,000 kilometers (248,548.5 miles) by François Lecot (1879–1949), an innkeeper from Rochetaillée, France, in a 1,900-c.c. 66-b.h.p. Citroën 11 sedan mainly between Paris and Monte Carlo, from July 22, 1935 to July 26, 1936. He drove on 363 of the 370 days allowed.

The world's duration record is 185,353 miles 1,741 yards in 133 days 17 hours 37 minutes 38.64 seconds (average speed 58.07 m.p.h.) by Marchand, Presalé and six others in a Citroën on the Montlhéry track near Paris, during March–July, 1933.

Most Successful Drivers

Based on the World Drivers' Championships, inaugurated in 1950, the most successful driver is Juan Manuel Fangio y Cia (born Balcarce, Argentina, June 24, 1911), who won five times in 1951–54–55–56–57. He retired in 1958, after having won 24 Grand Prix races (2 shared).

The most successful driver in terms of race wins is Richard Lee Petty (born Randleman, North Carolina, July 2, 1937) with 190 NASCAR Grand National wins from 1960 to December, 1979. His best year was 1967 with 27 victories.

The most Grand Prix victories is 27 by Jackie Stewart of Scotland between September 12, 1965 and August 5, 1973. Jim Clark, O.B.E. (1936–1968) of Scotland holds the record of Grand Prix victories in one year with 7 in 1963. He won 61 Formula One and Formula Libre races between 1959 and 1968. The most Grand Prix starts is 176 (out of a possible 184) between May 18, 1958, and Jan. 26, 1975, by Norman Graham Hill, O.B.E. (1929–1975). He took part in 90 *consecutive* Grands Prix between November 20, 1960 and October 5, 1969.

Oldest and Youngest World Champions. The oldest was Juan Manuel Fangio, who won his last World Championship on August 18, 1957, aged 46 years 55 days. The youngest was Emerson Fittipaldi (Brazil) who won his first World Championship on September 10, 1972, aged 25 years 273 days.

Oldest and Youngest Grand Prix Winners and Drivers. The youngest Grand Prix winner was Bruce Leslie McLaren (1937–70) of New Zealand, who won the US Grand Prix at Sebring, Florida, on December 12, 1959, aged 22 years 104 days. The oldest Grand

FASTEST LAND VEHICLE: The 48,000-h.p. Budweiser rocket car, boosted by a Sidewinder missile, reportedly achieved a peak speed of 739.666 m.p.h. in a one-way run at Rogers Lake, Mojave, California. Stuntman Stan Barrett was the driver for the December, 1979, ride.

Prix winner was Tazio Giorgio Nuvolari (1892–1953) of Italy, who won the Albi Grand Prix at Albi, France, on July 14, 1946, aged 53 years 240 days. The oldest Grand Prix driver was Louis Alexandre Ghiron (Monaco, 1899–1979), who finished 6th in the Monaco Grand Prix on May 22, 1955, aged 55 years 292 days.

The youngest Grand Prix driver was Christopher Arthur Amon (b. Bulls, New Zealand, July 20, 1943) who took part in the Belgian Grand Prix on June 9, 1963, aged 19 years 324 days.

Land Speed Records

The highest speed attained by any wheeled land vehicle is 739.666 m.p.h. or Mach 1.0106 in a one-way stretch by the rocket-engined *Budweiser Rocket*, designed by William Frederick, and driven by Stan Barrett at Edwards Air Force Base, Calif. on Dec. 17, 1979. The vehicle, owned by Hal Needham, has a 48,000-h.p. rocket engine with 6,000 lbs of extra thrust from a sidewinder missile. The rear wheels (100-lb solid discs) lifted 10 inches off the ground above Mach 0.95 acting as 7,500 r.p.m. gyroscopes.

The *official* world land speed record, which is for the average of a two-way run, remains that which was achieved by Gary Gabelich (b. San Pedro, California, August 29, 1950), at Bonneville Salt Flats, Utah, on October 23, 1970. He drove the Reaction Dynamics *The Blue Flame*, weighing 4,950 lbs. and measuring 37 feet long, powered by a liquid natural gas-hydrogen peroxide rocket engine developing a maximum static thrust of 22,000 lbs. On his first run, at 11:23 a.m. (local time), he covered the measured kilometer in 3.543 seconds (average speed 631.367 m.p.h.) and the mile in 5.829 seconds (617.602 m.p.h.). On the return run, at 12:11 p.m., his times were 3.554 seconds for the kilometer (629.413 m.p.h.) and 5.739 seconds for the mile (627.287 m.p.h.). The average times for the two runs were 3.5485 seconds for the kilometer (630.388 m.p.h.) and 5.784 seconds for the mile (622.407 m.p.h.). During the attempt only 13,000 lbs. s.t. was used and a peak speed of 650 m.p.h. was momentarily attained.

The most successful land speed record breaker was Major Malcolm Campbell (1885–1948) (UK). He broke the official record nine times between September 25, 1924, with 146.157 m.p.h. in a Sunbeam, and September 3, 1935, when he achieved 301.129 m.p.h. in the Rolls-Royce-engined *Bluebird*.

The world speed record for compression-ignition-engined cars is 190.344 m.p.h. (average of two runs over measured mile) by Robert Havemann of Eureka, California, driving his *Corsair* stream-

LIFE IN THE FAST LANE: Gary Gabelich (left) holds the land speed record, set in 1970 when he averaged 630.388 m.p.h. over two one-kilometer runs. Richard Petty (right) is the most successful stock car driver of all time. He has set marks for most career, season, and consecutive victories, and his six Daytona 500 wins are the most in NASCAR's premier race.

liner, powered by a turbocharged 6,981-c.c. 6-cylinder GMC 6-71 diesel engine developing 746 b.h.p., at Bonneville Salt Flats, Utah, in August, 1971. The faster run was made at 210 m.p.h.

Dragging

Piston-Engined. The lowest elapsed time recorded by a piston-engined dragster is 5.637 seconds by Donald Glenn "Big Daddy" Garlits (born 1932) of Seffner, Florida, driving his rear-engined AA-F dragster, powered by a 7,948-c.c. supercharged Dodge V8 engine, during the National Hot Rod Association's Supernationals at Ontario Motor Speedway, California, on October 11, 1975.

The highest terminal velocity recorded is 255.58 m.p.h. by Shirley Muldowney (US) at Pomona, California, in January, 1979.

The world record for two runs in opposite directions over 440 yards from a standing start is 6.70 seconds by Dennis Victor Priddle (b. 1945) of Yeovil, Somerset, England, driving his 6,424-c.c. supercharged Chrysler dragster, developing 1,700 b.h.p. using nitromethane and methanol, at Elvington Airfield, England, on October 7, 1972. The faster run took 6.65 seconds.

Rocket or Jet-Engined. The highest terminal velocity recorded by any dragster is 377.754 m.p.h. (elapsed time 4.65 seconds) by Norman Craig Breedlove (b. March 23, 1938) of Los Angeles, California, driving his *English Leather Special* rocket dragster at Bonneville Salt Flats, Utah, in Sept. 1973. The lowest elapsed time recorded by any dragster is 3.94 seconds by Sam Miller (b. April 15, 1945) of Wayne, New Jersey, in Miami, Florida, in February, 1979.

Terminal velocity is the speed attained at the end of a 440-yard run made from a standing start and elapsed time is the time taken for the run.

FIRST LONG RALLY: Prince Scipione Borghese won the 1907 Peking-to-Paris rally by covering the 7,500 miles in two months. Accompanying him in his 40-h.p. Itala were his chauffeur, Ettore, and Luigi Barzini.

Stock Car Racing

Richard Petty of Randleman, North Carolina, was the first stock car driver to attain $1,000,000 lifetime earnings on August 1, 1971. His earnings through the 1979 season were $3,633,502, including a record $531,292 for a year in 1979. Petty also holds the NASCAR records for most races won (190), most victories in a single season (27 in 1967), most consecutive wins (10 in 1967), most Winston Cup Championships (7), most career starts in Winston Cup competition (805), and most victories in the Daytona 500 (6). His 1979 victory at Daytona earned the highest ever purse for a single NASCAR race, $73,900.

Rallies

Earliest. The earliest long rally was promoted by the Parisian daily *Le Matin* in 1907 from Peking, China to Paris, over a route of about 7,500 miles. Five cars left Peking on June 10. The winner, Prince Scipione Borghese, arrived in Paris on August 10, 1907 in his 40 h.p. Itala accompanied by his chauffeur, Ettore, and Luigi Barzini.

Longest. The world's longest ever rally event was the *Singapore Airlines* London–Sydney Rally run over 19,329 miles starting from Covent Garden, Greater London, on August 14, 1977, ending at the Sydney Opera House, passing through 17 countries. It was won on September 28, 1977, by Andrew Cowan, Colin Malkin and Michael Broad in a Mercedes 280E.

The longest rally held annually is the East African Safari (first run 1953 through Kenya, Tanzania and Uganda), which is up to

3,874 miles long, as in the 17th Safari held on April 8–12, 1971. It has been won a record three times by Joginder Singh (Kenya) in 1965, 1974 and 1976.

Monte Carlo. The Monte Carlo Rally (first run 1911) has been won a record four times by Sandro Munari (Italy) in 1972, 1975–77. The smallest car to win was an 851-c.c. Saab driven by Erik Carlsson (b. Sweden, March 5, 1929) and Gunnar Häggbom of Sweden, on January 25, 1962, and by Carlsson and Gunnar Palm on January 24, 1963.

Pikes Peak Race

The Pikes Peak Auto Hill Climb, Colorado (instituted 1916) has been won by Bobby Unser 13 times between 1956 and 1974 (10 championship, 2 stock and 1 sports car title). On June 30, 1968, in the 46th race, he set an absolute record of 11 minutes 54.9 seconds in his 5,506-c.c. Chevrolet championship car over the 12.42-mile course, rising from 9,402 to 14,110 feet through 157 curves.

World Drivers' Championship

Inaugurated in 1950, the world drivers' championship is made up of specified Formula One Grand Prix races each season. Winners:

1950	Giuseppe Farina (Ita)	1957	Juan Manuel Fangio (Arg)
1951	Juan Manuel Fangio (Arg)	1958	Mike Hawthorn (GB)
1952	Alberto Ascari (Ita)	1959	Jack Brabham (Aus)
1953	Alberto Ascari (Ita)	1960	Jack Brabham (Aus)
1954	Juan Manuel Fangio (Arg)	1961	Phil Hill (US)
1955	Juan Manuel Fangio (Arg)	1962	Graham Hill (GB)
1956	Juan Manuel Fangio (Arg)	1963	Jim Clark (GB)

MOST SUCCESSFUL DRIVER: Juan Manuel Fangio (Argentina) won five World Drivers' Championships. He won 24 Grand Prix races before retiring in 1958.

World Driver's Championship (continued)

1964	John Surtees (GB)	1972	Emerson Fittipaldi (Bra)
1965	Jim Clark (GB)	1973	Jackie Stewart (GB)
1966	Jack Brabham (Aus)	1974	Emerson Fittipaldi (Bra)
1967	Denny Hulme (NZ)	1975	Niki Lauda (Aut)
1968	Graham Hill (GB)	1976	James Hunt (GB)
1969	Jackie Stewart (GB)	1977	Niki Lauda (Aut)
1970	Jochen Rindt (W Ger)	1978	Mario Andretti (US)
1971	Jackie Stewart (GB)	1979	Jody Scheckter (So Af)

Manufacturer's World Championship (Formula One)

1958	Vanwall	1966	Repco-Brabham	1974	McLaren
1959	Cooper-Climax	1967	Repco-Brabham	1975	Ferrari
1960	Cooper-Climax	1968	Lotus-Ford	1976	Ferrari
1961	Ferrari	1969	Matra-Ford	1977	Ferrari
1962	BRM	1970	Lotus-Ford	1978	J.P.S. Lotus
1963	Lotus-Climax	1971	Tyrell-Ford	1979	Ferrari
1964	Ferrari	1972	J.P.S. Lotus		
1965	Lotus-Climax	1973	J.P.S. Lotus		

Indianapolis 500

Winners since 1946 (all US except where stated):

	Driver	Car	Speed (mph)
1946	George Robson	Thorne Engineering	114.820
1947	Mauri Rose	Blue Crown Special	116.338
1948	Mauri Rose	Blue Crown Special	119.814
1949	Bill Holland	Blue Crown Special	121.327
1950	Johnny Parsons	Wynn Kurtis Kraft	124.002
1951	Lee Wallard	Belanger	126.224
1952	Troy Ruttman	Agajanian	128.922
1953	Bill Vukovich	Fuel Injection	128.740
1954	Bill Vukovich	Fuel Injection	130.840
1955	Bob Sweikert	John Zink Special	128.209
1956	Pat Flaherty	John Zink Special	128.490
1957	Sam Hanks	Belond Exhaust	135.601
1958	Jimmy Bryan	Belond A. P.	133.791
1959	Rodger Ward	Leader Card Special	135.857
1960	Jim Rathmann	Ken-Paul Special	138.767
1961	A. J. Foyt	Bowes Seal Fast	139.130
1962	Rodger Ward	Leader Card Special	140.293
1963	Parnelli Jones	Agajanian Special	143.137
1964	A. J. Foyt	Sheraton-Thompson Special	147.350
1965	Jim Clark (GB)	Lotus-Ford	150.686
1966	Graham Hill (GB)	American Red Ball	144.317
1967	A. J. Foyt	Sheraton-Thompson Special	151.207

FIRSTS AT INDY: Janet Guthrie (left) didn't win the Indianapolis 500, but she was the first woman to compete in the race. In 1977 she was unable to finish when her car broke down, but in 1978 she finished ninth. Mario Andretti (right) won the 1969 race in his "STP Oil Treatment Special."

	Driver	Car	Spe (mph)
1968	Bobby Unser	Rislone Special	152.882
1969	Mario Andretti	STP Oil Treatment Special	156.867
1970	Al Unser	Johnny Lightning Special	155.749
1971	Al Unser	Johnny Lightning Special	157.735
1972	Mark Donohue	Sunoco McLaren	162.962
1973	Gordon Johncock	STP Double Oil Filter	159.036
1974	Johnny Rutherford	McLaren	158.589
1975	Bobby Unser	Jorgensen Eagle	149.213
1976	Johnny Rutherford	Hygain McLaren	148.725
1977	A. J. Foyt	Gilmore Coyote-Foyt	161.331
1978	Al Unser	Lola-Chapparal Cosworth	161.331
1979	Rick Mears	Penske-Cosworth	158.899

Le Mans 24-Hour Race

The world's most important race for sports cars was first held in 1923. Winners since 1949 when the race was revived after the Second World War:

	Driver	Car	Speed (mph)
1949	Luigi Chinetti/Lord Peter Selsdon	Ferrari	82.27
1950	Louis Rosier/Jean-Louis Rosier	Talbot	89.73
1951	Peter Walker/Peter Whitehead	Jaguar	93.50
1952	Hermann Lang/Fritz Riess	Mercedes	96.67
1953	Anthony Rolt/Duncan Hamilton	Jaguar	105.85
1954	José Froilan Gonzalez/Maurice Trintignant	Ferrari	105.15
1955	Mike Hawthorn/Ivor Bueb	Jaguar	107.07
1956	Ron Flockhart/Ninian Sanderson	Jaguar	104.46
1957	Ron Flockhart/Ivor Bueb	Jaguar	113.85
1958	Phil Hill/Olivier Gendebien	Ferrari	106.20
1959	Roy Salvadori/Carroll Shelby	Aston Martin	112.57
1960	Paul Frère/Olivier Gendebien	Ferrari	109.19
1961	Phil Hill/Olivier Gendebien	Ferrari	115.90
1962	Phil Hill/Olivier Gendebien	Ferrari	115.24
1963	Ludovico Scarfiotti/Lorenzo Bandini	Ferrari	118.10
1964	Jean Guichet/Nino Vaccarella	Ferrari	121.55
1965	Masten Gregory/Jochen Rindt	Ferrari	121.09
1966	Bruce McLaren/Chris Amon	Ford	126.01
1967	Anthony Joseph Foyt/Dan Gurney	Ford	132.49
1968	Pedro Rodriguez/Lucien Bianchi	Ford	115.29
1969	Jackie Ickx/Jackie Oliver	Ford	125.44
1970	Hans Herrmann/Richard Attwood	Porsche	119.29
1971	Helmut Marko/Gijs van Lennep	Porsche	138.142
1972	Graham Hill/Henri Pescarolo	Matra-Simca	121.47
1973	Henri Pescarolo/Gerard Larrousse	Matra-Simca	125.68
1974	Henri Pescarolo/Gerard Larrousse	Matra-Simca	119.27
1975	Jackie Ickx/Derek Bell	Gulf Ford	118.99
1976	Jackie Ickx/Gijs van Lennep	Porsche	123.50
1977	Jackie Ickx/Jurgen Barth/Hurley Haywood	Porsche	120.95
1978	Didier Peroni/Jean-Pierre Jaussaud	Renault Alpine	130.60
1979	Klaus Ludwig/Bill and Don Whittington	Porsche	108.06

British Grand Prix

First run as the RAC Grand Prix at Brooklands in 1927, and later as the Donington Grand Prix in 1937 and 1938. The name British Grand Prix was first used in 1949. Full list of winners, circuits and distance:

	Driver	Car	Circuit	Disance (miles)	Speed (mph)
1926	Robert Sénéchal/Louis Wagner	Delage	Brooklands	287	71.61
1927	Robert Benoist	Delage	Brooklands	325	85.59
1935	Richard Shuttleworth	Alfa Romeo	Donington	306	63.97
1936	Hans Ruesch/Richard Seaman	Alfa Romeo	Donington	306	69.23
1937	Bernd Rosemeyer	Auto-Union	Donington	250	82.85
1938	Tazio Nuvolari	Auto-Union	Donington	250	80.49

MOST GRAND PRIX WINS:
Jackie Stewart (GB) is in the
lead in the Grand Prix of
Germany. He won the race
and 26 others to set the
record for most Grand Prix
victories.

British Grand Prix (continued)

	Driver	Car	Circuit	Disance (miles)	Speed (mph)
1948	Luigi Villoresi	Maserati	Silverstone	250	72.28
1949	Baron Emmanuel de Graffenried	Maserati	Silverstone	300	77.31
1950	Giuseppe Farina	Alfa Romeo	Silverstone	202	90.95
1951	Froilan Gonzalez	Ferrari	Silverstone	253	96.11
1952	Alberto Ascari	Ferrari	Silverstone	249	90.92
1953	Alberto Ascari	Ferrari	Silverstone	263	92.97
1954	Froilan Gonzalez	Ferrari	Silverstone	270	89.69
1955	Stirling Moss	Mercedes-Benz	Aintree	270	86.47
1956	Juan Manuel Fangio	Ferrari	Silverstone	300	98.65
1957	Tony Brooks/Stirling Moss	Vanwall	Aintree	270	86.80
1958	Peter Collins	Ferrari	Silverstone	225	102.05
1959	Jack Brabham	Cooper-Climax	Aintree	225	89.88
1960	Jack Brabham	Cooper-Climax	Silverstone	231	108.69
1961	Wolfgang von Trips	Ferrari	Aintree	225	83.91
1962	Jim Clark	Lotus-Climax	Aintree	225	92.25
1963	Jim Clark	Lotus-Climax	Silverstone	246	107.75
1964	Jim Clark	Lotus-Climax	Brands Hatch	212	94.14
1965	Jim Clark	Lotus-Climax	Silverstone	240	112.02
1966	Jack Brabham	Repco Brabham	Brands Hatch	212	95.48
1967	Jim Clark	Lotus-Ford	Silverstone	240	117.64
1968	Joseph Siffert	Lotus-Ford	Brands Hatch	212	104.83
1969	Jackie Stewart	Matra-Ford	Silverstone	246	127.25
1970	Jochen Rindt	Lotus-Ford	Brands Hatch	212	108.69
1971	Jackie Stewart	Tyrell-Ford	Silverstone	199	130.48
1972	Emerson Fittipaldi	JPS-Ford	Brands Hatch	201	112.06
1973	Peter Revson	McLaren-Ford	Silverstone	196	131.75
1974	Jody Scheckter	Tyrell-Ford	Brands Hatch	199	115.73
1975	Emerson Fittipaldi	McLaren-Ford	Silverstone	164	120.01
1976	Niki Lauda	Ferrari	Brands Hatch	198	114.24
1977	James Hunt	McLaren-Ford	Silverstone	199	130.36
1978	Carlos Reutemann	Ferrari	Brands Hatch	199	116.61
1979	'Clay' Regazzoni	Saudia-Williams	Silverstone	199	138.80

Monte Carlo Rally

1911	Henri Rougier	Turcat-Mery 25hp
1912	J. Beutler	Berliet 16hp
1924	Jean Ledure	Bignan 2 litre
1925	Francois Repusseau	Renault 40 CV
1926	Hon Victor Bruce	AC Bristol
1927	Lefebvre	Amilcar 1100cc
1928	Jacques Bignan	Fiat 990cc
1929	Dr Sprenger Van Eijk	Graham-Paige 4.7 litre
1930	Hector Petit	Licorne 904cc
1931	Donald Healey	Invicta 4.5 litre
1932	M. Vasselle	Hotchkiss 2.5 litre
1933	M. Vasselle	Hotchkiss 3.5 litre
1934	Gas	Hotchkiss 3.5 litre
1935	Christian Lahaye	Renault Neryasport 5.6 litre
1936	I. Zamfirescu	Ford 3.6 litre
1937	René le Begue	Delahaye 3.6 litre
1938	Bakker Shut	Ford 3.6 litre
	Jean Trevoux	Hotchkiss 3.5 litre
1939	Paul	Delahaye 3.6 litre
1949	Jean Trevoux	Hotchkiss 3.5 litre
1950	Marcel Becquart	Hotchkiss 3.5 litre
1951	Jean Trevoux	Delahaye 4.6 litre
1952	Sidney Allard	Allard P2 4.4 litre
1953	Maurice Gatsonides	Ford Zephyr 2.3 litre
1954	Louis Chiron	Lancia-Aurelia 2.5 litre
1955	Per Malling	Sunbeam-Talbot 2.3 litre
1956	Ronnie Adams	Jaguar Mk VII 3.4 litre
1957	No rally held due to Suez Crisis	
1958	Guy Monraisse	Renault Dauphine 845cc
1959	Paul Coltelloni	Citroën ID 19 1.9 litre
1960	Walter Schock	Mercedes 220 SE
1961	Maurice Martin	Panhard PL 17 848cc
1962	Erik Carlsson/Gunnar Haggbom	Saab 96 848cc
1963	Erik Carlsson/Gunnar Palm	Saab 96 848cc
1964	Paddy Hopkirk/Henry Liddon	Mini-Cooper 'S' 1071cc
1965	Timo Makinen/Paul Easter	Mini-Cooper 'S' 1275cc
1966	Pauli Toivonen/Ensio Mikander	Citroën DS 21
1967	Rauno Aaltonen/Henry Liddon	Mini-Cooper 'S' 1275cc
1968	Vic Elford/David Stone	Porsche 911T
1969	Bjorn Waldegaard/Lars Helmer	Porsche 911
1970	Bjorn Waldegaard/Lars Helmer	Porsche 911 S
1971	Ove Andersson/David Stone	Alpine Renault A110
1972	Sandro Munari/Mario Manucci	Lancia Fulvia 1.6
1973	Jean-Claude Andruet/'Biche'	Alpine Renault A110
1974	No rally due to fuel crisis	
1975	Sandro Munari/Mario Manucci	Lancia Stratos
1976	Sandro Munari/Silvio Maiga	Lancia Stratos

TOAST OF THE TOWN: Italy's Sandro Munari (right) has won the famous Monte Carlo Rally a record four times. He and partner Silvio Maiga are enjoying a champagne celebration after their victory in 1976.

1977	Sandro Munari/Mario Manucci	Lancia Stratos
1978	Jean-Pierre Nicolas/Vincent Laverne	Porsche Carrera
1979	Bernard Darniche/Alain Mahe	Lancia Stratos

(Co-drivers' names included after 1962 when special stages and pace notes used for first time)

World Rallying Championship

For makes of car.

1968	Ford GB		1972	Lancia		1976	Lancia
1969	Ford Europe		1973	Renault Alpine		1977	Fiat
1970	Porsche		1974	Lancia		1978	Fiat
1971	Renault Alpine		1975	Lancia		1979	Ford

BADMINTON

Origins. A game similar to badminton was played in China in the 2nd millennium B.C. The modern game was devised *c.* 1863 at Badminton Hall in Avon, England, the seat of the Dukes of Beaufort. The oldest club is the Newcastle Badminton Club, England, formed as the Armstrong College Club, on January 24, 1900.

Most Titles Won

The record number of All-England Championship (instituted 1899) titles won is 21 by Sir George Thomas (1881–1972) between 1903 and 1928. The record for men's singles is 8 by Rudy Hartono of Indonesia (1968–74, 76). The most, including doubles, by women

BIRD WATCHER: Noriko Takagi (Japan) won the quickest victory ever when she needed only 9 minutes to beat her opponent in 1969 Uber Cup competition. Her victory helped Japan win the cup that year.

MOST WINS:
Judy Hashman (US) smashes her way to the 1966 title. Her 10 singles wins are a record for both sexes.

is 17, a record shared by Muriel Lucas (1899–1910) and Mrs. G. C. K. Hashman (*née* Judy Devlin) (US), whose wins came from 1954 to 1967, including a record 10 singles titles.

Shortest Game

In the 1969 Uber Cup in Djakarta, Indonesia, Miss N. Takagi (Japan) beat Miss P. Tumengkol in 9 minutes.

Marathons

The longest singles match is 73 hours 20 minutes by Richard Cuthbert at Queen Elizabeth's Grammar School, Horncastle, Lincolnshire, England, April 23–26, 1979. Christopher Berry, Stephen Crilley, Christopher Southall, and Gary Wemyss played doubles for 60 hours 36 minutes at Arnold School, Blackpool, Lancashire, England, August 26–28, 1979.

Longest Hit

Frank Rugani drove a shuttlecock 79 feet 8½ inches in indoor tests at San Jose, California, on February 29, 1964.

Thomas Cup

First held in 1948–49, the Thomas Cup is the international men's team championship, and is contested every three years.

1948–49	Malaya	1960–61	Indonesia	1972–73	Indonesia
1951–52	Malaya	1963–64	Indonesia	1975–76	Indonesia
1954–55	Malaya	1966–67	Malaysia	1978–79	Indonesia
1957–58	Indonesia	1969–70	Indonesia		

Uber Cup

First held in 1956–57, the Uber Cup is the international women's team championship, and is held every three years.

1956–57	US	1965–66	Japan	1974–75	Indonesia
1959–60	US	1968–69	Japan	1977–78	Japan
1962–63	US	1971–72	Japan		

World Championships

The first ever world championships were held in 1977 and are intended to be held every three years. Winners were:

Men's Singles: Flemming Delfs (Den)
Women's Singles: Lene Köppen (Den)
Men's Doubles: Johan Wahjudi & Tjun-Tjun (Ind)
Women's Doubles: Etsuko Tuganoo & Emiko Ueno (Jap)
Mixed Doubles: Steen Skovgaard & Lene Köppen (Den)

All-England Championships

Singles winners since 1947:

MEN		WOMEN	
1947	Conny Jepsen (Swe)	1947	Marie Ussing (Den)
1948	Jorn Skaarup (Den)	1948	Kirsten Thorndahl (Den)
1949	David Freeman (US)	1949	Aase Schiött Jacobsen (Den)
1950	Wong Peng Soon (Mal)	1950	Tonny Ahm (Den)
1951	Wong Peng Soon (Mal)	1951	Aase Schiött Jacobsen (Den)
1952	Wong Peng Soon (Mal)	1952	Tony Ahm (Den)
1953	Eddie Choong (Mal)	1953	Marie Ussing (Den)
1954	Eddie Choong (Mal)	1954	Judy Devlin (US)
1955	Wong Peng Soon (Mal)	1955	Margaret Varner (US)
1956	Eddie Choong (Mal)	1956	Margaret Varner (US)
1957	Eddie Choong (Mal)	1957	Judy Devlin (US)
1958	Erland Kops (Den)	1958	Judy Devlin (US)
1959	Tan Joe Hok (Ind)	1959	Heather Ward (Eng)
1960	Erland Kops (Den)	1960	Judy Devlin (US)
1961	Erland Kops (Den)	1961	Judy Hashman (Devlin) (US)
1962	Erland Kops (Den)	1962	Judy Hashman (US)
1963	Erland Kops (Den)	1963	Judy Hashman (US)
1964	Knud Nielsen (Den)	1964	Judy Hashman (US)
1965	Erland Kops (Den)	1965	Ursula Smith (Eng)
1966	Tan Aik Huang (Mal)	1966	Judy Hashman (US)
1967	Erland Kops (Den)	1967	Judy Hashman (US)
1968	Rudy Hartono (Ind)	1968	Eva Twedberg (Swe)
1969	Rudy Hartono (Ind)	1969	Hiroe Yuki (Jap)
1970	Rudy Hartono (Ind)	1970	Etsuko Takenaka (Jap)
1971	Rudy Hartono (Ind)	1971	Eva Twedberg (Swe)
1972	Rudy Hartono (Ind)	1972	Noriko Nakayama (Jap)
1973	Rudy Hartono (Ind)	1973	Margaret Beck (Eng)
1974	Rudy Hartono (Ind)	1974	Hiroe Yuki (Jap)
1975	Svend Pri (Den)	1975	Hiroe Yuki (Jap)
1976	Rudy Hartono (Ind)	1976	Gillian Gilks (Eng)
1977	Flemming Delfs (Den)	1977	Hiroe Yuki (Jap)
1978	Liem Swie King (Ind)	1978	Gillian Gilks (Eng)
1979	Liem Swie King (Ind)	1979	Lene Köppen (Den)

BASEBALL

Origins. The Reverend Thomas Wilson, of Maidstone, Kent, England, wrote disapprovingly, in 1700, of baseball being played on Sundays. It is also referred to in *Northanger Abbey* by Jane Austen, *c.* 1798.

SLUGGING IT OUT: (Left), Babe Ruth's .690 lifetime slugging percentage is still tops in the major leagues. His 119 extra-base hits and 457 total bases in 1921 are still season records. Hank Aaron (right) holds career records for most games played and most runs batted in, but his most notable accomplishment was breaking Babe Ruth's lifetime home run mark.

Earliest Games

The earliest game on record under the Cartwright rules was on June 19, 1846, in Hoboken, N.J., where the "New York Nine" defeated the Knickerbockers 23 to 1 in 4 innings. The earliest all-professional team was the Cincinnati Red Stockings in 1869, who won 56 and tied one game that season.

Home Runs

Henry L. (Hank) Aaron (b. February 5, 1934) broke the major league record set by George H. (Babe) Ruth (1895–1948) of 714 home runs in a lifetime when he hit No. 715 on April 8, 1974. Between 1954 and 1974 he hit 733 home runs in the National League. In 1975, he switched over to the American League and in that year and 1976, when he finally retired, he hit 22 more, bringing his lifetime total to 755, the major league record.

The Japanese slugger Sadaharu Oh (b. May 20, 1940), of the Yomiuri Giants, has hit 838 home runs in his career through the 1979 season.

A North American record of almost 800 in a lifetime has been claimed for Josh Gibson (1911–47), mostly for the Homestead Grays of the Negro National League, who was elected in 1972 to the Baseball Hall of Fame in Cooperstown, New York. Gibson is said to have hit 75 round-trippers in one season, in 1931, but no official records were kept.

The most officially recorded home runs hit by a professional player in the United States in one season is 72, by Joe Bauman, of the Rosewell, New Mexico team, a minor league club, in 1954. The major league record is 61 by Roger Maris, of the New York Yankees, in 1961.

The most home runs in a professional game is 8, by Justin (Nig)

Clarke of the Corsicana, Texas, minor league team, on June 15, 1902. The major league record is four, by several players.

Frank Robinson (b. August 31, 1935) hit home runs in the most major league ballparks—at least one in 32 different stadiums during regular season games from 1956–1977.

The longest home run ever measured was one of 618 feet by Roy Edward "Dizzy" Carlyle (1900–56) in a minor league game at Emeryville Ball Park, California, on July 4, 1929. Babe Ruth hit a 587-foot homer in a Boston Red Sox vs. New York Giants game at Tampa, Florida, on April 4, 1919. The longest measured home run in a major league game (regular season) is 565 feet, by Mickey Mantle (b. October 20, 1931) of the New York Yankees. He hit it on April 17, 1953, at Griffith Stadium, in Washington, D.C.

Fastest Pitcher

The fastest pitcher in the world is L. Nolan Ryan, then of the California Angels, who, on August 20, 1974, in Anaheim Stadium, was electronically clocked at a speed of 100.9 m.p.h.

Longest Throw

The longest throw of a 5–5¼-oz. baseball is 445 feet 10 inches by Glen Gorbous (b. Canada) on August 1, 1957. Mildred "Babe" Didrikson (later Mrs. George Zaharias) (1914–56) threw a ball 296 feet at Jersey City, New Jersey, on July 25, 1931.

Do-Nothing Record

Toby Harrah of the Texas Rangers (AL) played an entire doubleheader at shortstop on June 26, 1976, without having a chance to make any fielding plays, assists or putouts.

POWER TO SPARE: Right-handed flamethrower Nolan Ryan (left) had his fastball measured at 100.9 m.p.h. He pitched in 1980 for the Houston Astros at a reported $1 million per year. Mickey Mantle (right) stunned his Yankee teammates with a measured 565-foot homer in Washington, D.C. The switch-hitter performed well under pressure, setting lifetime World Series marks for runs scored, runs batted in, and home runs.

Do-Everything Record

Two major league ballplayers, Bert Campaneris (b. March 12, 1942) and Cesar Tovar (b. July 3, 1940), have the distinction of playing each of the nine field positions in a single major league game. Campaneris did it first, on September 8, 1965, when his team, the Kansas City A's, announced he would. He played one inning at each position, including the full eighth inning as a pitcher and gave up just one run. Tovar duplicated the feat on September 22, 1968, when he played for the Minnesota Twins. He pitched a scoreless first inning, and retired the first batter, none other than Campaneris.

Hit by Pitch

National League infielder Ron Hunt led the league in getting hit by pitched balls for a record 7 consecutive years. He was hit a record 243 times in his 12-year career (1963–74).

Fastest Base Runner

Ernest Evar Swanson (1902–73) took only 13.3 seconds to circle the bases at Columbus, Ohio, in 1932, averaging 18.45 m.p.h.

Youngest and Oldest Players

The youngest major league player of all time was the Cincinnati pitcher Joe Nuxhall, who started his career in June, 1944, aged 15 years 10 months 11 days.

Leroy Satchel Paige pitched three scoreless innings for the Kansas City Athletics at age 59 in 1965. Baseball's color barrier had kept him out of the major leagues until 1948, when he was a 42-year-old "rookie," and his record of 6 wins and 1 loss helped the Cleveland Indians win the pennant. His birthday is listed as July 7, 1906, but many believed he was born earlier.

LITTLEST MAJOR LEAGUER: In their quest for a leadoff base runner, the St. Louis Browns sent 3-foot-7-inch Eddie Gaedel to the plate as a pinch hitter in the first inning of the second game of a doubleheader on August 19, 1951. The 26-year-old midget walked on four pitches. Nonetheless, the hapless Browns were unable to score against the Detroit Tigers that inning.

LONGEST HITTING STREAK: Three-time MVP Joe DiMaggio (Yankees) batted safely in 56 consecutive games from May 15 to July 16, 1941. Here he is stroking a ninth-inning home run in Chicago on June 7, 1939.

Shortest and Tallest Players

The shortest major league player was surely Eddie Gaedel, a 3-foot-7-inch, 65-pound midget who pinch hit for the St. Louis Browns on August 19, 1951. Wearing number ⅛, the batter with the world's smallest strike zone walked on four pitches. Following the game, major league rules were hastily rewritten to prevent the recurrence of such an affair.

Fastball pitcher James Rodney Richard (b. March 7, 1950) of the Houston Astros is reportedly the tallest major league ballplayer at 6 feet 8½ inches.

Major League All-Time Records

(including 1979 season)

Individual Batting

Highest percentage, lifetime (5,000 at-bats)
.367 Tyrus R. Cobb, Det. AL, 1905–26; Phil. AL, 1927–28

Highest percentage, season (500 at-bats)
(Leader in each league)
.438 Hugh Duffy, Bos. NL, 1894
.422 Napoleon Lajoie, Phil. AL, 1901

Most games played
3,298 Henry L. Aaron, Mil. NL, 1954–65; Atl. NL, 1966–74; Mil. AL, 1975–76

Most consecutive games played
2,130 Henry Louis Gehrig, N.Y. AL, June 1, 1925 through Apr. 30, 1939

Most runs, lifetime
2,244 Tyrus R. Cobb, Det. AL, 1905–1926; Phil. AL, 1927–28; 24 years

Most runs batted in, season
190 Lewis R. (Hack) Wilson, Chi. NL, 155 games, 1930

Most runs batted in, game
12 James L. Bottomley, St. L. NL, Sept. 16, 1924

Most runs batted in, inning
7 Edward Cartwright, St. L. AA, Sept. 23, 1890

Most base hits
4,191 Tyrus R. Cobb, Det. AL, 1905–26; Phil. AL, 1927–28; 24 years

Most runs, season
196 William R. Hamilton, Phil. NL, 131 games, 1894

Most runs batted in, lifetime
2,297 Henry L. Aaron, Mil. NL, 1954–65; p. 36 Atl. NL, 1966–74; Mil. AL, 1975–76

Most base hits, season
257 George H. Sisler, St. L. AL, 154 games, 1920

Most hits in succession
12 M. Frank (Pinky) Higgins, Bos. AL, June 19–21 (4 games), 1938; Walter Dropo, Det. AL, July 14, July 15, 2 games, 1952

Most base hits, consecutive, game
7 Wilbert Robinson, Balt. NL, June 10, 1892, 1st game (7-ab), 6-1b, 1-2b

Renaldo Stennett, Pitt. NL, Sept. 16, 1975 (7-ab), 4-1b, 2-2b, 1-3b

Cesar Gutierrez, Det. AL, June 21, 1970, 2nd game (7-ab) 6-1b, 1-2b (extra-inning game)

Most consecutive games batted safely, season
56 Joseph P. DiMaggio, N.Y. AL (91 hits—16-2b, 4-3b, 15 hr), May 15 to July 16, 1941

Most long hits, season
119 George H. (Babe) Ruth, N.Y. AL (44-2b, 16-3b, 59 hr), 152 games, 1921

Most total bases, lifetime
6,856 Henry L. Aaron, Mil. NL, 1954–65; Atl. NL, 1966–74; Mil. AL, 1975–76

Most total bases, season
457 George H. (Babe) Ruth, N.Y. AL, 152 g. (85 on 1b, 88 on 2b, 48 on 3b, 236 on hr), 1921

Most total bases, game
18 Joseph W. Adcock, Mil. NL (1-2b, 4-hr), July 31, 1954

Sluggers' percentage
(The percentage is obtained by dividing the "times at bat" into total bases.)
Highest slugging percentage, lifetime
.690 George H. (Babe) Ruth, Bos.-N.Y. AL, 1914–34; Bos. NL, 1935

Triple-Crown winners
(Most times leading league in batting, runs batted in and home runs.)
2 Rogers Hornsby, St. L. NL, 1922, 1925
Theodore S. Williams, Bos. AL, 1942, 1947

Most-one-base-hits (singles), season
202 William H. Keeler, Balt. NL, 128 games, 1898

Most two-base hits, season
67 Earl W. Webb, Bos. AL, 151 games, 1931

Most three-base hits, season
36 J. Owen Wilson, Pitts. NL, 152 games, 1912

Most home runs, season
61 Roger E. Maris, N.Y. AL (162-game schedule) (30 home, 31 away), 161 gs. 1961
60 George H. (Babe) Ruth, N.Y. AL (154-game schedule) (28 home, 32 away), 151 gs, 1927

HIT MEN: Hack Wilson (left) set a major league mark with 190 runs batted in for the Chicago Cubs in 1930. His 56 home runs in the same season still stand as the National League record. Ty Cobb (right) collected 4,191 hits in his 24-year career for a lifetime batting average of .367—records that have stood for over 50 years. The Detroit Tiger star also stole home a record 35 times.

Most home runs lifetime
755 Henry L. Aaron, Mil. NL, 1954 (13), 1955 (27), 1956 (26), 1957 (44), 1958 (30), 1959 (39), 1960 (40), 1961 (34), 1962 (45), 1963 (44), 1964 (24), 1965 (32); Atl. NL, 1966 (44), 1967 (39), 1968 (29), 1969 (44), 1970 (38), 1971 (47), 1972 (34), 1973 (40), 1974 (20); Mil. AL, 1975 (12), 1976 (10)

Most home runs, bases filled, lifetime
23 Henry Louis Gehrig, N.Y. AL, 1927–1938

Most home runs with bases filled, season
5 Ernest Banks, Chi. NL, May 11, 19, July 17 (1st game). Aug. 2, Sept. 19, 1955
James E. Gentile, Balt. AL, May 9 (2), July 2, 7, Sept. 22, 1961

Most home runs, with bases filled, same game
2 Anthony M. Lazzeri, N.Y. AL, May 24, 1936
James R. Tabor, Bos. AL (2nd game), July 4, 1939
Rudolph York, Bos. AL, July 27, 1946
James E. Gentile, Balt. AL, May 9, 1961 (consecutive at-bats)
Tony L. Cloninger, Atl. NL, July 3, 1966
James T. Northrup, Det. AL, June 24, 1968 (consecutive at-bats)
Frank Robinson, Balt. AL, June 26, 1970 (consecutive at-bats)

Most bases on balls, game
6 James E. Foxx, Bos. AL, June 16, 1938

Most bases on balls, season
170 George H. (Babe) Ruth, N.Y. AL, 152 games, 1923

Most home runs, one month
18 Rudolph York, Det. AL, Aug. 1937

Most consecutive games hitting home runs
8 R. Dale Long, Pitt. NL, May 19–28, 1956

Most home runs, one doubleheader
5 Stanley F. Musial, St. L. NL, 1st game (3), 2nd game (2), May 2, 1954
Nathan Colbert, S.D. NL, 1st game (2), 2nd game (3), Aug. 1, 1972

Most hits, pinch-hitter, lifetime
147 Manuel R. Mota, S.F. NL, 1962; Pitt. NL, 1963–1968; Mont. NL, 1969; L.A. NL, 1969–1979

Most consecutive pinch hits, lifetime
9 David E. Philley, Phil. NL, Sept. 9, 11, 12, 13, 19, 20, 27, 28, 1958; Apr. 16, 1959

Most home runs, pinch-hitter, consecutive plate appearances
3 Del Unser, Phil. NL, June 30, July 5, 10, 1979

Most Valuable Player, as voted by Baseball Writers Association
3 times James E. Foxx, Phil. AL, 1932, 33, 38
Joseph P. DiMaggio, N.Y. AL, 1939, 41, 47
Stanley F. Musial, St. L. NL, 1943, 46, 48
Lawrence P. (Yogi) Berra, N.Y. AL, 1951, 54, 55
Roy Campanella, Bklyn. NL, 1951, 53, 55
Mickey C. Mantle, N.Y. AL, 1956, 57, 62

MAN OF STEAL: Lou Brock (St. Louis Cardinals) concluded his major league career in 1979 by setting a lifetime mark of 938 stolen bases. In 1974, Brock set a season record of 118 successful steals. The classy outfielder also has the highest lifetime World Series batting average (.391) with 34 hits in 21 games during three World Series.

Base Running

Most stolen bases, lifetime
938 Louis C. Brock, Chi.-St. L. NL,
1961–79

Most stolen bases, season since 1900
118 Louis C. Brock, St. L. NL, 153
games, 1974

Most stolen bases, game
7 George F. (Piano Legs) Gore, Chi.
NL, June 25, 1881
William R. (Sliding Billy) Hamilton,
Phil. NL, 2nd game, 8 inn., Aug.
31, 1894

Most times stealing home, game
2 by 9 players

Most times stealing home, lifetime
35 Tyrus R. Cobb, Det.-Phil. AL, 1905–
28

**Fewest times caught stealing season (50 +
attempts)**
2 Max Carey, Pitt. NL, 1922 (53 atts.)

Pitching

Most games, lifetime
1,070 J. Hoyt Wilhelm, N.Y.-St. L.-Atl.-
Chi. L.A. (448) NL, 1952–57,
69–72; Clev.-Balt.-Chi.-Cal.
(622) AL, 1957–69

Most games, season
106 Mike Marshall, L.A. NL, 1974

Most complete games, lifetime
751 Denton T. (Cy) Young, Clev.-St.
L.-Bos. NL (428); Bos.-Clev. AL
(323), 1890–1911

Most complete games, season
74 William H. White, Cin. NL,
1879

Most innings pitched, game
26 Leon J. Cadore, Bklyn. NL, May
1, 1920
Joseph Oeschger, Bos. NL, May 1,
1920

Lowest earned run average, season
0.90 Ferdinand M. Schupp, N.Y. NL,
1916 (140 inn)
1.01 Hubert B. (Dutch) Leonard, Bos.
AL, 1914 (222 inn)
1.12 Robert Gibson, St. L. NL, 1968
(305 inn)

Most games won, lifetime
511 Denton T. (Cy) Young, Clev. NL
(239) 1890–98; St. L. NL 1899–
1900; Bos. AL (193) 1901–08;
Clev. AL (29) 1909–11; Bos. NL
(4) 1911

Most games won, season
60 Charles Radbourne, Providence
NL, 1884

Most consecutive games won, lifetime
24 Carl O. Hubbell, N.Y. NL, 1936
(16); 1937 (8)

**MOST PITCHING APPEARANCES:
Knuckleballer Hoyt Wilhelm pitched
in 1,070 games. In his first major
league at bat, Wilhelm hit a home
run—the only one of his career.
His second at bat was his only
triple.**

Most consecutive games won, season
19 Timothy J. Keefe, N.Y. NL, 1888
Richard W. Marquard, N.Y. NL,
1912

Most shutout games, season
16 George W. Bradley, St. L. NL,
1876
Grover C. Alexander, Phil. NL,
1916

Most shutout games, lifetime
113 Walter P. Johnson, Wash. AL, 21
years, 1907–27

Most consecutive shutout games, season
6 Donald S. Drysdale, L.A. NL, May
14, 18, 22, 26, 31, June 4, 1968

Most consecutive shutout innings
58 Donald S. Drysdale, L.A. NL, May
14–June 8, 1968

Most strikeouts, lifetime
3,508 Walter P. Johnson, Wash. AL,
1907–27

Most strikeouts, season
505 Matthew Kilroy, Balt. AA, 1886
(Distance 50 ft)
383 L. Nolan Ryan, Cal. AL, 1973 (Distance 60 ft 6 in.)

Most strikeouts, game (9 inn) since 1900:
19 Steven N. Carlton, St. L. NL vs.
N.Y., Sept. 15, 1969 (lost)
G. Thomas Seaver, N.Y. NL vs.
S.D., Apr. 22, 1970
L. Nolan Ryan, Cal. AL vs. Bos.,
Aug. 12, 1974

Most strikeouts, extra-inning game
  21 Thomas E. Cheney, Wash. AL vs.
      Balt. (16 inns), Sept. 12, 1962
      (night)

Most no-hit games, lifetime
  4   Sanford Koufax, L.A. NL, 1962–
      63–64–65
      L. Nolan Ryan, Cal. AL, 1973
      (2)-74-75

Most consecutive no-hit games
  2   John S. Vander Meer, Cin. NL,
      June 11–15, 1938

Perfect game—9 innings

  1880 John Lee Richmond Worcester
        vs. Cleve. NL, June 12 ... 1–0
        John M. Ward, Prov. vs. Buff.
        NL, June 17 AM 5–0

  1904 Denton T. (Cy) Young, Bos. vs.
        Phil. AL, May 5 3–0

  1908 Adrian C. Joss, Clev. vs. Chi. AL,
        Oct. 2 1–0

  †1917 Ernest G. Shore, Bos. vs. Wash.
        AL, June 23 (1st g.) 4–0

  1922 C.C. Robertson, Chi. vs. Det. AL,
        April 30 2–0

  **1956 Donald J. Larson, N.Y. AL vs.
        Bklyn. NL, Oct. 8 2–0

  1964 James P. Bunning, Phil. NL vs.
        N.Y., June 21 (1st g.) 6–0

  1965 Sanford Koufax, L.A. NL vs.
        Chi., Sept. 9 1–0

  1968 James A. Hunter, Oak. AL vs.
        Minn., May 8 4–0

Special mention
  1959 Harvey Haddix, Jr., Pitt. vs Mil.
        NL, May 26, pitched 12 "per-
        fect" innings, allowed hit in
        13th and lost.

† Starting pitcher, "Babe" Ruth, was
banished from game by Umpire Owens
after giving first batter, Morgan, a base
on balls. Shore relieved and while he
pitched to second batter, Morgan was caught
stealing. Shore then retired next 26 batters to complete "perfect" game.

** World Series game.

Club Batting

Highest percentage season
.343 Phil. NL, 132 games, 1894

Highest percentage, season since 1900
.319 N.Y. NL, 154 games, 1930

Most runs, one club, game
  36 Chi. NL (36) vs. Louisville (7), June
      29, 1897

Most runs, one club, inning
  18 Chi. NL, 7th inning, Sept. 6, 1883

Most runs, both clubs, inning
  19 Wash. AA (14), Balt. (5), 1st inn.,
      June 17, 1891
      Clev. AL (13), Bos. (6), 8th inn.,
      April 10, 1977

Most hits, one club, 9 inning game
  36 Phil. NL, Aug. 17, 1894

Most hits, one club, inning
  18 Chi. NL, 7th inning, Sept. 6, 1883

**FALL GUYS: Three-time MVP Yogi Berra (left) played in a record 14
World Series, during which the all-star catcher collected a career-high 71
hits. Whitey Ford (right), Berra's battery mate with the Yankees, pitched
in 11 World Series, also setting career records for the Fall Classic in
victories (10) and strikeouts (94).**

HOME RUN SWING: Reggie Jackson (Yankees) hit three first-pitch home runs in the sixth game of the 1977 World Series to tie Babe Ruth's single-game record. Jackson's 5 homers and 10 runs were records for one series.

Fewest hits, both clubs, game
   1 Chi. NL (0) vs. L.A. (1), Sept. 9, 1965

Most home runs, one club, season (154-game schedule)
221 N.Y. NL, 155 games, 1947
       Cin. NL, 155 games, 1956

Most home runs, one club, season (162-game schedule)
240 N.Y. AL, 163 games, 1961

Fewest home runs (135 or more games), one club, season
   3 Chi. AL, 156 games, 1908

Most stolen bases (1900 to date), one club, season
347 N.Y. NL, 154 games, 1911

Most stolen bases, one club, inning
   8 Wash. AL, 1st inning, July 19, 1915
      Phil. NL, 9th inning, 1st g., July 7, 1919

Club Fielding

Highest percentage, one club, season
.985 Balt. AL, 1964

Fewest errors, season
 95 Balt. AL, 163 games, 1964
      Cin. NL, 162 games, 1977

Most double plays, club, season
217 Phil. AL, 154 games, 1949

Most double plays, club, game
   7 N.Y. Al, Aug. 14, 1942
      Houst. NL, May 4, 1969

General Club Records

Shortest and longest game by time
51 minutes N.Y. NL (6), Phil. (1), 1st g., Sept. 28, 1919
7:23 S.F. NL (8) at N.Y. (6) 23 inn., 2nd g., May 31, 1964

Longest 9-inning game
4:18 S.F. NL (7) at L.A. (8), Oct. 2, 1962

Fewest times shutout, season
0 Bos. NL, 1894 (132 g.)
Phil. NL, 1894 (127 g.)
N.Y. AL, 1932 (155 g.)

Most consecutive innings shutting out opponents.
56 Pitt. NL, June 1–9, 1903

Highest percentage games won, season
.798 Chi. NL (won 67, lost 17), 1880
.763 Chi. NL (won 116, lost 36), 1906
.721 Clev. AL (won 111, lost 43), 1954

Most games won, season (154-game schedule)
116 Chi. NL, 1906

Most consecutive games won, season
26 N.Y. NL, Sept. 7 (1st g.) to Sept. 30 (1 tie), 1916

Most pitchers used in a game, 9 innings, one club
9 St. L. AL vs. Chi., Oct. 2, 1949

Managers' consecutive championship records
5 years Charles D. (Casey) Stengel, N.Y. AL, 1949–50–51–52–53

World Series Records

Most series played
14 Lawrence P. (Yogi) Berra, N.Y. AL, 1947, 49–53, 55–58, 60–63

Highest batting percentage (20 g. min.), total series
.391 Louis C. Brock, St. L. NL, 1964, 67–68 (g-21, ab-87, h-34)

Highest batting percentage, 4 or more games, one series
.625 4-game series, George H. (Babe) Ruth, N.Y. AL, 1928

Most runs, total series
42 Mickey C. Mantle, N.Y. AL, 1951–53, 55–58, 60–64

Most runs, one series
10 Reginald M. Jackson, N.Y. AL, 1977

Most runs batted in, total series
40 Mickey C. Mantle, N.Y. AL, 1951–53, 55–58, 60–64

Most runs batted in, game
6 Robert C. Richardson, N.Y. AL, (4) 1st inn., (2) 4th inn., Oct. 8, 1960

Most runs batted in, consecutive times at bat
7 James L. (Dusty) Rhodes, N.Y. NL, first 4 times at bat, 1954

Most base hits, total series
71 Lawrence P. (Yogi) Berra, N.Y. AL, 1947, 49–53, 55–58, 60–61

Most home runs, total series
18 Mickey C. Mantle, N.Y. AL, 1952 (2), 53 (2), 55, 56 (3), 57, 58 (2), 60 (3), 63, 64 (3)

Most home runs, one series
5 Reginald M. Jackson, N.Y. AL, 1977

Most home runs, game
3 George H. (Babe) Ruth, N.Y. AL, Oct. 6, 1926; Oct. 9, 1928
Reginald M. Jackson, N.Y. AL, 1977

Pitcher's Records

Pitching in most series
11 Edward C. (Whitey) Ford, N.Y. AL, 1950, 53, 55–58, 60–64

Most victories, total series
10 Edward C. (Whitey) Ford, N.Y. AL, 1950 (1), 55 (2), 56 (1), 57 (1), 57 (1), 60 (2), 61 (2), 62 (1)

All victories, no defeats
6 Vernon L. (Lefty) Gomez, N.Y. AL, 1932 (1), 36 (2), 37 (2), 38 (1)

Most games won, one series
3 games in 5-game series
Christy Mathewson, N.Y. NL, 1905
J.W. Coombs, Phil. AL, 1910
Many others won 3 games in series of more games.

Most shutout games, total series
4 Christy Mathewson, N.Y. NL, 1905 (3), 1913

Most shutout games, one series
3 Christy Mathewson, N.Y. NL, 1905

Most strikeouts, one pitcher, total series
94 Edward C. (Whitey) Ford, N.Y. AL, 1950, 53, 55–58, 60–64

Most strikeouts, one series
23 in 4 games Sanford Koufax, L.A. NL, 1963

18 in 5 games Christy Mathewson, N.Y. NL, 1905

20 in 6 games C. A. (Chief) Bender, Phil. AL, 1911

35 in 7 games Robert Gibson, St. L. NL, 1968

28 in 8 games W. H. Dinneen, Bos. AL, 1903

Most strikeouts, one pitcher, game
17 Robert Gibson, St. L. NL, Oct. 2, 1968

Most Series Won
22 New York AL, 1923, 1927, 1928, 1932, 1936, 1937, 1938, 1939, 1941, 1943, 1947, 1949, 1950, 1951, 1952, 1953, 1956, 1958, 1961, 1962, 1977, 1978

World Series Attendance

The World Series record attendance is 420,784 (6 games with total receipts of $2,626,973.44) when the Los Angeles Dodgers beat the Chicago White Sox 4 games to 2, October 1–8, 1959.

The single game record is 92,706 for the fifth game (receipts $552,774.77) at the Memorial Coliseum, Los Angeles, on October 6, 1959.

Major League Pennant Winners

The National League was founded in 1876 and the American League in 1901. In 1903 and each season since 1905 the winners of these two leagues have met in the World Series.

Winners of these major leagues since 1901, with the World Series winners identified by (WS) have been:

	National League	American League
1901	Pittsburgh Pirates	Chicago White Sox
1902	Pittsburgh Pirates	Philadelphia Athletics
1903	Pittsburgh Pirates	Boston Red Sox (WS)
1904	New York Giants	Boston Red Sox
1905	New York Giants (WS)	Philadelphia Athletics
1906	Chicago Cubs	Chicago White Sox (WS)
1907	Chicago Cubs (WS)	Detroit Tigers
1908	Chicago Cubs (WS)	Detroit Tigers
1909	Pittsburgh Pirates (WS)	Detroit Tigers
1910	Chicago Cubs	Philadelphia Athletics (WS)
1911	New York Giants	Philadelphia Athletics (WS)
1912	New York Giants	Boston Red Sox (WS)
1913	New York Giants	Philadelphia Athletics (WS)
1914	Boston (WS)	Philadelphia Athletics
1915	Philadelphia	Boston Red Sox (WS)
1916	Brooklyn	Boston Red Sox (WS)
1917	New York Giants	Chicago White Sox (WS)
1918	Chicago Cubs	Boston Red Sox (WS)
1919	Cincinnati (WS)	Chicago White Sox
1920	Brooklyn	Cleveland Indians (WS)
1921	New York Giants (WS)	New York Yankees

CAPTURE THE FLAG: Stan "the Man" Musial (left) helped the St. Louis Cardinals to 4 pennants in 5 years, and was selected as the National League MVP 3 times. Lou Gehrig (right) played in 2,130 consecutive games, helping the Yankees to 6 of their record 22 championships. The Iron Man's 23 grand-slam home runs are a career record.

National League	American League
1922 New York Giants (WS)	New York Yankees
1923 New York Giants	New York Yankees (WS)
1924 New York Giants	Washington (WS)
1925 Pittsburgh Pirates (WS)	Washington
1926 St Louis Cardinals (WS)	New York Yankees
1927 Pittsburgh Pirates	New York Yankees (WS)
1928 St Louis Cardinals	New York Yankees (WS)
1929 Chicago Cubs	Philadelphia Athletics (WS)
1930 St. Louis Cardinals	Philadelphia Athletics (WS)
1931 St. Louis Cardinals (WS)	Philadelphia Athletics
1932 Chicago Cubs	New York Yankees (WS)
1933 New York Giants (WS)	Washington
1934 St. Louis Cardinals (WS)	Detroit Tigers
1935 Chicago Cubs	Detroit Tigers (WS)
1936 New York Giants	New York Yankees (WS)
1937 New York Giants	New York Yankees (WS)
1938 Chicago Cubs	New York Yankees (WS)
1939 Cincinnati Reds	New York Yankees (WS)
1940 Cincinnati Reds (WS)	Detroit Tigers
1941 Brooklyn Dodgers	New York Yankees (WS)
1942 St Louis Cardinals (WS)	New York Yankees
1943 St Louis Cardinals	New York Yankees (WS)
1944 St Louis Cardinals (WS)	St Louis Browns
1945 Chicago Cubs	Detroit Tigers
1946 St Louis Cardinals (WS)	Boston Red Sox
1947 Brooklyn Dodgers	New York Yankees (WS)
1948 Boston Braves	Cleveland Indians (WS)
1949 Brooklyn Dodgers	New York Yankees (WS)
1950 Philadelphia Phillies	New York Yankees (WS)
1951 New York Giants	New York Yankees (WS)
1952 Brooklyn Dodgers	New York Yankees (WS)
1953 Brooklyn Dodgers	New York Yankees (WS)
1954 New York Giants (WS)	Cleveland Indians
1955 Brooklyn Dodgers (WS)	New York Yankees
1956 Brooklyn Dodgers	New York Yankees (WS)
1957 Milwaukee Braves (WS)	New York Yankees
1958 Milwaukee Braves	New York Yankees (WS)
1959 Los Angeles Dodgers (WS)	Chicago White Sox

REDHOTS: 1968 was a great year for pitcher Bob Gibson (left) of the St. Louis Cardinals. The Redbirds' ace posted a 1.12 earned run average (a modern record), set World Series strikeout records, and won the Cy Young and MVP awards. Frank Robinson (right) is the only man to win MVP honors in both leagues, with the Cincinnati Reds and Baltimore Orioles. He hit at least one homer in 32 different ballparks.

1960	Pittsburgh Pirates (WS)	New York Yankees
1961	Cincinnati Reds	New York Yankees (WS)
1962	San Francisco Giants	New York Yankees (WS)
1963	Los Angeles Dodgers (WS)	New York Yankees
1964	St Louis Cardinals (WS)	New York Yankees
1965	Los Angeles Dodgers (WS)	Minnesota Twins
1966	Los Angeles Dodgers	Baltimore Orioles (WS)
1967	St Louis Cardinals (WS)	Boston Red Sox
1968	St Louis Cardinals	Detroit Tigers (WS)
1969	New York Mets (WS)	Baltimore Orioles
1970	Cincinnati Reds	Baltimore Orioles (WS)
1971	Pittsburgh Pirates (WS)	Baltimore Orioles
1972	Cincinnati Reds	Oakland Athletics (WS)
1973	New York Mets	Oakland Athletics (WS)
1974	Los Angeles Dodgers	Oakland Athletics (WS)
1975	Cincinnati Reds (WS)	Boston Red Sox
1976	Cincinnati Reds (WS)	New York Yankees
1977	Los Angeles Dodgers	New York Yankees (WS)
1978	Los Angeles Dodgers	New York Yankees (WS)
1979	Pittsburgh Pirates (WS)	Baltimore Orioles

Most Valuable Player

Elected for each league by the Baseball Writers Association of America.

	American League	**National League**
1931	Robert M. Grove, Phil.	Frank F. Frisch, St. L.
1932	James E. Foxx, Phil.	Charles H. Klein, Phil.
1933	James E. Foxx, Phil.	Carl O. Hubbell, N.Y.
1934	Gordon Cochrane, Det.	Jerome H. Dean, St. L.
1935	Henry B. Greenberg, Det.	Charles L. Hartnett, Chi.
1936	Henry L. Gehrig, N.Y.	Carl O. Hubbell, N.Y.
1937	Charles L. Gehringer, Det.	Joseph M. Medwick, St. L.
1938	James E. Foxx, Bos.	Ernest N. Lombardi, Cin.
1939	Joseph P. DiMaggio, N.Y.	William H. Walters, Cin.
1940	Henry B. Greenberg, Det.	Frank A. McCormick, Cin.
1941	Joseph P. DiMaggio, N.Y.	Adolph L. Camilli, Bklyn.
1942	Joseph L. Gordon, N.Y.	Morton C. Cooper, St. L.
1943	Spurgeon F. Chandler, N.Y.	Stanley F. Musial, St. L.
1944	Harold Newhouser, Det.	Martin W. Marion, St. L.
1945	Harold Newhouser, Det.	Philip J. Cavarretta, Chi.
1946	Theodore S. Williams, Bos.	Stanley F. Musial, St. L.
1947	Joseph P. DiMaggio, N.Y.	Robert I. Elliott, Bos.
1948	Louis Boudreau, Clev.	Stanley F. Musial, St. L.
1949	Theodore S. Williams, Bos.	Jack C. Robinson, Bklyn.
1950	Philip F. Rizzuto, N.Y.	C. James Konstanty, Phil.
1951	Lawrence P. Berra, N.Y.	Roy Campanella, Bklyn.
1952	Robert C. Shantz, Phil.	Henry J. Sauer, Chi.
1953	Albert L. Rosen, Clev.	Roy Campanella, Bklyn.
1954	Lawrence P. Berra, N.Y.	Willie H. Mays, N.Y.
1955	Lawrence P. Berra, N.Y.	Roy Campanella, Bklyn.
1956	Mickey C. Mantle, N.Y.	Donald Newcombe, Bklyn.
1957	Mickey C. Mantle, N.Y.	Henry L. Aaron, Mil.
1958	Jack E. Jensen, Bos.	Ernest Banks, Chi.
1959	J. Nelson Fox, Chi.	Ernest Banks, Chi.
1960	Roger E. Maris, N.Y.	Richard M. Groat, Pitt.
1961	Roger E. Maris, N.Y.	Frank Robinson, Cin.
1962	Mickey C. Mantle, N.Y.	Maurice Wills, L.A.
1963	Elston G. Howard, N.Y.	Sanford Koufax, L.A.
1964	Brooks C. Robinson, Balt.	Kenton L. Boyer, St. L.
1965	Zoilo C. Versalles, Minn.	Willie H. Mays, S.F.
1966	Frank Robinson, Balt.	Roberto W. Clemente, Pitt.
1967	Carl M. Yastrzemski, Bos.	Orlando M. Cepeda, St. L.
1968	Dennis D. McLain, Det.	Robert Gibson, St. L.
1969	Harmon C. Killebrew, Minn.	Willie L. McCovey, S.F.
1970	John W. Powell, Balt.	Johnny L. Bench, Cin.
1971	Vida Blue, Oak.	Joseph P. Torre, St. L.
1972	Richard A. Allen, Chi.	Johnny L. Bench, Cin.
1973	Reginald M. Jackson, Oak.	Peter E. Rose, Cin.
1974	Jeffrey A. Burroughs, Tex.	Steven P. Garvey, L.A.

Most Valuable Player (continued)

American League

1975 Fredric M. Lynn, Bos.
1976 Thurman L. Munson, N.Y.
1977 Rodney C. Carew, Minn.
1978 James E. Rice, Bos.
1979 Donald E. Baylor, Cal.

National League

Joe L. Morgan, Cin.
Joe L. Morgan, Cin.
George A. Foster, Cin.
David G. Parker, Pitt.
Keith Hernandez, St. L. (tie)
Wilver D. Stargell, Pitt.

Cy Young Award

Originally awarded each year to the outstanding pitcher in the major leagues, the award was changed in 1967 to recognize the outstanding pitcher in each league.

1956 Donald Newcombe, Bklyn. NL
1957 Warren E. Spahn, Mil. NL
1958 Robert Turley, N.Y. AL
1959 Early Wynn, Chi. AL
1960 Vernon Law, Pitt. NL
1961 Edward C. Ford, N.Y. AL

1962 Donald S. Drysdale, L.A. NL
1963 Sanford Koufax, L.A. AL
1964 W. Dean Chance, L.A. AL
1965 Sanford Koufax, L.A. NL
1966 Sanford Koufax, L.A. NL

American League

1967 James R. Lonborg, Bos.
1968 Dennis D. McLain, Det.
1969 Miguel A. Cuellar, Balt. (tie)
     Dennis D. McLain, Det.
1970 James E. Perry, Minn.
1971 Vida Blue, Oak.
1972 Gaylord J. Perry, Clev.
1973 James A. Palmer, Balt.
1974 James A. Hunter, Oak.
1975 James A. Palmer, Balt.
1976 James A. Palmer, Balt.
1977 Albert W. Lyle, N.Y.
1978 Ronald A. Guidry, N.Y.
1979 Michael K. Flanagan, Balt.

National League

Michael F. McCormick, S.F.
Robert Gibson, St. L.
G. Thomas Seaver, N.Y.

Robert Gibson, St. L.
Ferguson A. Jenkins, Chi.
Steven N. Carlton, Phil.
G. Thomas Seaver, N.Y.
Michael G. Marshall, L.A.
G. Thomas Seaver, N.Y.
Randall L. Jones, S.D.
Steven N. Carlton, Phil.
Gaylord J. Perry, S.D.
H. Bruce Sutter, Chi.

WINNING PITCHERS: Baltimore's Jim Palmer (left), a consistent 20-game winner, is one of 3 pitchers to win the Cy Young Award 3 times. The eponymous hero of the pitching award, Cy (for "cyclone") Young (right), set the virtually unbreakable record of 511 career wins.

BASKETBALL

Origins. *Ollamalitzli* was a 16th-century Aztec precursor of basketball played in Mexico. If the solid rubber ball was put through a fixed stone ring placed high on one side of the stadium, the player was entitled to the clothing of all the spectators. The captain of the losing team often lost his head (by execution). Another game played much earlier, in the 10th century B.C. by the Olmecs in Mexico, called *Pok-ta-Pok,* also resembled basketball in its concept of a ring through which a round object was passed.

Modern basketball (which may have been based on the German game of *Korbball*) was devised by the Canadian-born Dr. James A. Naismith (1861–1939) at the Training School of the International Y.M.C.A. College at Springfield, Massachusetts, in December, 1891. The first game played under modified rules was on January 20, 1892. The first public contest was on March 11, 1892. The International Amateur Basketball Federation (F.I.B.A.) was founded in 1932.

Most Accurate Shooting

The greatest free-throw shooting demonstration was made by a professional, Ted St. Martin, now of Jacksonville, Florida, who, on June 25, 1977, scored 2,036 consecutive free throws.

SHOOTING STARS: Les Henson (left) sank an 89-foot-3-inch basket. Pearl Moore (right), now with the champion NY Stars, a women's pro team, holds the college scoring record with 4,061 career points.

In a 24-hour period, May 31–June 1, 1975, Fred L. Newman of San Jose, California, scored 12,874 baskets out of 13,116 attempts (98.15 per cent). Newman has also made 88 consecutive free throws while blindfolded at the Central Y.M.C.A., San Jose, California, on February 5, 1978.

The McKendree College team set a college record by sinking all 39 of their free throw attempts on February 2, 1980.

Longest Field Goal

The longest *measured* field goal in a college game was 89 feet 3 inches by Les Henson of Virginia Tech, on January 21, 1980. Henson, a left-handed shooter, heaved the ball almost the full length of the court with his right hand just as the final buzzer sounded to give Virginia Tech a 79–77 victory over Florida State. The N.C.A.A. does not officially recognize a record for the longest shot—there is no standard for measuring—but they did report that the measurement was made from Henson's back foot to the back of the rim (which is 6 inches from the backboard), where the ball first touched. Later, Les exclaimed, "All of this commotion over a ball going through a hole!"

In a professional game, Jerry Harkness scored a field goal from an *estimated* distance of 92 feet for the Indiana Pacers of the Old American Basketball Association, on November 13, 1967. Harkness' shot was also at the buzzer, and by A.B.A. rules was worth three points. The basket gave the Pacers a one-point victory over the Dallas Chaparrals.

In an AAU game at Pacific Lutheran University on January 16, 1970, Steve Myers sank a shot while standing out of bounds at the other end of the court. Though the basket was illegal, the officials gave in to crowd sentiment and allowed the points to count. The distance is claimed to be 92 feet 3½ inches from measurements made 10 years later.

Individual Scoring

Marie Boyd scored 156 points in a women's high school basketball game for Central H.S., Lonaconing, Maryland, vs. Ursaline Academy, on February 25, 1924. The men's high school record is 135 points by Danny Heater of Burnsville, West Virginia, on January 26, 1960.

In college play, Clarence (Bevo) Francis of Rio Grande College, Ohio, scored 113 points against Hillsdale on February 2, 1954. One year earlier, Francis scored 116 points in a game, but the record was disallowed because the competition was with a two-year school. The major college record for men is 100 points by Frank Selvey of Furman University vs. Newberry College, February 13, 1954.

Wilton Norman (Wilt) Chamberlain (b. August 21, 1936) holds the professional record with 100 points for the Philadelphia Warriors vs. New York Knicks, scored on March 2, 1962. During the same season, Wilt set the record for points in a season (4,029) and he also holds the career record (31,419).

Pearl Moore of Francis Marion College, Florence, South Carolina, scored a record 4,061 points during her college career,

CHILD'S PLAY:
Bill Willoughby
was only 18 years
old when he
played in his first
NBA game for
the Atlanta Hawks
in 1975.

1975–79. She also holds the A.I.A.W. (Association for Intercollegiate Athletics for Women) single-game tournament record with 60 points. The men's college career scoring record is 4,045 points by Travis Grant for Kentucky State, 1969–72.

Youngest and Oldest

Bill Willoughby (b. May 20, 1957) made his N.B.A. debut for the Atlanta Hawks on October 23, 1975, when he was 18 years 5 months 3 days old. The oldest N.B.A. player was Bob Cousy (b. August 9, 1928), who was 41 years 6 months 2 days old when he appeared in the last of seven games he played for the team he was coaching (Cincinnati Royals) during 1969–70.

Tallest Players

The tallest player of all time is reputed to be Suleiman Ali Nashnush (b. 1943) who played for the Libyan team in 1962 when he measured 8 feet tall. The tallest woman player is Iuliana Semenova (USSR) who is reputed to stand 7 feet 2 inches tall and weigh 281 lbs. The tallest N.B.A. player is Tom Burleson, who is 7 feet 4 inches tall.

Greatest Attendances

The Harlem Globetrotters played an exhibition to 75,000 in the Olympic Stadium, West Berlin, Germany, in 1951. The largest indoor basketball crowd was at the Astrodome, Houston, Texas, where 52,693 watched a game on January 20, 1968, between the University of Houston and U.C.L.A.

The Harlem Globetrotters have traveled over 6,000,000 miles, visited 94 countries on six continents, and have been watched by an estimated 80,000,000 spectators. They have won over 12,000 games, losing less than 350, but many were not truly competitive. The team was founded by Abraham M. Saperstein (1903–66) of Chicago, and their first game was played at Hinckley, Illinois, on January 7, 1927.

WINNING SMILES: The Harlem Globetrotters, as typified by Meadowlark Lemon (left), have attracted over 80 million fans with their witty basketball antics. Bill Sharman (right), 7-time NBA free throw percentage leader, coached the LA Lakers during their 33-game winning streak.

Longest Winning Streaks

The Los Angeles Lakers set the professional record with 33 consecutive victories from November 5, 1971, to January 7, 1972.

Spanning four seasons (1970–71 to 1973–74), the University of California at Los Angeles won 88 games in a row before losing to Notre Dame in South Bend, Indiana, in 1974. Perhaps more extraordinary was U.C.L.A.'s 38-game winning streak in N.C.A.A. tournament play, a streak that included 7 straight national championships, 1967–73.

The women's team of Baskin High School, Baskin, Louisiana, won 218 consecutive games, 1947–53. The men's high school record winning streak is 159 games, by Passaic H.S., New Jersey, 1919–25.

Olympic Champions

The US won all seven Olympic titles from the time the sport was introduced to the Games in 1936 until 1968, without losing a single match. In 1972, in Munich, their run of 63 consecutive victories was broken when they lost 51–50 to the USSR in a much-disputed final match. They regained the Olympic title in Montreal in 1976, again without losing a game.

World Champions

Brazil, the USSR and Yugoslavia are the only countries to win the World Men's Championship (instituted 1950) on more than one occasion. Brazil won in 1959 and 1963; the USSR in 1967 and 1974; Yugoslavia in 1970 and 1978.

In 1975, the USSR won the women's championship (instituted 1953) for the fifth consecutive time since 1959.

Marathon

The longest game is 89 hours by two teams of five at Kwinana High School, Western Australia, on May 18–21, 1979.

National Basketball Association

Regular Season Records. *Including* 1978–79 *Season.* The National Basketball Association's Championship series was established in 1947. Prior to 1949, when it joined with the National Basketball League, the professional circuit was known as the Basketball Association of America.

SERVICE

Most Games, Lifetime
1,270 John Havlicek, Bos. 1963–78

Most Games, Consecutive, Lifetime
844 John Kerr, Syr.-Phil.-Balt., Oct. 31, 1954–Nov. 4, 1965

Most Complete Games, Season
79 Wilt Chamberlain, Phil. 1962

Most Complete Games, Consecutive, Season
47 Wilt Chamberlain, Phil. 1962

Most Minutes, Lifetime
47,859 Wilt Chamberlain, Phil.-S.F.-L.A. 1960–73

Most Minutes, Season
3,882 Wilt Chamberlain, Phil. 1962

SCORING

Most Seasons Leading League
7 Wilt Chamberlain, Phil. 1960–62; S.F. 1963–64; S.F.-Phil. 1965; Phil. 1966

Most Points, Lifetime
31,419 Wilt Chamberlain, Phil.-S.F.-L.A. 1960–73

Most Points, Season
4,029 Wilt Chamberlain, Phil. 1962

Most Seasons 1000+ Points
16 John Havlicek, Bos. 1963–78

Most Points, Game
100 Wilt Chamberlain, Phil. vs. N.Y., Mar. 2, 1962

Most Points, Half
59 Wilt Chamberlain, Phil. vs. N.Y., Mar. 2, 1962

Most Points, Quarter
33 George Gervin, S.A. vs. N.O. Apr. 9, 1978

Most Points, Overtime Period
13 Earl Monroe, Balt. vs. Det., Feb. 6, 1970
Joe Caldwell, Atl. vs. Cin., Feb. 18, 1970

Highest Scoring Average, Lifetime (400+ games)
30.1 Wilt Chamberlain, Phil.-S.F.-L.A. 1960–73

Highest Scoring Average, Season
50.4 Wilt Chamberlain, Phil. 1962

MOST GAMES: John (Hondo) Havlicek played in 1,270 games for the Boston Celtics from 1963 to 1978. The Celtics won 7 championships during Hondo's career.

FREE THROW ACE: Rick Barry has the highest lifetime free throw percentage. He sank 60 in a row for the Golden State Warriors in 1976.

National Basketball Association (*continued*)

Field Goals Made

Most Field Goals, Lifetime
12,681 Wilt Chamberlain, Phil.-S.F.-L.A. 1960–73

Most Field Goals, Season
1,597 Wilt Chamberlain, Phil. 1962

Most Field Goals, Consecutive, Season
35 Wilt Chamberlain, Phil. Feb. 17–28, 1967

Most Field Goals, Game
36 Wilt Chamberlain, Phil. vs. N.Y., Mar. 2, 1962

Most Field Goals, Half
22 Wilt Chamberlain, Phil. vs. N.Y., Mar. 2, 1962

Most Field Goals, Quarter
13 David Thompson, Den. vs. Det., Apr. 9, 1978

Most Three-Point Field Goals, Game
7 Rick Barry, Hou. vs. N.J., Feb. 6, 1980.

Field Goals Attempted

Most Field Goal Attempts, Lifetime
23,930 John Havlicek, Bos. 1963–1978

Most Field Goal Attempts, Season
3,159 Wilt Chamberlain, Phil. 1962

Most Field Goal Attempts, Game
63 Wilt Chamberlain, Phil. vs. N.Y., Mar. 2, 1962

Most Field Goal Attempts, Half
37 Wilt Chamberlain, Phil. vs. N.Y., Mar. 2, 1962

Most Field Goal Attempts, Quarter
21 Wilt Chamberlain, Phil. vs. N.Y., Mar. 2, 1962

Field Goal Percentage

Most Seasons Leading League
9 Wilt Chamberlain, Phil. 1961; S.F. 1963; S.F.-Phil. 1965; Phil. 1966–68; L.A. 1969, 72–73

Highest Percentage, Lifetime
.554 Artis Gilmore, Chi. 1977–79

Highest Percentage, Season
.727 Wilt Chamberlain, L.A. 1973

Free Throws Made

Most Free Throws Made, Lifetime
7,694 Oscar Robertson, Cin.-Mil. 1961–74

Most Free Throws Made, Season
840 Jerry West, L.A. 1966

Most Free Throws Made, Consecutive, Season
60 Rick Barry, G.S. Oct. 22–Nov. 16, 1976

Most Free Throws Made, Game
28 Wilt Chamberlain, Phil. vs. N.Y., Mar. 2, 1962

Most Free Throws Made (No Misses), Game
19 Bob Pettit, St. L. vs. Bos., Nov. 22, 1961

Most Free Throws Made, Half
19 Oscar Robertson, Cin. vs. Balt., Dec. 27, 1964

Most Free Throws Made, Quarter
14 Rick Barry, S.F. vs. N.Y., Dec. 6, 1966

Free Throws Attempted

Most Free Throw Attempts, Lifetime
11,862 Wilt Chamberlain, Phil.-S.F.-L.A. 1960–73

Most Free Throw Attempts, Season
1,363 Wilt Chamberlain, Phil., 1962

Most Free Throw Attempts, Game
34 Wilt Chamberlain, S.F. vs. N.Y., Nov. 27, 1963

Most Free Throw Attempts, Half
22 Oscar Robertson, Cin. vs. Balt., Dec. 27, 1964

CENTERS OF ATTENTION: Wilt Chamberlain (#13) and Bill Russell battle it out in Boston Garden. The contests between these two men provided some of the most exciting moments in NBA history. Russell's name is hard to find in the record books, but he played on eleven championship teams with the Boston Celtics. Chamberlain holds over 30 records: for service, scoring, field goal percentage and rebounds. He scored 50 or more points in a game 122 times during his 14-year career. It took the rest of the league 31 years to pass Wilt's record when January 19, 1980 marked only the 123rd time a player other than Wilt scored 50 points. Incredibly, he never fouled out of a game. Still, he only played on 2 championship teams.

Most Free Throw Attempts, Quarter
16 Oscar Robertson, Cin. vs. Balt.,
    Dec. 27, 1964
    Stan McKenzie, Phoe. vs. Phil.,
    Feb. 15, 1970
    Pete Maravich, Atl. vs. Chi., Jan.
    2, 1973

Free Throw Percentage

Most Seasons Leading League
7 Bill Sharman, Bos. 1953–57, 59,
   61

Highest Percentage, Lifetime
.899 Rick Barry, S.F.-G.S.-Hou. 1966–
      67, 73–79

Highest Percentage, Season
.947 Rick Barry, Hou. 1979

REBOUNDS

Most Seasons Leading League
11 Wilt Chamberlain, Phil. 1960–62;
    S.F. 1963; Phil. 1966–68; L.A.
    1969, 71–73

Most Rebounds, Lifetime
23,924 Wilt Chamberlain, Phil.-S.F.-L.A.
        1960–73

Most Rebounds Season
2,149 Wilt Chamberlain, Phil. 1961

Most Rebounds, Game
55 Wilt Chamberlain, Phil. vs. Bos.,
    Nov. 24, 1960

Most Rebounds, Half
32 Bill Russell, Bos. vs. Phil., Nov.
    16, 1957

Most Rebounds, Quarter
18 Nate Thurmond, S.F. vs. Balt.,
    Feb. 28, 1965

Highest Average (per game), Lifetime
22.9 Wilt Chamberlain, Phil.-S.F.-L.A.,
      1960–73

Highest Average (per game), Season
27.2 Wilt Chamberlain, Phil. 1961

ASSISTS

Most Seasons Leading League
8 Bob Cousy, Bos. 1953–60

Most Assists, Lifetime
9,887 Oscar Robertson, Cin.-Mil. 1961–
       74

Most Assists, Season
1,099 Kevin Porter, Det. 1979

Most Assists, Game
29 Kevin Porter, N.J. vs. Hou., Feb.
    24, 1978

Most Assists, Half
19 Bob Cousy, Bos. vs. Minn., Feb.
    27, 1959

Most Assists, Quarter
12 Bob Cousy, Bos. vs. Minn., Feb.
    27, 1959
    John Lucas, Hou. vs. Mil., Oct.
    27, 1977

Highest Average (per game), Lifetime
9.5 Oscar Robertson, Cin.-Mil. 1961–
     74

Highest Average (per game), Season
13.4 Kevin Porter, Det. 1979

PERSONAL FOULS

Most Personal Fouls, Lifetime
3,855 Hal Greer, Syr.-Phil. 1959–73

Most Personal Fouls, Season
367 Bill Robinzine, K.C. 1979

Most Personal Fouls, Game
8 Don Otten, T.C. vs. Sheb., Nov.
   24, 1949

Most Personal Fouls, Half
6 By many. Last:
   Cedric Maxwell, Bos. vs. San
   Diego, March 2, 1979

Most Personal Fouls, Quarter
6 Connie Dierking, Syr. vs. Cin.,
   Nov. 17, 1959
   Henry Akin, Seattle vs. Phil. Dec.
   20, 1967
   Bud Ogden, Phil. vs. Phoe., Feb.
   15, 1970
   Don Smith, Hou. vs. Clev., Feb.
   8, 1974
   Roger Brown, Det. vs. G.S., Mar.
   25, 1977

PASSING FANCY: Oscar Robertson set career assist records by averaging 9.5 assists per game for a total of 9,887 in his 14-year career.

GO WEST: Jerry West was a key member of the championship LA Laker team that won a record 69 games, including 33 in a row, in 1971–72. In the 1965–66 season, West made a record 840 free throws.

DISQUALIFICATIONS
(Fouling Out of Game)

Most Disqualifications, Lifetime
   127 Vern Mikkelsen, Minn. 1950–59

Most Disqualifications, Season
   26 Don Meineke, Ft. W. 1953

Most Games No Disqualifications, Lifetime
  1,045 Wilt Chamberlain, Phil.-S.F.-L.A.
      1960–73 (Entire Career)

TEAM RECORDS
(ot = overtime)

Most Seasons, League Champion
   13 Boston 1957, 59–66, 68–69, 74,
     76

Most Seasons, Consecutive, League Champion
   8 Boston 1959–66

Most Seasons, Division Champion
   14 Boston 1957–65, 72–76

Most Seasons, Consecutive, Division Champion
   9 Boston 1957–65

Most Games Won, Season
   69 Los Angeles 1972

Most Games Won, Consecutive, Season
   33 Los Angeles Nov. 5, 1971–Jan.
     7, 1972

Most Games Won, Consecutive, Start of Season
   15 Washington Nov. 3–Dec. 4, 1948

Most Games Won, Consecutive, End of Season
   14 Milwaukee Feb. 28–Mar. 27, 1973

Most Games Lost, Season
   73 Philadelphia 1973

Most Games Lost, Consecutive, Season
   20 Philadelphia Jan. 9–Feb. 11, 1973

Most Games Lost, Consecutive, Start of Season
   15 Denver Oct. 29–Dec. 25, 1949
      Cleveland Oct. 14–Nov. 10, 1970
      Philadelphia Oct. 10–Nov. 10,
      1973

Highest Percentage, Games Won, Season
   .841 Los Angeles 1972

Lowest Percentage, Games Won, Season
   .110 Philadelphia 1973

Team Scoring

Most Points, Season
 10,143 Philadelphia 1967

Most Games, 100+ Points, Season
   81 Los Angeles 1972

Most Games, Consecutive, 100+ Points, Season
   77 New York 1967

Most Points, Game
   173 Boston vs. Minn. Feb. 27, 1959

Most Points, Both Teams, Game
   316 Phil. (169) vs. N.Y. (147) Mar. 2,
     1962
     Cin. (1965) vs. San Diego (151)
     Mar. 12, 1970

Most Points Half
   97 Atlanta vs. San Diego Feb. 11,
     1970

Most Points, Quarter
   58 Buffalo vs. Bos. Oct. 20, 1972

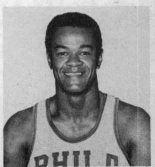

PERSONAL TOUCH: Hal Greer is the NBA lifetime leader in personal fouls with 3,855, but it was his 15 seasons of hustling play that caused him to collect that many.

Widest Victory Margin, Game
    63 Los Angeles (162) vs. Golden State (99) Mar. 19, 1972

Field Goals Made

Most Field Goals, Season
3,972 Milwaukee 1971

Most Field Goals, Game
    72 Boston vs. Minn. Feb. 27, 1959

Most Field Goals, Both Teams, Game
   134 Cin. (67) vs. San Diego (67) Mar. 12, 1970

Most Field Goals, Half
    40 Boston vs. Minn. Feb. 27, 1959
        Syracuse vs. Det. Jan. 13, 1963

Most Field Goals, Quarter
    23 Boston vs. Minn. Feb. 27, 1959
        Buffalo vs. Bos. Oct. 20, 1972

Field Goals Attempted

Most Field Goal Attempts, Season
9,295 Boston 1961

Most Field Goal Attempts, Game
   153 Philadelphia vs. L.A. Dec. 8, 1961 (3 ot)
   150 Boston vs Phil. Feb. 3, 1960

Most Field Goal Attempts, Both Teams, Game
   291 Phil. (153) vs. L.A. (138) Dec. 8, 1961 (3 ot)
   274 Bos. (149) vs. Det. (125) Jan. 27, 1961

Most Field Goal Attempts, Half
    83 Philadelphia vs. Syr. Nov. 4, 1959
        Boston vs. Phil. Dec. 27, 1960

Most Field Goal Attempts, Quarter
    47 Boston vs. Minn. Feb. 27, 1959

Highest Field Goal Percentage, Season
.517 Los Angeles 1979

Free Throws Made

Most Free Throws Made, Season
2,434 Phoenix 1970

Most Free Throws Made, Game
    59 Anderson vs. Syr. Nov. 24, 1949 (5 ot)

Most Free Throws Made, Both Teams, Game
   116 And. (59) vs. Syr. (57) Nov. 24, 1949 (5 ot)

Most Free Throws Made, Half
    36 Chicago vs. Phoe. Jan. 8, 1970

Most Free Throws Made, Quarter
    24 St. Louis vs. Syr. Dec. 21, 1957
        Cin. vs. Balt. Dec. 27, 1964

Free Throws Attempted

Most Free Throw Attempts, Season
3,411 Philadelphia 1967

Most Free Throw Attempts, Game
    86 Syracuse vs. And. Nov. 24, 1949 (5 ot)
    71 Chicago vs. Phoe. Jan. 8, 1970

Most Free Throw Attempts, Both Teams, Game
   160 Syr. (86) vs. And. (74), Nov. 24, 1949 (5 ot)
   127 Ft. W. (67) vs. Minn. (60) Dec. 31, 1954

Most Free Throw Attempts, Half
    48 Chicago vs. Phoe. Jan. 8, 1970

Most Free Throw Attempts, Quarter
    30 Boston vs. Chi. Jan. 9, 1963

Highest Free Throw Percentage, Season
.821 K.C.-Omaha 1975

Rebounds

Most Rebounds, Season
6,131 Boston 1961

Most Rebounds, Game
   112 Philadelphia vs. Cin. No. 8, 1959
        Boston vs. Det. Dec. 24, 1960

Most Rebounds, Both Teams, Game
   215 Phil. (110) vs. L.A. (105) Dec. 8, 1961 (3 ot)
   196 Bos. (106) vs. Det. (90) Jan. 27, 1961

Most Rebounds, Half
    62 Boston vs. Phil. Nov. 19, 1960
        New York vs. Phil. Nov. 19, 1960
        Philadelphia vs. Syr. Nov. 9, 1961

Most Rebounds, Quarter
    40 Philadelphia vs. Syr. Nov. 9, 1961

Assists

Most Assists, Season
2,562 Milwaukee 1979

Most Assists, Game
    60 Syracuse vs. Balt. Nov. 15, 1952 (1 ot)
    53 Milwaukee vs. Det. Dec. 26, 1978

Most Assists, Both Teams, Game
    89 Det. (48) vs. Clev. (41) Mar. 28, 1973 (1 ot)
    88 Phoe. (47) vs. San Diego (41) Mar. 15, 1969

Most Assists, Half
    30 Milwaukee vs. Det. Dec. 26, 1978

Most Assists, Quarter
    19 Milwaukee vs. Det. Dec. 26, 1978

Personal Fouls

Most Personal Fouls, Season
2,470 Atlanta 1978

Most Personal Fouls, Game
    66 Anderson vs. Syr. Nov. 24, 1949 (5 ot)

Most Personal Fouls, Both Teams, Game	Most Personal Fouls, Half
122 And. (66) vs. Syr. (56), Nov. 24, 1949 (5 ot)	30 Rochester vs. Syr. Jan. 15, 1953
97 Syr. (50) N.Y. (47) Feb. 15, 1953	Most Personal Fouls, Quarter
	18 Portland vs. Atl. Jan. 16, 1977

World Championships

First held in 1950, the World Championships for men are held between Olympic Games. Contested by amateur teams.

1950	Argentina	1959	Brazil	1967	USSR	1974	USSR
1954	US	1963	Brazil	1970	Yugoslavia	1978	Yugoslavia

Women's World Championships were first held in 1953.

1953	US	1959	USSR	1967	USSR	1975	USSR
1957	US	1964	USSR	1971	USSR	1979	Canada

Olympic Champions

Men

1936	US	1952	US	1960	US	1968	US	1976	US
1948	US	1956	US	1964	US	1972	USSR	1980	Yugoslavia

N.C.A.A. Championship

The most important amateur basketball competition in the US is the National Collegiate Athletic Association Championship. Winners have been:

Year	Champion	Score	Runner-Up	Year	Champion	Score	Runner-Up
1939	Oregon	46–33	Ohio State	1961	Cincinnati	70–65†	Ohio State
1940	Indiana	60–42‡	Kansas	1962	Cincinnati	71–59	Ohio State
1941	Wisconsin	39–34	Washington St.	1963	Loyola (Ill.)	60–58†	Cincinnati
1942	Stanford	53–38	Dartmouth	1964	UCLA	98–83	Duke
1943	Wyoming	46–34	Georgetown	1965	UCLA	91–80	Michigan
1944	Utah	42–40†	Dartmouth	1966	Texas-El Paso	72–65	Kentucky
1945	Oklahoma State	49–45	New York U.	1967	UCLA	79–64	Dayton
1946	Oklahoma State	43–40	North Carolina	1968	UCLA	78–55	North Carolina
1947	Holy Cross	58–47	Oklahoma	1969	UCLA	92–72	Purdue
1948	Kentucky	58–42	Baylor	1970	UCLA	80–69	Jacksonville
1949	Kentucky	46–36	Oklahoma State	1971	UCLA	68–62	Vacated
1950	CCNY	71–68	Bradley	1972	UCLA	81–76	Florida State
1951	Kentucky	68–58	Kansas State	1973	UCLA	87–66	Memphis State
1952	Kansas	80–63	St. John's	1974	North Carolina St.	76–64	Marquette
1953	Indiana	69–68	Kansas				
1954	LaSalle	92–76	Bradley	1975	UCLA	92–85	Kentucky
1955	San Francisco	77–63	LaSalle	1976	Indiana	86–68	Michigan
1956	San Francisco	83–71	Iowa	1977	Marquette	67–59	North Carolina
1957	North Carolina	54–53†	Kansas	1978	Kentucky	94–88	Duke
1958	Kentucky	84–72	Seattle	1979	Michigan State	75–64	Indiana State
1959	California	71–70	West Virginia	1980	Louisville	59–54	UCLA
1960	Ohio State	75–55	California				

† Overtime.

‡ Three overtimes.

NBA Champions

The major American professional competition is under the auspices of the National Basketball Association .(NBA), which was

formed in 1946 by a merger of the Basketball Association of
America and the National Basketball League. In 1976 the American Basketball Association merged with the NBA'. The teams are
currently divided into four divisions, Atlantic and Central in the
East, and Midwest and Pacific in the West. Winners of the Championship play-offs have been:

1947	Philadelphia	1956	Philadelphia	1965	Boston	1974	Boston
1948	Baltimore	1957	Boston	1966	Boston	1975	Golden State
1949	Minneapolis	1958	St. Louis	1967	Philadelphia	1976	Boston
1950	Minneapolis	1959	Boston	1968	Boston	1977	Portland
1951	Rochester	1960	Boston	1969	Boston	1978	Washington
1952	Minneapolis	1961	Boston	1970	New York	1979	Seattle
1953	Minneapolis	1962	Boston	1971	Milwaukee		
1954	Minneapolis	1963	Boston	1972	Los Angeles		
1955	Syracuse	1964	Boston	1973	New York		

A.I.A.W. Championship

The Association for Intercollegiate Athletics for Women instituted
playoff competition for a women's collegiate national championship in 1972.

1972	Immaculata	1975	Delta State	1978	UCLA
1973	Immaculata	1976	Delta State	1979	Old Dominion
1974	Immaculata	1977	Delta State	1980	Old Dominion

BILLIARDS

Earliest Mention. The earliest recorded mention of billiards was
in France in 1429, while Louis XI, King of France, 1461–83, is

ON CUE: William F.
(Willie) Hoppe
(1887–1959) won an
extraordinary 51
billiards champion-
ships between 1906
and 1952.

reported to have had a billiards table. The first recorded public room for billiards in England was the Piazza, Covent Garden, London, in the early part of the 19th century.

Rubber cushions were introduced in 1835 and slate beds in 1836.

Highest Breaks

Tom Reece (England) made an unfinished break of 499,135, including 249,152 cradle cannons (2 points each), in 85 hours 49 minutes against Joe Chapman at Burroughes' Hall, Soho Square, London, between June 3 and July 6, 1907. This was not recognized because press and public were not continuously present. The highest certified break made by the anchor cannon is 42,746 by W. Cook (England) from May 29 to June 7, 1907. The official world record under the then baulk-line rule is 1,784 by Joe Davis in the United Kingdom Championship on May 29, 1936. Walter Lindrum (Australia) made an official break of 4,137 in 2 hours 55 minutes against Joe Davis at Thurston's, London, on January 19–20, 1932, before the baulk-line rule was in force. The amateur record is 1,149 by Michael Ferreira (India) at Calcutta, India, on December 15, 1978.

Fastest Century

Walter Lindrum (1898–1960) of Australia made an unofficial 100 break in 27.5 seconds in Australia on October 10, 1952. His official record is 100 in 46.0 seconds, set in Sydney in 1941.

Most World Titles

The greatest number of world championship titles (instituted 1870) won by one player is eight by John Roberts, Jr. (1847–1919) (England) in 1870 (twice), 1871, 1875 (twice), 1877 and 1885 (twice). Willie Hoppe (US) won 51 "world" titles in the US variant of the game between 1906 and 1952.

Most Amateur Titles

The record for world amateur titles is four by Robert Marshall (Australia) in 1936–38–51–62. The record number of women's titles is eight by Vera Selby, 1970–78.

Pool

Pool or championship pocket billiards with numbered balls began to become standardized c. 1890. The greatest exponents were Ralph Greenleaf (US) (1899–1950), who won the "world" professional title 19 times (1919–1937), and William Mosconi (US), who dominated the game from 1941 to 1957.

Michael Eufemia holds the record for the greatest continuous run, pocketing 625 balls without a miss on February 2, 1960, before a large crowd at Logan's Billiard Academy, Brooklyn, New York.

Gary Mounsey (b. 1947) pocketed 11,700 balls in 24 hours, a rate of one per 7.5 seconds, in Hamilton, New Zealand, June 30–July 1, 1979.

HIGH POCKETS: Michael Eufemia pocketed 625 balls without a miss at Logan's Billiard Academy in Brooklyn, New York, in 1960.

The longest game is 175 hours by Graham Cooper and Tony Hillman at Nottingham, England, December 6–13, 1978.

3-Cushion Billiards

This pocketless variation dates back to 1878. The world governing body, *Union Mondiale de Billiard,* was formed in 1928. The most successful exponent, 1906–52, was William F. Hoppe (b. October 11, 1887, Cornwall-on-Hudson, New York; d. February 1, 1959) who won 51 billiards championships in all forms. The most U.M.B. titles have been won by Raymond Ceulemans (Belgium) (b. 1937) with 14 (1963–66, 1968–73, 1975–78) with a peak average of 1.679 in 1978.

BOBSLEDDING AND TOBAGGANING

Origins. The oldest known sled is dated *c.* 6500 B.C. and came from Heinola, Finland. The first known bobsled race took place at Davos, Switzerland, in 1889. The International Federation of Bobsleigh and Tobogganing was formed in 1923, followed by the International Bobsleigh Federation in 1957.

Olympic and World Titles

The Olympic four-man bob title (instituted 1924) has been won four times by Switzerland (1924, 36, 56, 72). The US (1932, 1936), Italy (1956, 1968) and West Germany (1952 and 1972) have won the Olympic boblet event (instituted 1932) twice. The most medals won by an individual is six (two gold, two silver, two bronze) by Eugenio Monti (Italy) from 1956 to 1968.

Monti (b. January 23, 1928) has been a member of 11 world championship crews, eight two-man and three four-man.

Tobogganing

The word toboggan comes from the Micmac American Indian word *Tobaakan*. The oldest tobogganing club in the world, founded in 1887, is at St. Moritz, Switzerland, home of the Cresta Run and site of the introduction of the skeleton one-man racing toboggan.

The skeleton one-man toboggan dates, in its present form, from 1892. On the Cresta Run at St. Moritz, dating from 1884, the record from the Junction (2,913 feet) is 42.96 seconds (average 63.08 m.p.h.) by Poldi Berchtold of Switzerland on February 22, 1975. The record from the top (3,977 feet long with a drop of 514 feet) is 53.24 seconds (average speed 50.92 m.p.h.), also by Berchtold on February 9, 1975. Speeds of 90 m.p.h. are occasionally attained.

The greatest number of wins in the Grand National (instituted 1885) is eight by the 1948 Olympic champion Nino Bibbia (Italy) (b. September 9, 1924) in 1960–61–62–63–64–66–68–73. The greatest number of wins in the Curzon Cup (instituted in 1910) is eight by Bibbia in 1950–57–58–60–62–63–64–69 who hence won the double in 1960–62–63–64. The most descents made in a season is 7,832 during 65 days in 1976.

Lugeing

In lugeing the rider adopts a sitting, as opposed to a prone position. Official international competition began at Klosters, Switzerland, in 1881. The first European championships were at Reichenberg (now East), Germany, in 1914, and the first world championships at Oslo, Norway, in 1953. The International Luge Federation was formed in 1957. Lugeing became an Olympic sport in 1964.

Most World Titles

The most successful rider in the world championships is Thomas Köhler (East Germany) (b. June 25, 1940), who won the single-seater title in 1962, 1964 (Olympic), 1966, 1967, and shared in the two-seater title in 1967 and 1968 (Olympic).

Highest Speed

The fastest luge run is at Krynica, Poland, where speeds of more than 80 m.p.h. have been recorded.

MOST MEDALS: Italian bobsledder Eugenio Monti has won six Olympic medals, including two gold. He has been a member of 11 world championship crews.

World and Olympic Champions

World Championships were first held for 4-man bobs in 1924 and 2-man bobs in 1931. In Olympic years the Olympic champions are recognized as world champions. (Olympic champions are identified by an *.)

2-Man World Champions—Bobsled

Most titles: Italy 14 (1954, 1956–63, 1966, 1968–69, 1971, 1975) (Eugenio Monti was on 8 of these teams) Winners since 1972:

1972*	W. Germany (Wolfgang Zimmerer and Peter Utzschneider)
1973	W. Germany (Wolfgang Zimmerer and Peter Utzschneider)
1974	W. Germany (Wolfgang Zimmerer and Peter Utzschneider)
1975	Italy (Giorgio Alvera and Franco Perrugat)
1976*	E. Germany (Meinhard Nehmer and Bernard Germeshausen)
1977	Switzerland (Hans Hiltebrand and Heinz Meier)
1978	Switzerland (Erich Schärer and Josef Benz)
1979	Switzerland (Erich Schärer and Josef Benz)
1980*	Switzerland (Erich Schäer and Josef Benz)

4-Man World Champions—Bobsled

Most titles: Switzerland 12 (1924, 1936, 1939, 1947, 1954–57, 1971–73, 1975) Winners since 1972:

1972*	Switzerland (J. Wicki, E. Hubacher, H. Leutenegger, W. Carmichel)
1973	Switzerland (R. Stadler, W. Camchel, K. Schärer, P. Schärer)
1974	W. Germany (W. Zimmerer, A. Wurzer, P. Utzschneider, M. Schumann)
1975	Switzerland (E. Schärer, M. Carmichel, J. Benz, P. Schärer)
1976*	E. Germany (M. Nehmer, J. Babok, B. Germeshausen, B. Lehmann)
1977	E. Germany (M. Nehmer, H. Gerhardt, B. Germeshausen, R. Bethge)
1978	E. Germany (H. Schönau, H. Bernhardt, B.Musiol, H. Seifert)
1979	W. Germany (S. Galsreiter, H. Wagner, H. Bosche, D. Gebhard)
1980*	E. Germany (M. Nehmer, B. Musiol, B. Germeshausen, H. Gerhardt)

World Champions—Luge Tobogganing—Women

Most titles first held 1955: 5 Margit Schumann (E Ger) 1973–77 Winners since 1972:

1972*	Anna-Maria Muller (E Ger)
1973–77	(inc. 1976*) Margit Schumann (E Ger)
1978	Vera Sosulya (USSR)
1979	Melitta Sollmann (E Ger)
1980*	Vera Sosulya (USSR)

World Champions—Luge Tobogganing—Men

Championships were first held in 1955. Most titles: 4 Thomas Köhler (E Ger) (1962, 1964*, 1966, 1967) Winners since 1972:

1972*	Wolfgang Scheidel (E Ger)
1973	Hans Rinn (E Ger)
1974	Josef Fendt (W Ger)
1975	Wolfram Fiedler (E Ger)
1976*	Detlef Günther (E Ger)
1977	Hans Rinn (E Ger)
1978	Paul Hildgartner (Ita)
1979	Detlef Günther (E Ger)
1980*	Bernhard Glass (E Ger)

World Champions—Luge Tobogganing—Men's Two-Seater

Winners since 1972:

1972*	Italy (Paul Hildgartner and Walter Plaikner) & E. Ger (Horst Hornlein and Reinhard Bredow) shared
1973	E Ger (Horst Hornlein and Reinhard Bredow)
1974	E Ger (Bernd Hahn and Ulli Hahn)
1975	E Ger (Bernd Hahn and Ulli Hahn)
1976*	E Ger (Hans Rinn and Norbert Hahn)
1977	E Ger (Hans Rinn and Norbert Hahn)
1978	USSR (Dainis Bremze and Aigars Krikis)
1979	E Ger (Hans Brandner and Balthasar Schwarm)
1980*	E Ger (Hans Rinn and Norbert Hahn)

BOWLING

Origins. Bowling can be traced to articles found in the tomb of an Egyptian child of 5200 B.C. where there were nine pieces of stone to be set up as pins at which a stone "ball" was rolled. The

PIN DROP: Anne Splain (left) rolled an 831 three-game series to set a women's record in 1979. Les Schissler (right) of Denver claps his hands as his 12th ball scatters the pins for the first 300 game in the team event in the history of the ABC Tournament, at Miami Beach in 1967.

ball first had to roll through an archway made of three pieces of marble. There is also resemblance to a Polynesian game called *ula maika* which utilized pins and balls of stone. The stones were rolled a distance of 60 feet. In the Italian Alps about 2,000 years ago, the underhand tossing of stones at an object is believed the beginnings of *bocci*, a game still widely played in Italy and similar to bowling. The ancient Germans played a game of nine-pins called *Heidenwerfen*—knock down pagans. Martin Luther is credited with the statement that nine was the ideal number of pins. In the British Isles, lawn bowls were preferred to bowling at pins. In the 16th century, bowling at pins was the national sport in Scotland. How bowling at pins came to the United States is a matter of controversy. Early British settlers probably brought lawn bowls and set up what is known as Bowling Green at the tip of Manhattan Island in New York but perhaps the Dutch under Henry Hudson were the ones to be credited. Some historians say that in Connecticut the tenth pin was added to evade a legal ban against the nine-pin game in 1845 but others say that ten pins was played in New York City before this and point to Washington Irving's "Rip Van Winkle," written about 1818, as evidence.

Lanes. In the US there was 8,699 bowling establishments with 154,077 lanes in 1979 and about 65,000,000 bowlers.

The world's largest bowling center (now closed) was the Tokyo World Lanes Center, Japan, with 252 lanes.

Organizations. The American Bowling Congress (ABC) comprises 4,800,000 men who bowl in leagues and tournaments. The Women's International Bowling Congress (WIBC) has a membership of 4,200,000. The Professional Bowlers Association (PBA), formed in 1958, numbers 2,000 of the world's best bowlers.

World Championships

The Fédération Internationale des Quilleurs world championships were instituted in 1954. The highest pinfall in the individual men's event is 5,963 for 28 games by Ed Luther (US) at Milwaukee, Wisconsin, on August 28, 1971.

In the women's event (instituted 1963) the record is 4,615 pins in 24 games by Annedore Haefker (West Germany) at Tolworth, Surrey, England, on October 11, 1975.

League Scores

Highest Men's. The highest individual score for three games in 886 by Allie Brandt of Lockport, New York, on October 25, 1939. Maximum possible is 900 (three perfect games). Highest team score is 3,858 by Budweisers of St. Louis on March 12, 1958.

The highest season average attained in sanctioned competition is 239 by Jim Lewis of Schenectady, New York, in 88 games in a 3-man league in 1975–76.

Highest Women's. The highest individual score for three games is 831 by Anne Splain in Boardman, Ohio, on December 7, 1979. Highest team score is 3,379 by Freeway Washer of Cleveland in 1960. (Highest in WIBC tournament plays is 737 by D. D. Jacobson in 1972.)

Consecutive Strikes. The record for consecutive strikes in sanctioned match play is 33 by John Pezzin (born 1930) at Toledo, Ohio, on March 4, 1976.

Most Perfect Scores. The highest number of sanctioned 300 games is 27 (through 1979) by Elvin Mesger of Sullivan, Missouri. The maximum 900 for a three-game series has been recorded three times in unsanctioned games—by Leo Bentley at Lorain, Ohio, on March 26, 1931; by Joe Sargent at Rochester, New York, in 1934; and by Jim Murgie in Philadelphia, on February 4, 1937.

ABC Tournament Scores

Highest Individual. Highest three-game series in singles is 801 by Mickey Higham of Kansas City, Missouri, in 1977. Best three-game total in any ABC event is 804 by Lou Veit of Milwaukee, Wisconsin, in team in 1977. Jim Godman of Lorain, Ohio, holds the record for a nine-game All-Events total with 2,184 (731–749–704) set in Indianapolis, Indiana, in 1974. ABC Hall of Famers Fred Bujack of Detroit, Michigan, Bill Lillard of Houston, Texas, and Nelson Burton Jr. of St. Louis, Missouri, have won the most championships with 8 each. Bujack shared in 3 team and 4 team All-Events titles between 1949 and 1955, and also won the individual All-Events title in 1955. Lillard bowled on Regular and team All-Events champions in 1955 and 1956, the Classic team champions in 1962 and 1971, and won regular doubles and All-Events titles in 1956. Burton shared in 3 Classic team titles, 2 Classic doubles titles and has won Classic singles twice and Classic All-Events.

Highest Doubles. The ABC record of 558 was set in 1976 by Les Zikes of Chicago and Tommy Hudson of Akron, Ohio. The record score in a doubles series is 1,453, set in 1952 by John Klares (755) and Steve Nagy (698) of Cleveland.

Perfect Scores. Les Schissler of Denver scored 300 in the Classic team event in 1967, and Ray Williams of Detroit scored 300 in Regular team play in 1974. In all, there have been only thirty-seven 300 games in the ABC tournament. There have been 20 perfect games in singles, 14 in doubles, and three in team play.

Best Finishes in One Tournament. Les Schissler of Denver won the singles, All-Events, and was on the winning team in 1966 to tie Ed Lubanski of Detroit and Bill Lillard of Houston as the only men to win three ABC crowns in one year. The best four finishes in one ABC tournament were third in singles, second in doubles, third in team and first in All-Events by Bob Strampe, Detroit, in 1967, and first in singles, third in team and doubles and second in All-Events by Paul Kulbaga, Cleveland, in 1960.

Most Tournament Appearances. Bill Doehrman of Fort Wayne, Indiana, has competed in 69 consecutive ABC tournaments, beginning in 1908. (No tournaments were held in 1943–45.)

Attendance. Largest attendance on one day for an ABC Tournament was 5,257 in Milwaukee in 1952. The total attendance record was set at Reno, Nevada, in 1977 with 174,953 in 89 days.

Youngest and Oldest Winners. The youngest champion was David Chilcott of Butler, Pennsylvania, who was a member of the 1970 Booster team champions. The oldest champion was Joe Detloff of Chicago, Illinois, who, at the age of 72, was a winner in the 1965 Booster team event. The oldest doubles team in ABC competition totaled 165 years in 1955: Jerry Ameling (83) and Joseph Lehnbeutter (82), both from St. Louis.

Strikes and Spares in a Row. In the greatest finish to win an ABC title, Ed Shay set a record of 12 strikes in a row in 1958, when he scored a perfect game for a total of 733 in the series.

The most spares in a row is 23, a record set by Lt. Hazen Sweet of Battle Creek, Michigan, in 1950.

Professional Bowlers Association Records

Most Titles. Earl Anthony of Kent, Washington, has won a lifetime total of 31 PBA titles. The record number of titles won in one PBA season is 8, by Mark Roth of North Arlington, New Jersey, in 1978.

Consecutive Titles. Only three bowlers have ever won three consecutive professional tournaments—Dick Weber in 1961, Johnny Petraglia in 1971, and Mark Roth in 1977.

Highest Earnings. The greatest lifetime earnings on the Professional Bowlers Association circuit have been won by Earl Anthony of Kent, Washington, who has taken home $719,141 through 1979. Mark Roth of North Arlington, New Jersey, won a record $134,500 in the 1978 season.

Perfect Games. A total of 119 perfect (300-point) games were bowled in PBA tournaments through 1979. Dick Weber rolled 3 perfect games in one tournament (Houston, Texas) in 1965, as did Billy Hardwick of Louisville, Kentucky (in the Japan Gold

FRAME AND FORTUNE: Earl Anthony (left) is the PBA career champion with a lifetime total of 31 titles and earnings of over $700,000. Mark Roth (right) set PBA season marks in 1978 when he won 8 titles and earned $134,500.

Cup competition) in 1968, Roy Buckley of Columbus, Ohio (at Chagrin Falls, Ohio) in 1971, John Wilcox (at Detroit), and Norm Meyers of St. Louis, Missouri (at Peoria, Illinois) in 1979.

Don Johnson of Las Vegas, Nevada, bowled at least one perfect game in 11 consecutive seasons (1965–1975). Guppy Troup, of Savannah, Georgia, rolled six perfect games on the 1979 tour.

Longest Career

William H. Bailey (born January 4, 1891) has been bowling in the Hamilton City Ten Pin League, Ontario, Canada, for 72 consecutive years.

Marathons

Tom Destowet bowled for 150 hours 15 minutes in Dublin, California, April 2–8, 1978. He bowled 709 games with a 16-lb. ball.

Firestone Tournament of Champions Winners

1965	Billy Hardwick	1970	Don Johnson	1975	Dave Davis
1966	Wayne Zahn	1971	Johnny Petraglia	1976	Marshall Holman
1967	Jim Stefanich	1972	Mike Durbin	1977	Mike Berlin
1968	Dave Davis	1973	Jim Godman	1978	Earl Anthony
1969	Jim Godman	1974	Earl Anthony	1979	George Pappas

PBA National Championship Winners

1960	Don Carter	1967	Dave Davis	1974	Earl Anthony
1961	Dave Soutar	1968	Wayne Zahn	1975	Earl Anthony
1962	Carmen Salvino	1969	Mike McGrath	1976	Paul Colwell
1963	Billy Hardwick	1970	Mike McGrath	1977	Tommy Hudson
1964	Bob Strampe	1971	Mike Limongello	1978	Warren Nelson
1965	Dave Davis	1972	Johnny Guenther	1979	Mike Aulby
1966	Wayne Zahn	1973	Earl Anthony		

Sporting News PBA Player of the Year

ABC Masters

	Year	Games	W	L	Ave.	MATCHES Prizes
Lee Jouglard, Detroit, Mich.	1951	21	6	1	201.38	$ 620
Willard Taylor, Charleston, W. Va.	1952	36	8	1	200.89	950
Rudy Habetler, Chicago, Ill.	1953	44	10	1	200.30	1,000
Red Elkins, San Mateo, Calif.	1954	28	7	0	205.68	925
Buzz Fazio, Detroit, Mich.	1955	28	7	0	204.46	1,175
Dick Hoover, Akron, Ohio	1956	32	7	1	209.28	1,175
Dick Hoover, Akron, Ohio	1957	40	9	1	216.98	1,225
Tom Hennessey, St. Louis, Mo.	1958	28	7	0	209.54	1,210
Ray Bluth, St. Louis, Mo.	1959	28	7	0	214.93	1,210
Billy Golembiewski, Detroit, Mich.	1960	28	7	0	206.46	2,280
Don Carter, St. Louis, Mo.	1961	36	8	1	211.50	2,820
Billy Golembiewski, Detroit, Mich.	1962	28	7	0	223.43	3,305
Harry Smith, St. Louis, Mo.	1963	28	7	0	219.11	4,400
Billy Welu, Houston, Texas	1964	28	7	0	227.00	4,400
Billy Welu, St. Louis, Mo.	1965	40	9	1	202.30	4,450
Bob Strampe, Detroit, Mich.	1966	28	7	0	219.18	4,400
Lou Scalia, Hollywood, Fla.	1967	28	7	0	216.32	4,400
Pete Tountas, Tucson, Ariz.	1968	40	9	1	220.38	4,500
Jim Chestney, Denver, Colo.	1969	44	10	1	223.05	4,650
Don Glover, Bakersfield, Calif.	1970	40	9	1	215.25	4,500
Jim Godman, Lorain, Ohio	1971	40	9	1	229.20	5,650
Bill Beach, Sharon, Pa.	1972	36	8	1	220.75	5,685
Dave Soutar, Kansas City, Mo.	1973	28	7	0	218.61	5,520
Paul Colwell, Tucson, Ariz.	1974	28	7	0	234.17	5,620
Ed Ressler, Allentown, Pa.	1975	40	9	1	213.57	5,650
Nelson Burton, Jr., St. Louis, Mo.	1976	28	7	0	220.79	5,645
Earl Anthony, Tacoma, Wash.	1977	28	7	0	218.21	6,520
Frank Ellenburg, Mesa, Ariz.	1978	36	8	1	200.61	7,675
Doug Myers, El Toro, Calif.	1979	32	7	1	202.90	7,600

BOXING

Earliest References. Boxing with gloves was depicted on a fresco from the Isle of Thera, Greece, which has been dated 1520 B.C. The earliest prize-ring code of rules was formulated in England on August 16, 1743, by the champion pugilist Jack Broughton (1704–89), who reigned from 1729 to 1750. Boxing, which had in 1867 come under the Queensberry Rules, formulated for John Sholto Douglas, 9th Marquess of Queensberry, was not established as a legal sport in Britain until after a ruling of Mr. Justice Grantham following the death of Billy Smith (Murray Livingstone) as the result of a fight on April 24, 1901, at Covent Garden, London.

Longest Fight

The longest recorded fight with gloves was between Andy Bowen of New Orleans and Jack Burke in New Orleans, on April 6–7, 1893. The fight lasted 110 rounds and 7 hours 19 minutes from

OLD GLORY: Jersey Joe Walcott (left) became the oldest man to win the heavyweight crown when he knocked out Ezzard Charles (right) in Pittsburgh in 1951. He was 37 at the time. He held the title for 14 months before losing to Rocky Marciano, making him the oldest heavyweight champ ever at 38 years 7 months 23 days.

9:15 p.m. to 4:34 a.m., but was declared a no contest (later changed to a draw) when both men were unable to continue. The longest recorded bare knuckle fight was one of 6 hours 15 minutes between James Kelly and Jack Smith at Fiery Creek, Dalesford, Victoria, Australia, on December 3, 1855. The greatest recorded number of rounds is 276 in 4 hours 30 minutes, when Jack Jones beat Patsy Tunney in Cheshire, England, in 1825.

Shortest Fight

There is a distinction between the quickest knockout and the shortest fight. A knockout in 10½ seconds (including a 10-second count) occurred on September 26, 1946, when Al Couture struck Ralph Walton while the latter was adjusting a gum shield in his corner at Lewiston, Maine. If the time was accurately taken it is clear that Couture must have been more than halfway across the ring from his own corner at the opening bell.

The fastest officially timed knockout in British boxing is 11 seconds (including a doubtless fast 10-second count) when Jack Cain beat Harry Deamer, both of Notting Hill, Greater London, at the National Sporting Club on February 20, 1922.

The shortest fight on record appears to be one in a Golden Gloves tournament in Minneapolis, Minnesota, on November 4, 1947, when Mike Collins floored Pat Brownson with his first punch and the contest was stopped, without a count, 4 seconds after the bell.

The shortest world heavyweight title fight occurred when Tommy Burns (1881–1955) (né Noah Brusso) of Canada knocked out Jem

Roche in 1 minute 28 seconds in Dublin, Ireland, on March 17, 1908. The duration of the Clay vs. Liston fight at Lewiston, Maine, on May 25, 1965, was 1 minute 52 seconds (including the count) as timed from the video tape recordings despite a ring-side announcement giving a time of 1 minute. The shortest world title fight was when Al McCoy knocked out George Chip in 45 seconds for the middleweight crown in New York on April 7, 1914.

Tallest

The tallest boxer to fight professionally was Gogea Mitu (born 1914) of Rumania in 1935. He was 7 feet 4 inches and weighed 327 lbs. John Rankin, who won a fight in New Orleans, in November, 1967, was reputedly also 7 feet 4 inches.

World Heavyweight Champions

Heaviest and Lightest. The heaviest world champion was Primo Carnera (Italy) (1906–67), the "Ambling Alp," who won the title from Jack Sharkey in 6 rounds in New York City, on June 29, 1933. He scaled 267 lbs. for this fight but his peak weight was 270 lbs. He had the longest reach at 85½ inches (fingertip to fingertip) and also the largest fists with a 14¾-inch circumference. He had an expanded chest measurement of 53 inches. The lightest champion was Robert James Fitzsimmons (1863–1917), who was born at Helston, Cornwall, England, and, at a weight of 167 lbs., won the title by knocking out James J. Corbett in 14 rounds at Carson City, Nevada, on March 17, 1897.

The greatest differential in a world title fight was 86 lbs. be-

LONGEST AND LARGEST: Joe Louis (left), here beating former champion Max Schmelling, was heavyweight champ longer than anyone else. His reign lasted over 11 years, including 25 defenses, before he retired in 1949. Primo Carnera (right) was the largest heavyweight champ at 6 feet 5.4 inches and 270 pounds.

tween Carnera (270 lbs.) and Tommy Loughran (184 lbs.) of the US, when the former won on points at Miami, Florida, on March 1, 1934.

Tallest and Shortest. The tallest world champion was Primo Carnera, who was measured at 6 feet 5.4 inches by the Physical Education Director at the Hemingway Gymnasium of Harvard, although he was widely reported and believed in 1933 to be 6 feet 8½ inches tall. Jess Willard (1881–1968), who won the title in 1915, often stated as 6 feet 6¼ inches tall, was in fact 6 feet 5¼ inches. The shortest was Tommy Burns (1881–1955) of Canada, world champion from February 23, 1906, to December 26, 1908, who stood 5 feet 7 inches, and weighed 179 lbs.

Oldest and Youngest. The oldest man to win the heavyweight crown was Jersey Joe Walcott (born Arnold Raymond Cream, January 31, 1914, at Merchantville, New Jersey), who knocked out Ezzard Charles on July 18, 1951, in Pittsburgh, when aged 37 years 5 months 18 days. Walcott was the oldest title holder at 38 years 7 months 23 days when he lost to Rocky Marciano on September 23, 1952. The youngest age at which the world title has been won is 21 years 331 days by Floyd Patterson (born Waco, North Carolina, January 4, 1935). After the retirement of Rocky Marciano, Patterson won the vacant title by beating Archie Moore in 5 rounds in Chicago, on November 30, 1956.

Most Recaptures. Muhammad Ali Haj is the only man to regain the heavyweight title twice. Ali first won the title on February 25, 1964, defeating Sonny Liston. He defeated George Foreman on October 30, 1974, having been stripped of his title by the world boxing authorities on April 26, 1967. He lost his title to Leon Spinks on February 15, 1978, but regained it on September 15, 1978, by defeating Spinks in New Orleans.

Undefeated. Rocky Marciano (b. Rocco Francis Marchegiano) (1923–69) is the only heavyweight champion to have been undefeated in his entire professional career (1947–56).

Longest-Lived. Jess Willard was born December 29, 1881, at St. Clere, Kansas, and died in Pacoima, California, on December 15, 1968, aged 86 years 351 days.

Earliest Title Fight. The first world heavyweight title fight, with gloves and 3-minute rounds, was between John L. Sullivan (1858–1918) and "Gentleman" James J. Corbett (1866–1933) in New Orleans, on September 7, 1892. Corbett won in 21 rounds.

World Champions (any weight)

Longest and Shortest Reigns. The longest reign of any world champion is 11 years 8 months 7 days by heavyweight Joe Louis (born Joseph Louis Barrow, in Lafayette, Alabama, May 13, 1914), from June 22, 1937, when he knocked out James J. Braddock in the 8th round at Chicago until announcing his retirement on March 1, 1949. During his reign Louis made a record 25 defenses of his heavyweight title.

The shortest reign has been 33 days by Tony Canzoneri (US)

WEIGHT WATCHING: "Hammerin'" Henry Armstrong (left) is the only man to hold world titles at three weights simultaneously: feather-weight, lightweight and welterweight. Pascual Perez (right) was the smallest world champion, winning the flyweight title at 107 pounds and 4 feet 11½ inches tall.

(1908–1959), junior welterweight champion from May 21 to June 23, 1933.

Youngest and Oldest. The youngest at which any world championship has been claimed is 17 years 180 days by Wilfredo Benitez (born September 8, 1958) of Puerto Rico, who won the W.B.A. light-welterweight title in San Juan on March 6, 1976.

The oldest world champion was Archie Moore (b. Archibald Lee Wright, Collinsville, Illinois, December 13, 1913 or 1916), who was recognized as a light-heavyweight champion up to February 10, 1962, when his title was removed. He was then between 45 and 48. Bob Fitzsimmons (1863–1917) had the longest career of any official world titleholder with over 32 years from 1882 to 1914. He won his last world title aged 40 years 183 days in San Francisco on November 25, 1903. He was an amateur from 1880 to 1882.

Greatest "Tonnage." The greatest "tonnage" recorded in any fight is 700 lbs., when Claude "Humphrey" McBride of Oklahoma at 340 lbs. knocked out Jimmy Black of Houston at 360 lbs. in the 3rd round at Oklahoma City on June 1, 1971.

The greatest "tonnage" in a world title fight was 488¾ lbs. when Carnera (259¼ lbs.) fought Paolino Uzcudun (229½ lbs.) of Spain in Rome, Italy, on October 22, 1933.

Smallest Champions. The smallest man to win any world title has been Pascual Perez (1926–1977) who won the flyweight title in Tokyo on November 26, 1954, at 107 lbs. and 4 feet 11½ inches tall. Jimmy Wilde (b. Merthyr Tydfil, 1892, d. 1969, UK) who held the flyweight title from 1916 to 1923 was reputed never to have fought above 108 lbs.

Longest Fight. The longest world title fight (under Queensberry Rules) was between the lightweights Joe Gans (1874–1910), of the US, and Oscar "Battling" Nelson (1882–1954), the "Durable Dane," at Goldfield, Nevada, on September 3, 1906. It was terminated in the 42nd round when Gans was declared the winner on a foul.

Most Recaptures. The only boxer to win a world title five times at one weight is Sugar Ray Robinson (b. Walker Smith, Jr., in Detroit, May 3, 1920) who beat Carmen Basilio (US) in the Chicago Stadium on March 25, 1958, to regain the world middleweight title for the fourth time. The other title wins were over Jake LaMotta (US) in Chicago on February 14, 1951, Randy Turpin (UK) in New York on September 12, 1951, Carl "Bobo" Olson (US) in Chicago on December 9, 1955, and Gene Fullmer (US) in Chicago on May 1, 1957. The record number of title bouts in a career is 33 or 34 (at bantam and featherweight) by George Dixon (1870–1909), *alias* "Little Chocolate," of Canada, between 1890 and 1901.

Most Titles Simultaneously. The only man to hold world titles at three weights simultaneously was "Hammerin' " Henry Armstrong (born December 12, 1912), now the Rev. Henry Jackson, of the US, at featherweight, lightweight and welterweight from August to December, 1938.

Most Knockdowns in Title Fights. Vic Toweel (South Africa) knocked down Danny O'Sullivan of London 14 times in 10 rounds in their world bantamweight fight at Johannesburg, on December 2, 1950, before the latter retired.

All Fights

Largest Purse. Muhammad Ali Haj (born Cassius Marcellus Clay, in Louisville, Kentucky, January 17, 1942) made a reported $6,500,000 in his successful defense of the heavyweight title against Ken Norton (US), held in Yankee Stadium, New York City, on September 28, 1976.

The largest stake ever fought for in the bare-knuckle era was $22,500 in a 27-round fight between Jack Cooper and Wolf Bendoff at Port Elizabeth, South Africa, on July 29, 1889.

Highest Attendances. The greatest paid attendance at any boxing fight has been 120,757 (with a ringside price of $27.50) for the Tunney vs. Dempsey world heavyweight title fight at the Sesquicentennial Stadium, Philadelphia, on September 23, 1926.

THE HARDER THEY FALL: Mu-hammad Ali is seated on the canvas (left) during his unsuccessful attempt to regain the heavyweight crown from Joe Frazier in New York's Madison Square Garden in 1971. Three years later, Ali knocked out George Foreman in the 8th round (right) in Zaire for the first of his record 2 recaptures.

The indoor record is 63,360 for the Spinks vs. Ali world heavy-weight title fight at the Louisiana Superdome in New Orleans, on September 15, 1978. The gate receipts exceeded $6,000,000, a record total. The highest non-paying attendance is 135,132 at the Tony Zale vs. Billy Pryor fight at Juneau Park, Milwaukee, Wisconsin, on August 18, 1941.

Lowest. The smallest attendance at a world heavyweight title fight was 2,434 at the Clay vs. Liston fight at Lewiston, Maine, on May 25, 1965.

Highest Earnings in Career. The largest known fortune ever made in a fighting career (or any sports career) is an estimated $60,000,000 (including exhibitions) amassed by Muhammad Ali from October, 1960 to August, 1979, in 59 fights comprising 529 rounds.

Most Knockouts. The greatest number of knockouts in a career is 141 by Archie Moore (1936 to 1963). The record for consecutive K.O.'s is 44, set by Lamar Clark of Utah at Las Vegas, Nevada, on January 11, 1960. He knocked out 6 in one night (5 in the first round) in Bingham, Utah, on December 1, 1958.

Most Fights. The greatest recorded number of fights in a career is 1,024 by Bobby Dobbs (US) (1858–1930), who is reported to have fought from 1875 to 1914, a period of 39 years. Abraham Hollandersky, *alias* Abe the Newsboy (US), is reputed to have had 1,309 fights in the fourteen years from 1905 to 1918, but many of them were exhibition bouts.

Most Fights Without Loss. Hal Bagwell, a lightweight, of Gloucester, England, was reputedly undefeated in 183 consecutive fights, of which only 5 were draws, between August 15, 1938, and November 29, 1948. His record of fights in the wartime period (1939–46) is very sketchy, however. Of boxers with complete records, Packey McFarland (1888–1936) went undefeated in 97 fights from 1905 to 1915.

Longest Career. The heavyweight Jem Mace, known as "the gypsy" (born at Norwich, England, April 8, 1831), had a career lasting 35 years from 1855 to 1890, but there were several years in which he had only one fight. He died, aged 79, in Jarrow on November 30, 1910. Walter Edgerton, the "Kentucky Rosebud," knocked out John Henry Johnson, aged 45, in 4 rounds at the Broadway A.C., New York City, on February 4, 1916, when aged 63. (See also *Most Fights*, above.)

Most Olympic Gold Medals. The only amateur boxers ever to win three Olympic gold medals are the southpaw László Papp (b 1926, Hungary), who took the middleweight (1948) and the light-middleweight titles (1952 and 1956), and Cuban heavyweight Teofilio Stevenson, who has won the gold medal in his division for three successive Games (1972, 1976 and 1980). The only man to win two titles in one meeting was Oliver L. Kirk (US), who took both the bantam and featherweight titles at St. Louis, Mo, in 1904, when the US won all the titles. Harry W. Mallin (GB) was in 1924 the first boxer ever to defend an Olympic title successfully when he retained the middleweight crown.

The oldest man to win an Olympic gold medal in boxing was Richard K. Gunn (b 1870) (GB), who won the featherweight title on October 27, 1908, in London, aged 38.

World Boxing Championships—Longest and Shortest Reigns

Heavyweight:	Longest: 11 yrs. 252 days	Joe Louis (US)	June 22, 1937– March 1, 1949
	Shortest: 212 days	Leon Spinks (US)	Feb. 15– Sept. 15, 1978
Light-Heavy:	Longest: 9 yrs. 55 days	Archie Moore (US)	Dec. 17, 1952– Feb. 10, 1962
	Shortest: 73 days	Jack Root (US)	April 22– July 4, 1903
Middleweight:	Longest: 8 yrs. 9 months	Tommy Ryan (US)	Feb. 25, 1898– March 1907 (rtd)
	Shortest: 64 days	Randolph Turpin (England)	July 10– Sept. 12, 1951
Junior Middle:	Longest: 2 yrs. 216 days	Koichi Wajima (Japan) (WBA)	Oct. 31, 1971– June 4, 1974
	Shortest: 143 days	Jose Duran (Spain) (WBA)	May 18, 1976– Oct. 8, 1976
Welterweight:	Longest: 4 yrs. 187 days	Freddie Cochrane (US)	July 29, 1941– Feb. 1, 1946
	Shortest: 65 days	Johnny Bratton (US) (NBA)	March 14– May 18, 1951
Junior Welter:	Longest: 3 yrs. 129 days	Antonio Cervantes (Colombia) (WBA)	Oct. 29, 1972– March 6, 1976
	Shortest: 33 days	Tony Canzoneri (US)	May 21– June 23, 1933
Lightweight:	Longest: 10 yrs.	Jack McAuliffe (Ireland)	Oct. 29, 1886– 1896 (rtd)
	Shortest: 56 days	Chango Carmona (Mexico) (WBC)	Sept. 15– Nov. 10, 1972
Junior Light:	Longest: 7 yrs. 106 days	Flash Elorde (Philippines)	March 16, 1960– June 30, 1967
	Shortest: 167 days	Yoshiaki Numata (Japan)	June 30– Dec. 14, 1967
Featherweight:	Longest: 11 yrs. 101 days	Johnny Kilbane (US)	Feb 22, 1912– June 2, 1923
	Shortest: 46 days	Dave Sullivan (Ireland)	Sept. 26– Nov. 11, 1898
Junior Feather: (Super-Bantamweight)	Longest: ———	Wilfredo Gomez (Puerto Rico) (WBC)	May 21, 1977– Current Champion
	Shortest: 54 days	Royal Kobayashi (Japan) (WBC)	Oct. 1– Nov. 24, 1976
Bantamweight:	Longest: 5 yrs. 348 days	Panama Al Brown (US)	June 18, 1929– June 1, 1935
	Shortest: 60 days	Pete Herman (US)	July 25– Sept. 23, 1921
Flyweight:	Longest: 7 yrs. 125 days	Jimmy Wilde (England)	Feb. 14, 1916– June 18, 1923
	Shortest: 47 days	Emile Pladner (France) (NBA) (IBU)	March 2– April 18, 1929
Junior Fly:	Longest: ———	Yoko Gushiken (Japan) (WBA)	Oct. 10, 1976– Current Champion
	Shortest: 76 days	Freddie Castillo (Mexico) (WBC)	Feb. 19– May 6, 1978

World Champions

Unfortunately it is by no means easy to draw up lists of boxing world champions as there have been different governing bodies that recognize champions. There are now two such governing bodies, the World Boxing Council (WBC) and the World Boxing Association (WBA).

Below is a full list of the Heavyweight World Champions since John L. Sullivan knocked out Paddy Ryan in 1882, and both WBA and WBC Champions at the other weights since 1965.

Heavyweight

1882	John L. Sullivan
1892	James J. Corbett
1897	Bob Fitzsimmons
1899	James J. Jeffries
1905	Marvin Hart
1906	Tommy Burns
1908	Jack Johnson
1915	Jess Willard
1919	Jack Dempsey
1926	Gene Tunney
1930	Max Schmeling
1932	Jack Sharkey
1933	Primo Carnera
1934	Max Baer
1935	James J. Braddock
1937	Joe Louis
1949	Ezzard Charles
1951	Jersey Joe Walcott
1952	Rocky Marciano
1956	Floyd Patterson
1959	Ingemar Johansson
1960	Floyd Patterson
1962	Sonny Liston
1964	Cassius Clay/Muhammad Ali
1965	Ernie Terrell (WBA only) (until 1967)
1968	Joe Frazier (NY State)
1968	Jimmy Ellis (WBA)
1970	Joe Frazier (undisputed)
1973	George Foreman
1974	Muhammad Ali
1978	Leon Spinks
1978	Ken Norton (WBC)
1978	Muhammad Ali (WBA)
1978	Larry Holmes (WBC)
1979	John Tate (WBA)

Most successful title defenses: 25 Joe Louis between 1937 and 1948, 19 Muhammad Ali between 1965 and 1978 (in addition to winning the title three times)

Light Heavyweight

1965	Jose Torres
1966	Dick Tiger
1968	Bob Foster
1971	Vincente Rondon (WBA) (1972)
1974	John Conteh (WBC)
1974	Victor Galindez (WBA)
1977	Miguel Cuello (WBC)
1978	Mate Parlov (WBC)
1978	Mike Rossman (WBA)
1978	Marvin Johnson (WBC)
1979	Matthew Franklin (WBC)
1979	Victor Galindez (WBA)
1979	Marvin Johnson (WBA)

Middleweight

1965	Dick Tiger
1966	Emile Griffith
1967	Nino Benvenuti
1967	Emile Griffith
1968	Nino Benvenuti
1970	Carlos Monzon
1974	Carlos Monzon (WBA)
1974	Rodrigo Valdes (WBC)
1976	Carlos Monzon (both)
1977	Rodrigo Valdes
1978	Hugo Corro
1979	Vito Antuofermo

Light Middleweight

1965	Nino Benvenuti
1966	Kim Ki-Soo
1968	Sandro Massinghi
1969	Freddie Little
1970	Carmelo Bossi
1971	Koichi Wajima
1974	Oscar Albarado
1975	Koichi Wajima
1975	Miguel De Oliveira (WBC)
1975	Jae Do Yuh (WBA)
1975	Elisha Obed (WBC)
1976	Eckhard Dagge (WBC)
1976	Koichi Wajima (WBA)
1976	José Duran (WBA)
1976	Miguel Castellini (WBA)
1977	Rocky Mattioli (WBC)
1977	Eddie Gazo (WBA)
1978	Masashi Kudo (WBA)
1979	Maurice Hope (WBC)
1979	Ayub Kalule (WBA)

Welterweight

1966	Curtis Cokes
1969	Jose Napoles
1970	Billy Backus
1971	Jose Napoles
1975	John H. Stracey (WBC)
1975	Angel Espada (WBA)
1976	Carlos Palomino (WBC)
1976	Jose Cuevas (WBA)
1979	Wilfredo Benitez (WBC)
1979	Sugar Ray Leonard (C)

Light Welterweight (or Super Lightweight)

1965	Carlos Hernandez
1966	Sandro Lopopolo
1967	Paul Fuji
1968	Pedro Adigue (WBC)
1968	Nicholas Loche (WBA)
1970	Bruno Arcari (WBC)

OLYMPIC GOLD GLOVES: Cuba's Teofilio Stevenson (right) lands a left to the head of Duane Bobick (US) enroute to the 1972 Olympic heavyweight gold medal. Stevenson also captured the gold in 1976 and 1980 to become only the second boxer to win 3 Olympic golds.

World Champions (continued)

1972	Alfonso Frazer (WBA)
1972	Antonio Cervantes (WBA)
1974	Perico Fernandez (WBC)
1975	Saensak Muangsurin (WBC)
1976	Miguel Velasquez (WBC)
1976	Wilfredo Benitez (WBA)
1976	Saensak Muangsurin (WBC)
1977	Antonio Cervantes (WBA)
1978	Him Sang-Hyun (WBC)

Lightweight

1965	Carlos Ortiz
1968	Carlos Teo Cruz
1969	Mando Ramos
1970	Ismael Laguna
1970	Ken Buchanan
1971	Pedro Carrasco (WBC)
1971	Ken Buchanan (WBA & UK)
1972	Mando Ramos (WBC)
1972	Roberto Duran (WBA & UK)
1972	Chango Carmona (WBC)
1972	Rodolfo Gonzalez (WBC)
1974	Guts Ishimatsu (WBC)
1974	Roberto Duran (WBA)
1976	Esteban de Jesus (WBC)
1978	Roberto Duran (both)
1979	Jim Watt (WBC)
1979	Ernesto Espana (WBA)

Junior Lightweight

1967	Yoshiaki Numata
1967	Hiroshi Kobayashi
1969	Rene Barrientos (WBC)
1969	Hiroshi Kobayashi (WBA)
1970	Yoshiaki Numata (WBC)
1971	Ricardo Arredondo (WBC)
1971	Alfredo Marcano (WBA)
1972	Ben Villaflor (WBA)
1973	Kuniaki Shibata (WBA)
1973	Ben Villaflor (WBA)
1974	Kuniaki Shibata (WBC)
1975	Alfredo Escalera (WBC)
1976	Sam Serrano (WBA)
1978	Alexis Arguello (WBC)

Featherweight

1964	Vincente Saldivar
1968	Howard Winstone (WBC)
1968	Raul Rojas (WBA)
1968	Jose Legra (WBC)
1968	Shozo Saijyo (WBA)
1969	Johnny Famechon (WBC)
1970	Vincente Saldivar (WBC)
1970	Kuniaki Shibata (WBC)
1971	Antonio Gomez (WBA)
1972	Clemente Sanchez (WBC)
1972	Ernesto Marcel (WBA)
1972	Jose Legra (WBC)
1973	Eder Jofre (WBC)
1974	Bobby Chacon (WBC)
1974	Ruben Olivares (WBA)
1974	Alexis Arguello (WBA)
1975	Ruben Olivares (WBC)
1975	David Kotey (WBC)
1976	Danny Lopez (WBC)
1977	Rafael Ortega (WBA)
1977	Cecilio Lastra (WBA)
1978	Eusebio Pedrosa (WBA)
1980	Salvador Sanchez (WBC)

Light Featherweight (Super Bantamweight)

1976	Rigoberto Riasco (WBC)
1976	Royal Kobayashi (WBC)
1976	Dong Kyun Yum (WBC)
1977	Wilfredo Gomez (WBC)
1977	Soo Hwan Hong (WBA)
1978	Ricardo Cardona (WBA)

Bantamweight

1965	Masahiko Herada
1968	Lionel Rose
1969	Ruben Olivares
1970	Jesus Castillo
1971	Ruben Olivares
1972	Rafael Herrera
1972	Enrique Pinder
1973	Rafael Herrera (WBC)
1973	Romero Anaya (WBA)

1973	Arnold Taylor (WBA)	1972	Venice Borkorsor (WBC)
1974	Rodolfo Martinez (WBC)	1973	Betulio Gonzalez (WBC)
1974	Soo Hwan Hong (WBA)	1973	Chartchai Chionoi (WBA)
1975	Alfonso Zamora (WBA)	1974	Shoji Oguma (WBC)
1976	Carlos Zarate (WBC)	1974	Susumu Hanagata (WBA)
1977	Jorge Lujan (WBA)	1975	Miguel Canto (WBC)
1979	Guadalupe Pintor (WBC)	1975	Erbito Salavarria (WBA)
		1976	Alfonso Lopez (WBA)
		1976	Gustavo Espadas (WBA)
Flyweight		1978	Betulio Gonzalez (WBA)
1965	Salvatore Burruni	1979	Park Chan-Hee (WBC)
1966	Walter McGowan (WBC)	1979	Luis Ibarra (WBA)
1966	Horacio Accavallo (WBA)		
1966	Chartchai Chionoi (WBC)		
1969	Efren Torres (WBC)	**Light Flyweight**	
1969	Hiroyuki Ebihara (WBA)	1975	Franco Udella (WBC)
1970	Chartchai Chionoi (WBC)	1975	Jaime Rios (WBC)
1970	Bernabe Villacampo (WBA)	1975	Luis Espada (WBC)
1970	Erbito Salavarria (WBC)	1976	Juan Guzman (WBA)
1970	Berkrerk Chartvanchai (WBA)	1976	Yoko Gushiken (WBA)
1970	Masao Ohba (WBA)	1978	Netranoi Vorasingh (WBC)
1971	Betulio Gonzalez (WBC)	1979	Sung Jun Kim (WBC)

World Amateur Boxing Championships

First held at Havana in 1974, the world amateur championships are held every four years, the second being held at Belgrade in 1978. Winners:

Heavy:	1974	Teofilio Stevenson (Cub)	1978	Teofilio Stevenson (Cub)
Light-Heavy:	1974	Mate Parlov (Yug)	1978	Sixto Soria (Cub)
Middle:	1974	Rufat Riskiev (USSR)	1978	Jose Gomez (Cub)
Light-Middle:	1974	Rolando Garbey (Cub)	1978	Viktor Savchenko (USSR)
Welter:	1974	Emilio Correa (Cub)	1978	Valeriy Rachkov (USSR)
Light-Welter:	1974	Ayub Kalule (Uga)	1978	Valeriy Lvov (USSR)
Light:	1974	Vasiliy Solomin (USSR)	1978	Andeh Davison (Nig)
Feather:	1974	Howard Davis (US)	1978	Angel Herrera (Cub)
Bantam:	1974	Wilfredo Gomez (PR)	1978	Adolfo Horta (Cub)
Fly:	1974	Douglas Rodriguez (Cub)	1978	Henryk Srednicki (Pol)
Light-Fly:	1974	Jorge Hernandez (Cub)	1978	Stephen Muchoki (Ken)

Olympic Games

Boxing has been included at each Olympic Games since 1904. Winners of two or more gold medals have been:

3 Laszlo Papp (Hun): Middle 1948, Light-Middle 1952 and 1956

3 Teofilio Stevenson (Cub): Heavy 1972, 1976 and 1980

2 Oliver Kirk (US): Feather and Bantam 1904

2 Harry Mallin (GB): Middle 1920 and 1924

2 Boris Lagutin (USSR): Light-Middle 1964 and 1968

2 Jerzy Kulej (Pol): Light-Welter 1964 and 1968

BULLFIGHTING

Origins. In the latter half of the second millennium B.C., bull leaping was practiced in Crete. Bullfighting in Spain was first reported by the Romans in Baetica (Andalusia) in the third century B.C.

The first renowned professional *espada* (bullfighter) was Francisco Romero of Ronda, in Andalusia, Spain, who introduced the *estoque* and the red *muleta c.* 1700. Spain now has some 190 active matadors. Since 1700, 42 major matadors have died in the ring.

HORNS OF A DILEMMA: El Cordobés is the highest paid bullfighter in history. In 1970, he received an estimated $1.8 million for 121 fights. He is here having a rough day; his skill and grace usually got the better of the bull.

Largest Stadiums

The world's largest bullfighting ring, the Plaza, Mexico City, with a capacity of 48,000, was closed in March, 1976. The largest of Spain's 312 bullrings in Las Ventas, Madrid, with a capacity of 24,000.

Most Successful Matadors

The most successful matador measured by bulls killed was Lagartijo (1841–1900), born Rafael Molina, whose lifetime total was 4,867.

The longest career of any full matador was that of Bienvenida (1922–75) (*né* Antonio Mejías) from 1942 to 1974. (Recent Spanish law requires compulsory retirement at age 55.)

Most Kills in a Day

In 1884, Romano set a record by killing 18 bulls in a day in Seville, and in 1949 El Litri (Miguel Báes) set a Spanish record with 114 *novilladas* in a season.

Highest Paid Matadors

The highest paid bullfighter in history is El Cordobés (born Manuel Benitez Pérez, probably on May 4, 1936, in Palma del Rio, Spain), who became a multimillionaire in 1965, during which year he fought 111 *corridas* up to October 4, receiving over $15,000 for each half hour in the ring. In 1970, he received an estimated $1,800,000 for 121 fights.

Paco Camino (b. December 19, 1941) has received $27,200 (2,000,000 *pesetas*) for a *corrida*. He retired in 1977.

CANOEING

Origins. The acknowledged pioneer of canoeing as a modern sport was John Macgregor, a British barrister, in 1865. The Canoe Club was formed on July 26, 1866.

Most Olympic Gold Medals

Gert Fredriksson (b. November 21, 1919) of Sweden has won the most Olympic gold medals with six in 1948–52–56–60. In addition to his Olympic titles he has won three other world titles in non-Olympic years.

The most by a woman is 3 by Ludmila Pinayeva (*née* Khvedosyuk, born January 14, 1936) (USSR) in the 500-meter K.1 in 1964 and 1968, and the 500-meter K.2 in 1972.

The Olympic 1,000-meter best performance of 3 minutes 06.46 seconds by the 1976 Spanish K.4 represents an average speed of 11.99 m.p.h., and a rate of about 125 strokes per minute.

Most World Titles

Yuri Lobanov (USSR) (b. September 29, 1952) won 11 world titles from 1972 to 1979. Ludmila Pinayeva added six world titles to her three Olympic golds, from 1966 to 1973, for a women's record total.

Longest Journey

The longest canoe journey in history was one of 7,516 miles around the eastern US by paddle and portage, from Lake Itasca, Minnesota, *via* New Orleans, Miami, New York and Lake Ontario, by Randy Bauer (born August 15, 1949) and Jerry Mimbach (born May 22, 1952) of Coon Rapids, Minnesota, from September 8, 1974, to August 30, 1976.

The longest journey without portage or aid of any kind is one

MOST GOLD MEDALS: Sweden's Gert Fredriksson has won 6 Olympic gold medals (1,000-meter Kayak Singles in 1948, 1952 and 1956; 10,000-meter Kayak Singles in 1948 and 1956; and the 1,000-meter Kayak Doubles in 1960), as well as three world titles in non-Olympic years. Here he is wearing the gold medal for the 10,000-meter race at the Melbourne Games in 1956.

GOLD IN MONTREAL: Russians Nina Glopova and Galina Kreft paddled their way to the women's Kayak Pairs gold medal at the 1976 Olympics in Montreal.

of 6,102 miles by Richard H. Grant and Ernest Lassey circumnavigating the eastern US from Chicago to New Orleans to Miami to New York, returning back to Chicago *via* the Great Lakes, from September 22, 1930, to August 15, 1931.

Eskimo Rolls

The record for Eskimo rolls is 1,000 in 65 minutes 39.3 seconds by Bruce Parry (b. September 25, 1960) on Lake Lismore, New South Wales, Australia, on December 17, 1977. A "hand-rolling" record of 100 rolls in 3 minutes 44 seconds was set in the Strathclyde University pool, Scotland, by Peter Turcan (21) on June 18, 1979.

English Channel Crossing

Andrew William Dougall Samuel (Scotland) paddled from Dover, England, to Wissant, France, in 3 hours 33 minutes 47 seconds on September 5, 1976.

The doubles record is 3 hours 20 minutes 30 seconds by Capt. William Stanley Crook and the late Ronald Ernest Rhodes, in their fiberglass K.2 *Accord*, from Dover, England, to Cap Blanc Nez, France, on September 20, 1961.

The record for a double crossing is 12 hours 47 minutes in K.1 canoes by nine members of the Canoe Camping Club of Great Britain on May 7, 1976.

Longest Open Sea Voyage

Beatrice and John Dowd, Ken Beard and Steve Benson (Richard Gillett replaced him midjourney) paddled 2,170 miles out of a total journey of 2,192 miles from Venezuela to Miami, Florida, via the West Indies from August 11, 1977, to April 29, 1978, in two Klepper Aerius 20 kayaks.

Highest Altitude

In September, 1976, Dr. Michael Jones (1951–78) and Michael Hopkinson of the British Everest Canoe Expedition canoed down the Dudh Kosi River in Nepal from an altitude of 17,500 feet.

Longest Race

The longest regularly held canoe race in the US is the Texas Water Safari (instituted 1963) which covers the 419 miles from San Marcos to Seadrift, Texas, on the San Marcos and Guadalupe rivers. Robert Chatham and Butch Hodges set the record of 37 hours 18 minutes on June 5–6, 1976.

Downstream Canoeing

River	Miles	Canoer	Location	Duration
Mississippi	2,320	Royal Air Force team of three two-man canoes (GB)	Lake Itasca, Minnesota, to Gulf of Mexico, Aug. 23–Oct. 4, 1978	42 days 5 hours
Mississippi-Missouri	3,810	Nicholas Francis (GB)	Three Forks, Montana, to New Orleans, July 13–Nov. 25, 1977	135 days
Congo	2,600	John and Julie Batchelor (GB)	Moasampanga to Banana, May 8–Sept. 12, 1974	128 days
Amazon	3,400	Stephan Z. Bezuk (US) (kayak)	Atalaya to Ponta do Céu, June 21–Nov. 4, 1970	136 days
Nile	4,000	John Goddard (US), Jean Laporte and André Davy (France)	Kagera to the Delta, Nov., 1953–July, 1954	9 months

ALL WET: Bruce Parry set the record for Eskimo rolls by performing 1,000 in 65 minutes 39.3 seconds in Australia in 1977.

Olympic Games

First held in the Olympic Games in 1936. Winners at each event in 1980 were:

MEN

Kayak Singles: 500m Vladimir Parfenovich (USSR) 1:43.43; 1000m Rüdiger Helm (E Ger) 3:48.77

Kayak Pairs: 500m: Vladimir Parfenovich & Sergei Chukhrai (USSR) 1:32.38 1000m Vladimir Parfenovich & Sergei Chukhrai (USSR) 3:26.72

Kayak Fours: 1000m Rüdiger Helm, Bernd Olbricht, Harald Marg, Bernd Duvigneau (E Ger) 3:13.76

Canadian Singles: 500m: Sergei Postrekhin (USSR) 1:53.37; 1000m: Lubomir Lubenov (Bul) 4:12.38

Canadian Pairs: 500m: Laszlo Foltan & Istvan Vaskuti (Hun) 1:43.39; 1000m Ivan Potzaichin & Toma Simionov (Rum) 3:47.65

WOMEN

Kayak Singles: 500m Birgit Fischer (E Ger) 1:57.96

Kayak Pairs: 500m Carsta Genauss & Martina Bischof (E Ger) 1:43.88

World Championships

Gert Fredriksson holds the record for the most world titles, as, in addition to his six Olympic Gold Medals, he also won three other world titles: 1000m Kayak Singles in 1950 and 1954; 500m Kayak Singles in 1954.

Double Gold medallists at the 1978 world championships were:
Rudiger Helm (E Ger): 1000m K1, 500m K2, 1000m K4—won most with 3
Rudiger Marg (E Ger): 500m K4, 1000m K4
Bernd Olbricht (E Ger): 500m K2, 1000m K4
Bernd Duvigneau (E Ger): 500m K4, 1000m K4
Tamas Buday (Hun): 1000m C2, 10,000m C2
Istvan Vaskuti (Hun): 500m C2, 10,000m C2
Marion Rosiger (E Ger): Women's 500m K2, 500m K4
Martina Fischer (E Ger): Women's 500m K2, 500m K4
Roswitha Eberl (E Ger): Women's 500m K1, 500m K4

CAVE EXPLORATION
(Spelunking)

Duration

The endurance record for staying in a cave is 463 days by Milutin Veljkovic (b. 1935) (Yugoslavia) in the Samar Cavern, Svrljig Mountains, northern Yugoslavia from June 24, 1969, to September 30, 1970.

Progressive Caving Depth Records

Feet	Cave	Cavers	Date	
453	Macocha, Moravia, Czech.	J. Nagel et al.		1748
741	Grotta di Padriciano, Trieste, Italy	Antonio Lindner et al.		1839
1,076	Grotta di Trebiciano, Trieste	Antonio Lindner et al.	April 6,	1841
1,509	Geldlöch, Austria	—		1923
1,574	Antro di Corchia, Tuscany, Italy	E. Fiorentino Club		1934
1,978	Trou du Glaz, Isère, France	P. Chevalier et al.		1947
2,418	Reseau de la Pierre St. Martin, Básses-Pyrénées, France	Georges Lépineux et al.	July,	1953
2,962	Gouffre Berger, Isère, France	*F. Petzl and 6 men	Sept. 25,	1954
3,123	Gouffre Berger, Isère, France	L. Potié, G. Garby et al.	Aug.,	1955
3,681	Gouffre Berger, Isère, France	F. Petzl and others	July,	1956
3,715	Gouffre Berger, Isère, France	K. Pearce	Aug.	1963

| 3,842 | Reseau de la Pierre Saint Martin | Ass. de Rech. Spéléo Internationale | Aug., 1966 |
| 4,370 | Reseau de la Pierre Saint Martin | A.R.S.I.P. | Aug., 1975 |

N.B.—The Reseau de la Pierre St. Martin was explored via a number of entrances, and was never entirely descended at any one time until 1978. Consequently, after Aug., 1963, the "sporting" records for greatest descent into a cave should read:

| 3,743 | Gouffre Berger, Isère, France | Spéléo Club de Seine | July, 1968 |
| 4,370 | Reseau de La Pierre St. Martin | P. Courbon *et al.* | Sept., 1978 |

CRICKET

Origins. The earliest evidence of the game of cricket is from a drawing depicting two men playing with a bat and ball dated *c.* 1250. The game was played in Guildford, Surrey, at least as early as 1550. The earliest major match of which the score survives was one in which a team representing England (40 and 70) was beaten by Kent (53 and 58 for 9) by one wicket at the Artillery Ground in Finsbury, London, on June 18, 1744. Cricket was played in Australia as early as 1803.

Cricket (First Class Matches Only)

Batting—Team Scores

Highest Innings
1,107 Victoria vs. N.S.W., Australia, Dec. 27–28, 1926

Highest Innings, Test
903 for 7 dec. England vs. Australia (5th Test), Aug. 20–23, 1938

Batting—Individual Scores

Highest Innings
499 Hanif Mohammad (Pakistan), Jan. 8–11, 1959

Highest Innings, Test
365 no Garfield Sobers (West Indies), Feb. 27–Mar. 1, 1958

TUNNEL VISION:
Milutin Veljkovic (being carried) stayed in a cave for 463 days in the Samar Cavern, Svrljig Mountains, Yugoslavia from June, 1969, to September, 1970.

BAT MAN: Garfield Sobers (West Indies) holds three major batting records in First Class competition.

Cricket (First Class Matches Only) (continued)

Most Runs, Over (6 ball)
  36 Garfield Sobers (Nottinghamshire), Aug. 31, 1968

Most Runs, Season
  3,816 Denis Compton (Middlesex and England), 1947

Most Runs, Career
  61,237 John (Jack) Hobbs (Surrey and England), 1905–34

Most Runs, Tests
  8,032 Garfield Sobers (West Indies), 1953–1974

Test Match Average
  99.94 (80 inn.) Donald Bradman (Australia), 1928–1948

Career Average
  95.14 (338 inn.) Donald Bradman (Australia), 1927–1949

Bowling

Most Wickets, Innings
  10 Numerous occasions

Most Wickets, Match
  19 Jim Laker (Surrey), July 26–31, 1956

Most Wickets, Season
  304 Alfred "Tich" Freeman (Kent), 1928

Most Wickets, Career
  4,187 Wilfred Rhodes, 1898–1930

Most Wickets, Tests
  309 Lance Gibbs (West Indies), 1958–1976

Wicket Keeping

Most Dismissals, Season
  127 Leslie Ames (Kent), 1929

Most Dismissals, Career
  1,527 John Murray (Middlesex), 1952–1975

Most Dismissals, Tests
  252 Alan Knott (England), 1967–1977

Miscellaneous

Fastest Century
  35 min. Percy Fender (Surrey), Aug. 26, 1920

Fastest Bowler
  99.7 m.p.h. Jeff Thompson (Australia), Dec. 1975

Most Test Appearances
  114 Colin Cowdrey (England), 1954–1975

Longest Cricket Ball Throw (5½ oz. ball)
  422 ft. Robert Percival, Apr. 18, 1881

CROQUET

Earliest references. Croquet was probably derived from the French game *Jeu de Mail* first mentioned in the 12th century. In its present-day form, it originated as a country-house lawn game in Ireland in the 1830's when it was called "crokey" and was introduced to Hampshire 20 years later. The first club was formed in the Steyne Gardens, Worthing, West Sussex, England.

Most Championships

The greatest number of victories in the Open Croquet Championships (instituted at Evesham, Hereford and Worcester, 1867) is ten by John William Solomon (b. 1932) (1953, 1956, 1959, 1961, 1963–68). He has also won the Men's Championship on ten occasions (1951, 1953, 1958–60, 1962, 1964, 1965, 1971 and 1972), the Open Doubles (with Edmond Patrick Charles Cotter) on ten occasions (1954–55, 1958–59, 1961–65 and 1969) and the Mixed Doubles once (with Mrs. N. Oddie) in 1954, making a total of 31 titles. Solomon has also won the President's Silver Cup (inst. 1934) on nine occasions (1955, 1957–59, 1962–64, 1968 and 1971). He has also been Champion of Champions on all four occasions that this competition has been run (1967–70).

WICKET SHOT: John Solomon won 10 Open Croquet Championships, and a total of 31 titles in all categories (men's, open doubles and mixed doubles). He also won the President's Silver Cup 9 times and was Champion of Champions in all 4 years of that competition.

OPEN WINNERS: Dorothy Dyne Steel (left) won 4 Open Croquet Championships, the most by a woman, and, like John Solomon, won a total of 31 titles in various categories. Humphrey Hicks (right) had the lowest handicap ever at minus 5½. He also won the Open Croquet Championship 7 times.

Dorothy Dyne Steel (1884–1965), fifteen times winner of the Women's Championship (1919–39), won the Open Croquet Championship four times (1925, 1933, 1935–36). She had also five Doubles and seven Mixed Doubles titles making a total of 31 titles.

International Trophy

The MacRobertson International Shield (instituted 1925) has been played for ten times. It has been won most often by Great Britain with six wins. The players to make five international appearances are J. C. Windsor (Australia) in 1925, 1928, 1930, 1935 and 1937 and John Solomon (GB) in 1951, 1956, 1963, 1969 and 1974.

Lowest Handicap

Historically the lowest playing handicap has been that of Humphrey Osmond Hicks (Devon) (b. 1904) with minus 5½. In 1974 the limit was however fixed at minus 5. The player holding the lowest handicap is G. Nigel Aspinall with minus 5.

Marathon

The longest croquet match on record is one of 100 hours by Peter Olsen, Julio Aznarez, Hazell Kelly and Donald Noack at Manly Croquet Club, N.S.W. Australia, May 14–18, 1978.

MacRobertson International Shield

Contested periodically by Great Britain, New Zealand and Australia.

1925	Great Britain	1937	Great Britain	1969	Great Britain
1928	Australia	1950	New Zealand	1974	Great Britain
1930	Australia	1956	Great Britain	1979	New Zealand
1935	Australia	1963	Great Britain		

The Open Croquet Championship

First held in 1867. Most wins:

10	John W. Solomon	(1953, 1956, 1959, 1961, 1963–68)
7	Humphrey Hicks	(1932, 1939, 1947–50, 1952)
5	Cyril Corbally	(1902–03, 1906, 1908, 1913)

Most wins by a woman:

4	Dorothy Steel	(1925, 1933,1935–36)

CROSS-COUNTRY RUNNING

International Championships

The earliest international cross-country race was run between England and France on a course 9 miles 18 yards long from Ville d'Avray, outside Paris, on March 20, 1898. The inaugural International Cross-Country Championships took place at the Hamilton Park Racecourse, Scotland, on March 28, 1903. Since 1973 the race has been run under the auspices of the International Amateur Athletic Federation.

The greatest margin of victory in the International Cross-Country Championships has been 56 seconds, or 390 yards, by Jack T. Holden (England) at Ayr Racecourse, Scotland, on March 24, 1934. The narrowest win was that of Jean-Claude Fayolle (France) at Ostend, Belgium, on March 20, 1965, when the timekeepers were unable to separate his time from that of Melvyn Richard Batty (England), who was placed second.

Most Appearances

The runner with the largest number of international championship appearances is Marcel Van de Wattyne of Belgium, who participated in 20 competitions in the years 1946–65.

OVER THE HILL: Italy's Paola Cacchi (left) was a 2-time cross-country world champion. Gaston Roelants (right) of Belgium shares a record with 4 titles.

Most Wins

The greatest number of victories in the International Cross-Country Race is four by Jack Holden (England) in 1933, 1934, 1935 and 1939, by Alain Mimoun-o-Kacha (France) in 1949, 1952, 1954 and 1956, and Gaston Roelants (Belgium) in 1962, 1967, 1969 and 1972. England has won 45 times to 1980. Doris Brown-Heritage (US) (b. September 17, 1942) has won the women's race five times, 1967–71.

Largest Field

The largest recorded field was one of 7,036 starters in the 18.6-mile Lidingöloppet, near Stockholm, Sweden, on October 10, 1978. There were 6,299 finishers.

International/World Cross-Country Championship

MEN

Year	Individual	Team	Year	Individual	Team
1903	Alfred Shrubb (Eng)	England	1949	Alain Mimoun (Fra)	France
1904	Alfred Shrubb (Eng)	England	1950	Lucien Theys (Bel)	France
1905	Albert Aldridge (Eng)	England	1951	Geoffrey Saunders (Eng)	England
1906	Charles Straw (Eng)	England	1952	Alain Mimoun (Fra)	France
1907	A. Underwood (Eng)	England	1953	Franjo Mihalic (Yug)	England
1908	Archie Robertson (Eng)	England	1954	Alain Mimoun (Fra)	England
1909	Edward Wood (Eng)	England	1955	Frank Sando (Eng)	England
1910	Edward Wood (Eng)	England	1956	Alain Mimoun (Fra)	France
1911	Jean Bouin (Fra)	England	1957	Frank Sando (Eng)	Belgium
1912	Jean Bouin (Fra)	England	1958	Stanley Eldon (Eng)	England
1913	Jean Bouin (Fra)	England	1959	Fred Norris (Eng)	England
1914	Arthur Nicholls (Eng)	England	1960	Abdesselem Rhadi (Fra)	England
1920	James Wilson (Sco)	England	1961	Basil Heatley (Eng)	Belgium
1921	W. Freeman (Eng)	England	1962	Gaston Roelants (Bel)	England
1922	Joseph Guillemot (Fra)	France	1963	Roy Fowler (Eng)	Belgium
1923	Charles Blewitt (Eng)	France	1964	Francesco Arizmendi (Spa)	England
1924	William Cotterell (Eng)	England	1965	Jean Fayolle (Fra)	England
1925	Jack Webster (Eng)	England	1966	Ben Asou El Ghazi (Mor)	England
1926	Ernest Harper (Eng)	France	1967	Gaston Roelants (Bel)	England
1927	L. Payne (Eng)	France	1968	Mohamed Gammoudi (Tun)	England
1928	H. Eckersley (Eng)	France	1969	Gaston Roelants (Bel)	England
1929	William Cotterell (Eng)	France	1970	Michael Tagg (Eng)	England
1930	Thomas Evenson (Eng)	England	1971	David Bedford (Eng)	England
1931	Tim Smythe (Ire)	England	1972	Gaston Roelants (Bel)	England
1932	Thomas Evenson (Eng)	England	1973	Pekka Paivarinta (Fin)	Belgium
1933	Jack Holden (Eng)	England	1974	Eric De Beck (Bel)	Belgium
1934	Jack Holden (Eng)	England	1975	Ian Stewart (Sco)	New Zealand
1935	Jack Holden (Eng)	England	1976	Carlos Lopes (Por)	England
1936	William Eaton (Eng)	England	1977	Leon Schots (Bel)	Belgium
1937	James Flockhart (Sco)	England	1978	John Treacy (Ire)	France
1938	John Emery (Eng)	England	1979	John Treacy (Ire)	England
1939	Jack Holden (Eng)	France			
1946	Raphael Pujazon (Fra)	France			
1947	Raphael Pujazon (Fra)	France			
1948	John Doms (Bel)	Belgium			

WOMEN (race first held 1967)

Year	Individual	Team
1967	Doris Brown (US)	England
1968	Doris Brown (US)	US

Year	Individual	Team		Year	Individual	Team
1969	Doris Brown (US)	US		1975	Julie Brown (US)	US
1970	Doris Brown (US)	England		1976	Carmen Valero (Spa)	USSR
1971	Doris Brown (US)	England		1977	Carmen Valero (Spa)	USSR
1972	Joyce Smith (Eng)	England		1978	Grete Waitz (Nor)	Rumania
1973	Paola Cacchi (Ita)	England		1979	Grete Waitz (Nor)	US
1974	Paola Cacchi (Ita)	England				

N.C.A.A. Team Champions

1938	Indiana		1952	Michigan State		1966	Villanova
1939	Michigan State		1953	Kansas		1967	Villanova
1940	Indiana		1954	Oklahoma State		1968	Villanova
1941	Rhode Island		1955	Michigan State		1969	Texas-El Paso
1942	Indiana		1956	Michigan State		1970	Villanova
	Penn State		1957	Notre Dame		1971	Oregon
1944	Drake		1958	Michigan State		1972	Tennessee
1945	Drake		1959	Michigan State		1973	Oregon
1946	Drake		1960	Houston		1974	Oregon
1947	Penn State		1961	Oregon State		1975	Texas-El Paso
1948	Michigan State		1962	San Jose State		1976	Texas-El Paso
1949	Michigan State		1963	San Jose State		1977	Oregon
1950	Penn State		1964	Western Michigan		1978	Texas-El Paso
1951	Syracuse		1965	Western Michigan		1979	Texas-El Paso

Note: No meet held in 1943.

A.I.A.W.

1975	Iowa State	1977	Iowa State	1979	No. Carolina State
1976	Iowa State	1978	Iowa State		

CURLING

Origins. Although a 15-century bronze figure in the Florence Museum appears to be holding a curling stone, the earliest illustration of the sport was in one of the winter scenes by the Flemish painter Pieter Brueghel, *c.* 1560. The club with the earliest records, dating back to 1716, is that at Kilsyth, Scotland. The game was introduced into Canada in 1759. Organized administration began in 1838 with the formation of the Grand (later Royal) Caledonian Curling Club, the international legislative body until the foundation of the International Curling Federation in 1966. The first indoor ice rink to introduce curling was at Southport, England, in 1879.

The US won the first Gordon International Medal series of matches, between Canada and the US, at Montreal in 1884. The first Strathcona Cup match between Canada and Scotland was won by Canada in 1903. Although demonstrated at the Winter Olympics of 1924, 1932 and 1964, curling has never been included in the official Olympic program.

Largest Rink

The world's largest curling rink is the Big Four Curling Rink, Calgary, Alberta, Canada, opened in 1959 at a cost of Can. $2,250,000. Each of the two floors has 24 sheets of ice, the total accommodating 96 teams and 384 players.

Most Titles

The record for the Air Canada Silver Broom is 13 wins by Canada. The most Strathcona Cup wins is seven by Canada (1903–09–12–12–23–38–57–65) against Scotland.

Perfect Games

A unique achievement is claimed by Mrs. Bernice Fekete of Edmonton, Alberta, Canada, who skipped her rink to two consecutive eight-enders on the same sheet of ice at the Derrick Club, Edmonton, on January 10 and February 6, 1973.

Marathon

The longest recorded curling match is one of 64 hours 28 minutes by eight members of the Pine Point Curling Club, N.W.T., Canada, on January 13–15, 1979. The duration record for 2 curlers is 24 hours 5 minutes by Eric Olesen and Warren Knuth at Racine Curling Club, Racine, Wisconsin on March 30–31, 1978. The weight handled was 27.72 tons each.

Longest Bonspiel

The longest bonspiel in the world is the Manitoba Bonspiel held in Winnipeg, Canada. There were 728 teams of 4 players in the February, 1977 tournament.

World Championships

Contested for the Scotch Cup from 1959 and for the Air Canada Silver Broom from 1968.

1959	Canada	1965	US	1971	Canada	1977	Sweden
1960	Canada	1966	Canada	1972	Canada	1978	US
1961	Canada	1967	Scotland	1973	Sweden	1979	Norway
1962	Canada	1968	Canada	1974	US		
1963	Canada	1969	Canada	1975	Switzerland		
1964	Canada	1970	Canada	1976	US		

CYCLING

Earliest Race

The earliest recorded bicycle race was a velocipede race over two kilometers (1.24 miles) at the Parc de St. Cloud, Paris, on May 31, 1868, won by James Moore (GB).

Stationary Cycling

David Steed of Tucson, Arizona, stayed stationary while balanced on a bike without support for 9 hours 15 minutes on November 25, 1977.

Highest Speed

The highest speed ever achieved on a bicycle is 140.5 m.p.h. by Dr. Allan V. Abbott, 29, of San Bernardino, California, behind a

PEDAL PUSHER: Dr. Allan Abbott attained the highest speed ever on a bicycle when he reached 140.5 m.p.h. behind a windshield mounted on a 1955 Chevrolet. His speed over a mile was 138.674 m.p.h.

windshield mounted on a 1955 Chevrolet over ¾ of a mile at Bonneville Salt Flats, Utah, on August 25, 1973. His speed over a mile was 138.674 m.p.h. Considerable help is provided by the slipstreaming effect of the lead vehicle. Charles Minthorne Murphy (born 1872) achieved the first mile-a-minute behind a pacing locomotive on the Long Island Railroad on June 30, 1899. He took only 57.8 seconds, so averaging 62.28 m.p.h.

Fred Markham recorded an official unpaced 8.80 sec. for 200 meters (50.84 m.p.h.) at Ontario, California, on May 6, 1979.

The greatest distance ever covered in one hour is 76 miles 604 yards by Leon Vanderstuyf (Belgium) on the Montlhéry Motor Circuit, France, on September 30, 1928. This was achieved from a standing start paced by a motorcycle. The 24-hour record behind pace is 860 miles 367 yards by Hubert Opperman in Australia in 1932.

The greatest distance covered in 60 minutes unpaced is 30 miles 1,258 yards by Eddy Merckx at Mexico City, Mexico, on October 25, 1972. The 24-hour record on the road is 515.8 miles by Teuvo Louhivuori of Finland on September 10, 1974.

Most Olympic Titles

Cycling has been on the Olympic program since the revival of the Games in 1896. The greatest number of gold medals ever won is three by Paul Masson (France) in 1896, Francisco Verri (Italy) in 1906 and Robert Charpentier (France) in 1936. Marcus Hurley (US) won four events in the "unofficial" cycling competition in the 1904 Games.

Tour de France

The greatest number of wins in the Tour de France (inaugurated 1903) is five by Jacques Anquetil (born January 8, 1934) of France, and Eddy Merckx (b. Belgium, June 17, 1945).

The closest race ever was that of 1968 when after 2,898.7 miles over 25 days (June 27–July 21) Jan Jannssen (Netherlands) (born May 19, 1940) beat Herman van Springel (Belgium) in Paris by 38 seconds. The longest course was 3,569 miles on June 20–July 18, 1926. The length of the course is usually about 3,000 miles, but varies from year to year.

The fastest average speed was 23.2 m.p.h. by Anquetil in 1962.

The longest race was 3,569 miles in 1926, and the greatest number of participants was in 1928, when 162 started and only 41 finished.

World Titles

The only four male cyclists to have won 7 world titles in any single world championship event are Leon Meredith (GB) who won the Amateur 100-kilometer paced event in 1904–05–07–08–09–11–13; Jeff Scherens (Belgium) who won the Professional sprint title in 1932–33–34–35–36–37 and 1947; Antonio Maspes (Italy) who won the Professional sprint title in 1955–56–59–60–61–62–64; and Daniel Morelon (France) who won the Amateur sprint title in 1966–67–69–70–71–73–75.

Yvonne Reynders (Belgium) won a total of 7 titles in women's events, the pursuits in 1961–64–65 and the road title in 1959–61–63–66. Beryl Burton (GB) equaled this total by winning the pursuits title in 1959–60–62–63–66 and the road title in 1960–67.

Endurance

Tommy Godwin (GB) in the 365 days of 1939 covered 75,065 miles or an average of 205.65 miles per day. He then completed 100,000 miles in 500 days to May 14, 1940.

ROUND TRIP: Richard DeBernardis bicycled around the perimeter of the continental United States in 180 days, beginning and finishing in Seattle. He used no other means of transportation during the 12,092-mile journey.

CYCLER OF THE YEAR: Tommy Godwin (GB) covered 75,065 miles in 1939. He averaged 205.65 miles per day in setting the mileage record for a year. He kept going for another 135 days for a total of 100,000 miles in 500 days.

The longest cycle tour on record is the more than 402,000 miles amassed by Walter Stolle (b. Sudetenland, 1926), an itinerant lecturer. From January 24, 1959 to December 12, 1976, he covered 159 countries, had 5 bicycles stolen and suffered 231 other robberies, along with over 1,000 flat tires. From 1922 to December 25, 1973, Tommy Chambers (b. 1903) of Glasgow, Scotland, had ridden a verified total of 799,405 miles. On Christmas Day he was badly injured and has not ridden since.

Ray Reece, 41, of Alverstoke, England, circumnavigated the world by bicycle (13,325 road miles) between June 14 and November 5 (143 days) in 1971.

John Hathaway of Vancouver, Canada, covered 50,600 miles, visiting every continent from November 10, 1974 to October 6, 1976.

Vivekananda Selva Kumar Anandan of Sri Lanka cycled for 187 hours 28 minutes non-stop around Vihara Maha Devi Park, Colombo, Sri Lanka, May 2–10, 1979.

U.S. Touring Records

The transcontinental record is 13 days 1 hour 20 minutes, from Santa Monica, California, to New York City by John Marino (b. 1948), August 13–26, 1978. He covered 2,956 miles.

Stan N. Kuhl (born December 31, 1955) and Steve Jeschien (born August 6, 1956) of Sunnyvale, California, traveled 8,026.7 miles on a tandem bicycle around the US from June 29 to October 3, 1976.

Richard J. DeBernardis of Los Angeles bicycled around the perimeter of the continental United States in 180 days, beginning in Seattle, Washington, on September 10, 1978, and returning on March 8, 1979. His 12,092-mile continuous journey was accomplished without resorting to other means of transportation at any point.

GEARING UP: Eddy Merckx (left), one of two men to win the Tour de France 5 times, holds professional speed records for 10 and 20 kilometers. He also holds the record for most distance in one hour. In fact, he set all three records on the same day. Patrick Sercu (right), here winning the Olympic gold medal for the 1,000-meter time trial in 1964, holds three indoor amateur and professional one-kilometer records.

World Cycling Records

(as of December 1, 1979)

Outdoor Tracks

MEN

Professional Unpaced Standing Start

1 km	1 min 7:49 sec	Peder Pedersen (Denmark)	Rome	June 27, 1974
5 km	5 min 51.6.sec	Ole Ritter (Denmark)	Mexico	Oct. 4, 1968
10 km	11 min 53.2 sec	Eddy Merckx (Belgium)	Mexico	Oct. 25, 1972
20 km	24 min 6.8 sec	Eddy Merckx (Belgium)	Mexico	Oct. 25, 1972
100 km	2 hr 14 min 2.5 sec	Ole Ritter (Denmark)	Mexico	Nov. 18, 1971
1 hr.	49 km 431.957 m (30 miles 1,258 yds)	Eddy Merckx (Belgium)	Mexico	Oct. 25, 1972

Professional Unpaced Flying Start

200 m	10.8 sec	Antonio Maspes (Italy)	Rome	July 21, 1960
500 m	28.8 sec	Marino Morettini (Italy)	Milan	Aug. 29, 1955
1,000 m	1 min 2.4 sec	Patrick Sercu (Belgium)	Milan	Sept. 17, 1973

Professional Motor-Paced

100 km	1 hr 3 min 40 sec	Walter Lohmann (West Germany)	Wuppertal	Oct. 24, 1955
1 hr	94 km 16 m (58 mi 737 yds)	Walter Lohmann (West Germany)	Wuppertal	Oct. 24, 1955

Amaetur Unpaced Standing Start

1 km	1 min 2.4 sec	Pierre Trentin (France)	Zurich	Nov. 15, 1970

4 km	4 min 40.24 sec	Hans-Henrik Oersted (Denmark)	Mexico	Oct. 31, 1979
5 km	5 min 50.06 sec	Hans-Henrik Oersted (Denmark)	Mexico	Oct. 31, 1979
10 km	11 min 54.91 sec	Hans-Henrik Oersted (Denmark)	Mexico	Oct. 31, 1979
20 km	24 min 35.63 sec	Hans-Henrik Oersted (Denmark)	Mexico	Nov. 2, 1979
100 km	2 hr 18 min 43.6 sec	Joern Lund (Denmark)	Rome	Sept. 19, 1971
1 hr	48 km 199.553 m (29 mi 1,671 yds)	Hans-Henrik Oersted (Denmark)	Mexico	Nov. 2, 1979

Amateur Unpaced Flying Start

200 m	10.61 sec	Omari Phakadze (USSR)	Mexico	Oct. 22, 1967
500 m	27.85 sec	Pierre Trentin (France)	Mexico	Oct. 21, 1967
1,000 m	1 min 1.14 sec	Luigi Borghetti (Italy)	Mexico	Oct. 21, 1967

WOMEN

Unpaced Standing Start

1 km	1 min 15.1 sec	Irena Kirichenko (USSR)	Yerevan	Oct. 8, 1966
5 km	6 min 44.75 sec	Keetie Van Oosten-Hage (Netherlands)	Munich	Sept. 16, 1978
10 km	13 min 34.39 sec	Keetie Van Oosten-Hage (Netherlands)	Munich	Sept. 16, 1978
20 km	27 min 26.66 sec	Keetie Van Oosten-Hage (Netherlands)	Munich	Sept. 16, 1978
100 km	2 hr 41 min 32.6 sec	Maria Cressari (Italy)	Milan	Oct. 17, 1974
1 hr	43 km 82 m (26 mi 1,355 yds)	Keetie Van Oosten-Hage (Netherlands)	Munich	Sept. 16, 1978

Unpaced Flying Start

200 m	12.3 sec	Lyubov Razuvayeva (USSR)	Irkutsk	July 17, 1955
500 m	31.7 sec	Galina Tzareva (USSR)	Tbilisi	Oct. 6, 1978
1,000 m	1 min 12.9 sec	Lyubov Razuvayeva (USSR)	Irkutsk	July 17, 1955

Indoor Tracks

MEN

Professional Unpaced Standing Start

1 km	1 min 7.35 sec	Patrick Sercu (Belgium)	Zurich	Dec. 2, 1972
5 km	6 min 5.6 sec	Ferdinand Bracke (Belgium)	Grenoble	Dec. 5, 1964
10 km	12 min 26.8 sec	Roger Riviere (France)	Paris	Oct. 19, 1958
20 km	25 min 18.0 sec	Siegfried Adler (West Germany)	Zurich	Aug. 2, 1968
1 hr	46 km 847 m (29 mi 192 yds)	Siegfried Adler (West Germany)	Zurich	Aug. 2, 1968

Professional Unpaced Flying Start

200 m	10.99 sec	Oscar Plattner (Switzerland)	Zurich	Dec. 1, 1961
500 m	28.6 sec	Oscar Plattner (Switzerland)	Zurich	Aug. 17, 1956
1,000 m	1 min 1.23 sec	Patrick Sercu (Belgium)	Antwerp	Feb. 3, 1967

Professional Motor-Paced

100 km	1 hr 23 min 59.8 sec	Guillermo Timoner (Spain)	San Sebastian	Sept. 12, 1965
1 hr	74 km 641 m (46 mi 669 yds)	Guy Solente (France)	Paris	Feb. 13, 1955

BRITISH BIKERS: Tom Simpson (left) won the 1965 professional road race title, the first of his countrymen to do so. Beryl Burton (right) collected 7 world titles during her racing career, including 5 pursuit titles in 1959, 60, 62, 63, and 66.

Indoor Track (continued)

Amateur Unpaced Standing Start

1 km	1 min 6.76 sec	Patrick Sercu (Belgium)	Brussels	Dec. 12, 1964
5 km	6 min 2.57 sec	Hans-Henrik Oersted (Denmark)	Copenhagen	Jan. 31, 1978
10 km	12 min 6.29 sec	Hans-Henrik Oersted (Denmark)	Copenhagen	Nov. 28, 1978
20 km	25 min 14.6 sec	Ole Ritter (Denmark)	Zurich	Oct. 30, 1966
1 hr	46 km 745 m (29 mi 81 yds)	Daniel Gisiger (Switzerland)	Zurich	June 14, 1977

Amateur Unpaced Flying Start

200 m	10.72 sec	Daniel Morelon (France)	Zurich	Nov. 4, 1966
500 m	28.75 sec	Daniel Morelon (France)	Zurich	June 12, 1976
1,000 m	1 min 1.44 sec	Hans Ledermann (Switzerland)	Zurich	Nov. 29, 1977

WOMEN

Unpaced Standing Start

1,000m	1 min 15.5 sec	Elizabeth Eicholz (East Germany)	East Berlin	March 4, 1964

Unpaced Flying Start

200 m	13.17 sec	Luigina Bissoli (Italy)	Milan	Dec. 6, 1978
500 m	34.32 sec	Luigina Bissoli (Italy)	Milan	Dec. 6, 1978
1,000 m	1 min 14.32 sec	Luigina Bissoli (Italy)	Milan	Dec. 6, 1978

World Championships

The first cycling world championships were held for amateurs in 1893, and the first for professionals in 1895.

Track champions at each event since 1965 (with the most wins at each event) have been:

MEN

Professional

	Sprint	Pursuit	Motor Paced (100 km)
1965	G. Beghetto (Ita)	L. Faggin (Ita)	G. Timoner (Spa)
1966	G. Beghetto (Ita)	L. Faggin (Ita)	R. de Loof (Bel)

	Sprint	Pursuit	Motor Paced (100 km)
1967	P. Sercu (Bel)	T. Groen (Hol)	L. Proost (Bel)
1968	G. Beghetto (Ita)	H. Porter (GB)	L. Proost (Bel)
1969	P. Sercu (Bel)	F. Bracke (Hol)	J. Oudkerk (Hol)
1970	G. Johnson (Aus)	H. Porter (GB)	E. Rudolph (W Ger)
1971	L. Loeveseijn (Hol)	D. Baert (Bel)	T. Verschueren (Bel)
1972	R. van Lancker (Bel)	H. Porter (GB)	T. Verschueren (Bel)
1973	R. van Lancker (Bel)	H. Porter (GB)	C. Stam (Hol)
1974	P. Pedersen (Den)	R. Schuiten (Hol)	C. Stam (Hol)
1975	J. Nicholson (Aus)	R. Schuiten (Hol)	D. Kemper (W Ger)
1976	J. Nicholson (Aus)	F. Moser (Ita)	W. Peffgen (W Ger)
1977	K. Nakano (Jap)	G. Braun (W Ger)	C. Stam (Hol)
1978	K. Nakano (Jap)	G. Braun (W Ger)	W. Peffgen (W Ger)
1979	K. Nakano (Jap)	B. Oosterbosch (Hol)	M. Venix (Hol)

Most: 7 Jeff Scherens (Bel) (1932–37, 1947) 7 Antonio Maspes (Ita) (1955–56, 1959–62, 1964) — 4 Hugh Porter (GB) *(as above)* — 6 Guillermo Timoner (Spa) (1955, 1959–60, 1962, 1964–65)

Amateur (* = Olympic champions)

	Sprint	Pursuit	Motor Paced
1965	O. Phakadze (USSR)	T. Groen (Hol)	M. Mas (Spa)
1966	D. Morelon (Fra)	T. Groen (Hol)	P. de Wit (Hol)
1967	D. Morelon (Fra)	G. Bongers (Hol)	P. de Wit (Hol)
1968	L. Borghetti (Ita)	M. Frey (Den)	G. Grassi (Ita)
1969	D. Morelon (Fra)	X. Kurmann (Swi)	A. Boom (Hol)
1970	D. Morelon (Fra)	X. Kurmann (Swi)	C. Stam (Hol)
1971	D. Morelon (Fra)	M. Rodriguez (Col)	H. Gnas (W Ger)
1972	*D. Morelon (Fra)	*K. Knudsen (Nor)	H. Gnas (W Ger)
1973	D. Morelon (Fra)	K. Knudsen (Nor)	H. Gnas (W Ger)
1974	A. Tkac (Cze)	H. Lutz (W Ger)	J. Breuer (W Ger)
1975	D. Morelon (Fra)	T. Huschke (E Ger)	G. Minneboo (Hol)
1976	*A. Tkac (Cze)	*G. Braun (W Ger)	G. Minneboo (Hol)
1977	H.-J. Geschke (E Ger)	N. Durpisch (E Ger)	G. Minneboo (Hol)
1978	A. Tkac (Cze)	D. Macha (E Ger)	G. Minneboo (Hol)
1979	L. Hesslich (E Ger)	N. Makarov (USSR)	M. Pronk (Hol)
1980	*Lutz Hesslich (E Ger)	*Robert Dill-Bundi (Swi)	

Most: 8 Daniel Morelon (Fra) *(as above)* — 3 Guido Messina (Ita) (1947–48, 1953) 3 Tiemen Groen (Hol) (1964–66) — Leon Meredith (GB) (1904–05, 1907–09, 1911, 1913)

Amateur * = Olympic champions)

1000 Meters Time Trial

1966	P. Trentin (Fra)	1971	E. Rapp (USSR)	1976	*K.-J. Grünke (E Ger)
1967	N. Fredborg (Den)	1972	*N. Fredborg (Den)	1977	L. Thoms (E Ger)
1968	N. Fredborg (Den)	1973	J. Kierzkowski (Pol)	1978	L. Thoms (E Ger)
1969	G. Sartori (Ita)	1974	E. Rapp (USSR)	1979	L. Thoms (E Ger)
1970	N. Fredborg (Den)	1975	K.-J. Grünke (E Ger)	1980	*L. Thoms (E Ger)

Amateur (* = Olympics)

	Team Pursuit	Tandem Sprint	Road Race
1965	USSR	not held	J. Botherell (Fra)
1966	Italy	Fra (D. Morelon, P. Trentin)	E. Dolman (Hol)
1967	USSR	Ita (D. Verzini, B. Gonzato)	G. Webb (GB)
1968	Italy	Ita (Gorini, G. Turrini)	V. Marcelli (Ita)
1969	USSR	E Ger (H.-J. Geschke, W. Otto)	L. Mortensen (Den)
1970	W. Germany	W Ger (J. Barth, R. Müller)	J. Schmidt (Den)
1971	Italy	E Ger (H.-J. Geschke, W. Otto)	R. Ovion (Fra)
1972	*W. Germany	USSR (V. Sements, I. Tselovalnikov)	*H. Kuiper (Hol)
1973	W. Germany	Cze (V. Vackar, M. Vymarzal)	R. Szurkowski (Pol)
1974	W. Germany	Cze (V. Vackar, M. Vymarzal)	J. Kowalski (Pol)
1975	W. Germany	not held	A. Gevers (Hol)
1976	*W. Germany	Pol (B. Kokot, J. Kotlinski)	*B. Johansson (Swe)
1977	E. Germany	Cze (V. Vackar, M. Vymarzal)	C. Corti (Ita)
1978	E. Germany	Cze (V. Vackar, M. Vymarzal)	G. Glaus (Swi)
1979	E. Germany	Fra (Y. Cahard, F. Depine)	G. Giacomini (Ita)
1980	*USSR	not held	*S. Sukhoruchenkov (USSR)

Professional Road Race

1965	T. Simpson (GB)	1970	J.-P. Monsere (Bel)	1975	H. Kuiper (Hol)
1966	R. Altig (W Ger)	1971	E. Merckx (Bel)	1976	F. Maertens (Bel)
1967	E. Merckx (Bel)	1972	M. Basso (Ita)	1977	F. Moser (Ita)
1968	V. Adorni (Ita)	1973	F. Gimondi (Ita)	1978	G. Kneteman (Hol)
1969	H. Ottenbroos (Hol)	1974	E. Merckx (Bel)	1979	J. Raas (Hol)

Most wins: 3 Alfredo Binda (Ita) (1927, 1930, 1932); 3 Henri van Steenbergen (Bel) (1949, 1956–57); 3 Eddy Merckx (Bel) (*as above*)

WOMEN

	Sprint	*Pursuit*	*Road Race*
1965	V. Savina (USSR)	Y. Reynders (Bel)	E. Eicholz (E Ger)
1966	I. Kirichenko (USSR)	B. Burton (GB)	Y. Reynders (Bel)
1967	V. Savina (USSR)	T. Garkushkina (USSR)	B. Burton (GB)
1968	I. Baguiniantz (USSR)	R. Obodovskaya (USSR)	K. Hage (Hol)
1969	G. Tsareva (USSR)	R. Obodovskaya (USSR)	A. McElmiry (US)
1970	G. Tsareva (USSR)	T. Garkushkina (USSR)	A. Konkina (USSR)
1971	G. Tsareva (USSR)	T. Garkushkina (USSR)	A. Konkina (USSR)
1972	G. Yermolayeva (USSR)	T. Garkushkina (USSR)	G. Gambillon (Fra)
1973	S. Young (US)	T. Garkushkina (USSR)	N. van den Broeck (Bel)
1974	T. Piltsikova (USSR)	T. Garkushkina (USSR)	G. Gambillon (Fra)
1975	S. Novarra (US)	K. van Oosten-Hage (Hol)	T. Fopma (Hol)
1976	S. Young (US)	K. van Oosten-Hage (Hol)	K. van Oosten-Hage (Hol)
1977	G. Tsareva (USSR)	V. Kuznyetsova (USSR)	J. Bost (Fra)
1978	G. Tsareva (USSR)	K. van Oosten-Hage (Hol)	B. Habetz (W Ger)
1979	G. Tsareva (USSR)	K. van Oosten-Hage (Hol)	P. de Bruin (Hol)
Most:	6 Galina Yermolayeva (USSR) 1958–61, 1963, 1972) Galina Tsareva (USSR) (*as above*)	6 Tamara Garkushkina (USSR) (*as above*)	4 Yvonne Reynders (Bel) (1959, 1961, 1963, 1966)

Tour de France

Perhaps the greatest French sporting event, the Tour de France is a stage race all round France, and in some cases into the surrounding countries. Individual winners since the race's inception in 1903:

FRANKLY ADMIRED: Jacques Anquetil, a Frenchman, has won the Tour de France on 5 occasions, a record he shares with Belgium's Eddy Merckx. The most protracted non-mechanical sporting event, the race takes place over 23 days and attracts more than 10 million spectators.

1903	Maurice Garin (Fra)	1947	Jean Robic (Fra)
1904	Henri Cornet (Fra)	1948	Gino Bartali (Ita)
1905	Louis Trousselier (Fra)	1949	Fausto Coppi (Ita)
1906	René Pottier (Fra)	1950	Ferdinand Kubler (Swi)
1907	Lucien Petit-Breton (Fra)	1951	Hugo Koblet (Swi)
1908	Lucien Petit-Breton (Fra)	1952	Fausto Coppi (Ita)
1909	François Faber (Lux)	1953	Louison Bobet (Fra)
1910	Octave Lapize (Fra)	1954	Louison Bobet (Fra)
1911	Gustave Garrigou (Fra)	1955	Louison Bobet (Fra)
1912	Odile Defraye (Bel)	1956	Roger Walkowiak (Fra)
1913	Philippe Thys (Bel)	1957	Jacques Anquetil (Fra)
1914	Philippe Thys (Bel)	1958	Charly Gaul (Lux)
1919	Firmin Lambot (Bel)	1959	Federico Bahamontes (Spa)
1920	Philippe Thys (Bel)	1960	Gastone Nencini (Ita)
1921	Léon Scieur (Bel)	1961	Jacques Anquetil (Fra)
1922	Firmin Lambot (Bel)	1962	Jacques Anquetil (Fra)
1923	Henri Pelissier (Fra)	1963	Jacques Anquetil (Fra)
1924	Ottavio Bottecchia (Ita)	1964	Jacques Anquetil (Fra)
1925	Ottavio Bottecchia (Ita)	1965	Felice Gimondi (Ita)
1926	Lucien Buysse (Bel)	1966	Lucien Aimar (Fra)
1927	Nicholas Frantz (Lux)	1967	Roger Pingeon (Fra)
1928	Nicholas Frantz (Lux)	1968	Jan Janssen (Hol)
1929	Maurice Dewaele (Bel)	1969	Eddy Merckx (Bel)
1930	André Leducq (Fra)	1970	Eddy Merckx (Bel)
1931	Antonin Magne (Fra)	1971	Eddy Merckx (Bel)
1932	André Leducq (Fra)	1972	Eddy Merckx (Bel)
1933	Georges Speicher (Fra)	1973	Luis Ocana (Spa)
1934	Antonin Magne (Fra)	1974	Eddy Merckx (Bel)
1935	Romain Maes (Bel)	1975	Bernard Thevenet (Fra)
1936	Sylvere Maes (Bel)	1976	Lucien van Impe (Bel)
1937	Roger Lapebie (Fra)	1977	Bernard Thevenet (Fra)
1938	Gino Bartali (Ita)	1978	Bernard Hinault (Fra)
1939	Sylvere Maes (Bel)	1979	Bernard Hinault (Fra)

Tour of Britain

The tour of Britain, first held in 1951, in a stage race for amateurs.

	Individual	Team		Individual	Team
1951	Ian Steel (GB)	Viking	1967	Les West (GB)	USSR
1952	Kenneth Russell (GB)	BSA	1968	Gosta Pettersson (Swe)	USSR
1953	Gordon Thomas (GB)	Wearwell	1969	Fedor Den Hertog (Hol)	Poland
1954	Eugene Tamburlini (Fra)	France	1970	Jiri Mainus (Cze)	Poland
1955	Anthony Hewson (GB)	Viking	1971	Fedor Den Hertog (Hol)	Holland
1956	Not held		1972	Hennie Kuiper (Hol)	Holland
1957	Not held		1973	Piet van Katwijk (Hol)	Sweden
1958	Richard Durlacher (Aut)	Belgium	1974	Roy Schuiten (Hol)	Holland
1959	Bill Bradley (GB)	Belgium	1975	Bernt Johansson (Swe)	Czecho-slovakia
1960	Bill Bradley (GB)	England			
1961	Billy Holmes (GB)	Northern	1976	Bill Nickson (GB)	Great Britain
1962	Eugen Pokorny (Pol)	England			
1963	Peter Chisman (GB)	Poland	1977	Said Gusseinov (USSR)	USSR
1964	Arthur Metcalfe (GB)	Emgland	1978	Jan Brzezny (Pol)	USSR
1965	Les West (GB)	Poland	1979	Yuriy Kachinine (USSR)	USSR
1966	Josef Gawliczek (Pol)	USSR			

Cyclo-Cross

The first cross-country world championships were held in 1950 and since 1967 have been divided into amateur and professional categories.

OPEN (1950–1966)

1950	Jean Robic (Fra)	1954	André Dufraisse (Fra)
1951	Roger Rondeaux (Fra)	1955	André Dufraisse (Fra)
1952	Roger Rondeaux (Fra)	1956	André Dufraisse (Fra)
1953	Roger Rondeaux (Fra)	1957	André Dufraisse (Fra)

1958	André Dufraisse (Fra)
1959	Renato Longo (Ita)
1960	Rolf Wolfshohl (W Ger)
1961	Rolf Wolfshohl (W Ger)
1962	Renato Longo (Ita)
1963	Rolf Wolfshohl (W Ger)
1964	Renato Longo (Ita)
1965	Renato Longo (Ita)
1966	Eric de Vlaeminck (Bel)

AMATEUR

1967	Michel Pelchat (Fra)
1968	Roger de Vlaeminck (Bel)
1969	René Declercq (Bel)
1970	Robert Vermeier (Bel)
1971	Robert Vermeier (Bel)
1972	Norbert de Deckere (Bel)
1973	Klaus-Peter Thaler (W Ger)
1974	Robert Vermeier (Bel)
1975	Robert Vermeier (Bel)

1976	Klaus-Peter Thaler (W Ger)
1977	Robert Vermeier (BeL)
1978	Roland Liboton (Bel)
1979	Vito di Tano (Ita)

PROFESSIONAL

1967	Renato Longo (Ita)
1968	Eric de Vlaeminck (Bel)
1969	Eric de Vlaeminck (Bel)
1970	Eric de Vlaeminck (Bel)
1971	Eric de Vlaeminck (Bel)
1972	Eric de Vlaeminck (Bel)
1973	Eric de Vlaeminck (Bel)
1974	Albert Van Damme (Bel)
1975	Roger de Vlaeminck (Bel)
1976	Albert Zweifel (Swi)
1977	Albert Zweifel (Swi)
1978	Albert Zweifel (Swi)
1979	Albert Zweifel (Swi)

EQUESTRIAN SPORTS

Origin. Evidence of horse riding dates from a Persian engraving dated *c.* 3000 B.C. Pignatelli's academy of horsemanship at Naples dates from the sixteenth century. The earliest jumping competition was at the Agricultural Hall, London, in 1869. Equestrian events have been included in the Olympic Games since 1912.

Most Olympic Medals

The greatest number of Olympic gold medals is 5 by Hans-Günter Winkler (West Germany), who won 4 team gold medals as captain in 1956, 1960, 1964 and 1972, and won the individual Grand Prix in 1956. The most team wins in the Prix des Nations is 5 by Germany in 1936, 1956, 1960, 1964, and 1972.

The lowest score obtained by a winner was no faults, by Frantisek Ventura (Czechoslovakia) on *Eliot* in 1928, and by Alwin Schockemöhle (West Germany) on *Warwick Rex* in 1976. Pierre Jonqueres d'Oriola (France) is the only two-time winner of the individual gold medal, in 1952 and 1964.

World Titles

The men's world championship (instituted 1953) has been won twice by Hans-Günter Winkler of West Germany in 1954 and 1955, and Raimondo d'Inzeo of Italy in 1956 and 1960. The women's title (instituted 1965) has been won twice by Jane "Janou" Tissot (*née* Lefebvre) of France on *Rocket* in 1970 and 1974.

Jumping Records

The official *Fédération Equestre Internationale* high jump record is 8 feet 1¼ inches by *Huasó*, ridden by Capt. A. Larraguibel Morales (Chile) at Santiago, Chile, on February 5, 1949, and 27 feet 2¾

MOST GOLD MEDALS: Hans-Günter Winkler (West Germany) has won 5 Olympic gold medals, 4 for team competition and the individual gold in 1956. The show-jumping champion has also won 2 world titles.

inches for long jump over water by *Amado Mio* ridden by Lt.-Col. Lopez del Hierro (Spain) at Barcelona, Spain, on November 12, 1951. *Heatherbloom*, ridden by Dick Donnelly, was reputed to have covered 37 feet in clearing an 8-foot-3-inch *puissance* jump at Richmond, Virginia, in 1903. H. Plant on *Solid Gold* cleared 36 feet 3 inches over water at the Wagga Show, N.S.W., Australia, on August 28, 1936. *Jerry M* allegedly cleared 40 feet over water at Aintree, Liverpool, England, in 1912.

At Cairns, Queensland, *Golden Meade* ridden by Jack Martin cleared an unofficially measured 8 feet 6 inches on July 25, 1946. *Ben Bolt* was credited with clearing 9 feet 6 inches at the 1938 Royal Horse Show, Sydney, Australia. The Australian record however is 8 feet 4 inches by C. Russell on *Flyaway* in 1939 and A. L. Payne on *Golden Meade* in 1946. The world's unofficial best for a woman is 7 feet 8 inches by Katrina Towns (now Musgrove) (Australia) on *Big John* at Cairns, Queensland, Australia, in 1978.

The greatest recorded height reached bareback is 6 feet 7 inches by *Silver Wood* at Heidelberg, Victoria, Australia, on December 10, 1938.

Longest Ride

Swiss-born Aimé Felix Tschiffely rode 10,000 miles from Buenos Aires, Argentina, to Washington, D.C., in 504 days, starting on April 23, 1925, with two horses, *Mancha* and *Gato*.

The Bicentennial "Great American Horse Race," begun in May 31, 1976, from Saratoga Springs, New York, to Sacramento, California (3,500 miles) was won by Virl Norton on *Lord Fauntleroy* —a mule—in 98 days. His actual riding time was 315.47 hours.

HORSE-FEATHERS: Flying like a bird, "Heatherbloom" was reputed to have covered 37 feet in clearing an 8-foot-3-inch jump in 1903. She is here making a demonstration jump of 8 feet 2 inches in 1905.

Marathon

Michael Grealy (Australia) rode at all paces (including jumping) for 55 hours 26 minutes at Blackwater, Queensland, Australia, on May 5–7, 1978.

Show Jumping

WORLD CHAMPIONS

Men
First held 1953. Team Championships first held 1978.

1953	Francisco Goyoago (Spa) on *Quorum*
1954	Hans-Günter Winkler (W Ger) on *Halla*
1955	Hans-Günter Winkler (W Ger) on *Halla*
1956	Raimondo d'Inzeo (Ita) on *Merano*
1960	Raimondo d'Inzeo (Ita) on *Gowran Girl*
1966	Pierre d'Oriola (Fra) on *Pomone*
1970	David Broome (GB) on *Beethoven*
1974	Hartwig Steenken (W Ger) on *Simona*
1978	Gerd Wiltfang (W Ger) on *Roman*

Women
First held 1965.

1965	Marion Coakes (GB) on *Stroller*
1970	Janou Lefebvre (Fra) on *Rocket*
1974	Janou Tissot (née Lefebvre) (Fra) on *Rocket*

Team
1978   Great Britain

OLYMPIC CHAMPIONS

First held 1900. Individual and Team winners since 1948 have been:

	Individual	Team
1948	Humberto Cortes (Mex) on *Arete*	Mexico
1952	Pierre d'Oriola (Fra) on *Ali Baba*	Great Britain
1956	Hans-Günter Winkler (W Ger) on *Halla*	W. Germany
1960	Raimondo d'Inzeo (Ita) on *Merano*	W. Germany
1964	Pierre d'Oriola (Fra) on *Lutteur*	W. Germany
1968	William Steinkraus (US) on *Snowbound*	Canada
1972	Graziano Mancinelli (Ita) on *Ambassador*	W. Germany
1976	Alwin Schockemöhle (W Ger) on *Warwick Rex*	France
1980	Jan Kowalczyk (Pol) on *Ariemor*	USSR

PRESIDENT'S CUP

The award for the world Team championship, based on each country's best six Nations Cup results in a season.

1965	Great Britain	1970	Great Britain	1975	W. Germany
1966	US	1971	W. Germany	1976	W. Germany
1967	Great Britain	1972	Great Britain	1977	Great Britain
1968	US	1973	Great Britain	1978	Great Britain
1969	W. Germany	1974	Great Britain	1979	Great Britain

Three-Day Event

WORLD CHAMPIONS

First held 1966

	Individual	Team		Individual	Team
1966	Carlos Moratorio (Arg) on *Chalan*		1974	Bruce Davidson (US) on *Irish Cap*	US
1970	Mary Gordon-Watson (GB) on *Cornishman V*	Ireland	1978	Bruce Davidson (US) on *Might Tango*	Canada
		Great Britain			

OLYMPIC CHAMPIONS

First held 1912. Winners since 1948 have been:

		Team			Team
1948	Bernard Chevallier (Fra) on *Aiglonne*	US	1968	Jean-Jacques Guyon (Fra) on *Pitou*	Great Britain
1952	Hans von Blixen-Finecke (Swe) on *Jubal*	Sweden	1972	Richard Meade (GB) on *Laurieston*	Great Britain
1956	Petrus Kastenman (Swe) on *Iluster*	Great Britain	1976	Edmund Coffin (US) on *Ballycor*	US
1960	Lawrence Morgan (Aus) on *Salad Days*	Australia	1980	Frederico Roman (Ita) on *Rossinan*	USSR
1964	Mauro Checcoli (Ita) on *Syrbean*	Italy			

Dressage

WORLD CHAMPIONS

First held 1966

1966	Josef Neckermann (W. Ger) on *Mariano*	W. Germany	1974	Reiner Klimke (W Ger) on *Dux*	W. Germany
1970	Elena Petouchkova (USSR) on *Pepel*	USSR	1978	Christine Stückelberger (Swi) on *Granat*	W. Germany

BROOK NO INTERFERENCE: Richard Meade (GB) has won 3 gold medals in the Three-Day Event, one individual and two team. He is shown here on "The Poacher" as a member of the winning world championship team in 1970.

NO FAULTS:
Alwin Schockemöhle (West Germany) rode "Warwick Rex" to the gold medal for Show Jumping in the 1976 Montreal Olympics. He is one of two riders to score no faults in Olympic competition. Schockemöhle has also won a gold, a silver and a bronze medal in team competition.

OLYMPIC CHAMPIONS

First held 1912. Team and individual winners since 1948 have been:

1948	Hans Moser (Swi) on *Hummer*	France	1968	Ivan Kizimov (USSR) on *Ichor*	W. Germany
1952	Henri St. Cyr (Swe) on *Master Rufus*	Sweden	1972	Liselott Linsenhoff (W Ger) on *Piaff*	USSR
1956	Henri St. Cyr (Swe) on *Juli*	Sweden	1976	Christine Stückelberger (Swi) on *Granat*	W. Germany
1960	Sergey Filatov (USSR) on *Absent*	Not held			
1964	Henri Chammartin (Swi) on *Woermann*	W. Germany	1980	Elizabeth Theurer (Aut) on *Man Chene*	USSR

FENCING

Origins. Fencing (fighting with single sticks) was practiced as a sport in Egypt as early as *c.* 1360 B.C. The first governing body for fencing in Britain was the Corporation of Masters of Defence founded by Henry VII before 1540 and fencing was practiced as sport, notably in prize fights, since that time. The foil was the practice weapon for the short court sword from the 17th century. The épée was established in the mid-19th century and the light sabre was introduced by the Italians in the late 19th century.

Most Olympic Titles

The greatest number of individual Olympic gold medals won is three by Ramón Fonst (Cuba) (b. 1883) in 1900 and 1904 (2) and Nedo Nadi (Italy) (1894–1952) in 1912 and 1920 (2). Nadi also won three team gold medals in 1920 making a then unprecedented total of five gold medals at one Olympic meet.

Edoardo Mangiarotti (Italy) (born April 7, 1919) holds the record of 13 Olympic medals (6 gold, 5 silver, 2 bronze), won in the foil and épée competitions from 1936 to 1960.

The most gold medals by a woman is four (one individual, three team) by Elena Novikova-Belova (USSR) (b. July 28, 1947) from 1968 to 1976, and the record for all medals is 7 (2 gold, 3 silver, 2 bronze) by Ildikó Sagine-Retjoo (formerly Ujlaki-Retjö) (Hungary) (b. May 11, 1937) from 1960 to 1976.

Most World Titles

The greatest number of individual world titles won is four by d'Oriola (see table below), but note that d'Oriola also won 2 individual Olympic titles. Likewise, of the three women foilists with 3 world titles (Helene Mayer, Ellen Müller-Preiss and Ilona Schacherer-Elek) only Elek also won 2 individual Olympic titles.

Ellen Müller-Preiss (Austria) won the women's foil in 1947 and 1949 and shared it in 1950. She also won the Olympic title in 1932.

Olympic Games and World Championships

Fencing has been included in each of the modern Olympic Games, and Olympic Championships are recognized as World Championships in Olympic years. World Championships are held annually, and have had official status since 1936, but followed European Championships which were first held in 1921. Women's events were first held in 1929.

Winners since 1965 (Olympic Champions identified by*):

INDIVIDUAL

Men's Foil

1965	Jean-Claude Magnan (Fra)
1966	Gherman Sveshnikov (USSR)
1967	Viktor Putyatin (USSR)
1968	*Ion Drimba (Rum)
1969	Friedrich Wessel (W Ger)
1970	Friedrich Wessel (W Ger)
1971	Vassily Stankovich (USSR)
1972	*Witold Woyda (Pol)
1973	Christian Nöel (Fra)
1974	Alexandr Romankov (USSR)
1975	Christian Nöel (Fra)
1976	*Fabio dal Zotto (Ita)
1977	Alexandr Romankov (USSR)
1978	Didier Flament (Fra)
1979	Alexandr Romankov (USSR)
1980	*Vladimir Smirnov (USSR)
Most: 6	Christian d'Oriola (Fra): 1947, *1948, 1949, *1952, 1953, 1954

FOILED AGAIN: Italy's Edoardo Mangiarotti (left) has won a record total of 13 medals (6 gold, 5 silver, 2 bronze) in Olympic foil and épée competition from 1936 to 1960. Helene Mayer (right) of Germany is one of 3 women foilists to win 3 world titles. Mayer was also the gold medalist in the 1928 Olympics and captured the bronze in 1936.

Men's Épée

1965	Zoltan Nemere (Hun)
1966	Aleksey Nikanchikov (USSR)
1967	Aleksey Nikanchikov (USSR)
1968	*Gyözö Kulcsar (Hun)
1969	Bogdan Andrzejewski (Pol)
1970	Aleksey Nikanchikov (USSR)
1971	Grigory Kriss (USSR)
1972	*Csaba Fenyvesi (Hun)
1973	Rolf Edling (Swe)
1974	Rolf Edling (Swe)
1975	Alexander Pusch (W Ger)
1976	*Alexander Pusch (W Ger)
1977	Johan Harmenberg (Swe)
1978	Alexander Pusch (W Ger)
1979	Philippe Riboud (Fra)
1980	*Johan Harmenberg (Swe)

3 Georges Buchard (Fra): 1927, 1931, 1933
3 Aleksey Nikanchikov: *as above*
3 Alexander Pusch: *as above*

Men's Sabre

1965	Jerzy Pawlowski (Pol)
1966	Jerzy Pawlowski (Pol)
1967	Mark Rakita (USSR)
1968	*Jerzy Pawlowski (Pol)
1969	Viktor Sidiak (USSR)
1970	Tibor Pezsa (Hun)
1971	Michele Maffei (Ita)
1972	*Viktor Sidiak (USSR)
1973	Mario Aldo Montano (Ita)
1974	Mario Aldo Montano (Ita)
1975	Vladimir Nazlimov (USSR)
1976	*Viktor Krovopouskov (USSR)
1977	Pal Gerevich (Hun)
1978	Viktor Krovopouskov (USSR)
1979	Vladimir Nazlimov (USSR)
1980	*Viktor Krovopouskov (USSR)

Most: 4 Rudolf Karpati (Hun): 1954, *1956, 1959, *1960
4 Aladar Gerevich (Hun): 1935, *1948, 1951, 1955
4 Jerzy Pawlowski (Pol): 1957, 1965, 1966, *1968

Women's Foil

1965	Galina Gorokhova (USSR)
1966	Tatyana Samusenko (USSR)
1967	Alexandra Zabelina (USSR)
1968	*Elena Novikova (USSR)
1969	Elena Novikova (USSR)
1970	Galina Gorokhova (USSR)
1971	Marie-Chantal Demaille (Fra)
1972	*Antonella Ragno-Lonzi (Ita)
1973	Valentina Nikonova (USSR)
1974	Ildiko Bobis (Hun)

1975	Ecaterina Stahl (Rum)
1976	*Ildiko Schwarczenberger (Hun)
1977	Valentina Sidorova (USSR)
1978	Valentina Sidorova (USSR)
1979	Cornelia Hanisch (W Ger)
1980	*Pascale Trinquet (Fra)

5 Ilona Elek (Hun): 1934, 1935, *1936, *1948, 1951

TEAM

	Men's Foil	Men's Épée	Men's Sabre	Women's Foil
1965	USSR	France	USSR	USSR
1966	USSR	France	Hungary	USSR
1967	Rumania	USSR	USSR	Hungary

GOLDEN TOUCH: Aladar Gerevich (right) is on his way to the gold medal in men's sabre competition in the 1948 Olympics. The Hungarian sabreur also collected 6 gold medals in team competition (1932–1960), a silver and 2 bronze, as well as three world titles in individual competition.

TEAM TERRIFIC: These men formed the 1908 gold medal Hungarian sabre team, the first team from that nation to win this event. Subsequent Hungarian teams won 8 more golds (including 7 in a row from 1928 to 1960), and a total of 24 world titles, including Olympic years.

	Men's Foil	Men's Épée	Men's Sabre	Women's Foil
1968	*France	*Hungary	*USSR	*USSR
1969	USSR	USSR	USSR	Rumania
1970	USSR	Hungary	USSR	USSR
1971	France	Hungary	USSR	USSR
1972	*Poland	*Hungary	*Italy	*USSR
1973	USSR	W. Germany	Hungary	Hungary
1974	USSR	Sweden	USSR	USSR
1975	France	Sweden	USSR	USSR
1976	*W. Germany	*Sweden	*USSR	*USSR
1977	W. Germany	Sweden	USSR	USSR
1978	Poland	Hungary	Hungary	USSR
1979	USSR	USSR	USSR	USSR
1980	*France	*France	*USSR	*France
Most:	17 USSR	16 Italy	24 Hungary	13 USSR

FIELD HOCKEY

Origins. A representation of two players with curved snagging sticks apparently in an orthodox "bully" position was found in Tomb No. 17 at Beni Hasan, Egypt, and has been dated to *c.* 2050 B.C. There is a reference to the game in Lincolnshire, England, in 1277. The first country to form a national association was England

(The Hockey Association) on April 16, 1875. The Fédération Internationale de Hockey was formed on January 7, 1924.

Earliest International

The first international match was the Wales vs. Ireland match on January 26, 1895. Ireland won 3–0.

Highest International Score

The highest score in international field hockey was when India defeated the US 24–1 at Los Angeles, in the 1932 Olympic Games. The Indians were Olympic Champions from the re-inception of Olympic hockey in 1928 until 1960, when Pakistan beat them 1–0 at Rome. They had their seventh win in 1964. Of the 6 Indians who have won 3 Olympic gold medals, two have also won a silver medal—Leslie Claudius in 1948, 1952, 1956 and 1960 (silver), and Udham Singh in 1952, 1956, 1964 and 1960 (silver).

The highest score in a women's international match occurred when England defeated France 23–0 at Merton, Surrey, on February 3, 1923.

Longest Game

The longest international game on record was one of 145 minutes (into the sixth period of extra time), when Netherlands beat Spain 1–0 in the Olympic tournament at Mexico City on October 25, 1968.

Marathon

Two terms of eleven from Richard Aldworth School, Basingstoke, Hampshire, England, played for 30 hours, October 12–13, 1979.

GREATEST DOMINATION: India has won 7 of the 13 Olympic field hockey competitions through 1976, including 6 in a row from 1928 to 1956. Here, Grahanandan Singh has scored a goal for India in their 4–0 victory over England in the 1948 finals.

Olympic Games

Winners of the men's Hockey title at the Olympic Games—first included in 1908:

1908	England	1948	India	1968	Pakistan
1920	Great Britain	1952	India	1972	West Germany
1928	India	1956	India	1976	New Zealand
1932	India	1960	Pakistan	1980	India
1936	India	1964	India		

World Cup

MEN

The first men's World Cup was held in 1971. Winners:

1971	Pakistan	1975	India
1973	Holland	1978	Pakistan

WOMEN

The FIH, the International Federation, governing Hockey for both men and women, organized the first official world championship for women—the World Cup—in 1974.

1974	Holland	1978	Holland
1976	West Germany		

A.I.A.W.

1975	West Chester State
1976	West Chester State
1977	West Chester State
1978	West Chester State
1979	California State-Long Beach

World Championship

The IFWHA, the International Federation of Women's Hockey Associations, organized a World Championship in 1975, and a second in August 1979.

1975	England
1979	Holland

FISHING

Largest Catches

The largest fish ever caught on a rod is an officially ratified man-eating great white shark (*Carcharodon carcharias*) weighing 2,664 lbs., and measuring 16 feet 10 inches long, caught by Alf Dean at Denial Bay, near Ceduna, South Australia, on April 21, 1959. Capt. Frank Mundus (US) harpooned and landed a 17-foot-long 4,500-lb. great white shark, after a 5-hour battle, off Montauk Point, Long Island, New York, on June 6, 1964. He was assisted by Peter Brandenberg, Gerald Mallow, Frank Bloom and Harvey Ferston.

A white pointer shark weighing 3,388 lbs. was caught on a rod by Clive Green off Albany, Western Australia, on April 26, 1976, but this will remain unratified as whale meat was used as bait.

The largest marine animal ever killed by *hand* harpoon was a blue whale 97 feet in length, killed by Archer Davidson in Two-fold Bay, New South Wales, Australia, in 1910. Its tail flukes measured 20 feet across and its jaw bone 23 feet 4 inches.

Smallest Catch

The smallest fish ever to win a competition was a smelt weighing 1/16 of an ounce, caught by Peter Christian at Buckenham Ferry, Norfolk, England, on January 9, 1977. This beat 107 other competitors.

THE ULTIMATE IN ANGLING: Alf Dean with the largest fish ever caught on a rod, a 2,664-pound man-eating great white shark. The 16-foot-10-inch fish was caught off Australia in 1959.

Spear-fishing

The largest fish ever taken underwater was an 804-lb. giant black grouper by Don Pinder of the Miami Triton Club, Florida, in 1955.

Freshwater Casting

The longest freshwater cast ratified under I.C.F. (International Casting Federation) rules is 574 feet 2 inches by Walter Kummerow (West Germany), for the Bait Distance Double-Handed 30-gram event held at Lenzerheide, Switzerland, in the 1968 Championships.

The longest Fly Distance Double-Handed cast is 257 feet 2 inches by S. Sheen of Norway, also set at Lenzerheide in 1968.

Longest Fight

The longest recorded fight with a fish by an individual is 32 hours 5 minutes by Donal Heatley (b. 1938) (New Zealand), with a black marlin (estimated length 20 feet and weight 1,500 lbs.) off Mayor Island off Tauranga, New Zealand, January 21–22, 1968. It towed the 12-ton launch 50 miles before breaking the line.

HEADS UP:
Capt. Frank
Mundus (US)
harpooned and
landed a
17-foot, 4,500-
pound great white
shark off
Montauk Point,
Long Island,
New York. It took
5 hours for
Mundus to land
the largest fish
ever caught.

**MARTIN'S
MARLIN:** Larry
Martin poses with
his record catch, a
1,282-pound
Atlantic blue
marlin which he
landed in the
Virgin Islands
in 1977.

IGFA Saltwater All-Tackle World Records

All-tackle records are kept for the heaviest saltwater fish of each species caught by an angler in any line class category up to 60 kg (130 lb). Following are the all-tackle records granted as of January 1, 1980.

Species	Scientific Name	Weight	Place	Date	Angler
Albacore	*Thunnus alalunga*	40.00 kg	Mogan Port, Gran Canaria, Canary I.	Nov. 19, 1977	Siegfried Dickemann
Amberjack greater	*Seriola dumerili*	88 lb 2 oz	Bermuda	June 21, 1964	Peter Simons
Barracuda, great	*Sphyraena barracuda*	67.58 kg	Lagos	Jan. 13, 1952	K. J. W. Hackett
Bass, black sea	*Centropristis striata*	149 lb	Nigeria		
		37.64 kg	Oregon Inlet, North Carolina	April 21, 1979	Joe W. Mizelle, Sr.
		83 lb			
		3.96 kg			
Bass, giant sea	*Stereolepis gigas*	8 lb 12 oz	Anacapa Island California	Aug. 20, 1968	James D. McAdam, Jr.
		255.60 kg			
		563 lb 8 oz			
Bass, striped	*Morone saxatilis*	32.65 kg	Cuttyhunk Massachusetts	Oct. 10, 1969	Edward J. Kirker
		72 lb			
Bluefish	*Pomatomus saltatrix*	14.40 kg	Hatteras North Carolina	Jan. 30, 1972	James M. Hussey
		31 lb 12 oz			
Bonefish	*Albula vulpes*	8.61 kg	Zululand South Africa	May 26, 1962	Brian W. Batchelor
		19 lb			
Bonito, Atlantic	*Sarda sarda*	6.00 kg	Fuerteventura Island Canary Islands	Aug. 22, 1979	Renate Reichel
		13 lb 3 oz			
Bonito, Pacific	*Sarda* spp.	10.65 kg	Victoria, Mahe Seychelles	Feb. 19, 1975	Mrs. Anne Cochain
		23 lb 8 oz			
Cobia	*Rachycentron canadum*	50.03 kg	Mombassa Kenya	Sept. 8, 1964	Eric Tinworth
		110 lb 5 oz			
Cod	*Gadus morhua*	44.79 kg	Isle of Shoals New Hampshire	June 8, 1969	Alphonse J. Bielevich
		98 lb 12 oz			
Dolphin	*Coryphaena hippurus*	39.46 kg	Papagallo Gulf Costa Rica	Sept. 25, 1976	Manuel Salazar
		87 lb			
Drum, black	*Pogonias cromis*	51.28 kg	Lewes Delaware	Sept. 15, 1975	Gerald M. Townsend
		113 lb 1 oz			
Drum, red	*Sciaenops ocellata*	40.82 kg	Rodanthe North Carolina	Nov. 7, 1973	Elvin Hooper
		90 lb			
Flounder, summer	*Paralichthys dentatus*	10.17 kg	Montauk New York	Sept. 15, 1975	Charles Nappi
		22 lb 7 oz			
Halibut,	*Paralichthys*	17.01 kg	San Diego	July 22, 1979	William E. Williams

Common Name	Scientific Name	Weight	Location	Date	Angler
Jack, California	*californicus*	37 lb 8 oz	California	June 20, 1978	Stephen V. Schwenk
Jack, crevalle	*Caranx hippos*	51 lb / 23.13 kg	Lake Worth, Florida	June 24, 1979	Tom Smith
Jack, horse-eye	*Caranx latus*	21 lb 5 oz / 9.66 kg	Arcus Bank, Bermuda		
Jewfish	*Epinephelus itajara*	680 lb / 308.44 kg	Fernandina Beach, Florida	May 20, 1961	Lynn Joyner
Kawakawa	*Euthynnus affinis*	21 lb / 9.52 kg	Kilauea, Kauai, Hawaii	Aug. 21, 1975	E. John O'Dell
Mackerel, king	*Scomberomorus cavalla*	90 lb / 40.82 kg	Key West, Florida	Feb. 16, 1976	Norton I. Thornton
Marlin, black	*Makaira indica*	1560 lb / 707.61 kg	Cabo Blanco, Peru	Aug. 4, 1953	Alfred C. Glassell, Jr.
Marlin, blue (Atl.)	*Makaira nigricans*	1282 lb / 581.51 kg	St. Thomas, Virgin Islands	Aug. 6, 1977	Larry Martin
Marlin, blue (Pac.)	*Makaira nigricans*	1153 lb / 522.99 kg	Ritidian Point, Guam	Aug. 21, 1969	Greg D. Perez
Marlin, striped	*Tetrapturus audax*	417 lb 8 oz / 189.37 kg	Cavalli Islands, New Zealand	Jan. 14, 1977	Phillip Bryers
Marlin, white	*Tetrapturus albidus*	174 lb 3 oz / 79.00 kg	Vitoria, Brazil	Nov. 1, 1975	Otavio Cunha Reboucas
Permit	*Trachinotus falcatus*	51 lb 8 oz / 23.35 kg	Lake Worth, Florida	Apr. 28, 1978	William M. Kenney
Pollock	*Pollachius virens*	46 lb 7 oz / 21.06 kg	Brielle, New Jersey	May 26, 1975	John Tomes Holton
Pompano, African	*Alectis ciliaris*	41 lb 8 oz / 18.82 kg	Fort Lauderdale, Florida	Feb. 15, 1979	Wayne Sommers
Roosterfish	*Nematistius pectoralis*	114 lb / 51.71 kg	La Paz, Baja, Mexico	June 1, 1960	Abe Sackheim
Runner, rainbow	*Elagatis bipinnulata*	33 lb 10 oz / 15.25 kg	Clarion Island, Mexico	Mar. 14, 1976	Ralph A. Mikkelsen
Sailfish (Atlantic)	*Istiophorus platypterus*	128 lb 1 oz / 58.10 kg	Luanda, Angola	Mar. 27, 1974	Harm Steyn
Sailfish (Pacific)	*Istiophorus platypterus*	221 lb / 100.24 kg	Santa Cruz Island, Ecuador	Feb. 12, 1947	C. W. Stewart
Seabass, white	*Cynoscion nobilis*	83 lb 12 oz / 37.98 kg	San Felipe, Mexico	Mar. 31, 1953	L. C. Baumgardner
Seatrout, spotted	*Cynoscion nebulosus*	16 lb / 7.25 kg	Mason's Beach, Virginia	May 28, 1977	William Katko

IGFA Saltwater All-Tackle World Records (continued)

Species	Scientific Name	Weight	Place	Date	Angler
Shark, blue	Prionace glauca	198.22 kg / 437 lb	Catherine Bay N.S.W., Australia	Oct. 2, 1976	Peter Hyde
Shark, hammerhead	Sphyrna spp.	318.87 kg / 703 lb	Jacksonville Beach Florida	July 5, 1975	H. B. "Blackie" Reasor
Shark, porbeagle	Lamna nasus	210.92 kg / 465 lb	Padstow, Cornwall England, U.K.	July 23, 1976	Jorge Potier
Shark, shortfin mako	Isurus oxyrinchus	498.88 kg / 1080 lb	Montauk New York	Aug. 26, 1979	James L. Melanson
Shark, thresher	Alopias spp.	335.20 kg / 739 lb	Tutukaka New Zealand	Feb. 17, 1975	Brian Galvin
Shark, tiger	Galeocerdo cuvieri	807.40 kg / 1780 lb	Cherry Grove S. Carolina	June 14, 1964	Walter Maxwell
Shark, white	Carcharodon carcharias	1208.38 kg / 2664 lb	Ceduna South Australia	Apr. 21, 1959	Alfred Dean
Skipjack, black	Euthynnus	6.57 kg / 14 lb 8 oz	Cabo San Lucas Baja, Mexico	May 24, 1977	Lorraine Carlton
Snook	Centropomus lineatus undecimalis	24.32 kg / 53 lb 10 oz	Rio de Parasmina Costa Rica	Oct. 18, 1978	Gilbert Ponzi
Spearfish	Tetrapturus spp.	36.00 kg / 79 lb 5 oz	Madeira Islands	May 25, 1979	Ronald Eckert
Swordfish	Xiphias gladius	536.15 kg / 1182 lb	Iquique Chile	May 7, 1953	L. Marron
Tanguigue	Scomberomorus commerson	38.75 kg / 85 lb 6 oz	Rottnest Island Western Australia	May 5, 1978	Barry Wrightson
Tarpon	Megalops atlantica	128.36 kg / 283 lb	Lake Maracaibo Venezuela	Mar. 19, 1956	M. Salazar
Tautog	Tautoga onitis	9.69 kg / 21 lb 6 oz	Cape May New Jersey	June 12, 1954	R. N. Sheafer
Trevally, lowly	Caranx ignobilis	52.61 kg / 116 lb	Pago Pago American Samoa	Feb 20, 1978	William G. Foster
Tuna, bigeye (Atl.)	Thunnus obesus	170.32 kg / 375 lb 8 oz	Ocean City Maryland	Aug. 26, 1977	Cecil Browne
Tuna, bigeye (Pac.)	Thunnus obesus	197.31 kg / 435 lb	Cabo Blanco Peru	Apr. 17, 1957	Dr. Russel V. A. Lee
Tuna, blackfin	Thunnus atlanticus	19.05 kg / 42 lb	Bermuda	June 2, 1978	Alan J. Card
	Thunnus	679.00 kg	Aulds Cove	Oct. 26, 1979	Ken Fraser

bluefin	*thynnus*	1496 lb	Nova Scotia, Canada	Nov. 12, 1978	Luke John Samaras
Tuna, dogtooth	*Gymnosarda unicolor*	85.80 kg / 189 lb 2 oz	Dar es Salaam, Tanzania	Apr. 20, 1978	Michael James
Tuna, longtail	*Thunnus tonggol*	29.50 kg / 65 lb	Port Stephens, N.S.W., Australia	Jan. 21, 1952	F. Drowley
Tuna, skipjack	*Katsuwonus pelamis*	18.11 kg / 39 lb 15 oz	Walker Cay, Bahamas	Apr. 19, 1971	Joseph R. P. Caboche, Jr.
TIE	*Katsuwonus pelamis*	40 lb	Baie du Tambeau, Mauritius	May 29, 1979	Rodney James Beard
Tuna, southern bluefin	*Thunnus maccoyii*	116.50 kg / 256 lb 13 oz	Hippolyte Rock, Tasmania, Australia	Apr. 1, 1977	Curt Wiesenhutter
Tuna, yellowfin	*Thunnus albacares*	176.35 kg / 388 lb 12 oz	San Benedico I., Mexico	Apr. 20, 1976	William E. Allison
Tunny, little	*Euthynnus alletteratus*	12.24 kg / 27 lb	Key Largo, Florida	June 15, 1962	John Pirovano
Wahoo	*Acanthocybium solandri*	67.58 kg / 149 lb	Cay Cay, Bahamas	Apr. 13, 1962	Dennis B. Hall
Weakfish	*Cynoscion regalis*	8.84 kg / 19 lb 8 oz	Trinidad, West Indies		
Yellowtail, California	*Seriola lalandi dorsalis*	32.64 kg / 71 lb 15 oz	Alijos Rocks, Mexico	June 24, 1979	Michael Carpenter
Yellowtail, southern	*Seriola lalandi lalandi*	50.34 kg / 111 lb	Bay of Islands, New Zealand	June 11, 1961	A. F. Plim

IGFA Freshwater All-Tackle World Records

All tackle records are kept for the heaviest freshwater fish of each species caught by an angler in any line class category up to 60 kg (130 lb). Following are the all-tackle records granted as of January, 1, 1980.

Species	Scientific Name	Weight	Place	Date	Angler
Bass, largemouth	*Micropterus salmoides*	10.09 kg / 22 lb 4 oz	Montgomery Lake, Georgia	June 2, 1932	George W. Perry
Bass, redeye	*Micropterus coosae*	3.71 kg / 8 lb 3 oz	Flint River, Georgia	Oct. 23, 1977	David A. Hubbard
Bass, rock	*Ambloplites rupestris*	1.36 kg / 3 lb	York River, Ontario, Canada	Aug. 1, 1974	Peter Gulgin
Bass, smallmouth	*Micropterus dolomieui*	5.41 kg / 11 lb 15 oz	Dale Hollow Lake, Kentucky	July 9, 1955	David L. Hayes

IGFA Freshwater All-Tackle World Records (continued)

Species	Scientific Name	Weight	Place	Date	Angler
Bass, spotted	*Micropterus punctulatus*	4.05 kg	Lewis Smith Lake	March 18, 1978	Philip C. Terry, Jr.
Bass, white	*Morone chrysops*	8 lb 15 oz	Alabama		
TIE	*Morone chrysops*	2.40 kg	Ferguson Lake California	March 8, 1972	Norman W. Mize
		5 lb 5 oz			
		2.43 kg	Grenada	April 21, 1979	William C. Mulvihill
		5 lb 6 oz	Mississippi		
Bass, whiterock	White X Striped	9.07 kg	Savannah River	May 5, 1977	Ron Raley
		20 lb	Georgia		
Bass, yellow	*Morone mississippiensis*	1.02 kg	Lake Monroe	March 27, 1977	Donald L. Stalker
		2 lb 4 oz	Indiana		
Bluegill	*Lepomis macrochirus*	2.15 kg	Ketona Lake	April 9, 1950	T. S. Hudson
		4 lb 12 oz	Alabama		
Bowfin	*Amia calva*	8.95 kg	Lake Marion	Nov. 5, 1972	M. R. Webster
		19 lb 12 oz	South Carolina		
Buffalo, bigmouth	*Ictiobus cyprinellus*	25.40 kg	Lock Loma Lake	Aug. 19, 1976	W. J. Long
		56 lb	Missouri		
Buffalo, smallmouth	*Ictiobus bubalus*	23.13 kg	Lawrence	May 2, 1979	Scott Butler
		51 lb	Kansas		
Bullhead, black	*Ictalurus melas*	3.62 kg	Lake Waccabuc	Aug. 1, 1951	Kani Evans
		8 lb	New York		
Carp	*Cyprinus carpio*	25.08 kg	Clearwater Lake	July 10, 1952	Frank J. Ledwein
		55 lb 5 oz	Minnesota		
Catfish, blue	*Ictalurus furcatus*	43.99 kg	Missouri River	Sept. 16, 1959	Edward B. Elliott
		97 lb	South Dakota		
Catfish, channel	*Ictalurus punctatus*	26.30 kg	Santee-Cooper Res.	July 7, 1964	W. B. Whaley
		58 lb	South Carolina		
Catfish, flathead	*Pylodictis olivaris*	36.06 kg	White River	Aug. 13, 1966	Glenn T. Simpson
		79 lb 8 oz	Indiana		
Catfish, white	*Ictalurus catus*	4.67 kg	Raritan River	June 23, 1976	Lewis W. Lomerson
		10 lb 5 oz	New Jersey		
Char, Arctic	*Salvelinus alpinus*	13.46 kg	Arctic River	Aug. 21, 1968	Jeanne P. Branson
		29 lb 11 oz	N.W. Terr., Canada		
Crappie, black	*Pomoxis nigromaculatus*	2.26 kg	Santee-Cooper Res.	March 15, 1957	Paul E. Foust
		5 lb	South Carolina		
Crappie, white	*Pomoxis annularis*	2.35 kg	Enid Dam	July 31, 1957	Fred L. Bright
		5 lb 3 oz	Mississippi		

Dolly Varden	*Salvelinus malma*	14.51 kg	Lake Pend Oreille Idaho	Oct. 27, 1949	N. L. Higgins
Drum, freshwater	*Aplodinotus grunniens*	32 lb	Nickajack Lake Tennessee	April 20, 1972	Benny E. Hull
Gar, alligator	*Lepisosteus spatula*	24.72 kg	Rio Grande River Texas	Dec. 2, 1951	Bill Valverde
Gar, longnose	*Lepisosteus osseus*	54 lb 8 oz	Trinity River Texas	July 30, 1954	Townsend Miller
Grayling, Arctic	*Thymallus arcticus*	126.55 kg	Katseyedie River N.W. Terr., Canada	Aug. 16, 1967	Jeanne P. Branson
Kokanee	*Oncorhynchus nerka*	279 lb	Priest Lake Idaho	June 9, 1975	Jerry Verge
Muskellunge	*Esox masquinongy*	22.82 kg	St. Lawrence River New York	Sept. 22, 1957	Arthur Lawton
Perch, white	*Morone americana*	50 lb 5 oz	Messalonskee Lake Maine	June 4, 1949	Mrs. Earl Small
Perch, yellow	*Perca flavescens*	2.69 kg	Bordentown New Jersey	May, 1865	Dr. C. C. Abbott
Pickerel, chain	*Esox niger*	5 lb 15 oz	Homerville Georgia	Feb. 17, 1961	Baxley McQuaig, Jr.
Pike, northern	*Esox lucius*	2.99 kg	Sacandaga Reservoir New York	Sept. 15, 1940	Peter Dubuc
Redhorse, silver	*Moxostoma anisurum*	6 lb 9 oz	Gasconade River Missouri	Oct. 5, 1974	C. Larry McKinney
Salmon, Atlantic	*Salmo salar*	31.72 kg	Tana River Norway	1928	Henrik Henriksen
Salmon, Chinook	*Oncorhynchus tshawytscha*	69 lb 15 oz	Help Bay Alaska	June 24, 1977	Howard C. Rider
Salmon, chum	*Oncorhynchus keta*	2.15 kg	Raymond Cove Alaska	June 11, 1977	Robert A. Jahnke
Salmon, coho	*Oncorhynchus kisutch*	4 lb 12 oz	Cowichan Bay B.C., Canada	Oct. 11, 1947	Mrs. Lee Hallberg
Salmon, landlocked	*Salmo salar*	1.91 kg	Sebago Lake Maine	Aug. 1, 1907	Edward Blakely
Sauger	*Stizostedion canadense*	4 lb 3 oz	Lake Sakakawea North Dakota	Oct. 6, 1971	Mike Fischer
Shad, American	*Alosa sapidissima*	4.25 kg	Delaware River Pennsylvania	April 26, 1979	J. Edward Whitman
Sturgeon, white	*Acipenser transmontanus*	9 lb 6 oz	Snake River Idaho	April 24, 1956	Willard Cravens

IGFA Freshwater All-Tackle World Records (continued)

Species	Scientific Name	Weight	Place	Date	Angler
Sunfish, green	Lepomis cyanellus	0.96 kg 2 lb 2 oz	Stockton Lake Missouri	June 18, 1971	Paul M. Dilley
Sunfish, redbreast	Lepomis auritus	0.69 kg 1 lb 8 oz	Suwannee River Florida	April 30, 1977	Tommy D. Cason, Jr.
Sunfish, redear	Lepomis macrolophus	2.04 kg 4 lb 8 oz	Chase City Virginia	June 19, 1970	Maurice E. Ball
Trout, brook	Salvelinus fontinalis	6.57 kg 14 lb 8 oz	Nipigon River Ontario, Canada	July, 1916	Dr. W. J. Cook
Trout, brown	Salmo trutta	16.30 kg 35 lb 15 oz	Nahuel Huapi Argentina	Dec. 16, 1952	Eugenio Cavaglia
Trout, cutthroat	Salmo clarki	18.59 kg 41 lb	Pyramid Lake Nevada	Dec., 1925	John Skimmerhorn
Trout, golden	Salmo aguabonita	4.98 kg 11 lb	Cook's Lake Wyoming	Aug. 5, 1948	Chas. S. Reed
Trout, lake	Salvelinus namaycush	29.48 kg 65 lb	Great Bear Lake N.W. Terr., Canada	Aug. 8, 1970	Larry Daunis
Trout (rainbow, steelhead, or kamloops)	Salmo gairdneri	19.10 kg 42 lb 2 oz	Bell Island Alaska	June 22, 1970	David Robert White
Trout, sunapee	Salvelinus aureolus	5.21 kg 11 lb 8 oz	Lake Sunapee New Hampshire	Aug. 1, 1954	Ernest Theoharis
Trout, tiger	Brown X Brook	7.71 kg 17 lb	Lake Michigan Wisconsin	Aug. 2, 1977	Edward Rudnicki
Walleye	Stizostedion vitreum vitreum	11.34 kg 25 lb	Old Hickory Lake Tennessee	Aug. 1, 1960	Mabry Harper
Warmouth	Lepomis gulosus	0.90 kg 2 lb	Sylvania Georgia	May 4, 1974	Carlton Robbins
Whitefish, lake	Coregonus clupeaformis	5.89 kg 13 lb	Great Bear Lake N.W. Terr., Canada	July 14, 1974	Robert L. Stinstman
Whitefish, mountain	Prosopium williamsoni	2.26 kg 5 lb	Athabasca River Alberta, Canada	June 3, 1963	Orville Welch

FOOTBALL

Origins. The origin of modern football stems from the "Boston Game" as played at Harvard. Harvard declined to participate in the inaugural meeting of the Intercollegiate Football Association in New York City in October, 1873, on the grounds that the proposed rules were based on the non-handling "Association" code of English football. Instead, Harvard accepted a proposal from McGill University of Montreal, Canada, who played the more closely akin English Rugby Football. The first football match under the Harvard Rules was thus played against McGill at Cambridge, Mass., in May, 1874. In November, 1876, a New Intercollegiate Football Association, based on modern football, was inaugurated at Springfield, Mass., with a pioneer membership of five colleges.

Professional football dates from the Latrobe, Pa. vs. Jeannette, Pa. match at Latrobe, in August, 1895. The National Football League was founded in Canton, Ohio, in 1920, although it did not adopt its present name until 1922. The year 1969 was the final year in which professional football was divided into separate National and American Leagues, for record purposes.

Longest Service Coach

The longest service head coach was Amos Alonzo Stagg (1862–1965), who served Springfield in 1890–91, Chicago from 1892 to 1932 and College of Pacific from 1933 to 1946, making a total of 57 years. He later served as an assistant coach to his son.

RUNNING BEAR: Gale Sayers, looking for his offensive line to open a hole, holds the NFL record for most TD's by a rookie (22) and most TD's in a game (6), both set in 1965. Watching the play is the winningest coach in NFL history, George Halas (center, in rain coat and baseball cap), whose Chicago Bears teams recorded 325 victories.

FULL GAINER: Jim Brown dives into the end zone in the 1964 NFL championship game. Brown, one of the greatest runners of all time, scored 43 points in one game for Syracuse Universi′y. As a professional with the Cleveland Browns, he set records for most career TD's, yards gained rushing, average gain rushing, and TD's rushing.

Winningest Coaches

Amos Alonzo Stagg's teams (see above) won 314 games, more than any other college coach. The record for most victories by a professional coach is 325, by George Halas (b. February 2, 1895), who coached the Chicago Bears, 1920–29, 1933–42, 1946–55, 1958–67. The most victorious high school coach is Gordon Wood who has guided teams in Texas to 367 wins (and only 43 defeats) since 1938.

Helmet Kicking

Fred (The Hammer) Williamson, formerly of the Kansas City Chiefs, kicked a football helmet 38 yards at the Palm Springs Hamilton/Avnet Competition on January 20, 1980.

College

College Series Records. The oldest collegiate series is that between Princeton and Rutgers dating from 1869, or 7 years before the passing of the Springfield rules. The most regularly contested series is between Lafayette and Lehigh, who have met 115 times between 1884 and the end of 1979.

Longest Streaks. The longest winning streak is 47 straight by Oklahoma. The longest unbeaten streak is 63 games (59 won, 4 tied) by Washington from 1907 to 1917.

Most Wins. Yale University became the only college to win more than 700 games when they finished the 1979 season with a total of 701 victories in 107 seasons.

Most Bowl Appearances. The University of Alabama has participated in 33 bowl games through January 1, 1980. Paul (Bear) Bryant, as coach of Alabama, produced teams that made 21 consecutive bowl appearances from 1960 to 1980.

Highest Score. The most points ever scored in a college football game was 222 by Georgia Tech, Atlanta, Georgia, against Cumberland University of Lebanon, Tennessee, on October 7, 1916. Tech also set records for the most points scored in one quarter (63), most touchdowns (32) and points after touchdown (30) in a game, and the largest victory margin (Cumberland did not score). There were no first downs.

Most Points in a Game. Joe Korshalla, halfback for West Liberty State, West Virginia, scored 71 points (and rushed for an all-time record high 504 yards in 20 carries) in a game against Cedarville College, Ohio, on November 19, 1932. He scored 11 touchdowns (none for less than 22 yards) and 5 extra points.

All-America Selections. The earliest All-America selections were made in 1889 by Caspar Whitney of *The Week's Sport* and later of *Harper's Weekly.*

The oldest All-America honoree was Al Wistert, University of

HIGH KICKERS: George Blanda (left) played in 340 pro games over 26 seasons and scored 2,002 points, including 943 PAT's and 335 field goals, all records. An excellent quarterback, he threw 36 TD passes, including 7 in one game, in 1961. Vince Rovetti (right), a San Francisco florist, kicked 1,035 20-yard field goals of 1,135 tries, barefoot, at Candlestick Park in 2½ hours 4 seconds, December, 1978.

Michigan tackle, who made the 1947 All-America team when he was 33 years old, Wistert, who had fought in World War II, never played high school football.

Modern Major-College Football Records (1938–1979)

Scoring

Most Points, Career
356 Tony Dorsett, Pittsburgh, 1973–76

Most Points, Season
174 Lydell Mitchell, Penn St., 1971

Most Points, Game
43 Jim Brown, Syracuse (vs. Colgate), 1956

Most Touchdowns, Career
59 Glenn Davis, Army, 1943–46
Tony Dorsett, Pittsburgh, 1973–76

Most Touchdowns, Season
29 Lydell Mitchell, Penn St., 1971

Most Touchdowns, Game
7 Arnold Boykin, Mississippi (vs. Miss. St.), 1951

Most Field Goals, Career
56 Tony Franklin, Texas A & M, 1975–78

Most Field Goals, Season
22 Matt Bahr, Penn St., 1978

Most Field Goals, Game
6 Vince Fusco, Duke (vs. Clemson), 1976
Frank Nester, W. Virginia (vs. Villanova), 1972
Charley Gogolak, Princeton (vs. Rutgers), 1965

Most Field Goals Made, Consecutive
15 Ish Odonez, Arkansas, 1978–79
Dale Castro, Maryland, 1979

Field Goal, Longest
67 yds. Joe Williams, Wichita St. (vs. So. Illinois), 1978
Steve Little, Arkansas (vs. Texas), 1977
Russell Erxleben, Texas (vs. Rice), 1977

Most Points After Touchdown, Consecutive
125 Uwe von Schamann, Oklahoma, 1976–78

Rushing

Most Yards Rushing, Career
6,048 Tony Dorsett, Pittsburgh, 1973–76

Most Yards Rushing, Season
1,948 Tony Dorsett, Pittsburgh, 1976

Most Yards Rushing, Game
356 Eddie Lee Ivery, Georgia Tech (vs. Air Force), 1978

Best Average per Carry, Career (minimum 300 attempts)
8.26 yds. Glenn Davis, Army, 1943–46

Best Average per Carry, Season (minimum 150 attempts)
9.35 yds. Greg Pruitt, Oklahoma, 1971

Longest Run from Scrimmage
99 yds. Kelsey Finch, Tennessee (vs. Florida), 1977
Ralph Thompson, West Texas St. (vs. Wichita St.), 1970
Max Anderson, Arizona St. (vs. Wyoming), 1967
Gale Sayers, Kansas (vs. Nebraska), 1963

Passing

Most Yards, Career
7,818 Jack Thompson, Wash. St., 1975–78

Most Yards, Season
3,720 Marc Wilson, Brigham Young, 1979

Most Yards, Game
571 Marc Wilson, Brigham Young (vs. Utah), 1977

Most Attempts, Career
1,128 John Reaves, Florida, 1969–71

Most Attempts, Season
509 Bill Anderson, Tulsa, 1965

Most Attempts, Game
69 Chuck Hixson, Southern Methodist (vs. Ohio St.), 1968

Most Completions, Career
642 Chuck Hixson, Southern Methodist, 1968–70

Most Completions, Season
296 Bill Anderson, Tulsa, 1965

Most Completions, Game
42 Bill Anderson, Tulsa (vs. So. Illinois), 1965

Most Touchdown Passes, Career
69 Steve Ramsey, N. Texas St., 1967–69

Most Touchdown Passes, Season
39 Dennis Shaw, San Diego St., 1969

Most Touchdown Passes, Game
9 Dennis Shaw, San Diego St. (vs. N. Mexico St.), 1969

PURPLE PEOPLE-EATER: Jim Marshall, a member of the fierce Minnesota Vikings' defensive line (whose purple jerseys caused them to be nicknamed the "purple people-eaters"), played in 282 consecutive regular-season games from 1960 to 1979. Including pre- and post-season play, Marshall played in every game in Viking history from their inception in 1961 to his retirement at the end of 1979. Along the way, Marshall scooped up 29 opponents' fumbles for another NFL record.

Most Consecutive Complete Passes, Game
15 Dave Humm, Nebraska (vs. Kansas), 1964
    Bill Anderson, Tulsa (vs. Colorado St.), 1965
    Tom Myers, Northwestern (vs. So. Carolina), 1962

Longest Pass from Scrimmage
99 yds. Cris Collinsworth to Derrick Gaffney, Florida (vs. Rice), 1977
    Terry Peel to Robert Ford, Houston (vs. San Diego St.), 1972
    Terry Peel to Robert Ford, Houston (vs. Syracuse), 1970
    Colin Clapton to Eddie Jenkins, Holy Cross (vs. Boston U.), 1970
    Bo Burris to Warren McVea, Houston (vs. Washington St.), 1966
    Fred Owens to Jack Ford, Portland (vs. St. Mary's), 1947

Receiving

Most Receptions, Career
261 Howard Twilley, Tulsa, 1963–65

Most Receptions, Season
134 Howard Twilley, Tulsa, 1965

Most Receptions, Game
22 Jay Miller, Brigham Young (vs. N. Mexico), 1973

Most Yards, Career
3,598 Ron Sellers, Florida St., 1966–68

Most Yards, Season
1,779 Howard Twilley, Tulsa, 1965

Most Yards, Game
349 Chuck Hughes, Texas-El Paso (vs. N. Texas St.), 1965

Most Touchdowns, Career
34 Elmo Wright, Houston, 1968–70

Most Touchdowns, Season
18 Tom Reynolds, San Diego St., 1969

Most Touchdowns, Game
6 Tim Delaney, San Diego St. (vs. N. Mexico St.), 1969

Interceptions

Most Interceptions, Career
29 Al Brosky, Illinois, 1950–52

Most Interceptions, Season
14 Al Worley, Washington, 1968

LONGEST PROFESSIONAL FIELD GOAL: Tom Dempsey (New Orleans Saints) kicked a 63-yard field goal on the last play of an NFL game to beat the Detroit Lions 19-17 on November 8, 1970. Dempsey, who was born with only half a right foot and only part of his right arm, wore a special shoe for placekicking. He reportedly once kicked a 57-yarder without a shoe in a semipro game.

Modern Major-College Football Records (1938-1979)

Most Interceptions, Game
    5 Dan Rebech, Miami, Ohio (vs. Western Michigan), 1972
        Byron Beaver, Houston (vs. Baylor), 1962
        Walt Pastuszak, Brown (vs. Rhode Island), 1949
        Lee Cook, Oklahoma St. (vs. Detroit), 1942

Punting

Best Average, Career (minimum 75 punts)
  46.9 yds. Marv Bateman, Utah, 1970–71

Best Average, Season (minimum 30 punts)
  49.3 yds. Kirk Wilson, U.C.L.A., 1956

Best Average, Game (minimum 5 punts)
  57.2 yds. Jack Jordan, Colorado (vs. Arizona St.), 1950

Longest Punt
  99 yds. Pat Brady, Nevada-Reno (vs. Loyola, Calif.), 1950

Kick Returns

Longest Punt Return
  100 yds. Richie Luzzi, Clemson (vs. Georgia), 1968 (return of field goal attempt)
        Don Guest, California (vs. Washington St.), 1966 (return of field goal attempt)
        Jimmy Campagna, Georgia (vs. Vanderbilt), 1952
        Hugh McElhenny, Washington (vs. So. California), 1951
        Frank Brady, Navy (vs. Maryland), 1951
        Bert Rechichar, Tennessee (vs. Wash. & Lee), 1950
        Eddie Macon, Pacific (vs. Boston U.), 1950

Longest Kickoff Return
  100 yds. by 118 players
        Ottis Anderson, Miami, had 2 100-yarders (vs. Utah State and Tulane) in the 1978 season

All-Time Professional Records

(Through 1979 Season)

Service

Most Seasons, Active Player
26 George Blanda, Chi. Bears, 1949–58; Balt., 1950; AFL: Hou., 1960–66; Oak., 1967–75

Most Games Played, Lifetime
340 George Blanda, Chi. Bears, 1949–58; Balt., 1950; AFL: Hou., 1960–66; Oak., 1967–75

Most Consecutive Games Played, Lifetime
282 Jim Marshall, Clev., 1960; Minn., 1961–79

Most Seasons, Head Coach
40 George Halas, Chi. Bears, 1920–29, 33–42, 46–55, 58–67

EFFICIENCY EXPERT: Washington Redskins star Sammy Baugh completed 70.3 per cent of his passes in 1945, a league record. The Hall of Fame quarterback led the league in passing a record 6 seasons.

Scoring

Most Seasons Leading League
5 Don Hutson, Green Bay, 1940–44
Gino Cappelletti, Bos., 1961, 63–66 (AFL)

Most Points, Lifetime
2,002 George Blanda, Chi. Bears, 1949–58; Balt., 1950; AFL: Hou., 1960–66; Oak., 1967–75 (9-td, 943-pat, 335-fg)

Most Points, Season
176 Paul Hornung, Green Bay, 1960 (15-td, 41-pat, 15-fg)

Most Points, Rookie Season
132 Gale Sayers, Chi., 1965 (22-td)

Most Points, Game
40 Ernie Nevers, Chi. Cards vs. Chi. Bears, Nov. 28, 1929 (6-td, 4-pat)

Most Points, One Quarter
29 Don Hutson, Green Bay vs. Det., Oct. 7, 1945 (4-td, 5-pat) 2nd Quarter

Touchdowns

Most Seasons Leading League
8 Don Hutson, Green Bay, 1935–38, 41–44

Most Touchdowns, Lifetime
126 Jim Brown, Cleve., 1957–65 (106-r, 20-p)

Most Touchdowns, Season
23 O. J. Simpson, Buff., 1975 (16-r, 7-p)

Most Touchdowns, Rookie Season
22 Gale Sayers, Chi., 1965 (14-r, 6-p, 1-prb, 1-krb)

Most Touchdowns, Game
6 Ernie Nevers, Chi. Cards vs. Chi. Bears, Nov. 28, 1929 (6-r)
William (Dub) Jones, Cleve. vs. Chi. Bears, Nov. 25, 1951 (4-r, 2-p)
Gale Sayers, Chi. vs. S. F., Dec. 12, 1965 (4-r, 1-p, 1-prb)

Most Consecutive Games Scoring Touchdowns
18 Lenny Moore, Balt., 1963–65

Points After Touchdown

Most Seasons Leading League
8 George Blanda, Chi. Bears, 1956; AFL: Hou., 1961–62; Oak., 1967–69, 72, 74

Most Points After Touchdown, Lifetime
943 George Blanda, Chi. Bears, 1949–58; Balt., 1950; AFL: Hou., 1960–66; Oak. 1967–75

GIANT STEPS: Y.A. Tittle (#14) shares NFL records for most TD passes in a game (7) and in a season (36). Here he has just handed off to NY Giant teammate Joe Morrison on a bad day for passing—a rainy Sunday afternoon.

All-Time Professional Records (continued)

Most Points After Touchdown, Lifetime
64   George Blanda, Hou., 1961 (AFL)

Most Points After Touchdown, Game
9   Marlin (Pat) Harder, Chi. Cards vs. N. Y., Oct. 17, 1948
Bob Waterfield, L. A. vs. Balt., Oct. 22, 1950
Charlie Gogolak, Wash. vs. N. Y., Nov. 27, 1966

Most Consecutive Points After Touchdown
234   Tommy Davis, S.F., 1959–65

Most Points After Touchdown (no misses), Game
9   Marlin (Pat) Harder, Chi. Cards vs. N. Y., Oct. 17, 1948
Bob Waterfield, L.A. vs. Balt., Oct. 22, 1950

Field Goals

Most Seasons Leading League
5   Lou Groza, Cleve., 1950, 52–54, 57

Most Field Goals, Lifetime
335   George Blanda, Chi. Bears, 1949–58; Balt., 1950; AFL: Hou., 1960–66; Oak., 1967–75

Most Field Goals, Season
34   Jim Turner, N. Y., 1968 (AFL)

Most Field Goals, Game
7   Jim Bakken, St. L. vs. Pitt., Sept. 24, 1967

Most Consecutive Games, Field Goals
31   Fred Cox, Minn., 1968–70

Most Consecutive Field Goals
16   Jan Stenerud, K.C., 1969 (AFL)
Don Cockroft, Clev., 1974–75
Garo Yepremian, Mia., 1978

Longest Field Goal
63 yds.   Tom Dempsey, New Orl. vs. Det., Nov. 8, 1970

Rushing

Most Seasons Leading League
8   Jim Brown, Cleve., 1957–61, 63–65

Most Yards Gained, Lifetime
12,312   Jim Brown, Cleve., 1957–65

Most Yards Gained, Season
2,003   O. J. Simpson, Buff., 1973

Most Yards Gained, Game
275   Walter Payton, Chi. vs. Minn., Nov. 20, 1977

Longest Run from Scrimmage
97 yards   Andy Uram, Green Bay vs. Chi. Cards, Oct. 8, 1939 (td)
Bob Gage, Pitt. vs. Chi. Bears, Dec. 4, 1949 (td)

Highest Average Gain, Lifetime (799 att.)
5.2   Jim Brown, Cleve., 1957–65 (2,-359–12,312)

Highest Average Gain, Season (100 att.)
9.9   Beattie Feathers, Chi. Bears, 1934 (101–1004)

Highest Average Gain, Game (10 att.)
17.1   Marion Motley, Cleve. vs. Pitt., Oct. 29, 1950 (11–188)

Most Touchdowns Rushing, Lifetime
  106 Jim Brown, Cleve., 1957–58

Most Touchdowns Rushing, Season
  19 Jim Taylor, Green Bay, 1962
      Earl Campbell, Houston, 1979

Most Touchdowns Rushing, Game
  6 Ernie Nevers, Chi. Cards vs. Chi.
     Bears, Nov. 28, 1929

Passing

Most Seasons Leading League
  6 Sammy Baugh, Wash., 1937, 40,
     43, 45, 47, 49

Most Passes Attempted, Lifetime
  6,467 Fran Tarkenton, Minn., 1961–66,
         72–78; N.Y. Giants, 1967–71
         (3,686 completions)

Most Passes Attempted, Season
  572 Fran Tarkenton, Minn., 1978
       (345 completions)

Most Passes Attempted, Game
  68 George Blanda, Hou. vs. Buff.,
      Nov. 1, 1964 (AFL) (37 comple-
      tions)

Most Passes Completed, Lifetime
  3,686 Fran Tarkenton, Minn., 1961–66,
         72–78; N.Y. Giants, 1967–71
         (6,467 attempts)

Most Passes Completed, Season
  345 Fran Tarkenton, Minn., 1978
       (572 attempts)

EAGLE EYE: 6-foot-8-inch Harold Carmichael (Philadelphia Eagles) set the NFL record for most consecutive games catching passes when he ran his streak to 112 at the end of 1979. The streak began in 1972.

Most Passes Completed, Game
  37 George Blanda, Hou. vs. Buff.,
      Nov. 1, 1964 (AFL) (68 at-
      tempts)

Most Consecutive Passes Completed
  17 Bert Jones, Balt. vs. N.Y. Jets,
      Dec. 15, 1974

Passing Efficiency, Lifetime (1,500 att.)
  59.9 Ken Stabler, Oak., 1970–78 (2,-
        481–1,486)

Passing Efficiency, Season (100 att.)
  70.3 Sammy Baugh, Wash., 1945 (182–
        129)

Passing Efficiency, Game (20 att.)
  90.9 Ken Anderson, Cin. vs. Pitt., Nov.
        10, 1974 (22–20)

Shortest Pass Completion for Touchdown
  2" Eddie LeBaron (to Bielski), Dall.
      vs. Wash., Oct. 9, 1960

Longest Pass Completion (all TDs)
  99 Frank Filchock (to Farkas), Wash.
      vs. Pitt. Oct. 15, 1939
      George Izo (to Mitchell), Wash.
      vs. Cleve., Sept. 15, 1963
      Karl Sweetan (to Studstill), Det.
      vs. Balt., Oct. 16, 1966
      C. A. Jurgensen (to Allen), Wash.
      vs. Chi., Sept. 15, 1968

Most Yards Gained Passing, Lifetime
  47,003 Fran Tarkenton, Minn., 1961–66,
          72–78; N.Y. Giants, 1967–71

Most Yards Gained Passing, Season
  4,082 Dan Fouts, S.D., 1979

Most Yards Gained Passing, Game
  554 Norm Van Brocklin, L. A. vs. N.
       Y. Yanks, Sept. 28, 1951 (41–27)

Most Touchdown Passes, Lifetime
  342 Fran Tarkenton, Minn., 1961–66,
       72–78; N.Y. Giants, 1967–71

Most Touchdown Passes, Season
  36 George Blanda, Hou., 1961 (AFL)
      Y.A. Tittle, N. Y., 1963

Most Touchdown Passes, Game
  7 Sid Luckman, Chi. Bears vs. N.
     Y., Nov. 14, 1943
     Adrian Burk, Phi. vs. Wash., Oct.
     17, 1954
     George Blanda, Hou. vs. N. Y.,
     Nov. 19, 1961 (AFL)
     Y. A. Tittle, N. Y. vs. Wash., Oct.
     28, 1962
     Joe Kapp, Minn. vs. Balt., Sept.
     28, 1969

Most Consecutive Games, Touchdown
Passes
  47 John Unitas, Balt., 1956–60

Passes Had Intercepted

Fewest Passes Intercepted, Season (Qualifiers)
  1 Joe Ferguson, Buff., 1976 (151
     attempts)

Most Consecutive Passes Attempted, None Intercepted
294 Bryan (Bart) Starr, Green Bay, 1964–65

Most Passes Intercepted, Game
8 Jim Hardy, Chi. Cards vs. Phil., Sept. 24, 1950 (39 attempts)

Lowest Percentage Passes Intercepted, Lifetime (1,500 att.)
3.31 Roman Gabriel, L.A., 1962–72; Phil., 1973–77 (4,498–149)

Lowest Percentage Passes Intercepted, Season (Qualifiers)
0.66 Joe Ferguson, Buff., 1976 (151–1)

Pass Receptions

Most Seasons Leading League
8 Don Hutson, Green Bay, 1936–37, 39, 41–45

Most Pass Receptions, Lifetime
649 Charley Taylor, Wash., 1964–75, 77

Most Pass Receptions, Season
101 Charley Hennigan, Hou., 1964 (AFL)

Most Pass Receptions, Game
18 Tom Fears, L.A. vs. Green Bay, Dec. 3, 1950 (189 yds.)

Most Pass Receptions by a Running Back, Game
15 Rickey Young, Minn. vs. N.E., Dec. 16, 1979

Longest Pass Reception (all TDs)
99 Andy Farkas (Filchock), Wash. vs. Pitt., Oct. 15, 1939
Bobby Mitchell (Izo), Wash. vs. Cleve., Sept. 15, 1963
Pat Studstill (Sweetan), Det. vs. Balt., Oct. 16, 1966
Gerry Allen (Jurgensen), Wash. vs. Chi., Sept. 15, 1968

Most Consecutive Games, Pass Receptions
112 Harold Carmichael, Phil., 1972–1979

Touchdowns Receiving

Most Touchdown Passes, Lifetime
99 Don Hutson, Green Bay, 1935–45

Most Touchdown Passes, Season
17 Don Hutson, Green Bay, 1942
Elroy (Crazy Legs) Hirsch, L.A., 1951
Bill Groman, Hou., 1961 (AFL)

Most Touchdown Passes, Game
5 Bob Shaw, Chi. Cards vs. Balt., Oct. 2, 1950

Most Consecutive Games, Touchdown Passes
11 Elroy (Crazy Legs) Hirsch, L.A., 1950–51
Gilbert (Buddy) Dial, Pitt., 1959–60

Pass Interceptions

Most Interceptions by, Lifetime
81 Paul Krause, Wash. (28), 1964–67; Minn. (53), 1968–79

Most Interceptions by, Season
14 Richard (Night Train) Lane, L. A., 1952

Most Interceptions by, Game
4 By many players

Interception Yardage

Most Yards Gained, Lifetime
1,282 Emlen Tunnell, N. Y., 1948–58; Green Bay, 1959–61

Most Yards Gained, Season
349 Charley McNeil, San Diego, 1961 (AFL)

Most Yards Gained, Game

177 Charley McNeil, San Diego vs. Hou., Sept. 24, 1961 (AFL)

Longest Gain (all TDs)
102 Bob Smith, Det. vs. Chi. Bears, Nov. 24 1949
Erich Barnes. N. Y. vs. Dall., Oct. 22, 1961
Gary Barbaro, K.C. vs. Sea., Dec. 11, 1977

Touchdowns on Interceptions

Most Touchdowns, Lifetime
9 Ken Houston, Hou., 1967–72; Wash. 1973–78

Most Touchdowns, Season
4 Ken Houston, Hou., 1971
Jim Kearney, K.C., 1972

Punting

Most Seasons Leading League
4 Sammy Baugh, Wash., 1940–43
Jerrel Wilson, AFL: K.C., 1965, 68; NFL: K.C., 1972–73

Most Punts, Lifetime
1,072 Jerrel Wilson, AFL: K.C., 1963–69; NFL: K.C., 1970–77; N.E., 1978

Most Punts, Season
109 John James, Atl., 1978

Most Punts, Game
14 Dick Nesbitt, Chi. Cards vs. Chi. Bears, Nov. 30, 1933
Keith Molesworth, Chi. Bears vs. G.B., Dec. 10, 1933
Sammy Baugh, Wash. vs. Phil., Nov. 5, 1939
John Kinscherf, N. Y. vs. Det., Nov. 7, 1943
George Taliaferro, N. Y. Yanks vs. L. A., Sept. 28, 1951

Longest Punt
98 yards Steve O'Neal, N. Y. Jets vs. Den., Sept. 21, 1969 (AFL)

Average Yardage Punting

Highest Punting Average, Lifetime (300 punts)
45.1 yards Sammy Baugh, Wash., 1937–52 (338)

Highest Punting Average, Season (20 punts)
51.4 yards Sammy Baugh, Wash., 1940 (35)

Highest Punting Average, Game (4 punts)
61.8 yards Bob Cifers, Det. vs. Chi. Bears, Nov. 24, 1946

Punt Returns
Yardage Returning Punts

Most Yards Gained, Lifetime
2,288 Rick Upchurch, Den., 1975–79

Most Yards Gained, Season
655 Neal Colzie, Oak., 1975

Most Yards Gained, Game
205 George Atkinson, Oak. vs. Buff., Sept. 15, 1968

Longest Punt Return (all TDs)
98 Gil LeFebvre, Cin. vs. Brk., Dec. 3, 1933
Charlie West, Minn. vs. Wash., Nov. 3, 1968
Dennis Morgan, Dall. vs St. L., Oct. 13, 1974

Average Yardage Returning Punts

Highest Average, Lifetime (75 returns)
13.4 Billy (White Shoes) Johnson, Hou., 1974–78

BEARING DOWN: Sid Luckman quarterbacked the Chicago Bears for 12 seasons from 1939 to 1950, during which time they won 4 championships (including a 73–0 walloping of the Washington Redskins in 1940). With Luckman, the Bears enjoyed a 24-game unbeaten streak from 1941 to 1943.

Highest Average, Season (Qualifiers)
23.0 Herb Rich, Balt., 1950

Highest Average, Game (3 returns)
47.7 Chuck Latourette, St. L. vs. N.O., Sept. 29, 1968

Touchdowns Returning Punts

Most Touchdowns, Lifetime
8 Jack Christiansen, Det., 1951–58

Most Touchdowns, Season
4 Jack Christiansen, Det., 1951
Rick Upchurch, Den., 1976

Most Touchdowns, Game
2 Jack Christiansen, Det. vs. L.A., Oct. 14, 1951; vs. G.B., Nov. 22, 1951
Dick Christy, N.Y. Titans vs. Den., Sept. 24, 1961
Rick Upchurch, Den. vs. Clev., Sept 26, 1976

Kickoff Returns
Yardage Returning Kickoffs

Most Yards Gained, Lifetime
6,922 Ron Smith, Chi., 1965, 70–72; Atl., 1966–67; L.A., 1968–69; S.D., 1973; Oak., 1974

Most Yards Gained, Season
1,317 Bobby Jancik, Hou., 1963 (AFL)

PUTTING THE FOOT IN FOOT-BALL: Steve O'Neal (NY Jets) came in to punt in the September 21, 1969 game against Denver in Mile High Stadium, Colorado, with the ball on the Jets' 1-yard line. Standing in his own end zone, O'Neal punted the ball to the Denver 30 where it hit and rolled to the Denver 1-yard line—a 98-yard punt!

Most Yards Gained, Game
294 Wally Triplett, Det. vs. L. A., Oct. 29, 1950 (4)

Longest Kickoff Return for Touchdown
106 Al Carmichael, Green Bay vs. Chi. Bears, Oct. 7, 1956
Noland Smith, K.C. vs. Den., Dec. 17, 1967 (AFL)
Roy Green, St. L. vs. Dall., Oct. 21, 1979

Average Yardage Returning Kickoffs

Highest Average, Lifetime (75 returns)
30.6 Gale Sayers, Chi., 1965–71

Highest Average, Season (15 returns)
41.1 Travis Williams, Green Bay, 1967 (18)

Highest Average, Game (3 returns)
73.5 Wally Triplett, Det. vs. L. A., Oct. 29, 1950 (4—294)

Touchdowns Returning Kickoffs

Most Touchdowns, Lifetime
6 Ollie Matson, Chi. Cards, 1952 (2), 54, 56, 58 (2)
Gale Sayers, Chi., 1965, 66 (2), 67 (3)
Travis Williams, G.B., 1967 (4), 69, 71

Most Touchdowns, Season
4 Travis Williams, Green Bay, 1967
Cecil Turner, Chi., 1970

Most Touchdowns, Game
2 Thomas (Tim) Brown, Phil. vs. Dall., Nov. 6, 1966
Travis Williams, Green Bay vs. Cleve., Nov. 12, 1967

Fumbles

Most Fumbles, Lifetime
105 Roman Gabriel, L.A., 1962–72; Phil., 1973–77

Most Fumbles, Season
17 Dan Pastorini, Hou., 1973

Most Fumbles, Game
7 Len Dawson, K.C. vs. San Diego, Nov. 15, 1964 (AFL)

Most Own Fumbles Recovered, Lifetime
43 Fran Tarkenton, Minn., 1961–66, 72–78; N.Y. Giants, 1967–71

Most Own Fumbles Recovered, Season
8 Paul Christman, Chi. Cards, 1945
Bill Butler, Minn., 1963

Most Own Fumbles Recovered, Game
4 Otto Graham, Cleve. vs. N. Y., Oct. 25, 1953
Sam Etcheverry, St. L. vs. N. Y., Sept 17, 1961
Roman Gabriel, L. A. vs. S. F., Oct. 12, 1969
Joe Ferguson, Buff. vs. Miami, Sept. 18, 1977

Most Opponents' Fumbles Recovered, Lifetime
29 Jim Marshall, Clev., 1960; Minn., 1961–79

Most Opponents' Fumbles Recovered, Season
9 Don Hultz, Minn., 1963

Most Opponents' Fumbles Recovered, Game
3 Corwin Clatt, Chi. Cards vs. Det., Nov. 6, 1949
Vic Sears, Phil. vs. Green Bay, Nov. 2, 1952
Ed Beatty, S. F. vs. L. A., Oct. 7, 1956
Ron Carroll, Hou. vs Cin., Oct. 27, 1974
Maurice Spencer, N.O. vs. Atl., Oct. 10, 1976
Steve Nelson, N. E. vs. Phil., Oct. 8, 1978

Longest Fumble Run
104 Jack Tatum, Oak., vs. G.B., Sept. 24, 1972

Miscellaneous

Most Dropkick Field Goals, Game
4 John (Paddy) Driscoll, Chi. Cards vs. Columbus, Oct. 11, 1925 (23, 18, 50, 35 yards)
Elbert Bloodgood, Kansas City vs. Duluth, Dec. 12, 1926 (35, 32, 20, 25 yards)

Longest Dropkick Field Goal
50 Wilbur (Pete) Henry, Canton vs. Toledo, Nov. 13, 1922
John (Paddy) Driscoll, Chi. Cards vs. Milwaukee, Sept. 28, 1924; vs. Columbus, Oct. 11, 1925

Most Yards Returned Missed Field Goal
101 Al Nelson, Phil. vs. Dall., Sept. 26, 1971 (td)

TEAM RECORDS—OFFENSE
(Playoff games not included)

Most Seasons League Champion
11 Green Bay, 1929–31, 36, 39, 44, 61–62, 65–67

Most Consecutive Games Without Defeat (Regular Season)
12 Canton, 1922–23 (Won–21, Tied–3)
Chicago Bears, 1941–43 (Won–23, Tied–1)

Most Consecutive Victories (All Games)
18 Chicago Bears (1933–34; 1941–42)
Miami (1972–73)

Most Consecutive Victories (Regular Season)
17 Chicago Bears, 1933–34

Most Consecutive Victories, One Season (All Games)
17 Miami, 1972

Most Consecutive Shutout Games Won
  7 Detroit, 1934

Scoring

Most Seasons Leading League
  9 Chicago Bears, 1934–35, 39, 41–43, 46–47, 56

Most Points, Season
  513 Houston, 1961 (AFL)

Most Points, Game
  72 Washington vs. N. Y., Nov. 27, 1966

Most Touchdowns, Season
  66 Houston, 1961 (AFL)

Most Touchdowns, Game
  10 Philadelphia vs. Cin., Nov. 6, 1934
      Los Angeles, vs. Balt., Oct. 22, 1950
      Washington vs. N. Y., Nov. 27, 1966

Most Touchdowns, Both Teams, Game
  16 Washington (10) vs. N. Y. (6), Nov. 27, 1966

Most Points After Touchdown, Season
  65 Houston, 1961 (AFL)

Most Points After Touchdown, Game
  10 Los Angeles, vs. Balt., Oct. 22, 1950

Most Points After Touchdown, Both Teams, Game
  14 Chicago Cards (9) vs. N. Y. (5), Oct. 17, 1948
      Houston (7) vs. Oakland (7), Dec. 22, 1963 (AFL)
      Washington (9) vs. N. Y. (5), Nov. 27, 1966

Most Field Goals Attempted, Season
  49 Los Angeles, 1966
      Washington, 1971

Most Field Goals Attempted, Game
  9 St. Louis vs. Pitt., Sept. 24, 1967

Most Field Goals Attempted, Both Teams, Game
  11 St. Louis (6) vs. Pitt. (5), Nov. 13, 1966
      Washington (6) vs. Chi. (5), Nov. 14, 1971
      Green Bay (6) vs. Det. (5), Sept. 29, 1974
      Washington (6) vs. N.Y. Giants (5), Nov. 14, 1976

Most Field Goals, Season
  34 New York, 1968 (AFL)

STRONG ARM: Fran Tarkenton set lifetime NFL records by attempting 6,467 passes and completing 3,686 of them during his 18-year career with the NY Giants and Minnesota Vikings. Tarkenton also holds career passing records for TD's and yards gained. In 1978, he and the Vikings set season records for attempts and completions.

ON THE RECEIVING END: Lynn Swann (left) and John Stallworth (right) are two good reasons the Pittsburgh Steelers have won more Super Bowls than any other team. Swann holds career Super Bowl records for most receptions and yards gained receiving. His 161 yards in the 1976 game is also tops. Stallworth tied a record with 2 TD catches in 1979. The two men share the record for career TD catches with 3 each.

All-Time Professional Records (continued)

Most Field Goals, Game
   7 St. Louis vs. Pitt., Sept. 24, 1967

Most Field Goals, Both Teams, Game
   8 Cleveland (4) vs. St. L., (4), Sept. 20, 1964
      Chicago (5) vs. Phil. (3), Oct. 20, 1968
      Washington (5) vs. Chi. (3), Nov. 14, 1971
      Kansas City (5) vs. Buff (3), Dec. 19, 1971
      Detroit (4) vs. G.B. (4), Sept. 29, 1974
      Cleveland (5) vs. Den. (3), Oct. 19, 1975
      New England (4) vs. S.D. (4), Nov. 9, 1975

Most Consecutive Games Scoring Field Goals
  31 Minnesota, 1968–70

First Downs

Most Seasons Leading League
   9 Chicago Bears, 1935, 39, 41, 43, 45, 47–49, 55

Most First Downs, Season
  345 Seattle, 1978

Most First Downs, Game
  38 Los Angeles vs. N.Y., Nov. 13, 1966

Most First Downs, Both Teams, Game
  58 Los Angeles (30) vs. Chi. Bears (28), Oct. 24, 1954
      Denver (34) vs. K.C. (24), Nov. 18, 1974

Most First Downs, Rushing, Season
  181 New England, 1978

Most First Downs, Rushing, Game
  25 Philadelphia vs. Wash., Dec. 2, 1951

Most First Downs, Passing, Season
  186 Houston, 1964 (AFL)
      Oakland, 1964 (AFL)

Most First Downs, Passing, Game
  25 Denver vs. K. C., Nov. 18, 1974

New Yards Gained (Rushes and Passes)

Most Seasons Leading League
  12 Chicago Bears, 1932, 34–35, 39, 41–44, 47, 49, 55–56

Most Yards Gained, Season
  6,288 Houston, 1961 (AFL)

Most Yards Gained, Game
  735 Los Angeles vs. N.Y. Yanks, Sept. 28, 1951
      (181-r, 554-p)

Most Yards Gained, Both Teams, Game
  1,133 Los Angeles (636) vs. N.Y. Yanks (497), Nov. 19, 1950

Rushing

Most Seasons Leading League
  12 Chicago Bears, 1932, 34–35, 39–42, 51, 55–56, 68, 77

Most Rushing Attempts, Season
  681 Oakland, 1977

Most Rushing Attempts, Game
72   Chicago Bears vs. Brk., Oct. 20, 1935

Most Rushing Attempts, Both Teams, Game
108   Chicago Cards (70) vs. Green Bay (38), Dec. 5, 1948

Most Yards Gained Rushing, Season
3,165   New England, 1978

Most Yards Gained Rushing, Game
426   Detroit vs. Pitt., Nov. 4, 1934

Most Yards Gained Rushing, Both Teams, Game
595   L.A. (371) vs. N.Y. Yanks (224), Nov. 18, 1951

Highest Average Gain Rushing, Season
5.7   Cleveland, 1963

Most Touchdowns Rushing, Season
36   Green Bay, 1962

Most Touchdowns Rushing, Game
7   Los Angeles vs. Atlanta, Dec. 4, 1976

Most Touchdowns Rushing, Both Teams, Game
8   Los Angeles (6) vs. N.Y. Yanks (2), Nov. 18, 1951
Cleveland (6) vs. L.A. (2), Nov. 24, 1957

ARMED FOR COMBAT: Pittsburgh Steeler quarterback Terry Bradshaw has led his team to a record 4 Super Bowl wins. In 1979, he passed for 318 yards and 4 TD's. His Super Bowl totals of 932 yards and 9 TD's are also records.

Passing

Most Seasons Leading League
10   Washington, 1937, 39–40, 42–45, 47, 67, 74

Most Passes Attempted, Season
592   Houston, 1964 (AFL)
Minnesota, 1978

Most Passes Attempted, Game
68   Houston vs. Buffalo, Nov. 1, 1964 (AFL) (37 comp.)

Most Passes Attempted, Both Teams, Game
98   Minn. (56) vs. Balt. (42), Sept. 28, 1969

Most Passes Completed, Season
352   Minnesota, 1978

Most Passes Completed, Game
37   Houston vs. Buffalo, Nov. 1, 1964 (AFL) (68 att.)

Most Passes Completed, Both Teams, Game
56   Minn. (36) vs. Balt. (20), Sept. 28, 1969

Most Yards Gained Passing, Season
4,392   Houston, 1961 (AFL)

Most Yards Gained Passing, Game
554   Los Angeles vs. N.Y. Yanks, Sept. 28, 1951

Most Yards Gained Passing, Both Teams, Game
834   Philadelphia (419) vs. St. L. (415), Dec. 16, 1962

Most Seasons Leading League (Completion Pct.)
11   Washington, 1937, 39–40, 42–45, 47–48, 69–70

Most Touchdowns Passing, Season
48   Houston, 1961 (AFL)

Most Touchdowns Passing, Game
7   Chicago Bears vs. N.Y., Nov. 14, 1943
Philadelphia vs. Wash., Oct. 17, 1954
Houston vs. N.Y., Nov. 19, 1961 and Oct. 14, 1962 (AFL)
New York vs. Wash., Oct 28, 1962
Minnesota vs. Balt., Sept. 28, 1969

Most Touchdowns Passing, Both Teams, Game
12   New Orleans (6) vs. St. Louis (6), Nov. 2, 1969

Most Passes Had Intercepted, Season
48   Houston, 1962 (AFL)

Fewest Passes Had Intercepted, Season
5   Cleveland, 1960 (264-att.)
Green Bay, 1966 (318-att.)

IN A RUSH: Franco Harris (Pittsburgh) holds 5 Super Bowl records: most career points (24); most career rushing attempts (101) and yards gained (354); and single-game records for rushing attempts (34) and yards gained (158), both set in 1975.

All-Time Professional Records (continued)

Most Passes Had Intercepted, Game
   9 Detroit vs. Green Bay, Oct 24, 1943
      Pittsburgh, vs. Phil., Dec. 12, 1965

Punting

Most Seasons Leading League (Avg. Distance)
   6 Washington, 1940–43, 45, 58

Highest Punting Average, Season
47.6 Detroit, 1961

Punt Returns

Most Seasons Leading League
   8 Detroit, 1943–45, 51–52, 62, 66, 69

Most Yards Gained Punt Returns, Season
781 Chicago Bears, 1948

Most Yards Gained Punt Returns, Game
231 Detroit vs. S.F., Oct. 6, 1963

Highest Average Punt Returns, Season
20.2 Chicago Bears, 1941

Most Touchdowns Punt Returns, Season
   5 Chicago Cards, 1959

Most Touchdowns Punt Returns, Game
   2 Detroit vs. L.A., Oct. 14; vs. Green Bay, Nov. 22, 1951
      Chicago Cards vs. Pitt., Nov. 1; vs. N.Y., Nov. 22, 1959
      New York Titans vs. Den., Sept. 24, 1961 (AFL)
      Denver vs. Clev., Sept. 26, 1976

Kickoff Returns

Most Seasons Leading League
   6 Washington, 1942, 47, 62–63, 73–74

Most Yards Gained Kickoff Returns, Season
1,824 Houston, 1963 (AFL)

Most Yards Gained Kickoff Returns, Game
362 Detroit vs. L.A., Oct. 29, 1950

Most Yards Gained Kickoff Returns, Both Teams, Game
560 Detroit (362) vs. L.A. (198), Oct. 29, 1950

Highest Average Kickoff Returns, Season
29.4 Chicago, 1972

Most Touchdowns Kickoff Returns, Season
   4 Green Bay, 1967
      Chicago, 1970

Most Touchdowns Kickoff Returns, Game
   2 Chicago Bears vs. Green Bay, Sept. 22, 1940–Nov. 9, 1952
      Philadelphia vs. Dall., Nov. 6, 1966
      Green Bay vs. Cleve., Nov. 12, 1967

Fumbles

Most Fumbles, Season
  56 Chicago Bears, 1938
      San Francisco, 1978

Fewest Fumbles, Season
    8   Cleveland, 1959

Most Fumbles, Game
    10   Phil/Pitts. vs. N.Y., Oct. 9, 1943
         Detroit vs. Minn., Nov. 12, 1967
         Kansas City vs. Hou., Oct. 12,
           1969 (AFL)
         San Francisco vs. Det., Dec. 17,
           1978

Most Fumbles, Both Teams, Game
    14   Chicago Bears (7) vs. Cleve. (7),
           Nov. 24, 1940
         St. Louis (8) vs. N.Y. (6), Sept.
           17, 1961
         Kansas City (10) vs. Hou. (4), Oct.
           12, 1969 (AFL)

**Most Opponents' Fumbles Recovered,
Season**
    31   Minnesota, 1963 (50 fumbles)

**Most Opponents' Fumbles Recovered,
Game**
    8   Washington vs. St. L., Oct. 25,
          1976

Most Own Fumbles Recovered, Season
    37   Chicago Bears, 1938 (56 fumbles)

**Most Fumbles (Opponents' and Own) Re-
covered, Season**
    58   Minnesota, 1963 (95 fumbles)

**Most Fumbles (Opponents' and Own), Re-
covered, Game**
    10   Denver vs. Buff., Dec. 13, 1964
           (AFL)
         Pittsburgh vs. Hou., Dec. 9, 1973
         Washington vs. St. L., Oct. 25,
           1976

Penalties

**Most Seasons Leading League, Fewest
Penalties**
    9   Pittsburgh, 1946–47, 50–52, 54,
          63, 65, 68

Most Penalties, Season
    133   Los Angeles, 1978

Fewest Penalties, Season
    19   Detroit, 1937 (139 yards)

Most Penalties, Game
    22   Brooklyn vs. Green Bay, Sept.
           17, 1944 (170 yards)
         Chicago Bears vs. Phil., Nov. 26,
           1944 (170 yards)

Fewest Penalties, Game
    0   By many teams

Fewest Penalties, Both Teams, Game
    0   Brooklyn vs. Pitt., Oct. 28, 1934;
          vs. Bos., Sept. 28, 1936
         Cleveland Rams vs. Chi. Bears,
           Oct. 9, 1938
         Pittsburgh vs. Phil., Nov. 10, 1940

Most Yards Penalized, Season
    1,274   Oakland, 1969 (AFL)

Fewest Yards Penalized, Season
    139   Detroit, 1937 (19 pen.)

Most Yards Penalized, Game
    209   Cleveland vs. Chi. Bears, Nov.
            25, 1951 (21 pen.)

DEFENSE

Fewest Points Allowed, Season (since 1932)
    44   Chicago Bears, 1932

**Fewest Touchdowns Allowed, Season (since
1932)**
    6   Chicago Bears, 1932
        Brooklyn, 1933

Fewest First Downs Allowed, Season
    77   Detroit, 1935

**Fewest First Downs Allowed, Rushing,
Season**
    35   Chicago Bears, 1942

**Fewest First Downs Allowed, Passing,
Season**
    33   Chicago Bears, 1943

Fewest Yards Allowed, Game
    −7   L.A. vs. Sea., Nov. 4, 1979

Fewest Yards Allowed, Season
    1,539   Chicago Cards, 1934

Fewest Yards Allowed Rushing, Season
    519   Chicago Bears, 1942

**Fewest Touchdowns Allowed, Rushing,
Season**
    2   Detroit, 1934
        Dallas, 1968
        Minnesota, 1971

**Fewest Yards Allowed Punt Returns,
Season**
    22   Green Bay, 1967

**Fewest Yards Allowed Kickoff Returns,
Season**
    225   Brooklyn, 1943

Fewest Yards Allowed Passing, Season
    545   Philadelphia, 1934

**Most Opponents Tackled Attempting Pass-
es, Season**
    67   Oakland, 1967 (AFL)

**Fewest Touchdowns Allowed, Passing,
Season**
    1   Portsmouth, 1932
        Philadelphia, 1934

**Most Seasons Leading League, Intercep-
tions Made**
    9   New York Giants, 1933, 1937–39,
          44, 48, 51, 54, 61

Most Pass Interceptions Made, Season
    49   San Diego, 1961 (AFL)

Most Yards Gained, Interceptions, Season
    929   San Diego, 1961 (AFL)

Most Yards Gained, Interceptions, Game
    314   Los Angeles vs. S.F., Oct. 18,
            1964

**Most Touchdowns, Interception Returns,
Season**
    9   San Diego, 1961 (AFL)

Most Touchdowns, Interception Returns,
Game
  3 Baltimore vs. Green Bay, Nov. 5,
     1950
     Cleveland vs. Chi., Dec. 11, 1960
     Philadelphia vs. Pitt., Dec. 12,
     1965
     Baltimore vs. Pitt., Sept. 29, 1968
     Buffalo vs. N.Y., Sept 29, 1968
     (AFL)
     Houston vs. S.D., Dec. 19, 1971
     Cincinnati vs. Hou., Dec. 17, 1972
     Tampa Bay vs. N.O., Dec., 11,
     1977

Selected Super Bowl Records

Most Points, Game
  15 Don Chandler, G.B., 1968

Most Points, Career
  24 Franco Harris, Pitt., 4 games

Most Rushing Attempts, Game
  34 Franco Harris, Pitt., 1975

Most Rushing Attempts, Career
  101 Franco Harris, Pitt., 4 games

Most Yards Rushing, Game
  158 Franco Harris, Pitt., 1975

Most Yards Rushing, Career
  354 Franco Harris, Pitt., 4 games

Longest Run from Scrimmage
  58 yds. Tom Matte, Balt., 1969

Most Passing Attempts, Game
  35 Fran Tarkenton, Minn., 1977

Most Passing Attempts, Career
  98 Roger Staubach, Dall., 5 games

Most Passes Completed, Game
  18 Fran Tarkenton, Minn., 1974

Most Passes Completed, Career
  61 Roger Staubach, Dall., 5 games

Most Yards Gained Passing, Game
  318 Terry Bradshaw, Pitt., 1979

Most Yards Gained Passing, Career
  932 Terry Bradshaw, Pitt., 4 games

Most Touchdown Passes, Game
  4 Terry Bradshaw, Pitt., 1979

Most Touchdown Passes, Career
  9 Terry Bradshaw, Pitt., 4 games

Longest Pass Completion
  75 yds. John Unitas to John Mackey,
     Balt., 1971
     Terry Bradshaw to John Stall-
     worth, Pitt., 1979

Most Pass Receptions, Game
  8 George Sauer, N.J. Jets, 1969

Most Pass Receptions, Career
  16 Lynn Swann, Pitt., 4 games

Most Yards, Pass Receiving, Game
  161 Lynn Swann, Pitt., 1976

Most Yards, Pass Receiving, Career
  364 Lynn Swann, Pitt., 4 games

Most Touchdowns, Pass Receiving, Game
  2 Max McGee, G.B., 1967
     Bill Miller, Oak., 1968
     John Stallworth, Pitt., 1979

Most Touchdowns, Pass Receiving, Career
  3 John Stallworth, Pitt., 4 games
     Lynn Swann, Pitt., 4 games

Most Interceptions, Game
  2 Randy Beverly, N.Y. Jets, 1969
     Chuck Howley, Dall., 1971
     Jake Scott, Miami, 1973

Most Interceptions, Career
  3 Chuck Howley, Dall., 2 games

Longest Punt
  61 yds. Jerrel Wilson, K.C., 1967

Longest Punt Return
  31 yds. Willie Wood, G.B., 1968

Longest Kickoff Return
  67 yds. Rick Upchurch, Den., 1978

National Football League

The American Professional Football Association was formed in 1920. Its name was changed in 1922 to the National Football League. In 1933 the National Football League (NFL) was divided into two divisions—Eastern and Western, with the winners of each division meeting in the championship play-off. From 1950 to 1952 the two divisions were named American and National, before reverting to Eastern and Western from 1953 to 1970.

Meanwhile in 1960 the American Football League (AFL) was formed and from 1970 under the umbrella of the National Football League there was a re-organization of teams. From then there were two conferences, the National Conference and the American Conference, each containing three divisions.

IT'S CATCHING:
"Crazy Legs" Hirsch
caught 17 TD passes
(a shared record) in 1951
to help give the LA
Rams their only
professional football
championship prior to
the 1979 NFC title.

1921	Chicago Bears
1922	Canton Bulldogs
1923	Canton Bulldogs
1924	Cleveland Bulldogs
1925	Chicago Cardinals
1926	Frankford Yellow Jackets
1927	New York Giants
1928	Providence Steamrollers
1929	Green Bay Packers
1930	Green Bay Packers
1931	Green Bay Packers
1932	Chicago Bears
1933	Chicago Bears
1934	New York Giants
1935	Detroit Lions
1936	Green Bay Packers
1937	Washington Redskins
1938	New York Giants
1939	Green Bay Packers
1940	Chicago Bears
1941	Chicago Bears
1942	Washington Redskins
1943	Chicago Bears
1944	Green Bay Packers
1945	Cleveland Rams
1946	Chicago Bears
1947	Chicago Cardinals
1948	Philadelphia Eagles
1949	Philadelphia Eagles
1950	Cleveland Browns
1951	Los Angeles Rams
1952	Detroit Lions
1953	Detroit Lions
1954	Cleveland Browns
1955	Cleveland Browns
1956	New York Giants
1957	Detroit Lions
1958	Baltimore Colts
1959	Baltimore Colts
1960	Philadelphia Eagles
1961	Green Bay Packers
1962	Green Bay Packers
1963	Chicago Bears
1964	Cleveland Browns
1965	Green Bay Packers
1966	Green Bay Packers
1967	Green Bay Packers
1968	Baltimore Colts
1969	Minnesota Vikings

National Football Conference

1970	Dallas Cowboys
1971	Dallas Cowboys
1972	Washington Redskins
1973	Minnesota Vikings
1974	Minnesota Vikings

American Football League

1960	Houston Oilers
1961	Houston Oilers
1962	Dallas Texans
1963	San Diego Chargers
1964	Buffalo Bills
1965	Buffalo Bills
1966	Kansas City Chiefs
1967	Oakland Raiders
1968	New York Jets
1969	Kansas City Chiefs

American Football Conference

1970	Baltimore Colts
1971	Miami Dolphins
1972	Miami Dolphins
1973	Miami Dolphins
1974	Pittsburgh Steelers

National Football Conference

1975	Dallas Cowboys
1976	Minnesota Vikings
1977	Dallas Cowboys
1978	Dallas Cowboys
1979	Los Angeles Rams

American Football Conference

1975	Pittsburgh Steelers
1976	Oakland Raiders
1977	Denver Broncos
1978	Pittsburgh Steelers
1979	Pittsburgh Steelers

Super Bowl

Contested each year in mid-January, the Super Bowl was originally a competition between champions of the NFL and AFL (1967–70). When the leagues merged, the Super Bowl became a play-off between the champions of the National and American Conferences.

1967	Green Bay (NFL)	35	Kansas City (AFL)	10
1968	Green Bay (NFL)	33	Oakland (AFL)	14
1969	New York (AFL)	16	Baltimore (NFL)	7
1970	Kansas City (AFL)	23	Minnesota (NFL)	7
1971	Baltimore (AFC)	16	Dallas (NFC)	13
1972	Dallas (NFC)	24	Miami (AFC)	3
1973	Miami (AFC)	14	Washington (NFC)	7
1974	Miami (AFC)	24	Minnesota (NFC)	7
1975	Pittsburgh (AFC)	16	Minnesota (NFC)	6
1976	Pittsburgh (AFC)	21	Dallas (NFC)	17
1977	Oakland (AFC)	32	Minnesota (NFC)	14
1978	Dallas (NFC)	27	Denver (AFC)	10
1979	Pittsburgh (AFC)	35	Dallas (NFC)	31
1980	Pittsburgh (AFC)	31	Los Angeles (NFC)	19

LEAGUE LEADERS: Quarterback Len Dawson of the Kansas City Chiefs looks to pass against the NY Jets in Shea Stadium, New York. Dawson led the AFL's Chiefs to a convincing 23–7 win over the Minnesota Vikings in the 1970 Super Bowl. One year earlier, the Jets, with Joe Namath, had stunned the NFL's Baltimore Colts with a 16–7 victory. These victories brought respectability to the AFL and helped insure an equitable merger with the NFL for the 1970 season.

N.C.A.A. National Champions

(Based on the Associated Press poll of sportswriters and the United Press International poll of coaches.)

	AP	UPI		AP	UPI
1936	Minnesota		1958	Louisiana St.	Louisiana St.
1937	Pittsburgh		1959	Syracuse	Syracuse
1938	Texas Christian		1960	Minnesota	Minnesota
1939	Texas A & M		1961	Alabama	Alabama
1940	Minnesota		1962	Southern Cal	Southern Cal
1941	Minnesota		1963	Texas	Texas
1942	Ohio State		1964	Alabama	Alabama
1943	Notre Dame		1965	Alabama	Michigan St.
1944	Army		1966	Notre Dame	Notre Dame
1945	Army		1967	Southern Cal	Southern Cal
1946	Notre Dame		1968	Ohio State	Ohio State
1947	Notre Dame		1969	Texas	Texas
1948	Michigan		1970	Nebraska	Texas
1949	Notre Dame		1971	Nebraska	Nebraska
1950	Oklahoma	Oklahoma	1972	Southern Cal	Southern Cal
1951	Tennessee	Tennessee	1973	Notre Dame	Alabama
1952	Michigan St.	Michigan St.	1974	Oklahoma	Southern Cal
1953	Maryland	Maryland	1975	Oklahoma	Oklahoma
1954	Ohio State	UCLA	1976	Pittsburgh	Pittsburgh
1955	Oklahoma	Oklahoma	1977	Notre Dame	Notre Dame
1956	Oklahoma	Oklahoma	1978	Alabama	Southern Cal
1957	Auburn	Ohio State	1979	Alabama	Alabama

Heisman Memorial Trophy

(Honoring the outstanding college football player in the United States, presented by the Downtown Athletic Club of New York.)

1935   Jay Berwanger, Chicago
1936   Larry Kelley, Yale
1937   Clint Frank, Yale
1938   Davey O'Brien, TCU
1939   Nile Kinnick, Iowa
1940   Tom Harmon, Michigan
1941   Bruce Smith, Minnesota
1942   Frank Sinkwich, Georgia
1943   Angelo Bertelli, Notre Dame
1944   Les Horvath, Ohio State
1945   Doc Blanchard, Army
1946   Glenn Davis, Army
1947   John Lujack, Notre Dame
1948   Doak Walker, SMU
1949   Leon Hart, Notre Dame
1950   Vic Janowicz, Ohio State
1951   Dick Kazmaier, Princeton
1952   Billy Vessels, Oklahoma
1953   John Lattner, Notre Dame
1954   Alan Ameche, Wisconsin
1955   Howard Cassady, Ohio State
1956   Paul Hornung, Notre Dame
1957   John Crow, Texas A & M
1958   Pete Dawkins, Army
1959   Billy Cannon, LSU
1960   Joe Bellino, Navy
1961   Ernie Davis, Syracuse
1962   Terry Baker, Oregon St.
1963   Roger Staubach, Navy
1964   John Huarte, Notre Dame
1965   Mike Garrett, Southern Cal
1966   Steve Spurrier, Florida
1967   Gary Beban, UCLA
1968   O. J. Simpson, Southern Cal
1969   Steve Owens, Oklahoma
1970   Jim Plunkett, Stanford

TURN ON THE JUICE: O.J. Simpson won the Heisman Trophy as the outstanding college player in 1968. He helped lead Southern Cal to the national championship in 1967 and played in 3 Rose Bowls. As a pro, Simpson smashed Jim Brown's season rushing record by gaining 2,003 yards in 1973 with the Buffalo Bills. In 1975, Simpson set a season TD record with 23.

Heisman Memorial Trophy (continued)

1971 Pat Sullivan, Auburn	1976 Tony Dorsett, Pittsburgh
1972 Johnny Rodgers, Nebraska	1977 Earl Campbell, Texas
1973 John Cappelletti, Penn State	1978 Billy Sims, Oklahoma
1974 Archie Griffin, Ohio State	1979 Charles White, Southern Cal
1975 Archie Griffin, Ohio State	

Annual Results of Major Bowl Games

Rose Bowl, Pasadena

1902 Michigan 49, Stanford 0	1948 Michigan 49, So. California 0
1916 Wash. State 14, Brown 0	1949 Northwestern 20, California 14
1917 Oregon 14, Pennsylvania 0	1950 Ohio State 17, California 14
1918–19 Service teams	1951 Michigan 14, California 6
1920 Harvard 7, Oregon 6	1952 Illinois 40, Stanford 7
1921 California 28, Ohio State 0	1953 So. California 7, Wisconsin 0
1922 Wash. & Jeff. 0, California 0	1954 Mich. State 28, UCLA 20
1923 So. California 14, Penn State 3	1955 Ohio State 20, So. California 7
1924 Navy 14, Washington 14	1956 Mich. State 17, UCLA 14
1925 Notre Dame 27, Stanford 10	1957 Iowa 35, Oregon St. 19
1926 Alabama 20, Washington 19	1958 Ohio State 10, Oregon 7
1927 Alabama 7, Stanford 7	1959 Iowa 38, California 12
1928 Stanford 7, Pittsburgh 6	1960 Washington 44, Wisconsin 8
1929 Georgia Tech 8, California 7	1961 Washington 17, Minnesota 7
1930 So. California 47, Pittsburgh 14	1962 Minnesota 21, UCLA 3
1931 Alabama 24, Wash. State 0	1963 So. California 42, Wisconsin 37
1932 So. California 21, Tulane 12	1964 Illinois 17, Washington 7
1933 So. California 35, Pittsburgh 0	1965 Michigan 34, Oregon St. 7
1934 Columbia 7, Stanford 0	1966 UCLA 14, Mich. State 12
1935 Alabama 29, Stanford 13	1967 Purdue 14, So. California 13
1936 Stanford 7, So. Methodist 0	1968 Southern Cal 14, Indiana 3
1937 Pittsburgh 21, Washington 0	1969 Ohio State 27, Southern Cal 16
1938 California 13, Alabama 0	1970 Southern Cal 10, Michigan 3
1939 So. California 7, Duke 3	1971 Stanford 27, Ohio State 17
1940 So. California 14, Tennessee 0	1972 Stanford 13, Michigan 12
1941 Stanford 21, Nebraska 13	1973 So. California 42, Ohio State 17
1942 Oregon St. 20, Duke 16	1974 Ohio State 42, So. California 21
(at Durham)	1975 So. California 18, Ohio State 17
1943 Georgia 9, UCLA 0	1976 UCLA 23, Ohio State 10
1944 So. California 29, Washington 0	1977 So. California 14, Michigan 5
1945 So. California 25, Tennessee 0	1978 Washington 27, Michigan 20
1946 Alabama 34, So. California 14	1979 So. California 17, Michigan 10
1947 Illinois 45, UCLA 14	1980 So. California 17, Ohio State 16

Orange Bowl, Miami

1933 Miami (Fla.) 7, Manhattan 0	1957 Colorado 27, Clemson 21
1934 Duquesne 33, Miami (Fla.) 7	1958 Oklahoma 48, Duke 21
1935 Bucknell 26, Miami (Fla.) 0	1959 Oklahoma 21, Syracuse 6
1936 Catholic U. 20, Mississippi 19	1960 Georgia 14, Missouri 0
1937 Duquesne 13, Miss. State 12	1961 Missouri 21, Navy 14
1938 Auburn 6, Mich. State 0	1962 LSU 25, Colorado 7
1939 Tennessee 17, Oklahoma 0	1963 Alabama 17, Oklahoma 0
1940 Georgia Tech 21, Missouri 7	1964 Nebraska 13, Auburn 7
1941 Miss. State 14, Georgetown 7	1965 Texas 21, Alabama 17
1942 Georgia 40, TCU 26	1966 Alabama 39, Nebraska 28
1943 Alabama 37, Boston Col. 21	1967 Florida 27, Georgia Tech 12
1944 LSU 19, Texas A & M 14	1968 Oklahoma 26, Tennessee 24
1945 Tulsa 26, Georgia Tech 12	1969 Penn State 15, Kansas 14
1946 Miami (Fla.) 13, Holy Cross 6	1970 Penn State 10, Missouri 3
1947 Rice 8, Tennessee 0	1971 Nebraska 17, Louisiana St. 12
1948 Georgia Tech 20, Kansas 14	1972 Nebraska 38, Alabama 6
1949 Texas 41, Georgia 28	1973 Nebraska 40, Notre Dame 6
1950 Santa Clara 21, Kentucky 13	1974 Penn State 16, Louisiana St. 9
1951 Clemson 14, Miami (Fla.) 14	1975 Notre Dame 13, Alabama 11
1952 Georgia Tech 17, Baylor 14	1976 Oklahoma 14, Michigan 6
1953 Alabama 61, Syracuse 6	1977 Ohio State 27, Colorado 10
1954 Oklahoma 7, Maryland 0	1978 Arkansas 31, Oklahoma 6
1955 Duke 34, Nebraska 7	1979 Oklahoma 31, Nebraska 24
1956 Oklahoma 20, Maryland 6	1980 Oklahoma 24, Florida State 7

Sugar Bowl, New Orleans

1935	Tulane 20, Temple 14	1959	LSU 7, Clemson 0
1936	TCU 3, LSU 2	1960	Mississippi 21, LSU 0
1937	Santa Clara 21, LSU 14	1961	Mississippi 14, Rice 6
1938	Santa Clara 6, LSU 0	1962	Alabama 10, Arkansas 3
1939	TCU 15, Carnegie Tech 7	1963	Mississippi 17, Arkansas 13
1940	Texas A & M 14, Tulane 13	1964	Alabama 12, Mississippi 7
1941	Boston Col. 19, Tennessee 13	1965	LSU 13, Syracuse 10
1942	Fordham 2, Missouri 0	1966	Missouri 20, Florida 18
1943	Tennessee 14, Tulsa 7	1967	Alabama 34, Nebraska 7
1944	Georgia Tech 20, Tulsa 18	1968	LSU 20, Wyoming 13
1945	Duke 29, Alabama 26	1969	Arkansas 16, Georgia 2
1946	Oklahoma A & M 33, St. Mary's 13	1970	Mississippi 27, Arkansas 22
1947	Georgia 20, No. Carolina 10	1971	Tennessee 34, Air Force 13
1948	Texas 27, Alabama 7	1972	Oklahoma 40, Auburn 22
1949	Oklahoma 14, No. Carolina 6	*1972	(Dec.) Oklahoma 14, Penn State 0
1950	Oklahoma 35, LSU 0	1973	Notre Dame 24, Alabama 23
1951	Kentucky 13, Oklahoma 7	1974	Nebraska 13, Florida 10
1952	Maryland 28, Tennessee 13	1975	Alabama 13, Penn State 6
1953	Georgia Tech 24, Mississippi 7	1977	(Jan.) Pittsburgh 27, Georgia 3
1954	Georgia Tech 42, West Virginia 19	1978	Alabama 35, Ohio State 6
1955	Navy 21, Mississippi 0	1979	Alabama 14, Penn State 7
1956	Georgia Tech 7, Pittsburgh 0	1980	Alabama 24, Arkansas 9
1957	Baylor 13, Tennessee 7		
1958	Mississippi 39, Texas 7		*Penn St. awarded game by forfeit

Cotton Bowl, Dallas

1937	TCU 16, Marquette 6	1959	TCU 0, Air Force 0
1938	Rice 28, Colorado 14	1960	Syracuse 23, Texas 14
1939	St. Mary's 20, Texas Tech 13	1961	Duke 7, Arkansas 6
1940	Clemson 6, Boston Col. 3	1962	Texas 12, Mississippi 7
1941	Texas A & M 13, Fordham 12	1963	LSU 13, Texas 0
1942	Alabama 29, Texas A & M 21	1964	Texas 28, Navy 6
1943	Texas 14, Georgia Tech 7	1965	Arkansas 10, Nebraska 7
1944	Randolph Field 7, Texas 7	1966	LSU 14, Arkansas 7
1945	Oklahoma A & M 34, TCU 0	1967	Georgia 24, So. Methodist 9
1946	Texas 40, Missouri 27	1968	Texas A & M 20, Alabama 16
1947	Arkansas 0, LSU 0	1969	Texas 36, Tennessee 13
1948	So. Methodist 13, Penn State 13	1970	Texas 21, Notre Dame 17
1949	So. Methodist 21, Oregon 13	1971	Notre Dame 24, Texas 11
1950	Rice 27, No. Carolina 13	1972	Penn State 30, Texas 6
1951	Tennessee 20, Texas 14	1973	Texas 17, Alabama 13
1952	Kentucky 20, TCU 7	1974	Nebraska 19, Texas 3
1953	Texas 16, Tennessee 0	1975	Penn State 41, Baylor 20
1954	Rice 28, Alabama 6	1976	Arkansas 31, Georgia 10
1955	Georgia Tech 14, Arkansas 6	1977	Houston 30, Maryland 21
1956	Mississippi 14, TCU 13	1978	Notre Dame 38, Texas 10
1957	TCU 28, Syracuse 17	1979	Notre Dame 35, Houston 34
1958	Navy 20, Rice 7	1980	Houston 17, Nebraska 14

GAMBLING

World's Biggest Win

The world's biggest gambling win is $2,451,549 for a bet of two cruzeiros ($.58) in the Brazilian football pools Loteria Esportiva by Miron Vieira de Sousa, 30, of Ivolandia, Brazil, on the results of 13 games in October, 1975. The first thing he bought was a set of false teeth.

By winning a state lottery in January, 1976, Eric C. Leek, of North Arlington, New Jersey, won $1,776 a week for life. Aged 26, he will receive a total of $4.6 million should he live a further 50 years.

BIG DEAL: Earl Arnall dealt blackjack for 190 hours at the King 8 Casino in Las Vegas, Nevada, June 22-30, 1977.

World's Biggest Loss

An unnamed Italian industrialist was reported to have lost $1,920,000 in five hours at roulette in Monte Carlo, Monaco, on March 6, 1974. A Saudi Arabian prince was reported to have lost more than $1 million in a single session at the Metro Club, Las Vegas, Nevada, in December, 1974.

Largest Casino

The largest casino in the world is the Casino, Mar del Plata, Argentina, with average daily attendances of 14,500 rising to 25,000 during carnivals. The Casino has more than 150 roulette tables running simultaneously.

Blackjack

Marathon. Earl Arnall, a dealer at the King 8 Casino in Las Vegas, Nevada, spent 190 hours at the blackjack table, 22-30, 1977. Ardeth Hardy set the women's mark of 169 hours 47 minutes of continuous dealing during the same period. Both took the 5-minute rest breaks within each hour.

Slot Machines

Largest. The world's biggest slot machine (or one-armed bandit) is Super Bertha (555 cubic feet) installed by Si Redd at the Four Queens Casino, Las Vegas, Nevada, in September, 1973. Once in every 25,000,000,000 plays it may yield $1 million for a $10 investment.

Biggest Win. The biggest beating handed to a "one-armed bandit" was $300,000 by Jerome A. Sommer of Ocean City, New Jersey, at the Flamingo Hilton, Las Vegas, Nevada, on January 4, 1980.

The total gambling "take" in 1978 in Nevada casinos was estimated at $1,800,000,000.

Bingo

Origins. Bingo is a lottery game which, as keno, was developed in the 1880's from lotto, whose origin is thought to be the 17th-century Italian game *tumbule*. It has long been known in the British Army (called Housey-Housey) and the Royal Navy (called Tombola). The winner was the first to complete a random selection of numbers from 1–90. The US version of Bingo differs in that the selection is from 1–75. There are six million players in the United Kingdom alone.

Largest House. The largest "house" in Bingo sessions was at the Empire Pool, Wembly, Brent, Greater London, on April 25, 1965, when 10,000 attended.

Most Cards. The highest recorded number of cards played simultaneously (with a call rate of 31.7 seconds per call) has been 346 by Robert A. Berg at Pacific Beach, California, on November 16, 1973.

Bingo-Calling Marathon. A session of 240 hours 30 minutes was held at the Top Rank Social Club, Kingston-upon-Thames, Surrey, England, on May 1–4, 1979, with Philip Carter and Timothy Mann calling.

Roulette

Longest Run. The longest run on an ungaffed (*i.e.* true) wheel reliably recorded is six successive coups (in No. 10) at El San Juan Hotel, Puerto Rico, on July 9, 1959. The odds with a double zero were 1 in 38^6 or 3,010,936,383 to 1.

BIGGEST "BANDIT" OF THEM ALL: When playing Super Bertha, the world's largest slot machine, eight 7's add up to much more than 56. Once in every 25 billion plays the 555-cubic-foot "one-armed bandit" may yield $1 million for a $10 investment.

Longest Marathon. The longest "marathon" on record is one of 31 days from April 10 to May 11, 1970, at the Casino de Macao, to test the validity or invalidity of certain contentions in 20,000 spins.

Horse Race Betting

Topmost Tipster. The only recorded instance of a racing correspondent forecasting ten out of ten winners on a race card was at Delaware Park, Wilmington, Delaware, on July 28, 1974, by Charles Lamb of the *Baltimore News American*.

Most Complicated Bet. The most complicated bet is the Harlequin, a British compound wager on four horses with 2,028 possible ways of winning. It was invented by Monty H. Preston of London who has been reputed to be the fastest settler of bets in the world. He once completed 3,000 bets in a 4½-hour test.

Largest Bookmaker. The world's largest bookmaker is Ladbrokes of London, with a turnover from gambling in 1978 of $780,000,000. See also *Harness Racing* and *Horse Racing*.

GAMES AND PASTIMES

Backgammon

Origins. Forerunners of the game have been traced back to a dice and a board game found in excavations at Ur, dated to 3000 B.C. Later the Romans played a game remarkably similar to the modern one. The name "Backgammon" is variously ascribed to Welsh "little battle," or Saxon "back game." Modern variations include the American Acey Deucey.

Championships. At present there are no world championships held, but a points rating system may soon be introduced internationally, thereby enabling players to be ranked. Tournaments in backgammon have been held but for too short a time to be significant in determining individual or team champions.

Marathon. Dick Newcomb and Greg Peterson of Rockford, Illinois, played for 151 hours 11 minutes, June 30–July 6, 1978.

Bridge (Contract)

Earliest References. Bridge (corruption of Biritch) is thought to be of Levantine origin, similar games having been played there in the early 1870's. The game was known in London in 1886 under the title of "Biritch or Russian Whist." Whist, first referred to in 1529, was the world's premier card game until 1930. Its rules had been standardized in 1742.

Auction bridge (highest bidder names trump) was invented *c.* 1902. The contract principle, present in several games (notably the French game *Plafond, c.* 1917), was introduced to bridge by Harold S. Vanderbilt (US) on November 1, 1925, during a Caribbean voyage aboard the *S.S. Finland*. The new version became a worldwide craze after the US vs. Great Britain challenge match between Rumanian-born Ely Culbertson (1891–1955) and Lt.-Col. Walter Thomas More Buller (1887–1938) at Almack's Club, London, September, 1930. The US won the 200-hand match by 4,845 points.

Most Master Points. In 1971, a new World Ranking List based on Master Points was instituted. The leading male player is Giorgio Belladonna (see below) with 1,712 points as of March, 1978, followed by 5 more Italians. The world's leading woman player is Mrs. Rixi Markus (GB) with 269 points to March, 1978.

World Titles. The world Championship (Bermuda Bowl) has been won most often by Italy's "Blue Team" (Squadra Azzurra) which also won the Olympiad in 1964, 1968 and 1972. Giorgio Belladonna was on all 16 winning teams.

World Championships. World Championships for the Bermuda Bowl were first held in 1951. Winners:

1951	US	1958	Italy	1967	Italy	1975	Italy
1952	US	1959	Italy	1968	Italy	1976	US
1953	US	1961	Italy	1969	Italy	1977	US
1954	US	1962	Italy	1970	North America	1978	Not held
1955	Great Britain	1963	Italy	1971	US	1979	US
1956	France	1965	Italy	1973	Italy		
1957	Italy	1966	Italy	1974	Italy		

Team (Four) Olympiad				Olympic Pairs Competition (Open)	
Men		**Women**		**Men**	
1960	France	1960	United Arab Republic	1962	France
1964	Italy	1964	Great Britain	1966	Holland
1968	Italy	1968	Sweden	1970	Austria
1972	Italy	1972	Italy	1974	US
1976	Brazil	1976	US	1978	Brazil

LONDON BRIDGE: Mrs. Rixi Markus of Great Britain is the leading woman bridge player with 269 Master Points to March, 1978.

MASTERMIND: Italy's Giorgio Belladonna (center) had the greatest accumulation of Master Points through March, 1978, with 1,712. Italy has the most Bermuda Bowl wins with 13 and also 3 Olympic titles. Belladonna has been on all 16 winning teams. Here he is during the 1965 World Championships. The challenging British team included Boris Schapiro (left) and Terence Reese (right).

Highest Possible Scores (excluding penalties for rules infractions)

Opponents bid 7 of any suit or no trump, doubled and redoubled and vulnerable.		Bid 1 no trump, doubled and redoubled, vulnerable.	
Opponents make no trick.		*Below Line* 1st trick (40 × 4)	160
Above Line 1st undertrick	400	*Above Line* 6 overtricks (400 × 6)	2,400
12 subsequent undertricks at 600 each	7,200	2nd game of 2-Game Rubber	*350
All Honors	150	All Honors (4 aces)	150
	7,750	Bonus for making redoubled contract	50
		(Highest Possible Positive Score)	3,110

*In practice, the full bonus of 700 points is awarded after the completion of the second game, rather than 350 after each game.

Perfect Deals. The mathematical odds against dealing 13 cards of one suit are 158,753,389,899 to 1, while the odds are 635,013,559,591 to 1 against receiving a "perfect hand" consisting of all 13 spades. The odds against each of the 4 players receiving a complete suit (a "perfect deal") are 2,235,197,406,895,366,368,301,559,999 to 1.

Bridge Marathon. The longest recorded bridge session is one of 180 hours by four students at Edinburgh University, Scotland, April 21–28, 1972.

Checkers

Origins. Checkers, known as draughts in some countries, has origins earlier than chess. It was played in Egypt in the second millennium B.C. The earliest book on the game was by Antonio Torquemada of Valencia, Spain in 1547.

There have been three US vs. Great Britain international matches. The earliest, in 1905, was won by the Scottish Masters, 73–34, with 284 draws. The US won in 1927 in New York, 96–20 with 364 draws, and won again in the most recent match, in 1973.

The only man to win 5 British Championships has been Jim Marshall (Fife, Scotland) in 1948–50–52–54–66. The longest tenure of invincibility was that of Melvin Pomeroy (US), who was internationally undefeated from 1914 until his death in 1933.

Longest and Shortest Games. In competition, the prescribed rate of play is not less than 30 moves per hour with the average game lasting about 90 minutes. In 1958 a match between Dr. Marian Tinsley (US) and Derek Oldbury (GB) lasted 7½ hours.

The shortest possible game is one of 20 moves composed by Alan M. Beckerson (GB) on November 2, 1977.

Most Opponents. Newell W. Banks (b. Detroit, October 10, 1887) played 140 games simultaneously, winning 133 and drawing 7 in Chicago in 1933. His playing time was 145 minutes, so averaging about one second per move.

Chess

Origins. The name chess is derived from the Persian word *shah*. It is a descendant of the game *Chaturanga*. The earliest reference is from the Middle Persian Karnamak (*c.* 590–628), though there are grounds for believing its origins are from the 2nd century, owing to the discovery, announced in December, 1972, of two ivory chessmen in the Uzbek Soviet Republic, datable to that century. The game reached Britain in *c.* 1255. The *Fédération Internationale des Echecs* was established in 1924. There were an estimated 7,000,000 registered players in the USSR in 1973.

World Champions. François André Danican, *alias* Philidor (1726–95), of France claimed the title of "world champion" from 1747 until his death. World champions have been generally recognized since 1886. The longest undisputed tenure was 27 years by Dr. Emanuel Lasker (1868–1941) of Germany, from 1894 to 1921. Robert J. (Bobby) Fischer (b. Chicago, March 9, 1943) is reckoned on the officially adopted Elo system to be the greatest Grandmaster of all time. He has an I.Q. of 187 and at 15 became the youngest ever International Grandmaster.

The women's world championship has been most often won by Russian-born Vera Menchik-Stevenson (1906–44) (GB) from 1927 till her death, and was successfully defended a record 7 times. Nona Gaprindasvili (USSR) held the title from 1962 to 1978, and defended 4 times.

Winning Streak. Bobby Fischer (see above) won 20 games in succession in Grandmaster chess from December 2, 1970 (vs. Jorge Rubinetti of Argentina) to September 30, 1971 (vs. Tigran Petrosian of the USSR). Anatoliy Karpov (USSR) lost only 4.3 per cent of his 597 games to December, 1977.

Longest Games. The most protracted master game on record was one drawn on the 191st move between H. Pilnik (Argentina) and Moshe Czerniak (Israel) at Mar del Plata, Argentina, in April, 1950. The total playing time was 20 hours. A game of 2½ hours, but drawn on the 171st move (average over 7½ minutes per move), was played between Makagonov and Chekhover at Baku, USSR, in 1945.

The slowest recorded move (before modern rules) was one of 11 hours between Paul Charles Morphy (1837–84), the US champion 1852–1862, and the German chess master Louis Paulsen (1833–91).

Marathon. The longest recorded session is one of 165 hours 9 minutes by Philip Thomas and Andrew Harris of Nottingham University, England, October 6–13, 1979.

Most Opponents. The record for most opponents tackled (with replacements as they are defeated) is held by Branimir Brebrich (Canada) who played 575 games (winning 533, drawing 27 and losing 15) in Edmonton, Alberta, Canada, January 27–28, 1978 in 28 hours of play.

Vlastimil Hort (b. January 12, 1944) (Czechoslovakia) in Seltjarnarnes, Iceland, on April 23–24, 1977, simultaneously tackled 201 opponents and did not lose a game.

Georges Koltanowski (Belgium, later of US) tackled 56 opponents "blindfold" and won 50, drew 6, lost 0 in 9¾ hours at the Fairmont Hotel, San Francisco, on December 13, 1960.

World Champions

The first officially recognized match was won by Wilhelm Steinitz in 1886, but included in this list are unofficially recognized champions before that date.

MEN

1851–58	Adolph Anderssen (Ger)	1862–66	Adolph Anderssen (Ger)
1858–62	Paul Morphy (US)	1866–94	Wilhelm Steinitz (Ger)

RUSSIAN KNIGHTS: Russian Elizaveta Bykova (right), who held the women's chess title for 4 years, is here successfully defending her title against countrywoman Nona Gaprindashvili. Gaprindashvili ultimately captured the title in 1962 and held on to it for 16 years.

GRANDEST GRAND-MASTER: Russia's Anatoliy Karpov (left) has been the world champion since 1975. He lost only 4.3 per cent of his 597 games to December, 1977. Here he defends against Victor Korchnoi.

1894–1921	Emanuel Lasker (Ger)	1972–75	Robert Fischer (US)
1921–27	José Capablanca (Cuba)	1975–	Anatoliy Karpov (USSR)
1927–35	Alexandre Alekhine (Fra)		
1935–37	Max Euwe (Hol)	**WOMEN**	
1937–47	Alexandre Alekhine (Fra)	1927–44	Vera Menchik (GB)
1948–57	Mikhail Botvinnik (USSR)	1950–53	Lyudmila Rudenko (USSR)
1957–58	Vassiliy Smyslov (USSR)	1953–56	Elizaveta Bykova (USSR)
1958–61	Mikhail Botvinnik (USSR)	1956–58	Olga Rubtsova (USSR)
1961–62	Mikhail Tal (USSR)	1958–62	Elizaveta Bykova (USSR)
1962–64	Mikhail Botvinnik (USSR)	1962–78	Nona Gaprindashvili (USSR)
1964–69	Tigran Petrosian (USSR)	1978–	Maya Chiburdanidze (USSR)
1969–72	Boris Spassky (USSR)		

World Team Championships (Chess Olympiad)

First held in 1927, and now held every two years. Winners:

MEN				**WOMEN**	
1927	Hungary	1956	USSR	1957	USSR
1928	Hungary	1958	USSR	1963	USSR
1930	Poland	1960	USSR	1966	USSR
1931	US	1962	USSR	1969	USSR
1933	US	1964	USSR	1972	USSR
1935	US	1966	USSR	1974	USSR
1937	US	1968	USSR	1976	Israel
1939	Germany	1970	USSR	1978	USSR
1950	Yugoslavia	1972	USSR		
1952	USSR	1974	USSR		
1954	USSR	1976	US		
		1978	Hungary		

Cribbage

Origins. The invention of this game (once called "Cribbidge") is credited to the English dramatist John Suckling (1609–42). It is played by an estimated 10 million people in the US alone.

Rare Hands. F. Art Skinner of Alberta, Canada, is reported to have had five maximum 29-point hands. Paul Nault of Athol, Massachusetts, had two such hands within eight games in a tournament on March 19, 1977. At Blackpool, England, Derek Hearne dealt two hands of six clubs with the remaining club being the turn-up on February 8, 1976. Bill Rogers of Burnaby, B.C., Canada, scored 29 in the crib in 1975.

Marathon. Four members of the Barley Mow Forever Legless Society of England played for 60 hours on February 6–8, 1979.

Darts

Origins. Darts date from the use by archers of heavily weighted 10-inch throwing arrows for self-defense in close fighting. "Dartes" were used in Ireland in the 16th century, and darts was played on the *Mayflower* by the Pilgrims in 1620. Today, more people in Great Britain (6,000,000) play darts than any other single sport.

Lowest Possible Scores. Under English rules, the lowest number of darts needed to achieve standard scores is: 201, four darts; 301, six darts; 401, seven darts; 501, nine darts; 1,001, seventeen darts. The four- and six-dart "possibles" have been achieved many times, the nine-dart 501 occasionally, but the seventeen-dart 1,001 has never been accomplished. The lowest number of darts thrown for a score of 1,001 is 19 by Cliff Inglish at the Bromfield Men's Club, Devon, England, on November 11, 1975.

Fastest Match. The fastest time taken for a match of 3 game of 301 is 1 minute 58 seconds by Ricky Fusco at the Perivale Residents Association Club, Middlesex, England, on December 30, 1976.

Million-and-One. Eight players from King's Lock, Middlewich, Cheshire, England, scored 1,000,001 with 40,968 darts in one session, August 3–5, 1979.

Marathon. Stephen Ablett and Chris Dare played for 101 hours at Nienburg Weser, West Germany, on March 29–April 2, 1975.

World Masters Individual

First held in the West Centre Hotel, London, December, 1974.

1974 Cliff Inglis (Eng)	1977 Eric Bristow (Eng)
1975 Alan Evans (Wal)	1978 Ronnie Davis (Eng)
1976 John Lowe (Eng)	

LOWE SCORES: John Lowe (England), holding a triple bull's-eye and a double armful of Danish fans, has won several of the most prestigious dart tournaments.

British Open Championship

First held in January 1975.

1975	Alan Evans (Wal)		1978	Eric Bristow (Eng)
1976	Jack North (Eng)		1979	Tony Brown (Eng)
1977	John Lowe (Eng)			

Embassy World Professional Championship

First held in February 1978 in Stoke-on-Trent.

1978	Leighton Rees (Wal)	1979	John Lowe (Eng)

Nations Cup

Team Championship first held in March 1977 at West Centre Hotel, London.

1977	Scotland	1978	Sweden	1979	England

US Open Darts Championship

1969	Kirk Dormeyer	1973	Al Lippman	1977	Rick Wobensmith
1970	Linn Garner	1974	Al Lippman	1978	John Zimnawoda
1971	Bob Thiede	1975	Conrad Daniels	1979	Jake Brestowski
1972	Joe Baltadonis	1976	Tony Money	1980	Ricky Ney

Dominoes

Origins. The National Museum in Baghdad, Iraq, contains artifacts from Ur called "dominoes" dated *c.* 2450 B.C. The game remains unstandardized. Eskimos play with 148 pieces, while the European game uses only 28.

Marathon. The longest session by 2 players is 123 hours 4 minutes by Alan Mannering and David Harrison of Stoke-on-Trent, England, on February 8–13, 1978.

Frisbee®

Origins. Competitive play began in 1957, and championships are supervised by the International Frisbee Disc Association.

Distance. The world record for outdoor distance is 444 feet on a throw by John Kirkland of Del Mar, California, on April 30,

DOGGING IT: "Martha Faye" and master John Pickerill display the form which gave "Martha" and Dave Johnson the world record for canine distance Frisbee throw and catch, a remarkable 334.6 feet on June 11, 1978, in Wilmette, Illinois.

FRIS-WHIZZES: John Kirkland (left) of Del Mar, California, set the Frisbee outdoor distance mark with a toss of 444 feet in Dallas, Texas. Monika Lou (right) holds a pair of women's records with an indoor toss of 222.5 feet and a time of 10.04 seconds in the maximum time aloft event.

1978, in Dallas, Texas. The indoor distance record is held by Joseph Youngman with a 296.3-foot toss on August 22, 1978, in Los Angeles.

Susane Lempert holds the women's outdoor distance record (283.5 feet, set in Boston on July 24, 1976), while the women's indoor distance record belongs to Monika Lou, who threw 222.5 feet on August 24, 1977, in Los Angeles.

The 24-hour group distance record is 428.02 miles set in Vernon, Connecticut, by the South Windsor Ultimate Frisbee Disc Team, July 8–9, 1977. Dan Roddick and Alan Bonopane of Pasadena, California, hold the world record for 24-hour pair distance with 250.02 miles, December 30–31, 1979.

Skills. Mark Vinchesi set the record for maximum time aloft by keeping a Frisbee disc in the air for 15.2 seconds in Amherst, Massachusetts, on August 20, 1978. For women, the time-aloft record is 10.04 seconds, set in Santa Barbara, California, by Monika Lou.

The greatest distance achieved for throwing a Frisbee disc, running, and catching it is 271.2 feet by Tom Monroe of Huntsville, Alabama, on August 24, 1979, in Irvine, California.

Fastest Guts Catch. Charles Duvall threw a professional model Frisbee disc at a speed of 60 miles per hour and his teammate Steve McClean made a clean catch of the throw on August 1, 1979, for the "Guinness Game" TV show in Los Angeles. The throw was electronically timed across a regulation 14-meter Guts court.

Marathons. The Alhambra Frisbee Disc Club of Alhambra, California, set the group marathon mark with 1001 hours, May 7–June

18, 1978. The two-person marathon record is held by Ken McDade and Chris Train of Mississauga, Ontario. They played for 100 hours 40 minutes, March 25–29, 1979, in Toronto.

Monopoly®

Origins. The patentee of Monopoly, the world's most popular proprietary board game of which Parker Bros. have sold 80,000,000 copies, was Charles Darrow (1889–1967). He invented the patented version of the game in 1933, while an unemployed heating engineer, using the street names of Atlantic City, New Jersey, where he spent his vacations.

Marathon. The longest game by four players ratified by Parker Bros. is 288 hours by Valerie Schmoltze, Karen and Bob Schmidt and Paul Boyer of Ashland, Pennsylvania, August 17–29, 1978.

Scrabble® Crossword Game

Origins. The crossword game was invented by Alfred M. Butts in 1931 and was developed, refined and trademarked as Scrabble ® Crossword Game by James Brunot in 1948. He sold the North American rights to Selchow & Richter Company, New York, the European rights to J. W. Spears & Sons, London, and the Australian rights to Murfett Pty. Ltd., Melbourne.

Highest scores. The highest competitive game score known is 730 by Ron K. Hendra (GB) on July 12, 1978. His opponent scored 360. Ralph Beaman (US) made an idealized game score of 4,153 in 1974. The highest competitive single turn score recorded is 380. Ronald E. Jerome, of Bracknell, Berkshire, England made an idealized single turn score of 1,961 in May, 1974.

Marathon. The longest Scrabble ® Crossword Game is 120 hours by Norman Hazeldean, Alan Giles, Tom Barton and Keith Ollett at Uckfield, East Sussex, England, August 4–9, 1975, and Mark Morris, Jean-Pierre Burdinat, Robert Emmanuel and Gary Dolton in Sydney, Australia, August 27–September 1, 1975.

Skateboarding

"World" skateboard championships have been staged intermittently since 1966. The highest recorded speed on a skateboard under US Skateboard Association rules is 71.79 m.p.h. on a course at Mt. Baldy, California, in a prone position, by Richard K. Brown, age 33, on June 17, 1979. The stand-up record is 53.45 m.p.h. by John Hutson, 23, at Signal Hill, Long Beach, California, on June 11, 1978. The high jump record is 5 feet by Bryan Beardsly (US) at Signal Hill, September 24–25, 1977.

At the US Skateboard Association championships, Tony Alva, 19, of Santa Monica, California, took off from a moving skateboard, jumped over 17 barrels (12-inch diameters) and landed on another skateboard.

Mike Kinney won a marathon contest at Reseda, California, on May 26, 1979, with 217.3 miles in 30 hours 35 minutes.

LOVE IT AND LEAP IT: Bryan Beardsly (left) holds the record at 5 feet for high jumping and landing on a skateboard. Tony Alva (right) took off from a moving skateboard, jumped over 17 barrels of 12-inch diameter, and landed on another skateboard.

SKATEBOARD SPEEDSTER: John Hutson set the stand-up speed record of 53.45 m.p.h. at Signal Hill in Long Beach, California, on June 11, 1978.

Tiddlywinks

Origins. This game was first espoused by adults in 1955, when Cambridge University (England) issued a challenge to Oxford.

Speed Records. The record for potting 24 winks from a distance of 18 inches is 21.8 seconds by Stephen Williams in May, 1966. Allen R. Astles of the University of Wales potted 10,000 winks in 3 hours 51 minutes 46 seconds in February, 1966.

Marathons. The most protracted game on record is one of 240 hours by six players from St. Anselm's College, Birkenhead, Merseyside, England, August 2–12, 1977.

GLIDING

Origins. Emanuel Swedenborg (1688–1772) of Sweden made sketches of gliders *c.* 1714.

The earliest man-carrying glider was designed by Sir George Cayley (1773–1857) and carried his coachman (possibly John Appleby) about 500 yards across a valley near Brompton Hall, Yorkshire, England, in the summer of 1853. Gliders now attain speeds of 168 m.p.h. and the Jastrzab aerobatic sailplane is designed to withstand vertical dives at up to 280 m.p.h.

Most World Titles

World individual championships (instituted 1948) have been won 5 times by West Germans.

EARLIEST GLIDER: This is a replica of Sir George Cayley's glider. The original flew 500 yards across a valley in England in 1853.

Hang-Gliding

In the 11th century, the monk Elmer is reported to have flown from the 60-foot-tall tower of Malmesbury Abbey, Wiltshire, England. The earliest modern pioneer was Otto Lilienthal (1848–96) of Germany who made numerous flights between 1893 and 1896. Professor Francis Rogallo of the US National Space Agency developed a "wing" in the 1950's from his research into space capsule re-entries.

The official F.A.I. record for the farthest distance covered in 95 miles by George Worthington (US) in an ASG-21 (Rogallo) over California, on July 21, 1977.

The official F.A.I. height gain record is 11,700 feet, recorded by George Worthington (US) over Bishop, California, on July 22, 1978.

The greatest altitude from which a hang-glider has descended is 31,600 feet by Bob McCaffrey, 18, who was released from a balloon over the Mojave Desert, California, on November 21, 1976.

Championships. The First World Team Championships, held at Chattanooga, Tennessee, in October, 1978, were won by Great Britain.

International Gliding Records (Correct as of Dec. 1, 1979)

SINGLE-SEATERS

Height Gain	12,894 m (42,303 ft)	P.F. Bikle, US	SGS 1-23E	Feb. 25, 1961
Absolute Altitude	14,102 m (42,666 ft)	P.F. Bikle, US	SGS 1-23 E	Feb. 25, 1961
Straight Distant	1,460.8 km (905.7 mi)	H.W. Grosse, W. Germany	ASW-12	April 25, 1972
Goal Flight	1,254.26 km (777.6 mi)	B.L. Drake, D.N. Speight, S.H. Georgeson, New Zealand	Nimbus 2	Jan. 14, 1978
Goal and Return	1,634.7 km (1,013.5 km)	K.H. Striedieck, US	ASW-17	May 9, 1977
Triangular Distance	1,229.25 km (762.1 mi)	H.W. Grosse, W. Germany (in Australia)	ASW-17	Jan. 4, 1979
100 km Triangle	165.3 km/h (102.5 mph)	K. Briegleb, US	Kestrel 17	July 18, 1974
300 km Triangle	153.43 km/h (95.1 mph)	W. Neubert, W. Germany (in Kenya)	Kestrel 604	March 3, 1972
500 km Triangle	143.04 km/h (88.7 mph)	E. Pearson, GB (in S.W. Africa)	Nimbus 2	Nov. 27, 1976
750 km Triangle	141.13 km/h (87.5 mph)	G. Eckle, W. Germany (in South Africa)	Nimbus 2	Jan. 7, 1978
1000 km Triangle	145.33 km/h (90.1 mph)	H.W. Grosse, W. Germany (in Australia)	ASW-17	Jan. 3, 1979

MULTI-SEATERS

Height Gain	11,680 m (38,320.1 ft)	S. Josefczak and J. Tarczon, Poland	Bocian	Nov. 5, 1966
Absolute Altitude	13,489 m (44,255.2 ft)	L. Edgar and H. Klieforth, US	Pratt Read G-1	March 19, 1952
Straight Distance	970.4 km (601.6 mi)	I. Renner and H. Geissler, Australia	Calif A-21	Jan. 27, 1975
Goal Flight	864.86 km (536.2 mi)	Isabella Gorokhova and Z. Koslova, USSR	Blanik	June 3, 1967
Goal and Return*	829.7 km (514.4 mi)	T. Knauff and R. Tawse, US	Janus	April 7, 1979

GLIDER AND RIDER: Walter Neubert piloted his Kestrel 604 to the world record for a 300-kilometer triangle. He soared at 95.1 m.p.h. in Kenya in 1972.

Triangular Distance*	850 km (527 mi)	E. Müller and O. Schäffner, W. Germany	Janus	Nov. 15, 1979
100 km Triangle	147.19 km/h (91.2 mph)	E. Mouat-Biggs and S. Murray, South Africa	Janus	Nov. 21, 1977
300 km Triangle	135.51 km/h (84 mph)	E. Mouat-Biggs and S. Murray, South Africa	Janus	Nov. 16, 1977
500 km Triangle	140.06 km/h (86.8 mph)	E. Mouat-Biggs and S. Murray, South Africa	Janus	Nov. 17, 1977
750 km Triangle	122.26 km/h (75.8 mph)	E. Müller and O. Schäffner, W. Germany (in South Africa)	Janus	Nov. 26, 1978

*Awaiting homologation.

SINGLE-SEATERS (WOMEN)

Height Gain	9,119 m (29,918 ft)	Anne Burns, GB (in South Africa)	Skylark 3B	Jan. 13, 1961
Absolute Altitude	12,637 m 41,459.9 ft)	Sabrina Jackintell, US	Astir CS	Feb. 14, 1979
Straight Distance	810 km (502.2 mi)	Adela Dankowska, Poland	Jantar 1	April 19, 1977
Goal Flight	731.6 km (453.6 mi)	Tamara Zaiganova, USSR	A-15	July 29, 1966
Goal and Return	801.7 km (497 mi)	Ranna Reitsch, W. Germany (in US)	ASW-20	April 7, 1979
Triangular Distance	779.68 km (483.4 mi)	Elizabeth Karel, Australia	LS-3	Jan. 24, 1979
100 km Triangle	139.45 km/h (86.5 mph)	Susan Martin, Australia	LS-3	Feb. 2, 1979
300 km Triangle	121.88 km/h (75.6 mph)	Elizabeth Karel, Australia	LS-3	Jan. 30, 1979
500 km Triangle	133.14 km/h (82.5 mph)	Susan Martin, Australia	LS-3	Jan. 29, 1979
750 km Triangle	95.42 km/h (59.2 mph)	Elizabeth Karel, Australia	LS-3	Jan. 24, 1979

MULTI-SEATERS (WOMEN)

Height Gain	8,430 m (27,657 ft)	Adela Dankowska and M. Mateliska, Poland	Bocian	Oct. 17, 1967
Absolute Altitude	10,809 m (35,462 ft)	Mary Nutt and H. Duncan, US	SGS 2-32	March 5, 1975
Straight Distance	864.85 km (536.2 mi)	Tatiana Pavlova and L. Filomechkina, USSR	Blanik	June 3, 1967
Goal Flight	864.86 km (536.2 mi)	Isabella Gorokhova and Z. Koslova, USSR	Blanik	June 3, 1967

International Gliding Records (continued)

Goal and Return*	593 km (367.7 mi)	Adele Orsi and M. Monti, Italy	—	June 18, 1978
100 km Triangle	124 km/h (76.9 mph)	Adela Dankowska and E. Grzelak, Poland	Halny	Aug. 1, 1978
300 km Triangle	97.74 km/h (60.6 mph)	Adele Orsi and F. Bellengeri, Italy	Calíf A-21	Aug. 18, 974
500 km Triangle	69.6 km/h (43.2 mph)	Tamara Zaiganova and V. Lobanova, USSR	Blanik	May 29, 1968

*Awaiting homologation.

International Motor Gliders (Correct as of Dec. 1, 1979)

SINGLE-SEATERS

Height Gain*	8,700 m (28,543 ft)	Gunther Cichon, W. Germany	Nimbus M	May 27, 1979
Absolute Altitude*	10,300 m (33,793 ft)	Gunther Cichon, W. Germany	Nimbus M	May 27, 1979
Goal and Return*	833 km (516.5 mi)	Gunther Cichon, W. Germany (in South Africa)	Nimbus M1	May 23, 1979
Triangular Distance*	850 km (527 mi)	Karl Abhau, W. Germany (in South Africa)	Nimbus M	Nov. 16, 1979
100 km Triangle	152.16 km/h (94.3 mph)	F. Rueb, W. Germany (in South Africa)	Nimbus 2M	Dec. 29, 1977
300 km Triangle	131.75 km/h (81.7 mph)	F. Rueb, W. Germany (in South Africa)	Nimbus 2M	Dec. 27, 1977
500 km Triangle	119.1 km/h (73.8 mph)	F. Rueb, W. Germany (in South Africa)	Nimbus 2M	Dec. 12, 1978
750 km Triangle	120.21 km/h (74.5 mph)	F. Rueb, W. Germany (in South Africa)	Nimbus 2M	Dec. 29, 1978

*Awaiting homologation.

SOARS AND SCORES: Heinz Huth (West Germany) was the first glider pilot to win two world titles with victories in the Standard category in 1960 and 1963.

Height	4,523 m	F. Jung and G. Marzinzik,	K-16	March 26, 1978
Gain	(14,839 ft)	W. Germany (in France)		
Absolute	7,000 m	D. Mayr and F. Adler, W.	K-16	March 22, 1977
Height*	(22,966 ft)	Germany		
Goal	646.42 km	G. Jacobs and G. Hüttel,	SF-25E	April 28, 1976
Flight	(400.8 mi)	W. Germany		
Goal and	394 km	G. Jacobs and W.	SF-25E	May 28,1977
Return*	(224.3 mi)	Sandermann, W.		
		Germany		
100 km	73.83 km/h	F. Kensche and H.	SF-25E	April 19, 1976
Triangle	(47.8 mph)	Schaffer. W. Germany		
300 km	73.8 km/h	W. Binder and V. Derau,	Janus BM	July 3, 1978
Triangle	(45.8 mph)	W. Germany		
500 km	67 km/h	W. Binder and K. Kerber,	Janus M	April 18, 1978
Triangle*	(41.5 mph)	W. Germany		

*Awaiting homologation.

World Championships

The first World Gliding (or Soaring) Championships were held in 1937. They are held biennially, and there are now three categories—Open, Standard and 15 meters. Winners at each category:

OPEN

1937 Heini Dittmar (Ger)
1948 Per Persson (Swe)
1950 Billy Nilsson (Swe)
1952 Phillip Wills (GB)
1954 Gerard Pierre (Fra)
1956 Paul MacCready (US)
1958 Ernst Haase (W Ger)
1960 Rudolf Hossinger (Arg)
1963 Edward Makula (Pol)
1965 Jan Wroblewski (Pol)
1968 Harro Wodl (Aut)
1970 George Moffat (US)
1972 Goran Ax (Swe)
1974 George Moffat (US)
1976 George Lee (GB)
1978 George Lee (GB)

2-Seater

1952 Luis Juez and J. Ara (Spa)
1954 Z. Rain and P. Komac (Yug)
1956 Nick Goodhard and Frank Foster (GB)

Standard

1958 Adam Witek (Pol)
1960 Heinz Huth (W Ger)
1963 Heinz Huth (W Ger)
1965 François Henry (Fra)
1968 A. J. Smith (US)
1970 Helmut Reichmann (W Ger)
1972 Jan Wroblewski (Pol)
1974 Helmut Reichmann (W Ger)
1976 Ingo Renner (Aus)
1978 Baer Selen (Hol)

15 meters

1978 Helmut Reichmann (W Ger)

GOLF

Origins. Although a stained glass window in Gloucester Cathedral, Scotland, dating from 1350 portrays a golfer-like figure, the earliest mention of golf occurs in a prohibiting law passed by the Scottish Parliament in March, 1457, under which "golff be utterly cryit doune and not usit." The Romans had a cognate game called *paganica*, which may have been carried to Britain before 400 A.D. The Chinese National Golf Association claims the game is of Chinese origin ("Ch'ui Wan—the ball-hitting game") from the 3rd or 2nd century B.C. Gutta-percha balls succeeded feather balls in 1848, and were in turn succeeded in 1902 by rubber-cored balls,

ON COURSE: "Slammin'" Sam Snead (left) carded a 59 for 18 holes and 122 for 36 in the 1959 Greenbrier Open. Snead has been credited with 134 tournament victories since 1934. Mickey Wright (right) celebrates her record-tying 4th US Women's Open title. Her 62 is the all-time women's best for a full-size 18-hole course, and her 82 pro tournament wins is also tops.

invented in 1899 by Coburn Haskell (US). Steel shafts were authorized in 1929.

Clubs

Oldest. The oldest club of which there is written evidence is the Gentleman Golfers (now the Honourable Company of Edinburgh Golfers) formed in March, 1744—10 years prior to the institution of the Royal and Ancient Club of St. Andrews, Fife, Scotland. The oldest existing club in North America is the Royal Montreal Club (November, 1873) and the oldest in the US is St. Andrews, Westchester County, New York (1888). An older claim is by the Foxbury Country Club, Clarion County, Pennsylvania (1887).

Courses

Highest. The highest golf course in the world is the Tuctu Golf Club in Morococha, Peru, which is 14,335 feet above sea level at its lowest point. Golf has, however, been played in Tibet at an altitude of over 16,000 feet.

Lowest. The lowest golf course in the world was that of the now defunct Sodom and Gomorrah Golfing Society at Kallia (Qulya), on the northern shores of the Dead Sea, 1,250 feet below sea level. Currently the lowest is in the Netherlands; the Rotterdam Golf Club's 9-hole course is 26 feet below sea level.

Longest Hole. The longest hole in the world is the 17th hole (par 6) of 745 yards at the Black Mountain Golf Club, North Carolina. It was opened in 1964. In August, 1927, the 6th hole at Prescott Country Club in Arkansas measured 838 yards.

Largest Green. Probably the largest green in the world is the 5th green at International, G.C., Bolton, Massachusetts, with an area greater than 28,000 square feet.

Biggest Bunker. The world's biggest trap is Hell's Half Acre on the 7th hole of the Pine Valley course, New Jersey, built in 1912 and generally regarded as the world's most trying course.

Longest Course. The world's longest course is the 8,101-yard Dub's Dread Golf Club course (par 78) in Piper, Kansas.

Longest "Course." Floyd Satterlee Rood used the whole United States as a course when he played from the Pacific surf to the Atlantic surf from September 14, 1963 to October 3, 1964, in 114,737 strokes. He lost 3,511 balls on the 3,397.7-mile trip.

Lowest Scores

9 holes and 18 holes—Men. The lowest recorded score on any 18-hole course with a par of 70 or more is 55 first achieved by Alfred Edward Smith (b. 1903), the English professional, at Woolacombe on January 1, 1936. The course measured 4,248 yards. The detail was 4, 2, 3, 4, 2, 4, 3, 4, 3 = 29 out, and 2, 3, 3, 3, 3, 2, 5, 4, 1 = 26 in.

At least three players are recorded to have played a long course (over 6,000 yards) in a score of 58.

Nine holes in 25 (4, 3, 3, 2, 3, 3, 1, 4, 2) was recorded by A. J. "Bill" Burke in a round of 57 (32 + 25) on the 6,389-yard par 71 Normandie course in St. Louis on May 20, 1970. The tournament record is 27 by Jose Maria Canizares (Spain) (b. February 18, 1947) for the first nine of the third round in the 1978 Swiss Open on the 6,811-yard Crans-Sur-Sierre course.

The United States P.G.A. tournament record for 18 holes is 59 (30 + 29) by Al Geiberger (b. September 1, 1937) in the second round of the Danny Thomas Classic, on the 72-par, 7,249-yard course at Memphis, Tennessee, on June 10, 1977.

In non-P.G.A. tournaments, Sam Snead had 59 in the Greenbrier Open (now called the Sam Snead Festival), at White Sulphur Springs, West Virginia, on May 16, 1959; Gary Player (South Africa) (born November 1, 1935) carded 59 in the second round of the Brazilian Open in Rio de Janeiro on November 29, 1974; and David Jagger (GB) also had 59 in a Pro-Am tournament prior to the 1973 Nigerian Open.

Women. The lowest recorded score on an 18-hole course (over 6,000 yards) for a woman is 62 (30 + 32) by Mary (Mickey) Kathryn Wright (born February 14, 1935), of Dallas, on the Hogan Park Course (6,282 yards) at Midland, Texas, in November, 1964.

Wanda Morgan (b. March 22, 1910) recorded a score of 60 (31 + 29) on the Westgate-on-Sea and Birchington Golf Club course (England) over 18 holes (5,002 yards) on July 11, 1929.

36 holes. The record of 36 holes is 122 (59 + 63) by Sam Snead in the 1959 Greenbrier Open (now called the Sam Snead Festival) (non-P.G.A.) (see above) May 16–17, 1959. Horton Smith (see below) scored 121 (63 + 58) on a short course on December 21, 1928.

72 holes. The lowest recorded score on a first-class course is 257 (27 under par) by Mike Souchak (born May 10, 1927) in the Texas Open at Brackenridge Park, San Antonio in February, 1955, made up of 60 (33 out and 27 in), 68, 64, 65 (average 64.25 per round), exhibiting, as one critic said, his "up and down form." Horton Smith (1908–63), twice US Masters Champion, scored 245 (63, 58, 61 and 63) for 72 holes on the 4,700-yard course (par 64) at Catalina Country Club, California, to win the Catalina Open on December 21–23, 1928.

The lowest 72 holes in a national championship is 262 by Percy Alliss (1897–1975) of Britain, with 67, 66, 66 and 63 in the Italian Open Championship at San Remo in 1932, and by Liang Huan Lu (b. 1936) (Taiwan) in the 1971 French Open at Biarritz. Kelvin D. G. Nagle (b. December 21, 1920) of Australia shot 261 in the Hong Kong Open in 1961.

Eclectic Record. The lowest recorded eclectic (from the Greek *eklecktikos*, meaning "choosing") score, i.e. the sum of a player's all-time personal low scores for each hole, for a course of more than 6,000 yards, is 33 by the club professional Jack McKinnon on the 6,538-yard Capilano Golf and Country Club course, Vancouver, British Columbia, Canada. This was compiled over the period 1937–1964 and reads 2-2-2-1-2-2-2-2-1 (16 out) and 2-1-2-2-1-2-2-2 -3 (17 in) = 33.

Highest Scores

Highest Round Score. It is recorded that Chevalier von Cittern went round 18 holes at Biarritz, France, in 1888 in 316 strokes—an average of 17.55 shots per hole.

Steven Ward took 222 strokes for the 6,212-yard Pecos Course, Reeves County, Texas, on June 18, 1976—but he was only aged 3 years 286 days.

Highest Single-Hole Scores. The highest score recorded for a single hole in the British Open is 21 by a player in the inaugural meeting at Prestwick in 1860. Double figures have been recorded on the card of the winner only once, when Willie Fernie (1851–1924) scored a 10 at Musselburgh, Lothian, Scotland, in 1833. Ray Ainsley of Ojai, California, took 19 strokes for the par-4 16th hole during the second round of the US Open at Cherry Hills Country Club, Denver, Colorado, on June 10, 1938. Most of the strokes were used in trying to extricate the ball from a brook. Hans Merrell of Mogadore, Ohio, took 19 strokes on the par-3 16th (222 yards) during the third round of the Bing Crosby National Tournament at the Cypress Point course, Del Monte, California, on January 17, 1959.

Most Shots—Women. A woman player in the qualifying round of the Shawnee Invitational for Ladies at Shawnee-on-Delaware, Pennsylvania, *c.* 1912, took 166 strokes for the 130-yard 16th hole. Her tee shot went into the Binniekill River and the ball floated. She put out in a boat with her exemplary, but statistically minded, husband at the oars. She eventually beached the ball 1½ miles downstream, but was not yet out of the woods. She had to play through a forest on the home stretch. In a competition at Peacehaven, Sussex, England, in 1890, A. J. Lewis had 156 putts on one green without holing out.

Throwing the Golf Ball

The lowest recorded score for throwing a golf ball around 18 holes (over 6,000 yards) is 82 by Joe Flynn, 21, at the 6,228-yard Port Royal Course, Bermuda, on March 27, 1975.

Longest Drive

In long-driving contests 330 yards is rarely surpassed at sea level.

The world record is 392 yards by a member of the Irish P.G.A., Tommie Campbell, made at Dun Laoghaire, Co. Dublin, in July, 1964.

The United States P.G.A. record is 341 yards by Jack William Nicklaus (born Columbus, Ohio, January 21, 1940), then weighing 206 lbs., in July, 1963.

Valentin Barrios (Spain) drove a ball 568½ yards on an airport runway at Palma, Majorca, on March 7, 1977.

The longest on an ordinary course is 515 yards by Michael Hoke Austin (born February 17, 1910) of Los Angeles, in the US National Seniors Open Championship at Las Vegas, Nevada, on September 25, 1974. Aided by an estimated 35-m.p.h. tailwind, the 6-foot-2-inch 210-lb. golfer drove the ball on the fly to within

DIFFERENT STROKES: Ireland's Tommie Campbell (left) holds the world record for the longest drive with a distance of 392 yards in Dublin in 1964. Cary Middlecoff (right) holed an 86-foot putt on the 13th green at the Augusta National, Georgia, in 1955. The record putt helped him to win the Masters.

a yard of the green on the part-4, 450-yard 5th hole of the Winterwood Course. The ball rolled 65 yards past the hole.

Arthur Lynskey claimed a drive of 200 yards out and 2 miles down off Pikes Peak, Colorado, on June 28, 1968.

A drive of 2,640 yards (1½ miles) across ice was achieved by an Australian meteorologist named Nils Lied at Mawson Base, Antarctica, in 1962. On the moon, the energy expended on a mundane 300-yard drive would achieve, craters permitting, a distance of a mile.

Longest Hitter. The golfer regarded the longest consistent hitter the game has ever known is the 6-foot-5-inch-tall, 230-lb. George Bayer (US), the 1957 Canadian Open Champion. His longest measured drive was one of 420 yards at the fourth in the Las Vegas Invitational in 1953. It was measured as a precaution against litigation since the ball struck a spectator. Bayer also drove a ball pin high on a 426-yard hole in Tucson, Arizona. Radar measurements show that an 87-m.p.h. impact velocity for a golf ball falls to 46 m.p.h. in 3.0 seconds.

Longest Putt

The longest recorded holed putt in a major tournament was one of 86 feet on the vast 13th green at the Augusta National, Georgia, by Cary Middlecoff (b. January, 1921) in the 1955 Masters Tournament.

Bobby Jones was reputed to have holed a putt in excess of 100 feet on the 5th green in the first round on the 1927 British Open at St. Andrews, Scotland.

Fastest and Slowest Rounds

With such variations in the lengths of courses, speed records, even for rounds under par, are of little comparative value.

Bob Williams at Eugene, Oregon, completed 18 holes (6,010 yds.) in 27 minutes 48.2 seconds in 1971, but this test permitted him to stroke the ball while it was moving. The record for a still ball is 3.0 minutes 10 seconds by Dick Kimbrough (US) (b. 1931) at North Platte C.C., Nebraska (6,068 yards), on August 8, 1972, using only a 3-iron.

On August 25, 1979, forty-two players from Ridgemont Country Club, Rochester, New York, completed the 18-hole 6,161-yard course in 8 minutes 53.8 seconds.

The slowest stroke-play tournament round was one of 6 hours 45 minutes by South Africa in the first round of the 1972 World Cup at the Royal Melbourne Golf Club, Australia. This was a 4-ball medal round, everything holed out.

Most Rounds in a Day

The greatest number of rounds played on foot in 24 hours is 22 rounds plus 5 holes (401 holes) by Ian Colston, 35, at Bendigo G.C., Victoria, Australia (6,061 yards) on November 27–28, 1971. He covered more than 100 miles.

The most holes played on foot in a week (158½ hours) is 1,123

BUCK SHOT: Jack Nicklaus is the all-time leading money winner of USPGA golf prizes with $3,408,827 to the end of 1979. Nicklaus is the only golfer who has won all 5 major titles while setting a record total 17 major tournament victories. His 5 wins is tops for the Masters Championship. He is shown here blasting out of a bunker off the 18th green during his winning effort in the 1970 World Match Play Tournament.

by Richard H. Stacey at Paxton Park Golf Club, Paducah, Kentucky, September 25–October 1, 1979.

Most Tournament Wins

The record for winning tournaments in a single season is 19, including a record 11 consecutively, by Byron Nelson (born February 4, 1912) (US) in 1945.

Sam Snead has won 84 official U.S.P.G.A. tour events to December, 1978, and has been credited with a total 134 tournament victories since 1934.

Mickey Wright (US) won 82 professional tournaments up to December, 1978.

Jack Nicklaus (US) is the only golfer who has won five major titles, including the US Amateur, twice, and a record total 17 major tournaments (1962–78). His remarkable record in the British Open is three firsts, five seconds and two thirds.

Most Titles

US Open	Willie Anderson (1880–1910)	4	1901–03–04–05
	Robert Tyre Jones, Jr. (1902–71)	4	123–26–29–30
	Ben W. Hogan (b. Aug. 13, 1912)	4	1948–50–51–53
US Amateur	R. T. Jones, Jr.	5	1924–25–27–28–30
British Open	Harry Vardon (1870–1937)	6	1896–98–99, 1903, 1911, 1914
British Amateur	John Ball (1861–1940)	8	1888–90–92–94–99, 1907–10, 1912

U.S. Open

This championship was inaugurated in 1894. The lowest 72-hole aggregate is 275 (71, 67, 72 and 65) by Jack Nicklaus on the Lower Course (7,015 yards) at Baltusrol Golf Club, Springfield, New Jersey, on June 15–18, 1967, and by Lee Trevino (b. Horizon City, Texas, December 1, 1939) at Oak Hill Country Club, Rochester, New York, on June 13–16, 1968. The lowest score for 18 holes is 63 by Johnny Miller (b. April 29, 1947) of California on the 6,921-yard, par-71 Oakmont (Pennsylvania) course on June 17, 1973.

U.S. Masters

The lowest score in the US Masters (instituted at the 6,980-yard Augusta National Golf Course, Georgia, in 1934) was 271 by Jack Nicklaus in 1965 and Raymond Floyd (born 1942) in 1976. The lowest rounds have been 64 by Lloyd Mangrum (1914–74) (1st round, 1940), Jack Nicklaus (3rd round, 1965), Maurice Bembridge (GB) (b. February 21, 1945) (4th round, 1974), Hale Irwin (b. June 3, 1945) (4th round, 1975), Gary Player (S. Africa) (4th round, 1978) and Miller Barber (b. March 31, 1931) (2nd round, 1979).

TOP TITLISTS: Glenna Collett Vare (left) won the US Women's Amateur title a record 6 times. Walter Hagen (right) has the most USPGA Championship victories with 5. Hagen also captured 3 British Open titles and 2 US Open Championships.

U.S. Amateur

This championship was inaugurated in 1893. The lowest score for 9 holes is 30 by Francis D. Ouimet (1893–1967) in 1932.

British Open

The Open Championship was inaugurated in 1860 at Prestwick, Strathclyde, Scotland. The lowest score for 9 holes is 29 by Tom Haliburton (Wentworth) and Peter W. Thomson (Australia), in the first round at the Open on the Royal Lytham and St. Anne's course at Lytham St. Anne's, Lancashire, England, on July 10, 1963. Tony Jacklin (GB, b. July, 1944) also shot a 29 in the first round of the 1970 Open at St. Andrews, Scotland.

The lowest scoring round in the Open itself is 63 by Mark Hayes (US, b. July 12, 1949) at Turnberry, Strathclyde, Scotland, in the second round on July 7, 1977. Henry Cotton (GB) at Royal St. George's, Sandwich, Kent, England, completed the first 36 holes in 132 (67 + 65) on June 27, 1934.

The lowest 72-hole aggregate is 268 (68, 70, 65, and 65) by Tom Watson (US) (b. September 4, 1949) at Turnberry, Scotland, on July 9, 1977.

British Amateur

The lowest score for nine holes in the British Championship (inaugurated in 1885) is 29 by Richard Davol Chapman (born March 23, 1911) of the US at Sandwich in 1948. Michael Francis Bonallack (b. 1934) shot a 61 (32 + 29) on the 6,905-yard par-71 course at Ganton, Yorkshire, on July 27, 1968, on the 1st 18 of the 36 holes in the final round.

World Cup (formerly Canada Cup)

The World Cup (instituted 1953) has been won most often by the US with 15 victories between 1955 and 1979. The only men on six winning teams have been Arnold Palmer (b. Sept. 10, 1929) (1960, 62–63–64, 66–67) and Jack Nicklaus (1963–4, 66–67, 71, 73). The only man to take the individual title three times is Jack Nicklaus (US) in 1963–64–71. The lowest aggregate score for 144 holes is 545 by Australia (Bruce Devlin and David Graham) at San Isidro, Buenos Aires, Argentina, on November 12–15, 1970, and the lowest score by an individual winner was 269 by Roberto de Vicenzo, 47, on the same occasion.

Walker Cup

The US versus Great Britain–Ireland series instituted in 1921 (for the Walker Cup since 1922), now biennial, has been won by the US 25½–2½ to date. Joe Carr (GB-I) played in 10 contests (1947–67).

Ryder Trophy

The biennial Ryder Cup (instituted 1927) professional match between the US and GB had been won by the US 18½–3½ to July, 1978. Billy Casper has the record of winning most matches, with

DRIVING FOR DOLLARS: Kathy Whitworth (left) is the all-time leading career money winner in women's golf with $858,460 through 1979. Her 80 official tournament wins through the 1978 season leave her only 2 behind Mickey Wright on the career victories list. Nancy Lopez-Melton (right) proudly displays one of many trophies the young sensation has earned. Her winnings of $197,488 in 1979 shattered the women's yearly earnings record that she herself had set the year before.

20 won (1961–75). In 1979, the US team played a team from Europe for the first time, and won for their 19th victory.

Curtis Cup

Contested every two years by teams of women golfers from the US and GB, the Curtis Cup (instituted 1932) has been won by the US 16–2 with 2 ties through 1978.

Biggest Victory Margin

Randall Colin Vines (b. June 22, 1945) of Australia won the Tasmanian Open in 1968 with a score of 274, with a margin of 17 strokes over the second-place finisher.

The same margin of 17 was achieved by Bernard Langer (W. Germany) in winning the World Under–25 tournament with a score of 274 at Nimes, France, on September 30, 1979.

Longest Tie

The longest delayed result in any National Open Championship occurred in the 1931 US Open at Toledo, Ohio. George von Elm and Billy Burke tied at 292, then tied the first playoff at 149. Burke won the second playoff by a single stroke after 72 extra holes.

Highest Earnings

The greatest amount ever won in official US P.G.A. golf prizes is $3,408,827 by Jack Nicklaus to the end of 1979.

The record for a year is $462,636 by Tom Watson (US) in 1979.

The highest career earnings by a woman is $858,460 by Kathy Whitworth (b. September 27, 1939) through the end of 1979.

Nancy Lopez (now Mrs. Tim Melton) (b. January 6, 1957) won a record $197,488 in the 1979 season.

Richest Prize

The greatest first-place prize money was $100,000 (total purse $500,000) in the 144-hole "World Open" played at Pinehurst, North Carolina, on November 8–17, 1973, won by Miller Barber, 42, of Texas. The World Series of Golf also carries a prize of $100,000.

Largest Tournament

The annual Ford Amateur Golf Tournament in Great Britain had a record 100,030 competitors in 1978.

Youngest and Oldest Champions

The youngest winner of the British Open was Tom Morris, Jr. (b. 1851, d. December 25, 1875) at Prestwick, Ayrshire, Scotland, in 1868, aged 17 years 5 months. The youngest winners of the British Amateur title were John Charles Beharrel (b. May 2, 1938) at Troon, Strathclyde, Scotland, on June 2, 1956, and Robert (Bobby) Cole (S. Africa) (b. May 11, 1948) at Carnoustie, Tayside, Scotland, on June 11, 1966, both aged 18 years 1 month. The oldest winner of the British Amateur was the Hon. Michael Scott at Hoylake, Cheshire, England, in 1933, when 54. The oldest Open Champion was "Old Tom" Morris (1821–1908) who was aged 46 years 99 days when he won in 1867. In modern times, the 1967 champion Roberto de Vicenzo (b. Buenos Aires, Argentina, April 14, 1923) was aged 44 years 93 days. The oldest US Amateur Champion was Jack Westland (born 1905) at Seattle, Washington, in 1952, aged 47.

Most Peripatetic Golfer

George S. Salter of Carmel, California, has played in 116 different "countries" around the world from 1964 to 1977.

Shooting Your Age

Sam Snead holds the record for shooting the lowest score in professional competition less than the player's age in years with a 64 on the Onion Creek Golf Club, Austin, Texas (par 70) of 6,585 yards in April, 1978, when he was one month short of his 66th birthday. He was also the first player on record to score his age on the P.G.A. tour, by hitting a 67 in the second round of the Ed McMahon Quad Cities Open at Oakwood Country Club, Coal Valley, Illinois, on June 20, 1979. He bettered this mark two days later, with a 66 in the final round. Snead turned 67 on May 27, 1979.

The oldest player to score his age is C. Arthur Thompson (1869–1975) of Victoria, British Columbia, Canada, who scored 103 on the Uplands course of 6,215 yards when aged 103 in 1973.

The youngest player to score his age is Robert Leroy Klingaman (born October 22, 1914) who shot a 58 when aged 58 on the 5,654-yard course at the Caledonia Golf Club, Fayetteville, Pennsylvania, on August 31, 1973. Bob Hamilton, age 59, shot 59 on the 6,233-yard blue course, Hamilton Golf Club, Evansville, Indiana, on June 3, 1975.

Holes-in-One

In 1979, *Golf Digest* was notified of 29,416 holes-in-one, so averaging over 80 per day.

Longest. The longest straight hole shot in one is the 10th hole (444 yards) at Miracle Hills Golf Club, Omaha, Nebraska. Robert Mitera achieved a hole-in-one there on October 7, 1965. Mitera, aged 21 and 5 feet 6 inches tall, weighed 165 lbs. A two-handicap player, he normally drove 245 yards. A 50-m.p.h. gust carried his shot over a 290-yard drop-off. The group in front testified to the remaining 154 yards.

The longest dogleg achieved in one is the 480-yard 5th hole at Hope Country Club, Arkansas, by L. Bruce on November 15, 1962.

The women's record is 393 yards by Marie Robie of Wollaston, Massachusetts, on the first hole of the Furnace Brook Golf Club. September 4, 1949.

HOLE TRUTH: Joseph Vitullo (left) has made 10 holes-in-one on the 130-yard 16th hole at the Hubbard Golf Course, Ohio. C. Arthur Thompson (right) became the oldest player to score his age when he carded a 103 on the 6,215-yard Uplands course when aged 103 in 1973.

Most. The greatest number of holes-in-one in a career is 44 by Norman L. Manley, 56 years old, of Long Beach, California.

Douglas Porteous, 28, aced 4 holes over 36 consecutive holes—the 3rd and 6th on September 26 and the 5th on September 28 at Ruchill Golf Club, Glasgow, Scotland and the 6th at the Clydebank and District Golf Club Course on September 30, 1974. Robert Taylor holed the 188-yard 16th hole at Hunstanton, Norfolk, England, on three successive days—May 31, June 1 and 2, 1974. Joseph F. Vitullo (b. April 1, 1916) aced the 130-yard 16th hole at the Hubbard Golf Course, Ohio, for the tenth time on June 26, 1979.

Consecutive. There is no recorded instance of a golfer performing three consecutive holes-in-one, but there are at least 15 cases of "aces" being achieved in two consecutive holes of which the greatest was Norman L. Manley's unique "double albatross" on two par-4 holes (330-yard 7th and 290-yard 8th) on the Del Valle Country Club course, Saugus, California, on September 2, 1964.

The only woman ever to card consecutive aces is Sue Prell, on the 13th and 14th holes at Chatswood Golf Club, Sydney, Australia, on May 29, 1977.

The closest recorded instances of a golfer getting 3 consecutive holes-in-one were by the Rev. Harold Snider (b. July 4, 1900) who aced the 8th, 13th and 14th holes of the par-3 Ironwood course in Phoenix, Arizona, on June 9, 1976, and Dr. Joseph Boydstone on the 3rd, 4th and 9th at Bakersfield G.C., California on October 10, 1962.

Youngest and Oldest. The youngest golfer recorded to have shot a hole-in-one was Coby Orr (aged 5) of Littleton, Colorado, on the 103-yard fifth hole at the Riverside Golf Course, San Antonio, Texas, in 1975.

The oldest golfers to have performed the feat are George Miller, 93, at the 11th (116 yards) at Anaheim Golf Club, California, on December 4, 1970, and Charles Youngman, 93, at the Tam O'Shanter Club, Toronto, in 1971. Maude Hutton became the oldest woman to make a hole-in-one when, at age 86, she aced the 102-yard 14th hole at Kings Inn Golf and Country Club, Sun City Center, Florida, on August 7, 1978.

British Open Championship

The first Championship was held at Prestwick in 1860. In 1892 the competition was extended from 36 to 72 holes. Winners (GB except where shown):

		Score			Score
1860	Willie Park, Sr.	174	1872	Tom Morris, Jr.	166
1861	Tom Morris, Sr.	163	1873	Tom Kidd	179
1862	Tom Morris, Sr.	163	1874	Mungo Park	159
1863	Willie Park, Sr.	168	1875	Willie Park, Sr.	166
1864	Tom Morris, Sr.	167	1876	Robert Martin	176
1865	Andrew Strath	162	1877	Jamie Anderson	160
1866	Willie Park, Sr.	169	1878	Jamie Anderson	157
1867	Tom Morris, Sr.	170	1879	Jamie Anderson	170
1868	Tom Morris, Jr.	170	1880	Robert Ferguson	162
1869	Tom Morris, Jr.	154	1881	Robert Ferguson	170
1870	Tom Morris, Jr.	149	1882	Robert Ferguson	171

DRIVING REIGN: Lee Trevino has won the British Open (twice), the US Open (twice), and the USPGA Championship (once).

British Open Championship (continued)

Year	Player	Score	Year	Player	Score
1883	Willie Fernie	159	1931	Tommy D. Armour (US)	296
1884	Jack Simpson	160	1932	Gene Sarazen (US)	283
1885	Bob Martin	171	1933	Denny Shute (US)	292
1886	David Brown	157	1934	Henry Cotton	283
1887	Willie Park, Jr.	161	1935	Alfred Perry	283
1888	Jack Burns	171	1936	Alfred Padgham	287
1889	Willie Park, Jr.	155	1937	Henry Cotton	290
1890	John Ball	164	1938	R. A. Whitcombe	295
1891	Hugh Kirkaldy	169	1939	Richard Burton	290
1892	Harold H. Hilton	305	1946	Sam Snead (US)	290
1893	William Auchterlonie	322	1947	Fred Daly	293
1894	John H. Taylor	326	1948	Henry Cotton	284
1895	John H. Taylor	322	1949	Bobby Locke (S Af)	283
1896	Harry Vardon	316	1950	Bobby Locke (S Af)	279
1897	Harold H. Hilton	314	1951	Max Faulkner	285
1898	Harry Vardon	307	1952	Bobby Locke (S Af)	287
1899	Harry Vardon	310	1953	Ben Hogan (US)	282
1900	John H. Taylor	309	1954	Peter Thomson (Aus)	283
1901	James Braid	309	1955	Peter Thomson (Aus)	281
1902	Alexander Herd	307	1956	Peter Thomson (Aus)	286
1903	Harry Vardon	300	1957	Bobby Locke (S Af)	279
1904	Jack White	296	1958	Peter Thomson (Aus)	278
1905	James Braid	318	1959	Gary Player (S Af)	284
1906	James Braid	300	1960	Kel Nagle (Aus)	278
1907	Arnaud Massy	312	1961	Arnold Palmer (US)	284
1908	James Braid	291	1962	Arnold Palmer (US)	276
1909	John H. Taylor	295	1963	Bob Charles (NZ)	277
1910	James Braid	299	1964	Tony Lema (US)	279
1911	Harry Vardon	303	1965	Peter Thomson (Aus)	285
1912	Edward (Ted) Ray	295	1966	Jack Nicklaus (US)	282
1913	John H. Taylor	304	1967	Roberto de Vincenzo (Arg)	278
1914	Harry Vardon	306	1968	Gary Player (S Af)	299
1920	George Duncan	303	1969	Tony Jacklin	280
1921	Jock Hutchison (US)	296	1970	Jack Nicklaus (US)	283
1922	Walter Hagen (US)	300	1971	Lee Trevino (US)	278
1923	Arthur G. Havers	295	1972	Lee Trevino (US)	278
1924	Walter Hagen (US)	301	1973	Tom Weiskopf (US)	276
1925	James M. Barnes (US)	300	1974	Gary Player (S Af)	282
1926	Robert T. Jones, Jr. (US)	291	1975	Tom Watson (US)	279
1927	Robert T. Jones, Jr., (US)	285	1976	Johnny Miller (US)	279
1928	Walter Hagen (US)	292	1977	Tom Watson (US)	268
1929	Walter Hagen (US)	292	1978	Jack Nicklaus (US)	281
1930	Robert T. Jones, Jr. (US)	291	1979	Severiano Ballesteros (Spa)	283

U.S. Masters Championship

Played each year at the Augusta National Golf Course, Augusta, Georgia. Instituted in 1934. Stroke play over 72 holes. Winners (US except where shown):

Year	Winner	Score	Year	Winner	Score
1934	Horton Smith	284	1959	Art Wall	284
1935	Gene Sarazen	282	1960	Arnold Palmer	282
1936	Horton Smith	285	1961	Gary Player (S Af)	280
1937	Byron Nelson	283	1962	Arnold Palmer	280
1938	Henry Picard	285	1963	Jack Nicklaus	286
1939	Ralph Guldahl	279	1964	Arnold Palmer	276
1940	Jimmy Demaret	280	1965	Jack Nicklaus	271
1941	Craig Wood	280	1966	Jack Nicklaus	288
1942	Byron Nelson	280	1967	Gay Brewer	280
1946	Herman Keiser	282	1968	Bob Goalby	277
1947	Jimmy Demaret	281	1969	George Archer	281
1948	Claude Harmon	279	1970	Billy Casper	279
1949	Sam Snead	282	1971	Charles Coody	279
1950	Jimmy Demaret	283	1972	Jack Nicklaus	286
1951	Ben Hogan	280	1973	Tommy Aaron	283
1952	Sam Snead	286	1974	Gary Player (S Af)	278
1953	Ben Hogan	274	1975	Jack Nicklaus	276
1954	Sam Snead	289	1976	Ray Floyd	271
1955	Cary Middlecoff	279	1977	Tom Watson	276
1956	Jack Burke	289	1978	Gary Player (S Af)	277
1957	Doug Ford	283	1979	Fuzzy Zoeller	280
1958	Arnold Palmer	284			

U.S. Open Championship

First held in 1894. Stroke play over 27 holes. Winners (US except where shown):

Year	Winner	Score	Year	Winner	Score
1895	Horace Rawling	173	1930	Robert T. Jones, Jr.	287
1896	James Foulis	152	1931	Billy Burke	292
1897	Joe Lloyd	162	1932	Gene Sarazen	286
1898	Fred Herd	328	1933	John Goodman	287
1899	Willie Smith	315	1934	Olin Dutra	293
1900	Harry Vardon (GB)	313	1935	Sam Parks, Jr.	299
1901	Willie Anderson	331	1936	Tony Manero	282
1902	Laurie Auchterlonie	307	1937	Ralph Guldahl	281
1903	Willie Anderson	307	1938	Ralph Guldahl	284
1904	Willie Anderson	303	1939	Byron Nelson	284
1905	Willie Anderson	314	1940	Lawson Little	287
1906	Alex Smith	295	1941	Craig Wood	284
1907	Alex Ross	302	1946	Lloyd Mangrum	284
1908	Fred McLeod	322	1947	Lew Worsnam	282
1909	George Sargent	290	1948	Ben Hogan	276
1910	Alex Smith	298	1949	Cary Middlecoff	286
1911	John McDermott	307	1950	Ben Hogan	287
1912	John McDermott	294	1951	Ben Hogan	287
1913	Francis Ouimet	304	1952	Julius Boros	281
1914	Walter Hagen	290	1953	Ben Hogan	283
1915	Jerome D. Travers	297	1954	Ed Furgol	284
1916	Charles Evans, Jr.	286	1955	Jack Fleck	287
1919	Walter Hagen	301	1956	Cary Middlecoff	281
1920	Edward Ray (GB)	295	1957	Dick Mayer	282
1921	Jim Barnes	289	1958	Tommy Bolt	283
1922	Gene Sarazen	288	1959	Billy Casper	282
1923	Robert T. Jones, Jr.	296	1960	Arnold Palmer	280
1924	Cyril Walker	297	1961	Gene Littler	281
1925	Willie Macfarlane	291	1962	Jack Nicklaus	283
1926	Robert T. Jones, Jr.	293	1963	Julius Boros	293
1927	Tommy Armour	301	1964	Ken Venturi	278
1928	Johnny Farrell	294	1965	Gary Player (S Af)	282
1929	Robert T. Jones, Jr.	294	1966	Billy Casper	278

SEASONED VETERANS: Arnold Palmer and Gary Player (left, Palmer in the white shirt) were two of the top golfers in the early 1960's. The immensely popular Palmer attracted many fans, known as "Arnie's Army," as he won titles in the British and US Opens, the Masters and many other tournaments. South African Gary Player has victories in 4 of the top tournaments (lacking only the US Amateur title to match Nicklaus), as well as a record 5 wins in the World Match Play Tournament. Byron Nelson (right) won a record 19 tournaments in one season (1945), including 11 in a row (also a record).

U.S. Open Championship (continued)

		Score			Score
1967	Jack Nicklaus	275	1974	Hale Irwin	287
1968	Lee Trevino	275	1975	Lou Graham	287
1969	Orville Moody	281	1976	Jerry Pate	277
1970	Tony Jacklin (GB)	281	1977	Hubert Green	278
1971	Lee Trevino	280	1978	Andy North	285
1972	Jack Nicklaus	290	1979	Hale Irwin	284
1973	Johnny Miller	279			

U.S. Professional Golfers' Association Championship

First played in 1916. From then until 1957 it was a knock-out match play tournament, but since 1958 has been decided over 36 holes of stroke play.

1916	James M. Barnes	1938	Paul Runyan	
1919	James M. Barnes	1939	Henry Picard	
1920	Jock Hutchinson	1940	Byron Nelson	
1921	Walter Hagen	1941	Vic Ghezzi	
1922	Gene Sarazen	1942	Sam Snead	
1923	Gene Sarazen	1944	Bob Hamilton	
1924	Walter Hagen	1945	Byron Nelson	
1925	Walter Hagen	1946	Ben Hogan	
1926	Walter Hagen	1947	Jim Ferrier	
1927	Walter Hagen	1948	Ben Hogan	
1928	Leo Diegel	1949	Sam Snead	
1929	Leo Diegel	1950	Chandler Harper	
1930	Tommy Armour	1951	Sam Snead	
1931	Tom Creavy	1952	Jim Turnesa	
1932	Olin Dutra	1953	Walter Burkemo	
1933	Gene Sarazen	1954	Chick Harbert	
1934	Paul Runyan	1955	Doug Ford	
1935	Johnny Revolta	1956	Jack Burke	
1936	Denny Shute	1957	Lionel Hebert	
1937	Denny Shute	1958	Dow Finsterwald	276

		Score				*Score*
1959	Bob Rosburg	277		1970	Dave Stockton	279
1960	Jay Hebert	281		1971	Jack Nicklaus	281
1961	Jerry Barber	277		1972	Gary Player (S Af)	281
1962	Gary Player (S Af)	278		1973	Jack Nicklaus	277
1963	Jack Nicklaus	279		1974	Lee Trevino	276
1964	Bob Nichols	271		1975	Jack Nicklaus	276
1965	Dave Marr	280		1976	Dave Stockton	281
1966	Al Geiberger	280		1977	Lanny Wadkinsz	282
1967	Don January	281		1978	John Mahaffey	276
1968	Julius Boros	281		1979	David Graham (Aus)	272
1969	Ray Floyd	276				

World Match Play Tournament

Sponsored by Piccadilly from 1964 to 1976, and by Colgate from 1977.

1964	Arnold Palmer (US)		1972	Tom Weiskopf (US)
1965	Gary Player (S Af)		1973	Gary Player (S Af)
1966	Gary Player (S Af)		1974	Hale Irwin (US)
1967	Arnold Palmer (US)		1975	Hale Irwin (US)
1968	Gary Player (S Af)		1976	David Graham (Aus)
1969	Bob Charles (NZ)		1977	Graham Marsh (Aus)
1970	Jack Nicklaus (US)		1978	Isao Aoki (Jap)
1971	Gary Player (S Af)		1979	William Rogers (US)

U.S. Women's Open Championship

First held in 1946 as match play, but since 1947 has been at 72 holes stroke play. Winners since 1965 (all US except where stated):

1965	Carol Mann 290		1973	Sue Maxwell Berning 290
1966	Sandra Spuzich 277		1974	Sandra Haynie 295
1967	Catherine Lacoste (Fra) 294		1975	Sandra Palmer 295
1968	Sue Maxwell Berning 289		1976	Jo Anne Carner 292
1969	Donna Caponi 294		1977	Hollis Stacy 292
1970	Donna Caponi 287		1978	Hollis Stacy 289
1971	Jo Anne Carner 288		1979	Jerilyn Britz
1972	Sue Maxwell Berning 299			

PITCHING IN: Carol Mann (left), winner of the 1965 US Women's Open, shot 54 holes in 200 strokes to tie Ruth Jessen for the LPGA record in 1968. Betsy Rawls (right), whose 4 US Women's Open wins share a record, had her best year in 1959, when she won 10 tournaments and set what was then a record for women's yearly winnings with $27,000. She now serves as LPGA Tournament Director.

Colgate European Women's Open Championship

First held in 1974. 72 holes stroke play. Winners:

1974	Judy Rankin (US) 218 (54 holes)	1977	Judy Rankin (US) 281
1975	Donna Caponi Young (US) 283	1978	Nancy Lopez (US) 289
1976	Chako Higuchi (Jap) 284	1979	Nancy Lopez (US) 282

British Amateur Championship

First played in 1885, the Amateur Championship is a knock-out match play event. Winners since 1965:

1965	Michael Bonallack (GB)	1973	Dick Siderowf (US)
1966	Bobby Cole (S Af)	1974	Trevor Homer (US)
1967	Bob Dickson (US)	1975	Marvin Giles (US)
1968	Michael Bonallack (GB)	1976	Dick Siderowf (US)
1969	Michael Bonallack (GB)	1977	Peter McAvoy (GB)
1970	Michael Bonallack (GB)	1978	Peter McAvoy (GB)
1971	Steve Melnyk (US)	1979	Jay Sigel (US)
1972	Trevor Homer (GB)		

U.S. Amateur Championship

First played in 1893, a match play tournament over 36 holes per round. Winners since 1965:

1965	Bob Murphy	1973	Craig Stadler
1966	Gary Cowan	1974	Jerry Pate
1967	Bob Dickson	1975	Fred Ridley
1968	Bruce Fleisher	1976	Bill Sander
1969	Steve Melnyk	1977	John Fought
1970	Lanny Wadkins	1978	John Cook
1971	Gary Cowan	1979	Mark O'Meara
1972	Marvin Giles		(all the above from the US)

World Cup

Contested by 2-man national teams of professionals. Instituted in 1953 as the Canada Cup.

1953	Argentina	1960	US	1967	US	1974	South Africa
1954	Australia	1961	US	1968	Canada	1975	US
1955	US	1962	US	1969	US	1976	Spain
1956	US	1963	US	1970	Australia	1977	Spain
1957	Japan	1964	US	1971	US	1978	US
1958	Ireland	1965	South Africa	1972	Taiwan	1979	US
1959	Australia	1966	US	1973	US		

Eisenhower Trophy

Contested by 4-man amateur national teams. First held in 1958.

1958	Australia	1966	Australia	1974	US
1960	US	1968	US	1976	GB and Ireland
1962	US	1970	US	1978	US
1964	GB and Ireland	1972	US		

World Women's Amateur Team Championship

Contested every two years for the Espirito Santo Trophy.

1964	France	1968	US	1972	US	1976	US
1966	US	1970	US	1974	US	1978	Australia

GREYHOUND RACING

Earliest Meeting. In September, 1876, a greyhound meeting was staged at Hendon, North London, England, with a railed hare operated by a windlass. Modern greyhound racing originated with the perfecting of the mechanical hare by Owen P. Smith at Emeryville, California, in 1919.

Fastest Dog

The highest speed at which any greyhound has been timed is 41.72 m.p.h. (410 yards in 20.1 secs.) by *The Shoe* for a track record at Richmond, New South Wales, Australia, on April 25, 1968. It is estimated that he covered the last 100 yards in 4.5 seconds or at 45.45 m.p.h. The fastest *photo*-timing over 500 meters is 28.99 seconds or 38.58 m.p.h. by *Linacre* on July 30, 1977, at Brighton and Hove Stadium, Sussex, England. The fastest photo-timing over hurdles is 29.71 seconds (37.64 m.p.h.) by *Watchit Buster* on August 22, 1978, also at Brighton.

Winning Streak

An American greyhound, *Real Huntsman*, won a world record 28 consecutive victories in 1950–51.

TOP DOG: "Sherry's Prince" was a 3-time winner of England's Grand National, and formerly held the record for the fastest time over hurdles with 29.10 seconds (36.90 m.p.h.) over 525 yards in 1971.

GYMNASTICS

Earliest References. A primitive form of gymnastics was widely practiced in ancient Greece and Rome during the period of the ancient Olympic Games (776 B.C. to 393 A.D.), but Johann Friedrich Simon, was the first teacher of modern gymnastics, at Basedow's School, Dessau, Germany, in 1776.

World Championships

The greatest number of individual titles won by a man in the World Championships is 10 by Boris Shakhlin (USSR) between 1954 and 1964. He was also on three winning teams. The women's record is 10 individual wins and 5 team titles by Larissa Semyonovna Latynina (born December 27, 1934, retired 1966) of the USSR, between 1956 and 1964.

Japan has won the men's team title a record five times and the USSR has won the women's title on six occasions.

Olympic Games

Japan has won the most men's titles with 5 victories. The USSR has won 7 women's team titles.

The only man to win six individual gold medals is Boris Shakhlin (USSR), with one in 1956, four (two shared) in 1960 and one in 1964. He was also a member of the winning Combined Exercises team in 1956.

The most successful woman has been Vera Caslavska-Odlozil (Czechoslovakia), with seven individual gold medals: three in 1964 and four (one shared) in 1968. Larissa Latynina of the USSR won six individual and three team gold medals, five silver, and four bronze for an all-time record total of 18 Olympic medals.

Nadia Comaneci (b. 1961, Rumania) became the first gymnast

A PERFECT "10": Nadia Comaneci (Rumania) was 14 years old when she made Olympic history as the first gymnast ever to be awarded a perfect score. Her unprecedented feat came during the 1976 Olympics in Montreal. She went on to earn 6 more 10's for a remarkable total of 7 flawless routines (4 on uneven parallel bars and 3 on the balance beam). Russian gymnast Nelli Kim achieved 2 scores of 10 in the same competition, but her achievement was overshadowed by Comaneci. Nadia came home with 3 gold medals (combined exercises, uneven bars, and balance beam) and 1 bronze (floor exercises).

to be awarded a perfect score of 10.00 in the Olympic Games, in the 1976 Montreal Olympics. She ended the competition with a total of seven such marks (four on the uneven parallel bars, three on the balance beam). Nelli Kim (USSR) (b. July 29, 1957) was also awarded two perfect scores during the same competition.

Youngest International Competitor

Anita Jokiel (Poland) was aged 11 years 2 days when she competed at Brighton, East Sussex, England, on December 6, 1977.

World Cup

In the first World Cup Competition in London in 1975, Ludmilla Tourisheva (now Mrs. Valery Borzov) (born October 7, 1952) of the USSR won all five available gold medals.

Chinning the Bar

The record for 2-arm chins from a dead hang position is 120 by Lee Chin-yong (b. August 15, 1925) at the YMCA Gym Hall, Seoul, Korea, on March 1, 1979. William Aaron Vaught (b. 1959) did 20 one-arm chin-ups at Finch's Gymnasium, Houston, Texas, on January 3, 1976. It is believed that only one person in 100,000 can chin a bar one-handed.

Francis Lewis (born 1896) of Beatrice, Nebraska, in May 1914, achieved 7 consecutive chins using only the middle finger of his left hand. His bodyweight was 158 lbs.

Rope Climbing

The US Amateur Athletic Union records are tantamount to world records: 20 feet (hands alone) 2.8 secs., Don Perry, at Champaign, Illinois, on April 3, 1954; 25 feet (hands alone), 4.7 secs., Garvin S. Smith at Los Angeles, on April 19, 1947.

Parallel Bar Dips

Peter Herbert (aged 33) performed a record 294 consecutive dips on July 11, 1979, at Haverfordwest Sports Centre, Dyfed, Wales. Jack LaLanne is reported to have done, 1,000 in Oakland, California, in 1945.

Push-Ups

Tommy Gildert did 9,105 consecutive push-ups at the Burnley Boys Club, Lancashire, England, on July 1, 1979. On the same day he also performed 269 one-arm push-ups in 10 minutes.

Noel Barry Mason of Burton-on-Trent, England, did 1,845 push-ups, the most in 30 minutes, on November 16, 1979. Noel Barry Mason of Burton-on-Trent, England did 267 fingertip push-ups in 1 minute 50 seconds on June 10, 1979. Robert Goldman of Arverne, New York, did 80 consecutive handstand push-ups in 43 seconds on August 31, 1978, at the Brickman Hotel in New York.

JUMP STEADY: Ashrita Furman (left) performed 27,000 jumping jacks in 6 hours 45 minutes 26 seconds (jumping for 95 per cent of the time) for a world record. Sixty-two students from Air Academy High School, Colorado, skipped a single long rope (below) for 11 turns to set the record for most children jumping a single rope.

Sit-Ups

The greatest recorded number of consecutive sit-ups on a hard surface without feet pinned or knees bent is 26,000 in 11 hours 44 minutes by Angel Bustamonte (b. February, 28, 1959) in Sacramento, California, on December 17, 1977. On November 7, 1979, Darryl Hyek recorded 141 sit-ups at the Golden Triangle Health Spa, Tarentum, Pennsylvania, in 2 minutes under the same conditions.

Jumping Jacks

The greatest number of side-straddle hops is 27,000, performed in 6 hours 45 minutes 26 seconds (jumping for 95 per cent of the time) by Ashrita Furman (b. September 16, 1954) at the Jack LaLanne Health Spa, New York, on August 14, 1979.

Vertical Jump

The greatest height reached in a vertical jump (the difference between standing and jumping fingertip reach against a wall) is 42 inches by David Thompson (6 feet 4 inches) of North Carolina in 1972. Higher jumps reported by athletes Franklin Jacobs (US) and Greg Joy (Canada) were probably made with an initial run.

LEAPING LADY: Mary Peters (GB) reportedly set a women's vertical jump record by leaping 30 inches in California in 1972. She is here wearing the gold medal she received for another outstanding feat— winning the 1972 Olympic Pentathlon with a record 4,801 points.

Olympic Pentathlon champion Mary E. Peters (GB) reportedly jumped 30 inches in California in 1972.

For a TV show, Shannon Faucher, a 23-year-old college student from Los Angeles, jumped from a flat standing position to a standing position on top of a refrigerator 55″ high to set a jumping stunt record.

Somersaults

James Chelich (b. Fairview, Alberta, Canada, March 12, 1957) performed 8,450 forward rolls in 8.3 miles on September 21, 1974.

Ian Michael Miles (born July 6, 1960) of Corsham, Wiltshire, England, made a successful diving front somersault with a tuck over 33 men at Harrogate, North Yorkshire, on July 27, 1977.

Four-time (1951–54) AAU tumbling champion Dick Browning of the University of Illinois (b. Indiana, May 10, 1933) set a high jumping somersault mark when he cleared a bar set at 7 feet 6 inches at Santa Barbara, California, in April, 1954. He is the younger brother of the 1952 Olympic diving champion.

Rope Jumping

The longest recorded non-stop rope-jumping marathon was one of 6 hours 15 minutes 12 seconds by Katsumi Suzuki of Saitama, Japan, on October 3, 1979.

Other rope-jumping records made without a break:

Most turns in one jump	5	Katsumi Suzuki	Saitama, Japan	May 29, 1975
Most turns in 1 minute	290	Brian D. Christensen	East Ridge, Tenn.	May 30, 1978
Most turns in 10 seconds	108	A. Rayner	Wakefield, Eng.	June 28, 1978
Most doubles (with cross)	386	K. A. Brooks	Queensland, Australia	Dec. 23, 1978
Double turns	6,851	Katsumi Suzuki (Japan)	Tokyo	July 4, 1976
Treble turns	381	Katsumi Suzuki (Japan)	Saitama	May 29, 1975
Quadruple turns	51	Katsumi Suzuki (Japan)	Saitama	May 29, 1975
Duration	1,264 miles	Tom Morris (Aust)	Brisbane-Cairns	1963
Most children single rope (11 turns)	62	from Air Academy High School	Colorado Springs, Colorado	Jan. 31, 1979

ROUTINE WINS: Japan's Akinori Nakayama (left) won 2 gold medals in the 1968 Olympics (for the rings and the parallel bars) and won another gold medal (on the rings, shown here) in Munich in 1972. He was a member of the gold medal Japanese team at both Games. Boris Shakhlin (right) is the top male gold medal winner with 6 individual gold medals and 1 team gold. Shakhlin (USSR) has the most wins in World Championship competition with 10 individual and 3 team titles.

Largest Gymnasium

The world's largest gymnasium is Yale University's Payne Whitney Gymnasium at New Haven, Connecticut, completed in 1932 and valued at $18,000,000. The building, known as the "Cathedral of Muscle," has nine stories with wings of five stories each. It is equipped with 4 basketball courts, 3 rowing tanks, 28 squash courts, 12 handball courts, a roof jogging track and a 25-yard by 14-yard swimming pool on the first floor and a 55-yard-long pool on the third floor.

Largest Crowd

The largest recorded crowd was some 18,000 people who packed the Forum, Montreal, Canada for the finals of the women's individual apparatus competitions at the XXI Olympic Games on July 22, 1976.

Comparable audiences are reported at the Shanghai Stadium, People's Republic of China.

Olympic Games

First held in the Olympics in 1896; since the 1948 Games the events have been: Men: Floor Exercises, Side Horse, Rings, Horse Vault, Parallel Bars, Horizontal Bar. Women: Horse Vault, Uneven Parallel Bars, Balance Beam, Floor Exercises. Competitors compete for medals in both these events and the Combined Exercises for which points in individual events are totalled. Winners of the Combined Exercises (Team and Individual) since 1948:

RED STARS: Russian Lyudmila Tourischeva won 4 gold medals in 3 games (1972 Combined Exercises and 3 team medals), as well as 3 silvers and 2 bronze from 1968 to 1976. Larissa Latynina (right), also Russian, has won an all-time record 18 Olympic medals, including 6 individual and 3 team golds. She also has the most world titles with 10 individual and 5 team wins in the World Championships.

MEN

	Team	Individual	Most Individual Gold Medals	
1948	Finland	Veikko Huhtanen (Fin)	2	Veikko Huhtanen and Paavo Aaltonen (Fin)
1952	USSR	Viktor Chukarin (USSR)	3	Viktor Chukarin
1956	USSR	Viktor Chukarin (USSR)	2	Viktor Chukarin and Valentin Muratov (USSR)
1960	Japan	Boris Shakhlin (USSR)	4	Boris Shakhlin
1964	Japan	Yukio Endo (Jap)	2	Yukio Endo
1968	Japan	Sawao Kato (Jap)	2	Kato, Akinori Nakayama (Jap), and Mikhail Voronin (USSR)
1972	Japan	Sawao Kato (Jap)	2	Sawao Kato (Jap)
1976	Japan	Nikolai Andrianov (USSR)	4	Nikolai Andrianov (USSR)
1980	USSR	Alexandr Dityatin (USSR)	2	Alexander Dityatin (USSR)

WOMEN

	Team	Individual	Most Individual Gold Medals	
1948	Czecho-slovakia	(Only a team competition)		
1952	USSR	Maria Gorokhovskaya (USSR)	1	by several women
1956	USSR	Larissa Latynina (USSR)	3	Latynina and Agnes Keleti (Hun)
1960	USSR	Larissa Latynina (USSR)	2	Larissa Latynina
1964	USSR	Vera Caslavska (Cze)	3	Vera Caslavska
1968	USSR	Vera Caslavska (Cze)	4	Vera Caslavska
1972	USSR	Lyudmila Tourischeva (USSR)	2	Olga Korbut (USSR) and Karin Janz (E Ger)
1976	USSR	Nadia Comaneci (Rum)	3	Nadia Comaneci (Rum)
1980	USSR	Yelena Davydova (USSR)	2	Nadia Comaneci (Rum)

World Championships

Combined Exercises World Champions since 1950:

MEN

	Team	Individual	Most Individual Gold Medals	
1950	Switzerland	Walter Lehmann (Swi)	2	Lehmann and Josef Stalder (Swi)
1954	USSR	Valentin Muratov (USSR) and Viktor Chukharin (USSR)	3	Valentin Muratov (USSR)
1958	USSR	Boris Shakhlin (USSR)	4	Boris Shakhlin (USSR)
1962	Japan	Yuriy Titov (USSR)	2	Titov and Miroslav Cerar (Yug)
1966	Japan	Mikhail Voronin (USSR)	2	Mikhail Voronin (USSR)
1970	Japan	Elizo Kenmotsu (Jap)	3	Akinori Nakayama (Jap)
1974	Japan	Shigeru Kasamatsu (Jap)	3	Shigeru Kasamatsu (Jap)
1978	Japan	Nikolai Andrianov (USSR)	2	Nikolai Andrianov (USSR)

WOMEN

	Team	Individual	Most Individual Gold Medals	
1950	Sweden	Helena Rakoczy (Pol)	4	Helena Rakoczy (Pol)
1954	USSR	Galina Roudiko (USSR)	2	Tamara Minina (USSR)
1958	USSR	Larissa Latynina (USSR)	4	Larissa Latynina (USSR)
1962	USSR	Larissa Latynina (USSR)	2	Larissa Latynina (USSR)
1966	Czechoslovakia	Vera Caslavska (Cze)	3	Natalia Kuchinskaya (USSR)
1970	USSR	Lyudmila Tourischeva (USSR)	2	Tourischeva and Erika Zuchold (E Ger)
1974	USSR	Lyudmila Tourischeva (USSR)	3	Tourischeva
1978	USSR	Elena Mukhina (USSR)	2	Nelli Kim (USSR)

N.C.A.A. Champions

1938	Chicago	1942	Illinois	1951	Florida State
1939	Illinois	1948	Penn State	1952	Florida State
1940	Illinois	1949	Temple	1953	Penn State
1941	Illinois	1950	Illinois	1954	Penn State

COLD FEAT: Shannon Faucher jumped from a flat standing position to a standing position on top of a refrigerator 55 inches high on the "Guinness Game" TV show in 1979.

1955	Illinois	1963	Michigan	1972	Southern Illinois
1956	Illinois	1964	Southern Illinois	1973	Iowa State
1957	Penn State	1965	Penn State	1974	Iowa State
1958	Michigan State	1966	Southern Illinois	1975	California
	Illinois	1967	Southern Illinois	1976	Penn State
1959	Penn State	1968	California	1977	Indiana State
1960	Penn State	1969	Iowa		Oklahoma
1961	Penn State	1970	Michigan	1978	Oklahoma
1962	Southern Cal	1971	Iowa State	1979	Nebraska

A.I.A.W.

1969	Springfield	1973	Massachusetts	1977	Clarion State
1970	So. Illinois	1974	So. Illinois	1978	Penn State
1971	Springfield	1975	So. Illinois	1979	California State-
1972	Springfield	1976	Clarion State		Fullerton

HANDBALL (Court)

Origin. Handball is a game of ancient Celtic origin. In the early 19th century only a front wall was used, but later side and back walls were added. The court is now standardized 60 feet by 30 feet in Ireland, Ghana and Australia, and 40 feet by 20 feet in Canada, Mexico and the US. The game is played with both a hard and soft ball in Ireland, and a soft ball only elsewhere.

The earliest international contest was in New York City in 1887, between the champions of the US and Ireland.

Championship

World championships were inaugurated in New York in October, 1964, with competitors from Australia, Canada, Ireland, Mexico and the US. The US is the only nation to have won twice, with victories in 1964 and 1967 (shared).

HANDY MAN: Jim Jacobs has been the most successful player in the USHA National Four-Wall Championships with 6 singles and 6 doubles titles.

Most Titles

The most successful player in the U.S.H.A. National Four-Wall Championships has been James Jacobs (US), who won a record 6 singles titles (1955–56–57–60–64–65) and shared in 6 doubles titles (1960–62–63–65–67–68). Martin Decatur has won 8 doubles titles (1962–63–65–67–68–75–78–79), 5 of these with Jacobs as his partner.

U.S.H.A. National Champions

PROFESSIONAL SINGLES		FOUR-WALL DOUBLES	
1951	Walter Plekan	1951–52	Frank Coyle and Bill Baier
1952	Vic Hershkowitz	1953	Sam Haber and Harry Dreyfus
1953	Bob Brady	1954–56	Sam Haber and Ken Schneider
1954	Vic Hershkowitz	1957–59	Phil Collins and John Sloan
1955–57	Jim Jacobs	1960	Jim Jacobs and Dick Weisman
1958–59	John Sloan	1961	John Sloan and Vic Hershkowitz
1960	Jim Jacobs	1962–63	Jim Jacobs and Marty Decatur
1961	John Sloan	1964	John Sloan and Phil Elbert
1962–63	Oscar Obert	1965	Jim Jacobs and Marty Decatur
1964–65	Jim Jacobs	1966	Pete Tyson and Bob Lindsay
1966–67	Paul Haber	1967–68	Jim Jacobs and Marty Decatur
1968	Simon (Stuffy) Singer	1969	Lou Kramberg and Lou Russo
1969–71	Paul Haber	1970	Carl Obert and Ruby Obert
1972	Fred Lewis	1971	Ray Neveau and Simie Fein
1973	Terry Mack	1972	Kent Fusselman and Al Drews
1974–76	Fred Lewis	1973–74	Ray Neveau and Simie Fein
1977	Naty Alvarado	1975	Steve Lott and Marty Decatur
1978	Fred Lewis	1976	Dan O'Connor and Gary Rohrer
1979	Naty Alvarado	1977	Matt Kelley and Skip McDowell
		1978–79	Marty Decatur and Simon (Stuffy) Singer

HANDBALL (Field)

Origins. Field handball was first played *c.* 1895. The earliest international match was when Sweden beat Denmark on March 8, 1935. It was introduced into the Olympic Games at Berlin in 1936 as an 11-a-side outdoor game, but when reintroduced in 1972 it was an indoor game with a 7-a-side, which has been the standard team size since 1952. Field handball is played somewhat like soccer but with hands instead of feet.

By 1977 there were some 70 countries affiliated with the International Handball Federation, a World Cup competition, and an estimated 10,000,000 participants.

World Titles

The most victories in the world championship (instituted 1938) competition are by Rumania with four men's and three women's titles from 1956 to 1974.

Olympic and World Champions

First held in the Olympic Games in 1936, the sport for men was re-introduced in 1972, and is now held indoors.

OLYMPIC CHAMPIONS

Men
1936 Germany
1972 Yugoslavia
1976 USSR
1980 E. Germany

Women
1976 USSR
1980 USSR

WORLD CHAMPIONS

Men		Women			
Outdoor	*Indoor*	*Outdoor*		*Indoor*	
1938 Germany	1954 Sweden	1949 Hungary		1957 Czechoslovakia	
1948 Sweden	1958 Sweden	1956 Rumania		1962 Rumania	
1952 W. Germany	1961 Rumania	1960 Rumania		1965 Hungary	
1955 W. Germany	1964 Rumania			1971 E. Germany	
1959 W. Germany	1967 Czechoslovakia			1973 Yugoslavia	
1963 E. Germany	1970 Rumania				
1966 W. Germany	1974 Rumania				
	1978 W. Germany				

PLAYING THE FIELD: Shown here is the 1972 Czechoslovakian team disposing of the Soviet team on their way to the silver medal in the Olympic Games in Munich.

HARNESS RACING

Origins. Trotting races were held in Valkenburg, Netherlands, in 1554. In England the trotting gait (the simultaneous use of the diagonally opposite legs) was known in the 16th century. The sulky first appeared in harness racing in 1829. Pacers thrust out their fore and hind legs simultaneously on one side.

Highest Price

The highest price paid for a trotter is $3,200,000 for *Green Speed* by the Pine Hollow Stud of New York from Beverly Lloyds of Florida, in 1977. The highest for a pacer is $3,600,000 for *Nero* in March, 1976, and *Falcon Almahurst* in 1978.

Greatest Winnings

The greatest amount won by a trotting horse is $1,960,945 by *Bellino II* (France) to retirement in 1977. The record for a pacing horse is $1,360,887 by *Rambling Willie* (US) to the end of the 1978 season.

Most Successful Driver

The most successful sulky driver in North America has been Herve Filion (Canada) (b. Quebec, February 1, 1940) who reached

HOT TO TROT: Canadian Herve Filion (left), 10-time winner of the North American championship, has career winnings of $29,115,826 (for 7,079 wins) through 1979. He set season records in 1974 with 637 victories for $3,474,315. Bea Farber (right) won the first International Women's Driving Tournament (a 16-race competition) in 1978. In the same year, she became the first woman to make harness racing's Top Ten list in the major category (300 or more drives).

a record of 7,079 wins by January 1, 1980, after a record 637 victories and winnings of $3,474,315 in the 1974 season. He has won a record $29,115,826 in his career to January 1, 1980. Filion won the North American championship for the tenth time in 1978.

Record Against Time

		TROTTING	
World (mile track)	1:54.8	Nevele Pride (U.S.), Indianapolis, Ind.	Aug. 31, 1969
		PACING	
World (mile track)	1:52.0	Steady Star (Canada), Lexington, Ky.	Oct. 1, 1971
		RECORDS SET IN RACES	
Trotting	1:55.0	Speedy Somolli (U.S.) at Du Quoin, Ill.	Sept. 2, 1978
	1:55.0	Florida Pro (U.S.) at Du Quoin, Ill.	Sept. 2, 1978
Pacing	1:53.0	Abercrombie (U.S.) at Meadowlands, N.J.	Aug. 4, 1979

HOCKEY

Origins. There is pictorial evidence of a hockey-like game being played on ice in the Netherlands in the early 16th century. The game probably was first played in 1855 at Kingston, Ontario, Canada, but Halifax also lays claim to priority.

The International Ice Hockey Federation was founded in 1908. The National Hockey League was inaugurated in 1917. The World

ROCKET MAN: Maurice (Rocket) Richard of the Montreal Canadiens scores a goal against the Boston Bruins in the finals of the 1953 Stanley Cup competition, won by the Canadiens 4 games to 1. Rocket Richard's 82 Stanley Cup goals is an NHL record. His brother, Henri (Pocket Rocket) Richard, played in 11 finals as part of his record 180 playoff games.

Hockey Association was formed in 1971 and disbanded in 1979 when four of its teams joined the N.H.L.

Olympic Games

Canada has won the Olympic title six times and the world title 19 times, the last being at Geneva in 1961. The longest Olympic career is that of Richard Torriani (Switzerland) from 1928 to 1948. The most gold medals won by any player is three; this was achieved by four USSR players in the 1964–68–72 Games—Vitaliy Davidov, Aleksandr Ragulin, Anatoliy Firssov and Viktor Kuzkin.

Stanley Cup

This cup, presented by the Governor-General Lord Stanley (original cost $48.67), became emblematic of world professional team supremacy 33 years after the first contest at Montreal in 1893. It has been won most often by the Montreal Canadiens, with 22 wins. Henri Richard played in his eleventh finals in 1973.

Longest Match

The longest match was 2 hours 56 minutes 30 seconds (playing time) when the Detroit Red Wings eventually beat the Montreal Maroons 1–0 in the 17th minute of the sixth period of overtime at the Forum, Montreal, at 2:25 a.m. on March 25, 1936, 5 hours 51 minutes after the opening faceoff.

Longest Career

Gordie Howe (b. March 31, 1928, Floral, Saskatchewan, Canada) skated a record 25 years for the Detroit Red Wings from 1946–47 through the 1970–71 season, playing in a record total of 1,687 N.H.L. games. During that time he also set records for most career goals, assists, and scoring points; was selected as an all-star a record 21 times; and collected 500 stitches in his face.

KNOWS THE SCORE: Gordie Howe's professional hockey career has spanned parts of 5 decades. The 22-time NHL all-star is the only man to net 800 goals in that league's regular season play, and his professional goal total is over 1,000. His additional career records include most seasons, most games, most assists, and most scoring points.

After leaving the Red Wings, he ended a two-year retirement to skate with his two sons as teammates and played for 6 more seasons with the Houston Aeros and the New England Whalers of the World Hockey Association, participating in 419 games.

With the incorporation of the (now Hartford) Whalers into the N.H.L. for the 1979–80 season, Gordie Howe is in his 26th year in that league, and the remarkable 52-year-old grandfather was again selected as an N.H.L. all-star. Howe is the first team athlete in modern North American professional sports to have a career that spanned parts of five decades.

Most Consecutive Games

Garry Unger, playing for Toronto, Detroit, St. Louis, and Atlanta, skated in 914 consecutive N.H.L. games without a miss during 13 seasons from February 24, 1968, through December 21, 1979, when a torn shoulder muscle kept him on the bench.

The most consecutive complete games by a goaltender is 502, set by Glenn Hall (Detroit, Chicago), beginning in 1955 and ending when he suffered a back injury in a game against Boston on November 7, 1962.

Longest Season

The only man ever to play 82 games in a 78-game season is Ross Lonsberry. He began the 1971–72 season with the Los Angeles Kings where he played 50 games. Then, in January, he was traded to the Philadelphia Flyers (who had played only 46 games at the time) where he finished out the season (32 more games).

Dennis Owchar (with Pittsburgh and Colorado) and Jerry Butler (with St. Louis and Toronto) played 82 games in an 80-game season in 1977–78.

Most Wins and Losses

The Montreal Canadiens had the winningest season in N.H.L. history in 1976–77. They ended the regular 80-game season with a record 132 points earned, with an all-time record of 60 victories and 12 ties against only 8 losses.

The Washington Capitols set the record for seasonal losses with 67 in their maiden season in the league (1974–75). They won only 8 games.

Longest Winning Streak. In the 1929–30 season, the Boston Bruins won 14 straight games. The longest a team has ever gone without a defeat is 35 games, set by the Philadelphia Flyers with 25 wins and ties from October 14, 1979, to January 6, 1980. The Flyers outscored their opponents 153 goals to 98 during the record unbeaten streak which was ended by the Minnesota North Stars on January 7, 1980.

Longest Losing Streak. The Washington Capitols went from February 18 to March 26, 1975, without gaining a point—a total of 17 straight defeats. The longest time a team has gone without a win was when the Kansas City Scouts played 27 games before scoring a victory. Starting February 12, 1976, they lost 21 games and tied 6 games before ending the drought on April 4, 1976.

Team Scoring

Most Goals. The greatest number of goals recorded in a World Championship match has been 47–0 when Canada beat Denmark on February 12, 1949.

The Boston Bruins set all-time records for goal production in the 1970–71 season with a total of 399. Added to a record 697 assists they tallied a record total of 1,096 points. One line alone (Esposito, Hodge, Cashman) accounted for 336 points—a record itself.

Guy Lafleur, Steve Shutt, and Jacques Lemaire of the Montreal Canadiens produced a total of 150 goals in the 1976–77 season—a record for a single line.

The N.H.L. record for both teams is 21 goals, scored when the Montreal Canadiens beat the Toronto St. Patricks at Montreal 14–7 on January 10, 1920. The most goals ever scored by one team in a single game was set by the Canadiens when they defeated the Quebec Bulldogs on March 3, 1920 by a score of 16–3.

The Detroit Red Wings scored 15 consecutive goals without an answering tally when they defeated the New York Rangers 15–0 on January 23, 1944.

Fastest Scoring. Toronto scored 8 goals against the New York Americans in 4 minutes 52 seconds on March 19, 1938.

The fastest goals that have ever been scored from the opening whistle both came at 6 seconds of the first period: by Henry

GOAL ORIENTED: Guy Lafleur (left, in white), star right wing of the Montreal Canadiens, has scored 50 or more goals for a record 6 consecutive seasons, and his 100 or more points in all of those seasons ties him with Bobby Orr for the NHL mark. Phil Esposito (right), now with the NY Rangers, scored an incredible 76 regular-season goals with Boston in 1970–71. With 76 assists that same season, he also set a record for points with 152. Espo's 32 career hat-tricks are also tops.

HIGH FLYER: Reggie Leach (Philadelphia Flyers) scored a total of 80 goals during the regular season and Stanley Cup playoffs in 1975–76. His scoring helped Philadelphia to their second straight Cup victory, and they are the only NHL modern-era "expansion team" to win the coveted prize. Leach also contributed to Philadelphia's record 35-game unbeaten streak in 1979–80.

Boucha of the Detroit Red Wings on January 28, 1973, against Montreal; and by Jean Pronovost of the Pittsburgh Penguins on March 25, 1976, against St. Louis. Claude Provost of the Canadiens scored a goal against Boston after 4 seconds of the opening of the second period on November 9, 1957.

Kim D. Miles scored a goal after only 3 seconds of play for the University of Guelph, playing the University of Western Ontario on February 11, 1975.

The fastest scoring record is held by Bill Mosienko (Chicago) who scored 3 goals in 21 seconds against the New York Rangers on March 23, 1952.

Gus Bodnar (Toronto Maple Leafs) scored a goal against the New York Rangers at 15 seconds of the first period of *his first N.H.L. game* on October 30, 1943. Later in his career, while with Chicago, Bodnar again entered the record book when he assisted on all 3 of Bill Mosienko's quick goals.

Individual Scoring

Most Goals and Points. The career record in the N.H.L. for goals is 800 (after 74 games of the 1979–80 season) by Gordie Howe of the Detroit Red Wings and Hartford Whalers. Howe has scored 1,848 points in his N.H.L. career, with 1,048 assists (also through 74 games of the 1979–80 season). With 67 goals, 91 assists, and 158 points in Stanley Cup competition; and 202 goals, 377 assists, and 579 points in W.H.A. season and playoff games, Howe's unequaled professional career scoring totals are 1,069 goals, 1,516 assists, and 2,585 points.

GETTING THE POINT: Swedish-born Anders Hedberg (left) scored 83 goals for the WHA's Winnipeg Jets in the 1976–77 season (including playoffs). The speedy, graceful skater is now with the NY Rangers in the NHL. Bobby Orr (right) scored more goals and had more points than any defenseman in NHL history. His 102 assists (1.31 per game) in 1970–71 are unequaled in all NHL play. Orr won more individual awards than any other player in a spectacular career cut short by knee injuries.

Reggie Leach (Philadelphia Flyers) scored a total of 80 goals in the 1975–76 season including the playoffs.

Phil Esposito (Boston Bruins) scored 76 goals on a record 550 shots in the 1970–71 regular season. Esposito also holds the record for most points in a season at 152 (76 goals, 76 assists), set in the same season.

Guy Lafleur (b. September 20, 1951), of the Montreal Canadiens, has had both 50 or more goals and 100 points for six consecutive seasons from 1974–75 through 1979–80.

Phil Esposito has also scored 100 or more points in 6 different seasons, and 50 or more goals in 5 consecutive years. Bobby Orr had 6 consecutive 100-or-more-point seasons from 1969–70 to 1974–75. Bobby Hull (Chicago) had five 50-or-more-goal years when he left the N.H.L., and is the only player besides Gordie Howe to collect over 1,000 goals, with 1,012 in N.H.L., Stanley Cup, and W.H.A. play through 1979.

Anders Hedberg (born in Sweden, February 24, 1951) set a W.H.A. mark, scoring 83 goals for the Winnipeg Jets in 1976–77.

Marc Tardif (b. June 12, 1949) set a W.H.A. record for most points in a season with 169 (71 goals and 98 assists) for the Quebec Nordiques in 1977–78.

The most goals ever scored in one game is 7 by Joe Malone of the Quebec Bulldogs against the Toronto St. Patricks on January 31, 1920. Four different men have scored 4 goals in one period—Harvey Jackson (Toronto), Max Bentley (Chicago), Clint Smith (Chicago), and Red Berenson (St. Louis).

The most points scored in one N.H.L. game is 10, a record set by Darryl Sittler of the Toronto Maple Leafs, on February 7, 1976, against the Boston Bruins. He had 6 goals and 4 assists.

Jim Harrison, playing for Alberta, set a W.H.A. record for points with 10 (3 goals, 7 assists) against Toronto on January 30, 1973.

In 1921–22, Harry (Punch) Broadbent of the Ottawa Senators scored 25 goals in 16 consecutive games to set an all-time "consecutive game goal-scoring streak" record.

Most Assists. Bobby Orr of Boston assisted on 102 goals in the 1970–71 season for a record. His average of 13.1 assists per game is also a league record.

The most assists recorded in one game is 7 by Billy Taylor of Detroit on March 16, 1947 against Chicago. Detroit won 10–6. Wayne Gretzky also had 7 assists in one game for Edmonton vs. Washington, February 15, 1980.

Most 3-Goal Games. In his 18-year N.H.L. career, Phil Esposito of Chicago, Boston and the New York Rangers has scored 3 or more goals in 32 games. Five of these were 4-goal efforts. The term "hat-trick" properly applies when 3 goals are scored consecutively by one player in a game without interruption by either an answering score by the other team or a goal by any other player on his own team. In general usage, a "hat-trick" is any 3-goal effort by a player in one game.

Goaltending

The longest any goalie has gone without a defeat is 33 games, a record set by Gerry Cheevers of Boston in 1971-72. The longest a goalie has ever kept successive opponents scoreless is 461 minutes 29 seconds by Alex Connell of the Ottawa Senators in 1927–28. He registered 6 consecutive shutouts in this time.

The most shutouts ever recorded in one season is 22 by George

THE PUCK STOPS HERE: Boston Bruins goaltender Gerry Cheevers (left) was unbeaten in 33 games during the 1971–72 season. Whenever a puck strikes Cheevers' mask, he draws stichmarks to remind himself of the mask's protective value. Terry Sawchuk (right) registered a record 103 career shutouts while appearing in a record 971 games during his 20 NHL seasons.

Hainsworth of Montreal in 1928–29 (this is also a team record). This feat is even more remarkable considering that the season was only 44 games long at that time, compared to the 80-game season currently used.

Terry Sawchuk registered a record 103 career shutouts in his 20 seasons in the N.H.L. He played for Detroit, Boston, Toronto, Los Angeles, and the New York Rangers during that time. He also appeared in a record 971 games.

The only goaltender to score a goal in an N.H.L. game is Bill Smith (New York Islanders), against the Colorado Rockies in Denver, November 28, 1979. After the Rockies had removed their goaltender in favor of an extra skater during a delayed penalty, a Colorado defenseman's errant centering pass skidded nearly 200 feet down the ice into his own untended goal. Goalie Smith was the last Islander to touch the puck and was credited with the goal even though he did not take the "shot."

Most Penalties

The most any team has been penalized in one season is the 1,980 minutes assessed against the Philadelphia Flyers in 1975–76.

The Los Angeles Kings and the Philadelphia Flyers set N.H.L. records for penalties (54) and penalty minutes (380) in a game on March 11, 1979. The Flyers were assessed 194 minutes in penalty time, a record for one team in a single game. Ten players, five from each team, were ejected from the game, including Randy Holt of the Kings, who accumulated 57 minutes in penalties, also a league record.

Bryan Watson (Montreal, Detroit, California, Pittsburgh, St. Louis and Washington) amassed a record total of 2,212 penalty minutes in 858 games over 16 seasons.

Dave Schultz of Philadelphia was called for a record 472 minutes in the 1974–75 season. Schultz averaged a record 346 minutes per year in penalties from 1972–73, through 1975–76 (1,386 minutes total).

Jim Dorey of the Toronto Maple Leafs set an all-time record in Toronto on October 16, 1968, in a game against the Pittsburgh Penguins. He was whistled down for a total of 9 penalties in the game, 7 of which came in the second period (also a record). The 4 minor penalties, 2 major penalties, 2 10-minute misconducts, and 1 game misconduct added up to a total of 48 minutes for one game.

Penalty Shots

Armand Mondou of the Montreal Canadiens was the first player in the N.H.L. to attempt a penalty shot on November 10, 1934. He did not score. Since then, about 40 per cent of those awarded have resulted in goals. The most penalty shots called in a single season was 29 in 1934–35.

Fastest Player

The highest speed measured for any player is 29.7 m.p.h. for Bobby Hull (Chicago Black Hawks) (b. January 3, 1939). The highest puck speed is also attributed to Hull, whose left-handed slap shot has been measured at 118.3 m.p.h.

Stanley Cup Winners

The first Stanley Cup competition was 1893, for the amateur hockey championship of Canada. In 1910, the National Hockey Association took possession of the cup, and the trophy has represented the professional hockey championship ever since. Beginning in 1926, the cup has been competed for by N.H.L. teams only, and has been under the exclusive control of the league since 1946.

SEASON	CHAMPIONS	SEASON	CHAMPIONS
1892–93	Montreal A.A.A.	1917–18	Toronto Arenas
1893–94	Montreal A.A.A.	1918–19	No decision.
1894–95	Montreal Victorias	1919–20	Ottawa Senators
1895–96	Winnipeg Victorias (February)	1920–21	Ottawa Senators
1895–96	Montreal Victorias (December, 1896)	1921–22	Toronto St. Pats
		1922–23	Ottawa Senators
1896–97	Montreal Victorias	1923–24	Montreal Canadiens
1897–98	Montreal Victorias	1924–25	Victoria Cougars
1898–99	Montreal Shamrocks	1925–26	Montreal Maroons
1899–1900	Montreal Shamrocks	1926–27	Ottawa Senators
1900–01	Winnipeg Victorias	1927–28	New York Rangers
1901–02	Montreal A.A.A.	1928–29	Boston Bruins
1902–03	Ottawa Silver Seven	1929–30	Montreal Canadiens
1903–04	Ottawa Silver Seven	1930–31	Montreal Canadiens
1904–05	Ottawa Silver Seven	1931–32	Toronto Maple Leafs
1905–06	Montreal Wanderers	1932–33	New York Rangers
1906–07	Kenora Thistles (January)	1933–34	Chicago Black Hawks
1906–07	Montreal Wanderers (March)	1934–35	Montreal Maroons
1907–08	Montreal Wanderers	1935–36	Detroit Red Wings
1908–09	Ottawa Senators	1936–37	Detroit Red Wings
1909–10	Montreal Wanderers	1937–38	Chicago Black Hawks
1910–11	Ottawa Senators	1938–39	Boston Bruins
1911–12	Quebec Bulldogs	1939–40	New York Rangers
1912–13	Quebec Bulldogs	1940–41	Boston Bruins
1913–14	Toronto Blueshirts	1941–42	Toronto Maple Leafs
1914–15	Vancouver Millionaires	1942–43	Detroit Red Wings
1915–16	Montreal Canadiens	1943–44	Montreal Canadiens
1916–17	Seattle Metropolitans	1944–45	Toronto Maple Leafs

NET RESULTS: Goaltender Ken Dryden typifies the high standard of excellence that brought the Montreal Canadiens 22 Stanley Cup championships. Dryden played on 6 Cup-winning teams. He is here lunging for a save against the Chicago Black Hawks in March, 1973.

SEASON	CHAMPIONS	SEASON	CHAMPIONS
1945–46	Montreal Canadiens	1962–63	Toronto Maple Leafs
1946–47	Toronto Maple Leafs	1963–64	Toronto Maple Leafs
1947–48	Toronto Maple Leafs	1964–65	Montreal Canadiens
1948–49	Toronto Maple Leafs	1965–66	Montreal Canadiens
1949–50	Detroit Red Wings	1966–67	Toronto Maple Leafs
1950–51	Toronto Maple Leafs	1967–68	Montreal Canadiens
1951–52	Detroit Red Wings	1968–69	Montreal Canadiens
1952–53	Montreal Canadiens	1969–70	Boston Bruins
1953–54	Detroit Red Wings	1970–71	Montreal Canadiens
1954–55	Detroit Red Wings	1971–72	Boston Bruins
1955–56	Montreal Canadiens	1972–73	Montreal Canadiens
1956–57	Montreal Canadiens	1973–74	Philadelphia Flyers
1957–58	Montreal Canadiens	1974–75	Philadelphia Flyers
1958–59	Montreal Canadiens	1975–76	Montreal Canadiens
1959–60	Montreal Canadiens	1976–77	Montreal Canadiens
1960–61	Chicago Black Hawks	1977–78	Montreal Canadiens
1961–62	Toronto Maple Leafs	1978–79	Montreal Canadiens

World Championship

First held in conjunction with the Olympics, and amateur only until 1976, but now held annually. Winners since 1965:

1965	USSR	1970	USSR	1975	USSR
1966	USSR	1971	USSR	1976	Czechoslovakia
1967	USSR	1972	Czechoslovakia	1977	Czechoslovakia
1968	USSR	1973	USSR	1978	USSR
1969	USSR	1974	USSR	1979	USSR

Most wins: Canada 19, USSR 15

GOLD RUSH: American hockey players wildly celebrate their 4–3 upset victory over the Soviet Union in the semi-finals of the 1980 Winter Olympics in Lake Placid, New York. The US Team went on to beat Finland 4–2 in the final round to capture the gold medal.

Olympic Champions

First held 1920.

1920	Canada	1936	Great Britain	1960	US	1976	USSR
1924	Canada	1948	Canada	1964	USSR	1980	US
1928	Canada	1952	Canada	1968	USSR		
1932	Canada	1956	USSR	1972	USSR		

N.C.A.A. Champions

1948	Michigan	1959	North Dakota	1970	Cornell
1949	Boston College	1960	Denver	1971	Boston Univ.
1950	Colorado College	1961	Denver	1972	Boston Univ.
1951	Michigan	1962	Michigan Tech	1973	Wisconsin
1952	Michigan	1963	North Dakota	1974	Minnesota
1953	Michigan	1964	Michigan	1975	Michigan Tech
1954	RPI	1965	Michigan Tech	1976	Minnesota
1955	Michigan	1966	Michigan State	1977	Wisconsin
1956	Michigan	1967	Cornell	1978	Boston Univ.
1957	Colorado College	1968	Denver	1979	Minnesota
1958	Denver	1969	Denver		

HORSE RACING

Origins. Horsemanship was an important part of the Hittite
culture of Anatolia, Turkey, dating from about 1400 B.C. The
33rd ancient Olympic Games of 648 B.C. featured horse racing. The
earliest horse race recorded in England was one held in *c.* 210 A.D.
at Netherby, Yorkshire, among Arabians brought to Britain by
Lucius Septimius Severus (146–211 A.D.), Emperor of Rome. The
oldest race still being run annually is the Lanark Silver Bell,
instituted in Scotland by William the Lion (1143–1214). Organized horse racing began in New York State at least as early as
March, 1668.

The original Charleston Jockey Club, Virginia, was the first in
the world, organized in 1734. Racing colors (silks) became compulsory in 1889.

Racecourses

The world's largest racecourse is the Newmarket course in
England (founded 1636), on which the Beacon Course, the longest
of the 19 courses, is 4 miles 397 yards long and the Rowley Mile is
167 feet wide. The border between Suffolk and Cambridgeshire
runs through the Newmarket course. The world's largest racecourse grandstand was opened in 1968 at Belmont Park, Long
Island, N.Y., at a cost of $30,700,000. It is 110 feet tall, 440 yards
long and contains 908 mutuel windows. The greatest seating capacity at any racetrack is 40,000 at the Atlantic City Audit, New
Jersey. The world's smallest is the Lebong racecourse, Darjeeling,
West Bengal, India (altitude 7,000 feet), where the complete lap is
481 yards. It was laid out *c.* 1885 and used as a parade ground.

Longest Race

The longest recorded horse race was one of 1,200 miles in
Portugal, won by *Emir*, a horse bred from Egyptian-bred Blunt

Arab stock. The holder of the world's record for long distance racing and speed is *Champion Crabbet,* who covered 300 miles in 52 hours 33 minutes, carrying 245 lbs., in 1920.

In 1831, Squire George Osbaldeston (1787–1866), M.P. of East Retford, England, covered 200 miles in 8 hours 42 minutes at Newmarket, using 50 mounts, so averaging 22.99 m.p.h.

Most Entrants

The most horses entered in a single race was 66, in the Grand National Steeplechase of March 22, 1929, held at Aintree, England. The record for flat racing is 58 in the Lincolnshire Handicap in England, on March 13, 1948.

Speed Records

Distance	Time	mph	Name	Course	Date
¼ mile	20.8s	43.26	*Big Racket* (Mex)	Mexico City, Mex.	Feb. 5, 1945
½ mile	44.4s	40.54	*Sonido* (Ven)	‡Caracas, Ven	June 28, 1970
⅝ mile	53.6s	41.98†	*Indigenous* (GB)	‡*Epsom, England	June 2, 1960
	53.89s	41.75††	*Raffingora* (GB)	‡*Epsom, England	June 5, 1970
	55.4s	40.61	*Zip Pocket* (US)	Phoenix, Arizona	Apr. 22, 1967
¾ mile	1m 06.2s	40.78	*Broken Tendril* (GB)	*Brighton, England	Aug. 6, 1929
	1m 07.2s	40.18	*Grey Papa* (US)	Longacres, Wash.	Sept. 4, 1972
Mile	1m 31.8s	39.21	*Soueida* (GB)	*Brighton, England	Sept. 19, 1963
	1m 31.8s	39.21	*Loose Cover* (GB)	*Brighton, England	June 9, 1966
	1m 32.2s	39.04	*Dr. Fager* (US)	Arlington, Ill.	Aug. 24, 1968
1¼ miles	1m 57.4s	38.33	*Double Discount*	Arcadia, Calif.	Oct. 9, 1977
1½ miles	2m 23.0s	37.76	*Fiddle Isle* (US)	Arcadia, Calif.	Mar. 21, 1970
2 miles**	3m 15.0s	36.93	*Polazel* (GB)	Salisbury, England	July 8, 1924
2½ miles	4m 14.6s	35.35	*Miss Grillo* (US)	Pimlico, Md.	Nov. 12, 1948
3 miles	5m 15.0s	34.29	*Farragut* (Mex)	Aguascalientes, Mex.	Mar. 9, 1941

* Course downhill for ¼ of a mile.

**A more reliable modern record is 3m 16.75 secs by *Il Tempo* (NZ) at Trentham, Wellington, New Zealand, on January 17, 1970.

†Hand-timed.   ††Electrically-timed.   ‡Straight courses.

Victories

The horse with the best recorded win-loss record was *Kincsem,* a Hungarian mare foaled in 1874, who was unbeaten in 54 races (1876–79), including the English Goodwood Cup of 1878.

Camarero, owned by Don José Coll Vidal of Puerto Rico, foaled in 1951, had a winning streak of 56 races, 1953–55, and 73 wins in 77 starts altogether.

Greatest Winnings

The greatest amount ever won by a horse is $2,393,818 by *Affirmed* from 1977 to 1979.

The most won by a mare is $1,535,443 by *Dahlia,* from 1972 to 1976.

The most won in a year is $1,279,334 by *Spectacular Bid* in 1979.

Triple Crown

Eleven horses have won all three races in one season which constitute the American Triple Crown (Kentucky Derby, Preakness Stakes and the Belmont Stakes). This feat was first achieved by *Sir*

HORSE CENTS: 1978 Triple Crown winner "Affirmed" (#6), ridden by Laffit Pincay, is shown winning the Jockey Club Gold Cup race by ¾ of a length on October 6, 1979, at Belmont Park. "Affirmed's" lifetime record of 22 1sts, 5 2nds, and 1 3rd in 29 starts made him the all-time money winner and Horse of the Year for the 2nd straight year. Jockey Pincay broke the yearly winnings record by passing $8 million. "Spectacular Bid" (#3), ridden by Willie Shoemaker, was syndicated for a record $22 million after setting a yearly winnings record in 1979. Shoemaker has won more races and prize money than any jockey in history.

Barton in 1919, and most recently by *Seattle Slew* in 1977 and *Affirmed* in 1978.

The only Triple Crown winner to sire another winner was *Gallant Fox,* the 1930 winner, who sired *Omaha,* who won in 1935.

Tallest

The tallest horse ever to race is *Fort d'Or,* owned by Lady Elizabeth (Eliza) Nugent (*née* Guinness) of Berkshire, England, which stands 18.2 hands. He was foaled in April, 1963.

Most Valuable Horse

Spectacular Bid, who set a yearly winnings record in 1979, was syndicated for $22,000,000, in 40 shares of $550,000 each, in March, 1980.

The highest price for a yearling is $1,500,000 for a colt by *Secretariat* out of *Charming Alibi,* subsequently named *Canadian Bound,* bought at Keeneland, Kentucky, on July 20, 1976.

Dead Heats

There is no recorded case in turf history of a quintuple dead heat. The nearest approach was in the Astley Stakes, at Lewes, England, on August 6, 1880, when *Mazurka, Wandering Nun,* and *Scobell* triple dead-heated for first place, just ahead of *Cumberland* and *Thora,* who dead-heated for fourth place. Each of the five jockeys thought he had won. The only three known examples of a quadruple dead heat were between *Honest Harry, Miss Decoy,* a filly

CROWN JEWELS: "Secretariat" (left) became the first horse in 25 years to capture the Triple Crown when he won the 1½-mile Belmont Stakes by 31 lengths on June 9, 1973. Jockey Willie Shoemaker (right, aboard "Lucky Debonair" in the 1965 Kentucky Derby) is in a familiar position—first across the finish line.

by *Beningbrough* (later named *Young Daffodil*) and *Peteria* at Bogside, England, on June 7, 1808; between *Defaulter, The Squire of Malton, Reindeer* and *Pulcherrima* in the Omnibus Stakes at The Hoo, England, on April 26, 1851; and between *Overreach, Lady Go-Lightly, Gamester* and *The Unexpected* at the Houghton Meeting at Newmarket, England, on October 22, 1855.

Since the introduction of the photo-finish, the highest number of horses in a dead heat has been three, on several occasions.

Funeral Wreath

The largest floral piece honoring a horse was the tribute to the racehorse *Ruffian*, an 8½-foot-high, 8-foot-wide horseshoe made of 1,362 white carnations. It was made by Jay W. Becker Florist Inc. of Floral Park, New York, and decorated the grave of the horse in the infield at Belmont Race Track where she was buried in July, 1975.

Jockeys

The most successful jockey of all time is Willie Shoemaker (b. weighing 2½ lbs. on August 19, 1931) now weighing 98 lbs. and standing 4 feet 11½ inches, who beat Johnny Longden's lifetime record of 6,032 winners on September 7, 1970. From March, 1949, to the end of 1979 he rode 7,766 winners. His winnings have aggregated some $74,504,570.

Chris McCarron (US), 19, won a total of 546 races in 1974.

The greatest amount ever won by any jockey in a year is $8,183,535 by Laffit Pincay (b. December 29, 1946) in the US in 1979. He beat the previous record by nearly $2 million.

The oldest jockey was Levi Barlingame (US), who rode his last race at Stafford, Kansas, in 1932, aged 80. The youngest jockey was Frank Wootton (English Champion jockey 1909–12), who rode his first winner in South Africa aged 9 years 10 months. The lightest recorded jockey was Kitchener (died 1872), who won the Chester Cup in England on *Red Deer* in 1844 at 49 lbs. He was said to have weighed only 40 lbs. in 1840.

Victor Morley Lawson won his first race at Warwick, England, on *Ocean King*, October 16, 1973, aged 67.

The most winners ridden on one card is 8 by Hubert S. Jones, 17, out of 13 mounts at Caliente, California, on June 11, 1944 (of which 5 were photo-finishes), and by Oscar Barattuci at Rosario City, Argentina, on December 15, 1957.

The longest winning streak is 12 races by Sir Gordon Richards (GB) who won the last race at Nottingham, England, on October

RACING'S SAD DAY: Shown here is the largest funeral wreath ever made to honor a horse. Assembled with 1,362 white carnations, it was made by Becker Florist Inc. and it decorated the grave of "Ruffian" at Belmont Park, New York. "Ruffian" had won Eclipse Awards as the outstanding 2-year-old and 3-year-old filly in 1974 and 1975. She was leading in a match race with "Foolish Pleasure," the 1975 Kentucky Derby winner, when she stumbled and pulled up lame with a broken leg. The break was irreparable and she had to be killed. She was buried in the Belmont Park infield.

3, 1933, six out of six at Chepstow on October 4, and the first five races the next day at Chepstow.

Shortest Odds

The shortest odds ever quoted for any racehorse are 1 to 10,000 for *Dragon Blood*, ridden by Lester Piggott (GB) in the Premio Naviglio in Milan, Italy, on June 1, 1967. He won. Odds of 1 to 100 were quoted for the American horse *Man o' War* (foaled March 29, 1917, died November 1, 1947) on three separate occasions in 1920. In 21 starts in 1919–20 he had 20 wins and one second (on August 13, 1919, in the Sanford Memorial Stakes).

Pari-Mutuel Record

The US pari-mutuel record pay-off is $941.75 to $1 on *Wishing Ring* at Latonia track, Kentucky, in 1912.

Trainers

The greatest number of wins by a trainer in one year is 494 by Jack Van Berg in 1976. The greatest amount won in a year is $3,563,147 by Lazaro S. Berrera in 1979.

Owners

The most winners by an owner in one year is 494 by Dan R. Lasater (US) in 1974, when he also won a record $3,022,960 in prize money.

Largest Prizes

The richest race ever held in the All-American Futurity, a race for quarter-horses over 440 yards at Ruidoso Downs, New Mexico. The prizes totaled $1,280,000 in both 1978 and 1979. Total prize money of $1,530,000 is planned for the 1981 race.

The richest first prize was $437,500, won by *Moon Lark*, the winner of the 1978 All-American Futurity, and *Pie in the Sky*, the winner in 1979.

Triple Crown

The Triple Crown is made up of three races for three-year-olds.

KENTUCKY DERBY

1¼ miles at Churchill Downs, Louisville, Kentucky; first held in 1875.

PREAKNESS

1¹³⁄₁₆ miles at Pimlico, Baltimore. Maryland; first held in 1873.

BELMONT STAKES

1½ miles at Belmont Park, New York; first held in 1867.

Horses to have won all three races have been:

1919	Sir Barton
1930	Gallant Fox
1935	Omaha
1937	War Admiral
1941	Whirlaway
1943	Count Fleet
1946	Assault
1948	Citation
1973	Secretariat
1977	Seattle Slew
1978	Affirmed

Eclipse Awards

Inaugurated in 1971, the Eclipse Awards are the results of voting by members of the Thoroughbred Racing Association, the National Turf Writers Association, and the Daily Racing Form.

HORSE OF THE YEAR

1971	Ack Ack
1972	Secretariat
1973	Secretariat
1974	Forego
1975	Forego
1976	Forego
1977	Seattle Slew
1978	Affirmed
1979	Affirmed

OLDER COLT, HORSE OR GELDING

1971	Ack Ack
1972	Autobiography
1973	Riva Ridge
1974	Forego
1975	Forego
1976	Forego
1977	Forego
1978	Seattle Slew
1979	Affirmed

3-YEAR-OLD COLT

1971	Canonero II
1972	Key to the Mint
1973	Secretariat
1974	Little Current
1975	Wajima
1976	Bold Forbes
1977	Seattle Slew
1978	Affirmed
1979	Spectacular Bid

2-YEAR-OLD COLT

1971	Riva Ridge
1972	Secretariat
1973	Protagonist
1974	Foolish Pleasure
1975	Honest Pleasure
1976	Seattle Slew
1977	Affirmed
1978	Spectacular Bid
1979	Rockhill Native

CHAMPION FEMALE TURF HORSE

1979	Trillion

CHAMPION TURF HORSE

1971	Run the Gauntlet
1972	Cougar II
1973	Secretariat
1974	Dahlia
1975	Snow Knight
1976	Youth
1977	Johnny D.
1978	Mac Diarmida
1979*	Bowl Game

*Award changed to Champion Male Turf Horse

WORKING WOMAN: Robyn Smith became the first woman jockey to win a major stakes race when she finished first in the $27,450 Paumanauk Handicap aboard "North Sea" at Aqueduct Race Track, New York, on March 1, 1973. Smith is shown here aboard "Remand" at Belmont Park in 1977. In the background is part of racing's largest grandstand. In the late 1960's, women overcame tremendous resistance from the male racing establishment to win the right to become licensed jockeys.

OLDER FILLY OR MARE

1971	Shuvee
1972	Typecast
1973	Susan's Girl
1974	Desert Vixen
1975	Susan's Girl
1976	Proud Delta
1977	Cascapedia
1978	Late Bloomer
1979	Waya

3-YEAR-OLD FILLY

1971	Turkish Trousers
1972	Susan's Girl
1973	Desert Vixen
1974	Chris Evert
1975	Ruffian
1976	Revidere
1977	Our Mims
1978	Tempest Queen
1979	Davona Dale

2-YEAR-OLD FILLY

1971	Numbered Account
1972	La Prevoyante
1973	Talking Picture
1974	Ruffian
1975	Dearly Precious
1976	Sensational
1977	Lakeville Miss
1978	Candy Eclair
	It's in the Air (tie)
1979	Smart Angle

SPRINTER

1971	Ack Ack
1972	Chou Croute
1973	Shecky Greene
1974	Forego
1975	Gallant Bob
1976	My Juliet
1977	What a Summer
1978	Dr. Patches
	J. O. Tobin (tie)
1979	Star de Naskra

OUTSTANDING TRAINER

1971	Charles Whittingham
1972	Lucien Laurin
1973	H. Allen Jerkens
1974	Sherrill Ward
1975	Steve DiMauro
1976	Lazaro Barrera
1977	Lazaro Barrera
1978	Lazaro Barrera
1979	Lazaro Barrera

OUTSTANDING JOCKEY

1971	Laffit Pincay, Jr.
1972	Braulio Baeza
1973	Laffit Pincay, Jr.
1974	Laffit Pincay, Jr.
1975	Braulio Baeza
1976	Sandy Hawley
1977	Steve Cauthen
1978	Darrel McHargue
1979	Laffit Pincay, Jr.

STEEPLECHASE OR HURDLE HORSE

1971	Shadow Brook
1972	Soothsayer
1973	Athenian Idol
1974	Gran Kan
1975	Life's Illusion
1976	Straight and True
1977	Cafe Prince
1978	Cafe Prince
1979	Martie's Anger

OUTSTANDING OWNER

1971	Mr. and Mrs. E. E. Fogelson
1974	Dan Lasater
1975	Dan Lasater
1976	Dan Lasater
1977	Maxwell Gluck
1978	Harbor View Farm
1979	Harbor View Farm

OUTSTANDING APPRENTICE JOCKEY

1971	Gene St. Leon
1972	Thomas Wallis
1973	Steve Valdez
1974	Chris McCarron
1975	Jimmy Edwards
1976	George Martens
1977	Steve Cauthen
1978	Ron Franklin
1979	Cash Asmussen

HORSESHOE PITCHING

Origin. This sport was derived by military farriers and is of great antiquity. The first formal World Championships were staged at Bronson, Kansas, in 1909.

Most Titles

The record for men's titles is 10 by Ted Allen (Boulder, Colorado) in 1933–34–35–40–46–53–55–56–57–59. The women's record is 9 titles by Vicki Chapelle Winston (LaMonte, Missouri) in 1956–58–59–61–63–66–67–69–75.

Highest Percentage

The record for percentage of ringers in one game is 95 by Ruth Hangen (Getzville, N.Y.) in 1973. The record for consecutive ringers is 72 by Ted Allen in 1951 for men, and 42 by Ruth Hangen in 1974 for women.

Most Ringers

The most ringers in a single game is 175 by Glen Henton of Maquoketa, Iowa, in 1965.

Marathon

The longest continuous session of a 4-man contest, two teams pitching continuously and without substitutions, is 76½ hours by Gary Alexander, Ralph Lewis, Steven Padgett and Stephen Moss, in Lakewood, Colorado, on July 1–4, 1979.

ICE SKATING

Origins. The earliest reference to ice skating is in Scandinavian literature of the 2nd century, although its origins are believed, on

GAY BLADES: Russian ice dancers Ludmilla Pakhomova and Aleksandr Gorshkov (left) won 6 world titles (including 5 in a row, 1970–74) and an Olympic gold medal. Sonja Henie (right) won 10 figure skating world titles and 3 Olympic gold medals. She parlayed her amateur success into earnings estimated in excess of $47 million appearing in ice shows and motion pictures.

JUMPS AND SPINS: Canada's Vern Taylor (left) performed the first ever triple Axel in competition in the 1978 World Championships. Turning completely around 31 times in 12 seconds, Elaine Ballace (right) of Los Angeles was the first to be electronically timed at this speed of 2.6 spins per second. Sonja Henie was known for her speed for spinning but was never timed electronically.

archeological evidence to be 10 centuries earlier still. The earliest account of 1180 refers to skates made of bone. The earliest known illustration is a Dutch woodcut of 1498. The earliest skating club was the Edinburgh Skating Club, Scotland, formed in 1742. The earliest artificial ice rink in the world was opened at the Baker Street Bazaar, Portman Square, London, on December 7, 1842. The International Skating Union was founded in 1892.

Longest Race

The longest race regularly held is the "Elfstedentocht" ("Tour of the Eleven Towns") in the Netherlands. It covers 200 kilometers (124 miles 483 yards) and the fastest time is 7 hours 35 minutes by Jeen van den Berg (born January 8, 1928) on February 3, 1954.

Largest Rink

The world's largest indoor artificial ice rink is in the Moscow Olympic indoor arena which has an ice area of 86,800 square feet. The largest artificial outdoor rink is the quintuple complex of the Fujiku Highland Promenade Rink, Japan (opened 1967), with an area of 285,244 square feet.

Figure Skating

World. The greatest number of individual world men's figure skating titles (instituted 1896) in ten by Ulrich Salchow (1877–1949), of Sweden, in 1901–05 and 1907–11. The women's record (instituted 1906) is also ten individual titles, by Sonja Henie (April 8, 1912–October 12, 1969), of Norway, between 1927 and 1936. Irina Rodnina (born September 12, 1949), of the USSR, has won ten pairs titles (instituted 1908)—four with Aleksiy Ulanov (1969–72) and six with her husband Aleksandr Zaitsev (1973–77). The most ice dance titles (instituted 1950) won in six by Aleksandr Gorshkov (born December 8, 1946) and Ludmilla Pakhomova (born December 31, 1946), both of the USSR, in 1970–71–72–73–74 and 1976.

Olympic. The most Olympic gold medals won by a figure skater is three by Gillis Grafstrom (1893–1938), of Sweden, in 1920, 1924, and 1928 (also silver medal in 1932); and by Sonja Henie (see above) in 1928, 1932 and 1936. Irina Rodnina (see above) have also won three gold medals in pairs skating in 1972, 1976 and 1980.

Most Difficult Jump. The first ever triple Axel performed in competition was by Vern Taylor (b. 1958) (Canada) in the World Championships at Ottawa on March 10, 1978.

A quadruple twist lift has been performed by only one pair, Sergei Shakrai (b. 1957) and Marina Tcherkasova (b. 1962) of the USSR, in an international championship at Helsinki, Finland, on January 26, 1977. They were also the first skaters to accomplish simultaneous triple jumps at that level, at Strasbourg, France, on February 1, 1978.

Highest Marks. The highest number of maximum six marks awarded for one performance in an international championship was 11 to Aleksandr Zaitsev and Irina Rodnina (USSR) in the European pairs competition in Zagreb, Yugoslavia, in 1974.

Donald Jackson (Canada) was awarded 7 "sixes" (the most by a soloist) in the world men's championship at Prague, Czechslovakia, in 1962.

Most Titles Speed Skating

World. The greatest number of world overall titles (instituted 1893) won by any skater is five by Oscar Mathisen (Norway) in 1908–09 and 1912–14, and Clas Thunberg (1893–1973) of Finland, in 1923, 1925, 1928–29 and 1931. The most titles won by a woman is four by Mrs. Inga Voronina, *née* Artomonova (1936–66) of Moscow, USSR, in 1957, 1958, 1962 and 1965, and Mrs. Atje Keulen-Deelstra of the Netherlands (b. 1938) in 1970 and 1972–73–74.

The highest score attained in the world combined title (comprising 500 m., 1,500 m., 5,000 m., and 10,000 m.) is 162.973 points achieved by Eric Heiden (US) at Oslo, Norway, February 10–11, 1979.

Olympic. The most Olympic gold medals won in speed skating is six by Lydia Skoblikova (born March 8, 1939), of Chelyabinsk, USSR, in 1960 (2) and 1964 (4). The male record is shared by Clas Thunberg (see above) with 5 gold (including 1 tied gold) and also 1 silver and 1 tied bronze in 1924–28, and Eric Heiden, who uniquely swept all 5 races in 1980 and set Olympic records in each of them.

ON ICE: Russian speed skater Lydia Skoblikova (left) has won 6 Olympic gold medals. She has also captured 2 world titles, and is shown here winning the 1,500 meters in the 1975 World Championships. Sheila Young (right) is the world record holder for 500 meters, making her the fastest woman on ice. Young picked up a gold medal in the 1976 Olympics for that distance, and she has also won 2 world cycling titles (see page 86).

World Speed Skating Records

(Ratified by the I.S.U.)

Distance	min sec	Name and Nationality	Place	Date
Men				
500 meters	37.00*	Evgeni Kulikov (USSR)	Medeo, USSR	Mar. 29, 1975
1,000 meters	1:13.60	Eric Heiden (US)	Davos, Switz.	Jan. 13, 1980
1,500 meters	1:54.79	Eric Heiden (US)	Davos, Switz.	Jan. 20, 1980
3,000 meters	4:04.06	Dmitri Ogloblin (USSR)	Medeo, USSR	Mar. 29, 1979
5,000 meters	6.56.90	Kay Stenshjemmel (Norway)	Medeo, USSR	Mar. 19, 1977
10,000 meters	14.28.13	Eric Heiden (US)	Lake Placid, NY	Feb. 23, 1980
Women				
500 meters	40.68	Sheila Young (US)	Inzell, W. Ger.	Mar. 13, 1976
1,000 meters	1:23.46	Tatiana Averina (USSR)	Medeo, USSR	Mar. 29, 1975
1,500 meters	2:07.18	Khalida Vorobyeva (USSR)	Medeo, USSR	Apr. 10, 1978
3,000 meters	4:31.00	Galina Stepanskaya (USSR)	Medeo, USSR	Mar. 23, 1976

*This represents an average speed of 30.22 m.p.h.

Longest Marathon

The longest recorded skating marathon is one of 109 hours 5 minutes by Austin McKinley of Christchurch, New Zealand, June 21–25, 1977.

Figure Skating

World Champions

World figure skating championships were first held in 1896 for men, and in 1906 for women. Pair skating titles have been decided since 1908 and Ice Dancing since 1952. The championships were not held in 1961.

MEN'S FIGURE SKATING

Winners since 1947:

1947	Hans Gerschwiler (Swi)	
1948	Richard Button (US)	
1949	Richard Button (US)	
1950	Richard Button (US)	
1951	Richard Button (US)	
1952	Richard Button (US)	
1953	Hayes Jenkins (US)	
1954	Hayes Jenkins (US)	
1955	Hayes Jenkins (US)	
1956	Hayes Jenkins (US)	
1957	David Jenkins (US)	
1958	David Jenkins (US)	
1959	David Jenkins (US)	
1960	Alain Giletti (Fra)	
1962	Donald Jackson (Can)	
1963	Donald McPherson (Can)	
1964	Manfred Schnelldorfer (W Ger)	
1965	Alain Calmat (Fra)	
1966	Emmerich Danzer (Aut)	
1967	Emmerich Danzer (Aut)	
1968	Emmerich Danzer (Aut)	
1969	Tim Wood (US)	
1970	Tim Wood (US)	
1971	Ondrej Nepela (Cze)	
1972	Ondrej Nepela (Cze)	
1973	Ondrej Nepela (Cze)	
1974	Jan Hoffmann (E Ger)	
1975	Sergei Volkov (USSR)	
1976	John Curry (GB)	
1977	Vladimir Kovalev (USSR)	
1978	Charles Tickner (US)	
1979	Vladimir Kovalev (USSR)	

Most titles: 10 Ulrich Salchow (Swe): 1901–05, 1907–11; 7 Karl Schäfer (Aut): 1930–36

WOMEN'S FIGURE SKATING

Winners since 1947:

1947	Barbara Ann Scott (Can)
1948	Barbara Ann Scott (Can)
1949	Aja Vrzanova (Cze)
1950	Aja Vrzanova (Cze)
1951	Jeanette Altwegg (GB)
1952	Jeanette Altwegg (GB)
1953	Tenley Albright (US)
1954	Gundi Busch (W Ger)
1955	Tenley Albright (US)
1956	Carol Heiss (US)
1957	Carol Heiss (US)
1958	Carol Heiss (US)
1959	Carol Heiss (US)
1960	Carol Heiss (US)
1962	Sjoukje Dijkstra (Hol)
1963	Sjoukje Dijkstra (Hol)
1964	Sjoukje Dijkstra (Hol)
1965	Petra Burka (Can)
1966	Peggy Fleming (US)
1967	Peggy Fleming (US)
1968	Peggy Fleming (US)
1969	Gabriele Seyfert (E Ger)
1970	Gabriele Seyfert (E Ger)
1971	Beatrix Schuba (Aut)
1972	Beatrix Schuba (Aut)
1973	Karen Magnussen (Can)
1974	Christine Errath (E Ger)
1975	Dianne de Leeuw (Hol)
1976	Dorothy Hamill (US)
1977	Linda Fratianne (US)
1978	Annette Pötzsch (E Ger)
1979	Linda Fratianne (US)

Most titles: 10 Sonja Henie (Nor) 1927–36

PAIRS SKATING

1947, 1948	Pierre Baugniet and Micheline Lannoy (Bel)
1949	Ede Király and Andrea Kékessy (Hun)
1950	Peter Kennedy and Karol Kennedy (US)
1951, 1952	Paul Faulk and Ria Baran/Falk (W Ger)
1953	John Nicks and Jennifer Nicks (GB)
1954, 1955	Norris Bowden and Frances Dafoe (Can)
1956	Kurt Oppelt and Sissy Schwarz (Aut)
1957–1960	Robert Paul and Barbara Wagner (Can)
1962	Otto Jelinek and Maria Jelinek (Can)
1963–1964	Hans-Jürgen Bäumler and Marika Kilius (W Ger)
1965–1968	Oleg Protopopov and Lyudmila Protopopov (USSR)
1969–1972	Alexei Ulanov and Irina Rodnina (USSR)
1973–1978	Aleksandr Zaitsev and Irina Rodnina (USSR)
1979	Randy Gardner and Tai Babilonia (US)

ICE DANCE SKATING

1952–1955	Lawrence Demmy and Jean Westwood (GB)
1956	Paul Thomas and Pamela Weight (GB)
1957–1958	Courtney Jones and June Markham (GB)
1959–1960	Courtney Jones and Doreen Denny (GB)
1962–1965	Pavel Roman and Eva Romanova (Cze)
1966–1969	Bernard Ford and Diane Towler (GB)
1970–1974	Aleksandr Gorshkov and Lyudmila Pakhomova (USSR)
1975	Andrei Minenkov and Irina Moiseyeva (USSR)
1976	Aleksandr Gorshlov and Lyudmila Pakhomova (USSR)
1977	Andrei Minenkov and Irina Moiseyeva (USSR)
1978–1979	Gennadiy Karponosov and Natalia Linichuk (USSR)

AMERICAN SWEEP SKATES: Eric Heiden, of Madison, Wisconsin, won all 5 speed skating races at the 1980 Winter Olympics in Lake Placid, New York. Heiden set Olympic records in every race, and he shattered the world record for 10,000 meters by 6.20 seconds. (The 4 women's races were also won in Olympic record time.) When Heiden set the 10,000-meter record for his unprecedented 5 individual gold medals in one Games, he also became the holder of 3 of the 6 men's world speed skating records.

Olympic Champions

Figure Skating was first included in the Olympic Games in 1908, and has been included at each celebration since 1920. Winners since 1948:

MEN'S FIGURE SKATING

1948	Richard Button (US)
1952	Richard Button (US)
1956	Hayes Jenkins (US)
1960	David Jenkins (US)
1964	Manfred Schnelldorfer (W Ger)
1968	Wolfgang Schwarz (Aut)
1972	Ondrej Nepela (Cze)
1976	John Curry (GB)
1980	Robin Cousins (GB)

WOMEN'S FIGURE SKATING

1948	Barbara Ann Scott (Can)
1952	Jeanette Altwegg (GB)
1956	Tenley Albright (US)
1960	Carol Heiss (US)
1964	Sjoukje Dijkstra (Hol)
1968	Peggy Fleming (US)
1972	Beatrix Schuba (Aut)
1976	Dorothy Hamill (US)
1980	Annette Pötzsch (E Ger)

PAIRS SKATING

1948	Pierre Baugniet and Micheline Lannoy (Bel)
1952	Paul Falk and Ria Falk (W Ger)
1956	Kurt Oppelt and Sissy Schwarz (Aut)
1960	Robert Paul and Barbara Wagner (Can)
1964	Oleg Protopopov and Lyudmila Protopopov (USSR)
1968	Oleg Protopopov and Lyudmila Belousova (Protopopov) (USSR)
1972	Alexei Ulanov and Irina Rodnina (USSR)
1976	Aleksandr Zaitsev and Irina Rodnina (USSR)
1980	Aleksandr Zaitsev and Irina Rodnina (USSR)

ICE DANCE

First held 1976

1976	Aleksandr Gorshkov and Lyudmila Pakhomova (USSR)
1980	Gennadiy Karponosov and Natalia Linichuk (USSR)

Speed Skating
World Champions

World championships were first held in 1893. For men they are contested at 500, 1,500, 5,000 and 10,000 meters and for women at 500, 1,000, 3,000 and 5,000 meters. Overall world champions

PERFECT PAIR: Irina Rodnina and Aleksandr Zaitsev (USSR) were awarded 11 perfect scores in the European pairs competition in 1974. Rodnina, skating with Zaitsev (her husband) and a previous partner, Alexei Ulanov, has won 10 world titles and 3 Olympic gold medals.

are determined over the four distances. Overall world champions since 1947 have been:

MEN

1947	Lauri Parkkinen (Fin)		1970	Atje Keulen-Deelstra (Hol)
1948	Odd Lundberg (Nor)		1971	Nina Statkevich (USSR)
1949	Kornel Pajor (Hun)		1972	Atje Keulen-Deelstra (Hol)
1950	Hjalmar Andersen (Nor)		1973	Atje Keulen-Deelstra (Hol)
1951	Hjalmar Andersen (Nor)		1974	Atje Keulen-Deelstra (Hol)
1952	Hjalmar Andersen (Nor)		1975	Karin Kessow (E Ger)
1953	Oleg Goncharenko (USSR)		1976	Sylvia Burka (Can)
1954	Boris Schilkov (USSR)		1977	Vera Bryndzey (USSR)
1955	Sigvard Ericsson (Swe)		1978	Tatiana Averina (USSR)
1956	Oleg Goncharenko (USSR)		1979	Elizabeth Heiden (US)
1957	Knut Johannesen (Nor)			
1958	Oleg Goncharenko (USSR)			
1959	Juhani Järvinen (Fin)			
1960	Boris Stenin (USSR)			
1961	Hendrik van der Grift (Hol)			
1962	Viktor Kosichkin (USSR)			
1963	Johnny Nilsson (Swe)			
1964	Knut Johannesen (Nor)			
1965	Per Moe (Nor)			
1966	Kees Verkerk (Hol)			
1967	Kees Verkerk (Hol)			
1968	Anton Maier (Nor)			
1969	Dag Fornaess (Nor)			
1970	Ard Schenk (Hol)			
1971	Ard Schenk (Hol)			
1972	Ard Schenk (Hol)			
1973	Goran Claesson (Swe)			
1974	Sten Stensen (Nor)			
1975	Harm Kuipers (Hol)			
1976	Piet Kleine (Hol)			
1977	Eric Heiden (US)			
1978	Eric Heiden (US)			
1979	Eric Heiden (US)			

WOMEN

1947	Verne Lesche (Fin)
1948	Maria Isakova (USSR)
1949	Maria Isakova (USSR)
1950	Maria Isakova (USSR)
1951	Eva Huttunen (Fin)
1952	Lydia Selichova (USSR)
1953	Khalida Schegoleyeva (USSR)
1954	Lydia Selichova (USSR)
1955	Rimma Zhukova (USSR)
1956	Sofia Kondakova (USSR)
1957	Inga Artamonova (USSR)
1958	Inga Antamonova (USSR)
1959	Tamara Rylova (USSR)
1960	Valentina Stenina (USSR)
1961	Valentina Stenina (USSR)
1962	Inga Voronina (née Artamonova) (USSR)
1963	Lydia Skoblikova (USSR)
1964	Lydia Skoblikova (USSR)
1965	Inga Voronina (USSR)
1966	Valentina Stenina (USSR)
1967	Stein Kaiser (Hol)
1968	Stein Kaiser (Hol)
1969	Lasma Kauniste (USSR)

GIVE IT A WHIRL: American Dorothy Hamill wears a confident smile as she spins her way to the gold medal during the free skating competition in the 1976 Winter Olympics at Innsbruck, Austria. She also won the world title that year.

Olympic Champions

Speed Skating has been included on the Olympic program since 1924 for men, and since 1960 for women. Winners since 1948:

DUTCH TREAT: Ard Schenk captured 3 gold medals at the 1972 Olympics in Sapporo, Japan. The Dutch speed skater, here leading in the 1972 Olympic 10,000 meters competition, also won 3 straight overall world titles, 1970–72.

MEN

500 meters
1948	Finn Helgesen (Nor) 43.1
1952	Kenneth Henry (US) 43.2
1956	Yevgeniy Grischin (USSR) 40.2
1960	Yevgeniy Grischin (USSR) 40.2
1964	Richard McDermott (US) 40.1
1968	Erhard Keller (W Ger) 40.3
1972	Erhard Keller (W Ger) 39.44
1976	Yevgeniy Kulikov (USSR) 39.17
1980	Eric Heiden (US) 38.03

1,000 meters
1976	Peter Muller (US) 1:19.32
1980	Eric Heiden (US) 1:15.18

1,500 meters
1948	Sverre Farstad (Nor) 2:17.6
1952	Hjalmar Andersen (Nor) 2:20.4
1956	Yevgeniy Grischin (USSR) and Yuriy Mikhailov (USSR) 2:08.6
1960	Roald Aas (Nor) and Yevgeniy Grischin (USSR) 2:10.4
1964	Ants Antson (USSR) 2:10.3
1968	Cornelis Verkerk (Hol) 2:03.4
1972	Ard Schenk (Hol) 2:02.96
1976	Jan Egil Storholt (Nor) 1:59.38
1980	Eric Heiden (US) 1:55.44

5,000 meters
1948	Reidar Liaklev (Nor) 8:29.4
1952	Hjalmar Andersen (Nor) 8:10.6
1956	Boris Schilkov (USSR) 7:48.7
1960	Viktor Kositschkin (USSR) 7:51.3
1964	Knut Johannesen (Nor) 7:38.4
1968	Anton Maier (Nor) 7:22.4
1972	Ard Schenk (Hol) 7:23.61
1976	Sten Stensen (Nor) 7:24.48
1980	Eric Heiden (US) 7:02.29

10,000 meters
1948	Åke Seyffarth (Swe) 17:26.3
1952	Hjalmar Andersen (Nor) 16:45.8
1956	Sigvard Ericsson (Swe) 16:35.9
1960	Knut Johannesen (Nor) 15:46.6
1964	Jonny Nilsson (Swe) 15:50.1
1968	Johnny Hoeglin (Swe) 15:23.6
1972	Ard Schenk (Hol) 15:01.35
1976	Piet Kleine (Hol) 14:50.59
1980	Eric Heiden (US) 14:28.13

WOMEN

500 meters
1960	Helga Haase (W Ger) 45.9
1964	Lydia Skoblikova (USSR) 45.0
1968	Lyudmila Titova (USSR) 46.1
1972	Anne Henning (US) 43.33
1976	Sheila Young (US) 42.76
1980	Karin Enke (E Ger) 41.78

1,000 meters
1960	Klala Guseva (USSR) 1:34.1
1964	Lydia Skoblikova (USSR) 1:33.2
1968	Corolina Geijssen (Hol) 1:32.6
1972	Monika Pflug (W Ger) 1:31.40
1976	Tatiana Averina (USSR) 1:28.43
1980	Natalya Petruseva (USSR) 1:24.10

1,500 meters
1960	Lydia Skoblikova (USSR) 2:25.2
1964	Lydia Skoblikova (USSR) 2:22.6
1968	Kaija Mustonen (Fin) 2:22.4
1972	Dianne Holum (US) 2:20.85
1976	Galina Stepanskaya (USSR) 2:16.58
1980	Annie Borckink (Hol) 2:10.95

3,000 meters
1960	Lydia Skoblikova (USSR) 5:14.3
1964	Lydia Skoblikova (USSR) 5:14.9
1968	Johanna Schut (Hol) 4:56.2
1972	Stein Bass-Kaiser (Hol) 4:52.14
1976	Tatiana Averina (USSR) 4:45.19
1980	Bjoerg Eva Jensen (Nor) 4:32.13

BLAZING BLADES: Tatiana Averina (USSR) won 2 gold medals at Innsbruck in the 1976 Olympics. The holder of the 1,000 meters world record, Averina also won the overall world title in 1978.

ICE AND SAND YACHTING

Origin. The sport originated in the Low Countries (earliest patent is dated 1600) and along the Baltic coast. The earliest authentic record is Dutch, dating from 1768. The largest ice yacht built was *Icicle,* built for Commodore John E. Roosevelt for racing on the Hudson River, New York, *c.* 1870. It was 68 feet 11 inches long and carried 1,070 square feet of canvas.

Highest Speed

The highest speed officially recorded is 143 m.p.h. by John D. Buckstaff in a Class A sternsteerer on Lake Winnebago, Wisconsin, in 1938. Such a speed is possible in a wind of 72 m.p.h.

GROUND SWELL: The fastest recorded speed for a sand yacht is 57.69 m.p.h. by "Coronation Year Mk. II," achieved in England in 1956.

Sand Yachting

Land or sand yachts of Dutch construction were first reported on beaches (now in Belgium) in 1595. The earliest international championship was staged in 1914.

The fastest recorded speed for a sand yacht is 57.69 m.p.h. (measured mile is 62.4 secs.) by *Coronation Year Mk. II,* owned by R. Millett Denning and crewed by J. Halliday, Bob Harding, J. Glassbrook and Cliff Martindale at Lytham St. Anne's, England, in 1956.

A speed of 77.47 m.p.h. was attained by Jan Paul Lowe (born April 15, 1936) (US) in *Sunkist,* at Ivanpaugh Dry Lake, California, on March 25, 1975.

JAI-ALAI (Pelota)

Origins. The game, which originated in Italy as *longue paume* and was introduced into France in the 13th century, is said to be the fastest of all ball games. Gloves were introduced *c.* 1840 and the *chistera* (basket-like glove) was invented *c.* 1860 by Jean "Gantchiki" Dithurbide of Ste. Pée. The long *grand chistera* was invented by Melchior Curuchague of Buenos Aires, Argentina, in 1888.

Various games are played in a *fronton* (enclosed stadium) the most popular being *main nue, remonte, rebot, pala, grand chistera* and *cesta punta.* The sport is governed by the Federación Internacional de Pelota Vasca in Madrid, Spain.

The world's largest *fronton* is the World Jai-Alai in Miami,

OFF THE WALL: Jai-alai features the highest projectile speed of any ball game, the fastest measured speed being 188 m.p.h. The exciting, acrobatic game is most often played on a 3-walled court (front, back and side), with the fourth side open for spectators.

Florida, which had a record attendance of 15,052 on December 27, 1975.

The fastest throw of a (*pelota*) ball was made by José Ramon Areitio at an electronically measured speed of 188 m.p.h., recorded at the Newport Jai-Alai, Rhode Island, on August 3, 1979.

Longest Domination

The longest domination as the world's No. 1 player was enjoyed by Chiquito de Cambo (*né* Joseph Apesteguy) (France) (b. May 10, 1881–d. 1955), from the beginning of the century until succeeded in 1938 by Jean Urruty (France) (b. October 19, 1913).

World Amateur Jai-Alai Championships

Under the auspices of the Federación Internacional de Pelota Vasca, which is based in Spain. First held in 1952. Recent winners:

1966	Mexico	1971	Spain	1976	France
1968	Spain	1974	France	1978	Spain
1970	France	1975	United States		

LACROSSE

Origin. The game is of American Indian origin, derived from the inter-tribal game *baggataway*, and was played by Iroquois Indians at lower Ontario, Canada, and upper New York State, before 1492. The French named it after their game of *Chouler à la crosse*, known in 1381. The game was included in the Olympic Games of 1908, and featured as an exhibition sport in 1928 and 1948 Games.

World Championship

The United States won the first two Men's World Championships, in 1967 and 1974. Canada won the third in 1978, beating the US 17–16 in overtime—this was the first drawn international match. World Championships for women were instituted in 1969, and have been contested twice. Great Britain won the first title and the United States the other in 1974.

Highest Score

The highest score in any international match was US over Canada, 28–4, at Stockport, England, on July 3, 1978.

Collegiate

Most Championships. Johns Hopkins University, Baltimore, Maryland, has won or shared 35 national championships.

Individual Scoring. John Cheek (Washington College) netted 200 career goals, while Doug Fry (Maryland-Baltimore County) holds the collegiate record with 70 goals in one season.

Rick Gilbert (Hobart) holds the USILA record for single season assists (88) and points (122). He also holds career records with 287 assists and a remarkable 444 points.

Goaltending. Jeff Singer made a record 909 career saves as goaltender for the Massachusetts Institute of Technology.

USILA National Champions

The Wingate Trophy, emblematic of the championship of the United States Intercollegiate Lacrosse Association, was first awarded in 1936. It is given each year in perpetual competition.

Since 1971, the NCAA assumed responsibility for national championship competition.

NATIVE SPORT: Lacrosse was derived from a game played by Iroquois Indians, whose contests would cover several miles and last several days. This illustration depicts a contest between Iroquois and early Canadian settlers.

Collegiate (continued)

1881	Harvard	1930	St. John's
1882	Harvard	1931	Johns Hopkins
1883	Yale	1932	No champion†
1884	Princeton	1933	No champion#
1885	Harvard	1934	No champion‡
1886	Harvard	1935	No champion§
1887	Harvard	1936	Maryland
1888	Princeton	1937	Maryland, Princeton
1889	Princeton	1938	Navy
1890	Lehigh	1939	Maryland
1891	Johns Hopkins	1940	Maryland
1892	Stevens	1941	Johns Hopkins
1893	Lehigh	1942	Princeton
1894	Stevens	1943	Navy
1895	Lehigh	1944	Army
1896	Lehigh	1945	Army, Navy
1897	Lehigh	1946	Navy
1898	Johns Hopkins	1947	Johns Hopkins
1899	Johns Hopkins	1948	Johns Hopkins
1900	Johns Hopkins	1949	Johns Hopkins, Navy
1901	no records	1950	Johns Hopkins
1902	Johns Hopkins	1951	Army, Princeton
1903	Johns Hopkins	1952	Virginia, RPI
1904	Swarthmore	1953	Princeton
1905	Columbia, Cornell, Harvard, Swarthmore	1954	Navy
		1955	Maryland
1906	Cornell, Johns Hopkins	1956	Maryland
1907	Cornell, Johns Hopkins	1957	Johns Hopkins
1908	Harvard, Johns Hopkins	1958	Army
1909	Harvard, Columbia, Johns Hopkins	1959	Army, Maryland, Johns Hopkins
1910	Harvard, Swarthmore	1960	Navy
1911	Harvard, Johns Hopkins	1961	Army, Navy
1912	Harvard	1962	Navy
1913	Harvard, Johns Hopkins	1963	Navy
1914	Cornell, Lehigh	1964	Navy
1915	Harvard, Johns Hopkins	1965	Navy
1916	Cornell, Lehigh	1966	Navy
1917	Stevens, Lehigh	1967	Maryland, Navy, Johns Hopkins
1918	Stevens, Johns Hopkins	1968	Johns Hopkins
1919	Johns Hopkins	1969	Johns Hopkins, Army
1920	Syracuse, Lehigh	1970	Johns Hopkins, Navy, Virginia
1921	Lehigh	1971	Cornell
1922	Syracuse	1972	Virginia
1923	Johns Hopkins	1973	Maryland
1924	Syracuse, Johns Hopkins	1974	Johns Hopkins
1925	Syracuse, Maryland	1975	Maryland
1926	Johns Hopkins	1976	Cornell
1927	Johns Hopkins	1977	Cornell
1928	Johns Hopkins, Maryland, Rutgers, Navy	1978	Johns Hopkins
		1979	Johns Hopkins
1929	Navy, Union*		

* St. John's, not a member of the USILA, generally was recognized as the national champion but was ineligible for official recognition.

† Johns Hopkins won Olympic playoff.

Johns Hopkins, Princeton, Dartmouth were undefeated. Hopkins played strongest schedule.

‡ Johns Hopkins, Maryland, St. John's each won all games but one.

§ St. John's, Maryland, Navy each won all games but one, while Princeton was unbeaten. St. John's played strongest schedule.

USWLA Championship

The United States Women's Lacrosse Association (founded 1931) is made up of Districts, Associations, Clubs, Allied Schools and Colleges. In 1975, their tournament was designated a national

BEST IN BALTIMORE: Johns Hopkins University in Baltimore, Maryland, has won the most collegiate championships. Lacrosse is so popular in Baltimore that Johns Hopkins games have often drawn more spectators than major league baseball's pennant-winning Baltimore Orioles. Here, a Johns Hopkins player takes a shot at the goal of another top college team, the University of Maryland.

championship. In 1980, the USWLA will hold a championship for colleges only, and in 1981 the college tournament will come under the jurisdiction of the AIAW.

1975	Philadelphia Association	1978	Philadelphia Association
1976	Philadelphia Association	1979	Philadelphia Association
1977	Philadelphia Association		

MARATHON

Origins. The inaugural marathon race was staged at the first modern Olympic Games in Athens, Greece, in 1896. The event commemorates the run of an unknown Greek courier who, in 490 B.C., ran some 24 miles from the Plains of Marathon to Athens with the news of a Greek victory over a numerically superior Persian army. Upon delivering his message ("Rejoice! We've won.") the heroic runner collapsed and died.

The Olympic marathons were run over courses of various lengths until 1924, when the official distance was set at 26 miles 385 yards. This distance was first instituted as a favor to the British monarchs during the 1908 Olympics in London, where the runners started from the royal residence at Windsor Castle and finished in front of the royal box at White City Stadium.

Most Spectators and Participants

The greatest number of live spectators for any sporting spectacle is the estimated 2,500,000 who lined the route of the New York City Marathon on October 21, 1979. The race is supervised by the New York Road Runners Club, which reported a field of 11,405 registered runners (of whom 10,477, or nearly 92 per cent, finished), reputedly the greatest number of participants for a marathon road race. The first New York City Marathon in 1970 attracted only 126 registered starters.

Fastest Runs

There is no official marathon record because of the varying severity of courses. The best time over 26 miles 385 yards is 2 hours 8 minutes 33.6 seconds (average 12.24 m.p.h.) by Derek Clayton (b. 1942 at Barrow-in-Furness, England) of Australia, at Antwerp, Belgium, on May 30, 1969.

The fastest time by a woman is 2 hours 27 minutes 33 seconds (average 10.70 m.p.h.) by Grete Waitz (Norway) (b. October 1, 1953) in the New York City Marathon on October 21, 1979.

Progressive Best Performances

MEN

2:55:18.4	John Hayes (US)	1908
2:52:45.4	Robert Fowler (US)	1909
2:46:52.6	James Clark (US)	1909
2:46:04.6	Albert Raines (US)	1909
2:42:31.0	Fred Barrett (GB)	1909
2:38:16.2	Harry Green (GB)	1913
2:36:06.6	Johannes Kolehmai-nen (Finland)	1913
2:29:01.8	Albert Michelsen (US)	1925
2:27:49.0	Fusashige Suzuki (Japan)	1925
2:26:44.0	Yasao Ikenaka (Japan)	1935
2:26:42.0	Kitei Son (Japan)	1935
2:25:39.0	Yun Bok Suh (Korea)	1947
2:20:42.2	Jim Peters (GB)	1952
2:18:40.2	Jim Peters (GB)	1953
2:18:34.8	Jim Peters (GB)	1953
2:17:39.4	Jim Peters (GB)	1954
2:15:17.0	Sergey Popov (USSR)	1958
2:15:16.2	Abebe Bikila (Ethiopia)	1960
2:15:15.8	Toru Terasawa (Japan)	1963
2:14:28.0*	Buddy Edelen (US)	1963
2:13:55.0	Basil Heatley (GB)	1964
2:12:11.2	Abebe Bikila (Ethiopia)	1964
2:12:00.0	Morio Shigematsu (Japan)	1965
2:09:36.4	Derek Clayton (Australia)	1967
2:08:33.6	Derek Clayton (Australia)	1969

* 36 yds. (about 6 sec.) under standard distance.

WOMEN

3:40:22.0	Violet Piercy (GB)	1926
3:37:07.0	Merry Lepper (US)	1963
3:27:45.0	Dale Greig (GB)	1966
3:19:33.0	Mildred Sampson (NZ)	1964
3:15:22.0	Maureen Wilton (Canada)	1967
3:07:26.0	Anni Pede-Erdkamp (Germany)	1967
3:02:53.0	Caroline Walker (US)	1970
3:01:42.0	Elizabeth Bonner (US)	1971
3:00:35.0	Sara Mae Berman (US)	1971
2:46:30.0	Adrienne Beames (Australia)	1971
2:46:24.0	Chantal Langlace (France)	1974

MARATHON MAN: Australia's Derek Clayton recorded the fastest time ever for a marathon in Belgium in 1969.

2:43:54.5	Jackie Hansen (US)	1974	2:35:10.4	Chantal Langlace	1977
2:42:24:0	Liane Winter	1975		(France)	
	(Germany)		2:34:47.5	Christa Vahlensieck	1977
2:40:15.8	Christa Vahlensieck	1975		(Germany)	
	(Germany)		2:32:30.0	Grete Waitz (Norway)	1978
2:38:19.0	Jackie Hansen (US)	1975	2:27:33.0	Grete Waitz (Norway)	1979

Statistics of Major Races

Boston Marathon

1897	John J. McDermott (US)	2:55:10
1898	Ronald J. McDonald (US)	2:42:00
1899	Lawrence J. Brignolia (US)	2:54:38
1900	James J Caffrey (Canada)	2:39:44.4
1901	James J. Caffrey (Canada)	2:29:23.6
1902	Samuel A. Mellor, Jr. (US)	2:43:12
1903	John C. Lorden (US)	2:41:29.8
1904	Michael Spring (US)	2:38:04.4
1905	Frederick Lorz (US)	2:38:25.4
1906	Timothy Ford (US)	2:45:45
1907	Thomas Longboat (Canada)	2:24:24
1908	Thomas P. Morrissey (US)	2:25:43.2
1909	Henri Renaud (US)	2:53:36.8
1910	Frederick Cameron (Canada)	2:28:52.4
1911	Clarence H. DeMar (US)	2:21:39.6
1912	Michael Ryan (US)	2:21:18.2
1913	Fritz Carlson (US)	2:25:14.8
1914	James Duffy (Canada)	2:25:01.2
1915	Edouard Fabre (Canada)	2:31:41.2
1916	Arthur V. Roth (US)	2:27:16.4
1917	William Kennedy (US)	2:28:37.2
1918	Camp Devens Service Team (US)	2:24:53
1919	Carl W. A. Linder (US)	2:29:13.4
1920	Peter Trivoulidas (US)	2:29:31
1921	Frank Zuna (US)	2:18:57.6
1922	Clarence H. DeMar (US)	2:18:10
1923	Clarence H. DeMar (US)	2:23:37.4

LONG RUNNING PERFORMER: Clarence DeMar is first at the finish line of the 1930 Boston Marathon. DeMar's 7 wins in the race are the most by any runner. The Boston Marathon has been held every year since 1897.

1924	Clarence H. DeMar (US)	2:29:40.2
1925	Charles L. Mellor (US)	2:33:00.6
1926	John C. Miles (Canada)	2:25:40.4
1927	Clarence H. DeMar (US)	2:40:22.2
1928	Clarence H. DeMar (US)	2:37:07.8
1929	John C. Miles (Canada)	2:33:08.6
1930	Clarence H. DeMar (US)	2:34:48.2
1931	James P. Henigan (US)	2:46:45.8
1932	Paul de Bruyn (Germany)	2:33:36.4
1933	Leslie S. Pawson (US)	2:31:01.6
1934	David Komonen (Canada)	2:32:53.8
1935	John A. Kelley (US)	2:32:07.4
1936	Ellison M. Brown (US)	2:33:40.8
1937	Walter Young (Canada)	2:33:20
1938	Leslie S. Pawson (US)	2:35:34.8
1939	Ellison M. Brown (US)	2:28:51.8
1940	Gerard Cote (Canada)	2:38:28.6
1941	Leslie S. Pawson (US)	2:30:38
1942	Bernard J. Smith (US)	2:26:51.2
1943	Gerard Cote (Canada)	2:28:25.8
1944	Gerard Cote (Canada)	2:31:50.4
1945	John A. Kelley (US)	2:30:40.2
1946	Stylianos Kyriakidis (Greece)	2:29:27
1947	Yun Bok Suh (Korea)	2:25:39
1948	Gerard Cote (Canada)	2:31:02
1949	Karl Gosta Leandersson (Sweden)	2:31:50.8
1950	Kee Yong Ham (South Korea)	2:32:39
1951	Shigeki Tanaka (Japan)	2:27:45
1952	Doroteo Flores (Guatemala)	2:31:53
1953	Keizo Yamada (Japan)	2:18:51
1954	Veikko Karvonen (Finland)	2:20:39
1955	Hideo Hamamura (Japan)	2:18:22
1956	Antti Viskari (Finland)	2:14:14
1957	John J. Kelley (US)	2:20:05
1958	Franjo Mihalic (Yugoslavia)	2:25:54
1959	Eino Oksanen (Finland)	2:22:42
1960	Paavo Kotila (Finland)	2:20:54
1961	Eino Oksanen (Finland)	2:23:39
1962	Eino Oksanen (Finland)	2:23:48
1963	Aurele Vandendriessche (Belgium)	2:18:58
1964	Aurele Vandendriessche (Belgium)	2:19:59
1965	Morio Shegematsu (Japan)	2:16:33
1966	Kenji Kimihara (Japan)	2:17:11
1967	David McKenzie (NZ)	2:15:45
1968	Ambrose Burfoot (US)	2:22:17
1969	Yoshiaki Unetani (Japan)	2:13:49
1970	Ronald Hill (GB)	2:10:30
1971	Alvaro Meiji (Colombia)	2:18:45
1972	Olavi Suomalainen (Finland)	2:15:39
1973	Jon Anderson (US)	2:16:03
1974	Neil Cusack (Ireland)	2:13:39
1975	William Rodgers (US)	2:09:55
1976	Jack Fultz (US)	2:20:19
1977	Jerome Drayton (Canada)	2:14:46
1978	William Rodgers (US)	2:10:13
1979	William Rodgers (US)	2:09:27
1980	William Rodgers (US)	2:12:11

Kosice Marathon (Czechoslovakia)

1924	Karol Halla (Czech)	3:01:35
1925	Pal Kiraly (Hungary)	2:41:55
1926	Paul Hempel (Germany)	2:57:02
1927	Jozsef Galambos (Hungary)	2:38:25.2
1928	Jozsef Galambos (Hungary)	2:55:45
1929	Paul Hempel (Germany)	2:51:31
1930	Istvan Zelenka (Hungary)	2:50:58.2
1931	Juan Carlos Zabala (Argentina)	2:33:19
1932	Jozsef Galambos (Hungary)	2:43:14.4

1933	Jozsef Galambos (Hungary)		2:37:53:2
1934	Josef Sulc (Czech)		2:41:26.3
1935	Arturs Motmillers (Latvia)		2:44:57.2
1936	Gyorgy Balaban (Austria)		2:41:08
1937	Desire Leriche (France)		2:43:41.7
1945	Antonin Spiroch (Czech)		2:47:21.8
1946	Mikko Hietanen (Finland)		2:35:02.4
1947	Charles Heirendt (Lux)		2:36:06
1948	Karl Gosta Leandersson (Sweden)		2:34:46.4
1949	Matti Urpalainen (Finland)		2:33:45.6
1950	Karl Gosta Leandersson (Sweden)		2:31:20.2
1951	Jaroslav Strupp (Czech)		2:41:07.8
1952	Erkki Puolakka (Finland)		2:29:10
1953	Walter Bednar (Czech)		2:53:32.8
1954	Erkki Puolakka (Finland)		2:27:21
1955	Evert Nyberg (Sweden)		2:25:40
1956	Tomas Nilsson (Sweden)		2:22:05.4
1957	Ivan Filin (USSR)		2:23:57.8
1958	Pavel Kantorek (Czech)		2:29:37.2
1959	Sergey Popov (USSR)		2:17:45.2
1960	Samuel Hardicker (GB)		2:26:46.8
1961	Abebe Bikila (Ethiopia)		2:20:12
1962	Pavel Kantorek (Czech)		2:28:29.8
1963	Leonard Edelen (US)		2:15:09.6
1964	Pavel Kantorek (Czech)		2:25:55.4
1965	Aurele Vandendriessche (Belgium)		2:23:47
1966	Gyula Toth (Hungary)		2:19:11.2
1967	Nedjalko Farcic (Yugoslavia)		2:20:53.8

ROAD RUNNER: Abebe Bikila (Ethiopia) won the 1961 Kosice Marathon in Czechoslovakia. Bikila is one of the two men to successfully defend the Olympic Marathon title, winning the gold medal in 1960 and 1964 (see page 346).

1968	Vaclav Chudomel (Czech)	2:26:28.4
1969	Demissie Wolde (Ethiopia)	2:15:37
1970	Mikhail Gorelov (USSR)	2;16:26.2
1971	Gyula Toth (Hungary)	2:21:43.6
1972	John Farrington (Australia)	2:17:34.4
1973	Vladimir Moiseyev (USSR)	2:19:01.2
1974	Keith Angus (GB)	2:20:09
1975	Chang Sop Choe (N Korea)	2:15:47.8
1976	Takeshi So (Japan)	2:18:42:4
1977	Chun Son Goe (N Korea)	2:15:19.4
1978	Chun Son Goe (N Korea)	2:13:34.5
1979	Jouni Kortelainen (Finland)	2:15:12

Asahi Marathon (Japan)

1947	Toshikazu Wada (Japan)	2:45:45
1948	Saburo Yamada (Japan)	2:37:25
1949	Shinzo Koga (Japan)	2:40:26
1950	Shunji Koyanagi (Japan)	2:30:47
1951	Hiroyoshi Haigo (Japan)	2:30:13
1952	Katsuo Nishida (Japa)	2:27:59
1953	Hideo Hamamura (Japan)	2:27:26
1954	Reinaldo Gorno (Argentina)	2:24:55
1955	Veikko Karvonen (Finland)	2:23:16
1956	Keizo Yamada (Japan)	2:25:15
1957	Kurao Hiroshima (Japan)	2:21:40
1958	Nobuyoshi Sadanaga (Japan)	2:24:01
1959	Kurao Hiroshima (Japan)	2:29:34
1960	Barrington Magee (NZ)	2:19:04
1961	Pavel Kantorek (Czech)	2:22:05

IN THE DISTANCE: In 1979, Norwegian school teacher Grete Waitz (#5, left) won the women's honors in the New York City Marathon for the 2nd straight year. Her best time broke the record she set a year earlier in the same race, and her 1979 time was faster than the men's best in the 1972 race. Frank Shorter (right), here winning the 1972 Olympic marathon, captured first place in the Asahi Marathon 4 straight times.

1962	Toru Terasawa (Japan)	2:16:18.4
1963	Jeffrey Julian (NZ)	2:18:00.6
1964	Toru Terasawa (Japan)	2:14:48.2
1965	Hidekuni Hiroshima (Japan)	2:18:35.8
1966	Michael Ryan (NZ)	2:14:04.6
1967	Derek Clayton (Australia)	2:09:36.4
1968	William Adcocks (GB)	2:10:47.8
1969	Jerome Drayton (Canada)	2:11:12.8
1970	Akio Usami (Japan)	2:10:37.8
1971	Frank Shorter (US)	2:12:50.4
1972	Frank Shorter (US)	2:10:30
1973	Frank Shorter (US)	2:11:45.0
1974	Frank Shorter (US)	2:11:31.2
1975	Jerome Drayton (Canada)	2:10:08.4
1976	Jerome Drayton (Canada)	2:12:35
1977	William Rodgers (US)	2:10:55.3
1978	Toshihiko Seko (Japan)	2:10:21
1979	Toshihiko Seko (Japan)	2:10:35

New York City Marathon

MEN

1970	Gary Muhrcke	2:31:38.2
1971	Norman Higgins	2:22:54.2
1972	Sheldon Karlin	2:27:52.8
1973	Tom Fleming	2:21:54.8
1974	Norbert Sander	2:26:30.2
1975	Tom Fleming	2:19:27.0
1976	Bill Rodgers	2:10:09.6
1977	Bill Rodgers	2:11:28.2
1978	Bill Rodgers	2:12:11.6
1979	Bill Rodgers	2:11:42.0

WOMEN

1970	No Finisher	—
1971	Beth Bonner	2:55:22
1972	Nina Kuscsik	3:18:41
1973	Nina Kuscsik	2:57:07
1974	Katherine Switzer	3:07:29
1975	Kim Merritt	2:46:14
1976	Miki Gorman	2:39:11
1977	Miki Gorman	2:43:10
1978	Grete Waitz	2:32:30
1979	Grete Waitz	2:27:33

MARTIAL ARTS

Judo

Origin. Judo is a modern combat sport which developed out of an amalgam of several old (pre-Christian era) Japanese fighting arts, the most popular of which was *ju-jitsu (jiu-jitsu)*, which is thought to be of pre-Christian Chinese origin. Judo has developed greatly since 1882, when it was first devised by Dr. Jigoro Kano (1860–1938): World Championships were inaugurated in Tokyo on May 5, 1956.

Highest Grades. The efficiency grades in Judo are divided into pupil *(kyu)* and master *(dan)* grades. The highest awarded is the extremely rare red belt *Judan* (10th *dan*), given only to seven men. The Judo protocol provides for a *Juichidan* (11th *dan*), who also would wear a red belt, and even a *Junidan* (12th *dan*), who would wear a white belt twice as wide as an ordinary belt, and even a *Shihan* (the highest of all), but these have never been bestowed.

Marathon. The longest recorded Judo marathon with continuous play by two of six Judoka is 5-minute stints is 200 hours by the Dufftown and District Judo Club, Banffshire, Scotland, on July 9–17, 1977.

Champion. Two men have won 4 world titles. Wilhelm Ruska of the Netherlands won the 1967 and the 1971 heavyweight and the 1972 Olympic heavyweight and Open titles, and Shozo Fujii (Japan) won the middleweight title in 1971, 1973, 1975, and 1979.

World Judo Championships

Judo World Championships were first held in 1956 and are now held biennially, but were cancelled in 1977. New weight categories were applied to the 1979 competition.

1979 CHAMPIONS

Sumio Endo (Jap) Open
Yamashita (Jap) +95 kg
Khouboulouri (USSR) 95 kg
Detlef Ultsch (E Ger) 86 kg

Shozo Fujii (Jap) 78 kg
Katzuki (Jap) 71 kg
Solodouchine (USSR) 65 kg
Thierry Rey (Fra) 60 kg

OPEN ARMS: Wilhelm Ruska rejoices his victory in the 1972 Olympic openweight finals. Ruska also won the gold medal in the heavyweight division that year, as well as 2 world titles, in 1967 and 1971.

FLIPPERS: Japan's Shinobu Sekine (left) beat Brian Jacks (GB) in the semi-finals of the 1972 Olympic middleweight competition and went on to win the gold medal. Jacks ended up sharing the bronze medal.

PREVIOUS WINNERS
OPEN

1956	Shokichi Natsui (Jap)
1958	Koji Sone (Jap)
1961	Anton Geesink (Hol)
1965	Isao Inokuma (Jap)
1967	Matsuo Matsunaga (Jap)
1969	Masatoshi Shinomaki (Jap)
1971	Masatoshi Shinomaki (Jap)
1973	Kazuhiro Nimomiya (Jap)
1975	Haruki Uemura (Jap)

HEAVYWEIGHT (over 93 kg)

1965	Anton Geesink (Hol)
1967	Wilhelm Ruska (Hol)
1969	Shuja Suma (Jap)
1971	Wilhelm Ruska (Hol)
1973	Chonofuhe Tagaki (Jap)
1975	Sumio Endo (Jap)

LIGHT HEAVYWEIGHT (over 80 kg)

1967	Nobuyaki Sato (Jap)
1969	Fumio Sasahara (Jap)
1971	Fumio Sasahara (Jap)
1973	Nobuyaki Sato (Jap)
1975	Jean-Luc Rouge (Fra)

MIDDLEWEIGHT (over 70 kg)

1965	Isao Okano (Jap)
1967	Eiji Maruki (Jap)
1969	Isomu Sonoda (Jap)
1971	Shozo Fujii (Jap)
1973	Shozo Fujii (Jap)
1975	Shozo Fujii (Jap)

LIGHT MIDDLEWEIGHT
(Welterweight) (over 63 kg)

1967	Hiroshi Minatoya (Jap)
1969	Hiroshi Minatoya (Jap)
1971	Hizashi Tsuzawa (Jap)
1973	Kazutoyo Nomura (Jap)
1975	Vladimir Nevzova (USSR)

LIGHTWEIGHT (under 63 kg)

1965	H. Matsuda (Jap)
1967	Takosumi Shigeoka (Jap)
1969	Yoshio Sonoda (Jap)
1971	Takao Kawaguchi (Jap)
1973	Yoshiharu Minamo (Jap)
1975	Yoshiharu Minamo (Jap)

Olympic Judo Champions

Judo was first held in the Olympic Games at Tokyo in 1964, but was not included in 1968. Winners:

OPEN

1964	Anton Geesink (Hol)
1972	Wilhelm Ruska (Hol)
1976	Haruko Uemura (Jap)
1980	Dietmar Lorenz (E. Ger)

HEAVY

1964	Isao Inokuma (Jap)
1972	Wilhelm Ruska (Hol)
1976	Sergei Novikov (USSR)
1980	Angelo Parisi (Fra)

LIGHT HEAVY

1972	Shota Chochoshvily (USSR)
1976	Kazuhiro Ninomiya (Jap)
1980	Robert Van de Walle (Bel)

MIDDLE

1964	Isao Okano (Jap)
1972	Shinobu Sekine (Jap)
1976	Isamu Sonoda (Jap)
1980	Juerg Roethlisberger (Swi)

MIDDLE LIGHT

1980	Nikolay Sobdukhin

LIGHT MIDDLE

1972	Kazutoyo Nomura (Jap)
1976	Vladimir Nevzorov (USSR)
1980	Shota Khabareli (USSR)

LIGHT

1964	Takehide Nakatani (Jap)
1972	Takao Kawaguchi (Jap)
1976	Hector Rodriguez (Cub)
1980	Ezio Gamba (Ita)

SUPER LIGHT

1980	Thierry Ray (Fra)

Karate

Origins. Originally *karate* (empty hand) is known to have been developed by the unarmed populace as a method of attack on, and defense against, armed Japanese aggressors in Okinawa, Ryukyu Islands, based on techniques devised from the 6th century Chinese art of Shaolin boxing (Kempo). Transmitted to Japan in the 1920's by Funakoshi Gichin, this method of combat was refined and organized into a sport with competitive rules.

The five major schools of *karate* in Japan are *Shotokan, Wado-ryu, Goju-ryu, Shito-ryu,* and *Kyokushinkai,* each of which places different emphasis on speed, power, etc. Other styles include *Sankukai, Shotokai* and *Shukokai.* The military form of *Tae-kwan-do* with 9 *dans* is a Korean equivalent of *karate. Kung fu* is believed to have originated in Nepal or Tibet but was adopted within Chinese temples *via* India, and has in recent years been widely popularized through various martial arts films.

Wu shu is a comprehensive term embracing all Chinese martial arts.

Most Titles. The only winner of 3 All-Japanese titles has been Takeshi Oishi, who won in 1969–70–71.

The leading exponents among karatekas are a number of 10th *dans* in Japan.

World Championships (Karate-do)

TEAM

First held in 1970. Winners:

1970	Japan
1972	France
1975	Great Britain
1977	Holland

INDIVIDUAL

1977 Otti Roethof (Hol)

Japan Karate Association (JKA) World Championships
(Shotoku style)

JUI-KUMITE (free-style fighting)

Individual — **Team**

1975 Masahiko Tanaka (Jap) Japan
1977 Masahiko Tanaka (Jap) Japan

KATA (training dances)

Team	*Men*	*Women*
1977	Japan	Japan

World Kendo Championships

First held in 1970 in Japan; and subsequently in the US in 1973 and in Britain in 1976.

Individual winners:		**Team prize:**	
1970	Kobayashi (Jap)	1970	Japan
1973	Sakuragi (Jap)	1973	Japan
1976	Eiji Yoko (Jap)	1976	Japan
1979	H. Yamada (Jap)	1979	Japan

MODERN PENTATHLON

Earliest. The Modern Pentathlon (Riding, Fencing, Shooting, Swimming and Running) was inaugurated into the Olympic Games at Stockholm in 1912.

Point scores in riding, fencing, cross country and hence overall scores have no comparative value between one competition and another. In shooting and swimming (300 meters), where measure-

RUN, SHOOT, SWIM, FENCE AND RIDE: Russian Igor Novikov (left) won the world title 4 times, 1957–61. András Bálczo (right) of Hungary won 5 world titles and the 1972 Olympic individual title. He has also won 2 team gold medals and 2 silver medals, an extraordinary feat in this multifaceted event.

ments are absolute, the point scores are of record significance. The records in these areas in major competition are listed below:

	Points			
Shooting	1,132	Danieli Massala (Italy)	Jönkoping, Sweden	Aug. 21, 1978
Swimming	1,324	Robert Nieman (US)	Montreal, Canada	July 21, 1976

Most World Titles

The record number of world titles won is 6 by András Balczó (Hungary) in 1963, 1965, 1966, 1967 and 1969, and the Olympic title in 1972, which also rates as a world title.

Olympic Titles

The greatest number of Olympic gold medals won in three by Balczó, a member of Hungary's winning team in 1960 and 1968, and the 1972 individual champion. Lars Hall (Sweden) uniquely has won two individual championships. Balczó has won a record number of five medals (3 gold and 2 silver).

INDIVIDUAL GOLD: Lars Hall (Sweden) is the only man to win 2 individual gold medals in the Olympic Pentathlon competition. His victories came in 1952 and 1956.

Olympic Champions

Since 1948:

	Individual	Team
1948	William Grut (Swe)	
1952	Lars Hall (Swe)	Hungary
1956	Lars Hall (Swe)	USSR
1960	Ferenc Németh (Hun)	Hungary
1964	Ferenc Török (Hun)	USSR
1968	Bjorn Ferm (Swe)	Hungary
1972	András Balczó (Hun)	USSR
1976	Janusz Pyciak-Peciak (Pol)	GB
1980	Anatoliy Starostin (USSR)	USSR

World Champions

MEN

	Individual	Team
1949	Tage Bjurefelt (Swe)	Sweden
1950	Lars Hall (Swe)	Sweden
1951	Lars Hall (Swe)	Sweden
1953	Dabor Benedek (Hun)	Sweden
1954	Björn Thofelt (Swe)	Hungary
1955	Konstantin Salnikov (USSR)	Hungary
1957	Igor Novikov (USSR)	USSR
1958	Igor Novikov (USSR)	USSR
1959	Igor Novikov (USSR)	USSR
1961	Igor Novikov (USSR)	USSR
1962	S. Dobnikov (USSR)	USSR
1963	András Balczó (Hun)	Hungary
1965	András Balczó (Hun)	Hungary
1966	András Balczó (Hun)	Hungary
1967	András Balczó (Hun)	Hungary
1969	András Balczó (Hun)	USSR
1970	Paul Kelemen (Hun)	Hungary
1971	Boris Onischenko (USSR)	USSR
1973	Pavel Lednev (USSR)	USSR
1974	Pavel Lednev (USSR)	USSR
1975	Pavel Lednev (USSR)	Hungary
1977	Janusz Pyciak-Peciak (Pol)	Poland
1978	Pavel Lednev (USSR)	Poland
1979	Robert Nieman (US)	US

WOMEN

First contested 1977.

1977	Virginia Swift (US)
1978	Wendy Norman (GB)
1979	Kathy Taylor (GB)

MOTORCYCLING

Earliest Races. The first motorcycle race was held on an oval track at Sheen House, Richmond, Surrey, England, on November 29, 1897, won by Charles Jarrott (1877–1944) on a Fournier. The oldest motorcycle races in the world are the Auto-Cycle Union Tourist Trophy (T.T.) series, first held on the 15.81-mile "Peel" ("St. John's") course on the Isle of Man on May 28, 1907, and still run on the island, on the "Mountain" circuit (37.73 miles).

Longest Circuits

The 37.73-mile "Mountain" circuit, over which the two main T.T. races have been run since 1911, has 264 curves and corners and is the longest used for any motorcycle race.

QUICK AS A VINK: Henk Vink recorded the world record average speed for two 1-kilometer runs with 16.68 seconds in 1977. The faster run was made in 16.09 seconds.

Fastest Circuits

The highest average lap speed attained on any closed circuit is 160.288 m.p.h. by Yvon du Hamel (Canada) on a modified 903-c.c. four-cylinder Kawasaki Z1 on the 31-degree banked 2.5-mile Daytona International Speedway, Florida, in March, 1973. His lap time was 56.149 seconds.

The fastest road circuit is the Francorchamps circuit near Spa, Belgium. It is 14.12 kilometers (8 miles 1,340 yards) in length and was lapped in 3 minutes 50.3 seconds (average speed of 137.150 m.p.h.) by Barry S. F. Sheene (born Holborn, London, England, September 11, 1950) on a 495-c.c. four-cylinder Suzuki during the Belgian Grand Prix on July 3, 1977.

Fastest Race

The fastest race in the world was held at Grenzlandring, West Germany, in 1939. It was won by Georg Meier (b. Germany, 1910) at an average speed of 134 m.p.h. on a supercharged 495-c.c. flat-twin B.M.W.

The fastest road race in the 500-c.c. Belgian Grand Prix on the Francorchamps circuit (see above). The record time for this 10-lap 87.74-mile race is 38 minutes 58.5 seconds (average speed of 135.068 m.p.h.) by Barry Sheene (UK) on a 495-c.c. four-cylinder Suzuki on July 3, 1977.

Longest Race

The longest race is the Liège 24 Hours. The greatest distance ever covered is 2,761.9 miles (average speed 115.08 m.p.h.) by Jean-Claude Chemarin and Christian Leon of France on a 941-c.c. four-cylinder Honda on the Francorchamps circuit (8 miles 1,340 yards) near Spa, Belgium, Angust 14–15, 1976.

World Championships

Most world championship titles (instituted by the *Fédération Internationale Motorcycliste* in 1949) won are 15 by Giacomo Agostini (Italy) in the 350-cc. class and in the 500-c.c. class. Agostini (b. 1942) is the only man to win two world championships in five consecutive years (350- and 500-c.c. titles in 1968–69–70–71–72). Agostini won 122 races in the world championship series between April 24, 1965, and August 29, 1976, including a record 19 in 1970, also achieved by Stanley Michael Bailey "Mike" Hailwood (b. Oxford, England, April 2, 1940) in 1966.

Klaus Enders (Germany) (b. 1937) won six world side-car titles.

Jöel Robert (b. Chatelet, Belgium, November 11, 1943) has won six 250-c.c. moto-cross (also known as "scrambles") world championships (1964, 68–72). Between April 25, 1964, and June 18, 1972, he won a record fifty 250-c.c. Grands Prix. He became the youngest moto-cross world champion on July 12, 1964, when he won the 250-c.c. championship aged 20 years 8 months.

Alberto "Johnny" Cecotto (born Caracas, Venezuela, January 1956) was the youngest person to win a world championship. He was aged 19 years 211 days when he won the 350-c.c. title on August 24, 1975.

The oldest was Hermann-Peter Müller (1909–76) of West Germany, who won the 250-c.c title in 1955, aged 46.

Most Successful Machines

Italian M.V.-Agusta motorcycles won 37 world championships between 1952 and 1973 and 276 world championship races between 1952 and 1976. Japanese Honda machines won 29 world championship races and five world championships in 1966. In the seven years Honda contested the championship (1961–67) its annual average was 20 race wins.

Speed Records

Official world speed records must be set with two runs over a measured distance within a time limit (one hour for F.I.M. records, two hours for A.M.A. records).

Donald Vesco (born 1939) of El Cajon, California, recorded an average speed of 303.810 m.p.h. over the measured mile at Bonneville Salt Flats, Utah, on September 28, 1975, to establish an A.M.A. record. Riding a 21-foot-long *Silver Bird* Streamliner powered by two 750-c.c. Yamaha TZ750 4-cylinder engines developing 180 b.h.p., he covered the first mile in 11.817 seconds (304.646 m.p.h.). On the second run his time was 11.882 seconds (302.979 m.p.h.). The average time for the two runs was 11.8495 (303.810 m.p.h.) for the A.M.A. record. On the same day, he set an F.I.M. record at an average speed of 302.928 m.p.h. Also on the same day, he covered a flying quarter mile in 2.925 seconds (307.692 m.p.h.), the highest speed ever achieved on a motorcycle.

The world record average speed for two runs over one kilometer (1,093.6 yards) from a standing start is 16.68 seconds by Henk Vink (Netherlands) on his supercharged 984-c.c. 4-cylinder

Kawasaki, at Elvington Airfield, Yorkshire, England, on July 24, 1977. The faster run was made in 16.09 seconds.

The world record for two runs over 440 yards from a standing start is 8.805 seconds by Henk Vink on his supercharged 1,132-c.c. 4-cylinder Kawasaki, at Elvington Airfield, Yorkshire, England, on July 23, 1977. The faster run was made in 8.55 seconds.

The fastest time for a single run over 440 yards from a standing start is 7.62 seconds by Russ Collins of Gardena, California, riding his nitro-burning 2000-c.c. 8-cylinder Honda, *Sorcerer*, at the National Hot Rod Association's World Finals at Ontario Speedway on October 7, 1978. The highest terminal velocity recorded at the end of a 440-yard run from a standing start is 199.55 m.p.h. by Russ Collins in the same run.

Marathon

The longest time a solo motorcycle has been kept in continuous motion is 500 hours by Owen Fitzgerald, Richard Kennett, and Donald Mitchell in Western Australia, on July 10–31, 1977. They covered 8,432 miles.

Moto-Cross

European Championships were held at 500 cc in 1952 and World Championships were first held at this category in 1957, at which time a 250 cc category was introduced as a European Championship. The latter was upgraded to World Championships status in 1962. Winners since 1957:

250 cc
European Championships

1957	Fritz Betzelbacher (W Ger)
1958	Jaromïr Cizek (Czech)
1959	Rolf Tibblin (Swe)
1960	Dave Bickers (GB)
1961	Dave Bickers (GB)

World Championships

1962	Torsten Hallman (Swe)
1963	Torsten Hallman (Swe)
1964	Joël Robert (Bel)
1965	Victor Arbekov (USSR)
1966	Torsten Hallman (Swe)
1967	Torsten Hallman (Swe)
1968	Joël Robert (Bel)
1969	Joël Robert (Bel)
1970	Joël Robert (Bel)
1971	Joël Robert (Bel)
1972	Joël Robert (Bel)
1973	Hakan Andersson (Swe)
1974	Gennadiy Moisseyev (USSR)
1975	Harry Everts (Bel)
1976	Heikki Mikkola (Fin)
1977	Gennadiy Moisseyev (USSR)
1978	Gennadiy Moisseyev (USSR)
1979	Hakan Calqvist (Swe)

500 cc
World Championships

1957	Bill Nilsson (Swe)
1958	René Baeten (Bel)
1959	Sten Lundin (Swe)
1960	Bill Nilsson (Swe)

FAST RIDE: In a 440-yard run from a standing start, Californian Russ Collins clocked 2 world bests on his bike, "Sorcerer." His time in the single run was 7.62 seconds and his terminal velocity was 199.55 m.p.h.

1961	Sten Lundin (Swe)	1975	Roger de Coster (Bel)
1962	Rolf Tibblin (Swe)	1976	Roger de Coster (Bel)
1963	Rolf Tibblin (Swe)	1977	Heikki Mikkola (Fin)
1964	Jeff Smith (GB)	1978	Heikki Mikkola (Fin)
1965	Jeff Smith (GB)	1979	Graham Noyce (GB)
1966	Paul Friedrichs (E Ger)		
1967	Paul Friedrichs (E Ger)		
1968	Paul Friedrichs (E Ger)	**125 cc**	
1969	Bengt Aberg (Swe)	**World Championships**	
1970	Bengt Aberg (Swe)		
1971	Roger de Coster (Bel)	1975	Gaston Rahier (Bel)
1972	Roger de Coster (Bel)	1976	Gaston Rahier (Bel)
1973	Roger de Coster (Bel)	1977	Gaston Rahier (Bel)
1974	Heikki Mikkola (Fin)	1978	Akira Watanabe (Jap)
		1979	Harry Everts (Bel)

TROPHÉE DES NATIONS

The international Team championship for 250 cc has been contested annually since 1961. Winning nations:
Great Britain: 1961–62, 1965
Sweden: 1963–64, 1966–68
Belgium: 1969–78
USSR: 1979

TRIALS

World Champions (first recognized 1975)
1975	Martin Lampkin (GB)
1976	Yrjo Vesterinen (Fin)
1977	Yrjo Vesterinen (Fin)
1978	Yyjo Vesterinen (Fin)
1979	Bernie Schreiber (US)

MOTO-CROSS DES NATIONS

The international Team championship for 500 cc has been contested annually since 1947. Winning nations:
Great Britain: 1947, 1949–50, 1952–54, 1956–57, 1959–60, 1963–67
Belgium: 1948, 1951, 1969, 1972–73, 1976–77, 1979
Sweden: 1955, 1958, 1961–62, 1971, 1974
USSR: 1968, 1978
Czechoslovakia: 1975

Motorcycling World Championship

The most important World Championship category is undoubtedly the 500 cc. For this and the other categories riders gain points based on their performances in a series of Grand Prix events. The World Championships were first held under the auspices of the FIM in 1949. Individual winners:

500 cc

1949	Leslie Graham (GB)
1950	Umberto Masetti (Ita)
1951	Geoff Duke (GB)
1952	Umberto Masetti (Ita)
1953	Geoff Duke (GB)
1954	Geoff Duke (GB)
1955	Geoff Duke (GB)
1956	John Surtees (GB)
1957	Liberto Liberati (Ita)
1958	John Surtees (GB)
1959	John Surtees (GB)
1960	John Surtees (GB)
1961	Gary Hocking (Rho)
1962	Mike Hailwood (GB)
1963	Mike Hailwood (GB)
1964	Mike Hailwood (GB)
1965	Mike Hailwood (GB)
1966	Giacomo Agostini (Ita)
1967	Giacomo Agostini (Ita)
1968	Giacomo Agostini (Ita)
1969	Giacomo Agostini (Ita)
1970	Giacomo Agostini (Ita)
1971	Giacomo Agostini (Ita)
1972	Giacomo Agostini (Ita)
1973	Phil Read (GB)
1974	Phil Read (GB)
1975	Giacomo Agostini (Ita)

TOP RACER: Giacomo Agostini (Italy) has won 15 world titles, including 5 straight in both the 500-c.c. and 300-c.c. classes.

1976 Barry Sheene (GB)
1977 Barry Sheene (GB)
1978 Kenny Roberts (US)
1979 Kenny Roberts (US)

250 cc
1949 Bruno Ruffo (Ita)
1950 Dario Ambrosini (Ita)
1951 Bruno Ruffo (Ita)
1952 Enrico Lorenzetti (Ita)
1953 Werner Haas (W Ger)
1954 Werner Haas (W Ger)
1955 Herman Müller (W Ger)
1956 Carlo Ubbiali (Ita)
1957 Cecil Sandford (GB)
1958 Tarquinio Provini (Ita)
1959 Carlo Ubbiali (Ita)
1960 Carlo Ubbiali (Ita)
1961 Mike Hailwood (GB)
1962 Jim Redman (Rho)
1963 Jim Redman (Rho)
1964 Phil Read (GB)
1965 Phil Read (GB)
1966 Mike Hailwood (GB)
1967 Mike Hailwood (GB)
1968 Phil Read (GB)
1969 Kel Carruthers (Aus)
1970 Rod Gould (GB)
1971 Phil Read (GB)
1972 Jarno Saarinen (Fin)
1973 Dieter Braun (W Ger)
1974 Walter Villa (Ita)
1975 Walter Villa (Ita)
1976 Walter Villa (Ita)
1977 Mario Lega (Ita)
1978 Kork Ballington (S Af)
1979 Kork Ballington (S Af)

350 cc
1949 Freddie Frith (GB)
1950 Bob Foster (GB)
1951 Geoff Duke (GB)
1952 Geoff Duke (GB)
1953 Fergus Anderson (GB)
1954 Fergus Anderson (GB)
1955 Bill Lomas (GB)
1956 Bill Lomas (GB)
1957 Keith Campbell (Aus)
1958 John Surtees (GB)
1959 John Surtees (GB)
1960 John Surtees (GB)
1961 Gary Hocking (Rho)
1962 Jim Redman (Rho)
1963 Jim Redman (Rho)
1964 Jim Redman (Rho)
1965 Jim Redman (Rho)
1966 Mike Hailwood (GB)
1967 Mike Hailwood (GB)
1968 Giacomo Agostini (Ita)
1969 Giacomo Agostini (Ita)
1970 Giacomo Agostini (Ita)
1971 Giacomo Agostini (Ita)
1972 Giacomo Agostini (Ita)
1973 Giacomo Agostini (Ita)
1974 Giacomo Agostini (Ita)
1975 Johnnie Cecotto (Ven)
1976 Walter Villa (Ita)
1977 Takazumi Katayama (Jap)
1978 Kork Ballington (S Af)
1979 Kork Ballington (S AF)

50 cc
1962 Ernst Degner (W Ger)
1963 Hugh Anderson (NZ)
1964 Hugh Anderson (NZ)
1965 Ralph Bryans (Ire)
1966 Hans-Georg Anscheidt (W Ger)
1967 Hans-Georg Anscheidt (W Ger)
1968 Hans-Georg Anscheidt (W Ger)
1969 Angel Nieto (Spa)
1970 Angel Nieto (Spa)
1971 Jan de Vries (Hol)
1972 Angel Nieto (Spa)
1973 Jan de Vries (Hol)
1974 Henk van Kessel (Hol)
1975 Angel Nieto (Spa)
1976 Angel Nieto (Spa)
1977 Angel Nieto (Spa)
1978 Rocardo Tormo (Spa)
1979 Eugenio Lazzarini (Ita)

FORMULA 750

1977 Steve Baker (US)
1978 Johnnie Cecotto (Ven)
1979 Patrick Pons (Fra)

125 cc
1949 Nello Pagani (Ita)
1950 Bruno Ruffo (Ita)
1951 Carlo Ubbiali (Ita)
1952 Cecil Sandford (GB)
1953 Werner Haas (W Ger)
1954 Rupert Hollaus (Aut)
1955 Carlo Ubbiali (Ita)
1956 Carlo Ubbiali (Ita)
1957 Tarquinio Provini (Ita)
1958 Carlo Ubbiali (Ita)
1959 Carlo Ubbiali (Ita)
1960 Carlo Ubbiali (Ita)
1961 Tom Phillis (Aus)
1962 Luigi Taveri (Swi)
1963 Hugh Anderson (NZ)
1964 Luigi Taveri (Swi)
1965 Hugh Anderson (NZ)
1966 Luigi Taveri (Swi)
1967 Bill Ivy (GB)

**MAN AND MACHINE: Jim Redman has
won world championships in both the
250-c.c. and 350-c.c. classes. In the latter
class, he captured 4 straight titles,
1962–65.**

TITLE RIDERS: Mike Hailwood (left) won 19 races in the 1966 world championship series, a season record he shares with Giacomo Agostini. Phil Read (right) has won world titles in the 550-c.c., 250-c.c. and 125-c.c. classes.

1968	Phil Read (GB)		1959	Walter Schneider (W Ger)
1969	Dave Simmonds (GB)		1960	Helmut Fath (W Ger)
1970	Dieter Braun (W Ger)		1961	Max Deubel (W Ger)
1971	Angel Nieto (Spa)		1962	Max Deubel (W Ger)
1972	Angel Nieto (Spa)		1963	Max Deubel (W Ger)
1973	Kent Andersson (Swe)		1964	Max Deubel (W Ger)
1974	Kent Andersson (Swe)		1965	Fritz Scheidegger (Swi)
1975	Paolo Pileri (Ita)		1966	Fritz Scheidegger (Swi)
1976	Pier-Paolo Bianchi (Ita)		1967	Klaus Enders (W Ger)
1977	Pier-Paolo Bianchi (Ita)		1968	Helmut Fath (W Ger)
1978	Eugenio Lazzarini (Ita)		1969	Klaus Enders (W Ger)
1979	Angel Nieto (Spa)		1970	Klaus Enders (W Ger)
			1971	Horst Owesle (W Ger)
SIDE-CARS			1972	Klaus Enders (W Ger)
			1973	Klaus Enders (W Ger)
1949	Eric Oliver (GB)		1974	Klaus Enders (W Ger)
1950	Eric Oliver (GB)		1975	Rolf Steinhausen (W Ger)
1951	Eric Oliver (GB)		1976	Rolf Steinhausen (W Ger)
1952	Cyril Smith (GB)		1977	George O'Dell (GB)
1953	Eric Oliver (GB)		1978	Rolf Biland (Swi)
1954	Wilhelm Noll (W Ger)		1979*	Rolf Biland (Swi)
1955	Wilhelm Faust (W Ger)			Bruno Holzer (Swi)
1956	Wilhelm Noll (W Ger)			
1957	Fritz Hillebrand (W Ger)			
1958	Walter Schneider (W Ger)		* Two championships held	

MOUNTAINEERING

Origins. Although bronze-age artifacts have been found on the summit (9,605 feet) of the Riffelhorn, Switzerland, mountaineering, as a sport, has a continuous history dating back only to 1854. Isolated instances of climbing for its own sake exist back to the

13th century. The Atacamenans built sacrificial platforms near the summit of Llullaillaco in South America (22,058 feet) in late pre-Columbian times, c. 1490.

Greatest Wall

The highest final stage in any wall climb is that on the south face of Annapurna I (26,545 feet). It was climbed by the British expedition led by Christian Bonington April 2–May 27, 1970, when Donald Whillans, 36, and Dougal Haston, 27, scaled to the summit. They used 18,000 feet of rope.

The longest wall climb is on the Rupal-Flank from the base camp at 11,680 feet to the South Point (26,384 feet) of Nanga Parbat—a vertical ascent of 14,704 feet. This was scaled by the Austro-Germano-Italian Expedition led by Dr. Herrligkoffer in April, 1970.

The world's most demanding free climbs are in the Yosemite Valley, California, with a severity rating of 5.12.

Mount Everest

Mount Everest (29,028 feet) was first climbed at 11:30 A.M. on May 29, 1953, when the summit was reached by Edmund Percival Hillary (born July 20, 1919), of New Zealand, and the Sherpa, Tenzing Norgay (born, as Namgyal Wangdi, in Nepal in 1914, formerly called Tenzing Khumjung Bhutia). The successful expedition was led by Col. (later Hon. Brigadier) Henry Cecil John Hunt (born June 22, 1910).

Up to October 2, 1979, Mt. Everest had been successfully climbed by 99 different climbers. These included four women.

Most Times. Three men have climbed Mt. Everest twice. Nwang Gombu (a Sherpa) in 1963 and 1965; Ang Phu (a Sherpa) in 1978 and 1979; Pertemba (a Sherpa) in 1975 and 1979.

Oldest. The oldest person to climb Mt. Everest is Dr. Gerhard Schmatz (W. Germany) (b. June 5, 1929) who was aged 50 years 118 days, when he reached the summit on October 1, 1979. His wife, Hannelore (b. February 16, 1940) was the oldest woman to succeed the following day, aged 39 years 229 days. Unfortunately, she was killed on the way down.

Successful Attempts. There have been 102 successful climbs of Mt. Everest, by 99 climbers as of December 1, 1979. Nepal has supplied the most with 15 men, three of them succeeding a second time (see above). After that, West Germany has 13, China 12, India 10 and the United States 8. The full list is as follows:

Ascents

NAME	NATION-ALITY	DATE ON SUMMIT	REMARKS
Edmund Hillary	NZ	May 29, 1953	First man on top (via South Ridge)
Tenzing Norgay (Sherpa)	India		
Ernst Schmied	Switz	May 23, 1956	
Juerg Marmet	Switz		
Adolf Reist	Switz	May 24, 1956	

PARTNERS IN CLIMB: Sherpa Tenzing Norgay stands atop 29,028-foot high Mount Everest (the highest mountain in the world) in this photograph taken by Edmund Hillary. Norgay and Hillary were the first men to reach the summit, arriving on May 29, 1953. Since their historic ascent, 99 climbers had reached the top as of October, 1979, and 3 of those climbers (all Sherpas) had done it twice. Sherpas are native to the Himalayas and are accustomed to living at high altitudes.

HIGH STEPPING: Japanese Women Climbing Expedition member Mrs. Junko Tabei, 35, became the first woman to conquer Mt. Everest when she scaled the peak on May 16, 1975. At right is the south wall aspect of the formidable mountain.

Mount Everest (continued)

NAME	NATION-ALITY	DATE ON SUMMIT	REMARKS
Hansrudolf von Gunten	Switz		
Wang Fu-chou	China	May 25, 1960	First via Northeast Ridge
Gonpa	China		
Chu Ying-hua	China		
James Warren Whittaker	US	May 1, 1963	
Nawang Gombu (Sherpa)	India		
Luther Jerstad	US	May 22, 1963	
Barry Bishop	US	May 22, 1963	
Dr. Willi Unsoeld	US	May 22, 1963	First via West Ridge
Dr. Tom Hornbein	US	May 22, 1963	
Capt. A. S. Cheema	India	May 20, 1965	
Nawang Gombu (Sherpa)	India	May 20, 1965	First man to scale Everest twice
Sonam Gyatso	India	May 22, 1965	
Sonam Wangyal	India		
C. P. Vohra	India	May 24, 1965	
Ang Kami (Sherpa)	India		
Capt. H. P. S. Ahluwalia	India	May 29, 1965	
H. C. S. Rawat	India		
Phu Dorje (Sherpa)	Nepal		
Teruo Matsuura	Japan	May 11, 1970	
Naomi Uermura	Japan		
Katsutoshi Hirabayashi	Japan	May 12, 1970	
Chotare (Sherpa)	Nepal		
Sgt. Rinaldo Carrel	Italy	May 5, 1973	
Sgt. Mirko Minuzzo	Italy		
Lhakpa Tenzing (Sherpa)	Nepal		
Shambu Tamang	Nepal		
Capt. Fabrizio Innamorati	Italy	May 7, 1973	
Virginio Epis	Italy		
Sgt. Maj. Claudio Benedetti	Italy		
Sonam Gyalgen (Sherpa)	Nepal		
Yasuo Kato	Japan	October 26, 1973	First autumn ascent of Everest
Hisashi Ishiguro	Japan		
Mrs. Junko Tabei	Japan	May 16, 1975	First woman to scale Everest

Name	Country	Date	Notes
Ang Tsering (Sherpa)	Nepal		
Mrs. Phanthog	China	May 27, 1975	
Sodnam Norbu	China		
Lotse	China		
Hou Sheng-fu	China		
Samdrub	China		
Darphuntso	China		
Kunga Pasang	China		
Tsering Tobgyal	China		
Ngapo Khyen	China		
Dougal Haston	GB	September 24, 1975	First via Southwest Face
Doug Scott	GB		
Peter Boardman	GB	September 26, 1975	
Pertemba (Sherpa)	Nepal		
Sgt. John Stokes	GB	May 16, 1976	
Cpl. Michael Lane	GB		
Dr. Chris Chandler	US	October 8, 1976	
Robert Cormack	US		
Sang-Don Ko	South Korea	September 15, 1977	
Pemba Norbu (Sherpa)	Nepal		
Wolfgang Nairz	Austria	May 3, 1978	
Robert Schauer	Austria		
Horst Bergmann	Austria		
Ang Phu (Sherpa)	Nepal		
Reinhold Messner	Italy	May 8, 1978	First persons to scale Everest without any use of oxygen
Peter Habeler	Austria		
Dr. Oswald Oelz	Austria	May 11, 1978	
Karl Reinhard	W Ger		
Franz Oppurg	Austria	May 14, 1978	First person to reach summit on last part of climb alone
Hubert Hillmaier	W Ger	October 14, 1978	
Josef Mack	W Ger		
Hans Engl	W Ger		
Jean Afanassief	France	October 15, 1978	
Nicolas Jaeger	France		
Pierre Mazeaud	France		
Kurt Diemberger	Austria		
Siegfried Hupfauer	W Ger	October 16, 1978	
Wilhelm Klimek	W Ger		
Robert Allenbach	Switz		
Miss Wanda Rutkiewicz	Poland		
Ang Kami (Sherpa)	Nepal		
Ang Dorje (Sherpa)	Nepal		
Mingma (Sherpa)	Nepal		
Georg Ritter	W Ger	October 17, 1978	
Bernd Kullmann	W Ger		
Jernej Zaplotnik	Yugo	May 13, 1979	
Andrej Stremfelj	Yugo		
Stipe Bozic	Yugo	May 15, 1979	
Stane Belak	Yugo		
Ang Phu (Sherpa)	Nepal		
Dr. Gerhard Schmatz	W Ger	October 1, 1979	
Dr. Hermann Warth	W Ger		
Hans Von Kaenel	Switz		
Pertemba (Sherpa)	Nepal		
Lhakpa Gyalu (Sherpa)	Nepal		
Tilman Fischbach	W Ger	October 2, 1979	
Guenter Kaempfe	W Ger		
Mrs. Hannelore Schmatz	W Ger		First woman to die on Everest
Nick Banks	NZ		
Ray Genet	US		
Sundare (Sherpa)	Nepal		
Ang Phurba (Sherpa)	Nepal		
Ang Jambu (Sherpa)	Nepal		

Note: The Sherpa people are a Tibetan race living on the slopes of the Himalayas.
Note: Gerhard and Hannelore Schmatz were the first married couple to climb Everest, and their expedition the first to put all its members on the summit.

OLYMPIC GAMES

Note: These records now include the un-numbered Games held at Athens in 1906, which some authorities ignore. Although inserted between the regular IIIrd Games in 1904 and the IV Games in 1908, the 1906 Games were both official and were of a higher standard than all three of those that preceded them.

Origins. The earliest celebration of the ancient Olympic Games of which there is a certain record is that of July, 776 B.C. (when Coroibos, a cook from Ellis, won a foot race), though their origin probably dates from *c.* 1370 B.C. The ancient Games were terminated by an order issued in Milan in 393 A.D. by Theodosius I, "the Great" (*c.* 346–395), Emperor of Rome. At the instigation of Pierre de Fredi, Baron de Coubertin (1863–1937), the Olympic Games of the modern era were inaugurated in Athens on April 6, 1896.

Most Medals

In the ancient Olympic Games, victors were given a chaplet (head garland) of olive leaves. Leonidas of Rhodes won 12 running titles from 164–152 B.C.

THE GOLD STANDARD: California swimmer Mark Spitz (left) won 7 gold medals (4 individual and 3 relay) in the 1972 Olympics in Munich, an unequaled achievement. American Indian Jim Thorpe (right), here pole vaulting in the decathlon, won 2 golds in 1912 that were later revoked for breaching the standards of amateurism. The question of amateurism has long been controversial as different nations have different policies concerning the subsidizing of athletes.

A FIRST LADY: Fanny Durack accepts the prize for her 1st-place finish in the women's 100 meters swimming competition in the 1912 Stockholm Olympics. Women first competed in incidental (and subsequently discontinued) Olympic sports such as tennis and golf, and later in the figure skating events held during the 1908 Games.

Individual. The most individual gold medals won by a male competitor in the modern Games is ten by Raymond Clarence Ewry (US) (b. October 14, 1874, at Lafayette, Indiana; d. September 27, 1937), a jumper (see *Track and Field*). The female record is seven by Veral Caslavska-Odlozil (b. May 3, 1942) of Czechoslovakia (also see *Gymnastics*).

The only Olympian to win 4 consecutive individual titles in the same event has been Alfred A. Oerter (b. September 19, 1936, New York City) who won the discus title in 1956–60–64–68.

Most Olympic Gold Medals at One Games. Mark Spitz (US), the swimmer who won 2 relay golds in Mexico in 1968, won 7 more (4 individual and 3 relay) at Munich in 1972. The latter figure is an absolute Olympic record for one celebration at any sport.

Youngest and Oldest Gold Medalists. The youngest woman to win a gold medal is Marjorie Gestring (US) (b. November 18, 1922) aged 13 years 267 days, in the 1936 women's springboard event. The youngest winner ever was a French boy (whose name is not recorded) who coxed the Netherlands coxed pair in 1900. He was not more than 10 and may have been as young as 7. He substituted for Dr. Hermanus Brockmann, who coxed in the heats but proved too heavy.

Oscar G. Swahn was a member of the winning Running Deer shooting team in 1912, aged 65 years 258 days.

National. The total figures for most medals and most gold metals for all Olympic events (including those now discontinued) for the Summer (1896–1980) and Winter Games (1924–1980) are:

	Gold	*Silver*	*Bronze*	*Total*
1. USA	664*	515½	443½	1,623
2. USSR (formerly Russia)	402	330	294	1,026
3. GB (including Ireland to 1920)	171½	209½	187	568

* The A.A.U. (US) reinstated James F. Thorpe (1888–1953), the disqualified high scorer in the 1912 decathlon and pentathlon events on October 12, 1973, but no issue of medals has yet been authorized by the International Olympic Committee. If allowed, this would give the U.S. 2 more gold medals.

Longest Span

The longest competitive span of any Olympic competitor is 40 years by Dr. Ivan Osiier (Denmark) (1888–1965), who competed as a fencer in 1908, 1912 (silver medal), 1920, 1924, 1928, 1932 and 1948, and by Magnus Konow (Norway) (1887–1972) in yachting, 1908–20 and 1936–48. The longest span for a woman is 24 years (1932–56) by the Austrian fencer Ellen Müller-Preiss. Raimondo d'Inzeo (born February 8, 1925) competed for Italy in equestrian events in a record eight celebrations (1948–1976), gaining one gold medal, two silver and three bronze medals. Janice Lee York Romary (born August 6, 1928), the US fencer, competed in all six Games from 1948 to 1968, and Lia Manoliu (Rumania) (born April 25, 1932) competed from 1952 to 1972, winning the discus title in 1968.

Largest Crowd

The largest crowd at any Olympic site was 150,000 at the 1952 ski-jumping at the Holmenkollen, outside Oslo, Norway. Estimates of the number of spectators of the marathon race through Tokyo, Japan, on October 21, 1964, have ranged from 500,000 to 1,500,000.

The greatest number of viewers for a televised event is an estimated 1,000,000,000 each for the live and recorded transmissions of the XXth Olympic Games in Munich, from August 26 to

OPENING DAY: The Olympic oath is sworn at the Opening Ceremony of the 1932 Winter Olympic Games at Lake Placid, New York.

September 11, 1972, and the XXIst Games in Montreal, from July 17 to August 1, 1976.

Most Competitors

The greatest number of competitors in any summer Olympic Games has been 7,147 at Munich in 1972. A record 122 countries competed in the 1972 Munich Games. The fewest was 311 competitors from 13 countries in 1896. In 1904 only 12 countries participated. The largest team was 880 men and 4 women from France at the 1900 Games in Paris.

Development of the Olympic Games

These figures relate to the Summer Games and exclude Demonstration Sports.

	Countries	Number of Sports	Competitors Male	Female
1896	13	9	311	0
1900	22	17	1,319	11
1904	12	14	617	8
1906	20	11	877	7
1908	22	21	1,999	36
1912	28	14	2,490	57
1920	29	22	2,543	64
1924	44	18	2,956	136
1928	46	15	2,724	290
1932	47	15	1,281	127
1936	49	20	3,738	328
1948	59	18	3,714	385
1952	69	17	4,407	518
1956	71	17	2,958	384
1960	83	17	4,738	610
1964	93	19	4,457	683
1968	112	18	4,750	781
1972	122	21	6,077	1,070
1976	88	21	4,915	1,274

FOUNDER: Pierre, Baron de Coubertin, founded the modern Olympic movement.

Most Participations

Four countries have never failed to be represented at the 20 Celebrations of the Games: Australia, Greece, Great Britain and Switzerland.

The Games

The first Olympic Games of the modern era were held in Athens, Greece, in 1896. Since then, with the exception of the war years (1916, 1940 and 1944), Games have been held every four years, and additionally in Athens in 1906. Separate Winter Olympics were first held in 1924.

SUMMER GAMES

I	Athens	Apr. 6–15, 1896
II	Paris	May 20–Nov. 23, 1900
III	St. Louis	July 1–Nov. 23, 1904
†	Athens	Apr. 22–May 2, 1906
IV	London	Apr. 27–Oct. 31, 1908

V	Stockholm	May 5–July 22, 1912
VI	*Berlin	1916
VII	Antwerp	Apr. 20–Sept. 12, 1920
VIII	Paris	May 4–July 27, 1924
IX	Amsterdam	May 17–Aug. 12, 1928

The Games (continued)

X	Los Angeles	July 30–Aug. 14, 1932		V	St. Moritz, Switz	Jan. 30–Feb. 8, 1948
XI	Berlin	Aug. 1–16, 1936		VI	Oslo, Norway	Feb. 14–25, 1952
XII	*Tokyo, then Helsinki 1940			VII	Cortina d' Ampezzo, Italy	Jan. 26–Feb. 5, 1956
XIII	*London	1944				
XIV	London	July 29–Aug. 14, 1948		VIII	Squaw Valley, Calif	Feb. 18–28, 1960
XV	Helsinki	July 19–Aug. 3, 1952		IX	Innsbruck, Austria	Jan. 29–Feb. 9, 1964
XVI	‡Melbourne	Nov. 22–Dec. 8, 1956				
XVII	Rome	Aug. 25–Sept. 11, 1960		X	Grenoble, France	Feb. 6–18, 1968
XVIII	Tokyo	Oct. 10–24, 1964		XI	Sapporo, Japan	Feb. 3–13, 1972
XIX	Mexico City	Oct. 12–27, 1968				
XX	Munich	Aug. 26–Sept. 10, 1972		XII	Innsbruck, Austria	Feb. 4–15, 1976
XXI	Montreal	July 17–Aug 1, 1976		XIII	Lake, Placid, NY	Feb. 13–24, 1980
XXII	Moscow	July 19–Aug. 3, 1980				
XXIII	Los Angeles	1984		XIV	Sarajevo, Yugoslavia	Feb. 1–12, 1984 (prov.)

WINTER GAMES

I	Chamonix, France	Jan. 25–Feb. 4, 1924
II	St. Moritz, Switz	Feb. 11–19, 1928
III	Lake Placid, NY	Feb. 4–15, 1932
IV	Garmisch-Partenkirchen, Germany	Feb. 6–16, 1936

* Cancelled due to World Wars

† Intercalated Celebration not numbered but officially organized by the IOC (International Olympic Committee)

‡ Equestrian events held in Stockholm, June 10–17, 1956

Olympic Records (as of XXIInd Games, Moscow, 1980)

ARCHERY

Men's Double F.I.T.A.	2,571	Darrel Pace (US)	1976
Women's Double F.I.T.A.	2,499	Luann Ryon (US)	1976

CYCLING

1,000 m Time Trial	1:02.95	Lothar Thoms (E. Germany)	1980
4,000 m Individual Pursuit	4:34.92	Robert Dill-Bundi (Switzerland)	1980
4,000 m Team Pursuit	4:15.70	USSR	1980

SHOOTING

	Points		
50 m Small Bore Rifle (3 positions)	1,173	Viktor Vigsov (USSR)	1980
50 m Small Bore Rifle (prone position)	599	Ho Jun Li (North Korea)	1972
	599	Karl Heinz Smieszek (West Germany)	1976
	599	Karoly Varga (Hungary)	1980
	599	Hellfried Heilfort (E. Germany)	1980
Free Rifle	1,157	Gary Anderson (US)	1972
Free Pistol	581	Alexander Melenter (USSR)	1980
Rapid Fire Pistol	597	Norbert Klaar (East Germany)	1976
Olympic Trench (Clay Pigeon)	199	Angelo Scalzone (Italy)	1972
Skeet	198	Evgeny Petrov (USSR)	1972
	198	Josef Panacek (Czechoslovakia)	1976
	198	Eric Swinkels (Netherlands)	1976
Running Boar	579	Alexander Gazov (USSR)	1976

SWIMMING

MEN

Event	Time	Name and/or Country	Date
Freestyle			
100 meters	49.99	James Montgomery (US)	1976
200 meters	1:49.81	Sergei Kopliakov (USSR)	1980
400 meters	3:51.31	Vladimir Salnikov (USSR)	1980
1,500 meters	14:58.27	Vladimir Salnikov (USSR)	1980
4 × 200 m Relay	7:23.22	United States	1976
Breaststroke			
100 meters	1:03.11	John Hencken (US)	1976
200 meters	2:15.11	David Andrew Wilkie (GB)	1976
Butterfly			
100 meters	54.3	Mark Spitz (US)	1972
200 meters	1:59.23	Michael Bruner (US)	1976
Backstroke			
100 meters	55.49	John Naber (US)	1976
200 meters	1:59.19	John Naber (US)	1976
Individual Medley			
400 meters	4:22.89	Alexander Sidovenko (USSR)	1980
Medley Relay	3:42.22	United States	1976

WOMEN

Event	Time	Name and/or Country	Date
Freestyle			
100 meters	54.79	Barbara Krause (E. Germany)	1980
200 meters	1:58.33	Barbara Krause (E. Germany)	1980
400 meters	4:08.76	Ines Diers (E. Germany)	1980
800 meters	8:28.90	Michelle Ford (Australia)	1980
4 × 100 m Relay	3:42.71	E. Germany	1980
Breaststroke			
100 meters	1:10.11	Ute Geweniger (E. Germany)	1980
200 meters	2:29.54	Lina Kachoshite (USSR)	1980
Butterfly			
100 meters	1:00.13	Kornelia Ender (East Germany)	1976
200 meters	2:10.44	Ines Geissler (E. Germany)	1980
Backstroke			
100 meters	1:00.86	Rica Reinisch (E. Germany)	1980
200 meters	2:11.77	Rica Reinisch (E. Germany)	1980
Individual Medley			
400 meters	4:36.29	Petra Schneider (E. Germany)	1980
Medley Relay	4:06.67	E. Germany	1980

JUMPING IN: Kornelia Ender (East Germany) won 4 gold medals in Montreal in 1976, winning each race (including the medley relay) in Olympic record time.

JUMPING OVER: Rosemarie Ackerman (East Germany) set an Olympic high jump record of 6 feet 4 inches in winning the gold medal for that event in the 1976 Montreal Games.

TRACK AND FIELD

MEN

Event	Time or Distance			Name and/or Country	Date
100 meters			9.95	James Ray Hines (US)	1968
200 meters			19.83	Tommie C. Smith (US)	1968
400 meters			43.86	Lee Edward Evans (US)	1968
800 meters			1:43.5	Alberto Juantorena (Cuba)	1976
1,500 meters			3:34.9	Hezekiah Kipchoe Keino (Kenya)	1968
5,000 meters			13:20.4*	Brendan Foster (GB)	1976
10,000 meters			27:38.4	Lasse Viren (Finland)	1972
Marathon			2H 09:55.0	Waldemar Cierpinski (East Germany)	1976
4 × 100 m relay			38.19	United States	1968
			38.19	United States	1972
4 × 400 m relay			2:56.1	United States	1968
20 km road walk			1hr.23:36.0	Maurizio Damilano (Italy)	1980
			3hr.49:24.0	Hartwig Gavder (E. Germany)	1980
100 m hurdles			13.24	Rodney Milburn Jr. (US)	1972
400 m hurdles			47.64	Edward Corley Moses (US)	1976
3,000 m steeplechase			8:08.0	Anders Garderud (Sweden)	1976

	ft	in	m		
High Jump	7	8¾	2.36	Gerd Wessig (E. Germany)	1980
Pole Vault	18	11½	5.78	Wladyslaw Kozakiewicz (Poland)	1980
Long Jump	29	2½	8.90	Robert Beamon (US)	1968
Triple Jump	57	0¾	17.39	Viktor Saneyev (USSR)	Oct. 17, 1968
Shot Putt	70	0½	21.35	Vladimir Kiselyev (USSR)	1980
Discus Throw	224	4	68.28*	Mac Maurice Wilkins (USA)	1976
Hammer Throw	268	4	81.80	Yuriy Sedykh (USSR)	1980
Javelin Throw	310	4	94.58	Miklos Nemeth (Hungary)	July 26, 1976
Decathlon	8,618 points			W. Bruce Jenner (US)	July 29–30, 1976

WOMEN

100 meters				11.01*	Annegret Richter (W. Germany)	1976
200 meters				22.03	Barbel Wockel (née Eckert) (E. Germany)	1980
400 meters				48.88	Marita Koch (E. Germany)	1980
800 meters				1:53.5	Nadezda Olizarenko (USSR)	1980
1500 meters				3:56.6	Tatyana Kazankina (USSR)	1980
4 × 100 m relay				41.60	E. Germany	1980
4 × 400 m relay				3:19.2	E. Germany	1976
100 m hurdles				12.56	Vera Komissova (USSR)	1980

	ft	in	m		
High Jump	6	5½	1.97	Sara Simeoni (Italy)	1980
Long Jump	23	2	7.06	Tatyana Kolpakova (USSR)	1980
Shot Putt	73	6¼	22.41	Ilona Slupianek (E. Germany)	1980
Discus Throw	229	6	69.96	Evelin Jahl (née Schlaak) (E. Germany)	1980
Javelin Throw	224	5	68.40	Maria Colon (Cuba)	1980
Pentathlon	5083 points			Nadezda Tkachenko (USSR)	1980

WEIGHTLIFTING

	Total Weight			
	Kilos	lb.		
Flyweight	245	540	Kanybek Osmonoliev (USSR)	1980
Bantamweight	275	606¼	Daniel Nunez (Cuba)	1980
Featherweight	290	639¼	Viktor Mazin (USSR)	1980
Lightweight	342.5	755	Yanko Rusev (Bulgaria)	1980
Middleweight	360	793½	Asen Zlatev (Bulgaria)	1980
Light Heavyweight	400	881¾	Yurik Vardanyan (USSR)	1980
Middle Heavyweight	382.5	843¼	David Rigert (USSR)	1976
100 kg	395	870¾	Ota Zaremba (Czechoslovakia)	1980
Heavyweight	422.5	931¼	Leonid Taranenko (USSR)	1980
Super Heavyweight	440.0	970	Vasili Alexeev (USSR)	1976

* In a semi-final

ORIENTEERING

Origins. Orienteering as now known was invented by Major Ernst Killander in Sweden in 1918. It was based on military exercises of the 1890's. The term was first used for an event at Oslo, Norway, on October 7, 1900.

World championships were inaugurated in 1966 and are held biennially under the auspices of the International Orienteering Federation (founded 1961), located in Sweden. The US Orienteering Federation was founded in 1971 to serve as the governing body for the sport in America and to choose teams for world championship competition.

World Champions

	Men's Individual	Women's Individual	Men's Relay	Women's Relay
1966	Aage Hadler (Nor)	Ulla Lindqvist (Swe)	Sweden	Sweden
1968	Karl Johansson (Swe)	Ulla Lindqvist (Swe)	Sweden	Norway
1970	Stig Berge (Nor)	Ingred Hadler (Nor)	Norway	Sweden
1972	Aage Hadler (Nor)	Sarolta Monspart (Fin)	Sweden	Finland
1974	Bernt Frilen (Swe)	Mona Norgaard (Den)	Sweden	Sweden
1976	Egil Johansen (Nor)	Liisa Veijalainen (Fin)	Sweden	Sweden
1978	Egil Johansen (Nor)	Anne Berit Eid (Nor)	Norway	Finland

OUT OF THE WOODS: Sweden's Ulla Lindqvist has won the women's orienteering world title twice, in 1966 and 1968.

PARACHUTING

Origins. Parachuting became a regulated sport with the institution of world championships in 1951. A team title was introduced in 1954, and women's events were included in 1956.

Most Titles

The USSR won the men's team titles in 1954–58–60–66–72–76 and the women's team titles in 1956–58–66–68–72–76. No individual has ever won a second world overall title.

Greatest Accuracy

Jacqueline Smith (GB) (b. March 29, 1951) scored ten consecutive dead center strikes (4-inch disk) in the World Championships at Zagreb, Yugoslavia, September 1, 1978. At Yuma, Arizona, in March, 1978, Dwight Reynolds scored a record 105 daytime dead centers, and Bill Wenger and Phil Munden tied with 43 nighttime DCs, competing as members of the US Army team, the Golden Knights.

Most Jumps

The greatest number of consecutive jumps completed in 24 hours is 233 by David Parchment at Shobdon Airfield, Hereford, England, on June 19, 1979.

HAPPY LANDINGS: Jacqueline Smith scored an incredible ten consecutive dead centers on a 4-inch target in the 1978 World Championships in Zagreb, Yugoslavia, to win the world accuracy title.

PIGEON RACING

Earliest References. Pigeon Racing developed from the use of homing pigeons for carrying messages—a quality utilized in the ancient Olympic Games (776 B.C.–393 A.D.). The sport originated in Belgium. The earliest major long-distance race was from London to Antwerp in 1819, involving 32 pigeons. The earliest recorded occasion on which 500 miles was flown in a day was by "Motor," owned by G. P. Pointer, which was released on June 30, 1896, from Thurso, Scotland, and covered 501 miles at an average speed of 49½ m.p.h.

Longest Flight

The greatest recorded homing flight by a pigeon was made by one owned by the 1st Duke of Wellington (1769–1852). Released from a sailing ship off the Ichabo Islands, West Africa, on April 8, it dropped dead a mile from its loft at Nine Elms, London, England, on June 1, 1845, 55 days later, having flown an airline route of 5,400 miles, but an actual distance of possibly 7,000 miles to avoid the Sahara Desert.

Highest Speeds

In level flight in windless conditions it is very doubtful if any pigeon can exceed 60 m.p.h. The highest race speed recorded is one of 3,229 yards per minute (110.07 m.p.h.) in East Anglia, England, on May 8, 1965, when 1,428 birds were backed by a powerful south southwest wind. The winner was owned by A. Vidgeon & Son.

FOR THE BIRDS: On July 30, 1976, these birds were released from the 86th floor of the Empire State Building in New York. One 2-month-old hen proceeded to fly the 6 miles to the New Jersey Meadowlands Sports Complex in 5 minutes 40 seconds—just over a mile a minute.

The highest race speed recorded over a distance of more than 1,000 kilometers is 82.93 m.p.h. by a hen pigeon in the Central Cumberland Combine Race over 683 miles 147 yards from Murray Bridge, South Australia, to North Ryde, Sydney, on October 2, 1971.

The world's longest reputed distance in 24 hours is 803 miles (velocity 1,525 yards per minute) by E. S. Petersen's winner of the 1941 San Antonio (Texas) Racing Club event.

Lowest Speed

Blue Clip, a pigeon belonging to Harold Hart, released in Rennes, France, arrived home in its loft in Leigh, England, on September 29, 1974, 7 years 2 months later. It had covered the 370 miles at an average speed of 0.00589 m.p.h., which is slower than the world's fastest snail.

Most First Prizes

Owned by R. Green, of Walsall Wood, West Midlands, England, *Champion Breakaway* had won a record 56 first prizes from 1972 to May, 1979.

Highest Priced Bird

The highest recorded price paid for a pigeon is approximately $48,000 by a Japanese fancier for *De Wittslager* to George Desender (Belgium) in October, 1978.

POLO

Earliest Games. Polo is usually regarded as being of Persian origin, having been played as *Pulu c.* 525 B.C. Other claims have come from Tibet and the Tang dynasty of China 250 A.D.

The earliest club of modern times was the Kachar Club (founded in 1859) in Assam, India. The game was introduced into England from India in 1869 by the 10th Hussars at Aldershot, Hampshire, and the earliest match was one between the 9th Lancers and the 10th Hussars on Hounslow Heath, west of London, in July, 1871. The earliest international match between England and the US was in 1886.

Playing Field

The game is played (by two teams of four) on the largest field of any ball game in the world. The ground measures 300 yards long by 160 yards wide with side-boards or, as in India, 200 yards wide without boards.

Highest Handicap

The highest handicap based on eight 7½-minute "chukkas" is 10 goals, introduced in the US in 1891 and in the United King-

dom and in Argentina in 1910. The latest of the 39 players to
have received 10-goal handicaps are Alberto Heguy and Alfredo
Harriot of Argentina, and in England, Eduardo Moore (Argentina). A match of two 40-goal handicap teams was staged for the
first time ever at Palermo, Buenos Aires, Argentina, in 1975.

Highest Scores

The highest aggregate number of goals scored in an international match is 30, when Argentina beat the US 21-9 at Meadow-
brook, Long Island, New York, in September, 1936.

Most Olympic Medals

Polo has been part of the Olympic program on five occasions:
1900, 1908, 1920, 1924 and 1936. Of the 21 gold medalists, a
1920 winner, John Wodehouse, the 3rd Earl of Kimberley (b.
1883–d. 1941) uniquely also won a silver medal (1908).

Most Internationals

Thomas Hitchcock, Jr. (1900–44) played five times for the US
vs. England (1921–24–27–30–39) and twice vs. Argentina (1928–36).

Oldest Pony

Rustum, a Barb gelding from Stourhead, England, was still playing
regularly at the age of 36.

Largest Trophy

Polo claims the world's largest sporting trophy—the Bangalore
Limited Handicap Polo Tournament Trophy. This massive cup
standing on its plinth is 6 feet tall and was presented in 1936 by
the Indian Raja of Kolanka.

HORSEPLAY: Of the 21 Olympic polo gold medalists, only John Wodehouse (2nd from left) has also won a silver medal. The rules of polo
prohibit players from playing left-handed.

Largest Crowd

Crowds of more than 50,000 have watched flood-lit matches at the Sydney, Australia, Agricultural Shows.

A crowd of 40,000 watched a game played at Jaipur, India, in 1976, when elephants were used instead of ponies. The length of the polo sticks used has not been ascertained.

POWERBOAT RACING

Origins. The earliest application of the gasoline engine to a boat was by Jean Joseph Etienne Lenoir (1822–1900) on the River Seine, Paris, in 1865. The sport was given impetus by the presentation of a championship cup by Sir Alfred Harmsworth of England in 1903, which was also the year of the first offshore race from Calais to Dover.

Harmsworth Cup

Of the 25 contests from 1903 to 1961, the US has won the most with 16.

The greatest number of wins has been achieved by Garfield A. Wood (US) with 8 (1920–21, 1926, 1928–29–30, 1932–33). The only boat to win three times is *Miss Supertest III*, owned by James C. Thompson (Canada), driven by Bob Hayward (Canada), in 1959–60–61. This boat also achieved the record speed of 119.27 m.p.h. at Picton, Ontario, Canada, in 1961. The trophy is now

LIVE AND LET FLY: Jerry Comeaux achieved the longest powerboat jump (110 feet) for a sequence in a James Bond movie. He jumped the Glastron GT-150 off a greased ramp at 56 m.p.h.

awarded to the British Commonwealth driver with the highest points in the World Offshore Championships.

Gold Cup

The Gold Cup (instituted 1903) has been won 8 times by Bill Muncey (1956–57–61–62–72–77–78–79). The record speed attained is 128.338 m.p.h. for a 2½-mile lap by the unlimited hydroplane *Atlas Van Lines*, driven by Bill Muncey in a qualifying round on the Columbia River, Washington, in July, 1977, and again in July, 1978.

Highest Speeds

The fastest offshore record, as recognized by the Union Internationale Montonautique, is 92.99 m.p.h. by a Class IIID Frode, driven by Mikael Frode (Sweden) on November 5, 1977.

The R6 inboard engine record of 128.375 m.p.h. was set by the hydroplane *Vladivar I*, driven by Toney Fahey (GB) on Lake Windermere, Cumbria, England, on May 23, 1977.

The Class ON record is 136.38 m.p.h. by J. F. Merten (US) in 1973.

Longest Race

The longest race has been the Port Richborough (London) to Monte Carlo Marathon Offshore International event. The race extended over 2,947 miles in 14 stages on June 10–25, 1972. It was won by *H.T.S.* (GB), driven by Mike Bellamy, Eddie Chater and Jim Brooks in 71 hours 35 minutes 56 seconds (average 41.15 m.p.h.).

Longest Jump

The longest jump achieved by a powerboat has been 110 feet by Jerry Comeaux, 29, in a Glastron GT-150 with a 135-h.p. Evinrude Starflite off a greased ramp on an isolated waterway in Louisiana, in mid-October, 1972. The takeoff speed was 56 m.p.h. The jump was required for a sequence in the eighth James Bond film, *Live and Let Die*.

Dragsters

The first drag boat to attain 200 m.p.h. was Sam Kurtovich's *Crisis* which attained 200.44 m.p.h. in California in October, 1969, at the end of a one-way run. *Climax* has since been reported to have attained 205.19 m.p.h.

Longest Journey

The Dane, Hans Tholstrup, 25, circumnavigated Australia (11,500 miles) in a 17-foot Caribbean Cougar fiberglass runabout with a single 80-h.p. Mercury outboard motor from May 11 to July 25, 1971.

REAL (ROYAL) TENNIS

Origins. The game originated as *jeu de paume* in French monasteries *c.* 1050. A tennis court is mentioned in the sale of the Hôtel de Nesle, Paris in 1308. The oldest court in the world is one built in Paris in 1496.

There are estimated to be 3,000 players and 32 active courts throughout the world. The latest court was opened at Bordeaux, France in 1979.

Most Titles

The first recorded World Tennis Champion was Clergé (France) *c.* 1740. Jacques Edmond Barre (France) (1802–73) held the title for a record 33 years from 1829 to 1862. Pierre Etchebaster (b. 1893) a Basque, holds the record for the greatest number of successful defenses of the title with eight between 1928 and 1952.

World Championship

The list of world champions at Real Tennis extends further back than just about any sport, as it begins with Clergé of France in 1740. Since then:

1765–85	Raymond Masson (Fra)	1908–12	Cecil Fairs (GB)
1785–1816	Joseph Barcellon (Fra)	1912–14	George Covey (GB)
1816–19	Marchesio (Ita)	1914–16	Jay Gould (US)
1819–29	Philip Cox (GB)	1916–28	George Covey (GB)
1829–62	Edmond Barre (Fra)	1928–55	Pierre Etchebaster (Fra)
1862–71	Edmund Tomkins (GB)	1955–57	James Dear (GB)
1871–85	George Lambert (GB)	1957–59	Albert Johnson (GB)
1885–90	Tom Pettitt (US)	1959–69	Northrup Knox (US)
1890–95	Charles Saunders (GB)	1969–72	George "Pete" Bostwick (US)
1895–1905	Peter Latham (GB)	1972–75	Jimmy Bostwick (US)
1905–07	Cecil Fairs (GB)	1976–	Howard Angus (GB)
1907–08	Peter Latham (GB)		

ROYAL TITLES: Pierre Etchebaster (left) successfully defended his championship a record 8 times. He held the title from 1928 to 1955. American Northrup Knox (right) was world champion from 1959 to 1969.

RODEO

Origins. Rodeo, which developed from 18th-century *fiestas*, came into being with the early days of the North American cattle industry. The earliest reference to the sport is at Santa Fe, New Mexico, on June 10, 1847. Steer wrestling began with Bill Pickett (Texas) in 1900. The other events are calf roping, bull riding, saddle and bareback bronc riding.

The largest rodeo in the world is the Calgary Exhibition and Stampede at Calgary, Alberta, Canada. The record attendance has been 1,069,830, July 8–17, 1977. The record for one day is 141,670 on July 13, 1974. The oldest continuously held rodeo is that at Payson, Arizona, first held in August, 1887.

In 1979, the Colorado-based Professional Rodeo Cowboys Association sanctioned a record 640 rodeos in 42 states and 4 Canadian provinces. Prize money for the year set an all-time mark ($8,800,000), membership rose to 4,820.

Champion Bull

The top bucking bull was probably *Honky Tonk*, an 11-year-old Brahma of the International Rodeo Association, who unseated

STAYING POWER: Larry Mahan shares the record for most all-round world titles with 6.

HORSING AROUND: Metha Brorsen of Perry, Oklahoma, was only 11 years old when she became the International Rodeo Association's champion cowgirl barrel racer in 1975. The young, 4-foot-9-inch, 66-pound rider earned over $15,000 that year.

187 riders in an undefeated eight-year career to his retirement in September, 1978.

Champion Bronc

Traditionally a bronc called *Midnight* owned by Jim McNab of Alberta, Canada, was never ridden in 12 appearances at the Calgary Stampede.

Most World Titles

The record number of all-round titles is 6 by Tom Ferguson (b. December 20, 1950) consecutively, 1974–79, and by Larry Mahan (b. November 21, 1943) (1966–67–68–69–70–73). Jim Shoulders (b. 1928) of Henryetta, Oklahoma, won a record 16 world championships between 1949 and 1959. The record figure for prize money (including bonuses) in a single season is $131,233 by Tom Ferguson, of Miami, Oklahoma, in 1978. Ferguson also holds the record for the most money won at one rodeo with $16,945 earned at Houston, Texas, in 1979.

Through the end of 1979, Dean Oliver was the leader in career winnings with $543,172. His career began in 1952, and he has won 11 world championships.

Single Events. The PRCA record for the most bareback riding world championships is 5 by Joe Alexander. Casey Tibbs won 6 saddle bronc titles, Jim Shoulders leads with 7 bull riding championships, and Dean Oliver has won 8 calf roping titles. Homer Pettigrew's 6 steer wrestling titles are the most for that event, and Everett Shaw has won 6 steer roping championships. The most team roping titles is 4 by Jim Rodriguez Jr. and Leo Camarillo. The most money won in one year in a single event is $80,260 by Bruce Ford for bareback riding in 1979.

Youngest and Oldest Champions

The youngest winner of a world title is Metha Brorsen of Oklahoma, who was only 11 years old when she won the International Rodeo Association Cowgirls barrel racing event in 1975. Ike Rude was 59 years old when he won the Professional Rodeo Cowboys Association's steer roping world championship in 1953.

Time Records

Records for timed events, such as calf roping and steer wrestling, are meaningless, because of the widely varying conditions due to the size of arenas and amount of start given the stock. The fastest time recently recorded for roping a calf is 5.7 seconds by Bill Reeder in Assiniboia, Saskatchewan, Canada, in 1978, and the fastest time for overcoming a steer is 2.4 seconds by James Bynum of Waxahachie, Texas, at Marietta, Oklahoma, in 1955.

The standard required time to stay on in bareback, saddle bronc and bull riding events is 8 seconds. In the now discontinued ride-to-a-finish events, rodeo riders have been recorded to have survived 90 minutes or more, until the mount had not a buck left in it.

Professional Rodeo Cowboys Association All-Round Champions

The title goes to the biggest money winner in America in two or more events. Winners since 1960:

Year	Name	Amount	Year	Name	Amount
1960	Harry Tompkins	$ 32,522	1971	Phil Lyne	$ 49,245
1961	Benny Reynolds	$ 31,309	1972	Phil Lyne	$ 60,852
1962	Tom Nesmith	$ 32,611	1973	Larry Mahan	$ 64,447
1963	Dean Oliver	$ 31,329	1974	Tom Ferguson	$ 66,929
1964	Dean Oliver	$ 31,150	1975	Leo Camarillo	$ 50,300 +
1965	Dean Oliver	$ 33,163		Tom Ferguson (tie)	
1966	Larry Mahan	$ 40,358	1976	Tom Ferguson	$ 96,913
1967	Larry Mahan	$ 51,996	1977	Tom Ferguson	$ 76,730
1968	Larry Mahan	$ 49,129	1978	Tom Ferguson	$103,733
1969	Larry Mahan	$ 57,726	1979	Tom Ferguson	$ 96,272
1970	Larry Mahan	$ 41,493			

POWER STEERING: Tim Ferguson has been the all-round champion for 6 straight years, 1974–1979 (shared in 1975). In 1978, he won a record $131,233 (including bonuses). A world steer wrestling champion in 1977 and 1978, Ferguson also holds the record for the greatest winnings in one rodeo.

ROLLER SKATING

Origin. The first roller skate was devised by Joseph Merlin of Huy, Belgium, in 1760, and was first worn by him in public in London. James L. Plimpton of New York City produced the present four-wheeled type and patented it in January, 1863. The first indoor rinks were opened in London in 1857. The great boom periods were 1870–75, 1908–12, 1948–54 and 1978 to the present, each originating in the US.

Largest Rink

The largest indoor rink ever to operate was located in the Grand Hall, Olympia, London, England. It had an actual skating area of 68,000 square feet. It first opened in 1890 for one season, then again from 1909 to 1912.

The largest rink now in operation is the Fireside Roll-Arena in Hoffman Estates, Illinois, which has a total skating surface of 29,859 square feet.

Roller Hockey

Roller hockey was first introduced in England as Rink Polo, at the old Lava rink, Denmark Hill, London, in the late 1870's. The Amateur Rink Hockey Association was formed in 1905, and in 1913 became the National Rink Hockey (now Roller Hockey) Association. Britain won the inaugural World Championship in

ROLLING ALONG: 1978 women's champions (left) were: 1st, Natalie Dunn; 2nd, Petra Schneider; and 3rd, Joanne Young. The 1978 pairs champions (right) were: 1st, Pat Jones and Robbie Coleman; 2nd, Paul Price and Tina Kreisley; and 3rd, Klaus Richter and Uta Brause.

1936, and since then Portugal has won the most with 11 titles from 1947 to 1973.

Most Titles

Most world speed titles have been won by Alberta Vianello (Italy) with 16 between 1953 and 1965.

Most world pair titles have been taken by Dieter Fingerle (W. Germany) with four. The records for figure titles are 5 by Karl Heinz Losch and 4 by Astrid Bader, both of West Germany.

Speed Records

The fastest speed (official world's record) is 25.78 m.p.h. by Giuseppe Cantarella (Italy) who recorded 34.9 seconds for 440 yards on a road at Catania, Italy, on September 28, 1963. The mile record on a rink is 2 minutes 25.1 seconds by Gianni Ferretti (Italy). The greatest distance skated in one hour on a rink by a woman is 21.995 miles by Marisa Danesi at Inzell, West Germany, on September 28, 1968. The men's record on a track is 23.133 miles by Alberto Civolani (Italy) at Inzell, West Germany, on September 28, 1968. He went on to skate 50 miles in 2 hours 20 minutes 33.1 seconds.

Marathon Record

The longest recorded continuous roller skating marathon was one of 322 hours 20 minutes by Randy Reed of Springfield, Oregon, June 12–26, 1977.

Endurance

Theodore J. Coombs (b. 1954) of Hermosa Beach, California, skated 5,193 miles from Los Angeles to New York and back to Yates Center, Kansas, from May 30 to September 14, 1979. His longest 24-hour distance was 120 miles, June 27–28.

World Champions

World Championships were first held in 1947. Just as in Ice Skating both speed skating and figure skating events are held.

FIGURE SKATING

Men
Winners since 1972:

1972	Michael Obrecht (W Ger)
1973	Randy Dayney (US)
1974	Michael Obrecht (W Ger)
1975	Leonardo Lienhard (Swi)
1976	Thomas Nieder (W Ger)
1977	Thomas Nieder (W Ger)
1978	Thomas Nieder (W Ger)
1979	Michael Butzke (W Ger)

Most titles: 5 Karl-Heinz Losch (W Ger) 1958, 1959, 1961, 1962, 1966

Women
Winners since 1972:

1972	Petra Hausler (W Ger)
1973	Sigrid Mullenbach (W Ger)
1974	Sigrid Mullenbach (W Ger)
1975	Sigrid Mullenbach (W Ger)
1976	Natalie Dunn (US)
1977	Natalie Dunn (US)
1978	Natalie Dunn (US)
1979	Petra Schneider (W Ger)

Most titles: 4 Astrid Bader (W Ger) 1965–68

Pairs
Winners since 1972:

1972	Ronald Robovitsky and Gail Robovitsky (US)
1973	Louis Stovel and Vicki Handyside (US)
1974	Ron Sabo and Susan McDonald (US)
1975	Ron Sabo and Darlene Waters (US)
1976	Ron Sabo and Darlene Waters (US)
1977	Ray Chapatta and Karen Mejia (US)
1978	Pat Jones and Rooie Coleman (US)
1979	Roy Chapatta and Karen Mejia (US)

Most titles: 3 Dieter Fingerle and Ute Keller (W Ger) 1965–67 (Fingerle also won in 1959 with S. Schneider)

Dance
Winners since 1972:

1972	Tom Straker and Bonnie Lambert (US)
1973	James Stephens and Jane Puracchio (US)
1974	Udo Donsdorf and Christine Henke (W Ger)
1975	Kerry Cavazzi and Jane Puracchio (US)
1976	Kerry Cavazzi and Jane Puracchio (US)
1977	Dan Littel and Fleurette Arsenault (US)
1978	Dan Littel and Fleurette Arsenault (US)
1979	Dan Littel and Fleurette Arsenault (US)

ROWING

Oldest Race. The Sphinx stela of Amenhotep II (1450–1425 B.C.) records that he *stroked* a boat for some three miles. The earliest established sculling race is the Doggett's Coat and Badge, first rowed on August 1, 1716 from London Bridge to Chelsea, and still contested annually. Although rowing regattas were held in Venice in 1300, the first English regatta probably took place on the Thames by the Ranelagh Gardens near Putney, London, in 1775. Boating began at Eton, England, in 1793. The oldest club, the Leander Club, was formed in *c.* 1818.

Olympic Medals

Since 1900 there have been 133 Olympic finals of which the US has won 26, E Germany 25, Germany (now W Germany) 15 and GB 14. Five oarsmen have won 3 gold medals: John B. Kelly (US) (1889–1960), father of Princess Grace of Monaco, in the sculls (1920) and double sculls (1920 and 1924); his cousin Paul V. Costello (US) (b Dec 17, 1899) in the double sculls (1920, 1924 and 1928); Jack Beresford, Jr. (GB) 1899–1977) in the sculls (1924), coxless fours (1932) and double sculls (1936); Vyacheslav Ivanov (USSR) (b July 30, 1938) in the sculls (1956, 1960 and 1964); and Siegfried Brietzke in the coxless pairs (1972) and the coxless fours (1976 and 1980).

Sculling

The record number of wins in the Wingfield Sculls (instituted on the Thames in 1830) is seven by Jack Beresford, Jr., from 1920 to 1926. The fastest time (Putney to Mortlake) has been 21 minutes 11 seconds by Leslie Southwood in 1933. The record number of world professional sculling titles (instituted 1831) won is seven by William Beach (Australia) between 1884 and 1887.

Highest Speed

Speeds in tidal or flowing water are of no comparative value. The highest recorded speed for 2,000 meters on non-tidal water

SCULL SKILLS; Russian Vyacheslav Ivanov (left), holding his 1960 gold medal, is the only man to win 3 Olympic single sculls titles (1956–64). Jack Beresford, Jr. (right) has won 3 Olympic gold medals; in the sculls, coxless fours, and double sculls. Beresford also has a record 7 wins in the Wingfield Sculls on the Thames River in England.

by an eight is 5 mins. 32.17 secs. (13.46 m.p.h.) by East Germany at the Montreal Olympics on July 18, 1976. A team from the Penn A.C. (US) was timed in 5 minutes 18.8 seconds (14.03 m.p.h.) in the F.I.S.A. Championships on the Meuse River, Liège, Belgium, on August 17, 1930.

Longest Race

The longest annual rowing race is the Ringvaart Regatta, a 62-mile contest for eights held at Delft, Netherlands. The record time is 7 hours 3 minutes 29 seconds by the Njord team on May 31, 1979.

The record for the 10-man ship's boat race over 65 miles from Gullmarsfjorden, Sweden, to the Norwegian border is 13 hours 8 minutes by a crew from the Swedish Royal Navy's Mine Hunter Diving Squadron on June 19, 1979.

Cross-Channel Row

The fastest row across the English Channel is 3 hours 50 minutes by Rev. Sidney Swann (b. 1862) on September 12, 1911.

World Records

MEN—Fastest times over 2,000 m course

	min sec	Country	Place	Date
Single Sculls	6:52.46	Sean Drea (Ireland)	Montreal, Canada	July 23, 1976
Double Sculls	6:12.48	Norway	Montreal, Canada	July 23, 1976
Coxed Pairs	6:56.94	East Germany	Copenhagen, Denmark	Aug.— 1971
Coxless Pairs	6:33.02	East Germany	Montreal, Canada	July 23, 1976
Coxed Fours	6:09.17	East Germany	Amsterdam, Netherlands	June 30, 1979
Coxless Fours	5:53.65	East Germany	Montreal, Canada	July 23, 1976
Quadruple Sculls	5:47.83	U.S.S.R.	Montreal, Canada	July 18, 1976
Eights	5:32:17	East Germany	Montreal, Canada	July 18, 1976

ALL IN A ROW: The US won a close finish in the eights race for a gold medal in the 1932 Olympics at Los Angeles.

WOMEN—Fastest times over 1,000 m course

	min sec	Country	Place	Date
Single Sculls	3:34.31	Christine Scheiblich (East Germany)	Amsterdam, Netherlands	Aug. 21, 1977
Double Sculls	3:15.95	East Germany	Bled, Yugoslavia	Sept. 2, 1979
Coxless Pairs	3:26.32	East Germany	Amsterdam, Netherlands	Aug. 21, 1977
Coxed Fours	3:14.5	U.S.S.R.	Mannheim, West Germany	May 20, 1979
Quadruple Sculls	3:06.75	East Germany	Bled, Yugoslavia	Sept. 2, 1979
Eights	2:57.79	United States	Bled, Yugoslavia	Sept. 1, 1979

World Championships

World Championships were first held in 1962 at Lucerne and have subsequently been held in 1966 at Bled, 1970 at St. Catherines, Canada, 1974 at Lucerne, 1975 at Nottingham, 1977 at Amsterdam and 1978 at Lake Karipiro, New Zealand. Women's world championships were first held in 1974.

Winners (*note*—in all coxed events, the name of the cox is shown last):

DOUBLE TROUBLE: Michael Hart and Chris Baillieu (GB) won the 1977 double sculls world title.

MEN

Single Sculls
1962 Vyacheslav Ivanov (USSR)
1966 Don Spero (US)
1970 Alberto Demiddi (Arg)
1974 Wolfgang Hönig (E Ger)
1975 Peter-Michael Kolbe (W Ger)
1977 Joachim Dreifke (E Ger)
1978 Peter-Michael Kolbe (W Ger)
1979 Pertti Karppinen (Fin)

Coxless Pairs
1962 W Ger (Bander, Z. Keller)
1966 E Ger (P. Kremitz, A. Göhler)
1970 W Ger (W. Klatt, P. Gorniv)
1974 E Ger (B. Landvoigt, J. Landvoigt)
1975 E Ger (B. Landvoigt, J. Landvoigt)
1977 USSR (V. Elisev, A. Kulagine)
1978 E Ger (B. Landvoigt, J. Landvoigt)
1979 E Ger (B. Landvoigt, J. Landvoigt)

Coxless Fours
1962 W Ger
1966 E Ger
1970 E Ger
1974 E Ger
1975 E Ger (S. Brietzke, A. Decker, S. Semmler, W. Mager)
1977 E Ger (S. Brietzke, A. Decker, S. Semmler, W. Mager)
1978 USSR (V. Preobrazneski, N. Kuznyetsov, V. Dolinin, A. Nemtirjov)
1979 E Ger (S. Brietzke, A. Decker, S. Semmler, W. Mager)

Double Sculls
1962 Fra (René Duhamel and Bernard Monnereau)
1966 Swi (Melchior Buergin and Martin Studach)
1970 Den (J. Engelbrecht and N. Secher)
1974 E Ger (Hans-Ulrich Schmied and Christof Kreuziger)
1975 Nor (Frank Hansen and Alf Hansen)
1977 GB (Chris Baillieu and Michael Hart)
1978 Nor (Frank Hansen and Alf Hansen)
1979 Nor (Frank Hansen and Alf Hansen)

Quadruple Sculls
1974 E Ger
1975 E Ger (S. Weisse, W. Guldenpfennig, W. Hönig, C. Kreuziger)
1977 E Ger (W. Guldenpfennig, K-H. Bussert, M. Winter, F. Dundr)
1978 E Ger (J. Dreifke, K-H. Bussert, M. Winter, F. Dundr)
1979 E Ger (P. Kersten, K. Kroppelin, K-H. Bussert, J. Dreifke)

Coxed Pairs
1962 W Ger (Jordan, Neuss)
1966 Hol (H. van Nes, J. van de Graaf)
1970 Rum (S. Tudor, P. Ceapura)
1974 USSR (V. Ivanov, V. Eshinov)
1975 E Ger (J. Lucke, W. Gunkel, B. Fritsch)
1977 Bul (T. Mrankov, S. Yanakiev, S. Stoykov)
1978 E Ger (J. Pfieffer, G. Uebeler, O. Beyer)
1979 E Ger (J. Pfieffer, G. Uebeler, G. Spohr)

Coxed Fours
1962 W Ger
1966 E Ger
1970 W Ger
1974 E Ger
1975 USSR (V. Eshiniv, N. Ivanov, A. Sema, A. Klepikov, A. Lukianov)
1977 E Ger (U. Diessner, G. Döhn, W. Diessner, D. Wendisch, A. Gregor)
1978 E Ger (U. Diessner, G. Döhn, W. Diessner, D. Wendisch, A. Gregor)
1979 E Ger (W. Schlufter, W. Diessner, J. Doberschutz, U. Diessner, W. Lutz)

Eights
1962 W Ger
1966 W Ger
1970 W Ger
1974 US
1975 E Ger
1977 E Ger
1978 E Ger
1979 E Ger

WOMEN

Single Sculls
1974 Christine Scheiblich (E Ger)
1975 Christine Scheiblich (E Ger)
1977 Christine Scheiblich (E Ger)
1978 Christine Hann (E Ger) (née Scheiblich)
1979 Sanda Toma (Rum)

Double Sculls
1974 USSR (G. Yermoleyeva, E. Antonova)
1975 USSR (G. Yermoleyeva, E. Antonova)
1977 E Ger (R. Zobelt, A. Borchmann)
1978 Bul (S. Olzetova, Z. Yordanova)
1979 E Ger (H. Westphal, C. Linse)

Coxless Pairs
1974 Rum (C. Neascu, M. Ghita)
1975 E Ger (A. Noack, S. Dähne)
1977 E Ger (A. Noack, S. Dähne)
1978 E Ger (C Bugel, U. Steindorf)
1979 E Ger (C. Bugel, U. Steindorf)

Quadruple Sculls
1974 E Ger
1975 E Ger
1977 E Ger
1978 Bul
1979 E Ger

Coxed Fours
1974 E Ger
1975 E Ger
1977 E Ger
1978 E Ger
1979 USSR

Eights
1974 E Ger
1975 E Ger
1977 E Ger
1978 USSR
1979 USSR

Olympic Games

Rowing has been included in each Olympic Games since 1900. Winners at each event since 1964 have been:

STROKED: East Germany leads a heat of the coxless fours at the 1972 Munich Olympics. The Germans went on to win the gold, repeating their success from 4 years earlier.

MEN

Single Sculls
1964 Vyacheslav Ivanov (USSR)
1968 Henri Wienese (Hol)
1972 Yuriy Malishev (USSR)
1976 Pertti Karppinen (Fin)
1980 Pertti Karppinen (Fin)

Coxless Pairs
1964 Can (G. Hungerford, R. Jackson)
1968 E Ger (J. Lucke, H-J Bothe)
1972 E Ger (S. Brietzke, W. Mager)
1976 E Ger (J. Landvoigt, B. Landvoigt)
1980 E Ger (J. Landvoigt, B. Landvoigt)

Coxless Fours
1964 Den (J. O. Hansen, B. Haslöv, E. Petersen, K. Helmudt)
1968 E Ger (F. Forberger, D. Grahn, F. Rühle, D. Schubert)
1972 E Ger (F. Forberger, F. Rühle, D. Grahn, D. Schubert)
1976 E Ger (S. Brietzke, A. Decker, S. Semmler, W. Mager)
1980 E Ger (J. Thiele, A. Decker, S. Semmler, S. Brietzke)

Quadruple Sculls
1976 E Ger (W. Guldenpfennig, R. Reiche, K.-H. Bussert, M. Wolfgramm)
1980 E Ger (F. Dundr, K. Burk, U. Heppner, M. Winter)

Double Sculls
1964 USSR (Oleg Tyurin ard Boris Dubrovsky)
1962 USSR (Anatoliy Sass and Aleksandr Timoshinin)
1972 USSR (Aleksandr Timoshinin and Gennadiy Korshikov)
1976 Nor (Frank Hansen and Alf Hansen)
1980 E. Ger (Joachim Dreifke and Klaus Kroppelien)

Coxed Pairs
1964 US (E. Ferry, C. Findlay, K. Mitchell)
1968 Ita (P. Baron, R. Sambo, B. Cipolla)
1972 E Ger (W. Gunkel, J. Lucke, K-D. Neubert)
1976 E Ger (H. Jahrling, F. Ulrich, G. Spohr)
1980 E Ger (H. Jahrling, F.W. Ulrich, G. Spohr)

Coxed Fours
1964 W Ger (P. Neusel, B. Britting, J. Werner, E. Hirschfelder, J. Oelke)
1968 NZ (R. Joyce, D. Storey, W. Cole, R. Collinge, S. Dickie)
1972 W Ger (P. Berger, H-J. Faerber, G. Auer, A. Bierl, U. Benter)
1976 USSR (V. Eshinov, N. Ivanov, M. Kuznyetsov, A. Klepikov, A. Lukianov)
1980 E Ger (D. Wendisch, U. Diessner, W. Diessner, G. Dohn, A. Gregor)

Eights
1964 US
1968 W Ger
1972 NZ
1976 E Ger
1980 E Ger

WOMEN (Women's events first included in 1976)

Single Sculls
1976 Christine Scheiblich (E Ger)
1980 Sanda Toma (Rum)

Double Sculls
1976 Bul (Svetla Otzetova, Zdravka Yordanova)
1980 USSR (Yelena Khloptseva, Larisa Popova)

Coxless Pairs
1976 Bul (Siika Kelbetcheva, S. Grouitcheva)
1980 E Ger (Ute Steindorf, Cornelia Klier)

Coxed Quadruple Sculls
1976 E Ger (A. Borchmann, J. Lau, V. Poley, R. Zobelt, L. Weigelt)
1980 E Ger (S. Reinhardt, J. Ploch, J. Lau, R. Zobelt, L. Buhr)

Coxed Fours
1976 E Ger (K. Metze, B. Schwede, G. Lohs, A. Kurth, S. Hess)
1980 E Ger (R. Kapheim, S. Frohlich, A. Noack, R. Saalfeld, K. Wenzel)

Eights
1976 E Ger
1980 E Ger

WHAT A CREW: This German team captured the gold medal in the coxed fours competition in the 1936 Olympics, held in Berlin before the Second World War.

Henley Royal Regatta

The annual regatta on the Thames at Henley was first held in 1839. Many events are held, but perhaps the two most famous are the Grand Challenge Cup for Eights, first held 1839 and the Diamond Challenge Sculls, first held in 1844. Winners of these events since 1965 have been:

GRAND CHALLENGE CUP		DIAMOND CHALLENGE SCULLS	
1965	Ratzeburg, W. Germany	1965	Don Spero (US)
1966	TSC Berlin	1966	Achim Hill (W Ger)
1967	SCW Leipzig	1967	Martin Studach (Switz)
1968	Univ. of London	1968	Hugh Wardell-Yerburgh (GB)
1969	SC Einheit, Dresden	1969	Hans-Joachim Böhmer (E Ger)
1970	ASK Rostock	1970	Jochen Meissner (W Ger)
1971	Tideway Scullers	1971	Alberto Demiddi (Arg)
1972	WMF Moscow	1972	Aleksandr Timoshinin (USSR)
1973	Trud Kolomna, USSR	1973	Sean Drea (Ire)
1974	Trud Kolomna, USSR	1974	Sean Drea (Ire)
1975	Leander/Thames Tradesmen	1975	Sean Drea (Ire)
1976	Thames Tradesmen	1976	Edward Hale (Aus)
1977	Univ. of Washington	1977	Tim Crooks (GB)
1978	Trakia Club, Bulgaria	1978	Tim Crooks (GB)
1979	Thames Tradesmen, London	1979	Hugh Matheron (GB)

Most wins: 6 Stuart Mackenzie (Aus) 1957–62

SHOOTING

Earliest Club. The Lucerne Shooting Guild (Switzerland) was formed *c.* 1466, and the first recorded shooting match was held at Zurich in 1472.

Olympic Medals

The record number of gold medals won is five by seven marksmen: Carl Osburn (US) (1912–1924); Konrad Stäheli (Switz.) (1900 and 1906); Willis Lee (US) (1920); Louis Richardet (Switz.) (1900 and 1906); Ole Andreas Lilloe-Olsen (Norway) (1920–1924);

Alfred Lane (US) (1912 and 1920) and Morris Fisher (US) (1920 and 1924). Osburn also won 4 silver and 2 bronze medals for a record total of 11. The only marksman to win 3 individual gold medals has been Gulbrandsen Skatteboe (Norway) (b. July 18, 1875) in 1906–1908–1912.

World Records

Possible Score

Free Pistol	50 m. 6 × 10 shot series	600–	577	Moritze Minder (Switz) Seoul, Korea, 1978
Free Rifle	300 m. 3 × 40 shot series	1,200–	1,160	Lones W. Wigger, Jr. (US) Seoul, Korea, 1978
Small-Bore Rifle	50 m. 3 × 40 shot series	1,200–	1,170*	Sven Johansson (Swe) Suhl, E. Germany, 1979
Small-Bore Rifle	50 m. 60 shots prone	600–	599	Eight men
Rapid-Fire Pistol	25 m. silhouettes 60 shots	600–	600	Weissenberger (W Ger) Suhl, E. Germany, 1979 Ion Corneliu (Rum) Bucharest, 1977
Running (Boar) Target	50 m. 60 shots "normal runs"	600–	581	Thomas Pfeffer (E Ger) Seoul, Korea, 1978
Trap	200 birds	200–	199	Angelo Scalzone (Ita) Munich, 1972 Michel Carrega (Fra) Thun, Switzerland, 1974
Skeet	200 birds	200–	200	Yevgeniy Petrov (USSR) Phoenix, Ariz., 1970 Yuri Tzuranov (USSR) Bologna, Italy, 1971 Tariel Zhgenti (USSR) Turin, Italy, 1973 Kield Rasmussen (Den) Vienna, 1975 Wieslaw Gawlikowski (Pol) Vienna, 1975
Center-Fire Pistol	25 m. 60 shots	600–	597	Thomas D. Smith (US) Sao Paulo, Brazil, 1963

* Awaiting ratification.

STRAIGHT SHOOTERS: Russian Yevgeniy Petrov (left) was the first of 5 men to score a perfect 200 for a trap shooting record. Annie Oakley (right) was the most renowned trick shot of all time. From age 27 to age 62, she demonstrated her ability to shoot 100 of 100 in trap shooting.

Record Heads

The world's finest head is the 23-pointer stag head in the Maritzburg collection, Germany. The outside span is 75½ inches, the length 47½ inches and the weight 41½ lbs. The greatest number of points is probably 33 (plus 29) on the stag shot in 1696 by Frederick III (1657–1713), the Elector of Brandenburg, later King Frederick I of Prussia.

Largest Shoulder Guns

The largest bore shoulder guns made were 2-bore. Less than a dozen of these were made by two English wildfowl gunmakers in c. 1885. Normally the largest guns made are double-barrelled 4-bore weighing up to 26 lbs. which can be handled only by men of exceptional physique. Larger smooth-bore guns have been made, but these are for use as punt-guns.

Bench Rest Shooting

The smallest group on record at 1,000 yards is 6.125 inches by Kenneth A. Keefer, Jr., with a 7 m.m.-300 Remington Action in Williamstown, Pennsylvania, on September 22, 1974.

Small-Bore Rifle Shooting

Richard Hansen shot 5,000 bull's-eyes in 24 hours at Fresno, California, on June 13, 1929.

Clay Pigeon Shooting

The record number of clay birds shot in an hour is 1,904 by Tom Kreckman, 36, at Cresco, Pennsylvania, on a Skeet range, September 28, 1975. Jerry Teynor shot 1,735 birds on a trap-shooting range at Bucyrus, Ohio, on July 30, 1977.

Most world titles have been won by Susan Nattrass (Canada) with five, 1974–5, 1977–9. The most by a man is four by Michel Carrega (France), 1970–1, 1974 and 1979.

Biggest Bag

The largest animal ever shot by any big game hunter was a bull African elephant (*Loxodonta africana africana*) shot by E. M. Nielsen of Columbus, Nebraska, 25 miles north-north-east of Mucusso, Angola, on November 7, 1974. The animal, brought down by a Westley Richards 0.425, stood 13 feet 8 inches at the shoulder.

In November, 1965, Simon Fletcher, 28, a Kenyan farmer, claims to have killed two elephants with one 0.458 bullet.

The greatest recorded lifetime bag is 556,000 birds, including 241,000 pheasants, by the 2nd Marquess of Ripon (1852–1923) of England. He himself dropped dead on a grouse moor after shooting his 52nd bird on the morning of September 22, 1923.

Trick Shooting

The greatest rapid-fire feat was that of Ed McGivern (US), who twice fired from 15 feet in 0.45 of a second 5 shots which could be covered by a silver half dollar piece at the Lead Club Range, South Dakota, on August 20, 1932.

McGivern also, on September 13, 1932, at Lewiston, Montana, fired 10 shots in 1.2 seconds from two guns at the same time double action (no draw), all 10 shots hitting two 2¼ by 3½ inch playing cards at 15 feet.

The most renowned trick shot of all time was Annie Oakley (*née* Mozee) (1860–1926). She demonstrated the ability to shoot 100 of 100 in trap shooting for 35 years, aged between 27 and 62. At 30 paces she could split a playing card end-on, hit a dime in mid-air or shoot a cigarette from the lips of her husband—one Frank Butler.

Air Weapons

The individual world record for air rifle (40 shots at 10 meters) is 393 by Olegario Vazquez (Mexico) at Mexico City in 1975, and for air pistol (40 shots at 10 meters) is 394 by Uwe Potteck (b. May 1, 1955) (East Germany) at Graz, Austria, in March, 1979.

Rapid Firing

Using a Soper single-loading rifle, Private John Warrick, 1st Berkshire Volunteers, loaded and fired 60 rounds in one minute at Basingstoke, England, in April, 1870.

Olympic Games

The events in the Olympics have varied considerably since Shooting was first included in 1908, and all events are now for individuals. Winners in 1980 were:

Free Pistol (50m):	Alexsandr Melemtev (USSR) 581/600
Small-Bore Rifle—Prone (50m):	Karoly Varga (Hun) 599/600
Small-Bore Rifle—3 Positions (50m):	Viktor Vlasov (USSR) 1173/1200
Rapid-Fire Pistol (25m):	Corneliu Ion (Rum) 596/600
Trap Shooting:	Luciano Giovanetti (Ita) 198/200
Skeet Shooting:	Hans-Kjeld Rasmussen (Den) 196/200
Running Game Target (50m):	Igor Sokolov (USSR) 589/600

World Championships

World Champions at the 1978 championships held in Seoul, South Korea, were:

MEN

Free Pistol (50m):	Moritz Minder (Swi) 577/600
Small-Bore Rifle—Prone (50m):	Alister Allan (GB) 599/600
Small-Bore Rifle—3 Positions (50m):	Lanny Bassham (US) 1165/1200
Rapid Fire Pistol (25m):	Ove Gunnarsson (Swe) 595/600
Trap Shooting:	Eladio Vallduvi (Spa) 198/200
Skeet Shooting:	Luciano Brunetti (Ita) 197/200
Running Game Target:	Guha Rannikko (Fin) 572/600

WOMEN

Small-Bore Rifle—Prone (50m):	Sue-Ann Sandusky (US) 596/600
Small-Bore Rifle—3 Positions (50m):	Wanda Oliver (US) 580/600
Trap Shooting:	Susan Nattrass (Can) 195/200
Skeet Shooting:	Bianca Hansberg (Ita) 189/200

(**Note:** in all cases the total possible score is shown last)

SKIING

Origins. The most ancient ski in existence was found well preserved in a peat bog at Höting, Sweden, dating from *c.* 2500 B.C. A rock carving of a skier at Bessovysledki, USSR, dates from 6000 B.C. The earliest recorded military use was in Norway, in 1199, though it did not grow into a sport until 1843 at Tromsø. The Trysil Shooting and Skiing Club (founded 1861), in Norway, claims to be the world's oldest. Skiing was not introduced in the Alps until 1883, though there is some evidence of earlier use in the Carniola district. The earliest formal downhill race was staged at Montana, Switzerland, in 1911. The first Slalom event was run at Mürren, Switzerland, on January 21, 1922. The International Ski Federation (F.I.S.) was founded on February 2, 1924. The Winter Olympics were inaugurated on January 25, 1924.

Highest Speed

The highest speed ever claimed for any skier is 124.412 m.p.h. by Steve McKinney (US) (b. 1953) at Portillo, Chile, on October 1, 1978. The fastest by a woman is 103.084 m.p.h. by Catherine Breyton (France) at Portillo on October 1, 1978.

The average race speed by 1976 Olympic Downhill champion Franz Klammer (b. December 3, 1953) of Austria on the Iglis-Patscherkofel course, Innsbruck, Austria, was 63.894 m.p.h. on February 5, 1976.

Duration

The longest non-stop Nordic skiing marathon was one that lasted 48 hours by Onni Savi, aged 35, of Padasjoki, Finland, who covered 305.9 kilometers (190.1 miles) between noon on April 19 and noon on April 21, 1966.

Ahti Nevada (Finland) covered 174.5 miles in 24 hours at Rovaniemi, Finland, on March 30, 1977.

Pat Purcell and John McGlynn (US) completed 81 hours 12 minutes of Alpine skiing at Holiday Mountain, Monticello, New York, on February 1–4, 1979.

Most World Titles

The World Alpine Championships were inaugurated at Mürren, Switzerland, in 1931. The greatest number of titles won is 12 by Christel Cranz (born July 1, 1914), of Germany, with four Slalom (1934–37–38–39), three Downhill (1935–37–39) and five Combined (1934–35–37–38–39). She also won the gold medal for the Combined in the 1936 Olympics. The most titles won by a man is seven by Anton ("Toni") Sailer (born November 17, 1935), of Austria, who won all four in 1956 (Giant Slalom, Slalom, Downhill

WORLD-BEATERS: Christel Cranz (left) won 12 world titles for Alpine skiing, as well as an Olympic gold medal in 1936. Toni Sailer (right) won 7 world titles including 3 Olympic gold medals. He made a clean sweep of all 4 titles in 1956.

and the non-Olympic Alpine Combination) and the Downhill, Giant Slalom and Combined in 1958.

In the Nordic events Sixten Jernberg (Sweden) (b. February 6, 1929) won eight titles, 4 at 50 km., one at 30 km., and 3 in relays, in 1956–64. Johan Grottumsbraaten (1899–1942), of Norway, won six individual titles (two at 18 kilometers and four Combined) in 1926–32. The most by a woman is nine by Galina Koulakova (USSR) (b. April 29, 1942) from 1968 to 1978. The record for a jumper is five by Birger Ruud (b. August 23, 1911), of Norway, in 1931–32 and 1935–36–37.

The Alpine World Cup, instituted in 1967, has been won four times by Gustavo Thoeni (Italy) (b. February 28, 1931). The women's cup has been won six times by the 5-foot-6-inch 150-lb. Annemarie Moser (née Pröll) (Austria). In 1973, she completed a record sequence of 11 consecutive downhill victories and in ten seasons, 1970–1979, has won a total of 62 individual events. The most individual events won by a man is 42 by Ingemar Stenmark (Sweden) in 1974–79, including a record 14 in one season in 1979.

The Nordic World Cup, instituted in 1979, was first won by Oddvar Braa (Norway) with the women's title won by Galina Koulakova (USSR).

Most Olympic Victories

The most Olympic gold medals won by an individual for skiing is four (including one for a relay) by Sixten Jernberg (born February 6, 1929), of Sweden, in 1956–60–64. In addition, Jernberg

SWEDE SUCCESS: Sweden's Sixten Jernberg is the most titled Nordic skier with 8 world titles and 4 Olympic gold medals. Here he is winning the Swedish Championship 15-kilometer race, his 7th straight national title.

has won three silver and two bronze medals. The only woman to win four gold medals is Galina Koulakova (b. 1942) of USSR, who won the 5 kilometers and 10 kilometers (1972) and was a member of the winning 3 × 5 kilometers relay team in 1972 and the 4 × 5 kilometers team in 1976. Koulakova also has won two silver and two bronze medals.

Aleksandr Tikhonov (USSR) has won four gold medals as a member of the winning team in the 4 × 7.5-kilometer biathlon relay (1968–80).

The most Olympic gold medals won in men's alpine skiing is three, by Anton ("Toni") Sailer in 1956 and Jean-Claude Killy in 1968.

Longest Jump

The longest ski jump ever recorded is one of 181 meters (593 feet 10 inches) by Bogdan Norcic (Yugoslavia) who fell on landing at Planica, Yugoslavia, in February 1977.

The official record is 176 meters (577 feet 5 inches) by Toni Innauer (Austria) (b. April 1, 1958) at Oberstdorf, West Germany, on March 6, 1976.

The women's record is 321 feet 6 inches by Anita Wold of Norway, at Okura, Sapporo, Japan, on January 14, 1975.

The longest jump achieved in the Olympics is 111 meters (364 feet) by Wojciech Fortuna (Poland) at Sapporo on February 11, 1972.

Cross-Country

The world's greatest Nordic ski race is the "Vasa Lopp," which commemorates an event of 1521 when Gustavus Vasa (1496–1560), later King of Sweden, skied 85.8 kilometers (53.3 miles) from Mora to Sälen, Sweden. The re-enactment of this journey in the reverse direction is an annual event, with a record 11,596 starters on March 5, 1978. The record time is 4 hours 5 minutes 58 seconds by Ola Hassis (Sweden) on March 4, 1979.

Steepest Descent

Sylvain Saudan (b. Lausanne, Switzerland, September 23, 1936) achieved a descent of Mont Blanc on the northeast side down the Couloir Gervasutti from 13,937 feet on October 17, 1967, skiing gradients in excess of 60 degrees.

Greatest Descent

The greatest reported elevation descended in 12 hours is 416,000 feet by Sarah Ludwig, Scott Ludwig, and Timothy B. Gaffney, at Mt. Brighton, Michigan, on February 16, 1974.

Sylvain Sudan (Switzerland) skied down the 23,400-foot Nun peak in the Ladakh Himalayas on June 26, 1977.

Highest Altitude

Yuichiro Miura (Japan) skied 1.6 miles down Mt. Everest on May 6, 1970, starting from 26,200 feet.

Longest Run

The longest all-downhill ski run in the world is the Weissfluhjoch-Küblis Parsenn course (7.6 miles long), near Davos, Switzerland. The run from the Aiguille du Midi top of the Chamonix lift (vertical lift, 8,176 feet) across the Vallée Blanche is 13 miles.

WINTER WONDERS: Italian Gustavo Thoeni (left) has won the Alpine World Cup a record 4 times. He has also won an Olympic gold and 4 other world titles. Galina Koulakova (right) has won 9 Nordic world titles with 4 Olympic gold medals. The Russian skier also won the inaugural Nordic World Cup in 1979.

SNOW JOB: Jean-Claude Killy (France) thrilled his countrymen when he swept all 3 Olympic gold medals in the 1968 Winter Olympics in Grenoble, France. Killy also won the Alpine Combination world title that year and 2 other world titles in 1966

Backflip on Skis

Twenty-one skiers at Mont St. Saveur, Quebec, Canada, performed a simultaneous back somersault while holding hands on March 2, 1977.

Longest Lift

The longest chair lift in the world is the Alpine Way to Kosciusko Châlet lift above Thredbo, near the Snowy Mountains, New South Wales, Australia. It takes from 45 to 75 minutes to ascend the 3.5 miles, according to the weather. The highest is at Chacaltaya, Bolivia, rising to 16,500 feet. The longest gondola ski lift, at Killington, Vermont, is 3.4 miles long.

Ski Parachuting

The greatest recorded vertical descent in parachute ski-jumping is 3,300 feet by Rick Sylvester (b. 1943) (US), who on July 28, 1976, skied off the 6,600-foot summit of Mt. Asgard in Auyuittuq National Park, Baffin Island, Canada, landing on the Turner Glacier. The jump was made for a sequence in the James Bond film "The Spy Who Loved Me."

Ski-Bob

The ski-bob was invented by a Mr. Stevens of Hartford, Connecticut, and patented (No. 47334) on April 19, 1892, as a "bicycle with ski-runners." The Fédération Internationale de Skibob was founded on January 14, 1961, in Innsbruck, Austria. The first World Championships were held at Bad Hofgastein, Austria, in 1967.

The highest speed has been 103.4 m.p.h. by Erich Brenter (Austria) at Cervinia, Italy, in 1964. The only ski-bobbers to retain world championships are Gerhilde Schiffkorn (Austria) who won the women's title in 1967 and 1969, Gertrude Geberth, who won in 1971 and 1973 and Alois Fischbauer (Austria) who won the men's title in 1973 and 1975.

Snowmobiling

The record speed for a snowmobile was increased to 135.93 m.p.h. by Donald J. Pitzen (US) at Union Lake, Michigan, on February 27, 1977.

The longest snowmobile journey to date was the cross-country trip from Westport, Washington to Lubec, Maine, a distance of 5,004.5 miles, completed by driver Fritz Sprandel of Schnecksville, Pennsylvania, on his Scorpion 440 Whip snowmobile, accompanied by mechanic Ed Kazmierski, from December 4, 1977 to February 6, 1978.

World and Olympic Champions—Alpine Skiing

Alpine Skiing has been included in the winter Olympic Games since 1948, and World Championships were first held in 1932. Winners at World Olympic (*) events since 1948 have been:

GOLD PROSPECTOR: Ingemar Stenmark (Sweden), despite an all-time record 42 World Cup event victories, had been unable to win an Olympic gold medal. He came to Lake Placid in 1980 looking to end the drought and succeeded, taking gold medals in both the slalom and giant slalom.

MEN

Alpine Combination
1948 Henri Oreiller (Fra)
1950 —
1952 —
1954 Stein Eriksen (Nor)
1956 Toni Sailer (Aut)
1958 Toni Sailer (Aut)
1960 Guy Perillat (Fra)
1962 Karl Schranz (Aut)
1964 Ludwig Leitner (W Ger)
1966 Jean-Claude Killy (Fra)
1968 Jean-Claude Killy (Fra)
1970 William Kidd (US)
1972 Gustavo Thoeni (Ita)
1974 Franz Klammer (Aut)
1976 Gustavo Thoeni (Ita)
1978 Andreas Wenzel (Lie)

Downhill
1948* Henri Oreiller (Fra)
1950 Zeno Colo (Ita)
1952* Zeno Colo (Ita)
1954 Christian Pravda (Aut)
1956* Toni Sailer (Aut)
1958 Toni Sailer (Aut)
1960* Jean Vuarnet (Fra)
1962 Karl Schranz (Aut)
1964* Egon Zimmermann (Aut)
1966 Jean-Claude Killy (Fra)
1968* Jean-Claude Killy (Fra)
1970 Bernhad Russi (Swi)
1972* Bernhard Russi (Swi)
1974 David Zwilling (Aut)
1976* Franz Klammer (Aut)
1978 Joseph Walcher (Aut)
1980* Leonhard Stock (Aut)

Slalom
1948* Edi Reinalter (Swi)
1950 Georges Schneider (Swi)
1952* Othmar Schneider (Aut)
1954 Stein Eriksen (Nor)
1956* Toni Sailer (Aut)
1958 Josl Rieder (Aut)
1960* Ernst Hinterseer (Aut)
1962 Charles Bozon (Fra)
1964* Josef Stiegler (Aut)
1966 Carlo Senoner (Ita)
1968* Jean-Claude Killy (Fra)
1970 Jean-Noel Augert (Fra)
1972* Francesco Ochoa (Spa)
1974 Gustavo Thoeni (Ita)
1976* Piero Gros (Ita)
1978 Ingemar Stenmark (Swe)
1980* Ingemar Stenmark (Swe)

Giant Slalom
1948* —
1950 Zeno Colo (Ita)
1952* Stein Eriksen (Nor)
1954 Stein Eriksen (Nor)
1956* Toni Sailer (Aut)
1958 Toni Sailer (Aut)
1960* Roger Staub (Swi)
1962 Egon Zimmermann (Aut)
1964* Francois Bonlieu (Fra)
1966 Guy Perillat (Fra)
1968* Jean-Claude Killy (Fra)
1970 Karl Schranz (Aut)
1972* Gustavo Thoeni (Ita)
1974 Gustavo Thoeni (Ita)
1976* Heini Hemmi (Swi)
1978 Ingemar Stenmark (Swe)
1980* Ingemar Stenmark (Swe)

ALPINE ACE: Annemarie Moser (Autria) has won a record 6 Alpine World Cups. She also came to Lake Placid in search of her first Olympic gold and left satisfied, with a victory in the 1980 downhill event.

FAST GATE: Gretchen Fraser (US) won the first gold medal for women's Olympic slalom skiing in 1948 in St. Moritz, Switzerland.

WOMEN

Alpine Combination

1948	Trude Jochum/Beiser (Aut)
1950	—
1952	—
1954	Ida Schöpfer (Swi)
1956	Madeleine Berthod (Swi)
1958	Frieda Danzer (Swi)
1960	Anne Heggtveit (Can)
1962	Marielle Goitschel (Fra)
1964	Marielle Goitschel (Fra)
1966	Marielle Goitschel (Fra)
1968	Nancy Greene (Can)
1970	Michele Jacot (Fra)
1972	Annemarie Pröll (Aut)
1974	Fabienne Serrat (Fra)
1976	Rosi Mittermaier (W Ger)
1978	Annemarie Moser (née Pröll) (Aut)

Downhill

1948*	Hedy Schlunegger (Swi)
1950*	Trude Jochum/Beiser (Aut)
1952*	Trude Jochum/Beiser (Aut)
1954	Ida Schöpfer (Aut)
1956*	Madeleine Berthod (Swi)
1958	Lucille Wheeler (Can)
1960*	Heidi Biebl (W Ger)
1962	Christl Haas (Aut)
1964*	Christl Haas (Aut)
1966	Erika Schinegger (Aut)
1968*	Olga Pall (Aut)
1970	Anneroesli Zyrd (Swi)
1972*	Marie-Therese Nadig (Swi)
1974	Annemarie Pröll (Aut)
1976*	Rosi Mittermaier (W Ger)
1978	Annemarie Moser (née Pröll) (Aut)
1980*	Annemarie Moser (Aut)

Slalom

1948*	Gretchen Fraser (US)
1950	Dagmar Rom (Aut)
1952*	Andrea Mead Lawrence (US)
1954	Trude Klecker (Aut)
1956*	Renée Colliard (Swi)
1958	Inger Björnbakken (Nor)
1960*	Anne Heggtveit (Can)
1962	Marianne Jahn (Aut)
1964*	Christine Goitschel (Fra)
1966	Annie Famose (Fra)
1968*	Marielle Goitschel (Fra)
1970	Ingrid Lafforgue (Fra)
1972*	Barbara Cochran (US)
1974	Hanni Wenzel (Lie)
1976*	Rosi Mittermaier (W Ger)
1978	Lea Sölkner (Aut)
1980*	Hanni Wenzel (Lie)

Giant Slalom

1948*	—
1950	Dagmar Rom (Aut)
1952*	Andrea Mead Lawrence (US)
1954	Lucienne Schmith (Fra)
1956*	Ossi Reichert (W Ger)
1958	Lucille Wheeler (Can)
1960*	Yvonne Rüegg (Swi)
1962	Marianne Jahn (Aut)
1964*	Marielle Goitschel (Fra)
1966	Marielle Goitschel (Fra)
1968*	Nancy Greene (Can)
1970	Betsy Clifford (Can)
1972*	Marie-Therese Nadig (Swi)
1974	Fabienne Serrat (Fra)
1976*	Kathy Kreiner (Can)
1978	Marie Epple (W Ger)
1980*	Hanni Wenzel (Lie)

GOING DOWNHILL: Hanni Wenzel, from the tiny Principality of Liechtenstein (66 sq. miles), won gold medals in both the women's slalom and giant slalom at Lake Placid in 1980. Here she is capturing the silver medal for the downhill in the same Games. Wenzel won the World Cup in 1978.

Alpine World Cup

The Alpine World Cup, a points competition involving the season's major events, was introduced in 1967.

MEN		WOMEN	
1967	Jean-Claude Killy (Fra)	1967	Nancy Greene (Can)
1968	Jean-Claude Killy (Fra)	1968	Nancy Greene (Can)
1969	Karl Schranz (Aut)	1969	Gertrud Gabl (Aut)
1970	Karl Schranz (Aut)	1970	Michele Jacot (Fra)
1971	Gustavo Thoeni (Ita)	1971	Annemarie Pröll (Aut)
1972	Gustavo Thoeni (Ita)	1972	Annemarie Pröll (Aut)
1973	Gustavo Thoeni (Ita)	1973	Annemarie Pröll (Aut)
1974	Piero Gros (Ita)	1974	Annemarie Pröll (Aut)
1975	Gustavo Thoeni (Ita)	1975	Annemarie Moser (née Pröll) (Aut)
1976	Ingemar Stenmark (Swe)	1976	Rosi Mittermaier (W Ger)
1977	Ingemar Stenmark (Swe)	1977	Lise-Marie Morerod (Swi)
1978	Ingemar Stenmark (Swe)	1978	Hanni Wenzel (Lie)
1979	Peter Luescher (Swi)	1979	Annemarie Moser (Aut)

World and Olympic Champions—Nordic Skiing

Nordic Skiing—Jumping and Cross-Country—was first included in the Olympic Games in 1924 and separate World Championships were first held in 1929. The *Nordic Combination* is for 15 kilometers cross-country and jumping. Winners since 1948 (* = Olympics):

MEN

1948*	Heikki Hasu (Fin)
1950	Heikki Hasu (Fin)
1952*	Simon Slättvik (Nor)
1954	Sverre Stenersen (Nor)
1956*	Sverre Stenersen (Nor)
1958	Paavo Korhonen (Fin)
1960*	Georg Thoma (W Ger)
1962	Arne Larsen (Nor)
1964*	Tormod Knutsen (Nor)
1966	Georg Thoma (W Ger)
1968*	Franz Keller (W Ger)
1970	Ladislav Rygl (Cze)
1972*	Ulrich Wehling (E Ger)
1974	Ulrich Wehling (E Ger)
1976*	Ulrich Wehling (E Ger)
1978	Konrad Winkler (E Ger)
1980*	Ulrich Wehling (E Ger)

TAKE FLIGHT: Austrian Karl Schnabl is flying to the gold medal in the 1976 Innsbruck Olympic ski-jump competition on the 90-meter hill. Schnabl also took the bronze on the 70-meter hill.

SKI-JUMPING

Since 1964 men have competed at the Olympic Games at Ski-Jumping on a 70-meter hill and on a 90-meter hill. Champions have been:

70-meter hill

1964	Veikko Kankkonen (Fin) 229.90m
1968	Jiri Raska (Cze) 216.5m
1972	Yukio Kasaya (Jap) 244.2m
1976	Hans-Georg Aschenbach (E Ger) 252.0m
1980*	Anton Innauer (Aut) 178.0m

90-meter hill

1964	Toralf Engen (Nor) 230.70m
1968	Vladimir Beloussov (USSR) 231.3m
1972	Wojciech Fortuna (Pol) 219.9m
1976	Karl Schnabl (Aut) 234.8m
1980*	Jouko Tormanen (Fin) 231.5m

World Champions

World ski-jumping championships were first held in 1929. Winners since 1966:

1966	Björn Wirkola (Nor) (70m and 90m)
1970	Gurij Napalkov (USSR) (70m and 90m)
1974	Hans-Georg Aschenbach (E Ger) (70m and 90m)
1978	Mathias Buse (E Ger) (70m)
	Tapio Räisänen (Fin) (90m)

BIATHLON

The Biathlon is a combination of Skiing and Shooting. World championships were first held in 1958 and Olympic championships in 1960. Champions (* = Olympics):

1958	Adolf Wiklund (Swe)
1959	Vladimir Melanin (USSR)
1960*	Klas Lestander (Swe)
1961	Kalevi Huuskonen (Fin)
1962	Vladimir Melanin (USSR)
1963	Vladimir Melanin (USSR)
1964*	Vladimir Melanin (USSR)
1965	Olav Jordet (Nor)
1966	Jan Istad (Nor)
1967	Viktor Mamatov (USSR)
1968*	Magnar Solberg (Nor)
1969	Aleksandr Tikhonov (USSR)
1970	Aleksandr Tikhonov (USSR)
1971	Heinz Dieter Speer (E Ger)
1972*	Magnar Solberg (Nor)
1973	Aleksandr Tikhonov (USSR)
1974	Juhani Suutarinen (Fin) (10km and 20km)

1975	Aleksandr Elisarov (USSR) (10km)		
	Heikki Ikola (Fin) (20km)		
1976*	Nikolay Kruglov (USSR) (20km)		
	Juhani Suutarinen (Fin) (10km)		
1977	Heikki Ikola (Fin) (20km)		
	Aleksandr Tikhonov (USSR) (10km)		
1978	Odd Lirhus (Nor) (20km)		
	Frank Ullrich (E Ger) (10km)		
1979	Klaus Siebert (E Ger) (20km)		
	Frank Ullrich (E Ger) (10km)		
1980*	Anatoly Alabyev (USSR) (20km)		
	Frank Ullrich (E Ger) (10km)		

Biathlon Team (Relay [4 × 7.5km] competition)

1958	Sweden	1971	USSR
1959	USSR	1972*	USSR
1961	Finland	1973	USSR
1962	USSR	1974	USSR
1963	USSR	1975	Finland
1965	Norway	1976*	USSR
1966	Norway	1977	USSR
1967	Norway	1978	E. Germany
1968*	USSR	1979	E. Germany
1969	USSR	1980*	USSR
1970	Norway		

SOCCER

Origins. A game with some similarities termed *Tsu-chu* was played in China in the 3rd and 4th centuries B.C. One of the earliest references to the game in England refers to the accidental death of a goalkeeper on February 23, 1582, in Essex. The earliest clear representation of the game is in a print from Edinburgh, Scotland, dated 1672–73. The game became standardized with the formation of the Football Association in England on October 26, 1863. A football game, *Calcio*, existed in Italy in 1410. The world's oldest club is Sheffield F. C. of England, formed on October 24, 1857. Eleven on a side was standardized in 1870.

Highest Scores

Teams. The highest score recorded in any first class match is 36. This occurred in the Scottish Cup match between Arbroath

WORLD CUP SCORES: The 1978 World Cup final drew the largest TV audience in sports history (excluding the Olympics) with 400,000,000 viewers. Here, Mario Kempes scores for Argentina in their 3–1 victory over Holland.

SCORING FEAT: Pelé celebrates one of his 1,281 goals, this one with the NY Cosmos of the North American Soccer League. One of the world's most famous and popular athletes, Pelé helped bring recognition to the NASL when he signed after his 18-year, 1,216-goal career in Brazil (during which Brazil won 3 World Cups).

and Bon Accord on September 5, 1885, when Arbroath won 36–0 on their home ground. But for the lack of nets, the playing time might have been longer and the score possibly even higher.

The highest goal margin recorded in any international match is 17. This occurred in the England vs. Australia match at Sydney on June 30, 1951, when England won 17–0. This match is not listed by England as a *full* international.

Individuals. The most goals scored by one player in a first-class match is 16 by Stephan Stanis (*né* Stanikowski, b. Poland, July 15, 1913) for Racing Club de Lens vs. Aubry-Asturies, in Lens, France, on December 13, 1942.

IN THEIR CUPS: Gerd Muller (left) scored 14 goals for West Germany in 2 World Cup final tournaments, with his country winning the second, in 1974. Geoffrey Hurst (right) holds the coveted World Cup trophy after his record 3 final-game goals helped England defeat West Germany in 1966.

The record number of goals scored by one player in an international match is 10 by Gottfried Fuchs for Germany, which beat Russia 16–0 in the 1912 Olympic tournament (consolation event) in Sweden.

Artur Friedenreich (1892–1969) (Brazil) scored an undocumented 1,329 goals in a 43-year first-class football career. The most goals scored in a specified period is 1,216 by Edson Arantes do Nascimento (b. Baurú, Brazil, October 23, 1940), known as Pelé, the Brazilian inside left, from September 7, 1956, to October 2, 1974 (1,254 games). His best year was 1958 with 139. His *milesimo* (1,000th) came in a penalty for his club, Santos, in the Maracaña Stadium, Rio de Janeiro, on November 19, 1969, when he was playing in his 909th first-class match. He came out of retirement in 1975 to add to his total with the New York Cosmos of the North American Soccer League. By his retirement on October 1, 1977 his total had reached 1,281 in 1,363 games. Franz ("Bimbo") Binder (b. 1911) scored 1,006 goals in 756 games in Austria and Germany between 1930 and 1950.

Fastest Goals

The record for an international match is 3 goals in 3½ minutes by Willie Hall (Tottenham Hotspur) for England against Ireland on November 16, 1938, at Old Trafford, Manchester, England.

The fastest goal in World Cup competition was one in 30 seconds by Ollie Nyberg for Sweden vs. Hungary, in Paris, June 16, 1938.

Most Appearances

Robert ("Bobby") Moore of West Ham United and Fulham set a new record of full international appearances by playing in his

108th game for England vs. Italy on November 14, 1973 at Wembley, London. His first appearance was vs. Peru on May 20, 1962, and he retired on May 14, 1977, on his 1,000th appearance.

Most Successful National Coach

Helmut Schoen (born 1915) of West Germany coached his teams to victory in the 1972 European championship and the 1974 World Cup, as well as finishing second in the 1966 World Cup and 1976 European championships, and third in the 1970 World Cup.

Longest Match

The world duration record for a first-class match was set in the Copa Libertadores championship in Santos, Brazil, on August 2–3, 1962, when Santos drew 3–3 with Penarol F.C. of Montevideo, Uruguay. The game lasted 3½ hours (with interruptions), from 9:30 P.M. to 1 A.M.

A match between the Simon Fraser University Clansmen and the Quincy College Hawks lasted 4 hours 25 minutes (221 minutes 43 seconds playing time) at Pasadena, California, in November, 1976.

Crowds

The greatest recorded crowd at any football match was 205,000 (199,854 paid) for the Brazil vs. Uruguay World Cup final in Rio de Janeiro, Brazil, on July 16, 1950.

World Cup

The *Fédération Internationale de Football* (F.I.F.A.) was founded in Paris on May 21, 1904, and instituted the World Cup Competition in 1930, in Montevideo, Uruguay.

The only country to win three times has been Brazil. Brazil was also third in 1938 and 1978, and second in 1950, and is the only one of the 45 participating countries to have played in all 11 competitions.

The record goal scorer has been Just Fontaine (France) with 13 goals in 6 games in the final stages of the 1958 competition. The most goals scored in a final is 3 by Geoffrey Hurst (West Ham United) for England vs. West Germany on July 30, 1966. Gerd Müller (West Germany) scored 14 goals in two World Cup finals (1970 and 1974).

Antonio Carbajal (b. 1923) played for Mexico in goal in the competitions of 1950–54–58–62 and 1966.

Receipts

The greatest receipts at a World Cup final were £204,805 ($573,454) from an attendance of 96,924 for the match between England and West Germany at the Empire Stadium, Wembley, Greater London, on July 30, 1966.

NET WEIGHT: Willie "Fatty" Foulke was the largest goalkeeper ever at 6 feet 3 inches and 311 pounds. The gigantic Englishman once stopped a game by snapping the crossbar.

Heaviest Goalkeeper

The biggest goalie on record was Willie J. ("Fatty") Foulke of England (1874–1916) who stood 6 feet 3 inches and weighed 311 lbs. By the time he died, he tipped the scales at 364 lbs. He once stopped a game by snapping the cross bar.

Soccer (Amateur)

Most Olympic Wins. The only country to have won the Olympic football title three times is Hungary in 1952, 1964 and 1968. The United Kingdom won in 1908 and 1912 and also the unofficial tournament of 1900. These contests have now virtually ceased to be amateur. The highest Olympic score is Denmark 17 vs. France "A" 1 in 1908.

Women's Championship. The first world invitational women's tournament was held in Taipei, Taiwan, during October, 1978. France and Finland were declared co-champions in a competition delayed by typhoons.

Largest Crowd. The highest attendance at any amateur match is 120,000 at Senayan Stadium, Djakarta, Indonesia, on February 26, 1976, for the Pre-Olympic Group II Final between North Korea and Indonesia.

Heading

The highest recorded number of repetitions for heading a ball is 12,374 in 79 minutes 24 seconds by Istvan Halaszi (b. Hungary, July 24, 1957) at the Jewish Community Center, Milwaukee, Wisconsin, on April 29, 1979.

Ball Control

Adrian Walsh (aged 34) juggled a regulation soccer ball for 4 hours 3 minutes 43 seconds non-stop at The Town Park, Mallow,

County Cork, Ireland, on June 24, 1979. He hit the ball 23,547 times with his feet, legs and head without ever letting the ball touch the ground.

Marathons

The longest recorded 11-a-side soccer marathon is 51 hours 30 minutes by two teams from Security Squadron, RAF Laarbruch, Germany, August 29–31, 1979.

The longest recorded authenticated 5-a-side games have been (outdoors) 62 hours 51 minutes by two teams (no substitutes) from St. Albans United F.C., at Belmont Hill, St. Albans, England, June 22–24, 1979, and (indoors) 92 hours 35 minutes by two teams (no substitutes) from Barton Villa AFC, of Eccles, Manchester, England, August 26–30, 1979.

NASL Records

History. The North American Soccer League was created in 1968 through the merger of the two competing professional soccer leagues: the United Soccer Association and the National Professional Soccer League. The fledgling 17-team league nearly collapsed in its second year when its membership dwindled to 5 teams. The ability of expansion teams to have winning seasons and the addition of internationally famous players (most notably Pelé) helped attendance to grow, and the league boasted 24 teams for its 1979 season.

Individual Scoring. Giorgio Chinaglia (b. January 24, 1947) of the New York Cosmos, scored a record 34 goals during the 1978 season. He also set the record for points that season with 79. (The

COSMOS TOPPER: Giorgio Chinaglia (NY Cosmos) set 2 scoring records in 1978 with 34 goals and 79 points, and helped his team to their second straight championship.

NASL awards 2 points for a goal and 1 point for an assist.) Alan Hinton (Vancouver) had the most assists in a season with 30 in 1978.

Several players share the record for goals in a game (5), as well as assists (4), but Chinaglia has the mark for most points in a game with 12 against Miami on August 10, 1976.

Steve Davis (Los Angeles) scored goals in 10 consecutive games in 1977.

Willie Mfum (New York) scored the fastest goal at 21 seconds against Rochester in 1971.

Goalkeeping. Claude Campos (Rochester) went 476 consecutive minutes without allowing a goal in 1972. The fewest goals allowed in a season is 8 by Bob Rigby (Philadelphia), in 1973. The record for most saves in a game is 22, by Mike Winter (St. Louis) vs. Rochester, May 27, 1973.

Attendance. The greatest crowd to see a soccer game in the United States and Canada was the 77,691 spectators at Giants Stadium, New Jersey, who watched an NASL playoff game between the New York Cosmos and Fort Lauderdale Strikers on August 14, 1977.

World Cup

First held in 1930 in Uruguay. Held every four years.

1930	Uruguay	1954	West Germany	1970	Brazil
1934	Italy	1958	Brazil	1974	West Germany
1938	Italy	1962	Brazil	1978	Argentina
1950	Uruguay	1966	England		

European Football Championship

First contested as the Nations Cup between 1958 and 1960, the European Football Championship is played every four years over a two-year period.

1960	USSR	1968	Italy	1976	Czechoslovakia
1964	Spain	1972	West Germany		

European Champion Clubs Cup (European Cup)

Contested annually since the 1955–56 season by the champion clubs of each member of the European Union (UEFA) together with the previous winner.

1955–56	Real Madrid	1963–64	Inter Milan	1971–72	Ajax (Amsterdam)
1956–57	Real Madrid	1964–65	Inter Milan	1972–73	Ajax (Amsterdam)
1957–58	Real Madrid	1965–66	Real Madrid	1973–74	Bayern Munich
1958–59	Real Madrid	1966–67	Celtic (Glasgow)	1974–75	Bayern Munich
1959–60	Real Madrid	1967–68	Manchester United	1975–76	Bayern Munich
1960–61	Benfica	1968–69	A C Milan	1976–77	Liverpool
1961–62	Benfica	1969–70	Feyenoord	1977–78	Liverpool
1962–63	A C Milan	1970–71	Ajax (Amsterdam)	1978–79	Nottingham Forest

European Cup Winners' Cup

Contested annually since the 1960–61 season by the winners of national cup competitions (or the runners-up, if the winners contest the European Cup).

1960–61	Florentina	1970–71	Chelsea
1961–62	Atletico Madrid	1971–72	Rangers (Glasgow)
1962–63	Tottenham Hotspur	1972–73	A C Milan
1963–64	Sporting Lisbon	1973–74	Magdeburg
1964–65	West Ham United	1974–75	Dynamo Kiev
1965–66	Borussia Dortmund	1975–76	Anderlecht
1966–67	Bayern Munich	1976–77	SV Hamburg
1967–68	A C Milan	1977–78	Anderlecht
1968–69	Slovan Bratislava	1978–79	Barcelona
1969–70	Manchester City		

European Super Cup

Held annually since 1972 between the winners of the European Champion Clubs Cup and the European Cup Winners' Cup.

1972	Ajax (Amsterdam)	1975	Dynamo Kiev	1977	Liverpool
1974	Ajax (Amsterdam)	1976	Anderlecht	1978	Anderlecht

World Club Cup

Contested by the winners of the European Cup and the Copa Libertadores de America, the South American Club Cup, since 1960.

1960	Real Madrid (Spa)	1969	A C Milan (Ita)
1961	Penarol (Uru)	1970	Feyenoord (Hol)
1962	Santos (Bra)	1971	Nacional (Uru)
1963	Santos (Bra)	1972	Ajax (Hol)
1964	Inter-Milan (Ita)	1973	Independiente (Arg)
1965	Inter-Milan (Ita)	1974	Atletico Madrid (Spa)
1966	Penarol (Uru)	1975	Not held
1967	Racing Club (Arg)	1976	Bayern Munich (W Ger)
1968	Estudiantes (Arg)	1977	Boca Juniors (Arg)

NASL Champions

1968	Atlanta Chiefs	1974	Los Angeles Aztecs
1969	Kansas City Spurs	1975	Tampa Bay Rowdies
1970	Rochester Lancers	1976	Toronto Metros
1971	Dallas Tornado	1977	New York Cosmos
1972	New York Cosmos	1978	New York Cosmos
1973	Philadelphia Atoms	1979	Vancouver Whitecaps

NASL Most Valuable Players

1968	John Kowalik, Chicago	1974	Peter Silvester, Baltimore
1969	Cirilio Fernandez, K.C.	1975	Steven David, Miami
1970	Carlos Metidieri, Rochester	1976	Pelé, N.Y.
1971	Carlos Metidieri, Rochester	1977	Franz Beckenbauer, N.Y.
1972	Randy Horton, N.Y.	1978	Mike Flanagan, New England
1973	Warren Archibald, Miami	1979	Johan Cruyff, Los Angeles

Olympic Games

Winners of the Olympic Games soccer competition have been:

1908	Great Britain	1952	Hungary
1912	Great Britain	1956	USSR
1920	Belgium	1960	Yugoslavia
1924	Uruguay	1964	Hungary
1928	Uruguay	1968	Hungary
1932	Not held	1972	Poland
1936	Italy	1976	E. Germany
1948	Sweden	1980	Czechoslovakia

POUND FOR POUND: The first transfer fee to approach £1 million was that paid by F. C. Barcelona of Spain for Johan Cruyff (left) of Ajax Amsterdam. In 1979, Cruyff was the NASL MVP with the LA Aztecs. Mike Flanagan (right) was the 1978 MVP for the New England Tea Men, but returned to England the next year.

N.C.A.A.

1959	St. Louis	1967	Michigan State	1973	St. Louis
1960	St. Louis		St. Louis	1974	Howard
1961	West Chester St.	1968	Maryland	1975	San Francisco
1962	St. Louis		Michigan State	1976	San Francisco
1963	St. Louis	1969	St. Louis	1977	Hartwick
1964	Navy	1970	St. Louis	1978	San Francisco
1965	St. Louis	1971	Vacated	1979	So. Illinois-Edwardsville
1966	San Francisco	1972	St. Louis		

SOFTBALL

Origins. Softball, as an indoor derivative of baseball, was invented by George Hancock at the Farragut Boat Club of Chicago, in 1887. Rules were codified in Minneapolis in 1895 as Kitten Ball. International rules were established in 1933 when the name Softball was officially adopted. The I.S.F. was formed in 1952 as governing body for both fast pitch and slow pitch.

World Championships

Most Titles. The US has won the men's world championship (instituted in 1966) three times, 1966, 68 and 76 (shared), and the women's title (instituted in 1965) twice, in 1974 and 1978.

Individual Records. Joan Joyce set a pair of records by pitching 2 perfect games and notching 76 strikeouts for the US women's team in the 1974 world championships at Stratford, Connecticut. In the same competition, Miyoko Naruse of Japan set three batting records with 17 hits, a .515 batting average and 11 RBIs

MAKING THE PITCH: Ty Stofflet (US) struck out a record 98 batters in the 1976 world championships. Stofflet also holds the pitching record for most consecutive wins in men's major fast pitch national tournament play with 14 for the York, Pennsylvania, team, 1977–79.

(shared with two others). In the men's competition at Wellington, New Zealand, in 1976, pitcher Ty Stofflet (US) struck out a record 98 batters. Bob Burrows of Canada hit the most-ever home runs with 4, and tied a record of 14 RBIs.

Marathon

The longest fast-pitch marathon is 55 hours 50 minutes by two teams of nine (no substitutes) from the Y.C.W. Softball Association, Melbourne, Australia, on December 16–18, 1978. The longest for slow pitch is 72 hours 3 seconds by two teams of 10 players from the US Navy in Singapore, December 28–31, 1977.

Men's Major Fast Pitch National Tournament Records

BATTING (INDIVIDUAL)

Highest Average: Ted Hicks (Springfield) 1978-.632
Most Hits: Ted Hicks (Springfield) 1978-12; Leon Wood (Clearwater) 1978-12
Most Home Runs: Bob McClish (Springfield, Mo.) 1973-5
Most Three Base Hits: Jim Henley (Chattanooga, Tn.) 1965-4
Most Two Base Hits: Al Linde (Midland, Mi.) 1951-5; George Bettineski (Seattle, Wa.) 1977-5
Most RBIs: Bob McClish (Springfield, Mo.) 1973-13

PITCHING (INDIVIDUAL)

Most Games Won: Harvey Sterkel (Aurora) 1959-8; Bonnie Jones (Detroit) 1961-8
Most Strikeouts: Herb Dudley (Clearwater) 1949-130
Most Strikeouts (Game): Herb Dudley (Clearwater) 1949-55 (21 innings); John Hunter (Clearwater) 1951-19 (7 innings); Harvey Sterkel (Aurora) 1959-19 (7 innings) and Richard Brubaker (Chicago) 1971-19 (7 innings)
Most Strikeouts (Game–Two Teams): Florida-Oklahoma—1949-81 (21 innings)
Most Strikeouts (Two Pitchers–Same Team): Harold Gears-Joe Witzigman (Kodak Park) 1936-21 (7 innings)
Most Innings Pitched: Harvey Sterkel (Aurora) 1959-92
Most Bases on Balls: Jack Hutchinson (Portland) 1959-19
Most Hits Allowed: Vern Grafton (Sunnyvale) 1964-33
Most Runs Given Up: G. Wesolowski (Baltimore) 1951-24

MISCELLANEOUS RECORDS

Longest Extra Inning Games: 31 innings—1963 Clearwater, Fl. (4) Haney, King (WP); Portland, Or. (3) Hutchinson, Ellison (LP); 24 innings—1959 Baltimore, Md. (2) Hampill (WP); Springfield, Mo. (0) Barr (LP); 1965 Chattanooga, Tn. (1) Providence, R.I. (0) 24 innings

Most National Championships: Clearwater, Fl.-10

Consecutive National Championships Ft. Wayne, In.-(1945–47)-3

Most Consecutive Wins by Team: Clearwater, Fl. (1962-63)-12; Reading, Pa. (1977–79)-12

Most Consecutive Wins by a Pitcher: Ty Stofflet (York, Pa.) 1977–78–79-14

Most Stolen Bases (Game): U.S. Army Forces 1969-7

Women's Major Fast Pitch National Tournament Records

BATTING (INDIVIDUAL)

Highest Average: Diane Kalliam (Santa Clara, Ca.) 1975-.632

Most Hits: Pat Guenzler (St. Louis, Mo.) 1975-14

Most Home Runs: Robbie Mulkey (Portland) 1949-4

Most Three Base Hits: Irene Huber (Fresno) 1949-3; Lu Flanagan (Seattle) 1971-3; Lana Svec (Ashland) 1977-3; Marilyn Rau (Sun City) 1978-3.

Most Two Base Hits: Joan Joyce (Stratford) 1968-5; Barbara Reinalda   (Stratford) 1976-5

Most RBIs: Kay Rich (Fresno) 1955-10

Most Runs Scored: Irene Shea (Stratford) 1975-9

BATTING (TEAM)

Most Hits: Stratford, Ct. 1974-69

Most Home Runs: Portland, Or. 1949-4

Most Three Base Hits: Phoenix, Az. 1955-7; Ashland, Oh. 1977-7

Most Two Base Hits: Stratford, Ct. 1968-12

Most RBIs: Fresno, Ca. 1955-30

PITCHING (INDIVIDUAL)

Most Innings Pitched: Joan Joyce (Stratford) 1974-70

Most Strike Outs: Joan Joyce (Stratford) 1973-134

Most Strike Outs (Game): Bertha Tickey (Orange) 1953-20 (7 innings); Joan Joyce (Stratford) 1961-40 (18 innings)

Most No-Hit Games: Louis Mazzucca (Portland) 1960-3

Most Perfect Games: Bertha Tickey (Orange-Stratford) 1950–1954–1968-3

Most National Tournament Wins: Bertha Tickey (Stratford)-69 (19 national tournaments)

Most Consecutive Strikeouts: Bertha Tickey (Stratford) 1968-11

MISCELLANEOUS RECORDS

Most Consecutive National Championships: Stratford-8

Most Total National Championships: Stratford-15

WINNING WAYS: The Raybestos Brakettes of Stratford, Connecticut, have won 15 women's national fast pitch tournaments. Here is the 1978 team that won the title for the 8th straight year.

National Fast Pitch Softball Champions

	MEN		WOMEN
1933	J. J. Gillis, Chicago, Ill.	1933	Great Northerns, Chicago, Ill.
1934	Ke Nash-A's, Kenosha, Wis.	1934	Hart Motors, Chicago, Ill.
1935	Crimson Coaches, Toledo, Ohio	1935	Bloomer Girls, Celveland, Ohio
1936	Kodak Park, Rochester, N.Y.	1936	National Mfg. Co., Cleveland, Ohio
1937	Briggs, Mfg. Co., Detroit, Mich.	1937	National Mfg. Co., Cleveland, Ohio
1938	Pohlers, Cincinnati, Ohio	1938	J. J. Krieg's Alameda, Ca.
1939	Carr's Covington, Ky.	1939	J. J. Krieg's, Alameda, Ca.
1940	Kodak Park, Rochester, N.Y.	1940	Arizona Ramblers, Phoenix, Az.
1941	Bendix Brakes, South Bend, In.	1941	Higgins "Midgets," Tulsa, Ok.
1942	Deep Rock Oilers, Tulsa, Ok.	1942	Jax Maids, New Orleans, La.
1943	Hammer Field, Fresno, Ca.	1943	Jax Maids, New Orleans. La
1944	Hammer Field, Fresno, Ca.	1944	Lind & Pomeroy, Portland, Or.
1945	Zollner's Pistons, Ft. Worth, Tx.	1945	Jax Maids, New Orleans, La.
1946	Zollner's Pistons, Ft. Worth, Tx.	1946	Jax Maids, New Orleans, La.
1947	Zollner's Pistons, Ft. Worth, Tx.	1947	Jax Maids, New Orleans, La.
1948	Briggs Beautyware, Detroit, Mich.	1948	Arizona Ramblers, Phoenix, Az.
1949	Tip-Top Clothiers, Toronto, Canada	1949	Arizona Ramblers, Phoenix, Az.
1950	Clearwater Bombers, Clearwater, Fl.	1950	Orange Lionettes, Orange, Ca.
1951	Dow Chemical Co., Midland, Mich.	1951	Orange Lionettes, Orange, Ca.
1952	Briggs Beautyware, Detroit, Mich.	1952	Orange Lionettes, Orange, Ca.
1953	Briggs Beautyware, Detroit, Mich.	1953	Betsy Ross Rockets, Fresno, Ca.
1954	Clearwater Bombers, Clearwater, Fl.	1954	Leach Motor Rockets, Fresno, Ca.
1955	Raybestos, Stratford, Ct.	1955	Orange Lionettes, Orange, Ca.
1956	Clearwater Bombers, Clearwater. Fl.	1956	Orange Lionettes, Orange, Ca.
1957	Clearwater Bombers, Clearwater, Fl.	1957	Betsy Ross Rockets, Fresno, Ca.
1958	Raybestos, Stratford, Ct.	1958	Raybestos Brakettes, Stratford, Ct.
1959	Sealmasters, Aurora, Ill.	1959	Raybestos Brakettes, Stratford, Ct.
1960	Clearwater Bombers, Clearwater, Fl.	1960	Raybestos Brakettes, Stratford, Ct.
1961	Sealmasters, Aurora, Ill.	1961	Gold Sox, Whittier, Ca.
1962	Clearwater Bombers, Clearwater, Fl.	1962	Orange Lionettes, Orange, Ca.
1963	Clearwater Bombers, Clearwater, Fl.	1963	Raybestos Brakettes, Stratford, Ct.
1964	Burch Tool, Detroit, Mich.	1964	Erv Lind Florists, Portland, Or.
1965	Sealmasters, Aurora, Ill.	1965	Orange Lionettes, Orange, Ca.
1966	Clearwater Bombers, Clearwater, Fla.	1966	Raybestos Brakettes, Stratford, Ct.
1967	Sealmasters, Aurora, Ill.	1967	Raybestos Brakettes, Stratford, Ct.
1968	Clearwater Bombers, Clearwater, Fl.	1968	Raybestos Brakettes, Stratford, Ct.
1969	Raybestos Cardinals, Stratford, Ct.	1969	Orange Lionettes, Orange, Ca.
1970	Raybestos Cardinals, Stratford, Ct.	1970	Orange Lionettes, Orange, Ca.
1971	Welty Way, Cedar Rapids, Iowa	1971	Raybestos Brakettes, Stratford, Ct.
1972	Raybestos Cardinals, Stratford, Ct.	1972	Raybestos Brakettes, Stratford, Ct.
1973	Clearwater Bombers, Clearwater, Fl.	1973	Raybestos Brakettes, Stratford, Ct.
1974	Guanella Bros., Santa Rosa, Ca.	1974	Raybestos Brakettes, Stratford, Ct.
1975	Rising Sun Hotel, Reading, Pa.	1975	Raybestos Brakettes, Stratford, Ct.
1976	Raybestos Cardinals, Stratford, Ct.	1976	Raybestos Brakettes, Stratford, Ct.
1977	Billard Barbell, Reading, Pa.	1977	Raybestos Brakettes, Stratford, Ct.
1978	Billard Barbell, Reading, Pa.	1978	Raybestos Brakettes, Stratford, Ct.
1979	McArdle Pontiac-Cadillac, Midland, Mich.	1979	Sun City Saints, Sun City, Az.

Collegiate

Women's college softball championships were first held in 1969 under the auspices of the Amateur Softball Association. The A.I.A.W. became a co-sponsor in 1977 and will be solely responsible for the tournament beginning in 1980. The competition is in fast pitch softball, and the A.I.A.W. plans to inaugurate slow pitch championships in 1981.

1969	John F. Kennedy	1973	Arizona State	1977	Northern Iowa
1970	John F. Kennedy	1974	Southwest Missouri St.	1978	UCLA
1971	John F. Kennedy	1975	Nebraska	1979	Texas Woman's U.
1972	Arizona State	1976	Michigan State		

BALL OF FIRE: Pitcher Joan Joyce holds a multitude of women's fast pitch softball records. Formerly with the national champion Raybestos Brakettes, Joyce now pitches for the Connecticut Falcons, a professional team. Joyce's pitches have reportedly been clocked at 116 m.p.h., and she has thrown more than 40 perfect games in her career. In exhibition play, Joyce struck out both Ted Williams (1962) and Hank Aaron (1978), although she had an edge with the women's softball pitcher's mound being much closer to home plate than the hardball mound.

Slow Pitch Records

BATTING

MEN'S MAJOR: Greg Furhman, York Barbells, York, Pa. 1978-.944
WOMEN'S MAJOR: Princess Carpenter, Rutenschroer Floral, Cincinnati, Oh. 1973-.857
MEN'S INDUSTRIAL: Bob Hurd, Sikorsky, Bridgeport, Ct. 1974-.933
16-INCH: Greg Fisele, Saints, St. Louis, Mo. 1973-.813

HOME RUNS

MEN'S MAJOR: Stan Harvey, Howard Furniture, Denver, N.C. 1978-23
WOMEN'S MAJOR: Patsy Danson, Carter's Rebel, Jacksonville, Fl. 1970-5
Sue Taylor, Huntington, N.Y. YMCA 1971-5
MEN'S INDUSTRIAL: Chris Cammack, Aetna, Charlotte, N.C. 1974-15
Bobby Height, Aetna, Charlotte, N.C. 1978-15

National Slow Pitch Champions

MEN'S OPEN DIVISION

1953 Shields Contractors, Newport, Ky.
1954 Waldeck's Tav., Cincinnati, Ohio
1955 Lang's Pet Shop, Covington, Ky.
1956 Gatliff Auto Sales, Newport, Ky.
1957 Gatliff Auto Sales, Newport, Ky.
1958 East Side Sports, Detroit, Mich.
1959 Yorkshire Rest., Dewport, Ky.
1960 Hamilton Tailoring, Cincinnati, Ohio
1961 Hamilton Tailoring, Cincinnati, Ohio
1962 Skip Hogan A.C., Pittsburgh, Pa.
1963 Gatliff Auto Sales, Newport, Ky.
1964 Skip Hogan A.C., Pittsburgh, Pa.
1965 Skip Hogan A.C., Pittsburgh, Pa.
1966 Michael's Lounge, Detroit, Mich.
1967 Jim's Sport Shop, Pittsburgh, Pa.
1968 County Sports, Levittown, N.Y.
1969 Copper Hearth, Milwaukee, Wis.
1970 Little Ceasar's, Southgate, Mich.
1971 Pile Drivers, Virginia Beach, Va.
1972 Jiffy Club, Louisville, Ky.
1973 Howard Furniture, Denver, N.C.
1974 Howard Furniture, Denver, N.C.
1975 Pyramid Cafe, Lakewood, Ohio
1976 Warren Motors, Jacksonville, Fla.
1977 Nelson Painting, Oklahoma City, Okla.
1978 Campbells Carpets, Concord, Ca.
1979 Nelco Manufacturing, Oklahoma City, Okla.

WOMEN'S DIVISION

1962 Dana Gardens, Cincinnati, Ohio
1963 Dana Gardens, Cincinnati, Ohio
1964 Dana Gardens, Cincinnati, Ohio
1965 Art's Aces, Omaha, Neb.
1966 Dana Gardens, Cincinnati, Ohio
1967 Ridge Maintenance, Cleveland, Ohio
1968 Escue Pontiac, Cincinnati, Ohio
1969 Converse Dots, Hialeah, Fl.
1970 Rutenschroer Floral, Cincinnati, Ohio
1971 Gators, Ft. Lauderdale, Fl.
1972 Riverside Ford, Cincinnati, Ohio
1973 Sweeney Chevrolet, Cincinnati, Ohio
1974 Marks Bros., No. Miami Dots, Miami, Fl.
1975 Marks Bros., No. Miami Dots, Miami, Fl.
1976 Sorrento's Pizza, Cincinnati, Ohio
1977 Fox Valley Lassies, St. Charles, Ill.
1978 Bob Hoffman's Dots, Miami, Fl.
1979 Bob Hoffman's Dots, Miami, Fl.

SQUASH

(Note: "1971," for example, refers to the 1971–72 season.)

Earliest Champions

Although racquets with a soft ball was played in 1817 at Harrow School (England), there was no recognized champion of any country until J. A. Miskey of Philadelphia won the American Amateur Singles Championship in 1906.

World Title

Australia has won the amateur team title four times. Geoffrey B. Hunt (Australia) took the amateur individual title in 1967, 1969, and 1971.

The World Open championship, instituted in 1976, has been won three times by Geoffrey B. Hunt (Australia).

Open Championship

The most wins in the Open Championship (amateur or professional), held annually in Britain, is seven by Hashim Khan (Pakistan). He also twice won the Vintage title, in 1977 and 78. Geoffrey B. Hunt (see above) matched Khan's record with his seventh championship in 1980.

Amateur Championship

The most wins in the Amateur Championship is six by Abdel Fattah Amr Bey (Egypt), later appointed Ambassador to London, who won in 1931–32–33 and 1935–36–37.

Longest and Shortest Championship Matches

The longest recorded match was one of 2 hours 35 minutes in the British Amateur Championships at Wembley, England, on December 12, 1976, when Murray Lilley (New Zealand) beat Barry O'Connor (GB) 9–3, 10–8, 2–9, 7–9, 10–8. The second game lasted 58 minutes and there was a total of 98 lets called in the match.

Sue Cogswell beat Teresa Lawes in only 16 minutes in a British Women's title match at Dallington, North Hampshire, on December 12, 1977.

Most Victories in the Women's Championship

The most wins in the Women's Squash Racquets Championship is 16 by Heather McKay (*née* Blundell) of Australia, 1961 to 1976. She also won the first World Open title in 1978. Since 1961 she has not lost a match.

Marathon

The longest squash marathon has been 120 hours 51 minutes by Peter Fairlie at Bridge of Allan Sports Club, Stirling, Scotland, June 30–July 5, 1979. George Deponselle and William de Bruin played for 106 hours 43 minutes at Sutterheim Country Club, Cape Province, South Africa, on October 1–5, 1978. (*This category will in the future be confined to two players only.*)

World Open Championship

First held in 1976 at Wembley.

MEN

1976	Geoff Hunt (Aus)
1977	Geoff Hunt (Aus)
1978	Postponed
1979	Geoff Hunt (Aus)

WOMEN

	Individual	Team
1976	Heather McKay (Aus)	Australia
1979	Heather McKay (Aus)	Great Britain

First held in 1976 in Australia.

World Amateur Championship

First held in 1967, it is contested every two years. Individual and team winners:

	Individual	Team
1967	Geoff Hunt (Aus)	Australia
1969	Geoff Hunt (Aus)	Australia
1971	Geoff Hunt (Aus)	Australia
1973	Cameron Nancarrow (Aus)	Australia
1975	Kevin Shawcross (Aus)	Great Britain
1977	Maqsood Ahmed (Pak)	Pakistan
1979	Jehangir Khan (Pak)	Great Britain

British Open Championship

First played in 1930, the British Open Championship, in which both amateurs and professionals may compete, was for years

HOLDING COURT: Australian Heather McKay won 16 consecutive women's squash titles, 1961–76. She has captured both women's World Open titles and has not lost a match since 1961.

regarded as the unofficial world championship. Until 1947 the event was held on a challenge system with two-leg matches between the holder and his challenger. Held annually.

1930–31	Don Butcher (GB) (2)	1962	Mohibullah Khan (Pak)
1932–37	Abdel Fattah Amr Bey (Egy) (5)	1963–66	Abou Taleb (Egy) (3)
1938	James Dear (GB)	1967–68	Jonah Barrington (GB) (2)
1946–49	Mahmoud el Karim (Egy) (4)	1969	Geoff Hunt (Aus)
1950–55	Hashim Khan (Pak) (6)	1970–73	Jonah Barrington (GB) (4)
1956	Roshan Khan (Pak)	1974	Geoff Hunt (Aus)
1957	Hashim Khan (Pak)	1975	Qamar Zaman (Pak)
1958–61	Azam Khan (Pak) (4)	1976–80	Geoff Hunt (Aus) (5)

British Women's Open Championship

First held in 1922.

1922	Joyce Cave (GB)	1960	Sheila Macintosh (GB)
1922	Sylvia Huntsman (GB)	1961	Fran Marshall (GB)
1923	Nancy Cave (GB)	1962–77	Heather McKay (Aus) (16)
1924	Joyce Cave (GB)	1978	Susan Newman/King (Aus)
1925–25	Cecily Fenwick (GB) (2)	1979	Barbara Wall (Aus)
1928	Joyce Cave (GB)		
1929–30	Nancy Cave (GB)	Note that there have occasionally been two championships in the same year, and that in other cases a year is missed. This is due to the championship being held in December or January.
1931	Cecily Fenwick (GB)	
1932–34	Susan Noel (GB) (3)	
1934–39	Margot Lumb (GB) (5)	
1947–49	Joan Curry (GB) (3)	
1950–58	Janet Morgan/Shardlow (GB) (10)	

British Amateur Championship

First held in 1922 and contested annually. Winners since 1963:

1963–66	Aftab Jawaid (Pak) (4)	1973–74	Mohibullah Khan (Pak) (2)
1967–69	Jonah Barrington (GB) (3)	1975/6	Kevin Shawcross (Aus)
1970	Geoff Hunt (Aus)	1976/7	Bruce Brownlee (NZ)
1971	Gogi Alauddin (Pak)	1977/8	Gamal Awad (Egy)
1972	Cameron Nancarrow (Aus)	1978/9	Gamal Awad (Egy)

KHAN GAME:
Hashim Khan
(Pakistan) shares
the record for most
wins in the
British Open with
7. He is the only
man to win 6 titles
consecutively.

SURFING

Origins. The traditional Polynesian sport of surfing in a canoe (*ehorooe*) was first recorded by the British explorer, Captain James Cook (1728–79) on his third voyage to Tahiti in December, 1771. Surfing on a board (*Amo Amo iluna ka lau oka nalu*) was first described ("most perilous and extraordinary . . . altogether astonishing, and is scarcely to be credited") by Lt. (later Capt.) James King of the Royal Navy in March, 1779, at Kealakekua Bay, Hawaii Island, A surfer was first depicted by the voyage's official artist, John Webber. The sport was revived at Waikiki by 1900. Hollow boards came in in 1929 and the plastic-foam type in 1956.

Highest Waves Ridden

Makaha Beach, Hawaii, provides reputedly the best consistently high waves for surfing, often reaching the rideable limit of 30–35 feet. The highest wave ever ridden was the *tsunami* of "perhaps 50 feet," which struck Minole, Hawaii, on April 3, 1868, and was ridden to save his life by a Hawaiian named Holua.

Longest Ride

About 4 to 6 times each year rideable surfing waves break in Matanchen Bay near San Blas, Nayarit, Mexico, which makes rides of *c.* 5,700 feet possible.

SURF'S UP: This surfer is riding the waves much as the Tahitians did when Captain Cook arrived at the island over 200 years ago. A wave of reportedly 50 feet was the highest ever ridden.

World Champions

World Championships were inaugurated in 1964 at Sydney, Australia. The first surfer to win two titles has been Joyce Hoffman (US) in 1965 and 1966.

SWIMMING

Earliest References. Swimming in schools in Japan was ordered by Imperial edict of Emperor Go-Yoozei as early as 1603, but competition was known from 36 B.C. Sea water bathing was fashionable at Scarborough, North Yorkshire, England, as early as 1660. Competitive swimming originated in London *c.* 1837, at which time there were five or more pools, the earliest of which had been opened at St. George's Pier Head, Liverpool, in 1828.

Largest Pools

The largest swimming pool in the world is the salt-water Orthlieb Pool in Casablanca, Morocco. It is 480 meters (1,547 feet) long, 75 meters (246 feet) wide, and has an area of 8.9 acres.

The largest land-locked swimming pool with heated water was the Fleishhacker Pool on Sloat Boulevard, near Great Highway, San Francisco. It measures 1,000 feet by 150 feet (3.44 acres), is up to 14 feet deep, and can contain 7,500,000 gallons of water. It was opened on May 2, 1925, but has now been abandoned to a few ducks.

The world's largest competition pool is at Osaka, Japan. It accommodates 13,614 spectators.

BOTTOM'S UP: American Joe Bottom reached a speed of 5.19 m.p.h. in a 50 yard swim in 1977. He set the world 100 meters butterfly record in 1977, and captured the world title for that event in 1978.

Fastest Swimmer

Excluding relay stages with their anticipatory starts, the highest speed reached by a swimmer is 5.19 m.p.h. by Joe Bottom (US), who recorded 19.70 seconds for 50 yards in a 25-yard pool at Cleveland, Ohio, on March 24, 1977.

The fastest by a woman is 4.42 m.p.h. by Sue Hinderaker (US) who clocked 23.14 seconds for 50 yards in Pittsburgh, Pennsylvania, on March 16, 1979.

Most World Records

Men: 32, Arne Borg (Sweden) (b. 1901), 1921–29. Women: 42, Ragnhild Hveger (Denmark) (b. December 10, 1920), 1936–42.

GOLD WATER: Mrs. Pat McCormick (left) and Dawn Fraser (right) share the record, along with Kornelia Ender, for the most gold medals won by a woman. McCormick (US) uniquely won all 4 in individual events while Fraser (Australia) is the only swimmer to win the same event at 3 consecutive games.

World Titles

In the world swimming championships (instituted in 1973), the greatest number of medals won is ten (3 gold, 2 silver) by Kornelia Ender of East Germany. The most by a man is seven (6 gold, 1 bronze) by James Montgomery (US).

The most medals in a single championships is six by Tracy Caulkins (US) (b. January 11, 1963) in 1978 with five golds and a silver.

Olympic Swimming Records

Most Olympic Gold Medals. The greatest number of Olympic gold medals won is 9 by Mark Andrew Spitz (US) (b. February 10, 1950), as follows:

100 meter freestyle	1972
200 meter freestyle	1972
100 meter butterfly	1972
200 meter butterfly	1972
4 × 100 meter freestyle relay	1968 and 1972
4 × 200 meter freestyle relay	1968 and 1972
4 × 100 meter medley relay	1972

All but one of these performances (the 4 × 200 meter relay of 1968) were also new world records at the time.

The record number of gold medals won by a woman is 4 shared by Mrs. Patricia McCormick (*née* Keller) (US) (b. May 12, 1930) with the High and Springboard Diving double in 1952 and 1956 (also the women's record for individual golds); by Dawn Fraser (later Mrs. Gary Ware) (Australia) (b. September 4, 1937) with the 100 meter freestyle (1956–60–64) and the 4 × 100 (meter freestyle relay (1956); and by Kornelia Ender (East Germany) with the 100 and 200 meter freestyle (1976), the 100 meter butterfly (1976) and the 4 × 100 meter medley relay (1976). Dawn Fraser is the only swimmer to win the same event on three successive occasions.

Most Olympic Medals. The most medals won is 11 by Spitz, who in addition to his 9 golds (see above), won a silver (100 m. butterfly) and a bronze (100 m. freestyle), both in 1968.

The most medals won by a woman is 8 by Dawn Fraser, who in addition to her 4 golds (see above) won 4 silvers (400 m. freestyle 1956, 4 × 100 m. freestyle relay 1960 and 1964, 4 × 100 m. medley relay 1960); by Shirley Babashoff (US) who won 2 golds (4 × 100 m. freestyle relay 1972 and 1976) and 6 silvers (100 m. freestyle 1972, 200 m. freestyle 1972 and 1976, 400 m. and 800 m. freestyle 1976, and 400 m. medley 1976); and by Kornelia Ender (E. Germany) who, in addition to her 4 golds (see above), won 4 silvers (200 m. individual medley 1972, 4 × 100 m. freestyle 1972 and 1976, 4 × 100 m. medley relay 1972).

Most Individual Gold Medals. The record number of individual gold medals won is 4 shared by four swimmers: Charles M. Daniels (US) (1884–1973) (100 m. freestyle 1906 and 1908, 220 yard freestyle 1904, 440 yard freestyle 1904); Roland Matthes (E. Germany) (b. November 17, 1950) with 100 m. and 200 m. backstroke 1968 and 1972 and Spitz and McCormick (see above).

TAKE A DIVE: Italy's Klaus Dibiasi won 5 Olympic diving medals (3 gold, 2 silver) and captured the highboard competition at 3 successive games.

Closest Verdict. The closest victory in the Olympic Games was in the Munich 400-meter individual medley final on August 30, 1972, when Gunnar Larson (Sweden) won by 2/1,000ths of a second in 4 minutes 31.981 seconds over Tim McKee (US)—a margin of less than ⅛ inch, or the length grown by a fingernail in 3 weeks.

Diving

Olympic Medals. Klaus Dibiasi (Italy) won a total of 5 medals (3 gold, 2 silver) in four Games from 1964 to 1976. He is also the only diver to win the same event (highboard) at three successive Games (1968, 1972, and 1976). Pat McCormick (see above) won 4 gold medals.

World Titles. Phil Boggs (US) (b. December 29, 1949) has won three gold medals in 1973, 75 and 78, but Klaus Dibiasi of Italy won four medals (2 gold and 2 silver) in 1973 and 1975. Trina Kalinina (USSR) (b. February 8, 1959) won five medals (three gold, one silver, one bronze) in 1973, 75 and 78.

Perfect Dive. In the 1972 US Olympic Trials, held in Chicago, Michael Finneran (b. September 21, 1948) was awarded a score of 10 by all seven judges for a backward 1½ somersault 2½ twist free dive from the 10-meter board, an achievement without precedent.

Long Distance Swimming

A unique achievement in long distance swimming was established in 1966 by the cross-Channel swimmer Mihir Sen of Calcutta, India. These were the Palk Strait from Sri Lanka to India (in 25 hours 36 minutes on April 5–6); the Straits of Gibraltar (Europe to Africa in 8 hours 1 minute on August 24); the Dardenelles (Gallipoli, Europe, to Sedulbahir, Asia Minor, in 13 hours 55 minutes on September 12) and the entire length of the Panama Canal in 34 hours 15 minutes on October 29–31. He had earlier swum the English Channel in 14 hours 45 minutes on September 27, 1958.

The longest recorded ocean swim is one of 128.8 miles by Walter Poenisch (US) (b. 1914) from Havana, Cuba to Little Duck Key, Florida (in a shark cage and wearing flippers) in 34 hours 15 minutes on July 11–13, 1978.

The greatest recorded distance ever swum is 1,826 miles down the Mississippi from Ford Dam, near Minneapolis, to Carrollton Avenue, New Orleans, July 6 to December 29, 1930, by Fred P. Newton, then 27, of Clinton, Oklahoma. He was in the water a total of 742 hours, and the water temperature fell as low as 47° F. He protected himself with petroleum jelly.

The longest duration swim ever achieved was one of 168 continuous hours, ending on February 24, 1941, by the legless Charles Zibbelman, *alias* Zimmy (born 1894), of the US, in a pool in Honolulu, Hawaii.

The longest duration swim by a woman was 87 hours 27 minutes in a salt water pool at Raven Hall, Coney Island, New York by Mrs. Myrtle Huddleston of New York City, in 1931. Margaret "Peggy" Byrne (US) (b. December 17, 1949), a Minnesota State Representative, swam 60 hours 15 minutes in a freshwater pool at Saint Paul, Minnesota, on December 18–20, 1978.

The greatest distance covered in a continuous swim is 292 miles by Joe Maciag (b. March 26, 1956) from Billings to Glendive, Montana, in the Yellowstone River in 64 hours 50 minutes, July 1–4, 1976.

Channel Swimming

Earliest Man. The first man to swim across the English Channel (without a life jacket) was the merchant navy captain Matthew Webb (1848–83) (GB), who swam breaststroke from Dover, England, to Calais Sands, France, in 21 hours 45 minutes on August

STERLING SWIMMER: Shirley Babashoff supplemented her 2 relay gold medals with 6 silvers (5 individual and 1 relay) in 1972 and 1976. The 8 total medals is a woman's record the American freestyler shares with 2 others.

CHANNEL ENERGY: Gertrude Ederle (left) was the first woman to successfully swim the English Channel. Ederle (US) earlier set a world record aged 12 years 298 days, making her the youngest record-breaker ever (see page xiii). Cynthia Nichols (right) holds the record for the fastest double crossing of the English Channel, faster by 10 hours than the previous mark.

24–25, 1875. Webb swam an estimated 38 miles to make the 21-mile crossing. Paul Boyton (US) had swum from Cap Gris Nez to the South Foreland in his patent lifesaving suit in 23 hours 30 minutes on May 28–29, 1875. There is good evidence that Jean-Marie Saletti, a French soldier, escaped from a British prison hulk off Dover by swimming to Boulogne in July or August, 1815. The first crossing from France to England was made by Enrico Tiraboschi, a wealthy Italian living in Argentina, who crossed in 16 hours 33 minutes on August 12, 1923, to win a $5,000 prize.

Woman. The first woman to succeed was Gertrude Ederle (US) who swam from Cap Gris Nez, France, to Deal, England, on August 6, 1926, in the then record time of 14 hours 39 minutes. The first woman to swim from England to France was Florence Chadwick of California, in 16 hours 19 minutes on September 11, 1951.

Youngest. The youngest conqueror is Markus Hopper (b. June 14, 1967) of Eltham, England, who swam from Dover to Sangatte, France, in 14 hours 37 minutes, when he was aged 12 years 53 days. The youngest woman was Abla Adel Khairi (b. Egypt, September 26, 1960), aged 13 years 326 days when she swam from England to France in 12 hours 30 minutes on August 17, 1974.

Oldest. The oldest conqueror of the 21-mile crossing has been James Edward "Doc" Counsilman (b. December 28, 1920), head coach of the 1976 US Olympic Swim team, who was 58 years 260 days when he swam from Dover to Cap Gris Nez on September 14, 1979. The oldest woman to conquer the Channel was Stella Taylor (born Bristol, Avon, England, December 20, 1929), aged 45 years 350 days when she swam it in 18 hours 15 minutes on August 26, 1975.

Fastest. The official Channel Swimming Association record is 7 hours 40 minutes by Penny Dean (b. March 21, 1955) of California, who swam from Shakespeare Beach, Dover, England to Cap Gris Nez, France on July 29, 1978.

Slowest. The slowest crossing was the third ever made, when Henry Sullivan (US) swam from England to France in 26 hours 50 minutes, August 5–6, 1923. It is estimated that he swam some 56 miles.

Relays. The two-way record is 16 hours 5½ minutes by six Saudi Arabian men on August 11, 1977. They completed the return journey from France to England in a record 7 hours 58 minutes.

Most Conquests. The greatest number of Channel conquests is 17 by Michael Reed (GB) to October 28, 1979. Cindy Nicholas made her first crossing of the Channel on July 29, 1975, and her eighth on August 5, 1979.

First Double Crossing. Antonio Abertondo (Argentina) aged 42, swam from England to France in 18 hours 50 minutes (8:35 a.m. on September 20 to 3:25 a.m. on September 21, 1961) and after about 4 minutes' rest returned to England in 24 hours 16 minutes, landing at St. Margaret's Bay at 3:45 a.m. on September 22, 1961, to complete the first "double crossing" in 43 hours 10 minutes.

Fastest Double Crossing. Cynthia Nicholas, a 19-year-old from Canada, became the first woman to complete a double crossing of the English Channel on September 7–8, 1977. Her astonishing time of 19 hours 55 minutes was more than 10 hours faster than the previous mark. She achieved a still faster time of 19 hours 12 minutes, August 4–5, 1979.

FAST FREESTYLE: Brian Goodell (US) set world records in both the 400 and 1,500 meters freestyle events to capture 2 gold medals in Montreal in 1976.

Underwater. The first underwater cross-Channel swim was achieved by Fred Baldasare (US), aged 38, who completed a 42-mile swim from France to England with scuba in 18 hours 1 minute on July 10–11, 1962.

Relay Records

The longest recorded mileage in a 24-hour relay swim (team of 5) is 85 miles 837.5 yards by a team from Hamline University, St. Paul, Minnesota, January 21–22, 1978.

The fastest time recorded for 100 miles in a pool by a team of 20 swimmers is 22 hours 38 minutes at the Atlantis Swim Centre, Plympton Park, Australia, on October 14–15, 1978.

Treading Water

The duration record of treading water (vertical posture in an 8-foot square without touching the lane markers) is 64 hours by Norman Albert at Pennsylvania State University on November 1–4, 1978.

GOOD NABER: John Naber (US) won 4 gold medals at the 1976 Montreal Olympics (2 individual, 2 relay). He set world records that still stand for both the 100 and 200 meters backstroke. Naber was also part of the US 4 × 100 meters medley relay team that set the world record in 1978.

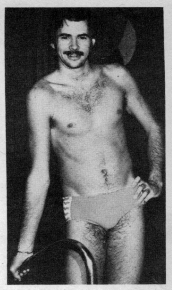

IN THE SWIM: American Cynthia Woodhead (left) smiles after setting the world record for the 200-meter freestyle in Tokyo in 1979. Britain's David Wilkie (right) captured the 200-meter breaststroke gold medal in Montreal in world record time.

FISH STORY: Michael Burton (US) won gold medals in the 400 and 1,500 freestyle in the 1968 Olympics, and won the 1,500 meters gold again in 1972.

World Records

At distances recognized by the Fédération Internationale de Natation Amateur as of August 1980. F.I.N.A. no longer recognizes any records made for non-metric distances. Only performances set in 50-meter pools are recognized as World Records.

MEN

Distance	min. sec.	Name and Nationality	Place	Date
FREESTYLE				
100 m	49.44	Jonty Skinner (S Africa)	Philadelphia, Pa.	Aug 14, 1976
200 m	1:49.16	Ambrose (Rowdy) Gaines (US)	Austin, Tex.	Apr 11, 1980
400 m	3:50.49	Peter Szmidt (Canada)	Toronto, Canada	July 17, 1980
800 m	7:56.49	Vladimir Salnikov (USSR)	Minsk, USSR	Mar 23, 1979
1,500 m	14:58.27	Vladimir Salnikov (USSR)	Moscow, USSR	July 22, 1980
4 × 100 Relay	3:19.74	US National Team	W. Berlin, W Germany	Aug 22, 1978
		(Jack Babashoff, Ambrose Gaines, David McCagg, James Montgomery)		
4 × 200 Relay	7:20.82	US National Team	W. Berlin, W Germany	Aug 24, 1978
		(Bruce Furniss, William Forrester, Bobby Hackett, Ambrose Gaines)		
BREASTSTROKE				
100 m	1:02.86	Gerald Moerken (W Germany)	Jönkoping, Sweden	Aug 17, 1977
200 m	2:15.11	David Wilkie (GB)	Montreal, Canada	July 24, 1976
BUTTERFLY STROKE				
100 m	54.15	Per Arvidsson (Sweden)	Austin, Tex.	Apr 11, 1980
200 m	1:58.21	Craig Beardsley (US)	Irvine, Calif	July 30, 1980
BACKSTROKE				
100 m	55.49	John Naber (US)	Montreal, Canada	July 19, 1976
200 m	1:59.19	John Naber (US)	Montreal, Canada	July 24, 1976
INDIVIDUAL MEDLEY				
200 m	2:03.24	Bill Barrett (US)	Irvine, Calif.	Aug 1, 1980
400 m	4:20.05	Jesse Vassallo (US)	W Berlin, W Germany	Aug 22, 1978

MEDLEY RELAY

(Backstroke, Breaststroke, Butterfly Stroke, Freestyle)

4 × 100 m   3:42.22   U.S. National Team .... W Berlin, W Germany .... Aug 22, 1978
(John Naber, John Hencken, Matthew Vogel, James Montgomery)

WOMEN

Distance	min. sec.	Name and Nationality	Place	Date

FREESTYLE

Distance	min. sec.	Name and Nationality	Place	Date
100 m	54.79	Barbara Krause (E Germany)	Moscow, USSR	July 21, 1980
200 m	1:58.23	Cynthia Woodhead (US)	Tokyo, Japan	Sept 3, 1979
400 m	4:06.28	Tracey Wickham (Australia)	W Berlin, W Germany	Aug 24, 1978
800 m	8:24.62	Tracey Wickham (Australia)	Edmonton, Canada	Aug 5, 1978
1,500 m	16:04.49	Kim Linehan (US)	Ft Lauderdale, Fla.	Aug 19, 1979
4 × 100 m Relay	3:42.71	E Germany	Moscow, USSR	July 27, 1980

(Barbara Krause, Caren Metshuck, Ines Diers, Sarina Hulsenbeck)

BREASTSTROKE

Distance	min. sec.	Name and Nationality	Place	Date
100 m	1:10.11	Ute Geweniger (E Germany)	Moscow, USSR	July 24, 1980
200 m	2:28.36	Lina Kachushite (USSR)	Potsdam, E Germany	Apr 6, 1979

BUTTERFLY STROKE

Distance	min. sec.	Name and Nationality	Place	Date
100 m	59.26	Mary Meagher (US)	Austin, Tex.	Apr 11, 1980
200 m	2:06.37	Mary Meagher (US)	Irvine, Calif.	July 30, 1980

BACKSTROKE

Distance	min. sec.	Name and Nationality	Place	Date
100 m	1:00.86	Rica Reinisch (E Germany)	Moscow, USSR	July 23, 1980
200 m	2:11.77	Rica Reinisch (E Germany)	Moscow, USSR	July 27, 1980

INDIVIDUAL MEDLEY

Distance	min. sec.	Name and Nationality	Place	Date
200 m	2:13.00	Petra Schneider (E Germany)	Magdeburg, E Germany	May 24, 1980
400 m	4:36.29	Petra Schneider (E Germany)	Moscow, USSR	July 26, 1980

MEDLEY RELAY

(Backstroke, Breaststroke, Butterfly Stroke, Freestyle)

Distance	min. sec.	Name and Nationality	Place	Date
4 × 100 m	4:06.67	E German National Team	Moscow, USSR	July 20, 1980

(Rica Reinisch, Ute Geweniger, Andrea Pollack, Sarina Hulsenbeck)

Olympic Games

Swimming events have been held at each Olympic Games since 1896, when three men's events were included—100, 500 and 1200 meters freestyle. Women's events were first included in 1912. Winners since 1948 have been:

MEN

100 Meters Freestyle
1948 Walter Ris (US) 57.3
1952 Clarke Scholes (US) 57.4
1956 Jon Henricks (Aus) 55.4
1960 John Devitt (Aus) 55.2
1964 Donald Schollander (US) 53.4
1968 Michael Wenden (Aus) 52.2
1972 Mark Spitz (US) 51.2
1976 Jim Montgomery (US) 49.99
1980 Jorg Weithe (E Ger) 50.40

200 Meters Freestyle
1968 Michael Wenden (Aus) 1:55.2
1972 Mark Spitz (US) 1:52.78
1976 Bruce Furniss (US) 1:50.29
1980 Sergei Kopliakov (USSR) 1:49.81

400 Meters Freestyle
1948 William Smith (US) 4:41.0
1952 Jean Boiteaux (Fra) 4:30.7
1956 Murray Rose (Aus) 4:27.3
1960 Murray Rose (Aus) 4:18.3
1964 Donald Schollander (US) 4:12.2
1968 Michael Burton (US) 4:09.0
1972 Bradford Cooper (Aus) 4:00.27
1976 Brian Goodell (US) 3:51.93
1980 Vladimir Salnikov (USSR) 3:51.31

1500 Meters Freestyle
1948 James McLane (US) 19:18.5
1952 Ford Konno (US) 18:30.0
1956 Murray Rose (Aus) 17:58.9
1960 John Konrads (Aus) 17:19.6
1964 Robert Windle (Aus) 17:01.7
1968 Michael Burton (US) 16:38.9
1972 Michael Burton (US) 15:52.58
1976 Brian Goodell (US) 15:02.40
1980 Vladimir Salnikov (USSR) 14:58.27

100 Meters Backstroke
1948 Allen Stack (US) 1:06.4
1952 Yoshinobu Oyakawa (US) 1:05.4
1956 David Thiele (Aus) 1:02.2
1960 David Thiele (Aus) 1:01.9
1968 Roland Matthes (E Ger) 58.7
1972 Roland Matthes (E Ger) 56.58
1976 John Naber (US) 55.49
1980 Bengt Baron (Swe) 56.53

200 Meters Backstroke
1964 Jed Graef (US) 2:10.3
1968 Roland Matthes (E Ger) 2:09.6
1972 Roland Matthes (E Ger) 2:02.82
1976 John Naber (US) 1:59.19
1980 Sandor Wladar (Hun) 2:01.93

100 Meters Butterfly
1968 Douglas Russell (US) 55.9
1972 Mark Spitz (US) 54.27
1976 Matt Vogel (US) 54.35
1980 Par Arvidsson (Swe) 54.92

200 Meters Butterfly
1956 William Yorzyk (US) 2:19.3
1960 Michael Troy (US) 2:12.8
1964 Kevin Berry (Aus) 2:06.6
1968 Carl Robie (US) 2:08.7
1972 Mark Spitz (US) 2:00.70
1976 Michael Bruner (US) 1:59.23
1980 Sergei Fesenko (USSR) 1:59.76

100 Meters Breaststroke
1968 Donald McKenzie (US) 1:07.7
1972 Nobutaka Taguchi (Jap) 1:04.94
1976 John Hencken (US) 1:03.11
1980 Duncan Goodhew (GB) 1:03.34

200 Meters Breaststroke
1948 Joseph Verdeur (US) 2:39.3
1952 John Davies (Aus) 2:34.4
1956 Masura Furukawa (Jap) 2:34.7
1960 William Mulliken (US) 2:37.4
1964 Ian O'Brien (Aus) 2:27.8
1968 Felipe Munoz (Mex) 2:28.7
1972 John Hencken (US) 2:21.55
1976 David Wilkie (GB) 2:15.11
1980 Robertas Zulpa (USSR) 2:15.85

200 Meters Individual Medley
1968 Charles Hickcox (US) 2:12.0
1972 Gunnar Larsson (Swe) 2:07.17

400 Meters Individual Medley
1964 Richard Roth (US) 4:45.4
1968 Charles Hickcox (US) 4:48.4
1972 Gunnar Larsson (Swe) 4:31:98
1976 Rod Strachan (US) 4:23.68
1980 Aleksandr Sidorenko (USSR) 4:22.89

4 × 100 Meters Freestyle Relay
1964 US 3:33.2
1968 US 3:31.7
1972 US 3:26.42

4 × 200 Meters Freestyle Relay
1948 US 8:46.0
1952 US 8:31.1
1956 Australia 8:23.6
1960 US 8:10.2
1964 US 7:52.1
1968 US 7:52.3
1972 US 7:35.78
1976 US 7:23.22
1980 USSR 7:23.50

4 × 100 Meters Medley Relay
1960 US 4:05.4
1964 US 3:58.4
1968 US 3:54.9
1972 US 3:48.16
1976 US 3:42.22
1980 Australia 3:45.70

Springboard Diving
1948 Bruce Harlan (US) 163.64
1952 David Browning (US) 205.29
1956 Robert Clotworthy (US) 159.56
1960 Gary Tobian (US) 170.00
1964 Kenneth Sitzberger (US) 159.90
1968 Bernard Wrightson (US) 170.15
1972 Vladimir Vasin (USSR) 594.09
1976 Philip Boggs (US) 619.05
1980 Aleksandr Portnov (USSR) 905.025

Platform Diving (Highboard)
1948 Samuel Lee (US) 130.05
1952 Samuel Lee (US) 156.28
1956 Joaquin Capilla (Mex) 152.44
1960 Robert Webster (US) 165.56
1964 Robert Webster (US) 148.58
1968 Klaus Dibiasi (Ita) 164.18
1972 Klaus Dibiasi (Ita) 504.12
1976 Klaus Dibiasi (Ita) 600.51
1980 Falk Hoffmann (E Ger) 835.650

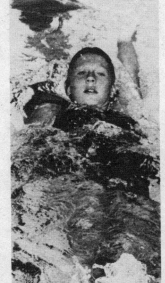

BACK IN THE RACE: American Cathy Ferguson won the gold medal for the 100 meters backstroke in the 1964 Tokyo Olympics.

WOMEN

100 Meters Freestyle
1948 Greta Andersen (Den) 1:06.3
1952 Katalin Szöke (Hun) 1:06.8
1956 Dawn Fraser (Aus) 1:02.0
1960 Dawn Fraser (Aus) 1:01.2
1964 Dawn Fraser (Aus) 59.5
1968 Jan Henne (US) 1:00.0
1972 Sandra Neilson (US) 58.59
1976 Kornelia Ender (E Ger) 55.65
1980 Barbara Krause (E Ger) 54.79

200 Meters Freestyle
1968 Debbie Meyer (US) 2:10 .5
1972 Shane Gould (Aus) 2:03.56
1976 Kornelia Ender (E Ger) 1:59.25
1980 Barbara Krause (E Ger) 1:58.33

400 Meters Freestyle
1948 Ann Curtis (US) 5:17.8
1952 Valeria Gyenge (Hun) 5:12.1
1956 Lorraine Crapp (Aus) 4:45.6
1960 Christine von Saltza (US) 4:50.6
1964 Virginia Duenkel (US) 4:43.3
1968 Debbie Meyer (US) 4:31.8
1972 Shane Gould (Aus) 4:19.04
1976 Petra Thuemer (E Ger) 4:09.89
1980 Ines Diers (E Ger) 4:08.76

800 Meters Freestyle
1968 Debbie Meyer (US) 9:24.0
1972 Keena Rothhammer (US) 8:53.68
1976 Petra Thuemer (E Ger) 8:37.14
1980 Michelle Ford (Aus) 8:28.90

100 Meters Backstroke
1948 Karen Harup (Den) 1:14.4
1952 Joan Harrison (S Af) 1:14.3
1956 Judy Grinham (GB) 1:12.9
1960 Lynn Burke (US) 1:09.3
1964 Cathy Ferguson (US) 1:07.7
1968 Kaye Hall (US) 1:06.2
1972 Melissa Belote (US) 1:05.78
1976 Ulrike Richter (E Ger) 1:01.83
1980 Rica Reinisch (E Ger) 1:00.86

200 Meters Backstroke
1968 Lillian Watson (US) 2:24.8
1972 Melissa Belote (US) 2:19.19
1976 Ulrike Richter (E Ger) 2:13.43
1980 Rica Reinisch (E Ger) 2:11.77

100 Meters Butterfly
1956 Shelley Mann (US) 1:11.0
1960 Carolyn Schuler (US) 1:09.5
1964 Sharon Stouder (US) 1:04.7
1968 Lynette McClements (US) 1:05.5
1972 Mayumi Aoki (Jap) 1:03.34
1976 Kornelia Ender (E Ger) 1:00.13
1980 Caren Metschuck (E Ger) 1:00.42

200 Meters Butterfly
1968 Ada Kok (Hol) 2:24.7
1972 Karen Moe (US) 2:15.57
1976 Andrea Pollack (E Ger) 2:11.41
1980 Ines Geissler (E Ger) 2:10.44

100 Meters Breaststroke
1968 Djurdica Bjedov (Yug) 1:15.8
1972 Catherine Carr (US) 1:13.58
1976 Hannelore Anke (E Ger) 1:11.16
1980 Ule Gewiniger (E Ger) 1:10.22

200 Meters Breaststroke
1948 Petronella van Vliet (Hol) 2:57.2
1952 Eva Székely (Hun) 2:51.7
1956 Ursula Happe (W Ger) 2:53.1
1960 Anita Lonsborough (GB) 2:49.5
1964 Galina Prozumenshchikova (USSR) 2:46.4
1968 Sharon Wichman (US) 2:44.4
1972 Beverley Whitfield (Aus) 2:41.71
1976 Marina Koshevaia (USSR) 2:33.35
1980 Lina Kachushite (USSR) 2:29.54

200 Meters Individual Medley
1968 Claudia Kolb (US) 2:24.7
1972 Shane Gould (Aus) 2:23.07

400 Meters Individual Medley
1964 Donna de Varona (US) 5:18.7
1968 Claudia Kolb (US) 5:08.5
1972 Gail Neall (Aus) 5:02.97
1976 Ulrike Tauber (E Ger) 4:42.77
1980 Petra Schneider (E Ger) 4:36.29

4 × 100 Meters Freestyle Relay
1948 US 4:29.2
1952 Hungary 4:24.4
1956 Australia 4:17.1
1960 US 4:08.9
1964 US 4:03.8
1968 US 4:02.5
1972 US 3:55.19
1976 US 3:44.82
1980 E Germany 3:42.71

4 × 100 Meters Medley Relay
1960 US 4:41.1
1964 US 4:33.9
1968 US 4:28.3
1972 US 4:20.75
1976 E Germany 4:07.95
1980 E Germany 4:06.67

Springboard Diving
1948 Victoria Draves (US) 108.74
1952 Patricia McCormick (US) 147.30
1956 Patricia McCormick (US) 142.36
1960 Ingrid Krämer (W Ger) 155.81
1964 Ingrid Engel (née Krämer) (W Ger) 145.00
1968 Sue Gossick (US) 150.77
1972 Micki King (US) 450.03
1976 Jennifer Chandler (US) 506.19
1980 Irina Kalinina (USSR) 725.910

Platform Diving (Highboard)
1948 Victoria Draves (US) 68.87
1952 Patricia McCormick (US) 79.37
1956 Patricia McCormick (US) 84.85
1960 Ingrid Krämer (W Ger) 91.28
1964 Lesley Bush (US) 99.80
1968 Milena Duchková (Cze) 109.59
1972 Ulrika Knape (Swe) 390.00
1976 Elena Vayteskhovskaya (USSR) 406.59
1980 Martina Jaschke (E Germany) 596.250

GOOD AS GOULD: Shane Gould (Australia) captured a pair of gold medals at the 1972 Olympics in Munich with victories in the 200 meters freestyle and 200 meters individual medley. Before she was 16 years old, Gould had broken every freestyle record from 100 to 1,500 meters.

DIFFERENT STROKES: American Sharon Wichman (left) overtakes Galina Prozumenshchikova (USSR) in the 1968 Olympic 200 meters breaststroke for the gold medal. The Russian swimmer had won the event in 1964. Roland Matthes (right) is one of 4 swimmers who have won 4 individual gold medals, capturing the 100 and 200 meters backstroke events in both 1968 and 1972.

World Championships

First held in Belgrade in 1973.

MEN

100 Meters Freestyle
1973   Jim Montgomery (US) 51.70
1975   Andrew Coan (US) 51.25
1978   David McCagg (US) 50.24

200 Meters Freestyle
1973   Jim Montgomery (US) 1:53.02
1975   Tim Shaw (US) 1:51.04
1978   William Forrester (US) 1:51.02

400 Meters Freestyle
1973   Rick DeMont (US) 3:58.18
1975   Tim Shaw (US) 3:54.88
1978   Vladimir Salnikov (USSR) 3:51.94

1500 Meters Freestyle
1973   Steve Holland (Aus) 15:31.85
1975   Tim Shaw (US) 15:28.92
1978   Vladimir Salnikov (USSR) 15:03.99

100 Meters Backstroke
1973   Roland Matthes (E Ger) 57.47
1975   Roland Matthes (E Ger) 58.15
1978   Robert Jackson (US) 56.36

200 Meters Backstroke
1973   Roland Matthes (E Ger) 2:01.87
1975   Zoltan Verraszto (Hun) 2:05.05
1978   Jesse Vassallo (US) 2:02.16

100 Meters Breaststroke
1973   John Hencken (US) 1:04.02
1975   David Wilkie (GB) 1:04.26
1978   Walter Kusch (E Ger) 1:03.56

200 Meters Breaststroke
1973   David Wilkie (GB) 2:19.28
1975   David Wilkie (GB) 2:18.23
1978   Nick Nevid (US) 2:18.37

100 Meters Butterfly
1973   Bruce Robertson (Can) 55.69
1975   Greg Jagenburg (US) 55.63
1978   Joseph Bottom (US) 54.30

200 Meters Butterfly
1973   Robin Backhaus (US) 2:03.32
1975   William Forrester (US) 2:01.95
1978   Michael Bruner (US) 1:59.38

200 Meters Individual Medley
1973   Gunnar Larsson (Swe) 2:08.36
1975   András Hargitay (Hun) 2:07.72
1978   Graham Smith (Can) 2:03.65

400 Meters Individual Medley
1973   András Hargitay (Hun) 4:31.11
1975   András Hargitay (Hun) 4:32.57
1978   Jesse Vassallo (US) 4:20.05

4 × 100 Meters Freestyle Relay
1973   US 3:27.18
1975   US 3:24.85
1978   US 3:19.74

4 × 200 Meters Freestyle Relay
1973   US 7:33.22
1975   West Germany 7:39.44
1978   US 7:20.82

4 × 100 Meters Medley Relay
1973   US 3:49.49
1975   US 3:49.00
1978   US 3:44.63

Springboard Diving
1973   Phil Boggs (US) 618.57
1975   Phil Boggs (US) 597.12
1978   Phil Boggs (US) 913.95

Platform Diving (Highboard)
1973   Klaus Dibiasi (Ita) 559.53
1975   Klaus Dibiasi (Ita) 547.98
1978   Greg Louganis (US) 844.11

WOMEN

100 Meters Freestyle
1973 Kornelia Ender (E Ger) 57.54
1975 Kornelia Ender (E Ger) 56.50
1978 Barbara Krause (E Ger) 55.68

200 Meters Freestyle
1973 Keena Rothhammer (US) 2:04.99
1975 Shirley Babashoff (Us) 2:02.50
1978 Cynthia Woodhead (US) 1:58.53

400 Meters Freestyle
1973 Heather Greenwood (US) 4:20.28
1975 Shirley Babashoff (US) 4:16.87
1978 Tracey Wickham (Aus) 4:06.28

800 Meters Freestyle
1973 Novella Calligaris (Ita) 8:52.97
1975 Jenny Turrall (Aus) 8:44.75
1978 Tracey Wickham (Aus) 8:24.94

100 Meters Backstroke
1973 Ulrike Richter (E Ger) 1:05.42
1975 Ulrike Richter (E Ger) 1:03.30
1978 Linda Jezek (US) 1:02.55

200 Meters Backstroke
1973 Melissa Belote (US) 2:20.52
1975 Birgit Treiber (E Ger) 2:15.46
1978 Linda Jezek (US) 2:11.93

100 Meters Breaststroke
1973 Renate Voge (E Ger) 1:13.74
1975 Hannelore Anke (E Ger) 1:12.72
1978 Julia Bogdanova (USSR) 1:10.31

200 Meters Breaststroke
1973 Renate Vogel (E Ger) 2:40.01
1975 Hannelore Anke (E Ger) 2:37.25
1978 Linda Kachushite (USSR) 2:31.42

100 Meters Butterfly
1973 Kornelia Ender (E Ger) 1:02.53
1975 Kornelia Ender (E Ger) 1:01.24
1978 Mary-Joan Pennington (US) 1:00.20

200 Meters Butterfly
1973 Rosemarie Kother (E Ger) 2:13.76
1975 Rosemarie Kother (E Ger) 2:13.82
1978 Tracy Caulkins (US) 2:09.87

200 Meters Individual Medley
1973 Angela Hubner (E Ger) 2:20.51
1975 Kathy Heddy (US) 2:19.80
1978 Tracy Caulkins (US) 2:14.07

400 Meters Individual Medley
1973 Gudrun Wegner (E Ger) 4:57.31
1975 Ulrike Tauber (E Ger) 4:52.76
1978 Tracy Caulkins (US) 4:40.83

4 × 100 Meters Freestyle Relay
1973 E. Germany 3:52.45
1975 E Germany 3:49.37
1978 US 3:43.43

4 × 100 Meters Medley Relay
1973 E. Germany 4:16.84
1975 E Germany 4:14.74
1978 US 4:08.21

Springboard Diving
1973 Christine Kohler (E Ger) 442.17
1975 Irina Kalinina (USSR) 489.81
1978 Irina Kalinina (USSR) 691.43

Platform Diving (Highboard)
1973 Ulrike Knape (Swe) 406.77
1975 Janet Ely (US) 403.89
1978 Irina Kalinina (USSR) 412.71

POOLED RESOURCES: Each member of this East German medley relay team won at least one individual world title in 1973. They are, from left to right: Renata Vogel, Ulrike Richter, Kornelia Ender and Rosemarie Kother. Richter also holds the 100 meters backstroke record and Ender is the all-time women's leader in gold and total medals in both Olympic and World Championship swimming.

CALIFORNIA SMILE: Heather Greenwood smiles after setting a 400 meters freestyle record in 1974. The young Californian had won the world title in that event a year earlier. Her world record was broken by Shirley Babashoff in 1975.

Synchronized Swimming

	Solo	Duet	Team
1973	Teresa Andersen (US) 120,460	US	US
1975	Gail Buzonas (US) 133.083	US	US
1978	Helen Vanderburg (Can) 186.249	Canada	US

N.C.A.A.

1937	Michigan	1952	Ohio State	1967	Stanford
1938	Michigan	1953	Yale	1968	Indiana
1939	Michigan	1954	Ohio State	1969	Indiana
1940	Michigan	1955	Ohio State	1970	Indiana
1941	Michigan	1956	Ohio State	1971	Indiana
1942	Yale	1957	Michigan	1972	Indiana
1943	Ohio State	1958	Michigan	1973	Indiana
1944	Yale	1959	Michigan	1974	Southern Cal
1945	Ohio State	1960	Southern Cal	1975	Southern Cal
1946	Ohio State	1961	Michigan	1976	Southern Cal
1947	Ohio State	1962	Ohio State	1977	Southern Cal
1948	Michigan	1963	Southern Cal	1978	Tennessee
1949	Ohio State	1964	Southern Cal	1979	California
1950	Ohio State	1965	Southern Cal		
1951	Yale	1966	Southern Cal		

A.I.A.W.

1970	Arizona State	1974	Arizona State	1978	Arizona State
1971	Arizona State	1975	Miami	1979	Florida
1972	West Chester State	1976	Miami		
1973	Arizona State	1977	Arizona State		

TABLE TENNIS

Earliest Reference. The earliest evidence relating to a game resembling table tennis has been found in the catalogues of London sporting goods manufacturers in the 1880's. The old Ping-Pong Association was formed there in 1902, but the game proved only a temporary craze until resuscitated in 1921.

Fastest Rallying

The record number of hits in 60 seconds is 162 by Nicky Jarvis and Desmond Douglas in London, England, on December 1, 1976. This was equaled by Douglas and Paul Day at Blackpool, England, on March 21, 1977. The most by women is 148 by Linda Howard and Melodi Ludi at Blackpool, Lancashire, England, on October 11, 1977.

With a paddle in each hand, Gary O. Fisher of Olympia, Washington, completed 5,000 consecutive volleys over the net in 44 minutes 28 seconds on June 25, 1979.

Longest Rally

In a 1936 Swaythling Cup match in Prague between Alex Ehrlich (Poland) and Paneth Farcas (Rumania), the opening rally lasted 2 hours 12 minutes.

Robert Siegel and Donald Peters of Stamford, Connecticut, staged a rally lasting 8 hours 33 minutes on July 30, 1978.

Longest Match

In the Swaythling Cup final match between Austria and Rumania in Prague, Czechoslovakia, in 1936, the play lasted for 25 or 26 hours, spread over three nights.

Marathon

The longest recorded time for a marathon singles match by two players is 132 hours 31 minutes by Danny Price and Randy Nunes in Cherry Hill, New Jersey, August 20–26, 1978.

The longest doubles marathon by 4 players is 101 hours 1 minute 11 seconds by Lance, Phil and Mark Warren and Bill Weir at Sacramento, California, on April 9–13, 1979.

Highest Speed

No conclusive measurements have been published, but in a lecture M. Sklorz (W. Germany) Stated that a smashed ball had been measured at speeds up to 105.6 m.p.h.

Youngest International

The youngest international (probably in any sport) was Joy Foster, aged 8, the 1958 Jamaican singles and mixed doubles champion.

Swaythling Cup

The Men's Team World Championship for the Swaythling Cup was first held in 1927, and from then until 1957, with the exception of the war years, it was contested annually; since then it has been held biennially.

1927–31	Hungary (5)	1949	Hungary	1965	China
1932	Czechoslovakia	1950–51	Czechoslovakia (2)	1967	Japan
1933–35	Hungary (3)	1952	Hungary	1969	Japan
1936	Austria	1953	England	1971	China
1937	US	1954–57	Japan (4)	1973	Sweden
1938	Hungary	1959	Japan	1975	China
1939	Czechoslovakia	1961	China	1977	China
1947–48	Czechoslovakia (2)	1963	China	1979	Hungary

Corbillon Cup

The Women's Team World Championship for the Marcel Corbillon Cup was first held in the 1933–34 season, and like the Swaythling Cup was contested annually until 1957 and biennially since then.

1934	Germany	1952	Japan	1965	China
1935–36	Czechoslovakia (2)	1953	Rumania	1967	Japan
1937	US	1954	Japan	1969	USSR
1938	Czechoslovakia	1955–56	Rumania (2)	1971	Japan
1939	Germany	1957	Japan	1973	South Korea
1937–48	England (2)	1959	Japan	1975	China
1949	US	1961	Japan	1977	China
1950–51	Rumania (2)	1963	Japan	1979	China

SMASHING SUCCESS: Chuang Tse-tung (China) smashes his way to the world title in Prague in 1963. He won the 1961 and 1965 titles also, for 3 straight. His smash was reputed to have been the fastest in table tennis in his time.

World Championships

First held in 1927. Singles winners have been:

MEN'S SINGLES

1927	Roland Jacobi (Hun)	1952	Hiroji Satoh (Jap)
1928	Zoltan Mechlovits (Hun)	1953	Ferenc Sido (Hun)
1929	Fred Perry (GB)	1954	Ichiro Ogimura (Jap)
1930	Viktor Barna (Hun)	1955	Toshiaki Tanaka (Jap)
1931	Miklos Szabados (Hun)	1956	Ichiro Ogimura (Jap)
1932	Viktor Barna (Hun)	1957	Toshiaki Tanaka (Jap)
1933	Viktor Barna (Hun)	1959	Jung Kuo-tuan (Chi)
1934	Viktor Barna (Hun)	1961	Chuang Tse-tung (Chi)
1935	Viktor Barna (Hun)	1963	Chuang Tse-tung (Chi)
1936	Standa Kolar (Cze)	1965	Chuang Tse-tung (Chi)
1937	Richard Bergmann (Aut)	1967	Nobuhiko Hasegawa (Jap)
1938	Bohumil Vana (Cze)	1969	Shigeo Ito (Jap)
1939	Richard Bergmann (Aut)	1971	Stellan Bengtsson (Swe)
1947	Bohumil Vana (Cze)	1973	Hsi En-ting (chi)
1948	Richard Bergmann (Eng)	1975	Istvan Jonyer (Hun)
1949	Johnny Leach (Eng)	1977	Mitsuru Kohno (Jap)
1950	Richard Bergmann (Eng)	1979	Seiji Ono (Jap)
1951	Johnny Leach (Eng)		

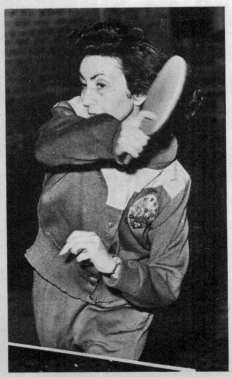

RUMANIAN RETURNS: Rumania's Angelica Rozeanu won 6 consecutive women's singles titles, 1950–55.

WOMEN'S SINGLES

1927–31	Maria Mednyanszky (Hun) (5)
1932–33	Anna Sipos (Hun) (2)
1934–35	Marie Kettnerova (Cze) (2)
1936	Ruth Aarons (US)
1937	vacant (Ruth Aarons and Trude Pritzi finalists)
1938	Trude Pritzi (Aut)
1939	Vlasha Depetrisova (Cze)
1947–49	Gizi Farkas (Hun) (3)
1950–55	Angelica Rozeanu (Rum) (6)
1956	Tomi Okawa (Jap)
1957	Fujie Eguchi (Jap)
1959	Kimiyo Matsuzaki (Jap)
1961	Chiu Chung-hui (Chi)
1963	Kimiyo Matsuzaki (Jap)
1965	Naoko Fukazu (Jap)
1967	Sachiko Morisawa (Jap)
1969	Toshiko Kowada (Jap)
1971	Lin Hui-ching (Chi)
1973	Hu Yu-lan (Chi)
1975	Pak Yung Sun (N Kor)
1977	Pak Yung Sun (N Kor)
1979	Ke Hsin-ai (Chi)

MEN'S DOUBLES

Winners since 1965:

1965	Chung Tse-tung and Hsu Yin-sheng (Chi)
1967	Hans Alser and Kjell Johansson (Swe)
1969	Hans Alser and Kjell Johansson (Swe)
1971	Istvan Jonyer and Tibor Klampar (Hun)
1973	Stellan Bengtsson and Kjell Johansson (Swe)
1975	Gabor Gergely and Istvan Jonyer (Hun)
1977	C hen-shih Li and Liang Ke-liang (Chi)
1979	Dragutin Surbek and Anton Stipancic (Yug)

Most wins have been achieved by:
8 Viktor Barna (Hun): 6 with Miklos Szabados 1929–32, 1934-35, with Sandor Glancz in 1933 and with Richard Bergmann 1939

WOMEN'S DOUBLES

Winners since 1965:

1965	Cheng Min-chih and Lin Hui-ching (Chi)
1967	Saeko Hirota and Sachiko Morisawa (Jap)
1969	Svyetlana Grinberg and Zoya Rudnova (USSR)
1971	Cheng Min-chih and Lin Hui-ching (Chi)
1973	Maria Alexandru (Rum) and Miho Hamada (Jap)
1975	Maria Alexandru (Rum) and Shoko Takashima (Jap)
1977	Yong Ok Pak (N Kor) and Ying Yang (Chi)
1979	Chang Li and Chang Te-ying (Chi)

MIXED DOUBLES

Winners since 1965:

1967	Koji Kimura and Masako Seki (Jap)
1967	Nobuhiko Hasegawa and Noriko Yamanaka (Jap)
1969	Nobuhiko Hasegawa and Yasuka Konno (Jap)
1971	Chang Shih-lin and Lin Hui-ching (Chi)
1973	Liang Ko-liang and Li Li (Chi)
1975	Stanislav Gomozkov and Anna Ferdman (USSR)
1977	Jacques Secretin and Claude Bergeret (Fra)
1979	Liang Ke-liang and Ke Hsin-ai (Chi)

Most wins have been achieved by:
7 Maria Mednyanszky (Hun): 6 with Anna Sipos 1930–35, 1 with Erika Flamm 1928

Most wins have been achieved by:
6 Maria Mednyanszky (Hun): 3 with Miklos Szabados 1930–31, 1934, 2 with Zoltan Mechlovits 1927–28, 1 with Istvan Kelen 1933
5 Ferenc Sido (Hun): 3 with Gizi Farkas 1947, 1949–50, 2 with Angelica Rozeanu 1952–53

TENNIS

Origins. The modern game of lawn tennis is generally agreed to have evolved as an outdoor form of Royal Tennis. "Field Tennis" was mentioned in an English magazine (*Sporting Magazine*) on September 29, 1793. The earliest club for such a game, variously called Pelota or Lawn Rackets, was the Leamington Club, founded in 1872 by Major Harry Gem. In February, 1874, Major Walter Clopton Wingfield of England (1833–1912) patented a form called "sphairistike," but the game soon became known as lawn tennis.

Amateurs were permitted to play with and against professionals in Open tournaments starting in 1968.

GRAND SLAMMERS: Rod Laver (left) and Don Budge (right) are the only men who have won the "grand slam" in tennis. Laver (Australia) is the only player to win it twice, as an amateur in 1962 and as a professional in 1969. Before 1969, professionals were barred from the tournaments. Budge (US) was the first player to win the grand slam, achieving it in 1938.

Greatest Crowd

The greatest crowd at a tennis match was the 30,472 who came to the Houston Astrodome in Houston, Texas, on September 20, 1973, to watch Billie Jean King beat Bobby Riggs, over 25 years her senior, in straight sets in the so-called "Tennis Match of the Century."

The record for an orthodox match is 25,578 at Sydney, Australia, on December 27, 1954, in the Davis Cup Challenge Round vs. the US (1st day).

Most Davis Cup Victories

The greatest number of wins in the Davis Cup (instituted 1900) has been (inclusive of 1979) by the United States with 26.

Individual Davis Cup Performance

Nicola Pietrangeli (Italy) played 164 rubbers, 1954 to 1972, winning 120. He played 110 singles (winning 78) and 54 doubles (winning 42). He took part in 66 ties.

Greatest Domination

The "grand slam" is to hold at the same time all four of the world's major championship titles: Wimbledon, the US Open, Australian and French championships. The first time this occurred was in 1935 when Frederick John Perry (UK) (b. 1909) won the French title, having won Wimbledon (1934), the US title (1933–34) and the Australian title (1934).

The first player to hold all four titles simultaneously was J.

Donald Budge (US) (b. 1915), who won the championships of Wimbledon (1937), the US (1937), Australia (1938), and France (1938). He subsequently retained Wimbledon (1938) and the US (1938). Rodney George Laver (Australia) (b. August 9, 1938) achieved this grand slam in 1962 as an amateur and repeated as a professional in 1969 to become the first two-time grand slammer.

Two women players also have won all these four titles in the same tennis year. The first was Maureen Catherine Connolly (US). She won the United States title in 1951, Wimbledon in 1952, retained the US title in 1952, won the Australian in 1953, the French in 1953, and Wimbledon again in 1953. She won her third US title in 1953, her second French title in 1954, and her third Wimbledon title in 1954. Miss Connolly (later Mrs. Norman Brinker) was seriously injured in a riding accident shortly before the 1954 US championships; she died in June, 1969, aged only 34.

The second woman to win the "grand slam" was Margaret Smith Court (Australia) (b. July 16, 1942) in 1970.

Olympic Medals

Lawn tennis was part of the program at the first eight celebrations of the Games (including 1906). The winner of the most medals was Max Decugis (1882–1978) of France, with six (a record four gold, one silver and one bronze) in the 1900, 1906 and 1920 tournaments.

The most medals won by a woman is five by Kitty McKane (later Mrs. L. A. Godfree) of Great Britain, with one gold, two silver and two bronze in 1920 and 1924. Five different women won a record two gold medals.

MORE GRAND SLAMMERS: The only women to win the tennis "grand slam" were Maureen Connolly (left) and Margaret Smith Court (right). Connolly (US) performed the feat in 1953, and might well have repeated had she not been injured in 1954. Court (Australia) won the grand slam in 1970.

Australian Championships

The greatest number of titles won is 22 by Margaret Court between 1960 and 1973. She also holds the record for the most women's singles titles with ten over the same period. The most men's singles titles won is six by Roy Stanley Emerson between 1961 and 1967.

United States Championships

The most US titles won is 18 (plus four "national" titles) by Margaret Court between 1961 and 1975. The record for women's singles is eight by Molla Mallory (*née* Bjurstedt) between 1915 and 1926. Three men have each won seven singles: Richard Dudley Sears, 1881–87, William A. Larned, 1901–11, and William Tatem Tilden, 1920–29.

French Championships

Margaret Court has won a record 13 titles, including a record five singles, between 1962 and 1973. The most men's singles victories is four, by Henri Cochet between 1926 and 1932, and Bjorn Borg between 1974 and 1979.

Wimbledon Records

The first Championship was in 1877. Professionals first played in 1968. From 1971 the tie-break system was introduced, which effectually prevents sets proceeding beyond a 17th game, i.e., 9–8.

AT YOUR SERVICE: Bill Tilden (left) won the US singles title 7 times in the 1920's. His serve was measured at 163.6 m.p.h. in 1931 (see page 316). Jean Borotra (right) made his 35th Wimbledon appearance in 1964. Here he is winning a semi-final match against the defending champion, Henri Cochet, in 1928.

Most Appearances. Arthur W. Gore (1968–1928) of the UK made 36 appearances between 1888 and 1927, and was in 1909, at 41 years, the oldest singles winner ever. In 1964, Jean Borotra (born August 13, 1898) of France made his 35th appearance since 1922. In 1977, he appeared in the Veterans' Doubles, aged 78.

Most Wins. Six-time singles champion Billie Jean King (*née* Moffitt) has also won ten women's doubles and four mixed doubles during the period 1961 to 1979, to total a record 20 titles.

The greatest number of singles wins was eight by Helen N. Moody (*née* Wills) (b. October 6, 1905) (US).

The greatest number of singles wins by a man since the Challenge Round (wherein the defending champion was given a bye until the final round) was abolished in 1922 is four, by Rod Laver, and consecutively by Bjorn Borg (Sweden) (b. June 6, 1956) in 1976–1979. The all-time men's record was seven by William C. Renshaw.

The greatest number of doubles wins by men was 8 by the brothers Doherty (GB)—Reginald Frank (1872–1919) and Hugh Lawrence (1875–1919). They won each year from 1897 to 1905 except for 1902. Hugh Doherty also won 5 singles titles (1902–06) and holds the record for most men's titles with 13.

THE WINNING MOMENT: Billie Jean King jubilantly tosses her racket in the air after scoring the winning point against Chris Evert in the 1975 women's singles finals at Wimbledon. The victory was her 19th at Wimbledon (6th in singles), tying her with "Bunny" Ryan for the most wins in that tournament. King's 1979 doubles victory established her as the winningest player in Wimbledon's history with 20 titles.

A PROFITABLE RACKET: Bjorn Borg (left) and Martina Navratilova (right) set yearly winnings records for men and women in 1979. Not including various exhibitions and restricted events, Borg (Sweden) won over $1 million. Navratilova, who was born in Czechoslovakia but recently became an American citizen, walked off with $747,548.

The most wins in women's doubles was 12 by Elizabeth "Bunny" Ryan (US) 1894–1979).

The greatest number of mixed doubles wins was 7 by Elizabeth Ryan (US), making a record total of 19 doubles victories from 1914 to 1934. The men's record is four wins, shared by Elias Victor Seixas (b. August 30, 1923) (US) in 1953–54–55–56, Kenneth N. Fletcher (b. June 15, 1940) (Australia) in 1963–65–66–68, and Owen Keir Davidson (Australia) (b. October 4, 1943) in 1967–71–73–74.

Youngest Champions. The youngest champion ever at Wimbledon was Charlotte Dod (1871–1960), who was 15 years 9 months old when she won in 1887.

The youngest male singles champion was Wilfred Baddeley (born January 11, 1872), who won the Wimbledon title in 1891 at the age of 19 years 175 days.

Richard Dennis Ralston (born July 27, 1942), of Bakersfield, California, was 25 days short of his 18th birthday when he won the men's doubles with Rafael H. Osuna (1938–69), of Mexico, in 1960.

The youngest-ever player at Wimbledon is reputedly Miss Mita Klima (Austria), who was 13 years old in the 1907 singles competition. The youngest of modern times is Tracy Austin (US) (b. December 12, 1962) who was only 14 years 7 months in the 1977 tournament.

Greatest Attendance. The record crowd for one day at Wimbledon is 38,295 on June 27, 1979. The total attendance record was set at the 1975 Championships with 388,591.

Professional Tennis

Highest Prize Money. The greatest reward for playing a single match is the $500,000 won by Jimmy Connors (US) (born September 2, 1952) when he beat John Newcombe (Australia) (born May 23, 1944) in a challenge match at Caesars Palace Hotel, Las Vegas, Nevada, April 26, 1975.

The record winnings for a year, according to the United States Tennis Association, is $1,019,345 by Bjorn Borg in 1979. The women's record is $747,548 by Martina Navratilova (b. Prague, Czechoslovakia, October 18, 1956), also in 1979.

Tennis Marathons

The longest recorded non-stop tennis singles match is one of 105 hours by Ricky Tolston and Jeff Sutton at Bill Faye Park, Kinston, North Carolina, on May 7–11, 1979.

The duration record for doubles is 80 hours by Paul Blackburn, Terry Mabbitt, Nigel Johnson, and Rod Wiley at Ilkley Tennis Club, Yorkshire, England, June 13–16, 1979.

Longest Game

The longest known singles game was one of 37 deuces (80 points) between Anthony Fawcett (Rhodesia) and Keith Glass (GB) in the

AMERICA'S TEAM: The victorious 1949 US Wightman Cup team, here receiving the cup from Mrs. H. Wightman, featured many of the best women tennis players of their era. From left to right, they are: Margaret Osborne duPont, Doris Hart, Beverley Baker, Mrs. Richard Buck, Mrs. Wightman, Patricia Todd, Gertrude Moran, Shirley Fry and Louise Brough. These women dominated the Wimbledon and US championships.

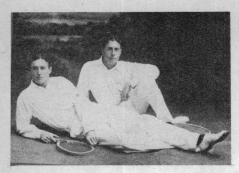

BROTHER ACT: Brothers Laurence and Reginald Doherty (GB) hold the record for most wins in men's doubles at Wimbledon with 8. The brothers also accounted for a total of 9 singles victories, with Reginald winning 4 (1897–1900) and Laurence winning 5 (1902–6).

first round of the Surrey championships at Surbiton, Surrey, England, on May 26, 1975. It lasted 31 minutes.

Fastest Service

The fastest service ever *measured* was one of 163.6 m.p.h. by William Tatem Tilden (1893–1953) (US) in 1931. The American professional Scott Carnahan, 22, was electronically clocked at 137 m.p.h. at Pauley Pavilion in Los Angeles, California, during the third annual "Cannonball Classic" sponsored by *Tennis* magazine, and reported in the fall of 1976. Some players consider the service of Robert Falkenburg (US) (born January 29, 1926), the 1948 Wimbledon champion, as the fastest ever produced.

Longest Career

The championship career of C. Alphonso Smith (born March 18, 1909) of Charlottesville, Virginia, extended from winning the US National Boys' title at Chicago on August 14, 1924, to winning the National 70-and-over title at Santa Barbara, California in August, 1979.

Davis Cup

The world's premier international team competition is contested on a best of five matches basis by men's teams. The Cup was first contested as a challenge match between the US and Great Britain in 1900.

Most Wins: US 26 (1900, 1902, 1913, 1920–26, 1937–38, 1946–49, 1954, 1958, 1963, 1968–72, 1978–79)
Australia/Australasia 24 (1907–09, 1911, 1914, 1919, 1939, 1950–53, 1955–57, 1959–62, 1964–67, 1973, 1977)
Great Britain/British Isles 9 (1903–06, 1912, 1933–36)
France 6 (1927–32)

Winners since 1974

1974	South Africa
1975	Sweden
1976	Italy
1977	Australia
1978	US
1979	US

Wightman Cup

Contested annually by women's teams from the US and Great Britain on a best of seven matches basis. First held in 1923, the

United States has won 42 times to 1979, Great Britain has won 10 times—1924, 1925, 1928, 1930, 1958, 1960, 1968, 1974, 1975, 1978.

Federation Cup

Contested by women's teams annually on a knock-out basis. First played in 1963.

1963	US	1969	US	1975	Czechoslovakia
1964	Australia	1970	Australia	1976	US
1965	Australia	1971	Australia	1977	US
1966	US	1972	South Africa	1978	US
1967	US	1973	Australia	1979	US
1968	Australia	1974	Australia		

Wimbledon Championships

The most celebrated of the world's major championships, the Wimbledon Championships were first played in 1877. Winners:

MEN'S SINGLES

1877	Spencer W. Gore (GB)
1878	Frank Hadow (GB)
1879	Rev. John Hartley (GB)
1880	Rev. John Hartley (GB)
1881	William Renshaw (GB)
1882	William Renshaw (GB)
1883	William Renshaw (GB)
1884	William Renshaw (GB)

LONGEST WIMBLEDON MATCH: Pancho Gonzales (US) played 112 games in 5 hours 12 minutes in an early round in 1969 before finally defeating Charles Pasarell: 22–24, 1–6, 16–14, 6–3, 11–9. The recently adopted "tie-breaker" system effectively eliminates such marathon matches.

1885	William Renshaw (GB)
1886	William Renshaw (GB)
1887	Herbert Lawford (GB)
1888	Ernest Renshaw (GB)
1889	William Renshaw (GB)
1890	Willoughby Hamilton (GB)
1891	Wilfred Baddeley (GB)
1892	Wilfred Baddeley (GB)
1893	Joshua Pim (GB)
1894	Joshua Pim (GB)
1895	Wilfred Baddeley (GB)
1896	Harold Mahony (GB)
1897	Reginald Doherty (GB)
1898	Reginald Doherty (GB)
1899	Reginald Doherty (GB)
1900	Reginald Doherty (GB)
1901	Arthur Gore (GB)
1902	Laurence Doherty (GB)
1903	Laurence Doherty (GB)
1904	Laurence Doherty (GB)
1905	Laurence Doherty (GB)
1906	Laurence Doherty (GB)
1907	Norman Brookes (Aus)
1908	Arthur W. Gore (GB)
1909	Arthur W. Gore (GB)
1910	Tony Wilding (NZ)
1911	Tony Wilding (NZ)
1912	Tony Wilding (NZ)
1913	Tony Wilding (NZ)
1914	Norman Brookes (Aus)
1919	Gerald Patterson (Aus)
1920	Bill Tilden (US)
1921	Bill Tilden (US)
1922	Gerald Patterson (Aus)
1923	William Johnston (US)
1924	Jean Borotra (Fra)
1925	René Lacoste (Fra)
1926	Jean Borotra (Fra)
1927	Henri Cochet (Fra)
1928	René Lacoste (Fra)
1929	Henri Cochet (Fra)
1930	Bill Tilden (US)
1931	Sidney Wood (US)
1932	Ellsworth Vines (US)
1933	Jack Crawford (Aus)
1934	Fred Perry (GB)

Wimbledon Championships (continued)

1935	Fred Perry (GB)
1936	Fred Perry (GB)
1937	Donald Budge (US)
1938	Donald Budge (US)
1939	Bobby Riggs (US)
1946	Yvon Petra (Fra)
1947	Jack Kramer (US)
1948	Bob Falkenburg (US)
1949	Ted Schroeder (US)
1950	Budge Patty (US)
1951	Dick Savitt (US)
1952	Frank Sedgman (Aus)
1953	Vic Seixas (US)
1954	Jaroslav Drobny (Cze)
1955	Tony Trabert (US)
1956	Lew Hoad (Aus)
1957	Lew Hoad (Aus)
1958	Ashley Cooper (Aus)
1959	Alex Olmedo (US)
1960	Neale Fraser (Aus)
1961	Rod Laver (Aus)
1962	Rod Laver (Aus)
1963	Chuck McKinley (US)
1964	Roy Emerson (Aus)
1965	Roy Emerson (Aus)
1966	Manuel Santana (Spa)
1967	John Newcombe (Aus)
1968	Rod Laver (Aus)
1969	Ron Laver (Aus)
1970	John Newcombe (Aus)
1971	John Newcombe (Aus)
1972	Stan Smith (US)
1973	Jan Kodes (Cze)
1974	Jimmy Connors (US)
1975	Arthur Ashe (US)
1976	Bjorn Borg (Swe)
1977	Bjorn Borg (Swe)
1978	Bjorn Borg (Swe)
1979	Bjorn Borg (Swe)

(Note: Hamilton, Pim and Mahony were Irish.)

WOMEN'S SINGLES

First played in 1884. Winners:

1884	Maud Watson (GB)
1885	Maud Watson (GB)
1886	Blanche Bingley (GB)
1887	Lottie Dod (GB)
1888	Lottie Dod (GB)
1889	Blanche Hillyard (née Bingley) (GB)
1890	Helene Rice (GB-Ire)
1891	Lottie Dod (GB)
1892	Lottie Dod (GB)
1893	Lottie Dod (GB)
1894	Blanche Hillyard (GB)
1895	Charlotte Cooper (GB)
1896	Charlotte Cooper (GB)
1897	Blanche Hillyard (GB)
1898	Charlotte Cooper (GB)
1899	Blanche Hillyard (GB)
1900	Blanche Hillyard (GB)
1901	Charlotte Sterry (née Cooper) (GB)
1902	Muriel Robb (GB)
1903	Dorothea Douglass (GB)
1904	Dorothea Douglass (GB)
1905	May Sutton (US)
1906	Dorothea Douglass (GB)
1907	May Sutton (US)
1908	Charlotte Sterry (GB)
1909	Dora Boothby (GB)
1910	Dorothea Lambert Chambers (née Douglass) (GB)
1911	Dorothea Lambert Chambers (GB)
1912	Ethel Larcombe (GB)
1913	Dorothea Lambert Chambers (GB)
1914	Dorothea Lambert Chambers (GB)
1919	Suzanne Lenglen (Fra)
1920	Suzanne Lenglen (Fra)
1921	Suzanne Lenglen (Fra)
1922	Suzanne Lenglen (Fra)
1923	Suzanne Lenglen (Fra)
1924	Kathleen McKane (GB)
1925	Suzanne Lenglen (Fra)
1926	Kathleen Godfree (née McKane) (GB)
1927	Helen Wills (US)
1928	Helen Wills (US)
1929	Helen Wills (US)
1930	Helen Wills Moody (US)
1931	Cilly Aussem (Ger)
1932	Helen Wills Moody (US)
1933	Helen Wills Moody (US)
1934	Dorothy Round (GB)
1935	Helen Wills Moody (US)
1936	Helen Jacobs (US)
1937	Dorothy Round (GB)
1938	Helen Wills Moody (US)

SEEING DOUBLE: "Bunny" Ryan is the all-time Wimbledon doubles champion with 19 wins (12 women's, 7 mixed). Her 19 victories were the overall record until Billie Jean King won the 1979 doubles title. Ryan, who had said she didn't want to live to see her record broken, died the night before King's 20th victory.

HOME COURT:
when Virginia
Wade won the
1977 Wimble-
don singles title,
she became
only the 7th
British woman
since 1914 to win
that champion-
ship.

1939	Alice Marble (US)
1946	Pauline Betz (US)
1947	Margaret Osborne (US)
1948	Louise Brough (US)
1949	Louise Brough (US)
1950	Louise Brough (US)
1951	Doris Hart (US)
1952	Maureen Connolly (US)
1953	Maureen Connolly (US)
1954	Maureen Connolly (US)
1955	Louise Brough (US)
1956	Shirley Fry (US)
1957	Althea Gibson (US)
1958	Althea Gibson (US)
1959	Maria Bueno (Bra)
1960	Maria Bueno (Bra)
1961	Angela Mortimer (GB)
1962	Karen Susman (US)
1963	Margaret Smith (Aus)
1964	Maria Bueno (Bra)
1965	Margaret Smith (Aus)
1966	Billie Jean King (US)
1967	Billie Jean King (US)
1968	Billie Jean King (US)
1969	Ann Jones (GB)
1970	Margaret Court (*née* Smith) (Aus)
1971	Evonne Goolagong (Aus)
1972	Billie Jean King (US)
1973	Billie Jean King (US)
1974	Christine Evert (US)
1975	Billie Jean King (US)
1976	Christine Evert (US)
1977	Virginia Wade (GB)
1978	Martina Navratilova (Cze)
1979	Martina Navratilova (Cze)

MEN'S DOUBLES

First held 1884.
Most wins: 8   Laurence Doherty and Reginald Doherty (GB): 1897–1901, 1903–05

Winners since 1965:

1965	John Newcombe and Tony Roche (Aus)
1966	Ken Fletcher and John Newcombe (Aus)
1967	Bob Hewitt and Frew McMillan (S Af)
1968	John Newcombe and Tony Roche (Aus)
1969	John Newcombe and Tony Roche (Aus)
1970	John Newcombe and Tony Roche (Aus)
1971	Roy Emerson and Rod Laver (Aus)
1972	Bob Hewitt and Frew McMillan (S Af)
1973	Jimmy Connors (US) and Ilie Nastase (Rum)
1974	John Newcombe and Tony Roche (Aus)
1975	Vitas Gerulaitis and Sandy Mayer (US)
1976	Brian Gottfried (US) and Raul Ramirez (Mex)
1977	Ross Case and Geoff Masters (Aus)
1978	Bob Hewitt and Frew McMillan (S Af)
1979	Peter Fleming and John McEnroe (US)

WOMEN'S DOUBLES

First held 1899, but not a championship event until 1913.

Most wins: 12 Elizabeth Ryan (US):1 with Agatha Morton 1914, 6 with Suzanne Lenglen (1919–23, 1925; 1 with Mary Browne 1926, 2 with Helen Wills Moody 1927, 1930; 2 with Simone Mathieu 1933–34

Winners since 1965:

1965	Maria Bueno (Bra) and Billie Jean Moffitt (US)
1966	Maria Bueno (Bra) and Nancy Richey (US)
1967	Rosemary Casals and Billie Jean King (*née* Moffitt) (US)
1968	Rosemary Casals and Billie Jean King (US)
1969	Margaret Court and Judy Tegart (Aus)
1970	Rosemary Casals and Billy Jean King (US)
1971	Rosemary Casals and Billie Jean King (US)
1972	Billie Jean King (US) and Betty Stove (Hol)
1973	Rosemary Casals and Billie Jean King (US)
1974	Evonne Goolagong (Aus) and Peggy Michel (US)
1975	Ann Kiyomura (US) and Kazuko Sawamatsu (Jap)
1976	Christine Evert (US) and Martina Navratilova (Cze)
1977	Helen Cawley (Aus) and Joanne Russell (US)
1978	Kerry Reid and Wendy Turnbull (Aus)
1979	Billie Jean King (US) and Martina Navratilova (Cze)

MIXED DOUBLES

First held 1900, but not a championship event until 1913.

Winners since 1965:

1965	Ken Fletcher and Margaret Smith (Aus)
1966	Ken Fletcher and Margaret Smith (Aus)
1967	Owen Davidson (Aus) and Billie Jean King (US)
1968	Ken Fletcher and Margaret Court (*née* Smith) (Aus)
1969	Fred Stolle (Aus) and Ann Jones (GB)
1970	Ilie Nastase (Rum) and Rosemary Casals (US)
1971	Owen Davidson (Aus) and Billie Jean King (US)

Most wins: 7 Elizabeth Ryan (US): 1919, 1921, 1923, 1927–28, 1930, 1932 with 5 different partners

1972	Ilie Nastase (Rum) and Rosemary Casals (US)
1973	Owen Davidson (Aus) and Billie Jean King (US)
1974	Owen Davidson (Aus) and Billie Jean King (US)
1975	Marty Reissen (US) and Margaret Court (Aus)
1976	Tony Roche (Aus) and Françoise Durr (Fra)
1977	Bob Hewitt and Greer Stevens (S Af)
1978	Frew McMillan (S Af) and Betty Stove (Hol)
1979	Bob Hewitt and Greer Stevens (US)

United States Championships

The USTA Championships were first held in 1881 and continued until 1969. The Tournament was superseded in 1970 by the US Open Championships which had first been held in 1968. Now held at Flushing Meadows, New York.

Most wins in the USTA Championships:
Men's Singles: 7 Richard D. Sears 1881–87; 7 William T. Tilden 1920–25, 1929
Women's Singles: 7 Helen Wills Moody 1923–25, 1927–29, 1931

MEN'S SINGLES

1920	Bill Tilden		1933	Fred Perry
1921	Bill Tilden		1934	Fred Perry
1922	Bill Tilden		1935	Wilmer Allison
1923	Bill Tilden		1936	Fred Perry
1924	Bill Tilden		1937	Don Budge
1925	Bill Tilden		1938	Don Budge
1926	René Lacoste		1939	Robert Riggs
1927	René Lacoste		1940	Don McNeill
1928	Henri Cochet		1941	Robert Riggs
1929	Bill Tilden		1942	F. R. Schroeder, Jr.
1930	John Doeg		1943	Joseph Hunt
1931	H. Ellsworth Vines		1944	Frank Parker
1932	H. Ellsworth Vines		1945	Frank Parker

OCEANS APART: Arthur Ashe (US) won the US championship at Forest Hills in 1968 and then the Wimbledon title 7 years later. Recovering from heart surgery, Ashe announced his retirement from competitive tennis in April, 1980.

1946 Jack Kramer	
1947 Jack Kramer	
1948 Pancho Gonzales	
1949 Pancho Gonzales	
1950 Arthur Larsen	
1951 Frank Sedgman	
1952 Frank Sedgman	
1953 Tony Trabert	
1954 E. Victor Seixas, Jr.	
1955 Tony Trabert	
1956 Ken Rosewall	
1957 Malcolm Anderson	
1958 Ashley Cooper	
1959 Neal A. Fraser	
1960 Neal A. Fraser	
1961 Roy Emerson	
1962 Rod Laver	
1963 Rafael Osuna	
1964 Ray Emerson	
1965 Manuel Santana	
1966 Fred Stolle	
1967 John Newcombe	
1968 Arthur Ashe	
1969 Rod Laver	
1970 Ken Rosewall	
1971 Stan Smith	
1972 Ilie Nastase	
1973 John Newcombe	
1974 Jimmy Connors	
1975 Manuel Orantes	
1976 Jimmy Connors	
1977 Guillermo Vilas	
1978 Jimmy Connors	
1979 John McEnroe	

MEN'S DOUBLES

1922	Bill Tilden—Vincent Richards
1923	Bill Tilden—Brian Norton
1924	Howard Kinsey—Robert Kinsey
1925	R. Norris Williams—Vincent Richards
1926	R. Norris Williams—Vincent Richards
1927	Bill Tilden—Francis Hunter
1928	George Lott—John Hennessey
1929	George Lott—John Doeg
1930	George Lott—John Doeg
1931	Wilmer Allison—John Van Ryan
1932	H. Ellsworth Vines—Keith Gledhill
1933	George Lott—Lester Stoefen
1934	George Lott—Lester Stoefen
1935	Wilmer Allison—John Van Ryn
1936	Don Budge—C. Gene Mako
1937	Baron G. von Cramm—Henner Henkel
1938	Don Budge—C. Gene Mako
1939	Adrian Quist—John Bromwich
1940	Jack Kramer—Frederick Schroeder, Jr.
1941	Jack Kramer—Frederick Schroeder, Jr.
1942	Gardnar Mulloy—William Talbert
1943	Jack Kramer—Frank Parker
1944	Don McNeill—Robert Falkenburg
1945	Gardnar Mulloy—William Talbert
1946	Gardnar Mulloy—William Talbert
1947	Jack Kramer—Frederick Schroeder, Jr.

1948	Gardnar Mulloy—William Talbert
1949	John Bromwich—William Sidwell
1950	John Bromwich—Frank Sedgman
1951	Frank Sedgman—Kenneth McGregor
1952	Mervyn Rose—E. Victor Seixas, Jr.
1953	Rex Hartwig—Mervyn Rose
1954	E. Victor Seixas, Jr.—Tony Trabert
1955	Kosel Kamo—Atsushi Miyagi
1956	Lewis Hoad—Ken Rosewall
1957	Ashley Cooper—Neale Fraser
1958	Hamilton Richardson—Alejandro Olmedo
1959	Neale A. Fraser—Roy Emerson
1960	Neale A. Fraser—Roy Emerson
1961	Dennis Ralston—Chuck McKinley
1962	Rafael Osuna—Antonio Palafox
1963	Dennis Ralston—Chuck McKinley
1964	Dennis Ralston—Chuck McKinley
1965	Roy Emerson—Fred Stolle
1966	Roy Emerson—Fred Stolle
1967	John Newcombe—Tony Roche
1968	Robert Lutz—Stan Smith
1969	Fred Stolle—Ken Rosewall
1970	Pierre Barthes—Nicki Pilic
1971	John Newcombe—Roger Taylor
1972	Cliff Drysdale—Roger Taylor
1973	John Newcombe—Owen Davidson
1974	Bob Lutz—Stan Smith
1975	Jimmy Connors—Ilie Nastase
1976	Marty Riessen—Tom Okker
1977	Bob Hewitt—Frew McMillan
1978	Stan Smith—Bob Lutz
1979	John McEnroe—Peter Fleming

MIXED DOUBLES

1946	Margaret Osborne—William Talbert
1947	A. Louise Brough—John Bromwich
1948	A. Louise Brough—Thomas Brown, Jr.
1949	A. Louise Brough—Eric Sturgess
1950	Mrs. M. O. duPont—Kenneth MacGregor
1951	Doris Hart—Frank Sedgman
1952	Doris Hart—Frank Sedgman
1953	Doris Hart—E. Victor Seixas, Jr.
1954	Doris Hart—E. Victor Seixas, Jr.
1955	Doris Hart—E. Victor Seixas, Jr.
1956	Mrs. M. O. duPont—Ken Rosewall
1957	Althea Gibson—Kurt Nielsen
1958	Mrs. M. O. duPont—Neale Fraser
1959	Mrs. M. O. duPont—Neale Fraser
1960	Mrs. M. O. duPont—Neale Fraser
1961	Margaret Smith—Robert Mark
1962	Margaret Smith—Fred Stolle
1963	Margaret Smith—Kenneth Fletcher
1964	Margaret Smith—John Newcombe
1965	Margaret Smith—Fred Stolle
1966	Donna Floyd Fales—Owen Davidson
1967	Billie Jean King—Owen Davidson
1968	Mary Ann Eisel—Peter Curtis
1969	Margaret S. Court—Marty Riessen
1970	Margaret S. Court—Marty Riessen
1971	Billie Jean King—Owen Davidson
1972	Margaret S. Court—Marty Riessen
1973	Billie Jean King—Owen Davidson
1974	Pam Teeguarden—Geoff Masters
1975	Rosemary Casals—Dick Stockton
1976	Billie Jean King—Phil Dent
1977	Betty Stove—Frew McMillan
1978	Betty Stove—Frew McMillan
1979	Greer Stevens—Bob Hewitt

WOMEN'S SINGLES

1935	Helen Jacobs
1936	Alice Marble
1937	Anita Lizana
1938	Alice Marble
1939	Alice Marble
1940	Alice Marble
1941	Mrs. Sarah P. Cooke
1942	Pauline Betz
1943	Pauline Betz
1944	Pauline Betz
1945	Sarah P. Cooke
1946	Pauline Betz
1947	A. Louise Brough
1948	Mrs. Margaret O. duPont
1949	Mrs. Margaret O. duPont
1950	Mrs. Margaret O. duPont

TOP OF HER GAME: Tracy Austin won the US Open singles title at age 16, making her the youngest singles champion ever in that tournament. In 1980, the talented 17-year-old Californian climbed to the No. 1 ranked position in women's tennis after beating Martina Navratilova in 2 successive tournaments. As of April 15, 1980, her career earnings were close to $1 million.

REPEAT PERFORMANCES: Althea Gibson (left) won the singles and mixed doubles titles in the US Championship in 1957 and repeated as the singles winner in 1958. Chris Evert Lloyd (right) won the US singles title 4 straight times, 1975–78. She has also captured 2 singles titles in both Wimbledon and the French Championships.

1951	Maureen Connolly
1952	Maureen Connolly
1953	Maureen Connolly
1954	Doris Hart
1955	Doris Hart
1956	Shirley J. Fry
1957	Althea Gibson
1958	Althea Gibson
1959	Maria Bueno
1960	Darlene Hard
1961	Darlene Hard
1962	Margaret Smith
1963	Maria Bueno
1964	Maria Bueno
1965	Margaret Smith
1966	Maria Bueno
1967	Billie Jean King
1968	Virginia Wade
1969	Margaret Smith Court
1970	Margaret Smith Court
1971	Billie Jean King
1972	Billie Jean King
1973	Margaret Smith Court
1974	Billie Jean King
1975	Chris Evert
1976	Chris Evert
1977	Chris Evert
1978	Chris Evert
1979	Tracy Austin

WOMEN'S DOUBLES

1936	Mrs. M. G. Van Ryn—Carolin Babcock
1937	Mrs. Sarah P. Fabyan—Alice Marble
1938	Alice Marble—Mrs. Sarah P. Fabyan
1939	Alice Marble—Mrs. Sarah P. Fabyan
1940	Alice Marble—Mrs. Sarah P. Fabyan
1941	Mrs. S. P. Cooke—Margaret Osborne
1942	A. Louise Brough—Margaret Osborne

1943	A. Louise Brough—Margaret Osborne
1944	A. Louise Brough—Margaret Osborne
1945	A. Louise Brough—Margaret Osborne
1946	A. Louise Brough—Margaret Osborne
1947	A. Louise Brough—Margaret Osborne
1948	A. Louise Brough—Mrs. M. O. duPont
1949	A. Louise Brough—Mrs. M. O. duPont
1950	A. Louise Brough—Mrs. M. O. duPont
1951	Doris Hart—Shirley Fry
1952	Doris Hart—Shirley Fry
1953	Doris Hart—Shirley Fry
1954	Doris Hart—Shirley Fry
1955	A. Louise Brough—Mrs. M. O. duPont
1956	A. Louise Brough—Mrs. M. O. duPont
1957	A. Louise Brough—Mrs. M. O. duPont
1958	Darlene Hard—Jeanne Arth
1959	Darlene Hard—Jeanne Arth
1960	Darlene Hard—Maria Bueno
1961	Darlene Hard—Lesley Turner
1962	Maria Bueno—Darlene Hard
1963	Margaret Smith—Robyn Ebbern
1964	Billie Jean Moffitt—Karen Susman
1965	Carole C. Graebner—Nancy Richey
1966	Maria Bueno—Nancy Richey
1967	Rosemary Casals—Billie Jean King
1968	Maria Bueno—Margaret S. Court
1969	Francoise Durr—Darlene Hard
1970	M. S. Court—Judy Tegart Dalton
1971	Rosemary Casals—Judy Tegart Dalton
1972	Françoise Durr—Betty Stove

Wimbledon Championships (continued)

1973 Margaret S. Court—Virginia Wade	1977 Betty Stove—Martina Navratilova
1974 Billie Jean King—Rosemary Casals	1978 Martina Navratilova—Billie Jean King
1975 Margaret Court—Virginia Wade	
1976 Linky Boshoff—Ilana Kloss	1979 Betty Stove—Wendy Turnbull

French Championships

First held in 1891. Held on hard courts at the Stade Roland Garros, near Paris. Singles winners since 1968:

MEN'S SINGLES	WOMEN'S SINGLES
1968 Ken Rosewall (Aus)	1968 Nancy Richey (US)
1969 Rod Laver (Aus)	1969 Margaret Court (Aus)
1970 Jan Kodes (Cze)	1970 Margaret Court (Aus)
1971 Jan Kodes (Cze)	1971 Evonne Goolagong (Aus)
1972 Andres Gimeno (Spa)	1972 Billie Jean King (US)
1973 Ilie Nastase (Rum)	1973 Margaret Court (Aus)
1974 Bjorn Borg (Swe)	1974 Christine Evert (US)
1975 Bjorn Borg (Swe)	1975 Christine Evert (US)
1976 Adriano Panatta (Ita)	1976 Susan Barker (GB)
1977 Guillermo Vilas (Arg)	1977 Mima Jausovec (Yug)
1978 Bjorn Borg (Swe)	1978 Virginia Ruzici (Rum)
1979 Bjorn Borg (Swe)	1979 Christine Evert-Lloyd (US)

Australian Championships

First held in 1905. Singles' winners since 1968 (year shown in second half of winter season):

MEN'S SINGLES	WOMEN'S SINGLES
1968 William Bowrey (Aus)	1968 Billie Jean King (US)
1969 Rod Laver (Aus)	1969 Margaret Court (Aus)
1970 Arthur Ashe (US)	1970 Margaret Court (Aus)
1971 Ken Rosewall (Aus)	1971 Margaret Court (Aus)
1972 Ken Rosewall (Aus)	1972 Virginia Wade (GB)
1973 John Newcombe (Aus)	1973 Margaret Court (Aus)
1974 Jimmy Connors (US)	1974 Evonne Goolagong (Aus)
1975 John Newcombe (Aus)	1975 Evonne Goolagong (Aus)
1976 Mark Edmondson (Aus)	1976 Evonne Cawley (née Goolagong) (Aus)
1977 Roscoe Tanner (US)	1977 Kerry Reid (Aus)
1978 Vitas Gerulaitis (US)	1978 Evonne Cawley (Aus)
1979 Guillermo Vilas (Arg)	1979 Christine O'Neill (Aus)

LOB STORY: Guillermo Vilas (Argentina) has won every major tournament except Wimbledon. He earned over $800,000 in 1977 (a record later broken by Bjorn Borg), and has won the Grand Prix 3 times.

WCT Champions

World Championship Tennis (WCT) has held a series of championships since 1971.

1971 Ken Rosewall (Aus)	1976 Bjorn Borg (Swe)
1972 Ken Rosewall (Aus)	1977 Jimmy Connors (US)
1973 Stan Smith (US)	1978 Vitas Gerulaitis (US)
1974 John Newcombe (Aus)	1979 John McEnroe (US)
1975 Arthur Ashe (US)	

Grand Prix

Winners on points gained in major tournaments since 1970:

1970 Cliff Richey (US)	1975 Guillermo Vilas (Arg)
1971 Stan Smith (US)	1976 Raul Ramirez (Mex)
1972 Ilie Nastase (Rum)	1977 Guillermo Vilas (Arg)
1973 Ilie Nastase (Rum)	1978 Jimmy Connors (US)
1974 Guillermo Vilas (Arg)	1979 John McEnroe (US)

Grand Prix Masters Tournament

Contested annually since 1970 by the top points scorers in the Grand Prix.

1970 Stan Smith (US)	1975 Ilie Nastase (Rum)
1971 Ilie Nastase (Rum)	1976 Manuel Orantes (Spa)
1972 Ilie Nastase (Rum)	1977 Jimmy Connors (US)
1973 Ilie Nastase (Rum)	1978 John McEnroe (US) (held in 1979)
1974 Guillermo Vilas (Arg)	1979 Bjorn Borg (Swe) (held in 1980)

TRACK AND FIELD

Earliest References. Track and field athletics date from the ancient Olympic Games. The earliest accurately known Olympiad dates from July, 776 B.C., at which celebration Coroibos won the foot race. The oldest surviving measurements are a long jump of 23 feet 1½ inches by Chionis of Sparta in *c.* 656 B.C. and a discus throw of 100 cubits (*c.* 152 feet) by Protesilaus.

Oldest Race

The oldest continuously held foot race is the "Red Hose Race" held at Carnwath, Scotland, since 1507. First prize is a pair of hand-knitted knee-length red stockings.

Earliest Landmarks

The first time 10 seconds ("even time") was bettered for 100 yards under championship conditions was when John Owen recorded 9⅕ seconds in the A.A.U. Championships at Analostan Island, Washington, D.C., on October 11, 1890. The first recorded instance of 6 feet being cleared on the high jump was when Marshall Jones Brooks jumped 6 feet 0⅛ inch at Marston, near Oxford, England, on March 17, 1876. The breaking of the "4 minute barrier" in the one mile was first achieved by Dr. Roger Gilbert Bannister (born Harrow, England, March 23, 1929), when

MAIN EVENTS: Czechoslovakian Dana Zátopkova (left) set a women's world javelin record when she was 35 years 255 days old. In 1970, Taiwan's Chi Cheng (right) became the first woman to run 100 yards in 10.0 seconds. In the same year, she won all 63 races she entered, setting 5 world records in the process.

he recorded 3 minutes 59.4 seconds on the Iffley Road track, Oxford, at 6:10 p.m. on May 6, 1954.

World Record Breakers

Oldest. The greatest age at which anyone has broken a standard world record is 41 years 196 days in the case of John J. Flanagan (1868–1938), who set a world record in the hammer throw on July 24, 1909. The female record is 35 years 255 days for Dana Zátopkova (*née* Ingrova) (born September 19, 1922) of Czechoslovakia, who broke the women's javelin record with 182 feet 10 inches at Prague, Czechoslovakia, on June 1, 1958.

Youngest. Ulrike Meyfarth (b. May 4, 1956) (W. Germany) equaled the world record for the women's high jump at 6 feet 3½ inches winning the gold medal at the Munich Olympics, 1972, when she was aged 16 years 123 days. Barbara Jones (see Oldest and Youngest Olympic Champions, page 332) was aged 15 years 123 days when she was part of a record-setting team.

Most Records in a Day

The only athlete to have his name entered in the record book 6 times in one day was J. C. "Jesse" Owens (US) (1913–1980) who at Ann Arbor, Michigan, on May 25, 1935, equaled the 100-yard running record with 9.4 secs. at 3:15 p.m.; long-jumped 26 feet 8¼ inches at 3:25 p.m.; ran 220 yards (straight away) in 20.3 secs. at 3:45 p.m.; and 220 yards over low hurdles in 22.6 secs. at 4 p.m. The two 220-yard runs were also ratified as 200-meter world records.

FOR THE RECORD: Ulrike Meyfarth (left) was only 16 years 123 days old when she equaled the women's high jump record to capture a gold medal at the 1972 Olympics. Jesse Owens (right), famous for winning 4 gold medals at the 1936 Berlin Olympics, collected 6 world records in only 45 minutes in Michigan in 1935.

Fastest Runners

Robert Lee Hayes (born December 20, 1942), of Jacksonville, Florida, may have reached a speed of over 27 m.p.h. at St. Louis, on June 21, 1963, in his world record 9.1 sec. 100 yards. Marlies Göhr (*née* Oelsner) (b. East Germany, March 21, 1958) reached a speed of over 24 m.p.h. in her world record 100 meters in 10.88 seconds at Dresden, East Germany, on July 1, 1977.

Running Backwards

The fastest time recorded for running 100 yards backwards is 13.1 seconds by Paul Wilson (New Zealand) in Tokyo, September 22, 1979.

Three-Legged Race

The fastest recorded time for 100-yard three-legged race is 11.0 seconds by Harry L. Hillman and Lawson Robertson in Brooklyn, New York City, on April 24, 1909.

Ambidextrous Shot Put

Allan Feuerbach (US) has put a 16-lb. shot a total of 121 feet 6¾ inches (51 feet 5 inches with his left hand and 70 feet 1¾ inches with his right) at Malmö, Sweden, on August 24, 1974.

Standing Long Jump

Joe Darby (1862–1937), the famous Victorian professional jumper from Dudley, Worcestershire, England, jumped a measured 12 feet 1½ inches *without* weights at Dudley Castle, on May 28, 1890. Johan Christian Evandt (Norway) achieved 11 feet 11¾ inches as an amateur in Reykjavik, Iceland, on March 11, 1962.

GET ON UP: American Franklin Jacobs (left) has high jumped 23¼ inches above his own height. The 5-foot-8-inch athlete cleared 7 feet 7¼ inches in January, 1978. Russian Vladimir Yaschenko (right) made the highest jump officially recorded when he cleared 7 feet 8½ inches indoors in Milan in 1978.

Standing High Jump

The best amateur standing high jump is 5 feet 10¾ inches by Rune Almen (Sweden) at Örebro, Sweden, on December 8, 1974. Joe Darby (see above), the professional, reportedly cleared 6 feet with his ankles tied at Church Cricket Ground, Dudley, England, on June 11, 1892.

Highest Jumper

There are several reported instances of high jumpers exceeding the official world record height of 7 feet 8 inches. The earliest of these came from unsubstantiated reports of Watusi tribesmen in Central Africa clearing up to 8 feet 2½ inches, definitely, however, from inclined take-offs. The greatest height cleared above an athlete's own head is 23¼ inches by Franklin Jacobs (US), who cleared 7 feet 7¼ inches despite a physical height of only 5 feet 8 inches at New York on January 28, 1978.

The greatest height cleared by a woman above her own head is 10¼ inches by Tamami Yagi (Japan) (b. November 15, 1958), who stands 5 feet 4½ inches tall and jumped 6 feet 2¾ inches at Matsumoto, Japan, on October 19, 1978.

Longest Career

Duncan McLean (born Gourock, Scotland, December 3, 1884) won the South African 100-yard title in February, 1904, in 9.9 seconds, and at age 91 set a world age-group record for 100 meters in 21.7 seconds in August, 1977—more than 72 years later.

Dimitrion Yordanidis completed a marathon race in 7 hours 33 minutes at the age of 98 in Athens, Greece, on October 10, 1976.

Blind 100 Meters

The fastest time recorded for 100 meters by a blind man is 11.4 seconds by Graham Henry Salmon (b. September 5, 1952) of Loughton, Essex, England, at Grangemouth, Scotland, on September 2, 1978.

One-Legged High Jump

Arnie Boldt (b. 1958), of Saskatchewan, Canada, cleared a height of 6 feet 6¾ inches indoors in 1977, in spite of the fact that he has only one leg.

Longest Race

The longest race ever staged was the 1929 Transcontinental Race (3,665 miles) from New York City to Los Angeles. The Finnish-born Johnny Salo (1893–1931) was the winner in 79 days, from March 31 to June 18. His elapsed time of 525 hours 57 minutes 20 seconds gave a running average of 6.97 m.p.h. His margin of victory was only 2 minutes 47 seconds.

Endurance

Mensen Ernst (1799–1846), of Norway, is reputed to have run from Istanbul, Turkey, to Calcutta, in West Bengal, India, and back in 59 days in 1836, so averaging an improbable 92.4 miles per day. The greatest non-stop run recorded is 186 miles in 31 hours 33 minutes 38 seconds by Max Telford (b. Hawick, Scotland, on February 2, 1935) of New Zealand at Wailuku, Hawaii, on March 19–20, 1977. No rest breaks were taken. Telford ran 5,110 miles from Anchorage, Alaska, to Halifax, Nova Scotia, in 106 days 18 hours, 45 minutes from July 25 to November 9, 1977.

The 24-hour running record (on a standard track) is 161 miles 545 yards by Ron Bentley, 43, at Walton-on-Thames, Surrey, England, November 3–4, 1973.

The fastest recorded time for 100 miles is 11 hours 30 minutes 51 seconds by Donald Ritchie (b. July 6, 1944) at Crystal Palace, London, on October 15, 1977. The best by a woman is 16 hours 50 minutes 47 seconds by Ruth Anderson (b. 1929) at Woodside, California, on June 15–16, 1978.

THE NEXT STEP: Earle Dilks recorded the greatest lifetime mileage of any runner with 195,855 miles through 1977.

FRONT FOUR: Fanny Blankers-Koen (left) and Betty Cuthbert (far right) share the women's record for most Olympic gold medals with 4 apiece. Blankers-Koen was 30 years old with 2 children when she captured her 4 golds, all in the 1948 Games. Cuthbert won 3 golds in 1956 and picked up her fourth 8 years later.

The greatest distance covered by a man in six days (*i.e.* the 144 permissible hours between Sundays in Victorian times) was 622¾ miles by George Littlewood (England), who required only 141 hours 57½ minutes for this feat on December 3–8, 1888, at the old Madison Square Garden, New York City.

The fastest time for the cross-American run is 53 days, 7 minutes for 3,046 miles by Tom McGrath (N. Ireland) from August 29 to October 21, 1977.

The greatest racing mileage is the 5,926 miles in 192 races of marathon distance or more by Ted Corbitt (US) (b. January 31, 1920) from April, 1951, to the end of 1978.

Jay F. Helgerson (b. February 3, 1955) of Foster City, California, ran a certified marathon (26 miles 385 yards) or longer, each week for 52 weeks from January 28, 1979 through January 19, 1980, totalling 1,418 racing miles. He claims the secret of his success is that he doesn't do much mileage during the rest of the week.

The greatest lifetime mileage recorded by any runner is 195,855 miles by Earle Littlewood Dilks (b. 1884) of New Castle, Pennsylvania, through 1977.

Most Olympic Gold Medals

The most Olympic gold medals won is 10 (an absolute Olympic record) by Ray C. Ewry (US) (b. October 14, 1873, d. September 29, 1837) with:

Standing High Jump	1900, 1904, 1906, 1908
Standing Long Jump	1900, 1904, 1906, 1908
Standing Triple Jump	1900, 1904

The most gold medals won by a woman is 4, a record shared by Francina E. Blankers-Koen (Netherlands) (b. April 26, 1918) with 100 m. 200 m., 80 m. hurdles and 4 × 100 m. relay (1948) and

Betty Cuthbert (Australia) (b. April 20, 1938) with 100 m., 200 m., 4 × 100 m. relay (1956) and 400 m. (1964).

Most Olympic Medals

The most medals won is 12 (9 gold and 3 silver) by Paavo Johannes Nurmi (Finland) (1897–1973) with:

1920   Gold: 10,000 m.; Cross-Country, Individual and Team; silver: 5,000 m.
1924   Gold: 1,500 m.; 5,000 m.; 3,000 m. Team; Cross-Country, Individual and Team.
1928   Gold: 10,000 m.; silver: 5,000 m.; 3,000 m. steeplechase.

The most medals won by a woman athlete is 7 by Shirley de la Hunty (*née* Strickland) (Australia) (b. July 18, 1925) with 3 gold, 1 silver and 3 bronze in the 1948, 1952 and 1956 Games. A recently discovered photo-finish indicates that she finished third, not fourth, in the 1948 200 m. event, this unofficially increasing her total to 8. Irena Szewinska (*née* Kirszenstein) of Poland has also won 7 medals (3 gold, 2 silver, 2 bronze) in 1964, 1968, 1972 and 1976. She is the only woman ever to win Olympic medals in track and field in four successive Games.

Most Wins at One Games

The most gold medals at one celebration is 5 by Nurmi in 1924 (see above) and the most individual is 4 by Alvin C. Kraenzlein (US) (1876–1928) in 1900 with 60 m., 110 m. hurdles, 200 m. hurdles and long jump.

Oldest and Youngest Olympic Champions

The oldest athlete to win an Olympic title was Irish-born Patrick J. "Babe" MacDonald (US) (1878–1954) who was aged 42

REVEALING PHOTO: This photo-finish from the 1948 Olympics 200 meters race indicates that Shirley Strickland (top left) came in third, not fourth as originally recorded, thus unofficially increasing her medal total to 8.

years 26 days when he won the 56-lb. weight throw at Antwerp, Belgium, on August 21, 1920. The oldest female champion was Lia Manoliu (Rumania) (b. April 25, 1932) aged 36 years 176 days when she won the discus at Mexico City on October 18, 1968.

The youngest gold medalist was Barbara Jones (US) (b. March 26, 1937) who was a member of the winning 4 × 100 meter relay team, aged 15 years 123 days, at Helsinki, Finland, on July 27, 1952. The youngest male champion was Robert Bruce Mathias (US) (b. November 17, 1930) aged 17 years 263 days when he won the decathlon at London on August 5–6, 1948.

Mass Relay Record

The record for 100 miles by 100 runners belonging to one club is 7 hours 56 minutes 55.6 seconds by Shore A.C. of New Jersey, on June 5, 1977.

The women's mark is 10 hours 47 minutes 9.3 seconds by a team from the San Francisco Dolphins Southend Running Club, on April 3, 1977.

The best time for a 100 × 400 meter relay is 1 hour 29 minutes 11.8 seconds (average 53.5 seconds) by the Physical Training Institute, Leuven, Belgium, on April 19, 1978.

Twelve runners from the Rochester Institute of Technology, New York, ran 2,846.5 miles in relay from Will Rogers State Beach Park, Santa Monica, California to Chesapeake Bay, at Annapolis, Maryland, in 14 days 4 hours 8 minutes from November 22 to December 6, 1979.

The longest relay ever run, and the one with the most participants, was by 1,607 students and teachers who covered 6,014.65 miles at Trondheim, Norway, from October 21 to November 23, 1977.

GAME COMPETITORS: Bob Mathias (left) became the youngest male gold medalist ever when he won the 1948 Olympic decathlon aged 17 years 283 days. Paavo Nurmi (right), known as the "Flying Finn," won a record 12 Olympic medals (9 gold, 3 silver) in 3 Games. He was barred from Olympic competition after 1928 for supposedly violating his amateur standing, a controversial decision that prevented him from possibly becoming the greatest all-time Olympic athlete.

DASHING FELLOW: Jim Hines (right) won the 1968 Olympic 100 meters dash in the world record time of 9.95 seconds, a record that has stood for over 10 years. The lower air resistance at Mexico City's high altitude may have helped the sprinters.

Pancake Race Record

The annual Housewives Pancake Race at Olney, Buckingham-shire, England, was first mentioned in 1445. The record for the winding 415-yard course (three tosses mandatory) is 61.0 seconds, set by Sally Ann Faulkner, 16, on February 26, 1974. The record for the counterpart race at Liberal, Kansas, is 58.5 seconds by Sheila Turner in the 1975 competition.

World Records (Outdoor)

The complete list of World Records for the 32 scheduled men's events (excluding the walking records, see under Walking) passed by the International Amateur Athletic Federation as of August, 1980. Those marked with an asterisk* are awaiting ratification. Note: On July 27, 1976, I.A.A.F. eliminated all records for races measured in yards, except for the mile (for sentimental reasons). All distances up to (and including) 400 meters must be electrically timed to be records. When a time is given to one-hundredth of a second, it represents the official electrically timed record. In one case, a professional performance has bettered or equaled the I.A.A.F. mark, but the same highly rigorous rules as to timing, measuring and weighing are not necessarily applied.

MEN

RUNNING

Event	min. sec.	Name and Nationality	Place	Date
100 m	9.95	James Ray Hines (US)	Mexico City	Oct 14, 1968
200 m (turn)	19.72	Pietro Mennea (Italy)	Mexico City	Sept 12, 1979
400 m	43.86	Lee Edward Evans (US)	Mexico City	Oct 18, 1968
800 m	1:42.4*	Sebastian Newbold Coe (GB)	Oslo	July 5, 1979
1,000 m	2:13.4*	Sebastian Newbold Coe (GB)	Oslo	July 1, 1980
1,500 m	3:32.1	Steven Michael James Ovett (GB)	Oslo	July 15, 1980
	3:32.1	Sebastian Newbold Coe (GB)	Zurich	Aug 15, 1979
1 mile	3:48.8*	Steven Michael James Ovett (GB)	Oslo	July 1, 1980
2,000 m	4:51.4	John Walker (NZ)	Oslo	June 30, 1976
3,000 m	7:32.1	Henry Rono (Kenya)	Oslo	June 27, 1978
5,000 m	13:08.4	Henry Rono (Kenya)	Berkeley, Calif	Apr 8, 1978
10,000 m	27:22.4	Henry Rono (Kenya)	Vienna	June 11, 1978
20,000 m	57:24.2	Jos Hermens (Netherlands)	Papendal, Netherlands	May 1, 1976
25,000 m	1 hr. 14:11.8	William Rodgers (US)	Saratoga, Calif	Feb 21, 1979
30,000 m	1 hr. 31:30.4	James Noel Carroll Alder (UK)	Crystal Palace, London	Sept 5, 1970
1 hour	13 miles 24⅔ yd	Jos Hermens (Netherlands)	Papendal, Netherlands	May 1, 1976

HURDLING

Event	min. sec.	Name and Nationality	Place	Date
100 m (3'6")	13.00	Renaldo Nehemiah (US)	Westwood, Ca.	May 6, 1979
400 m (3'0")	47.13	Edwin Corley Moses (US)	Milan	July 3, 1980
3,000 m Steeplechase	8:05.4	Henry Rono (Kenya)	Seattle	May 13, 1978

FIELD EVENTS

Event		ft	in	Name and Nationality	Place	Date
High Jump		7	8¾	Gerd Wessig (E Germany)	Moscow	Aug. 1, 1980
Pole Vault		18	11½*	Wladyslaw Kozakiewicz (Poland)	Moscow	July 30, 1980
Long Jump		29	2½	Robert Beamon (US)	Mexico City	Oct. 18, 1968
Triple Jump		58	8½	Joao de Oliveira (Brazil)	Mexico City	Oct. 15, 1975
Shot Put		72	8	Udo Beyer (E Germany)	Gothenburg, Sweden	July 6, 1978
Discus Throw		233	5	Wolfgang Schmidt (E Germany)	E. Berlin	Aug. 9, 1978
Hammer Throw		268	4½*	Yuri Sedykh (USSR)	Moscow	July 31, 1980
Javelin Throw		317	3	Ferenc Paragi (Hungary)	Tata, Hungary	Apr. 23, 1980

Note: One professional performance which was equal or superior to the IAAF marks, but where the same highly rigorous rules as to timing, measuring and weighing were not necessarily applied, was the Shot Put of 75 ft by Brian Ray Oldfield (US), at El Paso, Tex, on May 10, 1975.

RELAYS

Event	min. sec.	Team	Place	Date
4 × 100 m	38.03	United States Team (William Collins, Steven Earl Riddick, Clifford Wiley, Steven Williams)	Düsseldorf, W. Ger.	Sept. 3, 1977
4 × 200 m	1:20.3†	University of Southern California (US) (Joel Andrews, James Sanford, William Mullins, Clancy Edwards)	Tempe, Arizona	May 27, 1978
4 × 400 m	2:56.1	United States Olympic Team (Vincent Matthews, Ronald Freeman, G. Lawrence James, Lee Edward Evans)	Mexico City	Oct. 20, 1968
4 × 800 m	7:08.1	USSR Team (Vladimir Podoliakov, Nikolai Kirov, Vladimir Malosemlin, Anatoli Reschetniak)	Podolsk, USSR	Aug. 12, 1978
4 × 1,500 m	14:38.8	West German Team (Thomas Wessinghage, Harald Hudak, Michael Lederer, Karl Fleschen)	Cologne, W. Ger.	Aug. 17, 1977

†The time of 1:20.2 achieved by the Tobias Striders at Tempe, Arizona on May 27, 1978 was not ratified as the team was composed of varied nationalities.

DECATHLON

8,649 points*	Guido Kratschmer (W Germany)	Burghausen, W Germany	June 13–14, 1980

(First day: 100 m 10.58 sec, long jump 25 ft 7¼ in, shot put 50 ft 9¼ in, high jump 6 ft 6¾ in, 400 m 48.04 sec; second day: 110 m hurdles 13.92 sec, discus 149 ft 4 in, pole vault 15 ft 1 in, javelin 218 ft 0½ in, 1,500 m 4 min 24.15 sec.)

THE MARATHON

There is no official marathon record because of the varying severity of courses. The best time over 26 miles 385 yards (standardized in 1924) is 2 hours 08 minutes 33.6 seconds (av. 12.28 m.p.h.) by Derek Clayton (b. 1942 at Barrow-in-Furness, England) of Australia, at Antwerp, Belgium, on May 30, 1969.

The fastest time by a female is 2 hours 27 minutes 33 seconds (av. 10.31 m.p.h.) by Grete Waitz (Norway) (b. October 1, 1953) in New York City on October 21, 1979.

GOOD TIMES: Lee Evans (left) ran 400 meters in 43.86 seconds for a world record and a gold medal at the 1968 Olympics in Mexico City. Kenya's Henry Rono (right), a college student in the US, holds 4 world records. The long-distance ace has the top times for the 3,000, 5,000, and 10,000 meters runs, as well as the 3,000 meters steeplechase.

HUSTLING HURDLER: Ed Moses (US) broke Olympic and world records on his way to winning the gold medal at the 1968 Olympics in the 400 meters hurdles. In 1977 he broke his own record with a time of 47.45 seconds.

LAP HAPPY: This US Team set the world record for the 4 × 100 meters relay. From left to right, they are: Bill Collins, Cliff Wiley, Steve Williams and Steve Riddick.

JUMP FOR JOY: Bob Beamon stunned the sports world when he shattered the long-jump record by 2 feet in the 1968 Olympics in Mexico City for the gold medal. Beamon's distance of 29 feet 2½ inches will probably remain the world record for many years.

World Record (Outdoors) (continued)

WOMEN

RUNNING

Event	min. sec.	Name and Nationality	Place	Date
100 m	10.88	Marlies Oelsner (now Göhr) (E Germany)	Dresden	July 1, 1977
200 m (turn)	21.71	Marita Koch (E Germany)	Karl Marx, Stadt, E Germany	June 10, 1979
400 m	48.94	Marita Koch (E Germany)	Prague	Aug 31, 1978
800 m	1:53.5*	Nadyezda Olizarenko (née Mushta) (USSR)	Moscow	July 27, 1980
1,500 m	3:55.0*	Tatyana Kazankina (USSR)	Moscow	July 6, 1980
1 mile	4:21.71††	Mary Decker (US)	Auckland, NZ	Jan 26, 1980
3,000 m	8:27.2	Ludmila Bragina (USSR)	College Park, Md	Aug 7, 1976

HURDLES

Event	min. sec.	Name and Nationality	Place	Date
100 m (2'9")	12.36*	Grazyna Rabsztyn (Poland)	Warsaw	June 13, 1980
400 m (2'6")	54.28*	Karin Rossley (E Germany)	Jena, E Germany	May 17, 1980

FIELD EVENTS

Event	ft	in	Name and Nationality	Place	Date
High Jump	6	7	Sara Simeoni (Italy)	Brescia, Italy	Aug 4, 1978
Long Jump	23	3¼	Vilma Bardauskiene (USSR)	Prague	Aug 29, 1978
Shot Put	73	8†	Ilona Slupianek (née Schoknecht) (E Germany)	Potsdam	May 11, 1980
Discus Throw	235	7*	Marica Vergoni (Bulgaria)	Sofia	July 13, 1980
Javelin Throw	229	11*	Tatyana Biryulina (USSR)	Minsk, USSR	July 12, 1980

PENTATHLON

	Name and Nationality	Place	Date
5,083 points*	Nadyezhda Tkachenko (USSR)	Moscow	July 24, 1980

(100 m hurdles 13.29 sec, shot put 55 ft 3 in, high jump 6 ft 0¼ in, long jump 22 ft 1 in, 800 m 2 min 5.20 sec.)

† Helena Fibingerova (Czech) set an indoor record of 73 ft 10 in at Jablonec, Czechoslovakia, on Feb 19, 1977.
†† Decker ran an indoor mile in 4:17.6 in Houston, Feb. 16, 1980. No official record was set at the track was "oversize."

RELAYS

Event	min sec	Team	Place	Date
4 × 100 m	41.60*	E Germany (Romy Müller, Barbara Wöckel, Marlies Göhr, Ingrid Auerswold)	Moscow	Aug 1, 1980
4 × 200 m	1:28.2	E Germany (Marlies Göhr, Romy Müller, Barbara Wöckel, Marita Koch)	Jena, E Germany	Aug 10, 1980
4 × 400 m	3:19.2	E German National Team (Doris Maletzki, Brigitte Rohde, Ellen Streidt, Christina Brehmer)	Montreal	July 31, 1976
4 × 800 m	7:52.3	USSR National Team (Tatyana Providokhina, Valentina Gerasimova, Svetlana Styrkina, Tatyana Kazankina)	Podolsk, USSR	Aug 16, 1976

PASSING LANCE: Ruth Fuchs (East Germany) set a women's javelin record with a throw of 228 feet 1 inch in Dresden in 1979. Fuchs won the Olympic gold medal for throwing the javelin in both 1972 and 1976.

ON THE RUN: In 1976, Russia's Tatyana Kazankina (left, in the lead) set world records and won gold medals for both the 800 and 1,500 meters runs. East German Marita Koch (far right) holds the world record for the 200 and 400 meters dashes, as well as the indoor records at 100 and 400 meters. Here she is leading Polish runner Irena Szewinska, who has won 7 Olympic medals.

BAR BELLE: Italy's Sara Simeoni, winner of the Olympic silver medal in 1976, set the women's high jump record in August, 1978, when she cleared 6 feet 7 inches.

World Indoor Records

(Amateurs only) (as of January, 1980. Does not include records made on tracks in excess of 220 yards circumference.)

MEN

Event	min. sec.	Name and Nationality	Place	Date
50 yards	5.25	Houston Mc Tear (US)	Toronto	Feb. 10, 1978
50 meters	5.61	Manfret Kokot (E Ger)	Berlin	Jan. 31, 1973
60 yards	6.05	Houston McTear (US)	New York	Feb. 24, 1978
60 meters	6.38	Houston McTear (US)	Long Beach, Ca.	Jan. 5, 1980
100 yards	9.56	Manfret Kokot (E Ger)	East Berlin	Feb. 23, 1974
100 meters	10.16	Eugen Ray (E Ger)	East Berlin	Jan. 25, 1976
200 meters	21.05	Mauro Zuliani (Italy)	Genoa, Italy	Feb. 10, 1980
300 yards	29.47	William Snoddy (US)	Lincoln, Neb.	Feb. 25, 1978
300 meters	32.83	Pietro Mennea (Italy)	Milan, Italy	March 4, 1978
400 meters	46.21	Karel Kolar (Czech)	Vienna	Feb. 25, 1979
500 yards	54.4	Lee Evans (US)	College Park, Md.	Jan. 8, 1971
500 meters	1:01.2	Herman Frazier (US)	Long Beach, Ca.	Jan. 6, 1979
600 yards	1:07.6	Martin McGrady (US)	New York	Feb. 27, 1970
600 meters	1:17.3	Milovan Savic (Yugoslavia)	Nova Gorica, Yugo.	Jan. 25, 1976
800 meters	1:46.4	Carlo Grippo (Italy)	Milan, Italy	Feb. 24, 1977
880 yards	1:47.9	Ralph Doubell (Australia)	Albuquerque, N.M.	Jan. 25, 1969
1,000 yards	2:05.1	Mike Boit (Kenya)	San Diego, Ca.	Feb. 23, 1980
1,000 meters	2:19.1	Mark Winzenried (US)	Louisville, Ky.	Feb. 27, 1972
1,500 meters	3:37.4	Paul-Heinz Wellman (W Ger)	Dortmund, W. Ger.	Jan. 16, 1976
1 mile	3:52.6	John Walker (NZ)	Long Beach, Ca.	Jan. 6, 1979
2,000 meters	5:00.0	Eamonn Coghlan (Ireland)	San Diego, Ca.	Feb. 16, 1979
3,000 meters	7:39.2	Emiel Puttemans (Belgium)	Berlin	Feb. 18, 1973
2 miles	8:13.2	Emiel Puttemans (Belgium)	Berlin	Feb. 18, 1973
5,000 meters	13:20.8	Emiel Puttemans (Belgium)	Berlin	Feb. 10, 1976
50 yards hurdles	6:04	Renaldo Nehemiah (US)	Toronto	Feb. 2, 1979
50 meters hurdles	6.36	Renaldo Nehemiah (US)	Edmonton, Canada	Feb. 3, 1979
60 yards hurdles	6.89	Renaldo Nehemiah (US)	New York	Jan. 20, 1979
60 meters hurdles	7.54	Andre Prokofiev (USSR)	Vilnius, USSR	Feb. 3, 1979
60 meters hurdles		Yuri Tchernvanev (USSR)	Sindelfingen, W. Ger.	March 2, 1980

World Indoor Records (continued)

Event	meters	ft.	in.	Name and Nationality	Place	Date
High Jump	2.35	7	8½	Vladimir Yashchenko (USSR)	Milan, Italy	March 12, 1978
Long Jump	8.30	27	5¾	Larry Myricks (US)	Johnson City, Tn.	Jan. 12, 1980
Triple Jump	17.29	56	8¾	Gennadi Valyukevich (USSR)	Minsk, USSR	Feb. 12, 1979
Pole Vault	5.64	18	6	Konstantin Volkov (USSR)	Moscow	Feb. 9, 1980
Shot	22.02	72	2¾	George Woods (US)	Inglewood, Ca.	Feb. 8, 1974
35 lb. Weight	23.46	76	11¾	Yuri Syedikh (USSR)	Montreal	March 10, 1979

WOMEN

Event	min. sec.	Name and Nationality	Place	Date
50 yards	5.63	Sonia Lannaman (GB)	Montreal	March 5, 1976
50 meters	6.11	Marita Koch (E Ger)	Grenoble, France	Feb. 2, 1980
60 yards	6.63	Ludmila Storoshkova (USSR)	Ft. Worth, Tx.	March 3, 1979
60 meters	7.04	Evelyn Ashford (US)	Long Beach, Ca.	Jan. 5, 1980
100 yards	10.29	Marlies Gohr (E Ger)	Sentenberg, E. Ger.	Jan. 27, 1980
100 meters	11.15	Marita Koch (E Ger)	East Berlin	Jan. 12, 1980
200 meters	23.15	Angela Taylor (Jam)	Toronto	Feb. 23, 1980
300 yards	33.64	Marlene Otey (Jam)	Lincoln, Neb.	Feb. 2, 1980
300 meters	37.0	Angela Taylor (Can)	York, Canada	Jan. 26, 1980
400 meters	51.14	Marita Koch (E Ger)	San Sebastian, Spain	March 13, 1977
500 yards	1:03.3	Rosalyn Bryant (US)	San Diego, Ca.	Feb. 18, 1977
500 meters	1:10.5	Lorna Forde (Barbados)	Hanover, N.H.	Feb. 15, 1978
600 yards	1:18.4	Yvonne Saunders (Can)	Toronto	Feb. 15, 1974
600 meters	1:26.2	Anita Weiss (E Ger)	East Berlin	Jan. 12, 1980
800 meters	1:58.9	Mary Decker (US)	San Diego, Ca.	Feb. 22, 1980
880 yards	1:59.7	Mary Decker (US)	San Diego, Ca.	Feb. 22, 1974
1,000 yards	2:23.8	Mary Decker (US)	Inglewood, Ca.	Feb. 3, 1978
1,000 meters	2:34.8	Brigitte Kraus (W Ger)	Dortmund, W. Ger	Feb. 19, 1978
1,500 meters	4:00.8	Mary Decker (US)	New York	Feb. 8, 1980
1 mile	4:28.5	Francie Larrieu (US)	Richmond, Va.	March 3, 1975
3,000 meters	8:51.0	Grete Waitz (Norway)	San Francisco	Jan. 5, 1980
2 miles	9:31.7	Jan Merrill (US)	New London, Ct.	Jan. 27, 1979
50 yards hurdles	6.20	Johanna Klier (E Ger)	Toronto	Feb. 10, 1978

Event	meters	ft.	in.	Record Holder	Location	Date
50 meters hurdles	6.74			Annelie Ehrhardt (E Ger)	East Berlin	Feb. 4, 1973
60 yards	7.47			Stephanie Hightower (US)	New York	Feb. 8, 1980
60 meters hurdles	7.77			Zofia Bielczyk (Pol)	Sindelfingen, W. Ger.	March 1, 1980
100 meters hurdles	13.12			Annelie Ehrhardt (E Ger)	East Berlin	Jan. 14, 1976
High Jump	1.98	6	6	Andrea Matay (Hungary)	Budapest	Feb. 17, 1979
Long Jump	6.76	22	2 1/4	Angela Voigt (E Ger)	East Berlin	Jan. 24, 1976
Shot	22.50	73	9 3/4	Helena Fibingerova (Czech)	Jablonec, Czech.	Feb. 19, 1977

INSIDE STORY: Belgian Emiel Puttemans holds indoor records for 2,000, 3,000, and 5,000 meters and 2 miles. He set 3 of those records in one day in Berlin in 1973.

American sensation Mary Decker here breaks her 6-year-old record in the 880 yard run in San Diego. The holder of 3 indoor records, she set the outdoor women's mile record in January, 1980. On February 16, 1980, Decker ran the fastest mile ever by a woman in 4 minutes 17.6 seconds. The run is not an official record as the Houston indoor track was "oversize."

MILE HIGH: (Left) Filbert Bayi (#613) leads John Walker (#483) for a 1,500 meters record in 1974. In 1975, Bayi broke the 8-year-old mile record, only to have his record shattered by Walker 3 months later. Sebastian Coe (right) here breaks Walker's mile record in Oslo, Norway, in July, 1979. In addition to his 3-minute-49-second mile, Coe also set records for 800 and 1,500 meters during the summer.

Progressive World 1 Mile Record

Min. Sec.	Name and Nationality	Place	Date
4:55.0	J. Heaviside (Ireland)	Dublin	April 1, 1861
4:49.0	J. Heaviside (Ireland)	Dublin	May 27, 1861
4:46.0	N. Greene (Ireland)	Dublin	May 27, 1861
4:33.0	George Farran (Ireland)	Dublin	May 23, 1862
4:29.6	Walter Chinnery (GB)	Cambridge, UK	March 10, 1868
4:28.8	Walter Gibbs (GB)	London	April 3, 1868
4:28.6	Charles Gunton (GB)	London	March 31, 1873
4:26.0	Walter Slade (GB)	London	May 30, 1874
4:24.5	Walter Slade (GB)	London	June 19, 1875
4:23.2	Walter George (GB)	London	Aug. 16, 1880
4:19.4	Walter George (GB)	London	June 3, 1882
4:18.4	Walter George (GB)	Birmingham, UK	June 21, 1884
4:17.8	Thomas Conneff (Ireland/US)	Cambridge, Mass.	Aug. 26, 1893
4:17.0	Fred Bacon (GB)	London	July 6, 1895
4:15.6	Thomas Conneff (Ireland/US)	New York	Aug. 30, 1895
4:15.4	John Paul Jones (US)	Cambridge, Mass.	May 27, 1911
4:14.4	John Paul Jones (US)	Cambridge, Mass.	May 31, 1913
4:12.6	Norman Taber (US)	Cambridge, Mass.	July 16, 1915
4:10.4	Paavo Nurmi (Finland)	Stockholm	Aug. 23, 1923
4:09.2	Jules Ladoumegue (France)	Paris	Oct. 4, 1931
4:07.6	Jack Lovelock (N.Z.)	Princeton, N.J.	July 15, 1933
4:06.7**	Glenn Cunningham (US)	Princeton, N.J.	June 16, 1934
4:06.4	Sydney Wooderson (GB)	Mostpur Park, UK	Aug. 28, 1937
4:06.1**	Gunder Hägg (Sweden)	Gothenburg, Swe.	July 1, 1942
4:06.2	Arne Andersson (Sweden)	Stockholm	July 10, 1942
4:04.6	Gunder Hägg (Sweden)	Stockholm	Sept. 4, 1942
4:02.6	Arne Andersson (Sweden)	Gothenburg, Swe.	July 1, 1943
4:01.6	Arne Andersson (Sweden)	Malmo, Swe.	July 18, 1944
4:01.3**	Gunder Hägg (Sweden)	Malmo, Swe.	July 17, 1945
3:59.4	Roger Bannister (GB)	Oxford, Eng.	May 6, 1954
3:57.9**	John Landy (Australia)	Turku, Finland	June 21, 1954

**Ratified marks were 4:06:8, 4:06:2, 4:01:4 and 3:58:0 respectively.

Min. Sec.		Name and Nationality	Place	Date
3:57.2	....	Derek Ibbotson (GB)	London	July 19,1957
3:54.5	....	Herb Elliott (Australia)	Dublin	Aug. 6, 1958
3:54.4	....	Peter Snell (NZ)	Wanganvi, NZ ..	Jan. 27, 1962
3:54.1	....	Peter Snell (NZ)	Auckland, NZ ..	Nov. 17, 1964
3:53.6	....	Michel Jazy (France)	Rennes, France .	June 9, 1965
3:51.3	....	Jim Ryun (US)	Berkeley, Ca. ...	July 17, 1966
3:51.1	....	Jim Ryun (US)	Bakersfield, Ca.	June 23, 1967
3:51.0	....	Filbert Bayi (Tanzania)	Kingston, Jam. .	May 17, 1975
3:49.4	....	John Walker (NZ)	Gothenburg, Swe.	Aug. 12, 1975
3:49.0	....	Sebastian Coe (GB)	Oslo	July 17, 1979
3:48.8	....	Steve Ovett (GB)	Oslo	July 1, 1980

Note: The following professional times were superior to the then accepted amateur mark.

Min. Sec.		Name and Nationality	Place	Date
4:23.0	....	Thomas Horspool (GB)	—	— 1858
4:22¼	....	Siah Albison (GB)	Manchester, Eng.	Oct. 27, 1860
4:20.5	....	Edward Mills (GB)	—	April 23, 1863
4:20.0	....	Edward Mills (GB)	Manchester, Eng.	June 25, 1864
4:17¼	....	William Lang (GB)	Manchester, Eng.	Aug. 19, 1865
		William Richards (GB)		
4:16.2	....	William Cummings (GB)	Preston, UK ...	May 14, 1881
4:12¾	....	Walter George (GB)	London	Aug. 23, 1886

Olympic Champions

The first Olympics of the modern age were held in 1896 in Athens. They are still very much the pinnacle of track and field success, although World Championships have been announced by the I.A.A.F. for 1983, and for certain non-Olympic events at earlier dates.

Olympic champions since 1948 have been:

MEN

100 Meters
1948	Harrison Dillard (US) 10.3
1952	Lindy Remigino (US) 10.4
1956	Bobby-Joe Morrow (US) 10.5
1960	Armin Hary (W Ger) 10.2
1964	Robert Hayes (US) 10.05
1968	James Hines (US) 9.95
1972	Valeriy Borzov (USSR) 10.14
1976	Hasely Crawford (Tri) 10.06
1980	Allan Wells (GB) 10.25

200 Meters
1948	Melvin Patton (US) 21.1
1952	Andrew Stanfield (US) 20.7
1956	Bobby-Joe Morrow (US) 20.6
1960	Livio Berrutti (Ita) 20.2
1964	Henry Carr (US) 20.36
1968	Tommie Smith (US) 19.83
1972	Valeriy Borzov (USSR) 20.00
1976	Donald Quarrie (Jam) 20.23
1980	Pietro Mennea (Ita) 20.19

HUMAN RACE: New Zealand's John Lovelock (right) is congratulated by 2nd-place finisher Glenn Cunningham after setting a world record for 1,500 meters in the 1936 Olympics. Two years earlier, Cunningham had broken Lovelock's 11-month-old mile record.

RERUNS: Finland's Lasse Viren (above, #301) won the gold medals for the 5,000 and 10,000 meters runs in both 1972 and 1976. After winning the 10,000 meters in 1948, Emil Zatopek (right, #3) swept the 5,000 meters, 10,000 meters, and the marathon in 1952.

Olympic Champions (continued)

400 Meters

1948	Arthur Wint (Jam) 46.2
1952	George Rhoden (Jam) 45.9
1956	Charles Jenkins (US) 46.7
1960	Otis Davis (US) 44.9
1964	Michael Larrabee (US) 45.15
1968	Lee Evans (US) 43.86
1972	Vincent Matthews (US) 44.66
1976	Alberto Juantorena (Cub) 44.26
1980	Viktor Markin (USSR) 44.60

800 Meters

1948	Malvin Whitfield (US) 1:49.2
1952	Malvin Whitfield (US) 1:49.2
1956	Thomas Courtney (US) 1:47.7
1960	Peter Snell (NZ) 1:46.3
1964	Peter Snell (NZ) 1:45.1
1968	Ralph Doubell (Aus) 1:44.3
1972	David Wottle (US) 1:44.9
1976	Alberto Juantorena (Cub) 1:43.5
1980	Steven Ovett (GB) 1:45.4

1500 Meters

1948	Henry Eriksson (Swe) 3:49.8
1952	Josef Barthel (Lux) 3:45.1
1956	Ron Delany (Ire) 3:41.2
1960	Herbert Elliott (Aus) 3:35.6
1964	Peter Snell (NZ) 3:38.1
1968	Kipchoge Keino (Ken) 3:34.9
1972	Pekka Vasala (Fin) 3:36.3
1976	John Walker (NZ) 3:39.2
1980	Sebastian Coe (GB) 3:38.4

5000 Meters

1948	Gaston Reiff (Bel) 14:17.6
1952	Emil Zatopek (Cze) 14:06.6
1956	Vladimir Kuts (USSR) 13:39.6
1960	Murray Halberg (NZ) 13:43.4
1964	Robert Schul (US) 13:48.4
1968	Mohamed Gammoudi (Tun) 14:05.0
1972	Lasse Viren (Fin) 13:26.4
1976	Lasse Viren (Fin) 13:24.8
1980	Miruts Yifter (Eth) 13:21.0

10000 Meters

1948	Emil Zatopek (Cze) 29:59.6
1952	Emil Zatopek (Cze) 29:17.0
1956	Vladimir Kuts (USSR) 28:45.6
1960	Pyotr Bolotnikov (USSR) 28:32.2
1964	William Mills (US) 28:24.4
1968	Naftali Temu (Ken) 29:27.4
1972	Lasse Viren (Fin) 27:38.4
1976	Lasse Viren (Fin) 27:40.4
1980	Miruts Yifter (Eth) 27:42.7

Marathon

1948	Delfo Cabrera (Arg) 2:34:51.6
1952	Emil Zatopek (Cze) 2:23:03.2
1956	Alain Mimoun (Fra) 2:25:00.0
1960	Abebe Bikila (Eth) 2:15:16.2
1964	Abebe Bikila (Eth) 2:12:11.2
1968	Mamo Wolde (Eth) 2:20:26.4
1972	Frank Shorter (US) 2:12:19.8
1976	Waldemar Cierpinski (E Ger) 2:09:55.0
1980	Waldemar Cierpinski (E Ger) 2:11:03.0

4 × 100 Meters Relay

1948	US 40.6
1952	US 40.1
1956	US 39.5
1960	W. Germany 39.5
1964	US 39.06
1968	US 38.23
1972	US 38.19
1976	US 38.33
1980	USSR 38.26

4 × 400 Meters Relay

1948	US 3:10.4
1952	Jamaica 3:03.9
1956	US 3:04.8
1960	US 3:02.2
1964	US 3:00.7
1968	US 2:56.1
1972	Kenya 2:59.8
1976	US 2:58.7
1980	USSR 3:01.1

110 Meters Hurdles

1948	William Porter (US)	13.9
1952	Harrison Dillard (US)	13.7
1956	Lee Calhoun (US0	13.5
1960	Lee Calhoun (US)	13.8
1964	Hayes Jones (US)	13.67
1968	Willie Davenport (US)	13.33
1972	Rodney Milburn (US)	13.24
1976	Guy Drut (Fra)	13.30
1980	Thomas Munkelt (E Ger)	13.39

400 Meters Hurdles

1948	Roy Cochran (US)	51.1
1952	Charles Moore (US)	50.8
1956	Glenn Davis (US)	50.1
1960	Glenn Davis (US)	49.3
1964	Warren 'Rex' Cawley (US)	49.69
1968	David Hemery (GB)	48.12
1972	John Akii-Bua (Uga)	47.82
1976	Edwin Moses (US)	47.64
1980	Volker Beck (E Ger)	48.70

3000 Meters Steeplechase

1948	Torse Sjöstrand (Swe)	9:04.6
1952	Horace Ashenfelter (US)	8:45.4
1956	Christopher Brasher (GB)	8:41.2
1960	Zdzislaw Krzyzkowiak (Pol)	8:34.2
1964	Gaston Roelants (Bel)	8:30.8
1968	Amos Biwott (Ken)	8:23.6
1972	Kipchoge Keino (Ken)	8:23.6
1976	Anders Garderud (Swe)	8:08.0
1980	Bronislaw Malinowski (Pol)	8:09.7

10,000 Meters Walk

| 1948 | John Mikaelsson (Swe) | 45:13.2 |
| 1952 | John Mikaelsson (Swe) | 45:02.8 |

20,000 Meters Walk

1956	Leonid Spirin (USSR)	1:31:27.4
1960	Vladimir Golubnichiy (USSR)	1:34:07.2
1964	Kenneth Matthews (GB)	1:29:34.0
1968	Vladimir Golubnichiy (USSR)	1:33:58.4
1972	Peter Frenkel (E Ger)	1:26:424
1976	Daniel Bautista (Mex)	1:24:40.6
1980	Maunzio Da Milano (Ita)	1:23:35.5

IN THE FIRST PLACE: John Akii-bua of Uganda crosses the finish line to win the Olympic 400 meters hurdles in Munich in 1972. He set a world record to collect the gold medal.

OVER EASY: Valeriy Brumel (USSR) clears the bar at 7 feet 5¾ inches to break his own record during a US–USSR competition in Moscow in 1963. Brumel went on to capture the gold medal at the 1964 Olympics.

Olympic Champions (continued)

50,000 Meters Walk
1948	John Ljunggren (Swe)	4:41:52.0
1952	Giuseppe Dordoni (Ita)	4:28:07.8
1956	Norman Read (NZ)	4:30:42.8
1960	Don Thompson (GB)	4:25:30.0
1964	Abdon Pamich (Ita)	4:11:12.4
1968	Christophe Höhne (E Ger)	4:20:13.6
1972	Bernd Kannenberg (E Ger)	3:56:11.6
1976	Not held	
1980	Hartwig Gauder (E Ger)	3:49:24.0

High Jump
1948	John Winter (Aus)	1.98
1952	Walter Davis (US)	2.04
1956	Charles Dumas (US)	2.12
1960	Robert Shavlakadze (USSR)	2.16
1964	Valeriy Brumel (USSR)	2.18
1968	Richard Fosbury (US)	2.24
1972	Yuriy Tarmak (USSR)	2.23
1976	Jacek Wszola (Pol)	2.25
1980	Gerd Wessig (E Ger)	2.36

Pole Vault
1948	Guinn Smith (US)	4.30
1952	Robert Richards (US)	4.55
1956	Robert Richards (US)	4.56
1960	Donald Bragg (US)	4.70
1964	Frederick Hansen (US)	5.10
1968	Robert Seagren (US)	5.40
1972	Wolfgang Nordwig (E Ger)	5.50
1976	Tadeusz Slusarski (Pol)	5.50
1980	Wladyslaw Kozakiewicz (Pol)	5.78

Long Jump
1948	William Steele (US)	7.82
1952	Jerome Biffle (US)	7.57
1956	Gregory Bell (US)	7.83
1960	Ralph Boston (US)	8.12
1964	Lynn Davies (GB)	8.07
1968	Robert Beamon (US)	8.90
1972	Randy Williams (US)	8.24
1976	Arnie Robinson (US)	8.35
1980	Lutz Dombrowski (E Ger)	8.54

Triple Jump
1948	Arne Ahman (Swe)	15.40
1952	Adhemar Ferreira da Silva (Bra)	16.22
1956	Adhemar Ferreira da Silva (Bra)	16.35
1960	Jozef Schmidt (Pol)	16.81
1964	Jozef Schmidt	16.85
1968	Viktor Saneyev (USSR)	17.39
1972	Viktor Saneyev (USSR)	17.35
1976	Viktor Saneyev (USSR)	17.29
1980	Jaak Uudmae (USSR)	17.35

Shot
1948	Wilbur Thompson (US)	17.12
1952	Parry O'Brien (US)	17.41
1956	Parry O'Brien (US)	18.57
1960	William Nieder (US)	19.68
1964	Dallas Long (US)	20.33
1968	Randel Matson (US)	20.54
1972	Wladyslaw Komar (Pol)	21.18
1976	Udo Beyer (E Ger)	21.05
1980	Vladimir Kiselyov (USSR)	21.35

GOLD VAULT: Bob Seagren's 1968 pole vault gold medal was the last of a string of US victories that stretched all the way back to 1908.

ON THE RIGHT TRACK: Renate Stecher (left, in dark shirt) won the 100 and 200 meters sprint double in the 1972 Munich Olympics, making her the fifth woman to win both races. Ludmila Bragina (right), holder of the women's 3,000 meters world record, is on her way to the gold medal for 1,500 meters in 1972.

Discus

1948	Adolfo Consolini (Ita) 52.78
1952	Sim Iness (US) 55.03
1956	Alfred Oerter (US) 56.36
1960	Alfred Oerter (US) 59.18
1964	Alfred Oerter (US) 61.00
1968	Alfred Oerter (US) 64.78
1972	Ludvik Danek (Cze) 64.40
1976	Mac Wilkins (US) 67.50
1980	Viktor Rasshchupkin (USSR) 66.64

Hammer

1948	Imre Nemeth (Hun) 56.07
1952	Jozsef Csermak (Hun) 60.34
1956	Harold Connolly (US) 63.19
1960	Vasiliy Rudenkov (USSR) 67.10
1964	Romuald Klim (USSR) 69.74
1968	Gyula Zsivotzky (Hun) 73.36
1972	Anatoliy Bondarchuk (USSR) 75.50
1976	Yuriy Syedikh (USSR) 77.52
1980	Yuriy Syedikh (USSR) 81.80

Javelin

1948	Tapio Rautavaara (Fin) 69.77
1952	Cyrus Young (US) 73.78
1956	Egil Danielsen (Nor) 85.71
1960	Viktor Tsibulenko (USSR) 84.64
1964	Pauli Nevala (Fin) 82.66
1968	Janis Lusis (USSR) 90.10
1972	Klaus Wolfermann (W Ger) 90.48
1976	Mikos Nemeth (Hun) 94.58
1980	Dainis Kula (USSR) 91.20

Decathlon

1948	Robert Mathias (US) 6825
1952	Robert Mathias (US) 7731
1956	Milton Campbell (US) 7708
1960	Rafer Johnson (US) 8001
1964	Willi Holdorf (W Ger) 7887
1968	William Toomey (US) 8193
1972	Nikolai Avilov (USSR) 8454
1976	Bruce Jenner (US) 8618
1980	Daley Thompson (GB) 8495

WOMEN

100 Meters

1948	Fanny Blankers-Koen (Hol) 11.9
1952	Marjorie Jackson (Aus) 11.5
1956	Betty Cuthbert (Aus) 11.5
1960	Wilma Rudolph (US) 11.0
1964	Wyomia Tyus (US) 11.49
1968	Wyomia Tyus (US) 11.07
1972	Renate Stecher (E Ger) 11.07
1976	Annegret Richter (W Ger) 11.08
1980	Lyudmila Kondratyeva (USSR) 11.06

200 meters

1948	Fanny Blankers-Keon (Hol) 24.4
1952	Marjorie Jackson (Aus) 23.7
1956	Betty Cuthbert (Aus) 23.4
1960	Wilma Rudolph (US) 24.0
1964	Edith Maguire (US) 23.05
1968	Irena Szewinska (Pol) 22.58
1972	Renate Stecher (E Ger) 22.40
1976	Barbel Eckert (E Ger) 22.37
1980	Barbel Wockel (*née* Eckert) (E Ger) 22.03

400 Meters

1964	Betty Cuthbert (Aus) 52.01
1968	Colette Besson (Fra) 52.03
1972	Monika Zehrt (E Ger) 51.08
1976	Irena Szewinska (Pol) 49.29
1980	Marita Koch (E Ger) 48.88

800 Meters

1960	Lyudmila Shevtsova (USSR) 2:04.3
1964	Ann Packer (GB) 2:01.1
1968	Madeline Manning (US) 2:00.9
1972	Hildegard Falck (W Ger) 1:58.6
1976	Tatyana Kazankina (USSR) 1:54.9
1980	Nadyezhda Olizarenko (USSR) 1:53.5

1500 Meters

1972	Lyudmila Bragina (USSR) 4:01.4
1976	Tatyana Kazankina (USSR) 4:05.5
1980	Tatyana Kazankina (USSR) 3:56.6

80 Meters Hurdles
1948 Fanny Blankers-Keon (Hol) 11.2
1952 Shirley Strickland (Aus) 10.9
1956 Shirley Strickland (Aus) 10.7
1960 Irina Press (USSR) 10.8
1964 Karin Balzer (E Ger) 10.5
1968 Maureen Caird (Aus) 10.3

100 Meters Hurdles
1972 Annelie Ehrhardt (E Ger) 12.59
1976 Johanna Schaller (E Ger) 12.77
1980 Vera Kamisora (USSR) 12.56

4 × 100 Meters Relay
1948 Netherlands 47.5
1952 US 45.9
1956 Australia 44.5
1960 US 44.5
1964 Poland 43.69
1968 US 42.87
1972 W. Germany 42.81
1976 E. Germany 42.55
1980 E. Germany 41.60

4 × 400 Meters Relay
1972 E. Germany 3:23.0
1976 E. Germany 3:19.2
1980 USSR 3:20.2

High Jump
1948 Alice Coachman (US) 1.68
1952 Esther Brand (S Af) 1.67
1956 Mildred McDaniel (US) 1.76
1960 Iolanda Balas (Rum) 1.85
1964 Iolanda Balas (Rum) 1.90
1968 Miloslava Rezkova (Cze) 1.82
1972 Ulrike Meyfarth (W Ger) 1.92
1976 Rosi Ackermann (E Ger) 1.93
1980 Sara Simeoni (Ita) 1.97

Long Jump
1948 Olga Gyarmati (Hun) 5.69
1952 Yvette Williams (NZ) 6.24
1956 Elzbieta Krzesinska (Pol) 6.35
1960 Vyera Krepkina (USSR) 6.37
1964 Mary Rand (GB) 6.76
1968 Viorica Viscopoleanu (Rum) 6.82
1972 Heide Rosendahl (W Ger) 6.78
1976 Angela Voigt (E Ger) 6.72
1980 Tatyana Kolpakova (USSR) 7.06

Shot
1948 Micheline Ostermeyer (Fra) 13.75
1952 Galina Zybina (USSR) 15.28
1956 Tamara Tishkyevich (USSR) 16.59
1960 Tamara Press (USSR) 17.32
1964 Tamara Press (USSR) 18.14
1968 Margitta Gummel (E Ger) 19.61
1972 Nadyezhda Chizhova (USSR) 21.03
1976 Ivanka Khristova (Bul) 21.16
1980 Ilona Slupianek (E Ger) 22.41

Discus
1948 Micheline Ostermeyer (Fra) 41.92
1952 Nina Ponomaryeva (USSR) 51.42
1956 Olga Fikotova (Cze) 53.68
1960 Nina Ponomaryeva (USSR) 55.10
1964 Tamara Press (USSR) 57.26
1968 Lia Manoliu (Rum) 52.28
1972 Faina Melnik (USSR) 66.62
1976 Evelin Schlaak (now Jahl) (E Ger) 69.00
1980 Evelin Jahl (E Ger) 69.96

Javelin
1948 Herma Bouma (Aut) 45.56
1952 Dana Zatopkova (Cze) 50.46
1956 Inese Jaunzeme (USSR) 53.86
1960 Elvira Ozolina (USSR) 55.98
1964 Mihaela Penes (Rum) 60.54
1968 Angela Nemeth (Hun) 60.36
1972 Ruth Fuchs (E Ger) 63.88
1976 Ruth Fuchs (E Ger) 65.94
1980 Maria Colon (Cub) 68.40

Pentathlon
80m hurdles, Shot, High Jump. Long
Jump, 200m 1964–68: 100m
hurdles replaced
80m hurdles in 1972 and 800 meters
replaced 200m in 1976

1964 Irina Press (USSR) 4702
1968 Ingrid Becker (W Ger) 4559
1972 Mary Peters (GB) 4801
1976 Sigrun Siegl (E Ger) 4745
1980 Nadyezhda Tkachenko (USSR) 5083

(1964 and 1968 scores re-totalled on current scoring tables)

HAPPY LANDING: Viorica Viscopoleanu (Rumania) set a world record to win the long-jump gold medal in Mexico City in 1968.

TRAMPOLINING

Origin. The sport of trampolining (from the Spanish word *trampolin*, a springboard) dates from 1936, when the prototype "T" model trampoline was developed by George Nissen (US). Trampolines were used in show business at least as early as "The Walloons" of the period, 1910–12.

Marathon Record

The longest recorded trampoline bouncing marathon is one of 1,248 hours (52 days) set by a team of 6 in Phoenix, Arizona, from June 24 to August 15, 1974. The solo record is 179 hours (with 5-minute breaks per hour permissible) by Geoffrey Morton of Broken Hill, N.S.W., Australia, March 7–14, 1977.

World Champions

World Championships were first held in 1964; there are Individual Championships for men and women and synchronized events for men and women. There is also a team event awarded on the basis of each nation's individual performances.

INDIVIDUAL CHAMPIONS

Men		Women	
1964	Danny Millman (US)	1964	Judy Wills (US)
1965	George Irwin (US)	1965	Judy Wills (US)
1966	Wayne Miller (US)	1966	Judy Wills (US)
1967	Dave Jacobs (US)	1967	Judy Wills (US)
1968	Dave Jacobs (US)	1968	Judy Wills (US)
1970	Wayne Miller (US)	1970	Renée Ransom (US)
1972	Paul Luxon (GB)	1972	Alexandra Nicholson (US)
1974	Richard Tisson (Fra)	1974	Alexandra Nicholson (US)
1976	Richard Tisson (Fra)	1976	Svetlana Levina (USSR)
1978	Tonisch (USSR)	1978	Tatiana Anisimova (USSR)

BOUNCING BACK: American Judy Wills (left) won the individual trampolining title in the first 5 World Championships, 1964–68

VOLLEYBALL

Origin. The game was invented as Minnonette in 1895 by William G. Morgan at the Y.M.C.A. gymnasium at Holyoke, Massachusetts. The International Volleyball Association was formed in Paris in April, 1947. The ball travels at a speed of up to 70 m.p.h. when smashed over the net, which measures 7 feet 11½ inches. In the women's game it is 7 feet 4¼ inches.

World Titles

World Championships were instituted in 1949. The USSR has won five men's titles. The USSR won the women's championship on four occasions. The record crowd is 60,000 for the 1952 world title matches in Moscow, USSR.

Most Olympic Medals

The sport was introduced to the Olympic Games for both men and women in 1964. The only volleyball player to win four medals is Inna Ryskal (USSR) (b. June 15, 1944), who won a silver medal in 1964 and 1976 and golds in 1968 and 1972.

The record for medals for men is held by Yuriy Poyarkov (USSR), who won gold medals in 1964 and 1968, and a bronze in 1972.

Marathon

The longest recorded volleyball marathon by two teams of six is 75 hours by the Beta Theta Pi fraternity, Bethany College, West Virginia, October 3–6, 1979.

Olympic Champions

First contested in 1964.

MEN				WOMEN			
1964	USSR	1976	Poland	1964	Japan	1976	Japan
1968	USSR	1980	USSR	1968	USSR	1980	USSR
1972	Japan			1972	USSR		

World Champions

In addition to the Olympic Champions listed above.

MEN				WOMEN			
1949	USSR	1966	Czechoslovakia	1952	USSR	1970	USSR
1952	USSR	1970	E Germany	1956	USSR	1974	Japan
1956	Czechoslovakia	1974	Poland	1960	USSR	1978	Cuba
1960	USSR	1978	USSR	1962	Japan		
1962	USSR			1966	Japan		

N.C.A.A.

1970	UCLA	1974	UCLA	1978	Pepperdine
1971	UCLA	1975	UCLA	1979	UCLA
1972	UCLA	1976	UCLA		
1973	San Diego St.	1977	Southern Cal		

A.I.A.W.

NET RESULTS: Poland beat Japan 3 games to 2 in a semi-final in the 1976 Olympic volleyball competition in Montreal. The Polish team went on to win the gold medal. Championship volleyball competition is much faster and more precise than the street, beach, and schoolyard variety common in the US.

WALKING

Longest Annual Race

The Strasbourg-Paris event (instituted in 1926 in the reverse direction) over 313 to 344 miles is the world's longest annual walk event. Gilbert Roger (France) has won 6 times (1949–53–54–56–57–58). The fastest performance is by Robert Rinchard (Belgium) who walked 325 miles in the 1974 race in 63 hours 29 minutes, so (deducting 4 hours of compulsory stops) averaging 5.12 m.p.h.

Longest in 24 Hours

The best performance is 142 miles 448 yards by Jesse Castañeda (US) at the New Mexico State Fair in Albuquerque, September 18–19, 1976. The best by a woman is 116.6 miles by Ann Sayer (GB) at Rouen, France, on April 28–29, 1979.

Most Olympic Medals

Walking races have been included in the Olympic schedule since 1906, but walking matches have been known since 1589.

BEST FOOT FORWARD: East German Peter Frenkel (left) and West German Bernd Kannenberg (right) both set Olympic records in walking events at the 1972 Munich Games. Frenkel set his record at 20 kilometers, and it was broken by Daniel Bautista in 1976. Kannenberg's effort was at 50 kilometers, and the event was not held in the 1976 Games.

The only walker to win three gold medals has been Ugo Frigerio (Italy) (1901–68) with the 3,000 m. and 10,000 m. in 1920 and the 10,000 m. in 1924. He also holds the record of most medals with four (having additionally won the bronze medal in the 50,000 m. in 1932), which total is shared with Vladimir Golubnitschiy (USSR) (b. June 2, 1936), who won gold medals for the 10,000 m. in 1960 and 1968, the silver in 1972 and the bronze in 1964.

Most Titles

Four-time Olympian Ronald Owen Laird (b. May 31, 1938) of the New York Athletic Club, won a total of 65 US National titles from 1958 to 1976, plus 4 Canadian championships.

Official World Records (Track Walking)

(As recognized by the International Amateur Athletic Federation)

Distance	hr.	min.	sec.	Name and Nationality	Place	Date
20,000 meters	1	20	06.8	Daniel Bautista (Mexico)	Canada	Oct. 17, 1979
30,000 meters	2	08	00.0	José Marin (Spain)	Spain	Apr. 8, 1979
50,000 meters	3	41	39.0	Raul Gonzalez (Mexico)	Norway	Apr. 8, 1979
2 hours	17 miles 881 yards			José Marin (Spain)	Spain	May 25, 1979

Unofficial World Best (Track Walking)

(As of Dec. 20, 1979)

Distance	min.	sec.	Name and Nationality	Place	Date
Men					
1 mile	5 min.	55.8 sec.	Todd Scully (US)	New York	Feb. 9, 1979
3,000 m.	11 min.	05.0 sec.	Reina Salonen (Fin)	Turku, Finland	Feb. 2, 1977
5,000 m.	19 min.	03.3 sec.	Yevgeny Yevsyukov (USSR)	Fort Worth, Tex.	March 3, 1979
10,000 m.	39 min.	31.5 sec.	Daniel Bautista (Mex)	Grudziadz, Poland	May 30, 1979
1 hour	14,835 m.	(9 miles 383 yds.)	Daniel Bautista (Mex)	Monterey, Mexico	1979
Women					
1 mile	6 min.	58.4 sec.	Chris Shea (US)	New York	Feb. 23, 1979
3,000 m.	13 min.	25.25 sec.	Carol Tyson (GB)	Hofgangens, Sweden	July 6, 1979
5,000 m.	23 min.	11.2 sec.	Carol Tyson (GB)	Östersund, Sweden	June 30, 1979
10,000 m.	48 min.	11.0 sec.	Marion Fawkes (GB)	Harnosand, Sweden (GB)	July 8, 1979

Road Walking

The world's best road performances are: 20,000 meters, 1 hour 22 minutes 16 seconds by Daniel Bautista (Mexico) at Valencia, Spain, on May 19, 1979; 50,000 meters, 3 hours 41 minutes 19.2 seconds by Raul Gonzalez (Mexico) at Podebrady, Czechoslovakia on June 11, 1978.

Greatest Mileage

Dimitru Dan (born July 13, 1890, *fl.* 1976) of Rumania was the only man of 200 entrants to succeed in walking 100,000 kilometers (62,137 miles), in a contest organized by the Touring Club de France on April 1, 1910. By March 24, 1916, he had covered 96,000 kilometers (59,651 miles), averaging 27.24 miles per day.

"Non-Stop" Walking

Fred Jago (b. 1935) of Great Britain walked 317.15 miles at Vivary Park, Taunton, England, in 148 hours 31 minutes, July 13–19, 1979. He did not permit himself any stops for resting and was moving 98.3 per cent of the time.

Walking Around the World

The first person reported to have "walked around the world" is George M. Schilling (US) from August 3, 1897–1904, but the first verified achievement was by David Kunst, who started with his brother John from Waseca, Minnesota, on June 10, 1970. John was killed by Afghani bandits in 1972. David arrived home after walking 14,500 miles on October 5, 1974.

Tomas Carlos Pereira (b. Argentina, November 16, 1942) spent

CROSSWALK: John Lees (GB) walked 2,876 miles across the United States (Los Angeles to New York) in 53 days 12 hours 15 minutes to set the transcontinental walking record in 1972. Averaging 53.746 miles per day, Lees' cross-country time was 11 days better than the then current running record.

10 years, April 6, 1968, through April 8, 1978, walking 29,825 miles around all five continents.

The Trans-Asia record is 238 days for 6,800 miles from Riga, Latvia, to Vladivostok, USSR, by Georgyi Bushuyev, 50, in 1973–74.

Walking Across America

John Lees, 27, of Brighton, England, on April 11–June 3, 1972, walked 2,876 miles across the US from City Hall, Los Angeles, to City Hall, New York City, in 53 days 12 hours 15 minutes (53.746 miles per day).

Walking Across Canada

The record trans-Canada (Halifax to Vancouver) walk of 3,764 miles is 96 days by Clyde McRae, 23, from May 1 to August 4, 1973.

Walking Backwards

The greatest exponent of reverse pedestrianism has been Plennie L. Wingo (b. 1895) then of Abilene, Texas, who started on his 8,000-mile transcontinental walk on April 15, 1931, from Santa Monica, California, to Istanbul, Turkey, and arrived on October 24, 1932. He celebrated the walk's 45th anniversary by covering the 452 miles from Santa Monica to San Francisco, California, backwards, in 85 days, aged 81 years.

The longest distance recorded for walking backwards in 24 hours in 80.5 miles by Veikko Matias (b. April 23, 1941) of Kangasala, Finland, at Kankaapää Airfield, Niinisalo, Finland, on October 7–8, 1978.

WATER POLO

Origins. Water polo was developed in England as "Water Soccer" in 1869 and was first included in the Olympic Games in Paris in 1900.

Olympic Victories

Hungary has won the Olympic tournament most often with six wins, in 1932, 1936, 1952, 1956, 1964 and 1976. Five players share the record of three gold medals: George Wilkinson (1879–1946) in 1900–08–12, Paulo (Paul) Radmilovic (1886–1968) and Charles Sidney Smith (1879–1951) in 1908–12–20—all GB; and the Hungarians Deszö Gyarmati (b. October 23, 1927) and György Kárpáti (b. June 23, 1935) in 1952–56–64.

Radmilovic also won a gold medal for the 4 × 200 m. freestyle relay in 1908.

Most International Appearances

The greatest number of internationals is 244 by Ozren Bonacic for Yugoslavia between 1964 and September, 1975.

SLAM DUNK: Hungarian Gyorgy Karpati (#7) is one of the 5 players who have won 3 Olympic gold medals in water polo.

Marathon

The longest match on record is one of 70 hours 17 minutes between two teams of 15 from the Sedbergh School Swimming and Water Polo Club, Cumbria, England, July 14–17, 1979.

Olympic Champions

First contested in 1900 although the teams in 1900 and 1904 were club rather than national teams. Winners (men) since 1948:

1948	Italy	1960	Italy	1972	USSR
1952	Hungary	1964	Hungary	1976	Hungary
1956	Hungary	1968	Yugoslavia	1980	USSR

World Champions

1973	Hungary	1978	Italy
1975	USSR		

N.C.A.A.

1969	UCLA	1973	California	1977	California
1970	California-Irvine	1974	California	1978	Stanford
1971	UCLA	1975	California	1979	California-Santa Barbara
1972	UCLA	1976	Stanford		

WATER SKIING

Origins. The origins of water skiing lie in plank gliding or aquaplaning. A 19th-century treatise on sorcerers refers to Eliseo of Tarentum who, in the 14th century, "walks and dances" on the water. The first report of aquaplaning was from the Pacific coast of the US in the early 1900's.

A photograph exists of a "plank-riding" contest in a regatta won by a Mr. H. Storry at Scarborough, Yorkshire, England, on July 15, 1914. Competitors were towed on a *single* plank by a motor launch. The present-day sport of water skiing was pioneered by Ralph W. Samuelson on Lake Pepin, Minnesota, on two curved pine boards in the summer of 1922, though claims have been made for the birth of the sport on Lake Annecy (Haute Savoie), France, in 1920. The first World Water Ski Organization was formed in Geneva, Switzerland, on July 27, 1946.

Jumps

The first recorded jump on water skis was by Ralph W. Samuelson, off a greased ramp at Lake Pepin in 1925. The longest jump record is one of 197 feet by Michael Hazelwood (GB) at Moomba, Australia, on March 9, 1980. A minimum margin of 8 inches is required for sole possession of the world record.

The women's record is 129 feet by Deena Brush (US) at Tyler, Texas, on July 9, 1979.

Slalom

The world record for slalom on a particular pass is 4 buoys (with a 37-foot rope) at 36 m.p.h. by Kris LaPoint (US) at Horton Lake, near Barstow, California, on July 15, 1975, and also by his brother, Bob LaPoint, in Miami in August, 1976.

SPRAY HITTERS: American Mike Suyderhoud (left) has won 2 world overall titles, a record he shares with 2 other men. Venezuelan Carlos Suarez (right) was the overall champion in 1975.

The women's record is 4 buoys on a 39-foot line at 34 m.p.h. by Cindy Hutcherson Todd (US) at Callaway Gardens, Georgia, in 1978.

Tricks

The highest official point score for tricks is 8,140 points by Patrice Martin (France) at Toronto, Canada, on September 21, 1979.

The women's record of 6,200 points was set by Natalia Rumyantzeva (USSR) at Castelgandolfo, Italy, on September 2, 1979.

Longest Run

The greatest distance traveled non-stop is 1,124 miles by Will Coughey (New Zealand) on Lake Karapiro, New Zealand, in 30 hours 34 minutes, February 26–27, 1977.

Highest Speed

The water skiing speed record is 125.69 m.p.h. recorded by Danny Churchill (US) at the Oakland Marine Stadium, California, in 1971. A claim of 128.16 m.p.h. by Craig Wendt (US) at Long Beach on August 19, 1979, is awaiting ratification. Donna Patterson Brice (b. 1953) set a feminine record of 111.11 m.p.h. at Long Beach, California, on August 21, 1977.

Barefoot

The first person to water ski barefoot is reported to be Dick Pope, Jr., at Lake Eloise, Florida, on March 6, 1947. The barefoot duration record is 2 hours 42 minutes 39 seconds by Billy Nichols (US) (born 1964) on Lake Weir, Florida, on November 19, 1978. The backwards barefoot record is 39 minutes by Paul McManus (Australia). The best officially recorded barefoot jump is 52 feet by Keith Donnelly at Baronscourt, Northern Ireland, on July 9, 1978. The official barefoot speed record (two runs) is 110.02 m.p.h. by Lee Kirk (US) at Firebird Lake, Phoenix, Arizona, on June 11, 1977. His fastest run was 113.67 m.p.h. The fastest by a woman is 61.39 by Haidee Jones (now Lance) (Australia).

Most Titles

World overall championships (instituted 1949) have been twice won by Alfredo Mendoza (US) in 1953–55, Mike Suyderhoud (US) in 1967–69, and George Athans (Canada) in 1971 and 1973, and three times by Mrs. Willa McGuire (*née* Worthington) of the US, in 1949–50 and 1955, and Elizabeth Allan-Shetter (US) in 1965, 1969, and 1975.

Allan-Shetter has also won a record eight individual championship events.

World Championships

The first World Championships were held at Juan Les Pins, France, in 1949. Championships are now contested biennially in three parts—Slalom, Tricks and Jumping, with a separate contest

for the best overall performer. Overall Men's and Women's World
Champions have been:

MEN		WOMEN	
1949	Christian Jourdan (Fra) and	1949	Willa Worthington (US)
	Guy de Clercq (Bel)	1950	Willa McGuire (née Worthington)
1950	Dick Pope, Jr. (US)		(US)
1953	Alfredo Mendoza (US)	1953	Leah Marie Rawls (US)
1955	Alfredo Mendoza (US)	1955	Willa McGuire (US)
1957	Joe Cash (US)	1957	Marina Doria (Swi)
1959	Chuck Stearns (US)	1959	Vickie Van Hook (US)
1961	Bruno Zaccardi (Ita)	1961	Sylvie Hulsemann (Lux)
1963	Billy Spencer (US)	1963	Jeanette Brown (US)
1965	Roland Hillier (US)	1965	Liz Allan (US)
1967	Mike Suyderhoud (US)	1967	Jeanette Stewart-Wood (GB)
1969	Mike Suyderhoud (US)	1969	Liz Allan (US)
1971	George Athans (Can)	1971	Christy Weir (US)
1973	George Athans (Can)	1973	Lisa St John (US)
1975	Carlos Suarez (Ven)	1975	Liz Shetter (née Allan) (US)
1977	Mike Hazelwood (GB)	1977	Cindy Todd (US)
1979	Joel McClintock (Can)	1979	Cindy Todd (US)

TEAM competition has been won by the US for the 12 successive World Championships
from 1957.

WEIGHTLIFTING

Origins. Amateur weightlifting is of comparatively modern origin, and the first "world" championship was staged at the Café
Monico, Piccadilly, London, on March 28, 1891. Prior to that
time, weightlifting consisted of professional exhibitions in which

PICKUPS: American Norbert Schemansky (left) won 4 Olympic medals,
the most by any lifter. He became the oldest man to break a world record
when, aged 37 years 10 months, he set a heavyweight snatch mark. Jan
Todd (right), possibly the strongest woman in the world, holds the wom-
en's records for the 2-handed dead lift (463 lbs.) and the 3-lift total (1,125
lbs.).

some of the advertised poundages were open to doubt. The first to raise 400 lbs. was Karl Swoboda (1882–1933) (Austria) in Vienna, with 401¼ lbs. in 1910, using the Continental clean and jerk style.

Greatest Lift

The greatest weight ever raised by a human being is 6,270 lbs. in a back lift (weight raised off trestles) by the 364-lb. Paul Anderson (US) (b. 1932), the 1956 Olympic heavyweight champion, at Toccoa, Georgia, on June 12, 1957. (The heaviest Rolls-Royce, the Phantom VI, weighs 5,936 lbs.) The greatest by a woman is 3,564 lbs. with a hip and harness lift by Mrs. Josephine Blatt (née Schauer), (US) (1869–1923) at the Bijou Theatre, Hoboken, New Jersey, on April 15, 1895.

The greatest overhead lifts made from the ground are the clean and jerks achieved by superheavyweights which now exceed 560 lbs.

The greatest overhead lift ever made by a woman is 286 lbs. in a continental jerk by Katie Sandwina (née Brummbach) (Germany) (born January 21, 1884, died as Mrs. Max Heymann in New York City, in 1952) in c. 1911. This is equivalent to seven 40-pound office typewriters. She stood 5 feet 11 inches tall, weighed 210 lbs. and is reputed to have unofficially lifted 312½ lbs. and to have once shouldered a 1,200-lb. cannon taken from the tailboard of a Barnum & Bailey circus wagon.

Power Lifts

Paul Anderson as a professional has bench-pressed 627 lbs., achieved 1,200 lbs. in a deep-knee bend, and dead-lifted 820 lbs., making a career aggregate of 2,647 lbs.

Ronald Collins (GB) with a 1,655-lb. lift in Liverpool, England, on December 15, 1973, when his body weight was 165 lbs., became the first man to lift a total 10 times his own body weight. Since then 9 other lifters have achieved this, but only Collins has repeated in more than one weight division.

The newly instituted two-man dead lift record was raised to 1,439 lbs. by Clay and Doug Patterson in El Dorado, Arkansas, on March 3, 1979.

Hermann Görner (Germany) performed a one-handed dead lift of 734½ lbs. in Dresden on July 20, 1920. He once raised 24 men weighing 4,123 lbs. on a plank with the soles of his feet and also carried on his back a 1,444-lb. piano for a distance of 52½ feet on June 3, 1921. Görner is also reputed to have once lifted 14 bricks weighing 123½ lbs. horizontally, using only lateral pressure.

Peter B. Cortese (US) achieved a one-arm dead lift of 370 lbs.—22 lbs. over triple his body weight—at York, Pennsylvania, on September 4, 1954.

The highest competitive two-handed dead lift by a woman is 463 lbs. by Jan Suffolk Todd (born May 22, 1952) (US) at Honolulu, Hawaii, on May 4, 1979. She also holds the three-lift record total of 1,125 lbs. set at Stephenville Crossing, Newfoundland, Canada, on June 24, 1978.

It was reported that a hysterical 123-lb. woman, Mrs. Maxwell

TWO-TIMER: Leonid Zhabotinsky (USSR) won Olympic gold medals in the heavyweight class in 1976 and 1968, making him one of 10 lifters who have won gold medals in successive games. He held the superheavyweight clean and jerk record from 1964 until 1968.

Rogers, lifted one end of a 3,600-lb. car which, after the collapse of a jack, had fallen on top of her son at Tampa, Florida, on April 24, 1960. She cracked some vertebrae.

A dead lift record of 2,100,000 lbs. in 24 hours was set by a 10-man team in relay at the Darwen Weightlifting Club, Darwen, England, on August 19, 1978.

Most Olympic Gold Medals

Of the 90 Olympic titles at stake, the USSR has won 26, the US 15 and France 9. Ten lifters have succeeded in winning an Olympic gold medal in successive Games. Of these, three have also won a silver medal.

Most Olympic Medals

Winner of most Olympic medals is Norbert Schemansky (US) with four: gold, middle-heavyweight 1952; silver, heavyweight 1948; bronze, heavyweight 1960 and 1964.

Schemansky achieved a world record (heavyweight snatch of 361½ lbs. on April 28, 1962, at Detroit) at the record age of 37 years 10 months.

Official World Weightlifting Records

(As of August 4, 1980)

Flyweight
(114½ lb—52 kg)

Snatch	249¾	Han Gyong Si (N Korea)	USSR	July 20, 1980
Jerk	314	Alexander Senchine (USSR)	USSR	May 14, 1980
Total	545½	Alexander Voronin (USSR)	W Germany	Sept 18, 1979

Bantamweight
(123¼ lb—56 kg)

Snatch	275½	Daniel Nunez (Cuba)	USSR	July 21, 1980
Jerk	347	Yuri Sarkisian (USSR)	USSR	July 21, 1980
Total	606¼	Daniel Nunez (Cuba)	USSR	July 21, 1980

Featherweight
(132¼ lb—60 kg)

Snatch	292	Viktor Mazin (USSR)	USSR	July 6, 1980
Jerk	368	Viktor Mazin (USSR)	USSR	July 6, 1980
Total	655¾	Viktor Mazin (USSR)	USSR	July 6, 1980

Lightweight
(148¾ lb—67.5 kg)

Snatch	326¼	Yanko Rusev (Bulgaria)	Yugoslavia	Apr 28, 1980
Jerk	429¾	Yanko Rusev (Bulgaria)	USSR	July 23, 1980
Total	755	Yanko Rusev (Bulgaria)	USSR	July 23, 1980

Middleweight
(165¼ lb—75 kg)

Snatch	354¾	Nedelcho Kolev (Bulgaria)	Bulgaria	Feb 3, 1980
Jerk	453	Asen Zlatev (Bulgaria)	USSR	July 24, 1980
Total	793½	Asen Zlatev (Bulgaria)	USSR	July 24, 1980

Light-heavyweight
(181¾ lb—82.5 kg)

Snatch	391¼	Yurik Vardanyan (USSR)	USSR	July 26, 1979
Jerk	490½	Yurik Vardanyan (USSR)	USSR	July 26, 1980
Total	881¾	Yurik Vardanyan (USSR)	USSR	July 26, 1980

Middle-heavyweight
(198¼ lb—90 kg)

Snatch	398	David Rigert (USSR)	Czech	June 16, 1978
Jerk	491½	Yurik Vardanyan (USSR)	USSR	July 6, 1980
Total	881¾	David Rigert (USSR)	USSR	May 14, 1976

(220½ lb—100 kg)

Snatch	403¼	Igor Nikitine (USSR)	USSR	June 27, 1980
Jerk	506¾	David Rigert (USSR)	USSR	July 6, 1980
Total	892¾	David Rigert (USSR)	USSR	Nov 23, 1979

Heavyweight
(242½ lb—110 kg)

Snatch	419¾	Vyacheslav Klokov (USSR)	USSR	July 6, 1980
Jerk	529	Leonid Taranenko (USSR)	USSR	July 29, 1979
Total	931¼	Leonid Taranenko (USSR)	USSR	July 29, 1980

EXTREMISTS: Russian Alexander Voronin (left) won a gold medal in 1976 and holds the jerk and total weight record in the flyweight class, the lightest class of all. Vasili Alexeyev (right) has broken 80 official and world superheavyweight records, making him the world's most prolific recordbreaker. He won gold medals in 1972 and 1976.

Super-heavyweight
(Over 242½ lb—110 kg)

Snatch	442	Sultan Rakhamov (USSR)	USSR	Apr 25, 1978
Jerk	564¼	Vasili Alexeyev (USSR)	USSR	Nov 1, 1977
Total	981	Vasili Alexeyev (USSR)	USSR	Sept 1, 1977

Most Successful Olympic Weightlifters

Louis Hostin (France)	Gold, light-heavyweight 1932 and 1936; Silver, 1928.
John Davis (US)	Gold, heavyweight 1948 and 1952.
Tommy Kono (Hawaii/US)	Gold, lightweight 1952; Gold, light-heavyweight 1956; Silver, 1960.
Charles Vinci (US)	Gold, bantamweight 1956 and 1960.
Arkady Vorobyov (USSR)	Gold, middle-heavyweight 1956 and 1960.
Yoshinobu Miyake (Japan)	Gold, featherweight 1964 and 1968; Silver, bantamweight 1960.
Waldemar Baszanowski (Poland)	Gold, lightweight 1964 and 1968.
Leonid Zhabotinsky (USSR)	Gold, heavyweight 1964 and 1968.
Vasili Alexeyev (USSR)	Gold, super-heavyweight 1972 and 1976.
Norair Nourikian (Bulgaria)	Gold, featherweight 1972; Gold, bantamweight 1976.

World Powerlifting Records

(International Powerlifting Federation) Effective: November 5, 1979)

		Nation	Kg	Lbs	Date	Place
	52 Kg					
SQT	Chuck Dunbar	US	220	485	Aug. 18, 1979	Bay St. Louis, Mo.
BP	Chuck Dunbar	US	137.5	303	Aug. 18, 1979	Bay St. Louis, Mo.
DL	Hideaki Inaba	Japan	225	496	Nov. 2, 1979	Dayton, Ohio
TOT	Hideaki Inaba	Japan	565	1245.5	Nov. 2, 1979	Dayton, Ohio
	56 g					
SQT	Precious McKenzie	NZ	230	507	May 5, 1979	Honolulu, Hawaii
BP	Scott Frostbaum	US	140.5	309.5	Apr. 13, 1979	Ft. Worth, Tx.
DL	Lamar Gant	US	280	617	Nov. 2, 1979	Dayton, Ohio
TOT	Lamar Gant	US	610	1344.5	Nov. 2, 1979	Dayton, Ohio
	60 Kg					
SQT	Eddie Pengelly	GB	242.5	534.5	June 17, 1979	Birmingham, Eng.
BP	Yoshinobu Tominaga	Japan	162.5	358	May 28, 1979	Tokyo, Japan
DL	Lamar Grant	US	282.5	622.5	Nov. 3, 1978	Turku, Finland
TOT	Eddie Pengelly	GB	645	1421.5	June 17, 1979	Birmingham, Eng.
	67.5 Kg					
SQT	Mike Bridges	US	282.5	622.5	Nov. 3, 1978	Turku, Finland
BP	Roger Gorumba	US	187.5	413	July 14, 1979	Inglewood, Ca.
DL	Troy Hicks	US	290	639	Jan. 27, 1979	Cleveland, Tenn.
TOT	Mike Bridges	US	730	1609	Nov. 3, 1978	Turku, Finland
	75 Kg					
SQT	Mike Bridges	US	325	716.5	Nov. 3, 1979	Dayton, Ohio
BP	Mike Bridges	US	207.5	457	Nov. 3, 1979	Dayton, Ohio
DL	Rick Gaugler	US	315	694	Feb. 10, 1979	Ft. Worth, Tx.
TOT	Mike Bridges	US	830	1829.5	Nov. 3, 1979	Dayton, Ohio
	82.5 Kg					
SQT	Ron Collins	GB	332.5	733	June 17, 1979	Birmingham, Eng.
BP	Mike MacDonald	US	232.5	512.5	Feb. 17, 1979	Brookings, S.D.
DL	Veli Kumpunieni	Finland	345	760.5	May 19, 1979	Humppila, Finland
TOT	Ron Collins	GB	842.5	1857	June 12, 1979	Birmingham, Eng.
	90 Kg					
SQT	Jerry Jones	US	335	782.5	May 5, 1979	Honolulu, Hawaii
BP	Mike MacDonald	US	250	551	May 5, 1979	Honolulu, Hawaii
DL	Vince Anello	US	370	815.5	Nov. 4, 1978	Turku, Finland
TOT	Roger Estep	US	880	1940	Dec. 10, 1978	Sandusky, Ohio
	100 Kg					
SQT	Chip McCain	US	356.6	785.5	Aug. 18, 1979	Bay St. Louis, Mo.
BP	Mike MacDonald	US	260	573	Aug. 21, 1977	Santa Monica, Ca.
DL	Vince Anello	US	365	804.5	June 29, 1977	Culver City, Ca.
TOT	Larry Pacifico	US	935	2061	Nov. 4, 1977	Perth, Australia

110 Kg

SQT	Marvin Phillips	US	367.5	810	Apr. 10, 1978	Honolulu Hawaii
BP	Mike MacDonald	US	260	573	Nov. 22, 1975	Duluth, Minn.
DL	John Kuc	US	390	859.5	Nov. 4, 1979	Dayton, Ohio
TOT	John Kuc	US	965	2127	Nov. 4, 1979	Dayton, Ohio

125 Kg

SQT	Ernie Hackett	US	400.5	822.5	Aug. 19, 1979	Bay St. Louis, Mo.
BP	Tom Hardman	US	265.5	586	Dec. 17, 1979	Jasper, Canada
DL	Dave Shaw	US	366	806.5	July 15, 1979	Inglewood, Ca.
TOT	Larry Kidney	US	972.5	2143.5	Aug. 19, 1979	Bay St. Louis, Mo.

Over 125 Kg

SQT	Paul Wrenn	US	433	954.5	Aug. 19, 1979	Bay St. Louis, Mo.
BP	Bill Kazmaier	US	282.5	622.5	Nov. 4, 1979	Dayton, Ohio
DL	Don Reinhoudt	US	400	881.5	May 3, 1975	Chattanooga, Tenn.
TOT	Don Reinhoudt	US	1097.5	2420	May 3, 1975	Chattanooga, Tenn.

Note: SQT = Squat; BP = Bench Press; DL = Dead Lift

Superheavyweight Clean and Jerk Progressive World Record

Kg	Name and Nationality	Place	Date
147.5	Charles Rigoulot (France)	Paris	1924
152.5	Charles Rigoulot (France)	Paris	1924
157.5	Charles Rigoulot (France)	Paris	1925
160.5	Charles Rigoulot (France)	Paris	1925
161.5	Charles Rigoulot (France)	Paris	June 28, 1925
167.0	El Sayed Nosseir (Egypt)	Luxembourg	March 1, 1931
167.5	Arnold Luhaäär (Est)	Revel, USSR	Aug. 8, 1937
170.5	Ahmed Geissa (Egypt)		April 9, 1945
171.0	Jakov Kucenko (USSR)		Oct. 25, 1946
173.0	Jakov Kucenko (USSR)		May 8, 1947
174.0	Jakov Kucenko (USSR)		July 20, 1947
174.5	John Davis (US)		Sept. 27, 1947
177.5	John Davis (US)	London	Aug. 11 , 1948
180.0	John Davis (US)	Buenos Aires	March 11, 1951
182.0	John Davis (US)	Los Angeles	June 16, 1951
185.0	Norbert Schemansky (US)		1952
187.5	Norbert Schemansky (US)		Feb. 15, 1953
188.5	Norbert Schemansky (US)	Vienna	June 26, 1954
189.0	Norbert Schemansky (US)		1954
190.0	Norbert Schemansky (US)	Copenhagen	1954
192.5	Norbert Schemansky (US)	Lille, France	Oct. 17, 1954
196.5	Paul Anderson (US)	Cleveland	April 24, 1955
197.0	Paul Anderson (US)		Sept. 1, 1955
197.5	Juri Vlasov (USSR)	Leningrad	April 22, 1959
202.0	Juri Vlasov (USSR)	Rome	Sept. 10, 1960
205.0	Juri Vlasov (USSR)	Kislovodsk, USSR	June 27, 1961
206.0	Juri Vlasov (USSR)	London	July 29, 1961
208.0	Juri Vlasov (USSR)	Vienna	Sept. 28, 1961
210.5	Juri Vlasov (USSR)	Dnepropetrovsk, USSR	Dec. 22, 1961
211.0	Juri Vlasov (USSR)	Hämeenlinna, Finland	May 30, 1962
212.5	Juri Vlasov (USSR)	Stockholm	Sept. 13, 1963
213.0	Leonid Zhabotinsky (USSR)	Moscow	March 22, 1964
215.5	Juri Vlasov (USSR)	Podolsk, USSR	Aug. 3, 1964
217.5	Leonid Zhabotinsky (USSR)	Tokyo	Oct. 18, 1964
218.0	Leonid Zhabotinsky (USSR)	Berlin	Oct. 21, 1966
218.5	Leonid Zhabotinsky (USSR)	Sofia, Bulg.	June 18, 1967
219.0	Leonid Zhabotinsky (USSR)	Moscow	Aug. 3, 1967
220.0	Leonid Zhabotinsky (USSR)	Lugansk, USSR	May 19, 1968
220.5	Robert Bednarski (US)	York, Eng.	June 9, 1968
221.5	Vasili Alexeyev (USSR)	Velikie Luki, USSR	Jan. 24, 1970
222.0	Serge Reding (Belgium)	Herbeumont, Bel.	April 18, 1970
223.5	Vasili Alexeyev (USSR)	Vilnius, USSR	April 26, 1970
225.5	Vasili Alexeyev (USSR)	Szombathely, Hun.	June 28, 1970
226.5	Serge Reding (Belgium)	La Roche, Bel.	Aug. 28, 1970
227.5	Vasili Alexeyev (USSR)	Columbus, Oh.	Sept. 20, 1970
228.0	Vasili Alexeyev (USSR)	Volgograd, USSR	Nov. 17, 1970
228.5	Vasili Alexeyev (USSR)	Shakhti, USSR	Dec. 4, 1970
229.5	Vasili Alexeyev (USSR)	Dnepropetrovsk, USSR	Dec. 26, 1970
230.0	Vasili Alexeyev (USSR)	Paris	Feb. 14, 1971
230.5	Vasili Alexeyev (USSR)	Taganrog, USSR	April 18, 1971

231.0	Vasili Alexeyev (USSR)	Sofia, Bul.	June 27, 1971
232.5	Vasili Alexeyev (USSR)	Sofia, Bul.	June 27, 1971
233.0	Vasili Alexeyev (USSR)	Moscow	July 24, 1971
235.0	Vasili Alexeyev (USSR)	Moscow	July 24, 1971
235.5	Vasili Alexeyev (USSR)	Lima, Peru	Sept. 26, 1971
236.0	Vasili Alexeyev (USSR)	Tallinn, USSR	April 15, 1972
237.5	Vasili Alexeyev (USSR)	Tallinn, USSR	April 15, 1972
238.0	Vasili Alexeyev (USSR)	Donetsk, USSR	April 29, 1973
240.0	Vasili Alexeyev (USSR)	Madrid	June 18 1973
240.5	Vasili Alexeyev (USSR)	Erivan, USSR	March 20, 1974
241.0	Vasili Alexeyev (USSR)	Tbilisi, USSR	April 28, 1974
241.5	Vasili Alexeyev (USSR)	Manila, Phil.	Sept. 29, 1974
242.0	Vasili Alexeyev (USSR)	Glazov, USSR	Nov. 3, 1974
242.5	Vasili Alexeyev (USSR)	London	Nov. 27, 1974
243.0	Vasili Alexeyev (USSR)	Zaporozhe, USSR	Dec. 15, 1974
243.5	Vasili Alexeyev (USSR)	Lipetsk, USSR	Dec. 29, 1974
245.0	Vasili Alexeyev (USSR)	Vilnius, USSR	July 11, 1975
245.5	Vasili Alexeyev (USSR)	Moscow	Sept. 23, 1975
246.5	Gerd Bonk (E Ger)	Karl-Marx Stadt, E. Ger.	Nov. 28, 1975
247.5	Vasili Alexeyev (USSR)	Montreal	Dec. 7, 1975
252.5	Gerd Bonk (E Ger)	Berlin	April 11, 1976
255.0	Vasili Alexeyev (USSR)	Montreal	July 27, 1976
255.5	Vasili Alexeyev (USSR)	Moscow	Sept. 1, 1977
256.0	Vasili Alexeyev (USSR)	Moscow	Nov. 1, 1977

World and Olympic Champions

The first weightlifting World Championships were held in 1891 and weightlifting was included in the first modern Olympic Games in 1896. From 1928 to 1972 the recognized lifts (all two-handed) were Clean and Press, Snatch, and Clean and Jerk. In 1972 the Clean and Press was dropped from the international program. At the World Championships medals are awarded both for the individual lifts and for the aggregate total achieved in each weight category.

CHAMPIONS FOR AGGREGATE SINCE 1973
(*=Olympic champion) (with totals in kg)

Flyweight (52.0kg)
1973	Mohammad Nassiri (Iran) 240.0
1974	Mohammad Nassiri (Iran) 232.5
1975	Zigmunt Smalczerz (Pol) 237.5
1976*	Aleksandr Voronin (USSR) 242.5
1977	Aleksandr Voronin (USSR) 247.5
1978	Kanybek Osmonaliev (USSR) 240.0
1979	Kanybek Osmonaliev (USSR) 242.5
1980*	Kanybek Osmonaliev (USSR) 245.0

Bantamweight (56.0kg)
1973	Atanas Kirov (USSR) 257.5
1974	Atanas Kirov (USSR) 255.0
1975	Atanas Kirov (Bul) 255.0
1976*	Norair Nurikyan (Bul) 262.5
1977	Jiro Hosotani (Jap) 252.5
1978	Daniel Nunez (Cuba) 260.0
1979	Anton Kodiabashev (USSR) 267.5
1980*	Daniel Nunez (Cuba) 275.0

Featherweight (60.0kg)
1973	Dito Shanidze (USSR) 272.5
1974	Georgi Todorov (Bul) 280.0
1975	Georgi Todorov (Bul) 285.0
1976*	Nikolai Kolesnikov (USSR) 285.0
1977	Nikolai Kolesnikov (USSR) 280.0
1978	Nikolai Kolesnikov (USSR) 270.0
1979	Marek Seweryn (Pol) 282.5
1980*	Viktor Mazin (USSR) 290.0

UPLIFTING: Lifting in 3 different weight classes, American Tommy Kono won 8 world titles, including 2 Olympic gold medals, and shares the record for most championships with Vasili Alexeyev and John Davis (US).

Lightweight (67.5kg)
1973	Muharbi Kirzhinov (USSR)	305.0
1974	Peter Korol (USSR)	305.0
1975	Peter Korol (USSR)	312.5
1976*	Peter Korol (USSR)	305.0
1977	Roberto Urrutia (Cuba)	315.0
1978	Yanko Russev (Bul)	310.0
1979	Yanko Russev (Bul)	332.5
1980*	Yanko Russev (Bul)	342.5

Middleweight (75.0kg)
1973	Nedelcho Kolev (Bul)	337.5
1974	Nedelcho Kolev (Bul)	335.0
1975	Peter Wenzel (E Ger)	335.0
1976*	Jordan Mitkov (Bul)	335.0
1977	Yuriy Vardanian (USSR)	345.0
1978	Roberto Urrutia (Cuba)	347.5
1979	Roberto Urrutia (Cuba)	345.0
1980*	Lassen Zlatev (Bul)	360.0

Light Heavyweight (82.5kg)
1973	Vladimir Rizhenkov (USSR)	350.0
1974	Trendafil Stojchev (Bul)	350.0
1975	Valeriy Shary (USSR)	357.5
1976*	Valeriy Shary (USSR)	365.0
1977	Gennadiy Bessonov (USSR)	352.5
1978	Yuriy Vardanyan (USSR)	377.5
1979	Yuriy Vardanyan (USSR)	370.0
1980*	Yuriy Vardanyan (USSR)	400.00

Middle Heavyweight (90.0kg)
1973	David Rigert (USSR)	365.0
1974	David Rigert (USSR)	387.5
1975	David Rigert (USSR)	377.5
1976*	David Rigert (USSR)	382.5
1977	Sergei Poltoratski (USSR)	375.0
1978	Rolf Milser (W Ger)	377.5
1979	Gennadiy Bessonov (USSR)	380.0
1980*	Peter Baczako (Hun)	377.5

Heavyweight 1 (100.0kg)
First held 1977.
1977	Anatoliy Kozlov (USSR)	367.5
1978	David Rigert (USSR)	390.0
1979	Pavel Sirchine (USSR)	385.0
1980*	Ota Zaremba (Cze)	395.0

Heavyweight 2 (110.0kg)
1973	Pavel Pervushine (USSR)	385.0
1974	Vladimir Ustyuzhin (USSR)	380.0
1975	Valentin Khristov (Bul)	417.5
1976*	Yuriy Zaitsev (USSR)	385.0
1977	Valentin Khristov (Bul)	405.0
1978	Yuriy Zaitsev (USSR)	402.5
1979	Sergei Arakelov (USSR)	410.0
1980*	Leonid Taranenko (USSR)	422.5

Super Heavyweight (over 110kg)
1973	Vasiliy Alexeyev (USSR)	402.5
1974	Vasiliy Alexeyev (USSR)	425.0
1975	Vasiliy Alexeyev (USSR)	427.5
1976*	Vasiliy Alexeyev (USSR)	440.0
1977	Vasiliy Alexeyev (USSR)	430.0
1978	Jurgen Heuser (E Ger)	417.5
1979	Sultan Rakhmanov (USSR)	430.0
1980*	Sultan Rakhamanov (USSR)	440.0

Most years as World or Olympic Champion (OG = Olympic Games)
8	Vasiliy Alexeyev (USSR) 110.0 + : 1970–77 (inc. 2 OG)
8	John Davis (US) 82.5: 1938; 82.5 + : 1946–52 (inc. 2 OG)
8	Tommy Kono (US) 67.5: 1952 (OG); 75.0: 1953, 1957–59; 82.5: 1954–56 (inc. 1 OG)
7	Arkadiy Vorobyev (USSR) 82.5: 1953; 90.0: 1954–58, 1960 (inc. 2 OG)

WRESTLING

Earliest References. The earliest depictions of wrestling holds and falls on the walls of the tomb of Ptahhotep (5th Dynasty Egypt) indicate that organized wrestling dates from before *c.* 2350 B.C. It was introduced into the ancient Olympic Games in the 18th Olympiad in *c.* 708 B.C. The Graeco-Roman style is of French origin and arose about 1860. The International Amateur Wrestling Federation (F.I.L.A.) was founded in 1912.

Best Records

In international competition, Osamu Watanabe (b. October 21, 1950) (Japan), the 1964 Olympic free-style featherweight champion, was unbeaten and unscored-upon in 187 consecutive matches.

Wade Schalles (US) has won 615 bouts from 1964 to the end of 1977.

Most World Championships

The greatest number of world championships won by a wrestler is ten by the free-styler Aleksandr Medved (USSR), with the light-

FALL SPORT: Russian Aleksandr Medved (here taking down India's Maruti Mane) holds the record for most world titles with 10. Three of his championships were in Olympic competition, bringing him a record for gold medals he shares with 2 others.

heavyweight titles in 1962, 1963, 1964 (Olympic) and 1966, the heavyweight 1967 and 1968 (Olympic), and the super-heavyweight title 1969, 1970, 1971 and 1972 (Olympic). The only wrestler to win the same title in 6 successive years has been Abdollah Movahed (Iran) in the lightweight division in 1965–70. The record for successive Graeco-Roman titles is five by Roman Rurua (USSR) with the featherweight 1966, 1967, 1968 (Olympic), 1969 and 1970.

Most Olympic Titles

Three wrestlers have won three Olympic titles. They are:

Carl Westergren (Sweden) (1895–1958)		Aleksandr Medved (USSR) (b. Sept. 16, 1937)	
Graeco-Roman Middleweight A	1920	Free-style Light-heavyweight	1964
Graeco-Roman Middleweight B	1924	Free-style Heavyweight	1968
Graeco-Roman Heavyweight	1932	Free-style Super-heavyweight	1972

Ivar Johansson (Sweden) (1903–79)	
Free-style Middleweight	1932
Graeco-Roman Welterweight	1932
Graeco-Roman Middleweight	1936

The only wrestler with more medals is Imre Polyák (Hungary) who won the silver medal for the Graeco-Roman featherweight class in 1952, 56–60 and the gold in 1964.

Heaviest Heavyweight

The heaviest wrestler in Olympic history is Chris Taylor (US) (1950–79), bronze medalist in the super-heavyweight class in 1972, who stood 6 feet 5 inches tall and weighed over 420 lbs.

Longest Bout

The longest recorded bout was one of 11 hours 40 minutes between Martin Klein (Estonia, representing Russia) and Alfred Asikáinen (Finland) in the Graeco-Roman middleweight "A" event in the 1912 Olympic Games in Stockholm, Sweden. Klein won.

Sumo Wrestling

The sport's origins in Japan certainly date from *c.* 23 B.C. The heaviest performers were probably Dewagatake, a wrestler of the 1920's who was 6 feet 7¾ inches tall and weighed up to 430 lbs., and Odachi, of the 1950's, who stood 6 feet 7½ inches and weighed about 441 lbs. Weight is amassed by over-eating a high protein stew called *chankonabe*. The tallest was probably Ozora, an early 19th-century performer, who stood 7 feet 3 inches tall. The most successful wrestlers have been Koki Naya (born 1940), *alias* Taiho ("Great Bird"), who won 32 Emperor's Cups until his retirement in 1971; Sadaji Akiyoshi (b. 1912), *alias* Futabayama, who won 69 consecutive bouts in the 1930's; Totaro Koe, *alias* Umegatani I, who had the highest winning percentage among grand champions of .951 in the 1880's; and the *ozeki* Torokichi, *alias* Raiden, who in 21 years (1789–1810) won 240 bouts and lost only ten.

The youngest of the 56 men to attain the rank of *Yokozuna* (Grand Champion) was Toshimitsu Obata (*alias* Kitanoumi) in July, 1974, aged 21 years 2 months. Jesse Kuhaulva (b. Hawaii, June 16, 1944), *alias* Takamiyama, was the first non-Japanese to win an official tournament, in July, 1972.

N.C.A.A.

1928	*Oklahoma State	1932	*Indiana	1935	Oklahoma State
1929	Oklahoma State	1933	*Oklahoma State	1936	Oklahoma
1930	Oklahoma State		*Iowa State	1937	Oklahoma State
1931	*Oklahoma State	1934	Oklahoma State	1938	Oklahoma State

HEAVY MEDAL: Chris Taylor (US) was the heaviest wrestler in Olympic history. At 6 feet 5 inches tall, Taylor weighed over 420 pounds when he won the 1972 superheavyweight bronze medal.

LONE GOLD: Middleweight John Peterson hoists Turkey's Mehmet Uzon in a semi-final bout in the 1976 Olympics. Peterson went on to become the only American wrestler to win a gold medal in Montreal.

1939	Oklahoma State	1955	Oklahoma State	1968	Oklahoma State
1940	Oklahoma State	1956	Oklahoma State	1969	Iowa State
1941	Oklahoma State	1957	Oklahoma	1970	Iowa State
1942	Oklahoma State	1958	Oklahoma State	1971	Oklahoma State
1946	Oklahoma State	1959	Oklahoma State	1972	Iowa State
1947	Cornell College	1960	Oklahoma	1973	Iowa State
1948	Oklahoma State	1961	Oklahoma State	1974	Oklahoma
1949	Oklahoma State	1962	Oklahoma State	1975	Iowa
1950	Northern Iowa	1963	Oklahoma	1976	Iowa
1951	Oklahoma	1964	Oklahoma State	1977	Iowa State
1952	Oklahoma	1965	Iowa State	1978	Iowa
1953	Penn State	1966	Oklahoma State	1979	Iowa
1954	Oklahoma State	1967	Michigan State		

Note: No tournament held, 1943–45
*Unofficial champions.

YACHTING

Origin. Yachting in England dates from the £100 (now $200) stake race between King Charles II of England and his brother, James, Duke of York, on the Thames River, on September 1, 1661, over 23 miles, from Greenwich to Gravesend. The earliest club is the Royal Cork Yacht Club (formerly the Cork Harbour Water Club), established in Ireland in 1720. The word "yacht" is from the Dutch, meaning to hunt or chase.

SET SAIL: Crossbow II set the official world speed record of 33.4 knots (38.46 m.p.h.) over a 500 meters course off Portland Harbor, Dorset, England, in 1977. The 73½-foot boat is reported to have attained a speed of 45 knots (51 m.p.h.) momentarily in an unsuccessful attempt on its own record in 1978.

Most Successful

The most successful racing yacht in history was the British Royal Yacht *Britannia* (1893–1935), owned by King Edward VII while Prince of Wales, and subsequently by King George V, which won 231 races in 625 starts.

Highest Speed

The official world sailing speed record is 33.4 knots (38.46 m.p.h.) achieved by the 73½-foot *Crossbow II* over a 500-meter

(547-yard) course off Portland Harbor, Dorset, England, on October 4, 1977. The vessel, with a sail area of 1,400 square feet, was designed by Rod McAlpine-Downie and owned and steered by Timothy Colman. In an unsuccessful attempt on the record in October, 1978, *Crossbow II* is reported to have momentarily attained a speed of 45 knots (51 m.p.h.).

The fastest 24-hour single-handed run by a sailing yacht was recorded by Nick Keig (b. June 13, 1936), of the Isle of Man, who covered 340 nautical miles in a 37½-foot trimaran, *Three Legs of Mann I,* during the Falmouth to Punta, Azores, race on June 9–10, 1975, averaging 14.16 knots (16.30 m.p.h.). The fastest bursts of speed reached were about 25 knots (28.78 m.p.h.).

Most Competitors

1,261 sailing boats started the 233-mile Round Zealand (Denmark) race in June, 1976.

America's Cup

The America's Cup was originally won as an outright prize by the schooner *America* on August 22, 1851, at Cowes, England, but was later offered by the New York Yacht Club as a challenge trophy. On August 8, 1870, J. Ashbury's *Cambria* (GB) failed to capture the trophy from the *Magic,* owned by F. Osgood (US). Since then the Cup has been challenged by Great Britain in 15 contests, by Canada in two contests, and by Australia four times,

WIND BAGS: Denmark's Paul Elvstrom (left) won individual gold medals in Olympic yachting competition in 4 successive Games, 1948–60. Yachting's coveted trophy, the America's Cup (right), has been successfully defended 23 times by US sailors.

BIG VICTORY: Harold Vanderbilt's "Ranger," winner of the America's Cup in 1937, boasted the largest sail ever made. The championship yacht's parachute spinnaker had an area of 18,000 square feet.

but the United States holders have never been defeated. The closest race ever was the fourth race of the 1962 series, when the 12-meter sloop *Weatherly* beat her Australian challenger *Gretel* by about 3½ lengths (75 yards), a margin of only 26 seconds, on September 22, 1962. The fastest time ever recorded by a 12-meter boat for the triangular course of 24 miles is 2 hours 46 minutes 58 seconds by *Gretel* in 1962.

Little America's Cup

The catamaran counterpart to the America's Cup was instituted in 1961 for International C-class catamarans. Great Britain has won 8 times from 1961 to 1968.

Admiral's Cup

The ocean racing series to have attracted the largest number of participating nations (three boats allowed to each nation) is the Admiral's Cup held by the Royal Ocean Racing Club in the English Channel in alternate years. Up to 1979, Britain had won 7 times, US and Australia twice, and West Germany once. A record 19 nations competed in 1975, 1977 and 1979.

Olympic Victories

The first sportsman ever to win individual gold medals in four successive Olympic Games has been Paul B. Elvström (b. February 24, 1928) (Denmark) in the Firefly class in 1948 and the Finn class in 1952, 1956 and 1960. He has also won 8 other world titles in a total of 6 classes.

The lowest number of penalty points by the winner of any class in Olympic regatta is 3 points [6 wins (1 disqualified) and 1 second in 7 starts] by *Superdocius* of the Flying Dutchman class sailed by Lt. Rodney Stuart Pattison (b. August 5, 1943), British Royal Navy, and Ian Somerled Macdonald-Smith (b. July 3, 1945), in Acapulco Bay, Mexico, in October, 1968.

Largest Sail

The largest sail ever made was a parachute spinnaker with an area of 18,000 square feet (more than two-fifths of an acre) for Harold S. Vanderbilt's *Ranger* in 1937.

Largest Marina

The largest marina in the world is that of Marina Del Rey, Los Angeles, California, which has 7,500 berths.

Highest Altitude

The greatest altitude at which sailing has been conducted is 16,109 feet on Laguna Huallatani, Bolivia, by Peter Williams, Brian Barrett, Gordon Siddeley and Keith Robinson in *Mirror Dinghy No. 55448* on November 19, 1977.

THREE SHEETS TO THE WIND: Full sails abound in this photograph from the 1979 Admiral's Cup competition. These boats are, from left to right: "Vanina" (Italy), "Golden Apple of the Sun" (Ireland), and "Police Car" (Australia).

America's Cup Winners

The America's Cup is an international challenge trophy, named after the schooner *America*, the winner of a race around the Isle of Wight in 1851. All the winning yachts listed here have come from the US.

1870	*Magic*	1895	*Defender*	1958	*Columbia*
1871	*Columbia & Sappho*	1899	*Columbia*	1962	*Weatherly*
1876	*Madelaine*	1901	*Columbia*	1964	*Constellation*
1881	*Mischief*	1903	*Reliance*	1967	*Intrepid*
1885	*Puritan*	1920	*Resolute*	1970	*Intrepid*
1886	*Mayflower*	1930	*Enterprise*	1974	*Courageous*
1887	*Volunteer*	1934	*Rainbow*	1977	*Courageous*
1893	*Vigilant*	1937	*Ranger*		

Singlehanded Trans-Atlantic Crossing Race

1960	*Gipsy Moth III*—Francis Chichester (GB) 40d 12hr 30min	1968	*Sir Thomas Lipton*—Geoffrey Williams (GB) 25d 20hr 33min
1962	*Gypsy Moth III*—Francis Chichester (GB) 33d 15hr 7min	1972	*Pen Duick IV*—Alain Colas (Fra) 20d 13hr 15min
1964	*Pen Duick II*—Eric Tabarly (Fra) 27d 3hr 56min	1976	*Pen Duick VI*—Eric Tabarly (Fra) 23d 20hr 12min

Whitbread Round the World Race

1973–74	Raymond Carlin, *Sayula II* Mexico	1977–78	Cornelius van Rietschoten, *Flyer* Dutch

Admiral's Cup Winners

The Admiral's Cup is contested biennially by national 3-yacht teams. The competition comprises four races—a 200-mile Channel race, two inshore races held during Cowes Week, and finally the 605-mile Fastnet race from Cowes to the Fastnet Rock, off Southern Ireland, and back to Plymouth. First held 1957.

1957	Great Britain	1965	Great Britain	1973	W. Germany
1959	Great Britain	1967	Australia	1975	Great Britain
1961	US	1969	US	1977	Great Britain
1963	Great Britain	1971	Great Britain	1979	Australia

INDEX

PICTURE CREDITS

The editors and publishers wish to thank the following people and organizations for pictures which they supplied:

Acme Agency; Action Photos by H. W. Neale; Aitken, Ltd.; All-Sport Photographic; Amateur Softball Association; American Bowling Congress; Anglia Television, Ltd.; Associated Newspapers, Ltd.; Associated Press, London; Atlanta Braves; Tom Austin; Baltimore Orioles; Jim Benagh; Franklin Berger; William Berry; B.G.A.; David Bier; Boston Garden; Boston Bruins; Peter A. Brandenburg; Buffalo Bills; California Angels; Central Press Photos, Ltd.; Chicago Bears; Gerry Cranham; *Cycling;* Detroit Tigers; Tony Duffy; John Eagle; Embassy of the Czechoslovak Socialist Republic, London; Mary Evans; Farleigh Dickinson University; *The Gateway;* Global Olympic Picture Association; Golden State Warriors; Greyhound Racing Association; *Guardian;* Guy Gurney; Hartford Whalers; International Frisbee-disc Association; International Rodeo Association; Jim Jacobs; Marion Kaplan; Keystone Press Agency, Ltd.; George Konig; Kwolek's Studio; E. D. Lacey; Ladies Professional Golf Association; Las Vegas News Bureau; Los Angeles Lakers; Bob Madden; Alfredo MacDondo; Milwaukee Bucks; Minnesota Vikings; Montreal Canadiens; Don Morley; *La Moto;* Mark Moylan; NASCAR; National Association of Jai-Alai Frontons, Inc.; New Hungary; *News Chronicle;* New York Cosmos; New York Racing Association; New York Rangers; New York Stars; *The New York Times;* New York Yankees; NFL Properties, Inc.; North American Soccer League; *Northern Star,* Australia; Novosti Press Agency, Moscow; Oakland Raiders; Philadelphia Eagles; Philadelphia Flyers; Philadelphia 76ers; Photo Communications; Pittsburgh Steelers; *Planet News;* Popperfoto; Press Association; Professional Bowlers Association; Professional Rodeo Cowboys Association; Pro Football Hall of Fame; Provincial Sports Photography; Race Course Technical Services; Radio Times Hulton Picture Library; Trudy Rosen; *Rowing* Magazine; Al Ruelle; St. Louis Cardinals; *St. Thomas Daily News;* San Diego Convention and Visitors Bureau; Leon Serchuk; Jerry Soalt; Sonja Henie Og Niels Onstads Stiftelser; Anne Splain; Sport and General Press Agency; Sporting Pictures; *Sun;* Syndication International; Thomson Newspapers, Ltd.; United Press International, London and New York; United States Intercollegiate Lacrosse Association; United States Tennis Association; United States Trotting Association; Universal Pictorial Press; Verldens Gang; Virginia Tech; Wide World Photos, London and New York; World Sports.

Hey there sports fans

The makers of OLD SPICE after shave and cologne have more Great Moments in Sports to bring to you at better than book store prices!

THE UMPIRE STRIKES BACK

By Ron Luciano and David Fisher — Ron Luciano, the funniest ump ever to call balls and strikes, takes you out on the ballfield and into the clubhouse in the biggest and funniest baseball bestseller ever! Eighteen weeks on the *New York Times* Bestseller list.

Suggested Retail: $3.50   With OLD SPICE $2.50

GUINNESS BOOK OF OLYMPIC RECORDS

1984 Edition by Norris McWhirter — A Complete Roll of Olympic medal winners (from 1896 to 1980) as well as an explanation of each game and scoring system. In short, everything you need to fully enjoy the 1984 Olympics.

Suggested Retail: $3.50   With OLD SPICE $2.50

RULES OF THE GAME

By the Diagram Group — An invaluable and enjoyable reference to the rules, procedures, techniques, equipment, timing, and scoring of more than 400 national and international sporting events.

Suggested Retail: $12.95   With OLD SPICE $6.95

These three books have a total suggested retail price of $19.95. All three can be yours for only $9.95 and two proofs-of-purchase (UPC codes) from any OLD SPICE after shave or cologne boxes. Or, you can order any one book at our special offer price and one proof-of-purchase.

To get your OLD SPICE Sports Book offer, fill in the order form on the other side of this page.

Indicate the book(s) desired and total amount enclosed.

_____ ***UMPIRE STRIKES BACK***
@ $2.50 plus one proof of purchase $_____

_____ ***GUINNESS BOOK OF OLYMPIC RECORDS***
@ $2.50 plus one proof of purchase $_____

_____ ***RULES OF THE GAME***
@ $6.95 plus one proof of purchase $_____

All three books for $9.95 plus two proof of purchase $_____

Make checks payable to:
OLD SPICE Sports Book Offer.

Print your name and address

_____
NAME

_____
ADDRESS

_____
CITY

_____
STATE   ZIP

MAIL TO: OLD SPICE Sports Book Offer
P.O. Box 1066
Des Plaines, IL 60018

Offer expires June 30, 1984. Please add any applicable State and/or Sales Taxes. Allow 6 to 8 weeks for delivery. Offer good only in U.S.A. and is void where prohibited, taxed or restricted by law.